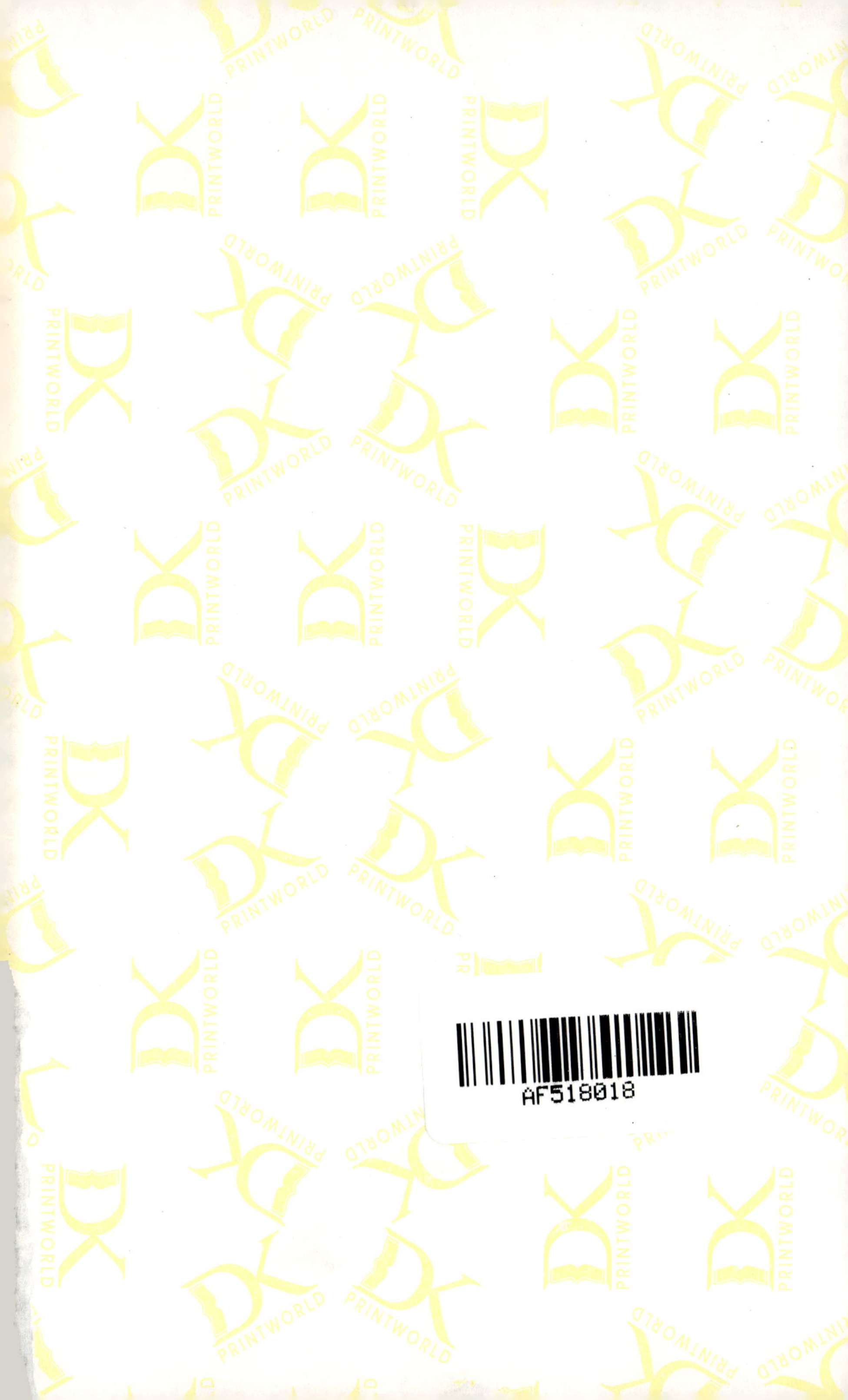
AF518018

Revisiting

Literature, Criticism and Aesthetics in India

Revisiting

Literature, Criticism and Aesthetics in India

Avadhesh Kumar Singh

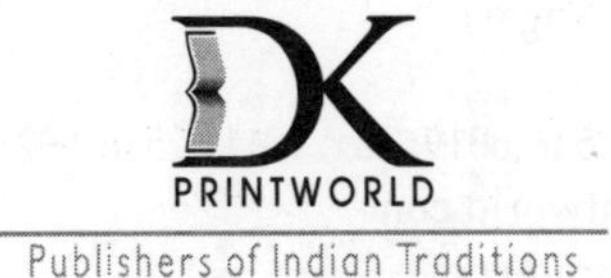

Cataloging in Publication Data — DK
Courtesy: D.K. Agencies (P) Ltd. <docinfo@dkagencies.com>

Singh, Avadhesh K.
Revisiting literature, criticism and aesthetics in India / Avadhesh Kumar Singh.
p. cm.
Includes bibliographical references (p.) and index.
ISBN 13: 9788124606278

1. Indic literature — 19th century — History and criticism — Theory, etc. 2. Indic literature — 20th century — History and criticism — Theory, etc. 3. Criticism — India. 4. Aesthetics, Indic. I. Title.

DDC 891.209 23

ISBN 13: 978-81-246-0627-8 **ISBN 10: 81-246-0627-7**
First published in India in 2012

Published and printed by:
D.K. Printworld (P) Ltd.
Regd. Office: '*Vedaśrī*', F-395, Sudarshan Park
(Metro Station: Ramesh Nagar)
New Delhi - 110 015
Phones: (011) 2545 3975; 2546 6019; *Fax*: (011) 2546 5926
E-mail: indology@dkprintworld.com
Website: www.dkprintworld.com

Acknowledgement

BEFORE I acknowledge my gratitude to individuals and institutions that supported me during the course of writing the book, *Re-visiting Literature, Criticism and Aesthetics in India*, I must share the cause(s) that went in its making.

The book is a consequence of my engagement with a few disturbing questions that I faced about India, its literature, culture, knowledge systems, their reception and representation in India and beyond, particularly in the English-speaking world. Since I am a product of India, I have my emotional attachments to it, yet I strove with full sincerity to be objective by exorcising them. The questions by their enormity and ubiquity encompassed various disciplines, and my limitations as a student of literature limited my responses, though my exposure to and practice of comparative study of literature and poetics helped me.

The questions included: What are Indian literary, critical and cultural realities? How has Indian culture survived? Why should there be single language/literature departments in a multilingual society like India in which almost everyone can operate in at least more than one language or dialect? What was the impact of colonization on Indian consciousness? What were the strategies of colonizers? How did India resist them? How should post-colonial India respond to new categories, floated either to measure or subsume it in the era of globalization? How should India re-orient literary studies in it in consonance with its linguistic and literary realities? Why have Indian knowledge systems in general and language of knowledge or learned composition, i.e. Sanskrit in particular, been expelled from the mainstream education system?

What have been its consequences? What happened to the symbiotic relationship between oral and written literature, and Sanskrit, and *Prākṛt* (natural) dialects and language? Why did a system building civilization like India not have aesthetics and ethics? Was there no formulation of theories of the creative process in India that can boast of epics like the *Rāmāyaṇa* and the *Mahābhārata*?

Is it not ironical that the scholars of Hindi, Gujarati, Marathi, Sanskrit and other Indian languages are at least aware of Western literature and critical theories but do not read or even know their sister literatures and critical traditions, for instance *Tolkappiyam* in Tamil? Is there some truth in the pronouncements like the end, death, or amnesia of/in Indian critical tradition? How should we respond to the proliferation of Western critical theories? How can and should we receive them? Can we theorize our own versions of Western critical theories like feminism or post-colonialism? If so, then how? How can we write/right them in India?

All four sections of the book "Word, World and Perception," "Colonialism and After," "Literature and Theorizing in India" and "Criticism and India" deal with these questions. In the process of responding to these questions I consciously related them to Indian realities. During the period, I encountered many trapped between those who at best were ignorant and indifferent and at worst contemptuous of Indian knowledge systems in general and Indian critical traditions in particular. Ironically, most of those, I realized later, who were lavish either in their appreciation or vituperation, did so on the basis of reading about them, without reading texts or verifying facts about them.

Two basic premises that formed the backdrop of my interaction with these issues were: India's rich cultural and knowledge traditions and its colonization which impacted it during and after. India is one of the world's foremost knowledge civilizations. There have been other knowledge civilizations in the world as well, but they, i.e. Greek, Arab, Chinese, Mayans and Incans among others, were either annihilated or converted into new folds. The consequent conversion did change the attitude of their inheritors towards knowledge and its construction and particularly towards the others. Indian tradition survived, perhaps, because it allowed questioning from within and prestiged and prioritized learning to teaching so much so that there is no word for teaching in most of the Indian languages in which the word for teaching is made after transforming the word for learning into the causative. Hence, the Indian civilization was a knowledge civilization because it was a learning civilization. But what happened to the culture of learning in it?

System-making came naturally to Indians. Indian culture had a natural wont for constructing Śāstra (system), for there are Śāstras in it for almost every activity — human and animal — things in motion and motionless. Critical thinking prospered in India for centuries much before colonization, till non-native traditions in the form of the Greek, the Muslim, and the Christian civilizations of knowledge intervened in it. The first was a fleeting interface of the cultural kind, the second had socio-political, religious and cultural connotations, but the last had the most lasting systematic political, religious, cultural and intellectual (academic) impact, as the Indian encounter with the British was a clash of two knowledge systems, if not civilizations, for it would be a gross over-estimation to term British/English culture as civilization. In the book, colonization emerges as the lynchpin around which, i.e. before, during and after it, responses revolve. But whatever happened to system building during and after colonization?

Colonialism, all its evils notwithstanding, had at least one positive attribute in it. It yoked different nations and continents, different civilizations and cultures, knowledge systems as well as literary and critical discourses together in an unprecedented manner in human history. Apart from being a clash of civilizations and different knowledge systems, it led to a new synthesis of cultural and critical discourses as a consequence of the confluence of two antithetical discourses. In the case of India, colonialism expanded and consolidated itself in the nineteenth and the first half of the twentieth century, though the declining years of the second quarter of the twentieth century witnessed the melting of the empire coinciding with the end of World War II.

During the initial phase of the rule of the East India Company in India, the Orientalists/Indologists appropriated India's intellectual and cultural resources to their advantage before their influence waned, and the advocates of Anglicization of India led by William Wilberforce and Thomas Babington Macaulay took over. The establishment of universities in India and emergence of a new class of educated people (mostly in the Western mode) and writers facilitated interaction between the Western/English and Indian critical traditions. In collaboration with other factors, the new generation resisted colonization through violent and non-violent ways and India attained its political independence. Its intellectual independence, however, is yet to take place . . . . If it has not till now, none other than Indians, their disorientation from their traditions and uncritical acceptance of other traditions are, to a good measure, responsible. Human history has lessons of hope for it, as R.W. Emerson pronounced intellectual independence of America in his lecture "American Scholar" on 31 August 1837 at the Phi Beta Kappa Society after its political independence in 1776. Freedom is a prerequisite for liberation — political, cultural, intellectual and spiritual. "Indian Scholar" will follow it. And all "scholars" put together would lead to the formation of the United Nations of Scholars without super powers.

Before I conclude, I must express my gratitude to individuals and institutions that helped me during the course of my study and provided space for interaction with scholars. Their interventions and observations deserve my sincere gratitude, as they enriched my understanding. Countless as they are in the form of my colleagues and students at the Department of English and Comparative Literary Studies, Saurashtra University, I must mention, among them, the names of Hans Breunig (Magdeburg), Sridhar Rajeshwaran (Mumbai), Subha Dasgupta (Jadavpur), Sunil Sagar and Maulik Vyas (Rajkot) in particular for going through the manuscript in parts at different points of time. The University Grants Commission, New Delhi supported the project and the publication of the book in particular. Shri Susheel Mittal, D.K. Printworld, has earned my gratitude for his keen interest in the publication of the book and its issues.

Moreover, I must state that my responses to the questions enumerated above were spread over a period of time. Different occasions necessitated use of the same argument for related frames of thought. I have retained them for the sake of continuity. If it leaves a jarring effect at times, I seek forgiveness for my indulgence. The institutions that provided space for me to share with them included Indian Institute of Advanced Studies, Shimla (Himachal Pradesh); Sahitya Akademi, New Delhi; Centre for Languages and Cultural Studies, Jawaharlal Nehru University, New Delhi; Department of Comparative Literature, Jadavpur University, Jadavpur; Banaras Hindu University, Varansai (UP); Department of English, University of Pune, Pune (Maharashtra); Department of English, University of Mumbai, Mumbai (Maharashtra); and Department of English and Comparative Literary Studies, Saurashtra University, Rajkot (Gujarat). I express my gratitude to all of them for giving me an opportunity to present my arguments before distinguished scholars of the country. Also my sincere acknowledgements are due to Professor K.D. Verma, Professor Rajnath, Professor Kapil Kapoor, Professor Makarand Paranjape, Professor Subha Dasgupta, Professor Jasbir Jain, Professor Chandrakala Padia, and Professor B.L. Chakkoo, the editors of various journals and anthologies in which my responses appeared from time to time in the form of papers. Apart from them, I have tried to acknowledge the source wherever needed. But more often than not I realized that whatever I thought as mine or new was what I had learnt from others. In the process I heard more and read less. And it is difficult for me to acknowledge all those from whom I heard so much. Also I do not want to embarrass them by mentioning their names for embellishing my arguments with them.

Acknowledgements are at times used as embellishments. In

the present case they are genuine and need to be respected. I do so wordlessly for my own satisfaction and peace, for words tend to hinder understanding and peace as well. Ironically enough whatever little I learnt and understood I did so by listening and reading. So I conclude this piece by not causing violence to words and people behind them because of my limitations, and therefore leave them in their worlds.

avadhesh kumar singh

Contents

PART III: LITERATURE AND THEORIZING IN INDIA

PART IV: CRITICISM AND INDIA

Lead in
Negotiating Little Questions

Responses to some natural questions are best avoided, as they tend to be repetititive of what has already been stated. Since they cannot be wished away, they are left in a state of suspension. Hence, before responding to the first legitimate question, 'What is criticism?' it would be appropriate for me to respond to, 'What is criticism all about?' Criticism is all about questions. It is not so much about answers. Answers always vary and change from time to time. All answers are provisional, questions are eternal. Moreover, all questions are not significant. Only 'different' questions matter, for they lend a different/new direction to the given tradition. That is why it is more difficult to ask good questions than answering them. For that a simple, innocent and yet different question, not volumes, is needed. And along with the faculty of reasoning are needed instinct and inspiration. For instance, in English critical tradition, William Wordsworth's contribution to critical writing is not so voluminous. He was a critic not by qualifications but compulsions. S.T. Coleridge did not oblige him by writing the 'Preface' to the *Lyrical Ballads*, so he had to. He capitalized on the compulsion by asking simple, natural and different questions. But in the process of asking hitherto unasked question, 'What is the process of poetic creation?', he gave a new direction to English critical tradition. In all critical traditions, good critics have asked 'different' questions, or repeated old questions at least differently.

With the word 'criticism,' a few other terms like idea, theory, knowledge, and interpretation come to our mind. Idea is an act of seeing, for etymologically speaking it originated in Greek and came to English via Latin. The root of the term 'idea' means 'seeing.' In this sense, it comes close to theory which too means seeing. Seeing is a multidimensional activity. It involves seeing, being seen, and seeing being seen.[1]

Seeing is an essential pre-condition of observation. Methodical observations with necessary substantiation are a necessary stage of criticism, i.e. judgement. Let us understand it in terms of various stages:

To begin with, there are things, in existence, in the world. Whether they are known or knowable is a moot question, but that would be dealt with in discussion of knowledge. After things, comes in existence reality. Things are real, not reality. Reality is a tentative rudimentary hypothesis about world or things around us. Observation of things around us leads to accumulation of experiences that constitute our consciousness which keeps expanding with every new experience — real or imaginary or both. Logical and a-logical, i.e. instinct or inspiration, both play their roles in it. Experiences lead to creation of world, around them. World of experiences/ observation is a world about the world, not the world itself. A writer responds to it with articulation of his experiences — factual or fictitious or both. A good writer responds to the given experience or situation, in a way different from his compatriots. S/he is like Hamlet, a prince later but a human being first. So many mothers must have married after their husbands' death in the world, rather many of them must have given up their husbands or even murdered them to marry someone else. So many sons must have passed through the torrid experience like Hamlet. But they did not become Hamlet. Hamlet is remembered as an integral part of literary memory because he reacted

1. For the discussion of "seeing" and theory, please see "Word and Beyond . . ." in Section I of the book. Also for discussion of "violence" in creative and critical acts, please see "Violence in Creative and Critical Acts," *Critical Practice*, vol. 1, no. 1, 1994, pp. 49-56.

differently, as he articulated through his questions first, and through his ideas and actions later. Hamlet's tragedy does not take place when he dies but it begins with his realization of his mother's infidelity, not only to his father but also to his memory just after his death, or in the last scene of the last act of *Hamlet*, but all through the play in the form of pertinent but different questions, hitherto unasked by his counterparts in human history. (Hamlet, as often stated, is his own critic, but more than that he is critics' critic.)

The preceding discussion about world and its observation can be schematized and extended thus:

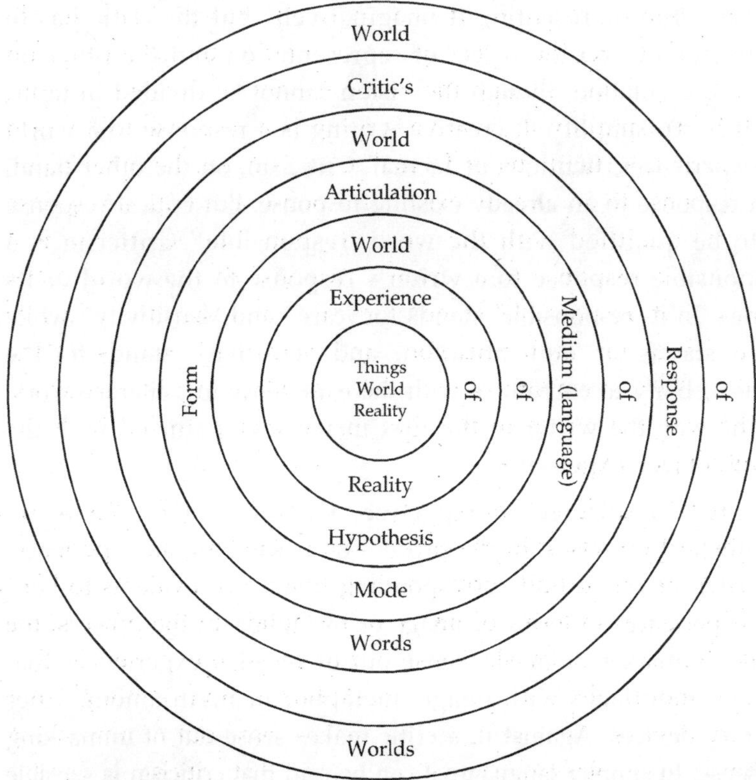

In the above scheme, the writer is considerably limited by enormity or ubiquity of experience and urge for articulation but has some choices to exercise, so s/he is not really powerless, for true powerlessness is absence of choices. These choices are in terms of world of words, medium, manner, and mode of expression. Above all, s/he has the choice about the very issue of articulation — whether to articulate or not at all. In comparison, a critic has limited space of choices, as s/he has to respond to an already given world of words, constructed on the basis of her/his experience with words by the writer. Moreover, in comparison to a writer who has to 'see' or focus only at the object of representation, the critic has to fix her/his eyes on the object of representation and its literary representation in the writing. Loosely speaking, a writer keeps both of his eyes on the object while representing it imaginatively, but the critic has to focus one eye on the object of representation and the other on its representation, though the vision cannot be divided in terms of eyes. To simplify it, creative writing is a response to a world of experiences, fictitious or factual. Criticism, on the other hand, is a response to an already existing response. But critical response is to be qualified with the word 'responsible.' Criticism is a responsible response to a writer's response to the world or its things. In it 'responsible' stands for 'care,' and 'sensitivity'; while 'care' stands for 'authentication,' and 'sensitivity' stands for the critic's ability to empathize with the experience in a literary work, in the way the writer in the first instance empathized with the thing/object/experience.

From a different perspective, writing and criticism are antithetical exercises. In the process of articulating an experience, a writer strives to find corresponding literary equivalents to her/his experiences in terms of image or metaphor. In the process, the writer unmakes or masks sense out of sensible experiences that s/he camouflages with image, metaphor or myth among other literary devices. Against it, a critic makes sense out of unmasking of sense. In simpler language, it can be said that criticism is sensible intellectualism whereas creative work is intellectual sensibility.

In this order of things, what is the position or sphere of

existence of criticism? After Roland Barthes it has become common-place to term criticism as an act of creation. In a sense it is true. (In a sense, for that matter, everything is true). If so, then in which sense? Criticism is not an act of creation in the sense a creative act is. Both of them use language but differently. Language as a medium behaves differently. Creative work makes use of media like metaphors, myths, symbols, and images among others, and it does so in the manner of representation. One relies heavily on plurality of meaning and the other strives to reduce the play of language. Creative writing is a movement away from abstract (experience being transformed into an idea or ideas) to concrete, whereas criticism is a movement from concrete to abstract. Creative writing is an interpretation of idea(s) in concrete idiom, and criticism is a re-interpretation of an interpretation, often in abstract, referential language. All these positions notwithstanding, the sphere of existence of criticism in relation to creative act can best be understood in terms of the Hindi word *anuśāsana* used as an equivalent of discipline. Studied in terms of prefix and the root word, the word *anu* means 'subsequent' and *śāsana* means 'discipline,' and criticism is *anuśāsana,* for as a discipline it is subsequent to creativity. Literary criticism in particular owes its existence to literature. Literary and critical theory, however, can exist in isolation, as they did in the 1960s and afterwards. But a question arises here: if it (theory) does not help in going even an inch closer to our understanding of literary text and its world, is it of any use?

Criticism is knowledge. It is knowledge about things through literature. As knowledge, criticism is different from other forms of knowledge. It uses the same medium that had gone in the making of literature but with the difference that literature uses language for understanding things by making non-referential use of language and thereby ostensibly unmaking sense; whereas critical discourse makes referential use of language. They are different in terms of functions: as the primary function of literature is pleasure and of criticism, knowledge; and whatsoever else is subordinate to it. Writers and critics of inordinate proficiency challenge the systems in which they operate and in the process expose their limitations. The scandalization of the system brings the best out of the human creativity, as all good creative writers have had critical sense, and good critics, at their best, if not always, made the most creative use of language in reaching out to meanings lying underneath the web of words.

Criticism is knowledge which is the relationship between the knower and the object to be known through the knowing faculty or mind, i.e. the thing known, or what he knows in the present case literary work or imaginative representation of things in it. The knower (critic) establishes relationship between her/himself and the object in a certain way. In this manner s/he examines the relationship between the writer, i.e. the knower, and the object, i.e. things, and the way this relationship is established. Propositions about things as they are, are known as truth, and if they are attested by many or all, become facts.

Let me now turn attention to the issue of critical faculty. Like the instincts of imitation and music, seeking harmony of things, sounds, colours, physical movements, and arrangements, the instinct of criticism comes naturally to human beings. What is to be imitated, and how it is to be imitated in terms of modes, manner, and even matter, is judged and decided in terms of one's capabilities and predilections, though the system building and methodology required for critical discourse are not developed at the stage in all beings equally.

Imitation is a natural human instinct, and so is the instinct of judgement. Human beings love to judge others, for it satisfies two basic human instincts — (i) of jealousy (though Bharatamuni did not include it directly in his discussion of *rasa* in the *Nāṭyaśāstra,* as he considered it in the category of *sañcārī bhāva* or transient emotions), and (ii) of power either by controlling directly or indirectly; by knowing the true measure of things through comparison. For that matter, all of us are critics in the original Greek sense of the term *kṛtikośa,* i.e. to judge, as human beings pass judgements in all spheres of life. To judge is to exercise power on others.

To extend the answer to above question further would almost lead to the question as to why people write at all. At the root of all human activity is the instinct of desire. At the root of all desires is *ātma-prema* (self-love) that is the cause of ego or to use a proper word *ahaṁkāra* i.e. *ahaṁ* + *kāra* = form or extension of ego, or *ahaṁ* + *kāra* = the cause of egoism.[2] The genetic endowment of self-love is the cause of instinct of survival, and ambition to excel others. When the ambition exceeds moderation, it leads to destruction of the self and others, the victims of the ambitious self. Whatever supports the fulfilment of desire and is not contrary to it (*anukūla*) gives happiness. Its opposite becomes the cause of absence of happiness, for *duḥkha* is the absence of *sukha*. The fulfilled desires lead to pride and inflation of ego, and thus the cycle goes on. With the exception of *bhaktas* or devotional poets, it is applicable to all forms of human art and critical activity with the stress on the fact that the latter is more egocentric than the former.

A critic's association with the act of judging brings in the element of responsibility. S/he has to consider all evidences, as revealed in the text, and reject or accept the preceding judgement on the text with proper substantiation. The power associated or at times as perceived by others is in fact weighed down by responsibility and 'responsability'.

Critics play their roles according to their ability to perform the task properly or manipulate by joining or making a group or association. Some people come to criticism with a certain role in their mind and they end up becoming something else. Certain

---

2. *Ahaṁkāra* is always not a negative term. As a technical term in Sāṁkhya, it means a principle of individuation. More than egoism, it indicates the consciousness of being distinct. In that sense, all inanimate five *mahābhūtas*, semi-conscious vegetation, and animate beings have *ahaṁkāra*. Besides *ahaṁkāra* is the substratum of *mahat* which cases *tamas* → *moha* → *mahāmoha* → *tamisra* → *andha tamisra*. In *Yoga-Sūtra* these five stages are recognized with a little difference as *avidyā, asmita, rāga, dveṣa,* and *abhiveṣa*.

roles or tags are attached to them. The roles that a person (critic here) plays and the way s/he behaves exposes different aspects of his individual self. In another context, Gajanan Madhav Muktibodh deals with different roles of a critic/writer as a king, judge, watch keeper (*praharī*), danseuse (*nartakī*), seer (*ṛṣi*), learned seer (*maharṣi*), revolutionary, world teacher (*jagatguru*), scientific experimenter, nation builder, and cultural elite (*sāṁskṛtik bhama sajjana*) (Muktibodh 1985: 10-19). The moment a critic begins to speak or write, s/he indulges in harangue after decking her/himself with the crown of a critic on her/his head holding the sceptre of truth in her/his hands. The fact is that all these roles are false, as s/he is true to none in the pursuit of power. The language or idiom that s/he has learnt, nay, mugged up, or acquired is recycled for all purposes. At times the language of criticism becomes so codified that it is understood and spoken by a minuscule minority of subscribers or members of a particular group. It becomes a language of thieves, used and spoken by thieves and understood by thieves only.

Different critics play different roles in different times. At times s/he is subservient to the author, as s/he follows the author or the work that s/he needs as stimulus. In another role, s/he becomes equal to a creative writer, as s/he interprets or creates meanings out of the text. S/he acts as precursor, as s/he prepares context for the text's reception. And the travesty of situation at times is that s/he becomes superior to a creative writer. S/he goes to the temple of the goddess of literary creativity as a devotee for the purpose of worshipping it but finding the temple dirty s/he begins to sweep it. So while some become priests in the temple of the goddess of learning, others become sweepers or both. Some might find that there is no idol in the temple and become one or replace the idol.

The moot question here is, do we need someone to explain a work of art? The answer to the question would depend on as to who asks the question and what is the location of the person. The critics would certainly need an answer to this question for establishing the validity of their existence. But if we need someone else to explain a work of art to us, who could be better than the artist him/herself? The fact, however, is that even if an artist explains a work of art, she/he would speak more for her/himself or about her/his poetic process than about the work. But it is not necessary that the writer by the very design or action is the best reader or critic of his/her own work. By doing so, she/he might re-write the work than explain it because she/he has already explained or interpreted her/his idea or experience in a given time and space. Only pretentious writers would lay claim to their ability to explain their creations. They would at best become translators — bad or otherwise, as in case of Gurudev Rabindranath Tagore's translation of his *Gītāñjalī*. Though he translated his *Gītāñjalī* from Bengali to English, the fact is that his *Gītāñjalī* in English is more than mere translation, as it is almost a new text for which the source text acted as a motor of creation. With the change in time and space, the writer does not remain the same. So though the principal thematic pre-occupations of the writer remain the same, the articulation and its orientation would be different. Moreover, the target readership also conditions the work. The *Gītāñjalī* for the Bengali and its translated version for English readership would affect the language and the use of literary devices like symbols, images, metaphors, and myths. Moreover, the concerned writer/critic/translator has to knowingly or otherwise foreground his critical faculty and subordinate his/her creative faculty to it.

What is the real issue in creative and critical discourses? The real issue in writing — creative or critical — is as to what a discourse tries to do or achieve. The writer imaginatively represents reality or things not as they are or appear to be but the way he sees them, and the way s/he employs the manner and medium of articulation. The issue, however, is not as simple as might appear to be on the surface. The writer does not represent things in his work; rather s/he represents his experience of things. One has to go a step further and state that at the point of articulation one represents experience of the experience which turns out to be his/her interpretation of experience. The interpretation is to a good measure conditioned by consciousness of the writer or by the ideology of the author, choice of form, nature of language, and processes and institutions of production.

The issue of location of criticism is equally significant, for it determines the orientation of criticism and the attitude of the critic towards the object of criticism. It matters because a critic is a human being who changes with change in his location, as it denotes change in temporal and spatial terms. Along with them matters the way a critic establishes relationship with things around him, and the way s/he keeps himself in and around the centre of things. His attitudes and motives become prime factors in critical enterprise. The location may be local (nativistic) or global (metro), though one must bear in mind the distinction between local, nativistic, and indigenous. Since the critic frequently shuffles at least physically, if not mentally or intellectually between the local and global, his perception gets hybridized with hybrid location. Hybridization is no issue; purity is a myth, hybridity a reality, and there is nothing like sacred or profane in Indian view, as it is often made out.

However, there emerge two perceptions — 'global+local' and 'local+global' in an age of their convergence. Both terms have their hierarchy, as the former prioritizes global and the latter local. Given a choice I would prefer the latter to former, for it brings local in the centre of discourse at least in principle. The fact of the matter is that local is real and global or universal parasitic, as it (metro/city/global) thrives by sapping the life force of non-metro, non-city, and non-global local; and under the pretext of achieving convergence between the two, the former strives to convert the latter into its image.

Criticism often tends to become a burden. It is so because it is associated with scholarship that creates a body of jargonsome words and tends to take recourse to its use as a matter of habit or convenience. Thus, a heavily codified world of language of 'thieves' comes into existence. Such critical scholars indulge in verbicide and instead of making sense out of unmaking of sense further unmake it. Such scholars talk only to ghosts and that is the fate of critics too. In his *Hamlet,* Shakespeare makes this point in the conversation between the uneducated soldiers and Horatio, the scholar. On seeing the ghost they ask Horatio, 'Talk to him, Horatio.' The ghosts are selective in appearance and often speak in dead classical languages that remain beyond the comprehension of common people. Criticism thus unconcerned with literature and life of people meets the same fate of ghosts.

Criticism is concerned with life and the way it is represented in literature. A writer can focus on the object of imitation; however, a critic keeps one eye on the object of imitation and the other on the way it is represented in the literary work. This concern brings the issue of commitment in its fold. What should be the commitment of criticism? In the case of literature, its worth lies in its commitment and ability to stand with and by all those who have been victims and spurned by the centre of power or configuration of circumstances. Some might call it 'ideology,' while for others it might be an issue of basic orientation of the discourse. Commitment, however, is best articulated when unstated like affection whose public demonstration leads to vulgarity. One of the best examples might be seen in Kālidāsa's *Raghuvaṁśam* in which King Dilip serves the cow Nandinī, the daughter of Kāmadhenu, for being blessed with a son. The king served the cow by following it like its shadow. The king's service or commitment is performed without any exhibitionism or even knowledge of the object of the service. But his basic objective is served. In the end the cow would be pleased. Against the king's commitment, what and where is the commitment of Nandinī, the cow? Nandinī's commitment is neither to the king nor to his power. Not even to the outcome of the king's service, i.e. an heir for him. Her commitment is towards her own calf. Her existence is primarily for the calf so much so that whatever she eats and drinks is converted into milk or food for nurturing the calf. Dilip is a critic who despite all powers cannot have an issue without the service of the cow which is a trope for literature. Literature is committed not to the critic but to its own issues that sustain it and its subsequent discursive practices including criticism by which it resists falsehood or non-truths lest they get established as truth or true truths. And the final word not to be forgotten by a critic is that a poet or a writer has 'poetic licence,' but s/he has no 'critical licence.'

II

Let me spare some space exclusively for literature, as the preceding dovetailing of critical and literary interaction centred more on criticism and less around literature.

Literature as a system of signs is science and a source of knowledge which is different from other systems of knowledge like: social sciences or pure sciences, as it employs the medium of language differently; and the principal purpose of literary discourse is pleasure to which knowledge is subordinate. It is however about seeing and articulating pattern or harmony in things that might on the surface appear chaotic. Criticism is realizing this pattern lying camouflaged underneath a heap of words in a system called literature.

Is literature an art or science? If it is an art, its literariness depends on its ability to suggest and attract the attention towards it through de-familiarization and distinct/marked use of language. It does not state the whole but suggests a part what it proposes to portray. By dealing with half a village, for instance, Hindi novelist Rahi Masoom Raza in his *Ādhā Gāon* portrayed whole of the village and used it as a trope for the Indian subcontinent and metaphorized the vivisected psyche of humanity. Its artisticness lies in its ability to transcend the self, deal with a part and contain the whole in it through suggestion.

The function of literature deserves some attention. It is commonplace to hear that literature is the mirror of the society. The concern that literature mirrors society is associated with the function of literature that formed the basis of mimetic theory of literature and the anxiety of authenticity. The position is based on the assumption that the mirroring is an innocent activity. It is not so because the mirror is not innocent. This can best be understood by visiting a mirror house. Reflection depends on the quality of mirror. If the mirror is dirty or clean, so would be the reflection. Also the kind of mirror determines the quality of reflection. The fact may be ascertained by a visit to a mirror house. And an equally important question here is: who holds the mirror? Rather who manufactures the mirror?

It is at times said that literature is not just a mirror of the society but a lamp as well. It is an old argument re-worded through the metaphor highlighting the instructive aspect of literature. But the lamp imparts light but does not control light. Its light is conditioned by innumerable factors. It would depend on hands holding it or on the location of the lamp. Its duration depends on the quantity of fuel in it.

Literature deserves a few words about its consequentiality. With the extension of meaning of literature and currency of the term 'writing' in place of literature and arbitrariness of the values as such, the very question regarding the value or relevance of literature has become redundant. However, even the relevance of irrelevance interests human mind. The *mūlya* (value) of literature can best be understood by knowing the *mūla* (root) of literature. The *mūlatva* (rootness, non-rootedness) of literature lies in its ability to please for long, to sustain life and subscribe to its values which are of utmost significance to it. Literature divorced from life and its values has no value or significance. This issue can be understood by asking the question as to with whom does literature stand? The production of literature in the present context might give the impression that the publishing houses control the writing. They do so, as can be discerned in the present when publishing houses decide what should be published, and as a consequence fiction, not poetry, finds favour with publishers. Word even after being produced or manufactured is received under the conditions and forces shaped by those who control process of production of literary discourse. However, it cannot be discounted that word is manufactured in no rich person's factory but in a heart or mind or both on which even the concerned person has modest control. So the relevance of word lies in response to: with whom it stands and for what. Does it stand for the poor, suppressed, exploited and wretched of the society with whom no one stands? Its voice is of some consequence if it employs its art and devices to speak with and for the voiceless. It disturbs none other than the perpetuators of violence — physical, psychological or verbal. Else it courts the risk of being at best an instrument of an individual's flights of fancy and at worst as the stooge of the power. The hype created around literature that it can bring about revolution is misplaced, for it can at best supplement the revolution, not cause or sustain it. Like all art forms, literature is a *bhāvamaya jagat* (a world full of emotions) whose duration is limited, for fretful realities of life puncture it soon after one would step out of it. The fact of life is that one cannot afford to be in this world of *bhāvamaya* for ever.

The whole process can be understood by metaphorizing it in terms of a sugar cane. The farmer prepares the field for the plantation of sugar cane. The farmer cannot produce water or soil or sun rays. S/he uses them as they are received by him/her. The plant makes juice out of it as it grows but this juice is the *sattva* or essence of soil, water and other elements of nature. The farmer relishes its growth and juice thereafter. So do others who have capacity to peel and squeeze juice out of the plant. The field is the context, the sugar cane the text or art, the farmer an artist or poet, and others are critics or *rasika*s who receive the cane and make others enjoy and appreciate it. The *rasa* is the beauty of the plant. The plant in its external appearance is beautiful but its real beauty lies hidden in the plant. Without the reception of the *rasika*, however, the plant and its *rasa* would dry up unnoticed in the field.

These proposals about literary and critical discourses would, it is expected, help in entering and thereafter meandering in the world and processes of literature, criticism and aesthetics in India.

Part I

Word, World and Perception

1

Word and Beyond

Questions of Meaning and Interpretation

> When, Lord of our prayer! The first of Speech, and the foremost, the sages uttered, giving the unnamed a name, which was their best, and their most stainless, when they with love revealed the divine secret in their souls. Where the sages formed the Speech with their mind, straining it as they strain flour with the sieve, therein have friends discovered bonds of friendship, whose holy beauty lies hidden in that Speech.
>
> With worship they followed the steps of the Speech and found it installed in the hearts of sages. They acquired it and gave it at many places, and seven singers intone it together.
>
> — *R̥gveda* X.71.1-3

In the beginning was the word. The pre-word world was not a world, for it was unnamed and whatever is unnamed remains unknown because knowing demands naming. Naming needs words to capture experience or the object of experience either through sense or speculative instruments. The world comes into existence with the word, the most sophisticated of all speculative instruments ever invented by human beings. As Bhartr̥hari, the philosopher-king, remarked, *sarvam śabden bhāṣate*, we take cognizance of the world with the word. The *sphoṭa* of the word, the means of cognizance, and formation of the world, took place simultaneously.

Word is an image of an idea. It is an immortal living being. It is *śabda* and *akṣara*, i.e. non-eroding or beyond erosion. Being an image of the idea the word is an interpretation of the idea. Word interprets, as it articulates it. That is why all acts of articulation are interpretative in themselves. Literary discourse composed of words is an interpretation of ideas in the author's mind. So what we call interpretation is, in fact, interpretation of an already existing interpretation. Michel Montaigne whose words, "We need to interpret interpretation more than to interpret things," Derrida used as the epigraphical note to his interpretation of Claude Lévi-Strauss' structuralism in "Structure, Sign and Play in the Discourse of the Human Sciences," bears evidence to it (Lodge: 108). The difference between the word as the interpretation of an idea of the author and the word as the interpretation of the interpretation of the idea and of the word is that of the *paddhati* or methodology and attitude (towards) and ideology of the medium, i.e. language of the user at the levels of articulators and receivers.

Śabda (sound or word) is *khaga* (*kh* = sky or space; *ga* = going). After being spoken it becomes a part of the sky, and it stays there as a part of it. Of three kinds of actions — mental, verbal and actual or physical — it is a verbal action, though there is nothing like purely verbal, mental or actual action because all actions involve their other counterparts in smaller or larger measure. Once one gets tuned to it, one receives it. Depending upon appropriate frequency and wavelength, word descends on its recipients.

Word, as a living being, is either dormant or in motion or at times in hibernation. When in motion, it moves either vertically or horizontally or both. When word moves vertically, like a seed in motion that unseeds itself to become a plant, it is poetry. When it moves horizontally, it is narrative. If the narrative is short, it is short story, and if long, it is epic (in verse) or novel (in prose). (There is always some space for exceptions like *Eugene Onegin* or *The Golden Gate*.) To carry the analogy further, it can be said that the novel is a river and the epic an ocean. Further, prose or verse narratives can have vertical and horizontal movements simultaneously in certain works. The motion of word(s) in terms of matter and manner demands its interpretation(s).[1]

1. The Sanskrit grammarians focused on *śabda* (word) and then on sentence as the units of interpretation. The Sanskrit rhetoricians realized the need for an →

II

Criticism is more about asking pertinent questions and less about answering questions because in human existence, only questions are eternal. All answers are provisional. However, if there are some who are convinced and pronounce that they have found eternal answers, they are gods or prophets. True criticism has no space either for them or their devotees, as it begins with questions and ends with questions. Like the *śara-śayyā* (bed of arrows), it is *praśna-śayyā* (bed of questions) with the difference that the *śara-śayyā* was only for Bhīṣma, but the *praśna-śayyā* is for all — the text, the author and reader-critic as well.

→ explicitly formulated theory of language for meaning as a base for the theory of poetics. Throughout the development of Indian linguistic thought the relationship between word and sentence, between word-meaning and sentence-meaning, remains a central problem.

Most of the serious discussions of meaning confined themselves to a relatively small portion or unit of language or language behaviour: namely statements to describe or report a state of affairs in the proposition of the natural sciences or statements, as are traditionally handled by logic. For the sake of brevity, it would be better for me to give the gist of discussion of Indian theory of meaning by John Brough from his piece "Some Indian Theories of Meaning."

"A sentence is *nirākāṁṣam*": something which has no requirement or expectation of words outside itself to complete its meaning. Half a sentence was a collection of words possessing *ākāṁkṣā*, *yogyatā* and *āsatti*. In effect, however, it is only the first, which is of real linguistic importance. It is the desire or requirement of an individual word or words in the sentence for others to complete the meaning, the factor that distinguishes a sentence from a string of words: cow, horse, and elephant. The second factor, *yogyatā*, really involves judgement on the truth or falsity of a statement or the sense or nonsense of a sentence. (Examples: "He wets it with fire" or "the round square"). The third condition *āsatti* or *samādhi* is that the word should be contiguous in time.

Of the two schools of the later Mimāṁsā (i) the Bhāṭṭa School which considered that words have meaning in them, and as the words are uttered, the words perform their own task of explaining their meaning, and the sentence is the summation of their meaning, and (ii) the Prābhākara School, more sophisticated than the former, proposed that the individual words did not explain any meaning until they were united together into a sentence.

→

Coming to the issue of interpretation, let me state that I have also been concerned with the question of the hegemony of the Western/American modes of interpretation, as it perpetuates the tradition that perceives the West as the donor and the rest of the world as the receiver. After the Second World War, one notices that the centre of creativity shifted to the so-called Third World in the absence of any 'great' moving communal/continental experience. This is discernible in the fact that most of the literary awards, though they hardly are the criteria for judging the true worth of a literary work, in the post-Second World War have gone to the people from the Third World. The West, in such a situation, sought to "control" the creativity of the Third World with its theory. Among other reasons, it accounts for the ascendence of theory and its growth as a separate discipline in the West in the 1960s and after.

The West gleefully said to the non-West, "O.K. You have creativity. But we have yardsticks for measuring you, for you cannot do so yourselves." And the Indian academia, barring a few exceptions, in the so-called post-colonial period genuflected to theories and 'isms.' This is/was the base of Western theoretical imperialism. This imperialism flourished, and still does so, for it pre-empts its criticism, constructs its response in advance, and

---

→ The utmost that can be said of a sentence, according to Bhartṛhari, is that it is grasped by *pratibhā* (an instantaneous flash of insight) (*Vākyapadīya* II.151-52).

Here, the role of word and word-potency and its division as *abhidhā* (primary or literal meaning), *lakṣaṇā* (transferred or metaphorical sense of words), and *vyañjanā* (the capacity to imply or reveal a meaning other than the literal meaning) also come into consideration.

Ignoring these aspects in Bhartṛhari and Ānandavardhana, the term *artha* (meaning) was later enlarged to include all that was conveyed by a poetic work, for instance the *rasa* (414-21).

It would be congruous to mention here that I. A. Richards was among the few English critics who came close to such a study when he asked the readers in *Principles of Literary Criticism*, "What does this sentence do?" instead of "What does this sentence mean?", for according to him a text is made in the act of reading.

→

spares some space for other voices. And if nothing works then it co-opts compelling voices like Edward Said, Homi Bhabha or Gayatri Chakravorty Spivak who are ingenious enough to justify whatever they do or say. The Western/American theory is the handmaid of Western/American intellectual imperialism. Let me mention here that I have no hesitation in accepting the virtues of its disciplinary rigour, but its hegemony ignores other existing traditions and kills the possibility of other alternatives. In India, we have committed intellectual suicide by linking Sanskrit, the principal culture bearing language of India for more than three millennia to a caste. And in the process of rejecting the caste, we abandoned the most unparalleled reservoir of knowledge systems. What an irony that when nineteenth-century Europe raved about Indian knowledge systems and revolutionized itself through them, we were either inveigled upon or compelled to drive these knowledge systems out of our own mainstream education system. Despite being an oral tradition, the manuscripts in Sanskrit exceed those in Greek and Latin combined, by a large number.[2]

The moot question then is: Could such a rich tradition of diverse knowledge systems with so many manuscripts in all Indian languages particularly Sanskrit as the language of learned composition have survived and continued without theories of interpretation and a well-defined methodology? Certainly not! Credit must be given to the Western academic and theoretical industry for establishing its supremacy, currency and consequent acceptance in such a manner outside its shores that we have been convinced about the non-existence of our own traditions. To know more about it we will go a little closer to the indigenous traditions with the help and guidance of our distinguished predecessors. Neither terms, nor categories, nor idiom is mine in whatever I say on the issue. All I say is what I have learnt from others and what is already there in the tradition. Quite a few distinguished

2. The statement is not a figment of my imagination. For verification please refer to Peter Scharf, "Preface," *Rāmopākhyāna, The Story of Rāma in the Mahābhārata: An Independent-study Reader in Sanskrit* (London: Routledge, 2003), ix.

scholars have worked on this particular aspect, as the references will indicate.

Indian intellectual knowledge systems, unlike its counterparts elsewhere, were unique in constructing their discourse by the *pūrva-pakṣa* without whose cognizance the *pakṣa* or *uttara-pakṣa* was inconceivable.[3] The congnition of *pūrva-pakṣa* did not mean mentioning page number(s) and publication details, for its need did not arise. It became part of the argument, and all those initiated, interested and participated in it knew it. Those without *pātratā* (competence) or who did not have access to it had no right or qualification to participate in the process. For example, as a student of literature I have no right to intervene in the debate pertaining to nuclear physics, for I lack *pātratā,* as I do not have knowledge either of physics or of the *pūrva-pakṣa* of the topic of debate.

However, the Indian tradition valued interpretation. And no civilization has more varied and powerful traditions of interpretations as the Indian. However, it did not consider interpretation as the core concern of literary discourse. Its primary *prayojana* (objective) was *rasāsvādana* (relish). But no one was ever prevented from inferring theories of interpretations of literature from theories of interpreting reality in *darśana* (philosophy). By considering some of the theories of interpretation in Indian tradition, it shall be possible for us to see its richness, relevance and the possibility of inferring a methodology of interpretation.

In the Indian tradition the *puruṣārtha catuṣṭaya,* i.e. the four *puruṣārtha*s called *dharma* (righteous conduct), *artha* (material well-being), *kāma* (gratification of desires), and *mokṣa* (emancipation from the cause of sorrow) form the core of all human endeavours including literary discourse. In other words, critical pursuit or interpretation of literary discourse should also have these objectives. (This is not a religious business or organized religion but it does not exclude worship as a part of life because the Indian tradition looks at life holistically, not in compartments.) As regards

3. For discussion of the term *siddhānta,* please see footnote no. 1 of "Continuity and Change in Indian Critical Tradition" in the book.

an individual's conduct in life, there are three guiding paths in life: *karma* (action), *upāsanā* (worship in general sense), and *jñāna* (knowledge). The last is superior to all, yet *dharma* is the super-ordinate principle of life and it determines the validity and value of knowledge and conduct. The Indian mind accorded sanctity to properly acquired valid knowledge. The confluence of *jñāna* and *dharma* led to the scholarly pursuit of interpretation and its system as Darśana or Mīmāṁsā that can be traced in the third century BCE to Jaiminī's *Mīmāṁsā-Sūtra*. The interpretative pursuit included determining and explaining the meaning of the text; establishing the relevance and significance of, and sometimes to amend, the rules of conduct or the thesis of a Śāstra, whatever is applicable, in cases where they grow out of tune with either the usage or the knowledge of the time; and articulating the rationale or/and rationality of the assertions to defend against counter philosophies or objections. Various types of discourses existing in ancient India were interpreted differently. For instance, the interpretations of Śrutis dealt with metaphysical questions leading to the emergence of different philosophical schools. The Smṛtis or sociological texts and their interpretations were concerned with framing and modulating the rules of conduct in accordance with time and place. The interpretation of the Śāstras dealt with the rigorous determination of the meaning of words, sentences and their referential domains. And the interpretation of *kāvya* concerned itself with the problem of indirect language.

The tradition of interpretation branched out in the various forms as annotations, paraphrase, elaboration/elucidation and exposition or *vyākhyāna*. (At times an altogether new text was born out of a section from the original, e.g. the Upaniṣad.) The first four came to be called *ṭīkā* (commentary) and its different schools came into existence in the course of time. In the cumulative tradition of *ṭīkā* each succeeding *ṭīkā* took note of all preceding *ṭīkā*s. These *ṭīkā*s were either interlaced (interpreting and building meaning of the object text from within a single school of thought) or chronologically sequential *ṭīkā* considering the preceding commentaries but differing in their basic assertions from each other in some ontological categories and epistemologically in the relative ordering of the means of knowledge. Jaiminī's *Mīmāṁsā-Sūtra* and Pāṇini's *Aṣṭādhyāyī*, 'the greatest monument of human intelligence', are the prime examples of diverse texts in the *ṭīkā paramparā* and also of methodology in the tradition.

Different types of *ṭīkā*s included *vṛtti* that analyses the rules and explains their operations and their domain, and comments on the rule bringing out their implicit contents. They together constitute *vyākhyā* or explanation that is close to *vārttika*, e.g. Kātyāyana's *Vārttika*s. The *vyākhyā*, when expanded, in the Pāṇinian school becomes *bhāṣya*, e.g. *Śābara-bhāṣya*. The *Śabara-bhāṣya* is divided into *adhikaraṇa*s (topic-divisions) and each *adhikaraṇa* is further given head-notes. Each *adhikaraṇa* is logically explained and discussed for and against the author's view. Further, he has given lucid and copious notes on each *sūtra*.

These categories and definitions were re-arranged and modified in the course of time. In his *Kāvyamīmāṁsā*, Rājaśekhara enlists eight kinds of commentaries: the commentary that explains the ideational contents of *sūtra* is called *vṛtti*; analysis of a *vṛtti* is *paddhati*; *bhāṣya* is a detailed analysis that takes into account the possible arguments and counter-arguments; *samīkṣā* is an explanation of intended and implicit issues in a *bhāṣya* analysis; *ṭīkā* is mere indication of meaning in the simplest and briefest language; *pañjikā* is an explanation of difficult words; *kārikā* is a brief statement of the meaning of a *sūtra*; and *vārttika* is an analysis of the unexpressed or suggested meanings and implication of a *sūtra*.

Leaving the types of interpretation, let me move to the core concern of interpretation. Interpretation is concerned with meaning — determining it and establishing its rationality. The whole endeavour of *vyākhyāna* pertains to *arthanirdhāraṇa* (determination of meaning). The *artha* is of two kinds: *yathārtha* (meaning as it is), and *tattvārtha* (the significance or purport). The interpreter has to establish both kinds of meanings. To achieve this, he has to bring in *prasaṅga* (context) as an instrument of exegesis along with other instruments like grammar, metarules, evidence, etymology, metaphysics, and symbolic nature of language. (For the study of the symbolics of meaning please refer to the ninth-century Indian poetician Ānandavardhana.) However, it is not easy to determine the *yathārtha*, for texts make varied use of figurative language, and the use of recurrent symbols is difficult to decipher. The old texts may use archaic language and the ideas involved may be abstract making the meaning esoteric, as Shrimant Anirvan has remarked:

> In all such cases when the *yathārtha* has been stated and we find that it does not make sense, it is the "suggestion that lies behind it" that is exclusive, and when the nature of experience or ideas that have been expressed are metaphysical or mystic — as is the case with the Vedas for example — "we need canons of interpretation (other) than mere intellectual ones." — 312

After establishing the *yathārtha*, the interpreter shifts his attention to *tattvārtha*, an interpretative exercise in which s/he uncovers deeper layers of purport or meanings by invoking the multiple complex context(s) existing in the text. Thus, the *arthanirdhāraṇa* consists of the *explication* of a clearly worded statement, focusing on particular lexical use, if necessary; *establishment* of the meaning of a seemingly clear or of a multivalent statement; and *determination* of the symbolical meaning of a transparent statement.

Moving further in our endeavour of alternative methodology or *śodha-paddhati*, we can take recourse to *śāstra-paddhati*, a universally accepted method of reading texts.

For centuries there existed simultaneously as well as relatively, two traditions of interpretation in India — (i) *loka-paddhati* (the popular tradition), and (ii) *śāstra-paddhati* (the learned tradition). The former existed, and still does rather more vigorously with the advent of electronic media particularly channels, in the form of *kathā* (narration of stories with commentary from/on a text like the *Rāmacaritamānasa* or the *Bhāgavata–Saptāha–Kathā* (*kathā* organized for a week), *akhaṇḍapāṭha* (continuous recitation of a text) and *pravacana* (lecture with elucidation from the learned tradition).

The *śāstra-paddhati*, referred sporadically, needs to be inferred and constructed. From references available in different texts, it can be seen as having four parts: (i) the formal organization of the discourse in terms of *prakaraṇa* and *adhikaraṇa*, (ii) the logical mode of discussion and argument or *tarka-paddhati*, (iii) *pramāṇa*s and epistemologies including the nature of evidence(s), and (iv) strategies or instruments of interpretation or *upakaraṇa*. The learned tradition strives to determine the meaning of the text in accordance with the accepted *paddhati* or method in shared metalanguage. It puts a certain premium on the interpreter, as s/he has to be an *adhikārī* or be equipped with the *adhikāra* or competence to interpret. For Anirvan, it is "a process of saturation, resulting in *participation mystique*" that "must set in before the eyes are ready to see and the mind to grasp" (326). This "process of saturation" demands acquiring all related and relevant knowledge because no decision can be taken by studying just one domain of knowledge, as Suśruta, in his *Suśruta Saṁhitā*, a treatise of medicine, states, *ekamśāstram adhīyāno na vidya śāstra niscayam."* ('Sūtrasthāna', Prabhāṣnīya Adhyāya IV, śloka 7). "One should not reach any conclusion by studying just one *śāstra* or discipline or domain of knowledge." Rājaśekhara, the ninth-century poetician, in the second chapter "Śāstranirdeśaḥ" of his *Kāvyamīmāṁsā*, drew the boundaries of this universe of knowledge that included the four Vedas — *Ṛgveda* (study of scriptures), *Yajurveda* (study of various *yajña*/practices), *Sāmaveda* (devotional cults based on music), and *Atharvaveda* (source-book of worldly knowledge); the five Upa-Vedas or sub-Vedas — Itihāsaveda (historical narratives), Dhanurveda (science of archery then, now military science), Gandharvaveda (science of fine arts), Āyurveda (medicine and surgery in common usage but in reality "science of life"), Gānaveda (singing and music); seven auxiliary sciences/disciplines or Upāṅgas — Śikṣā (the science of proper articulation and pronunciation of phonetics), Kalpa (rituals), Vyākaraṇa (grammar), Chhandas (the science of prosody or metrics), Jyotiṣa (astrology), Nirukta (etymology or explanation of difficult words particularly from the Vedas) and Alaṁkāraśāstra (rhetoric); and six Vidyās or disciplines —

Vārttāśāstra (in general, study of common usage, and in particular commerce, agriculture and husbandry), Kāmasūtra (erotics), Śilpaśāstra (sculpture, painting and architecture), Arthaśāstra (study of law or polity), Aṇvikṣikī (philosophical disputations) and Sāhityavidyā (poetics or study of literary discourse). Further, Aṇvikṣikī is of two kinds — Pūrva-pakṣa comprising three philosophical schools, i.e. Cārvāka, Buddhists and Jaina, and Uttara-pakṣa comprising Sāṁkhya (based on numerical discriminative tendencies), Nyāya (Logic), and Vaiśeṣika (Atomic School). These six schools of philosophy are collectively known as Tarka. The arguments on which Tarka relies are of three kinds — *vāda, jalpa* and *vitaṇḍa*. They are respectively 'exposition,' 'disputation adopted to gain victory over the opponent,' and 'fallacious controversy used for finding faults with the opponents of defence.' A learned man has to master all this universe of knowledge, if s/he is to interpret a Śāstra and make a lasting contribution to knowledge. About the nature of Śāstra, Rājaśekhara remarks:

saritāmiva pravāhāstucchāḥ prathamaṁ yathottaraṁ vipulāḥ ।
ye śāstrasamārambhā bhavanti lokasya te vandyāḥ ॥

— *Kāvyamīmāṁsā*, ch. II

Just as rivers are thin and narrow in the beginning and gradually widen, similarly Śāstras are brief and in the passage of time gradually increase in dimension, and are revered by one and all.

A learned scholar's exegetical pursuit of the exegetical literature, i.e. Bhāṣya, Vṛtti, Ṭīkā, Samīkṣā, Pañjikā, Kārikā and Vārttikā, leads to refinement, extension, precision and profundity of knowledge, as was achieved by great Indian minds like Yāska, Pāṇini, Patañjali, Śabara, Kumārila Bhaṭṭa, Ādi Śaṅkarācārya, Rāmānuja and Mādhavācārya among others.

However, keeping the present topic of methodology for literary discourse in view, it is congruous to know Rājaśekhara's views on literature and its interpretation. In the second chapter he defines *sāhityavidyā* or literature as *śabdārthayoarthavatsahabhāven vidyā sāhityavidyā*; 'The literary discourse is a discipline that studies the co-extension of words and meanings.' The Śāstra of literature in particular as a work is organized in different parts or sections. He states that a part of the Śāstra is called a *prakaraṇa* or a subject. The subjects of extrananeous subjects are denoted by means of words like *adhyāya, sarga,* and *pariccheda*. Different *ācāryas* have named them differently, for the texts are constructed differently and they are indescribable as well. It is possible to infer a methodology of constructing or composing a thesis, as one appreciates Rājaśekhara's acceptance of multiplicity of ways and approaches of/to (hypo)theses. He describes the function of his *śāstrakavi* (poetic interpreter) of *śāstra*:

> *bhavati prāthyannartham līnam samābhiplutam sphuṭikurvan* ।
> *alpamanalapam racayannanalpam ca śāstrakavi* ॥

> A *śāstrakavi* is one who expounds the profound meaning of words. He clarifies the difficult discourse, details the brevity of matter and concentrates the detailed exposition.

A word is the core unit of composition; its extension is *pada*, or phrase. Phrases (arranged grammatically) make a sentence, sentences or a paragraph. Paragraphs lead to a chapter, and chapters to a thesis, dissertation, book or text. The stages and attributes of a good thesis are exposition of meaning, clarification of difficult discourse, detailed consideration of the subject matter. However, it would be a gross injustice to the immense contribution of Rājaśekhara to concentrate on a chapter of one of his texts and consider him a research methodologist.

Besides Rājaśekhara, it is possible to find a general pattern for conducting (research) inquiry for an interpreter (researcher) by understanding *vyākhyāna-prakriyā*, a part of *śāstra-paddhati* (*śodha-paddhati* in our case). Interpretation as a self-contained act includes (a) what has already been said by the earlier thinkers of the same school, (b) *matāntara* or the differing opinion or idea, (c) *prasaṅga* or context. It includes in it paraphrase, explanation, example, and counter-example/point. Interpretation necessitates *vivāda* or controversy, but the *śāstra-paddhati* allows only one kind of *kathā*, the *vāda* or controversy at a time. The *vāda-kathā* continues till the truth is reached. On the other hand, *vijigiṣukathā,* i.e. discussion for winning over the opponent, includes *jalpa* and *vitaṇḍa* that have been discussed above. It is used not to ascertain truth but to expose the contrary conviction of the opposite disputant. (Refer to Bagchi (1937: 563-65) for this discussion.) Thus, *vāda* is a well-reasoned controversy, a postulation of a thesis, and a counter-thesis in relation to the object of inquiry. Since contradictory qualities should not exist in the object, an argument follows and continues till the resolution of the contradiction. To quote Bagchi:

> When Indian philosophers write treatise or expound certain truths in the seclusion of their seminaries, even then they present the *prima facie* objections of their opponent (*pūrva-pakṣa*) and meet them. While doing so, they assume the presence of these opponents and invest them with the freedom of advancing contrary arguments. They also assume the presence of neutral persons, give expression to the latter's doubts, and suggest solutions. When an author writes a "treatise, he thus imagines himself to be present in an assembly of the enlightened." — 564

This tradition of *vāda* in the *śāstra-paddhati*, according to Vācaspati Miśra, produces (i) knowledge of unknown truths, (ii) removal of doubts, and (iii) confirmation of previous knowledge (*Nyāyavārttikatātparyaṭīkā* I.2.1).

The structure of argument takes a given logical process. The process or pattern would change from school to school, for example, in the Mīmāṁsā, Buddhist or Nyāya school. The school of Nyāya formulates it as (i) *saṁśaya*, (ii) *hetu-sthāpanā*, (ii) *vyāpti*, (iv) *upanaya*, and (v) *nigamana*. Dealing with them, Bagchi says: ". . . after the presentation of the point at issue, the disputant will take one of the *pakṣa*s and his opponent will take up the other." That is to say, two contrary positions in the *vipratipatti-vākya* will be taken up by them. The disputant after having taken his position, should state the *hetu* (reason or middle term) that is capable of establishing his own position. This is called *sthāpanā*. To do this the disputant has to adduce a fact which is to be 'a case of,' and which has to be in the 'locus' of what is sought to be proved. For instance, when a doubt has been generated by the *vipratipatti-vākya*, 'Is sound non-eternal or not?' the disputant seeking to prove 'non-eternality' will employ the *hetu* 'having an origin.' That which has an origin is called *kr̥taka*. This *hetu* (having an origin) is 'a case of non-eternality' and exists in sound, which has been accepted as the 'locus' of non-eternality. These two facts represent what is called *vyāpti* (invariable concomitance) and *pakṣadharma* (condition of being an attribute to the subject), which constitute the strength of a *hetu*. With the help of these two, the *hetu* establishes what is to be proved (the *sādhya*). That the *hetu* is 'a case of' the *sādhya* has also to be demonstrated and this is to be done by citing instances from experience, as for example, 'whatever has an origin is non-eternal, e.g. a pot.' This example shows that there is an invariable relation of the *sādhya* to the *hetu*. Now a *sādhya* comes to be established in a *pakṣa* (subject of syllogism), if the *hetu* with the *vyāpti* of that *sādhya* is found in that *pakṣa*. The disputant, therefore, will have to employ the *upanaya* (application). This will be done by saying that the *hetu* (here, 'having an origin') with the *vyāpti* of the *sādhya* (here, 'non-eternality') is actually found in the *pakṣa* (here, 'sound'). The disputant will next end with the *nigamana* (conclusion). 'Therefore sound is non-eternal.' The original thesis regarding the non-eternal character of sound is thus established on the grounds of *kr̥takatva*, i.e. 'having an origin,' for the mark *kr̥takatva* establishes *anityatva*, i.e. non-eternality. These statements constitute the five parts (*avayava*) of the comprehensive statement called the *nyāya* (567-68).

This structure of logical disputation is invariably followed, in determining controversial prepositional meetings. Evidently, the syllogistic reasoning in India is different from that of the West: syllogism itself has five parts, as against the three of Aristotelian logic, and more importantly:

> the Indian syllogism is not, as with us (the Western logicians) an affair of pure deduction, but a sequence of inductions and it

> is characteristic of India's practical outlook and its practical conception of proof that not only some positive example, but generally one or more negative examples also, are inserted to demonstrate that *hetu* "is a case of *sādhya*." — Heimann 87

Speaking of the significance of the traditions of *śāstra-paddhati*, Heimann continues,

> . . . their importance arises from their applicability and use . . . from the earliest period of Indian thought discussion has been considered the most effective of all means of scientific research. — 89

Apart from the mode of discussion, the *śāstra-paddhati* deals with the structuring of argument as well, discernible as it is in the formal textual divisions — (a) *viṣaya* (subject matter), (b) *samasyā* (doubt arising in relation to the matter), (c) *pūrva-pakṣa* (the point of the opponent), (d) *uttara* (demonstration of the validity of that standpoint), and *siddhānta* and *nirṇaya* (demonstration of the validity of the standpoint being upheld or accepted and the conclusion). Pandit Ganganath Jha opines that this system of discussion "is adopted, more or less, in all the Sanskrit philosophical systems" (Jha, 1900). It can further be put as (i) *pakṣāntropanyāsa* (explication of the other opinion), (ii) *khaṇḍana* (rejection of the posited opinion), and (iii) *sarvamatasthāpanā* (establishment of the *siddhānta*, the accepted position) or the goal of *yathārthanirdhāraṇa* (determination of meaning as truth).

After the structure of disputation or argument comes the question of *pramāṇa* or evidence. In Indian discourse, *pramāṇa* includes *pratyakṣa* (perception or memories of knowledge acquired through perception), *anumāna* (inference, the secondary measure), *upamāna* (analogy), and *āpta-vacana* (testimony of the texts). (It does not ignore either *abhyāsa* or experience or *antarjñāna* or intuition.) Here, I avoid discussing the ten strategies or instruments of exegesis in the practice of the exegetes. These strategies can be employed as instruments in our interpretations.

Here two questions arise: why is that the mainstream Indian academia is still unaware of its rich Indian traditions of interpretation? And why have the knowledge and practices of those who were/are aware of their traditions not resulted in the currency and supremacy of our interpretative pursuits? If this *paddhati* can effectively and successfully work in case of Śāstras, can it not work in case of *śodha-paddhati* and *praṇālī* that is a mere trickle of the river called *śāstra*?

III

To construct and illustrate my discourse pertaining to interpretation, I would like to take recourse to a narrative or *dṛṣṭānta* (illustration). The narrative pertaining to Kālidāsa is located in Ujjayinī whose king had a daughter named Vidyottamā. As the name speaks for itself, she was *uttama* (par excellence) in *vidyā* (knowledge) and so she made a pledge that she would marry a person who would defeat her in *śāstrārtha* (intellectual disputation). As a consequence, many young suitors came forward and entered into a debate with her. They were, however, no match for her. In the course of time, the number of such defeated disgruntled souls increased. They then got together and decided to teach her a lesson. And the best way to teach her a lesson, they thought, was to get her married to a fool. So all of them set out to find a fool. Perhaps fools were not easily available those days, so it took them a few days. Ultimately they found a person who was hacking the branch of the tree he was sitting on. They immediately came to the conclusion that this was the person they had sought for so long. They requested him to come down and accompany them. They promised him good food, clothes, ornaments and above all a beautiful wife, if he followed their instructions. Since fools too have human weaknesses, he agreed.

Reaching Ujjayinī they informed the king that their *guru* who had been away had come back and wanted to have *śāstrārtha* with the princess who had defeated his students. They asked the king to arrange the *śāstrārtha* at the earliest. However, they had a condition. Since the *guru* was observing the vow of silence or *mauna-vrata*, he would respond only in gestures. To facilitate the communication it would be better that the princess too used gestures to communicate her questions or propositions. The gestures would later be interpreted by a group of scholars to decide the winner. The princess was so confident of her abilities that she agreed.

On the appointed day the *śāstrārtha* was held. On the one hand was Vidyottamā and facing her was the unnamed person whom we can for our convenience call X or the pre-Kālidāsa person. (At least I have not come across the name of the person who later became Kālidāsa). The third group was of the defeated scholars — facing both Vidyottamā and pre-Kālidāsa, for they were to interpret the language of gestures. And then there was the fourth group consisting of the king, the queen, the ministers and the courtiers. Beginning the debate, Vidyottamā raised a finger. Seeing it, pre-Kālidāsa pointed two fingers. Vidyottamā then showed her open palm. Pre-Kālidāsa thought for a while then showed his fist to the princess. The jury declared pre-Kālidāsa victorious.

Now let us examine the layers of interpretation that the signifiers the above text contains, leading to the defeat of the princess. Vidyottamā by raising a finger had proposed that there is nothing but just one *Brahman* (1). Pre-Kālidāsa thought that the princess wanted to blind him in one eye. If she so thinks, he thought, then he would blind her in both the eyes (2). That is why he pointed two fingers. The Jury interpreted the gestures in an altogether different manner. It said that the princess proposed that there is just one *Brahman*. However, our guru says that apart from the *Brahman* there is *jīva* (creature) as well (3). Further, the princess by showing five fingers of her palm proposed that there are five elements in nature (1). Pre-Kālidāsa thought that the princess wanted to slap him. Considering it he proposed that if she wanted to slap him, he would strike her with a punch (2). Interpreting this the jury said that the princess proposed that there are five elements in the nature and that pre-Kālidāsa with the gesture of his fist had on the other hand stated that though it is true that there are five elements, these elements in themselves can do nothing. Creation takes place only when they come together

(3). The jury proved that their *guru* was right and declared him victorious in the debate. As a consequence of the stratagem of the defeated scholars the most intelligent maiden was married to the greatest fool. Vidyottamā was, thus, the first victim of the theory of interpretaion.

Let me now discuss the narrative to make my point.

If gesture is a text, what determines interpretation is context or background that in fact is nothing but foreground because the moment the context comes under discussion, it gets fore-grounded. Apart from the context, the interpreters bring with them pre-texts that exist between the context and the text, including the knowledge of the systems, i.e. languages, literature and criticism, and attitudes and ideologies of their users and receivers. The context and pre-text in combination condition the interpretation. The text in such a situation becomes a pretext to generate an interpretation that has already been decided by torturing signifiers. Or else how do judging scholars conclude that Vidyottamā by pointing a finger or by showing her palm meant that there is only one *Brahman* or there are five elements in nature. It is context and pretext that determine the given interpretation. They know that Vidyottamā, the invincible scholar, would pose only a pregnant proposition such as the present one. Vidyottamā's acceptance of the interpretation validates it. Their contextual and pretextual meanings inform them that in reality pre-Kālidāsa meant that he would have interpreted Vidyottamā's text that she wanted to blind him in one eye. And so in response he constructed his text stating that if she did, so he would fully blind her. What is interpretation for him is in fact a misinterpretation. The jury knows it. But they ignore it knowingly, and using his signifying gestures as a pretext they impose desired interpretations, or fallacious interpretations, for its constructor has no cognizance of these. Since the concerned parties accept it, Vidyottamā by the given context that the teacher of all the scholars would have meant what she has been told, and pre-Kālidāsa had no option, the given misinterpretation emerged as a 'super-text.'

The language of gestures is the art of seeing and that of interpretation. It is an act of theorization as well. Vidyottamā sees her idea, expresses it through the medium of a gesture. She, i.e. her act of seeing, is seen by others, i.e. the *guru* and the jury. Further, she sees her seeing being seen by others. The problem here is that the same text, seen differently by so many, has different interpretations. These interpretations are conditioned by (i) competence and (ii) attitudinal prejudices of their proponents. The interpretation is a case of involuntary misinterpretation caused by incompetence and the interpretation of deliberation (in understanding Vidyottamā's proposition), over-interpretation (in reading the *guru*'s gesture in the way they wanted it), and super-imposition of their intended interpretation, which involves under/over-interpretation. It is so because the scholar-members of the Jury knew what Vidyottamā and pre-Kālidāsa intended to state through their gesture(s), but ignored whatever did not suit their desired conclusion and took whatever was of use for their end of defeating Vidyottamā.[4]

The narrative on the one hand seems implausible because it is not in accordance with the *śāstra-paddhati* in its spirit. On the other hand, the question arises: how could Vidyottamā, who had defeated so many scholars, be fooled by the same people? The discussion accepts multiplicity of interpretations, as many as are

4. Leave aside the case of Vidyottamā, even the goddess of learning Sarasvatī was, if stated rather loosely, a victim of misunderstanding or interpretation as regards Kālidāsa. The extended version of the narrative continues the story that after the marriage, Vidyottamā, once in a fit of anger at some mistake in the pronunciation of a ceratin word, pushed Kālidāsa. He fell down and in the process hurt his tongue with his teeth. Driven out of the house, he could do nothing but shout the name of his wife. Since his tongue was injured, he could not pronounce the name of his wife correctly, and so the sound that came out was similar to Vidyadomā. Sarasvatī went by the phonic similarity of the utterance and thought that Kālidāsa requested her to bestow knowledge upon him (*vidyā* = knowledge, *do* = give, *mā* = mother). In the post-Sanskrit (modern) Hindi version, located in a time when Hindi was not even in existence, suggests that if the goddess of learning is vulnerable to misinterpretation caused by mis-pronunciation, why can't an ordinary being, however intelligent, suffer from it?

the interpreters. The next question then is: Is the multiplicity of interpretations a problem? The problem is with invalid imposed interpretations. Moreover, among all interpretations that come into existence there are some that are more valid than others, leading to a preparation of the hierarchy of interpretations, though this hierarchy is determined to an extent by attitudes, predilections and the competence of interpreters.

The narrative scandalizes Reader Response theory, the theory found (in Meyers Abrams' terms) in 'New Readers' like Harold Bloom, Hillis Miller and Stanley Fish without excluding Jacques Derrida, in the light of Derrida's proposition about the decentring of the centre. The primary function of the centre in Western metaphysics was not only "to orient, balance and organize the structure" but also "to make sure that the organizing principle of the structure would limit what we might call the *play* of the structure" (Derrida, 1988: 109). The inability of the centre to hold itself leads to indeterminacy, unfixity and play. He proves it with his deconstruction of the concept of sign and interpreted structuralism. Apart from writing the manifesto of post-structuralim, Derrida became an apostle of indeterminacy and undecidability of meanings or interpretations, and asked his Derridean followers to celebrate the carnival of indeterminacy of meanings in the Nietzschean manner.

Stanley Fish shared the post-structuralists' enthusiasm for multiplicity of meanings without being a relativist, for he does not think that human mind can on its own either comprehend or apprehend and that all understanding is related to the context, though he does not subscribe to the deconstructionists' rejection of the 'presence' of meaning in a text. Context for Fish is inevitable; and within it every reader, on whom he squarely shifts the responsibility of interpretation, constructs a sentence or text. It, i.e. the context, is almost always the present context (original historical context and authorial intention that determine a readers' choice of interpretative strategies) of what he calls 'the interpretative community.' He shows his faith in 'the interpretative communities' for determining the 'horizons of expectations.' The term 'interpretative communities' becomes a core word in Fish. Ironically, he does not define it clearly.

Singularity of interpretation is as fallacious as indeterminacy or existence of as many interpretations as are interpreters. The Sanskrit poeticians took cognizance of the issue in terms of meaning, its multiplicity (*anekārthatā*) and invalid or faulty meaning (*arthadoṣa*). Ācārya Viśvanātha has this to say about *anekārthatā*:

> *anekārthaśabdasya saṁyogādhyeniyantrite* ।
> *ekārtheanyadhihetuvyañjanasābhidhāśraya* ॥
> — *Sāhitya-Darpaṇa* II.14

With the determination of one particular meaning (other) emergent multiple meanings of words that become inexpressible are revealed with the *vyañjanā*, and not with *abhidhā*. However, it is possible to determine one meaning by taking recourse to the following fifteen ways — *saṁyoga, viprayoga, sāhacarya, virodha, artha, prakaraṇa, liṅga, anyasannidhi, sāmarthya, aucitya, deśa, kāla, vyakti, svara,* and *ceṣṭā.*

Moreover, the validity of meaning can be ascertained by knowing invalid or faulty meanings. In the larger context Bhāmaha discusses the faults of poetic discourse (*kāvya doṣa*s) at the level of text itself. He enumerates them as *apa-artha* (absence of meaning in an incomplete utterance), *vyartha* (vain or contradictory meaning), *ekārtha* (redundancy of meaning), *samasyā* (doubt or unintended ambiguity), *apakrama* (absence of co-related sequence), *śabdahīna* (ungrammatical), *yatibhraṣṭa* (misplaced caesura), *bhinnavratta* (against metre or unmetrical), *visandhika* (absence of coalescence or *Saṁhitā*), *deśavirodhī* (contrary to facts or spirit of space or country), *kālavirodhī* (against the propriety of time or seasons), *kalāvirodhī* (against the facts and principles of art), *lokavirodhī* (against *loka* or common experience), *nyāyavirodhī* (not in conformity with Nyāya or judgement or popular maxims here), and *āgamavirodhī* (in opposition with Dharmaśāstras or sociological texts).

Further, it is possible to control the play of meaning by taking note of *artha-doṣa* (faults pertaining to meaning), as they are discussed in Sanskrit poetics. Mammaṭa in his *Kāvyaprakāśa* (7.55-57) states:

artho 'apuṣṭa kaṣṭo vyahat punarukat-duṣkram-grāmya ।
saṅdigdhonirhetuḥ prasiddhi vidyāviruddhaśca ॥
anavikrat saniyamaniyamaviśeṣaviśeṣaparivr̥ttaḥ ।
śakanśo apayuktaḥ sahacarbhinnāḥ prakiśitviruddhaḥ ॥
vidyānuvādayuktasyaktapunaḥ svīkratoślīlaḥ ।

The twenty-three faults as mentioned above are:

Apuṣṭa: Use of a phrase in whose absence the meaning would not suffer;

Kaṣṭārtha: When meaning is derived with difficulty;

Vyahata: When the object of expression is run down after expressing its significance;

Punarukta: Repetition of a word or phrase repeatedly;

Duṣkramtva: Violation of codes and practices of *śāstra* and *loka*;

Grāmya: Use of uncultured language;

Saṅdigdha: Uncertainty of meaning;

Nirhetutva: Absence of cause;

Prasiddhiviruddhatā: use of a socially unacceptable statement against a school;

Vidyāviruddhatā: Against the discipline of knowledge;

Anavikrata: When multiple meanings are stated in one particular manner leading to absence of uniqueness;

Saniyamparivr̥ttatā: Making a statement without mentioning the concerned fact or principle when it should be mentioned;

Aniyamparivr̥ttatā: Evoking meaning by making a statement with fact or principle when it should not be mentioned;

Viṣeṣaparivr̥ttatā: Stating about an object in general terms when it should be stated in particular terms;

Aviśeṣaparivr̥ttatā: Stating about an object in particular terms when it should be stated in general terms;

Sakaṅśa: When another phrase(s) or word(s) is/are desired for deriving meaning;

Apadayuktatā: Using phrases unnecessarily in an unwanted place;

Sahacarabhinna: Describing sublime and slimy objects and attributes together;

Prakiśtviruddhatā: Emergence of meaning contrary to the metaphorical meaning;

Vidyāyukta: Impropriety of *vidhi* or injunction;

Anuvāda ayukta: When a meaning is replete with some improper or illogical statement;

Tyaktapunaḥsvīkṛta: Starting a subject again after ending it once; and

Aślīla: Statement connoting vulgar or obscene meanings.

Bringing our focus back on the interpretations of the Vidyottamā and pre-Kālidāsa narratives, it becomes evident that the interpretations of gestures by the scholars suffered at least from *prakāśitviruddhatā* and *vidyāyukta*. By choosing gesture as signifier they created *sandigdhatā* or space of indeterminacy and/or doubt about the text generated by pre-Kālidāsa in Vidyottamā's mind. Then they wallowed in a pool of indeterminacy and imposed a pre-determined interpretation on her. For that they reached Vidyottamā's intended meaning and articulated it, and it became easier for them to earn her approval for their mis/over-interpretation of the gestures of pre-Kālidāsa. The irony of the whole discourse pertaining to Vidyottamā and also to *artha-doṣa* is that one comes to know of them only after they have been articulated. Fortunately for us, the Gresham's Law according to which 'bad currency drives good currency out of market' does not apply in literary and critical discourses. Faulty interpretations come into existence and gain currency also for some time, but in the end only valid interpretations sustain themselves in the long run. And that is something critical discourse has to ensure in order to validate the existence of not only literary discourse but also its own.[5]

Moreover, using another category of *kavi* (poet), the constructor of meaning or interpreter of an idea in his work, it is possible to know the nature of a problem. Rājaśekhara in the chapter on *Arthaharaṇam* (Appropriation of Meaning) in *Kāvyamīmāṁsā* speaks of five kinds of poets:

> *Bhrāmaka*: Who give a new twist even to the old familiar material and try to prove it as their own, and thus create confusion in the minds of the people;
>
> *Cumbaka*: Who delicately retouch old material but add their own beauty to it;
>
> *Karkaśa*: Who use their own originality and render old ideas into a new framework;
>
> *Drāvaka*: Who transform the original to such an extent that it is beyond recognition; and
>
> *Cintāmaṇi*: Whose works are imbued with unprecedented originality and inherent faculty of imagination.
>
> — *Kāvyamīmāṁsā*, Chapter XII

These categories can be applied to interpreters as well. From this viewpoint, the scholars of the narrative would fall in the first category of *bhrāmaka* reader-interpreters, for they use the space created by a cluster of signifiers used by pre-Kālidāsa to confuse the victim of the interpretation, i.e. Vidyottamā.

5. I have used the terms "interpretation" and "meaning" almost interchangeably deliberately and out of compulsion. The Indian tradition considered that the primary function of literary discourse was *ānanda* (delight) or *rasāsvādana* (relish) and the eradication of *avidyā* (ignorance), the root cause of suffering, and not interpretation, which is the concern of the discourse of philosophy of language and logic (*darśana, bhāṣāśāstra* and *śāstras*). Therefore, Sanskrit poeticians deliberated upon meaning. However, these schools, their texts and *paddhati* or methodology are so potent and pregnant with potential paradigms that theories of interpretation can be inferred from them. (For further discussion please refer to Kapoor, "Interpretation," *Literary Theory: Indian Conceptual Framework*, 39-43).

Postscript as Conclusion

In our tradition, the *śabda* is called *Brahman*, if *śabda* is *Brahman*, what is beyond *Śabda-brahman*? *Brahman* is non-*Brahman* that is finite. *Brahman*, knowing no other or difference, is infinite. So is Word. Word is infinite. Word is all. All interpretations, present and prospective, are already in existence in it. There is nothing beyond it. Different receivers — individuals and generations in different periods have to go close to it and find interpretations embedded in it.

2

Theory of the Creative Process in Narratives about the Rāmāyaṇa and the Mahābhārata

Mythic Narrative as a Mode of Constituting Knowledge

Who authored the Vedas?
Who composed the *Rāmāyaṇa*?
Who was the author of the *Mahābhārata*?

*R̥ṣi*s "heard" the Vedas.
Ādikavi Vālmīkī composed the *Rāmāyaṇa*.
Veda Vyāsa, the compiler, was the author of the *Mahābhārata*.

THE response to the three questions mentioned above is so commonplace that the very act of posing them may sound ridiculous to many. The answers, however, deal with "cooked" as against "raw" aspects of creativity. The questions and responses emphasize pre-cooked or pre-creative aspects. If we, however, examine them, there are quite a few answers to the questions pertaining to the creative process. *R̥ṣi*s were *dr̥ṣṭā*s (seers) who saw through the inner eyes, heard (*śruti*) the hymns with their inner ears and stored it in their memory (*smr̥ti*). The contemplation and meditation on what was heard and stored in memory led to articulation that took the form of text or Vedic discourse (*kr̥ti*). The paradigm of *śruti, smr̥ti* and *kr̥ti* despite being of some significance for constructing a "formula" of creative process is rather generalized,[1] for the Vedic literature is so dense, snugly woven, esoteric and metaphorical even in its ritualistic discourse that even the best of our hermeneutical endeavours fail to suggest a comprehensive theory of creative process.

Moving ahead one can see the analogy between Yoga and art, particularly in Patañjali's *Yoga-Sūtra*, a text of psychology and education. Yoga is the science of mind and also of *yoga*, i.e. union of mind and body and of making them one. Since mind is the site of creative process, *yoga*, the science of mind, can help in understanding the process. The eight parts of *yoga* can be considered as eight *aṅga*s (limbs or parts) — *yama, niyama, āsana, prāṇāyāma, pratyāhāra, dhyāna, dhāraṇā* and *samādhi* — of creative process (*Yoga-Sūtra*, II: 29). Apart from them, Patañjali writes about removing hindrances to *yoga* by dwelling on knowledge that presents itself in a dream or sleep. The insights, suggestions or knowledge obtained in dreams or sleep underscore the importance attached to instinct, intuition and inspiration by the Indian mind. This is attested by the *Agni Purāṇa*:

> Thou Lord of all gods, teach me in dreams how to carry out all the work, I have in my mind. (chapter 43)

This forms a part of the prayer uttered by the imager or the artist on the night before beginning his work, and after the ceremonial purification. Further it speaks about the significance of meditative aspect of creativity that I propose to take up for discussion later.

---

1. Here, *śruti* and *smṛti* are used in their literal sense, and *kṛti* is added by me for completing the paradigm. It (*smṛti*) is in consonance with the Platonic concept that memory is knowledge. Its echoes might be heard in William Wordsworth's much maligned theory of poetic process in "Preface" to *Lyrical Ballads* (1800). In "Tradition and Individual Talent" T.S. Eliot questioned Wordsworth's theory but Wordsworth's views cannot be rejected altogether. Moreover, Wordsworth's theory might have some resemblance with the Vedaic theory, yet their yoking together suffers from impropriety (*anaucitya*), for there is no evidence of Wordsworth's reading of the Vedaic or Upaniṣadic texts or tradition.

Buddhism in the post-*Rāmāyaṇa* and the post-*Mahābhārata* period received and appropriated the yogic traditions of *dhāraṇā, dhyāna, samādhi* and *saṁśaya,* as may be discerned in Buddha's postures in different art forms, and changed them from within. The imager's or artist's ritual is the Buddhist theory of creation. On the basis of his study of tāntric texts of the twelfth century summarized by M. Foucher in his *Iconographique Bouddhique* (Part II), Ananda K. Coomaraswamy summed it up thus:

> The artist then, or the magician (*sādhaka, mantrin,* or *yogin*) as he is called, is to proceed to a solitary place, after purificatory ablutions, and wearing newly washed garments. There he is to perform the "Seven-fold office" beginning with the invocation of the hosts of Buddha and Bodhisattvas in the open space before him, and the offering to them of real or imaginary flowers, and ending with a dictation of the merit acquired, to the welfare of all beings. Then he has to realize in thought the four infinite qualities (love, compassion, sympathy, same-sightedness). Then he must meditate on the original purity of the first principles of things, and on (what comes to the same thing) their emptiness or obsolete non-existence. "By the fire of the idea of emptiness, it is said, there are destroyed beyond recovery the five elements" which compose the individual consciousness. Only when the personality of the individual is thus set aside is he able to invoke the divinity desired to be represented, and to attain identity with this divinity, which last condition is strictly enjoined. For complete comprehension is only possible when the consciousness is thus identified with an object of cognition. All this takes place in the imagination. The divinity appears "like a reflection" or "as in a dream." Very rarely indeed is any drawing made use of, even in the most complicated conception, where the principal personage is surrounded by disciples in the centre of a *maṇḍala*. It is only when the mental image is thus defined that the artist begins to mould or paint.
>
> — Coomaraswamy, 1981: 52-53

These stages would have become mere ritual, if this "sevenfold office" was followed literally without subscribing to spirit or meaning lying underneath the meatphorical language. Here I must add that the meditative aspect of creation has been stressed in the Indian tradition. Coomaraswamy illustrated it with an example comparing Greek and Indian attitudes towards creation. Since paraphrasing would impair the inherent succinct form, I will quote him:

> We are told that Zeuxis, when commissioned to paint a figure of Helen for the people of Croton, stipulated to be allowed to use as models five of the most beautiful virgins of the city. The Indian artist, on the other hand, would have demanded opportunity for meditation and mental concentration, in order that he might visualize the idea of Helen in his inner consciousness, among discovery rather than creation, desiring rather to draw back the veil from the face of superwoman than to combine visible perfections by a process of intellectual selection. The result would be a work suggesting, more or less perfectly in accordance with his keenness of inner vision and technical capacity for its material embodiment, the real Helen as she lived in the national consciousness, a Helen more real than she who in the flesh brought death and sorrow to the Greek and Trojan heroes.
>
> — Coomaraswamy, 1981: 87

Against the above propositions about creative process in the Vedic, Yogic and Buddhist traditions, one feels surprised about the near absence of any theoretical formulations about the creative process of Vālmīki's *Rāmāyaṇa* and Veda Vyāsa's *Mahābhārata*, the two encyclopaedic patronymic texts, which are amongst the rarest creative treasures of the entire human civilization. It is in no way obligatory on the part of creative writers like Vālmīki and Veda Vyāsa to speak about the process of creation, yet human curiosity loves to peep into the minds of the greatest. But all authors of substance of yore have avoided speaking about theoretical aspects of their creativity. Since there was neither any inclination nor compulsion for it, it has to be deciphered from their works or from the mode of constructing knowledge. To find a tentative answer, one has to investigate different modes of constructing knowledge in the Indian tradition.

Among different ways of construction of knowledge in India

it is the *dṛṣṭānta* or narrative mode more than any other that is employed. In construction of knowledge the perception of time plays a crucial part. The Indian mind perceived time differently, as may be evident in different calendars prevalent in India even now. It, however, subscribed to cyclicity of time. And the culture that subscribes to cyclicity of time, as against linear mode of time, uses mythic narrative mode to construct knowledge. This is the reason why Bharatamuni's *Nāṭyaśāstra* despite being a Śāstra which is supposed to be formulatic, scientific (systematic), concise and comprehensive, begins with a mythic narrative mode about the origin of *nāṭya* (performative act) and ends with the same.[2] Keeping the traditional definition of śāstra in mind the *Nāṭyaśāstra* is a contradiction in itself as it is descriptive and in narrative mode. To denounce it for not being a Śāstra merely on the basis of traditional definition of Śāstra or to take the narrative at its face value would amount to trivialization of the mythic narrative and the mode of constructing knowledge because the narrative mode is used as a canopy for the meaning camouflaged underneath.

In Indian tradition, literature has a different function to serve. In Aristotle, its main function was restorative (re-attaining the state of psychological equipoise after going through a state of arousal of feelings and emotions), whereas in Indian tradition it is primarily illustrative (*dṛṣṭānta*). *Dṛṣṭānta* is not just to give

---

2. *sūtradibhihiḥ cesām praṇayam*
alpākṣaramasandigdham sāravadviśvatomukham
aṣṭobhamanavadyam ca sūtram sūtrakṛto viduḥ

The Śāstra is composed of *sūtra* (a string or thread) a rule or aphorism. These are pithy aphorism strung together. *Sūtra* can be defined as statements containing very few words, free from ambiguity, concise, devoid of superfluity, meaningful and far-reaching in its implications. (Rājaśekhara's *Kāvyamīmāṁsā*, Ch. II, "Śāstra-Nirdeśaḥ") A Śāstra is considered *apauruṣeya* when it is not possible to attribute it to a particular author.

On the other hand, *Padma Purāṇa* defines *sūtra* thus:

alpākṣaram asiṅdigdham sāravad viśvatomukham
aṣṭobhamanvadyam ca sūtram sūtrevido viduḥ

→

pleasure but to hold attention and impart knowledge through narrative (*dṛṣṭānta*). And the purpose of all discourses in Indian tradition is *puruṣārtha catuṣṭaya*, i.e. *dharma, artha, kāma* and *mokṣa*. For *dharma,* i.e. righteous action the tradition has Dharmaśāstra; for *artha* (economic prosperity through righteous means) there is Arthaśāstra; for *kāma* (gratification of human desires) there is Kāmaśāstra; and for *mokṣa,* i.e. liberation or emancipation attended by the first three, there are Upaniṣads. Literary discourse serves all these purposes through narrative illustrative mode.

In the light of the above observations it is possible to deconstruct the narratives about the origin of the *Rāmāyaṇa* and the *Mahābhārata*. The story about the *Rāmāyaṇa* is known to most of us. Vālmīki, the *ṛṣi,* had gone to take bath and for completing his daily ablutions in the river Tamasā. While performing his routine chores he saw a pair of heron (*kauñca*) in a blissful amorous union. A hunter shot at one of the herons. The sage saw the female counterpart wailing over the death of its mate. The scene moved the sage so much that the following words flowed naturally from him:

> *mā niṣāda pratiṣṭhām tvamāgamaḥ sāśvatī samāḥ* ।
> *yat krauñcamithunād ekamavadhiḥ kāmamohitam* ॥
>
> (1:II:15)

> Niṣāda (O hunter!) your fame will not be eternal, you who have killed one heron of the two in union blissful.

The pronouncement of these words transfigured Vālmīki, the sage to Vālmīki, the *Ādikavi* (the first poet), who composed the *Rāmāyaṇa* by making use of his creative faculty. Ironical it is that the first composition was in the form of a curse, and made the hunter's fame eternal along with the pair of herons.

In this narrative, the river stands for the unconscious in which Vālmīki, the conscious self, bathes for purification. The river further suggests continuity of flow of the unconscious self that would get merged ultimately with the collective unconscious. The confluence of the sage and river allows meeting of the vertical and horizontal flow of energy. The meeting between the vertical (man) and the horizontal (river) brings about a definitive change in the horizontal motion of the river's existence, when Vālmīki, the best among men lifts some water in his palm and offers it to Nature, the Sun God in particular. The river, at least a certain part of it, becomes vertical. It is not a state of conflict but a symbiotic relationship between man and river, in which man in the form of Vālmīki offers tribute to Nature with his hands as mere instruments. The river flows incontinently and Vālmīki's eyes flood with tears at the sight of the mourning she-heron. The river keeps flowing; so do the tears from the eyes of the sage and the heron. In other words, the pain of an individual understood the pain of the language-less other and flowed together and thus was immortalized in language. Though it was difficult for anyone to decipher the gender of the bird,[3] despite all debates of Sanskrit scholars, I would, if allowed, propose that it was a male heron that was killed and the she-heron lamented. I have reasons to believe so, as the following discussion would strive to prove.

This narrative of Vālmīki hides a paradigm of the creative process. In the narrative one can discern many Vālmīkis — Vālmīki, the plunderer and Vālmīki, the sage. Vālmīki, the plunderer has two aspects of his personality — before meeting the sages in the forest and afterwards, one who was given the word *mārā* by wandering sages, and whose repetition in the end leads to the recitation of "Rāma." By reciting it repetitively he becomes Vālmīki, the *r̥ṣi*. Vālmīki, the *r̥ṣi*, can also be seen as Vālmīki, the pre-*Ādikavi*, i.e. before he experienced the pain of the death of the heron to be followed by Vālmīki, the *Ādikavi*, as the composer of the *Rāmāyaṇa*,

---

→ A *sūtra* is one which, in a few words of no ambiguity or repetition, expresses in gist a vast idea; such a *sūtra* cannot be substituted nor does it contain any fault.

3. Vālmīki was a sage, not an ornithologist with binoculars who could decipher the gender of the living bird from a distance. In fact, every discipline has its truth. Poetic/literary discourse has its own poetic/literary truth. That the surviving bird was a female is a poetic truth for mourning comes to women more naturally than men.

and Vālmīki the participant in his own composition, as he played his role of Sītā's sustainer after her exile by Rāma.

Here it is possible to see a paradigm of the creative process clearly. It begins with purity, both physical and mental. It needs identification of an individual with all elements — be it human or non-human. Moreover, it needs the sublime, an all-comprehensive soul that empathizes with others, for only great minds and souls can breed great thoughts and represent them in their compositions. Vālmīki was going through his sacred rituals, and he could have very well avoided the incident as the killing of a mere bird. But Vālmīki, the plunderer who was cruelty incarnate, was now a *ṛṣi*, and so his transformed conscious self was moved by the cruelty inflicted upon a bird in such a way that the moment made him oblivious of his performing of rituals and even of existence. Thus, the narrative suggests centrality of ability to empathize with others and feeling their pain as one's own in the creative process.

The pain of the she-heron not only moved him but became an integral part of his unconscious self, which became the story of Rāma (the *Rāmāyaṇa*), which in fact is Sītā's song of sighs. The epic had its roots in pathos and the seer poet returns to it again and again in different forms leading ultimately to the arrival of Sītā in the *āśrama* of Vālmīki after having a brief interlude of happiness in Ayodhyā as the queen. Ayodhyā, in case of Sītā, is a site of pain where different turns of events gave her more pain than happiness. Sītā is Vālmīki's literary representation of the she-heron whose pain haunted Vālmīki throughout his life, and articulated through Sītā it was exorcised.

All works of art are cocoons around a major idea, expressed through corresponding artistic instruments, metaphor or character through which the writer unburdens his/her personal burdens. Sub-ideas act as threads running vertically and horizontally and thereby form the outer layer. Vālmīki sheds off multiple layers of his pain that had become a part of his cerebral system through Sītā's character, not through Rāma's. Various folk versions of *Rāmāyaṇa* in Marathi portray a few women wandering in the forest.

On being asked, they inform that they were doing so to share the pain that princess Sītā suffered during her exile.

Exile is a metaphysical murder. The first exile in the case of Sītā was a voluntary one to accompany her husband. Then there was the involuntary exile within the voluntary one, as she was abducted by Rāvaṇa. And the third was forced on her by her husband. The ultimate disappearance in the crevice of the earth is her voluntary exile forever, a metaphysical suicide. Sītā's exiles personify her pain whose linkage might be traced to the first experience of pain by the first poet. In fact, Sītā's last exile is not exile in the real sense of the term, for it marks her return to the mother's womb, the original home. In that sense, birth, as for all human beings, is an exile for Sītā from the safe, caring comfort of the mother's womb. Her final act of disappearance completes the eternal fivefold cycle of being — conception, deliverance from a mother's womb, initiation into the human world, confrontation with crises or coexistence with pain, and return to the original fold.

Baldly speaking, Sītā's pathetic story suggests pain to be the foundation of human existence and also the fountain of creativity. Poetry is an unfortunate product of pain and misery. Happiness, more often than not, is a strange interlude in the general drama of pain. Thus, purity, empathy, association with experiences — particularly painful ones of others — and making one's own creations or characters as part of one's own being are essential components of the creative process.[4] The narrative further suggests that poetry is an event, an accidental event which needs to be captured verbally. That the poet's certain specific objectives act as cause(s) is often not true.

---

4. Vālmīki and Veda Vyāsa are not just narrators but characters playing their roles in the drama of life created by them. Tulasīdāsa's *Rāmacaritamānasa* is an exception to this. As an aside, the *Rāmāyaṇa* is an epic with one hero (*nāyaka*). The *Mahābhārata* has many heroes in it. According to Rājaśekhara, the first *itihāsa* (historical narrative) is *parakriyā,* i.e. having only one protagonist and the latter is *purākalpa,* i.e. having two or more protagonists. However, both of them share the quality of their authors being as characters.

→

On the other hand, Veda Vyāsa's *Mahābhārata* has a more interesting and intricate narrative. Vyāsa composed the *Mahābhārata* after collecting and editing one Veda into four Saṁhitās. Prior to writing the epic he had composed it in his mind in terms of words and the order of events. But he did not give it a written form. He thought of the difficulty of how to teach this *ākhyāna variṣṭha* (grand narrative) to his students. Sensing his dilemma, Brahmā, the creator and teacher of all (*prajāpati* and *lokaguru*) appeared before him. Vyāsa paid his respect to him and seated him comfortably. He himself kept standing. He sat only after Brahmā asked him to do so. Vyāsa said to Brahmā that he had composed an epic in his mind. It contained the essence of the Vedas, Upaniṣads, Itihāsa, Purāṇas, old narratives dealing with education, medicine, present, past and future, having understanding of various *bhāva*s (the states of being like fear, compassion, life, death, grammar and war). He further added that it has everything that might be useful for all kinds of people but he said, *'param na lekhakaḥ kaścid etasyām bhūvi'*. (But there is no one on this earth who can write it in words.) Brahmā understood Vyāsa's dilemma, and knew full well that there was no exaggeration in Vyāsa's statement, so he blessed him and said, *'tvayā ca kāvyam ityuktam tasmāt kāvyam bhaviṣyati'* (since you have termed your verbal composition as *kāvya* (poetry), so it will be *kāvya* which will serve as foundation for all subsequent writers). Vyāsa himself called his work a *kāvya, kṛtam mayedam bhagavān kāvyam paramapūjitam*. Here I must take note of the typological/ genealogical sphere of existence of the *Mahābhārata*. Despite Brahmā's and Vyāsa's pronouncement regarding the epic as *kāvya*, Rājaśekhara puts it in the category of itihāsa. Ānandavardhana, on the other hand, regards it as a Śāstra-kāvya (Ānandavardhana,

→ The *Rāmacaritamānasa* of Tulasīdāsa is an epic with one hero but without the participation of its author in it, for which Tulasīdāsa's *bhakti* and elevated stature of Rāma might have been responsible. Vālmīki's Rāma is Puruṣottama but Tulasīdāsa's Rāma becomes his lord Maryādā-puruṣottama and the creator-*bhakta*, i.e. Tulasīdāsa had to maintain the distance between higher self and his lower personal self.

Udyota IV, *Dhvanyāloka*). According to him the *Mahābhārata* despite having poetic beauty has a form of Śāstra (didactic work). As a *śāstranaye* (didactic work) it considers *mokṣa* (liberation) as the supreme goal, as a *kāvyanaye* (a work of poetry) it proposes *śānta* (peace) as a *rasa* which is cessation of desires as the cause of strengthening of happiness. The predominance of *śānta* and *mokṣa* over other human aims is not explicitly stated but suggested in the epic.

To resolve Vyāsa's dilemma, Brahmā asked him to seek Lord Gaṇeśa's shelter and thereafter disappeared. After his departure, Vyāsa remembered Gaṇeśa who appeared before him. Vyāsa narrated his problem and requested Gaṇeśa to help him by becoming his amanuensis. Gaṇeśa accepted the offer but with the condition that he would have to dictate the epic continuously without halting at any point. Vyāsa accepted Gaṇeśa's condition but put forward his as well that Gaṇeśa would write whatever he would dictate only after understanding it. So whenever Vyāsa felt that Gaṇeśa was about to be faster than his verbal articulation, he would dictate a complex *śloka*. Gaṇeśa would take some time in understanding it, and in the intervening period Vyāsa would compose the next *śloka*. Thus, there are about eight thousand eight hundred complex *śloka*s in the epic of more than one lakh *śloka*s. About these eight thousand eight hundred *śloka*s, Veda Vyāsa said, *'aham vedmi, suko vetti, sañjayo vetti va nā va'* (I know, Śuka knows, and I don't know if Sañjaya knows it or not).

The mythical narrative is about a creative process, and its allegorical meaning can be interpreted in different ways. In the narrative Brahmā is no ordinary being but one of the three attributes of Brahmā, the infinite Supreme Being who is creative (Brahmā), protective (Viṣṇu) and destructive (Śiva). He is the creator or *prajāpati*, so he represents creativity — its collective unconscious containing all cultural forces to whom Ved Vyāsa, the conscious self, pays homage. Ved Vyāsa is the experiencing self as well as the organizing self of experiences at the verbal level. Gaṇeśa is the writing self that organizes the creative experiences but not without understanding them. Śukadeva is a competent reader/receiver who has aquired the tradition through inheritance and diligence of a constructed discourse. Sañjaya represents a receiver who can see the spectacle but it is not necessary that he should understand it. Veda Vyāsa's students are common receivers of the text who need organization of an experience in a certain way so that they can understand the discourse. In this paradigm, Brahmā, Veda Vyāsa and Gaṇeśa stand for different aspects of creative processes. All of them put together represent different layers or selves of the same writer. The other three, Śuka, Sañjaya and Ved Vyāsa's students are recipients or reader-critics or receiving selves of a discourse. Along with Ved Vyāsa, they are the knowing selves. In his statement Ved Vyāsa surprisingly dropped Gaṇeśa from the list of the knowers of the meaning of the *Mahābhārata*. It means that Gaṇeśa understood the *Mahābhārata* but did not know it as he was busy with the process of receiving the dictation of the *Mahābhārata* from Veda Vyāsa.

The narrative distinguishes between the experiencing and speaking self (speech) and the organizing self (writing) of the same creative being. Moreover, it goes beyond it, as it contains an act of reception in it as well. First, it makes a distinction between understanding and knowing and charts out four levels of creation and its reception: idea, its articulation at verbal level and organization at the level of writing, and reception. Reception is an act of negotiation between the two main processes of creation and criticism and in the process, attaining knowledge which is the relation between the knower and the object of knowing (the *Mahābhārata*, the creative work). The knowers are of multiple kinds, for the author, i.e. Ved Vyāsa himself is a knower of his own creation. Other than Vyāsa is Śukadeva who knows, for he has inherited and acquired the tradition with diligence. Sañjaya has the ability to see. But seeing is not knowing.[5] Hence, Vyāsa, the author, does not know whether Sañjaya knows it or not despite

5. Sañjaya can see the war from a distance but he is a spectator not a seer. All spectators see things or forms but know not the essence of the spectacle. Though English has only one word "know," Sanskrit has *jānāmi* and *vedmi*: →

having divine insight with which he narrated the epical war to blind Dhr̥tarāṣṭra.[6] Insight and blindness together see the war of Kurukṣetra. Sañjaya saw it and made it seen through the act of speech having received it to Dhr̥tarāṣṭra who was visually challenged from outside and inside as well, for his excessive love for Duryodhana blinded his inner vision.[7] The author of the *Mahābhārata* proposes to state that divine eyes/insight do not necessarily make one the knower of a creative act. Seeing is believing but not knowing. The students of Veda Vyāsa are inquisitive souls trying to know but just being students of Vyāsa

---

→ For instance, Ved Vyāsa knows (*vedmi*) and Duryodhana knows (*jānāmi*). The only difference, moreover, between Duryodhana and Arjuna is that the former knew what was *dharma* but could not practise it. He knew what was *adharma* but could not disengage himself from it. Arjuna did not know what to do even after entering the battlefield of Kurukṣetra so he sought the shelter of Kr̥ṣṇa, the *jagatguru*. And once he comes to know what is worth upholding and doing, he is freed from indecision and follows the path of action.

6. Vyāsa does not know if Sañjaya knew the meaning of the *Mahābhārata* or not. Ironically Sañjaya was provided with divine eyes by Vyāsa himself so that he could narrate the war to blind Dhr̥tarāṣṭra. If Vyāsa is unsure of Sañjaya's knowledge of the *Mahābhārata*, it becomes almost inconceivable for us to state anything with certainty about other narrators' knowledge of the *Mahābhārata*.

7. Dhr̥tarāṣṭra's love for his eldest son is natural. However, Indian culture saw him as a negative influence, for he failed in his duty as he discriminated between his son(s) and younger brother Pāṇḍava's sons whose caretaker he was supposed to be after the death of the latter. In fact, it can be seen as the major cause of the *Mahābhārata* war, as in the very first *śloka* of the *Śrīmad Bhagavad-Gītā*, he is concerned to know about *māmakā* (my own) and *pāṇḍavāśca* (of Pāṇḍava). The acts of making distinction among his own and his younger brother's sons and his order of preference have earned him the place of an unworthy head of the family.

   As far as "seeing" is concerned, *Śrīmad Bhagavad-Gītā* in its *śloka*s 27 to 30 of ch. XIII deals with it, and says that one who performs all his duties and considers himself a mere instrument, is a true seer. He who sees God manifested in all beings, and sees the indestructible (*avināśa*) among all dying elements really sees.

does not ensure that they would know what their teacher had mentally and verbally composed. It needs natural ability and diligence along with intervention[8] of the teacher, nay *guru* who knows what his students are incapable of knowing. And so he arranges and organizes the narrative in such a way that they would also comprehend. In the process, there emerges a meta-knowledge in narrative or narrative about narrative, its origin to be precise.[9]

All these notes regarding the creative process notwithstanding, it can certainly be said that the narrative of Veda Vyāsa and Gaṇeśa in the *Mahābhārata* resolves the debate about binary opposition of "speech" and "writing" which has dominated Western metaphysical and philosophical discourses for long from Plato to Jacques Derrida, as Vyāsa and Gaṇeśa — "speech" and "writing" — combine and become one in the act of creation despite being different, as they are faculties of the same being.

The narratives, thus, are a comprehensive and systematic study of creative and critical processes. Vālmīki and Ved Vyāsa did not theorize about creative processes, despite composing the encyclopaedia of Indian culture and civilization. Rather they constructed mythical narratives as a vehicle of constructing and communicating knowledge and left it for posterity to speculate about them. After all, speculation is an act of criticism. For that matter, all discourses are speculations.

---

8. For discussion of "intervention," please see Avdhesh Kumar Singh, "Preface" to *Interventions: Literary and Critical Discourses*. New Delhi: Creative, 2007.

9. In ch. X, *śloka* 1 of *Śrīmad Bhagavad-Gītā* Lord Kṛṣṇa calls himself Vāsudeva among the Yādavas, Arjuna among the Pāṇḍavas, and Vyāsa among *munis*, as Vyāsa knows the true essence of all things and their attributes and is by nature meditative.

3

Aesthetics, Ethics and Indian Culture

All that is beautiful is difficult. — Plato

Śāstric (scriptural) knowledge is unlimited, and the arts to be learned are many; the time we have is short, and our opportunities to learn are beset with obstacles. Therefore select for learning that which is most important, just as the swan drinks only the milk in water. — Cāṇakya, *Nītiśāstra*, XV. 10

Beauty is a symbol of morality. — Immanuel Kant

The rules are all very well up to a certain limit. . . . One should be able to follow them, but also to reject them and take them up again. . . . Woe to the impassive artist clinging to the narrow regulations of his art . . .. — Jean Georges Noverre

Hamein sundaratā kī kasauṭī badalanī hogī aur hamein niścaya hī vilāsitā ke mīnāra se utarakara us bacconvālī rūpavatī kā citra khīñcanā hogā jo bacce ko meṅḍa par sulākar pasīnā bahā rahī hai.

We will have to change the criteria of beauty, and come down from the minarets of luxury and draw a picture of a beautiful mother who sweats while working in a field after making her child sleep on the boundary (of the field).

— Munshi Premchand

BEFORE I dwell upon the topic, "Aesthetics, Ethics and Indian Literature," let me submit that I have chosen to write on the topic to understand the issue, not to make others understand, as might appear, on the basis of my little understanding that I acquired in the process of listening to and reading others. I acknowledge my gratitude to all who contributed to my understanding, and I seek their blessings so that I can do justice to the topic because more often than not the discussion of aesthetics and ethics tends to be ugly and immoral, as I have seen people quarrelling on the issue of ethics and their discourses have on many occasions led to verbal and even physical violence. I wish to discuss aesthetics and ethics in Indian traditions, but would like not to commit these two crimes as such. I would primarily concern myself with three propositions. (i) Are aesthetics and ethics Indian categories? (ii) And if they are not Indian categories, what did Indian tradition have, or what happened in it? (iii) And last but not least, I would strive to relate the entire issue of aesthetics and ethics to literary practice in India.

Let me forward my conclusion first and substantiate it later. Aesthetics and ethics are not Indian categories; they come from the West. Aesthetics has a long and continuous history in the West with a long tradition of discussion of beauty and aesthetic experience from Plato to Immanuel Kant, John Ruskin, Leo Tolstoy and Thomas Munro. In the Greek tradition particularly by the time of Plato, five major domains of knowledge were established: Epistemology, Ethics, Aesthetics, Poetics and Politics. Plato contributed to all of them. As far as aesthetics was concerned, Pythagoras and his followers viewed it as a part of philosophy that served to present a picture of the world as it was. For Socrates, it bordered on ethics, and Plato added the state control over art and the role played by art in educating (wo)man. By the time of Aristotle, it concerned itself with poetics and the nature of beauty and art. During this period, the concept of *kalokgotheia,* i.e. beautiful and goodness combined in one came to be established. The basic proposition was that whatever is beautiful has to be good and whatever is good, would in the course of time become beautiful.

Plato's consideration of beauty is unrivalled for its depth and subtlety. So Plato's discussion of "beauty" and "beautiful" particularly in his *Greater Hippias* and *Hippias Minor* demands attention. The discussion is facilitated by dialogue between Socrates and the interlocutors. During the discussion Socrates forwarded an interesting illustration. In order to avoid abstraction or monotony of philosophy of aesthetics and ethics, I would like to share an example from the *Rāmāyaṇa* tradition first and then return to Socrates because both the discussions are interrelated.

One of the narratives in the *Rāmāyaṇa* tradition mentions that while Sītā was in Rāvaṇa's captivity in Aśoka-Vāṭikā, on one fine day Rāvaṇa came with his entourage to the Aśoka-Vāṭikā with the purpose of persuading Sītā to accept his proposal. Hanumān, hiding himself on the *aśoka* tree, saw Rāvaṇa trying to inveigle upon, persuade, and threaten Sītā, but she did not budge. Hanumān saw the whole spectacle from above and heard the entire discourse between the two. Dejected Rāvaṇa went back to his palace in Laṅkā. On the same *aśoka* tree with Hanumān were a couple of monkeys sitting and talking to each other. Hanumān could understand their language because he belonged to the same tribe. In the course of the interaction, one monkey told the other as to why Rāvaṇa should not come again and again to the Aśoka-Vāṭikā to plead and persuade and even threaten Sītā. It was natural for him to do so because she was so beautiful. The other monkey conceded the fact to his counterpart but added to it that it is true that she is extremely beautiful. However, she would have been more beautiful if she had a little tail. See the irony here that Sītā who was such a paragon of beauty as would make Rāvaṇa ignore all the beautiful dames of his harem and pine for her, was less than beautiful from the viewpoint of a monkey. The Aśoka-Vāṭikā thus was a site of convergence of different aesthetics co-existing simultaneously at one particular point of time. One is the aesthetics of human beings who have their own concept of beauty, and the other is the aesthetics of other beings, other tribes or animals that were there.

Human predilections and tastes are as varied and relative as they themselves are. It is subject to change according to time and space. Plato is said to have remarked, 'Everyone chooses his love out of the objects of beauty according to his taste.' It is exemplified in the narrative of Lailā and Majanū, the two individuals who are referred to as one, for their love unified them into one soul. To

Majanū, Lailā was the most beautiful creature in the world; the world, however, thought otherwise. He is said to have pitied such people for their inability to see the beauty of Lailā because to see the beauty of Lailā one required the eyes of Majanū. Both of these illustrations prove that all statements about beauty or otherwise are statements of individual or collective prejudices or congeniality and there is nothing like the aesthetics.

I cited the examples not to tickle but primarily for the fact that Socrates, quoting Heraclitus, says that the most beautiful of all apes would be ugly in comparison to any human being. And the most beautiful of human beings would be less beautiful and less wise in comparison to the gods. The point that emerges here is that there is nothing like aesthetics. Also against our general perception whatever we understand by the term beauty, it (beauty) is not universal. Time and space and the ability to perceive the beauty determine what is beautiful or otherwise.

Plato in his dialogues discussed the question about beauty in the *Greater Hippias.* The interlocutors Hippias and Socrates asked the question, "What is beautiful?"(96) The latter tried to show the former how to resolve the problem pertaining to beauty.

Socrates: "What is beauty?"

Hippias: "I assure you, Socrates, if I must speak the truth, that a beautiful maiden is a beauty."(97)

The reply is a departure in the analysis of the beautiful: its concrete quality. However, the fact is that beauty is not only concrete and individual but is a characteristic of whole categories of phenomena. Socrates pointed it by saying:

> Is not a beautiful mare a beauty . . . but what about a beautiful lyre ?. . . what about a beautiful pot? . . . Is not that a beauty?(97)

He gradually persuaded Hippias to arrive at the conclusion that the beautiful is something individual inherent in a multitude, something concrete which is nevertheless universal. Even then Hippias could not digest the fact that a beautiful woman and a beautiful pot should be either compared or discussed in the same breath. However, Socrates drew his attention to the relativity of the beautiful. To determine the measure of the object's beauty, a comparison with another object is necessary. Socrates went on to cite Heraclitus:

> . . . the most beautiful of apes is ugly compared with the human race. . . . The wisest of men, when compared to a god will appear but an ape in wisdom and beauty and all else. (98)

In an attempt to find absolute beauty, Hippias suggested that this may be a property of gold: 'For I suppose we all know that if anything has gold added to it, it will appear beautiful when so adorned even though it appeared only before.' But Socrates objected to it on the ground that Phidias has carved a beautiful sculpture of Athena not out of gold but of ivory. Moreover, to supplement a clay pot, a fig spoon is beautiful while a gold one is ugly. But in that case the beautiful is the humdrum routine, the normal, the common, the age-old and sanctified by tradition. Hippias stated:

> Then I maintain that always, everywhere, and for every man it is most beautiful to be rich, healthy, honoured by the Greeks, to reach old-age and, after burying his parents nobly, himself to be borne to the tomb with solemn ceremony by his own children. (101)

Socrates however noted that this did not embrace the exceptional: heroes born from immortal gods or the gods themselves.

In the end, a definition is developed: the beautiful is that which is beneficial, useful and has power to produce something good. Socrates told his adversary, however, that there are things which are quite useful for perpetrating an evil deed, and these are far removed from the beautiful. Is not then the beautiful that which is useful for a good deed, i.e. the useful itself? This supposition, introducing a utilitarian element into the definition of beauty, is also rejected. 'It looks as if the view which a little while ago we thought the finest result of our discussions, the view that the beneficial, and the useful, and the power to produce something good, is beautiful, is in fact wrong. . . .' A new, sensualist approach to the beautiful emerges, which explains the significance of the latter as a source of pleasure: 'Beauty is the pleasant which comes through the senses of hearing and sight,' while the designation 'beautiful' is denied to that which is pleasant according to the other senses, that is, the senses which have to do with food, and drink, and sexual intercourse, and all such things. Thus, using Socrates as his mouthpiece, and asking reasonable questions Plato demarcated a line between physical and spiritual beauty. He added another dimension to the issue when he asked about virtuous actions and laws. Hearing and vision have nothing to do with the pleasure one derives from these.

Plato strove to confluence the utilitarian, the sensualist and the ethical issues of beauty: 'Beauty is that which is both useful and powerful for some good purpose.' He distinguished between the good and the beautiful. His Socrates remarked, "Then most certainly beauty is not good nor the good beautiful."

The dispute between Hippias and Socrates did not evolve a final definition of beauty. It should, however, not at all mean that it was theoretically fruitless. In the course of it, a comprehensive and dialectical analysis of the beautiful is made, while the last sentence summarized the outcome of the polemical discourse. He conceded that beautiful is difficult. But he did not mean by beauty of form such beauty as that of animals or pictures, which many would suppose to be his meaning. By them he meant straight lines and circles, and the plane or solid figures which are formed out of them by turning-lathes and rulers and measures of angles. He affirmed them to be not only relatively beautiful, like other things, but also eternally and absolutely beautiful, and they have peculiar pleasures.

The geometrician in Plato sought beauty in solids, in the quality of being proportionate. Plato's beauty is a specific aesthetic idea man can grasp only in a state of obsession or inspiration, through the memories the immortal soul has of the time when it has not yet inhabited the mortal body but existed in the world of ideas.

Noting the beauty of a concrete object, Plato seemed to opine that it emerges in the soul of man in the presence of beauty. He was the first to treat the beautiful as the product of man's aesthetic and spiritual relation to the object and not as an innate property of objects. This interpretation of the beautiful leads us to the supra-sensual nature of beauty. However, Plato saw the source of this quality of the beautiful not in social life or history but in the primacy of the spiritual.

Plato termed beauty, as cited earlier, 'difficult.' By doing so he suggested that beauty is difficult to measure but not impossible, for it is not a myth. The beauty of Plato's doctrine is that aesthetic experience has features which are all its own, and contemplation of the beautiful is the source of a number of unique 'pleasures.' Moreover, his interpretation of the beautiful is significant, for he saw it as the product of man's spiritual, specifically human approach to the world.

Departing from his teacher, Aristotle observed the beautiful not as an objective idea but as an objective property of things, and proposed that beauty is a matter of size and order; and to be beautiful, a living creature, must not only present a certain order in its arrangement of parts, but also to be of a certain definite magnitude. He discussed a structural characteristic of beauty stressing on the size, proportions and order as the elements of the beautiful. Subscribing to the Pythagorean tradition, Aristotle proposed that these properties are measurable in terms of mathematics. He suggested the principle of comparability of man and a beautiful object, saying that beauty is impossible either (i) in a very minute creature, since our perception becomes indistinct as it approaches instantaneity; or (ii) in a creature of vast size, as in that case, instead of the object being seen all at once, the unity and wholeness of it is lost to the beholder.

Relating beauty to proportion, Aristotle in his *Poetics* observed that the beautiful should be neither too small nor too large. This idea is apparently naïve but in reality a masterstroke of an analytical mind who considered things ontologically. Beauty, thus, becomes a measure, and the measure of all things is man. It is in comparison with man that the beautiful object should not be out of proportion. This centrality of man in the measurement of beauty is Aristotelian contribution to the discussion of beauty that Plato had already discussed in depth. But Aristotle's concept of beauty was not something altogether new, for it was in consonance with the Greek humanitarian character of the art. As distinct from a pyramid, the Parthenon is neither too small nor too large; it is small enough not to overwhelm man but large enough to convey the greatness of the Athenians who created it.

The subsequent discussion can be seen in terms of paradigmatic departure in terms of perception of beauty. In the Middle Ages, the dominating doctrine of the divine origin of beauty was proposed by Thomas Aquinas and Francis of Assisi. During the period, it became a branch of theology that used it (aesthetics) to persuade man to serve god with the help of art. Sensual beauty was looked upon as sinful; and enjoyment of it was prohibited. They believed that in the process of animating the inert matter, god renders it aesthetic. The Renaissance period valourized the beauty of nature and the pleasure it gave to wo/man. For the neoclassic critic like Charles Boileau in France, its endeavour was to set standards for art. He reduced the beautiful to the refined. The luxurious flowering in the wild forest was not considered as beautiful as the trimmed and groomed lawn in a garden.

The discussion of the aesthetic and aesthetics gained momentum in the eighteenth century. In the progression of history of human ideas in Europe, the Germans contributed to good extent to the discussion. Alexander Baumgarten used the term *asthetisch* which led to the emergence of the term *esthetics* by 1790. Immanuel Kant's aesthetic view lent a new direction to the tradition. He saw beauty as an object of disinterested relationship. To him, it is objective and universal, and so certain things are beautiful to everyone. In 1796 he observed of a man, 'If he says that canary wine is agreeable he is quite content if someone else corrects his terms and reminds him to say instead: It is agreeable to me,'

Everyone has own (sense of) taste: 'The case of beauty' is different from mere 'agreeableness' because, 'If he proclaims something to be beautiful, then he requires the same liking from others; he then judges not just for himself but for everyone, and speaks of beauty as if it were a property of things.' He considered the case of aesthetic judgement that usually lies beyond sensory discrimination which is linked to capacity for pleasure. To Kant, enjoyment is consequence of pleasure arising from sensation. However, judging something as 'beautiful' would require a third requisite, i.e. sensation must give rise to pleasure by engaging our capacities of reflective contemplation. It means that in judgements of beauty three things — sensation, emotional and intellectual responses take place simultaneously.

The interpretation of beauty from viewer's perspective brings in concepts of aesthetics and taste. The former is the philosophical notion of beauty (as aesthetic is related to philosophy and logic as well); the latter is acquired as a consequence of social milieu, education, and cultural values. That is why taste varies in accordance with class, culture and milieu. Among Kant's interpreters Hegel and Arthur Schopenhauer took diametrically opposite views regarding India. Hegel had no sympathy for Indian world-view. On the other hand, under the influence of the Upaniṣads and Buddhist philosophy, Schopenhauer saw human desiring, willing, and craving as the cause of suffering and pain. Aesthetic contemplation is a temporary way to escape this pain. The best way to escape is not willing at all but that is not possible for all. So aesthetic contemplation is the next best to not willing. A person is saved from suffering the world as well by total absorption in the world as representation. In Schopenhauerean aesthetics music had a special place, for it did not depend on the medium of phenomenal representation. Aesthetically, music presents the will or self, not the way the will appears to an individual observer. "Schopenhauer thought that the music was the art that did not copy ideas but actually embodied the will itself" (Daniel Albright, *Modernism and Music,* 2004: 39). In a way

Schopenhauer suggested that neither art nor aesthetics was the ultimate way, as some would think. It comes close to the fact that the entire world is *māyā* (illusion), and so art is a temporary escape. Though influenced by the Upaniṣads and Buddhist philosophy, as a philosophical mind he did not swallow the influence as a lump. Also he was more empirical and less speculative and transcendental than the sources of influence. In the process he emerged as the first real meeting point of convergence of Indian and Western aesthetics.

To Kant, beauty was objective and universal but contemporary scholars disagree with him, as they consider that beauty is not based on innate qualities but on culture specifics and individual interpretation. Pierre Bourdieu in the twentieth century contested Kant's views on aesthetics that beauty represents an experience that it is the product of an elevated class *habitus* and scholarly leisure.

In nineteenth century it (aesthetics) became a fad in Europe. Benedetto Croce, who had delivered three lectures on aesthetic in Naples in 1900, arranged them in his famous book *Aesthetic as Science of Expression and General Linguistics* (1902). It was translated in English in two volumes in 1909, the first volume discussing theoretical aspect of aesthetic and the second with its history. He proposed that expression is central in the way beauty was once thought to be central. With the ascendency of colonization the societies that came in touch with the European colonizer contracted the seductive discourse of aesthetics. In the twentieth century, I.A. Richards, an English critic, overshadowed by his more visible contemporaries like T.S. Eliot and F.R. Leavis, stated in *The Principles of Literary Criticism* about the apparition of beauty and referred to the phantom of aesthetics. Thomas Munro's *Toward Science in Aesthetics: Selected Essays* (New York: Liberal Press, 1956) made the scope of art boundless, beyond its traditional meaning and included, apart from literature, theatre, painting and music around 400 arts like cattle-breeding, perfumery, cooking, wine making, cloth-designing, hair-dressing, tattooing, beauty treatment and plastic surgery. This was based on the basic premise that human activities such as tattooing performed social, psychological and aesthetic functions in the early stages of human history. By considering art as boundless, Munro was subscribing to the ancient Greeks who used the word *techne* for arts and crafts both and the first artists for them were carpenters, potters, masons and other craftsmen who made articles for daily use.

With the rise of Marxism, its subscribers proposed, like other schools, to have a Marxist aesthetics. Why should Marxism lag behind in having its own system of analysing beauty? The result was Georg Lukācs's voluminous book on *Aesthetics.* But the fate of the endeavour was that the Marxist Lukācs had to take recourse to Aristotle rather than Marx for considering literary forms. The lure of having aesthetics persuaded Marxists in Hindi to start a movement for constructing their own aesthetics. The absurdity of their endeavour was exposed by Namvar Singh, a perspicacious Marxist critic, with his essay on the issue entitled "Mārxvāda kā Saundrayaśāstra" (Aesthetics of Marxism) in his book, *Vāda Vivāda aur Saṁvāda*.

II

The discussion on beauty brings in a few ancillary terms like the 'ugly,' 'base,' and 'horrible' with it, as the oppositional relationship among them adds to our understanding of them.

The ugly is what repels and the beautiful is what delights with its mere presence. To the ancient Egyptians, the ugly was a consequence of the progression of time known as ageing, and they noted that everything 'which is sound grows rotten and the flavour is lost,' and through ageing healthy and beautiful become ill and ugly. The 'base' is ugliness carried to extremes. However, ugliness attended by good or virtues becomes beautiful. For instance, Socrates, was one of the ugliest faces in Greece but he was not ugly but beautiful because of the truth that he espoused till his death. Apart from it, individual predilections or choices also play their roles. Moreover, good and virtuous earn attention and reverence by being so. In this sense, the beautiful is to which our mind is attached with reverence. For a child, his/her grandmother with no teeth in her mouth, wrinkled face and hollowed eyes is the most beautiful lady on the earth. The 'horrible' is optimistic only about hopelessness. It is close to tragic and yet opposite to it because it lacks in optimism that the tragic has in it. The tragic is beautiful because it can see life even in death.

Of these terms, beauty is 'difficult' but not a myth. Purity is a myth. In this universe, things are interrelated in so many intricate ways that exclusivity, a pre-condition for purity, is impossible because the air that all — pure or impure, beautiful and ugly — breathe is the same. And the pure air that the so-called pure inhale has already been rendered impure by the impure by breathing it. The subscribers of so-called purity, despite all scientific innovations, still have no control on elements of nature. Only the spirit underlying all elements or the ideas can lay claim to purity. All forms which are their manifestations are subject to moods of time, so corruptible, impure and ugly. Purity is a dirty concept. It is exclusive and has led to many an act of mayhem and wars. The Second World War and the vivisections of continents and partitions of nations on racial, regional, religious and ideological lines are some of its bloodiest manifestations in human history.

In the Indian, particularly Hindu, tradition, nothing is sacred or profane. Even *sat* (truth) does not exclude *asat* (non-truth). The Vedic hymn states, *asato sat jāyeta* (*sat* or truth is borne out of *asat* or non-truth). There is no space for negation in it. Everything, however diverse, is harmonized in it. Various forces, processes and manifestations of life — similar and dissimilar — co-exist in it, as one finds it in the metaphor of Lord Śiva's dance, i.e. the *tāṇḍava nṛtya* which combines *nṛtya* (dance) and *mṛtyu* (death) in one, simultaneous celebration of dance and death.

Moving towards the discussion of aesthetics in Indian tradition beyond the oppositional relationship between beauty and ugly, it needs to be stated that the opposite of 'good' is not 'bad' but 'a bit.' Similarly the opposite of 'beautiful' is not ugly, for there is nothing really ugly in the universe. The opposite of beautiful is 'vulgar.' The term vulgar has had its history, for *vulgus* in Latin stood for the general public. Popular was vulgar. What is liked by all cannot be genuinely good or refined in taste. It came to mean lacking in taste, good breeding, or refinement. Now it is used in the sense of indecent or lewd. The vulgar is a consequence of unjustifiable indulgence for some extraneous reasons. For instance, beauty pageants are vulgar, not because they are sites of exposure but because they over expose and use body as an object. A thing becomes vulgar when it is commodified and price tag is attached to it or if it is used to arouse baser instincts. All this is put in the category of *aślīla*, Sanskrit or Hindi word for 'vulgar.' The word *aślīla* can be traced to *R̥gveda* where it is used. Sāyaṇa interpreted it as *aślīla* first and later as *śrī-hīna*, *guṇavihīna* and *kutsit*. The poeticians considered it in aesthetic terms and put it in the category of poetic demerit (*kāvyadoṣa*) and propriety (*aucitya*). In the present context, the term vulgar or *aślīla* is associated with morality associated with sex. Since *kāma* was a category among the four goals of life in the *puruṣārtha catuṣṭaya*, the Indian society revered the author of *Kāmasūtra* as an *ācārya* and *r̥ṣi* (sage). But it has to be borne in mind that it should not be ever simplified because *kāma* was qualified by *dharma* (righteous conduct worth holding) and *artha* (material prosperity qualified by *dharma*). What is beautiful and what and how much is the impact of beautiful are determined by the context, culture and *deśa* and *kāla*, and individual preferences and predilections. The perception of beautiful is determined and conditioned by cultural traditions. For instance, in India, the flower of lotus is considered beautiful whereas in England and Europe it is the flower of lily. In the West golden hair is beautiful, in India curly black hair.

There was/is nothing like aesthetics in Indian tradition. What was/is there then? Why was/is it not there? In the ordinary sense of the term, aesthetics is a systematic study of sensory perception. In that sense, aesthetics is about beauty, often about surface beauty or form. Since Indian mind was more concerned with spirit, so it did not consider it important to construct a science of what is transitory.

There is no word like *sundara* or *saundarya* in Upaniṣadic or Vedic literature to the best of my knowledge. One of the words used is *vāja* that stands not for *sundara* but for grace, speed and energy. The words used later in the Indian tradition are *rūpa, manohara, ramaṇīyatā,* used by Sanskrit poeticians. For *external* appearance and for external beautification the word was/is *śṛṅgāra.* Ādi Śaṅkarācārya was among the first ones to use the word *saundarya* and wrote *Saundaryalaharī* (Waves of Beauty) which is about the Mother Goddess. Spirituality is a journey from gross to subtle, from the external to the internal, from the form to the formless and ultimately, as Śaṅkarācārya stated from the limited to the Infinite, non-dual consciousness. The forms give the impression of duality and of reality. That the self and the Infinite are one is realized by one-differentiating intellect. *Aham Brahmāsmi* (I am that!). Along with I, the other, i.e. you are also that. *Tat tvamasi* (That Thou art!). Here you are not you but Thou. In this state of realization, one begins to appreciate the other — ranging from a flower to thorn and from the sea to a snail because all are forms of the Infinite. In this state, one starts seeing beauty in ugliness and life in lifelessness, and demarcating line between/among things — sacred or profane — does not come into existence.

The centrality of Infinite and spirituality should lead to the destination of 'dispassion of one's self' that persuades one to think beyond self to other and society or God, for they are one and the same. It extends the statement, 'Love Thy Neighbour like Thyself,' for Thy neighbour is not the other but Thyself. Moreover, it frees the object from possession whose worst manifestations have been witnessed in the form of colonization — internal and external. Possession turns beauty into a mirage. But for that, one has to come out of the rut of individualism and identity of all sorts, e.g. class, caste or community, for they are inflated individualism. In the traditional Indian worldview, identity (*asmitā*) has been considered a negative property, as it leads to ego-centricism.

The non-differentiating soul cognizes beauty in all forms of creation as did Ādi Śaṅkara in *Saundaryalaharī*. The term *saundarya* is made from *sundara* (beautiful), one of the three attributes of the self, i.e. *satyam* (truth), *śivam* (tranquillity), auspicious and benevolence and *sundaram* (beauty). The first is truth, unchanging in time and space and the substratum of entire creation; the second *Śivam* is benevolence and inseparable from Śakti; and the third is *sundaram* (beauty). The human beings remain snared in the external form of beauty and the higher souls move from outside to beauty within after its recognition. Ādi Śaṅkara's *Saundaryalaharī* glorifies the incomparable beauty of the Mother, i.e. Śakti, the primordial energy responsible for feminine aspect and inseparable from Śiva. She is also addressed as the Devī or Mother Divine: Śaṅkara, while glorifying the beauty of the Divine Mother mentioned Kāma who is portrayed as archer with a bow and five senses. When Kāma shoots one with his arrows of flower, a wave of beauty arises deep inside through senses. Thus, one moves from external senses to formless inside. The philosopher king Bhartṛhari's *Śṛṅgāraśataka* and *Nītiśataka* deal with *śṛṅgāra* and *nīti* (either/moral) but they are more transcendental, and *alaukika*. Bhoja wrote *Saundarya Prakāśa* which literally means a treatise on beauty and is a work of poetics but the issues undertaken in poetics have their bearing on other systems dealing with all art forms and with consideration of beauty or aesthetic in them. The amorous feeling find their expression in Kālidāsa's works particularly in *Kumārsambhavam* and *Abhijñānśākuntalam*. In Kālidāsa, the beauty of nature and human world in physical and spiritual sense find their expression in his plays and poetry. In *Śākuntalam*, the poet almost presented a different notion of the beauty of form as it is and contrasted natural with spiritual/inner. Before leaving Kaṇva's *āśrama* for the palace of Duṣyanta, Śakuntalā is being beautified with the flowers. At that point of time, recognizing the natural beauty of Śakuntalā, the poet says that a natural beauty like hers needs no ornamentation. His words in *Abhijñānaśākuntalam* (1:18) read: *kimiva hi madhurāṇām maṇḍanam nākṛtinam* (Those who are naturally beautiful need no embellishment). The word used by Kālidāsa is not *sundara* but *madhura*. It further suggests that the poet puts naturally beautiful in the category of *madhura*. Those who have not been so generously bestowed by nature or are still discontented with how they are, try to compensate with embellishment. The term *madhura* signified the highest form of beauty, as can be seen from Mahāprabhu Vallabhācārya's *Madhuraśataka*, one of the precursors of *bhakti* movement pertaining to Kr̥ṣṇa's devotion. (It means sweet, pleasant, charming, delightful, and mellifluous. Suśruta used it in his *Saṁhitā*, a treatise of medicine, having positive therapeutic effect.) By the *bhakti* period, the terms *sundara* and *śrī* (having grace and splendour) came into usage. Later on *śrī* became a cultural term, added before names to show respect and cultural propriety. His contemporary Tulsīdās called a canto of his *Rāmacaritamānasa* as "Sundara-Kāṇḍa" which is recited by devotees as a prayer to Hanumān, for it is considered as a confluence of three ideals: *satyam*, *śivam*, and *sundaram*. Rāma stands for *satyam*, Hanumān for *śivam* as the son of Śiva and doer and harbinger of good deeds and news of Sītā's whereabouts, and Sītā for *sundaram* for her *saṁskāra*s (disposition). Who/What is/are *sundara* being(s) and object(s) in the "Sundara-Kāṇḍa"? In the canto, the word *sundara* appears nine times. *Sundara* includes Rāma's *mudrikā* (ring), given as an object of recognition, Sītā's *cūḍāmaṇi*, the Aśoka-Vāṭikā, the golden Laṅkā, Vibhīṣaṇa, and Trijaṭā, a she-demon, kept by Rāvaṇa as the guard in the Aśoka-Vāṭikā who coincidently was a devotee of Rāma. (Incidentally the house in which Sītā lived in Mithilā was called Sundara-dhāma.) Above all, Hanumān is *sundara*, for he is the cause of all *sundara* deeds in the sense of beautiful and auspicious as well. The canto really belongs to Hanumān, for he is the instrument of *sundara* deeds performed in the canto. Moreover, the canto belongs to Hanumān literally as well, for the term *sundara* is used for monkey as well.

III

Shifting focus from the early part of the Western and Indian history and texts to not so distant Indian past, one finds that the East India Company's occupation of India after its victory in the battle of Plassey in 1757 was paralleled with the discussion of aesthetical concerns in England in the form of writings like "Pleasures of the Imagination" in *The Spectator* by Joseph Addison in 1712 and later in the second half of the eighteenth century by Edmund Burke's discussion of the sublime. With the take-over of the Company by the Queen after 1857, the colonial master's way of understanding and appreciating the beautiful attracted the psyche of the subjects. The new class of educated people in the universities began to participate in aesthetics. This impacted all Indian languages in varying measures. Modern Indian languages like Hindi began discussion on aesthetics in the second half of the nineteenth century particularly in the writings of academic critics like Shyam Sunder Shukla and Babu Gulab Rai. Benedetto Croce's book *Aesthetic as Science of Expression and General Linguistics* (1902), translated into English in 1909, earned the attention of Hindi critics including Acharya Ramchandra Shukla who critiqued it competently and saw it as the Western incarnation of Kuntaka's *vakrokti*. He opposed Croce's position that the work of art is always internal and what is external is no longer a work of art because of Croce's over insistence on formal or artistic aspects of poetry/literature. Shukla viewed that there are a few things that captivate and control our inner being after coming in touch with them and our knowledge becomes helpless spectator of the situation and we get merged with them. This merging of our inner being with the object of attraction is the state of aesthetic experience. He conceived a general/common ideal of beauty by avoiding extremes of subjectivity and objectivity as well. However, he found the word *sundara* incapable of manifesting the true form of poetry, for the word points to external aspects and limits the nature of poetic experience. In this sense of the terms' figures of speech, love may be called "beautiful" but that would demean sublime poetry and be indicative of low taste.

Whether aesthetics is an Indian category or not, the fact is that it is accepted as a category and attained currency in modern Indian critical discourse so we must take cognizance of it and discuss it accordingly. For this I must take note of Ananda Kentish Coomaraswamy, Sri Aurobindo, Mahatma Gandhi and M.

Hiriyanna among others. M.K. Gandhi, not a critic or aesthetician in the traditional sense of the term, is important for the present discourse because he underscored the significance of what is termed as *rasa* (relish) or aesthetic experience but did not see any need for either critic, or system of criticism or aesthetics. Gandhi wrote some letters and some fragments here and there. I will give illustrations from two of his small pieces. One is related to criticism and the other is related to aesthetics. In two sentences, he wrote off the institution of criticism. In *Harijan* (14 November, 1936, p. 315) he wrote, "Why should I need an artist to explain a work of art to me? Why should it not speak out to me itself?" Here "artist" stands for the ideal critic who, it is supposed, knows his/her work of art better than anyone else. At another place when he referred to some beautiful painting, he said about his experience:

> . . . so far as I was concerned, I had no need of arts like painting for my own inspiration. For I myself find enough satisfaction in the view of starry vault. Perhaps Europe needs paintings to satisfy her. She has not our sky. — *Among the Great,* 1950: 87

The views of Munshi Premchand, a famous Hindi novelist, demand attention here. He wrote in Urdu and Hindi as well. In vol. III of *Vividha Prasaṅga* he said that India cannot afford "Art-for-Art's sake" because there was so much poverty and exploitation of poor farmers. Art-for-art's sake presupposes certain amount of prosperity in society that he saw India did not have in his period. So he proposed a new form of creativity and standards of measuring and appreciating beauty. He proposed that standards of measuring beauty must change in the new age. What kind of change would be there? From where would these standards come? He said, *kaśmakaśe-hayāt meiṅ husna kā mayāra hai* (The standards of beauty lie in the struggle for existence of our life). For him, struggle for existence and human values are significant and not aesthetical values because ultimately human life, human values and the struggle for existence matter more than criteria or crucible of art. In other words, the standards of beauty lie in the struggle for existence and should emerge from it. In the "Introduction" to his *Mansarovar* he stated it in a short sentence: *saralatā paidā kījiye* (create simplicity). He did not say *saralatā lāīye* because it has the connotations of importing it from outside. This simplicity is to be produced from within and it should replace the already existing complexity. With no aim of imposing my views I would submit that creativity is more important than the endeavour of constructing aesthetics. Poetics, aesthetics and their principles would follow creativity. And when there shall be a rich body of creativity, the principles can be inferred from it. There should be no undue haste for aesthetics because subscription to aesthetics would at best lead to faultless mediocrity but not even faulty sublime.

Aesthetic is such a seductive, yet equally fatal discourse that all those who had literary output of even small consequence either pronounced or proposed to construct their aesthetics. It was the kind of anxiety that we have in our academic literary practices at the moment, as everyday witnesses pronouncements about a new or alternative aesthetics or poetics, though they remain unrealized. All these attempts have proved to be mere ugly pronouncements. I am happy with these failures, for they suggest the success of creativity or art that defies being defined or standardized. Whenever a Śāstra comes into existence, it heralds, if not the end of creativity, then at least the best of creativity. The system of aesthetics or poetics is often preceded by an elongated period of creativity. For instance, in Greece by the time Aristotle wrote the *Poetics*, the best period of Greek literature in drama and poetry — in particular poetry and drama — was over. Similarly, by the time we reach to Bhāmaha in Sanskrit, the best of Sanskrit literature was written. So to me, the construction of Śāstra — call it aesthetics or ethics or whatever name, signals the end of real or great creativity in that domain. Among dalit creative writers and critics, Sharan Kumar Limbale wrote *Towards an Aesthetic of Dalit Literature: History, Controversies and Considerations* (2004) as an alternative to the classical poetics and added new *rasa* based on *ākrośa* (wrath caused by suffering and exploitation) just after 40-50 years of dalit writing (Limbale 101-16). He questioned the existing standards of evaluating dalit literature, and proposed a new dalit aesthetics. Another dalit writer and critic in Hindi, Omprakash Valmiki rejected Hindi aesthetics based on Sanskrit and Western aesthetics in his *Dalit Sāhitya kā Saundryaśāstra*. According to him, both of them are incapable of evaluating dalit writing because Sanskrit aesthetics is primarily feudalistic and Brāhmanical, and the Western aesthetics is capitalistic and feudalistic. It is true to good extent that *varṇa vyavasthā* or caste system conditioned Sanskrit literature but it would be wrong to obliterate the fact that the best of the Sanskrit poets Vālmīki and Veda Vyāsa were "dalits" from our present-day definitions. Kālidāsa too was casteless till he was fooled by pseudo-pundits for their advantage. It can be argued that they were co-opted or appropriated by the feudal or Brāhmanical systems. But the same can be forwarded against some of the present dalit writers who serve the present government system or private capitalist/system in different capacities.

Like Sharan Kumar Limbale, Omprakash Valmiki relying on Rajendra Yadav, proposes that dalit aesthetics relies on *prahāra* (attack or assault) and not on *sammohana* (fascination or ecstacy). It attacks age-old, rotten traditions of casteism, religion and exploitation. Rajendra Yadav, cited by Valmiki, saw alternative aesthetics beginning with *saṁgharṣa* (struggle), and leads to *yātanā* (suffering) and ultimately to a vision or dream of alternative society. Dalit literature, according to Valmiki, has all three of them. Dr Ambedkar's philosophy provided impetus to struggle in dalit literature. Inhuman torture inflicted on them has made dalits realize their suffering and need for its articulation, and dalit creativity provides them vision. To Valmiki's credit it must be stated that he gives new dimension to two words *ākāra* (form) and *āśaya* (tone) for considering a text according to aesthetics of dalit literature. The form is the work/text, as we see, and whatever is understood in terms of essence and message of a work is *āśaya*. Both of these terms, however, are not originally contributed by

Valmiki, as they are Hindi translation of 'form' and 'tone.' The rest of his arguments are oft repeated ones or taken from others with acknowledgement of course. The traditional literature is formalist, as it subscribes to the *ākāra,* so formalist criticism cannot do justice to dalit literature.

All Śāstras point towards the culmination or end of creativity in the given field. To me, dalit writing in itself is more important than aesthetics because aesthetics tries to condition creativity. Another fact is that artists or writers have written works on aesthetics and poetics but no aesthetician or poet has ever authored a creative work of significance. Bharata, Bhāmaha, Kuntaka, Kṣemendra, Ānandavardhana, Plato, Aristotle, Longinus or Kant have no significant creative work to their credit that either set new standard of new creativity or subscribed to best standards of creativity discussed by them. One can counter the argument by saying that all poets were poeticians first and poets later. It is like asking what came out first, the egg or chicken. Admittedly, in all artists and poets of significance creative and critical faculties dovetail simultaneously but the critical faculty is subsequent to creative, notwithstanding the post-structuralist rejection of hierarchy between them after 1960s. It is impossible to draw a line of demarcation between the two but only in state of mortgaging of critical sense, they can be termed the same.

Having argued against the need for aesthetics, I must return to the dalit aesthetic, as proposed by Limbale. The need for dalit aesthetics arose out of the failure of the mainstream Marathi criticism to do justice to *dalit* literature which flourished under the new consciousness brought about by Dr Ambedkar. As a reaction against the mainstream criticism by B.S. Mardhekar, R.B. Patankar, Surendra, Barlinge, Narhar Kurundkar, D.B. Kulkarni and Prabhakar Padhye among others, Sharad Patil wrote *Abrāhmaṇī Sāhitya kā Saundaryaśāstra*. Literature of rebellion wished to use the Śāstra of Saundaryaśāstra. As a consequence, this new aesthetics replaced *ānanda* (state of bliss) with *vedanā* (suffering), and proposed *svatantratā* (freedom) or *mukti* (emancipation) as its aesthetic values. Its nature is essentially materialist, and not spiritualist or esoteric. It subscribes to the position that the beauty of a work of art lies in artistic expression of reality. The standards of evaluation of *dalit* literature propose that the experience of an artist should attest a work; the experience of artist(s) should be made public; the experience of the artist should have the ability of transcending the limits of region; and the experience of the artist should appear new and fresh in all ages. The most significant contribution of dalit aesthetics is not in mere questioning of the mainstream aesthetics but in contributing to it in the light of *rasa* theory. Yadunath Thatte had proposed that Acharya Javdekar had termed *krānti* (revolution) as the tenth *rasa*. In the same sequence Thatte considered that *ākrośa* should be added as the next *rasa*. According to Limbale, it is an unending process because then *vidroha* will also be *rasa*. The problem is that *rasa* theory is very fixable but preconditions that by becoming a participant of the intricacies of a Śāstra one has to take care of *bhāva, vibhāva, ālambana* and *uddīpana*. And if dalit writers get trapped in them, their entire wrath, suffering and rebellion will be sapped by them.

Among the twentieth-century aestheticians, Ananda K. Coomaraswamy and M. Hiriyanna, who examined the issue of aesthetics and perception of beauty in India seriously, deserve discussion here. Coomaraswamy undertook "the task of working for the union of Eastern and Western thoughts for the good of humanity" (Romain Rolland, "Foreword" 1948: 6) and interpreted Indian art to the West in an age in which the Indians had lost faith in their own knowledge traditions. He wrote extensively on Indian philosophy, art and culture in different books. However, his views on Indian poetics are presented in two of his well-written essays "The Theory of Art in Asia" and "Hindu View of Art: Theory of Beauty."

As one of the most distinguished scholars with Indian orientation in his aesthetics and art criticism, Coomaraswamy was concerned with discovering and establishing the language of the spirit, 'the common universe of discourse' transcending the difference in tongue. Plainly speaking, his vision can be summed up in the fact that the Ultimate Truth is one. The language of truth necessarily consists of many dialects, adapted to the needs of different races and individuals. The Divine Ground, the Godhead, is the source of all that is. The Logos is the paradigm of all created things. Man, like nature, is composed of conjoint principle — divine and human, the invisible and the visible. There are two selves in man: one, the individual self (the psyche or the soul); two, the divine self (the pneuma or the spirit). All the proper activities of man — the production of works of art and literature among them — are ultimate means for the supreme realization in which the many become one in us as it is in Him. Supreme identity of many and One, the visible and the invisible, the appearances and the reality, in a state of non-differentiated awareness, wherein the knower and the known are one, is the end and perfection of man. All true arts are imitative of the art of the Divine Artificer. Art imitates nature in her mode of operation. The nature designated here is Mother Nature (*natura, naturans* God, *creatrix universalis*) rather than created nature (*natura naturata*), which is itself God's work of art. True art is symbolic and anagogic: it is a means to draw men's powers and attention away from attachment to the changing phenomenal world so that men can conceive the real world in its intelligible aspect.

Coomaraswamy has discussed Indian aesthetics with the ancient views on sculpture and painting. On the basis of his study of Hindu and Buddhist iconography and *Śukranītisāra* he has made three observations: (i) The formal element in art represents *cittasanna* (a purely mental activity). An icon-maker or imager has to practise yoga until he has conceived the *jñāna sattva rūpa* as if in a dream, i.e. *dhyātva yajet.* Thereafter having attained concentration he should begin the work *dhyātavya kuryāt.* (ii) Behind this all-pervading concept of art is the view that all arts have a divine origin. The artist is often considered as visiting heaven and observing the form of the angel or architecture to be reproduced on the earth under the guidance of the supreme artificer

Viśvakarman. (iii) In the end he discussed the terms like *sadṛṣya*, *anukaraṇa* or *anukṛti*, and *pramāṇa*.

Regarding the work of art, Coomaraswamy stated that "the work of art is determined . . . in the same way, proximately with regard to immediate use, and ultimately with regard to aesthetic experience" (Coomaraswamy, 1934: 46). He then defined art thus: "Art is then defined as follows: *vākyam rasātmakam kāvyam*, that is, "Art is Expression Informed by Ideal Beauty" (Idem). Here it is to be borne in mind that Coomaraswamy's Indian theory of art is derived from the discussion pertaining to making of images of deities, and that his interpretation of *anukṛti* is Platonic in attitude. Moreover, Coomaraswamy's rendering of *rasa* into "Ideal Beauty" seems incorrect because *rasa* is generally translated as 'emotional appeal,' 'aesthetic emotion,' or 'aesthetic experience.' Interestingly enough, he has equated *rasāsvādana* with *brahmānanda*, and this he did through his interpretation of two verses in *Sāhitya-Darpaṇa* (II. 2-3).

Coomaraswamy's view of Indian aesthetics is coloured by his monistic philosophy, consequently reducing Indian aesthetics not only in its range but also in its importance. Surprisingly he confined himself to Viśvanātha, a compiler, and Dhanañjaya and did not concentrate on Bharata, Bhāmaha, Ānandavardhana, Abhinavagupta, Mammaṭa and Jagannātha.

The basic tenets of Coomaraswamy's views on Indian poetics included: (a) Art is religion. (b) Art gives 'a state of non-differentiated awareness, wherein the knower and the known are one,' and this is the state when you realize the supreme identity of many and one. Artistic delight is identical with *brahmānanda*. A work of art is an excuse, so the details that go into a work of art are not all that significant. (c) Art is essentially symbolic and anagogic and not naturalistic. (d) A *rasika*, like a poet, is born. He has an innate knowledge of absolute values. He did not devote much of his energy in discussing Sanskrit poetics, as he did in case of Indian art, philosophy and aesthetics. But whatever he wrote bears enough evidence of his ability to analyse and formulate theoretically in the context of the tradition.

Following Ananda Coomaraswamy, the beauty and its discussion may be seen in terms of time. Beauty remains unwithered and unravished by time. But time encompasses momentary and eternal as well. So there is nothing concrete in the universe that is eternal. Coomaraswamy in his book, *Time and Eternity*, cited from the *Yoga-Sūtra-Bhāṣya* (3.52) in which a moment (*kṣaṇa*) is the "ultimate minimum of time, and cannot be further divided up . . . and the continuous flow of such moments is their 'course' (*karma*). . . . Their uninterrupted course is what is called 'time.' . . . The whole world passes through a mutation in any one moment; so all the external qualities of the world are relative to this present moment." The control of the moments and their sequence leads to a discriminative gnosis, of which the final development (ibid.: 54), "the Deliverer" (*tāraka*), "has all things for its object, and all times, without regard to their course (*akrama*) as its object." In this sense we must make a distinction between beauty and loveliness. The former is timeless and in that sense it would exist only at the level of ideas. The latter is measured in terms of its ability to attract attention, not necessarily hold it. Both of them, as they refer to eternal and momentary, appear opposite but are not so because every moment is a part of eternal. What we know as loveliness is an inflexion of idea in the concrete form: *kṣaṇe kṣaṇe yannavatamupaiti tadaiva rūpam ramaṇīyatāya* (Beautiful form or loveliness is what attains newness at every moment).

The answer to the question pertaining to beauty might be found in Coomaraswamy who saw it as *rasa.* To him, beauty and beautiful are different because the moment we use the word beautiful as an adjective for a woman and beautiful monkey and beautiful hair, the connotations are altogether different. He used the term *rasavanta* for beautiful.

M. Hiriyanna (1871-1950) considered aesthetics in his book, *Art Experience*, largely ignored in the Indian critical discussion.

The book deals with the central issue of the experience of art which forms the basis of entire critical discourse and aesthetic perception. He discussed nature and purpose of art experience in the light of Indian poetics and established its relevance in contemporary period with his own arguments. He treated Indian aesthetics as the branch of Indian philosophy, articulated as it is in the Upaniṣadic discourse. As a scholar entrenched in Indian philosophy and poetics, he saw the parallel development of Indian aesthetic and spiritual odyssey. The interweaving of the two flummoxed the Western scholars like Hegel in the nineteenth century but Hiriyanna saw the movements of the two from the external to internal without over-sighting the balance between the two. The *mantra*s, the Brāhmaṇas and the Upaniṣads provide an understanding of the unity underlying the diversity in the universe — from belief in supernatural gods in the skies with a promise for reward in virtuous life to the belief in the concept of *ātman* of the Vedānta. This doctrine of immanence emphasizes the "here-now" "in me" philosophy. According to him, the theory of evolution of art in Sanskrit poetics is primarily religious in its evolution. He divided the practice of Sanskrit poetics in two schools. The *Prācīna* (Old) School focused on the external expression of poetry, i.e. on *śabda* and *artha* dealing with *guṇa*s (excellences) and *doṣa*s (defects). The *Navīna* (Modern) School proposed departure from the old school of judging the experience and worth of art. In the ninth century, Ānandavardhana critiqued the *rasa* theory of the *Nāṭyaśāstra* in *Dhvanyāloka*. According to him, Ānandavardhana brought a major shift in Sanskrit poetics because earlier a poetic composition was considered good or bad on the basis of *guṇa*s (excellences/merits) and *doṣa*s (demerits/defects). From the new perspective the implicit meaning constitutes the real essence of all poetry. Whatever subserves the poetic end is *guṇa* and the otherwise is *doṣa*. It means *doṣa*s and *guṇa*s are relative in character and not absolute as was often thought. The inner meaning is the criterion and constitutes the truly poetical.

The artist never really feels concerned about them; for a thought

> or feeling experienced with poetic intensity is sure to find expression. The expression is also likely to be more or less imperfect, but the question is not whether it is perfect, but whether it is adequate to convey the thought or emotion to others. If it is adequate it is good poetry, otherwise it is not.
>
> — Hiriyanna, 1954: 6

The shift from the outer to the inner and from the absolute to relative was a major step in the development of theory of art, its creation and perception in India. It was related to spirituality as well. However, it did not mean that the outer was of no use. Aesthetic satisfaction, like its spiritual counterpart, lies in the balance between outer (in terms of explicit) form and meaning or *sthūla śarīra* in the form of idol or physical body and *sūkṣma śarīra* (inner reality or *ātman* of the human being manifesting itself in vitality, health, grace and contentment in art or human body). He then contrasted two attitudes of appreciation of the externals of true art in terms of two attitudes — one that looks on a statue of Buddha in meditative posture and remains satisfied with the admiration of beauty, naturalness and proportions of its external features, and the other which realizes the ideal of serenity and calm depicted there which constitutes its ultimate meaning. (Hiriyanna, 1954: 41).

Concerning the issue about the soul of art according to the *Navīna* School, *rasa* is the *ātman* of art. The *rasānanda* (bliss of taste of true beauty) is inscrutable which is neither expressible in words nor knowable objectively; it can only be realized. (Hiriyanna 1954:9). Whether we relish good food or contemplate the relationship between *ātman* (human soul) or *Paramātmā* (divine soil), the aesthetic experience (*rasānubhava*) or the realization dawns in those rare moments when the narrow ego-centric distinction between the self and the object breaks down, and human beings transcend narrow egocentric distinction temporarily at least so that a sense of detachment from desire ensues. This mood of detachment leads to the experience of delight. "It is this transcending of self-consciousness — this migrating from our narrow self, to put it otherwise — that constitutes the secret of aesthetic delight. The highest function of the poet who easily rises to these moods is to communicate the same to us" (Hiriyanna, 1954: 20).

To Hiriyanna, *rasa* is a metaphor, signifying both "a process and that the process is, in neither, sundered from the result"(1954: 81). At the level of a deeper implication, it points out the unity of aesthetic experience and its uniqueness also because there might be blending of various tastes but the result is one single taste surpassing all in its flavour. Here we must remember that *rasa* applies equally to all forms of literature and art, though it has been more discussed and refined with regard to poetry and drama.

Hiriyanna further discussed relationship between art and morality, art and life, the aesthete and aesthetics and ethics. The realization of harmony of art in terms of our own experience seems to snap our connection with the work-a-day world. "We do not really realize then, like the knower, the unity of all." According to him, "The knower is the *jñānin* or saint who knows the true source of this delight; the aesthete is one who through art experience enjoys the delight even while she or he is not privileged, by virtue of the nature of art experience, to knowledge of true enlightenment"(Hiriyanna 1954:9). The saint and the aesthete both realize unity in diversity. However, the difference between the detachment and delight brought about by art experience, when compared to the joyful detachment which the *jñānin* experiences, is one not to be forgotten in the long run although not evident in the moment of art experience.

While in the one case what is realized is the truth of Nature, it is in the other the truth of art. The latter, no doubt, is a lower truth; but there is yet a close resemblance between the two attitudes; and we may well compare the person appreciating art to a *jīvanamukta* [one that has realized the goal of life]. He does indeed get a foretaste of *mokṣa* [true freedom] then; but it is not *mokṣa* in fact because it is transient, not being based upon perfect knowledge (1954:10).

The fact is that even perfect knowledge is not enough for *mokṣa*. In other words, Indian philosophy does not put much premium on aesthetics, and puts art in its proper place, even the knowledge of spirituality in its proper place. He explained the place of *jñāna* (knowledge) in Indian philosophy:

> The most noticeable feature of Indian philosophy is the stress which it lays upon the influence which knowledge ought to have on life. None of the systems that developed in the course of centuries in India stopped short at the discovery of truth; but each followed it up by an inquiry as to how the discovered truth could be best applied to the practical problems of life. The ultimate goal of philosophic quest was not knowledge (*tattvajñāna*) so much as the achievement of true freedom (*mokṣa*).
> (Hiriyanna, 1954: 1)

The need for art and philosophy exists irrespective of what we consider to be the origins of the evil. Hiriyanna referred to the *Sāṁkhya* system which sees evil as an intrinsic part of nature, and the Advaita Vedānta belief which by contrast holds evil to be the result of our own imperfect vision of nature. The Indian view holds, like the Greek, that both art and philosophy arise out of a sense of the presence of evil in natural life. When we view it from the Sāṁkhya perspective, the function of art is to fashion something better than nature (1954:16), something which will serve as a relief from the troubles of life (1954:28); whereas from the Advaita Vedānta perspective, art could help us to see the best in nature, often unnoticed in quotidian life, and serve as a pathway to reality. From the latter perspective, "art is much more than a means to secure for man a temporary escape from the imperfections of common life; it is an 'intimation' to him of the possibility of rising permanently above those "imperfection" (1954:28); although, as Hiriyanna discussed in his essay on "Art and Morality," self-forgetfulness rather than self-realization is more often the hallmark of art experience as commonly pursued (1954:57).

Hiriyanna did not consider aesthetics of great consequence in the context of daily life, and in the scheme of Indian philosophy.

He believed that appreciating art allows us to experience the state of *mokṣa* for the short time, as we forget ourselves in the work of art. But it does not endure long but passes away sooner or later, for it depends for its continuance upon the presence of the external stimulus which has evoked it. The ideal state, on the other hand, if it should answer to that description at all, must, when attained, necessarily become a permanent feature of life" (1954:25). Art experience can arouse our interest in the ideal state by giving us a foretaste of it, and thus serve as a powerful incentive to the pursuit of that state, for which however it can in the long run never substitute.

There are two other ways in which art experience is inferior to the experience of the ideal state. Art experience has inherent in it the possibility of escapism, for there is nothing in aesthetic experience itself to guarantee against a life of self-centred satisfaction" (1954:26). This is in contrast to the ideal state which never forgets social responsibility:

> The ideal state will never be thus divorced from sympathy for fellow beings because, in the Indian view, it cannot be attained by anyone who has not learnt to render loving service to other as the result of a thorough training in social morality. — 26

Art experience, further, differs from experience of the ideal state in that it is induced artificially from outside, while that ideal state springs naturally from within. Hiriyanna made distinction between the experience of art and of the ideal state:

> . . . art experience does not require as a necessary condition of its attainment either philosophic knowledge or moral worth. It can be brought into being, even in their absence, by the power which all true works of art possess. That aesthetic contemplation can lead to the same kind of exalted experience as that of the ideal state, without all the arduous discipline — moral as well intellectual — required for the latter, may appear to be an excellence of it. In a sense, no doubt, it is; and an old Indian art critic has declared, with exultation, that the bliss of *mokṣa*, which the *yogin* has to strain himself for long to win, is no match for it.

> But we should remember that art experience is woefully fugitive, and that the enduring character of the satisfaction that attends the ideal experience more than compensates for all the trouble and the exertion involved in attaining it.
>
> — (1954:27-28)

It should however not be construed that *rasa* theory makes no distinction between good and bad. It is clear about what are the constituents of the best poetry and/or inferior art. To Hiriyanna's credit it must be stated that he discussed aesthetics in terms of Indian philosophical and cultural context. Moreover, he was among the Indian critics who did not lay excessive emphasis upon aesthetics. His estimate corrected the mistake or over-estimate of literature and aesthetics that arose out of Aristotle's statement that poetry is superior to history and philosophy, and thereby he put them to their right place.

IV

Like other domains of knowledge, the Greeks built the system of ethics. According to Plato, Socrates was the wisest of all Greeks because he was of the opinion that his knowledge was of no use. Socrates persuaded his countrymen to shift attention from external world to wo/man and his/her condition. In this configuration, knowledge with ability to impact human life was on the highest pedestal and the other was subordinate to it. Self-knowledge was imperative for success and a good life. He correlated knowledge with virtual and engrafted virtual with happiness. A wise man will know what is right, do what is good and therefore be happy. Aristotle saw man in terms of nature — physical (vegetable), emotional (animal) and mental (rational). The last was more important for him, for it is a necessity for philosophical cognition. Moderation was the principle for his world-view and ethics as well. Virtue lay in moderation (as a virtual). Moderate virtue denotes doing the right thing to the right person, at the right time to the proper extent in the correct fashion, for the right reason. Man, according to him, should not just live but live well with moderate virtues.

The West also, as in India, paid attention to duty-oriented ethics. Along with virtue theories, and consequential theories, duty theories (called as non-consequential theories because consequences of following these duties are of no consequence, and at times called deontological theories from the Greek word *deon,* i.e. duty) were developed in the West. Samuel Pufendorf, a seventeenth century German philosopher, saw three principal duties — to God, to oneself and to others. The first included the critical duty to know the existence and nature of God, the practical duty to worship God inwardly and outwardly. The second was of two kinds: duties of the soul including duties of one's skill and talent and duties of the body. The third involved absolute duties, i.e. treat people as equal and promote the good of other, and conditional duties including duty to keep one's promises and agreements.

Following Pufendorf, Kant agreed with duties to oneself and others. But he forwarded the foundational principle of duty encompassing duties. He called it the "categorical imperative," a single, self-evident principle of reason. The categorical imperative is different from hypothetical imperative, depending upon personal desire. The categorical imperative mandates a duty in the form of an action irrespective of personal desire. By subscribing to the single principle of duty, the morality of all actions can be determined. Critiquing Kant, Arthur Schopenhauer proposed his moral theory and primary incentives: compassion, malice and egoism. Compassion is the major motivator to moral expression. Malice and egoism are corrupt alternatives. By bringing in compassion Schopenhauer again became the point of convergence of Indian and Western ethical values of *karuṇā* (compassion) and *dayā* (mercy) of Buddhism, as they found space and new dimension more than five hundred years after Buddha in Jesus Christ and his order.

The right theory also had its relation with duty based approach, as they are interrelated. John Locke, the seventeenth-century British philosopher, proposed that laws of nature mandate that none should harm anyone's life, wealth, liberty or possessions, which Locke opined, were natural rights, given by God to man. Thomas Jefferson followed these three foundational rights, i.e. life, liberty and pursuit of happiness — in authoring the United States Declaration of Independence. Right theorists associate these rights to moral rights and propose their four features — that they are natural, universal, equal and inalienable. Rights of one person are duties of other. Recently British philosopher W.D. Ross enlisted *prima facie* duties which are 'part of the fundamental nature of the universe.' The duties, according to him, include: fidelity (to keep promises), reparation (to compensate when we harm others), gratitude (the duty to thank those who help us), justice (to recognize merit), beneficence (to improve others' conditions), self-improvement (to improve virtual and intelligence) and non-malaficence (not to injure others). The last one is more important as it is actual duty and other(s) may be *prima facie* or apparent duty.

The absence of ethics as a system in India that boasts of constructing Śāstras in the fields of almost all conceivable human activities may surprise those uninitiated in Indian knowledge systems. The verbal Upaniṣadic and Brāhmaṇa discourse and later on the texts like *Pañcatantra* and *Hitopadeśa* served the purpose of guiding moral behaviour. The later text Kamadiki's *Nītiśāstra* falls in this category. Cāṇakya's *Nītiśāstra* is another text on the subject. Apart from the texts like *Nītiśāstra*, sociological texts like Dharmaśāstra and Smṛtis served the function, as they detailed the issues of individual and group conduct in different ages. In southern India, the text like *Thirukkuraḷ* served the same function. These texts puzzle modern mind, for they are interdisciplinary in nature and thereby they defy being categorized according to the modern categories of specialization.

Apart from the sociological texts the cultural encyclopaedic texts like the *Rāmāyaṇa* and the *Mahābhārata* that exist at multiple levels and therefore cannot be put in one particular category, for they contain everything that pertains to the human life and its manifestations in different ways, served the multiple functions — literary, aesthetics, ethical, and religious among others. In Indian tradition they can be put under the category of *vāṅgmaya* (discourse) or *sāhitya* in general. The Indian *vāṅgmaya, dṛṣṭānta* is used to constitute, manifest, illustrate, and disseminate knowledge of different kinds — moral or ethical conduct. In the *Mahābhārata,* the concept of *dharma* determines ethical conduct. The concept of *dharma* (righteous conduct) is related to the concept of *satya* (truth) and *nīti* or ethical behaviour. I would with the concept of *satya,* point out the concept of *ṛta* which was considered superior to *satya*. The difference is discernible in the *Taittirīya Upaniṣad,* (chapṭer I) *ṛtam vadisyāmī, satyam vadisyāmī.*

If allowed to translate I would say that *satya* is factual truth and *ṛta* is truth as value, and both these words find their manifestations in the *Mahābhārata.* In his statement, *naro vā kuñjaro vā* (either man or elephant) Yudhiṣṭhira is in a way factually true but it is not *ṛta*. Moreover, this *ṛta* is to be seen in the light of *puruṣārtha catuṣṭaya.* The *puruṣārtha catuṣṭaya,* i.e. attainment of four goals, forms the crux of human life in all its manifestations in Indian culture. The goals of *puruṣārtha catuṣṭaya,* i.e. *dharma, artha, kāma* and *mokṣa* are not metaphysical but physical categories, as the first stands for righteous conduct, the second for economic well-being attained through righteous conduct, the third for graṭification of desires in the light of *dharma* and *artha,* and the *mokṣa* is emancipation from the cause of pain. It means that death is not a precondition for *mokṣa,* which might take place in the present life and world. Each one of them, if taken out of context and proportion, can be perverted, as *dharma* can become ritualism, *artha* (greed), *kāma* (lust) and *mokṣa* (escapism). Also, if one goes directly to the last by ignoring the first three, it can be fraught with spiritual disasters.

Dharma (righteous conduct) is the first of all four goals. As an ideal it is to be pursued individually and collectively, by family and society, within the four walls of the house and outside. If *dharma* is not practised, the society degenerates, and when it is beyond repair, there arises the need of the Kurukṣetra War to cleanse the society.

The concept of *dharma* needs to be seen in the perspective of another concept of *ṛṇa,* as discussed in many texts including the *Mahābhārata.* Literally *ṛṇa* means debt but it is not financial debt repayable in monetary terms but a set of duties emanating from the concept of ethical debt repayable through performance of duties. They include (i) *deva-ṛṇa* (debt to nature), (ii) *pitṛ-ṛṇa* (to the parents and forefathers), (iii) *ṛṣi-ṛṇa* (to the great teachers in the tradition one is born into), (iv) *nṛ-ṛṇa* (to the humanity at large), and (v) *bhūta-ṛṇa* (to all living beings). (*Manu-Saṁhitā* 3.70-71, *Śatapatha Brāhmaṇa* 1.7.2.1, *Rāmāyaṇa* 2.4.14, *Mahābhārata* 12.7.17-18, 12,63.20, 12.65.19 and 21). These are innate debts and their awareness and the capacity to resolve them emerges gradually in life. Their fulfilment rejects the question of human rights, for if all of us are conscious of our duties and fulfil them, the rights are naturally taken care of, and there is no imposition by any external agency or system like ethics.

If we take care of these five *ṛṇa*s, entire human orientation shifts from rights to duties leading to emancipation from what we would ask for, but what we must do to these five because in these five categories, all elements — living or dead — in all forms and time are taken care of. The concern for others in consonance with the holistic spirit can be seen in the "Bhūmipūjana" in *Taittirīyopniṣad* in the form of prayer for forgiveness of the mother Earth before constructing a house:

> *Oṁ*! May all the creatures who live here forgive me! May they plan to live elsewhere from now on! This formal offering is dedicated to please them.

Let us now move to the *Rāmāyaṇa* to seek response to the issue of social obligations and responsibilities. One of the questions that has bothered me for quite some time (and I don't think I have found a proper answer to it) is: why did Rāma abandon Sītā? Why did he send her to the forest after becoming the king of Ayodhyā? Many responses are forwarded to answer it. One of them is that Rāma was a human being and so he naturally felt that Sītā had been in Rāvaṇa's Laṅkā for so many months, so he doubted her chastity. Another response in the form of a narrative is that on one fine day while pregnant Sītā was sitting in some desolate mood in her palace in Ayodhyā, one of the sisters of Rāma asked her to describe Rāvaṇa, for she would have seen Rāvaṇa. Sītā replied that she did not see Rāvaṇa clearly. Only once she saw Rāvaṇa's shadow. She persuaded her to prepare a sketch of Rāvaṇa with a piece of charcoal. While Sītā prepared a sketch, her sister called Rāma complaining that Sītā loved Rāvaṇa and still remained in his thoughts. Rāma conceded to his sister's conspiracy, and abandoned her. The third one related to the washerman is known to all of us. Rāma's detectives heard the washerman telling his wife that he was not Rāma who would accept his wife after she had stayed in some other man's house. He cast aspersions more on Rāma's gullibility than on Sītā's chastity. The question that arises here is: what were the options before Rāma at that particular moment? Apart from abdicating the throne, one of the options available to Rāma was that he could have asked Hanumān to 'take care of' this petty *dhobī* for spreading canard about him. There was one more option of abdicating his throne. But why did he continue to be the king? In our tradition of *bahuśruta* (well-heard), against the tradition of the well-read of the West, I have heard from some commentators on the *Rāmāyaṇa* and *Mahābhārata* that in Indian tradition the answers to the issues, left unresolved in the preceding text, might be found in the subsequent texts. So for the answer to the question of the *Rāmāyaṇa* we must go to the subsequent texts in the tradition, i.e. the *Mahābhārata*. There is a narrative in the *Mahābhārata* about a sage who sat under a tree, did *tapa* and accumulated it. There was a crane sitting on the tree. The crane excreted and it fell on the head of the sage who looked at the bird in rage, the crane was burnt to ashes. It filled him with a sense of pride. With inflated pride he went to a home for alms. The lady did not come out to open the door, for she was busy tending to her husband. He knocked again and again. When she came out after finishing her duty, he stared angrily at her. But nothing happened to her; not even a hair of the lady was damaged. The lady told him, *nāham balaka* (I am not the crane). The sage was astonished as to how did she know about the incident. The sage was full of pride but not an unwise fellow. On being inquired by him, she said that society and family have given certain responsibilities to us, and whatever responsibility is given to us, we must perform it with utmost fidelity, commitment and sincerity. Therefore, I did not disrespect you knowingly because I was performing the duties, assigned to me by the society and the family because I was attending to my sick husband. The answer to the question of the *Rāmāyaṇa* is in the response of the lady in the *Mahābhārata*. Rāma was assigned the duty as the king, and he had accepted the responsibility in accordance with the prevailing custom. Therefore, he had no right to abdicate the throne. The only option left for him was to abandon Sītā. This is not to defend Rāma's act, for he needs not me at least, but to state that every individual has his/her *dharma* to be followed in all conditions. Rāma followed his *dharma* and gave precedence to his higher duty as the king to his subjects than to his duty as a husband. In all Indian traditions, *dharma* is the cornerstone of ethical conduct that needs no science or system. In brief, *dharma* is the soul of Indian ethics and *kāma* of aesthetics. These systems being extraneous impositions need not be fetishized in Indian civilization just because the West had them, for they form an integral part of human conduct and ideals in it.

V

Aesthetics is about beauty and its perception and ethics about moral code of conduct to be observed by an individual and society. I have no issue with them. The problem is that both of them as Śāstra are extraneous impositions. A Śāstra like aesthetics in particular strives to limit or condition creativity and beauty with its norms and prescriptions. In practice, it becomes an instrument of exclusivity, suppression and exploitation. Śāstra is seductive because of its power and that explains the cause of power and lays down principles that go into the making of the system. Who will not like to hold or wield power? This explains the anxiety for acquisition for aesthetics or ethics, as critics in almost every literature in India claim to construct one, in case they accept that it does not have one. But they are mere proposals. We accepted and began to discuss them in a state of civilizational degeneration that either constructed walls, or the well of self-satisfied indifference or accepted whatever was fashionable.

Against the above observations the fact is that Indian mind is essentially religio-philosophical. The classical Indian arts and enunciation of their principles evolved out of them. This religio-philosophicality made it spiritual and interdisciplinary, for religion touches all aspects of life. Not so inclement climate and natural generosity allowed it space to ponder over symbiotic relationship with elements of nature and metaphysical meditation. After centuries of meditations about life and its objectives, it concluded *puruṣārtha catuṣṭaya* as the governing principle of life and all human pursuits. It took note of outward, material and earthly (*laukika*) but valued it inferior to inward, spiritual and divine (*alaukika*). [Here, the Sanskrit word for spiritual is *adhyātma* which means to think beyond one's own self. Moreover, *alaukika* is not a metaphysical category, for it (*alaukika*) does not stand for absence of *loka*. Rather it means something that transcends this world, without not being of the world.] Forms or external aspects of things which are transitory, subject to change and corruptible did not deserve serious attention. So why waste time and energy in constructing a Śāstra of forms. The immanent spirit that pervades all forms deserves serious study. Indian mind did so, and accordingly put art and aesthetics to their proper place.

Indian mind considered what falls under aesthetics as science of sense perception or systematic study of philosophical notion of beauty under *puruṣārtha* (*kāma*) and in *rasa* (*śṛṅgāra*). To substantiate and illustrate the ways of the four ends of life, it composed Dharmaśāstras (sociological texts and *mahākāvya*s) for *dharma*, Kāmaśāstra for *kāma*, *Arthaśāstra* for *artha*, and diverse spiritual texts like the Upaniṣads and the *Gītā* for *mokṣa*. The first was the overarching principle for all human activities and took care of ethical code of conduct. The *kāma* included the issues pertaining to the beautiful and its relish. Since it was attended by *dharma* and *artha,* it can be considered as the ethical aesthetics, not aesthetic ethics. It is different from John Dewey's 'aesthetic ethics' which proposed unity of aesthetics and ethics marked by 'fair' (meaning 'attractive' and 'acceptable'). It provides a philosophical rationale for peace education, according to James Page.

Kāma included aesthetic pleasure including sexual pleasure and divine spiritual bliss. Its refined practice and formulation culminated in the composition of *Kāmasūtra* by Ācārya Vātsyāyana in seventh country CE (?) that deals with 64 arts (Raghavan: 460-64) in which a cultured person or a courtesan was supposed to be educated. Indian mind approximated them in the principles of *rasa, dharma, ṛta/satya* later in the form of *satyam, śivam, sundaram* translated earlier as truth, tranquillity and beauty. The triad sums up Indian view of life and attitude towards life but is a later development. In modern terms, *satyam, śivam, sundaram* can be considered as the trinity of science, ethics and art. Incidentally, Greek and early Christian authors also believed in this triad of *satyam, śivam, sundaram* much before the principle was worked out in India. In Greek philosophy Socrates, Plato and Aristotle had also considered the issues pertaining to truth, beauty, and goodness in their discourses. St. Augustine discussed them at length in *The City of God*. The classical triad of virtues, i.e. truth, beauty, and goodness became a part of the Christian world-view in the Augustinian synthesis of Christ and Plato.

Experience is soul and testimony of life. The cessation of experience signals end of life. Beauty is not the soul. The soul of experience is *rasa*. The *rasatva* (relish) of things and ability to relish (*rasikatā*) mattered more than anything else to Indian mind. The centrality of *rasa* would have reverberated for long in the air before it was formulated in the *Nāṭyaśāstra.* Rasa theory is suitable for considering all kinds of experiences and their articulation in different art forms. Bhoja remarks that there are as many *bhāvas* (states of being) as may be leaves on a tree. Hence in different ages there can be different and new *rasas* accordingly. There is nothing profane in either questioning the adequacy of the *rasa* theory or adding a new *rasa*. The acolytes of the *rasa* theory needs not get alarmed by individuality of new experiences and try to thrust them under the given frameworks and kinds of *rasas*.

Moreover, the Rasa School admits the fitness of all kinds of themes and topics for poetic/artistic treatment. It is a consequence of suitable transformation of emotions or mood of emotional exaltation which is impersonal yet inward, detached yet subjective. Also, the aesthetic experience, i.e. *rasānubhava* is unique because each individual experiences it her/himself as in the case of an individual relishing the taste of a dish. The harmony of aesthetic experience is realized in one's own experiences and apprehended merely intellectually.

The tradition of sustained commentary on *rasa* continued for about twelve centuries or even more till Ānandavardhana, who theorized the *dhvani* (suggestion) school and wedded it to the *rasa* theory, capable of analysing all artistic manifestations, in the ninth century, and added *śānta rasa* to the existing eight *rasas*. The *rasa-dhvani* was the culmination of all comprehensive theorization of understanding or receiving art. With the *rasadhvani* formulation, there was no need of a new system like aesthetics. It (*rasadhvani*) makes the judging of a work of art objective and comprehensive and flexible because different competent readers/receivers can read the work differently according to their tastes and competence. In fact, it would allow the same reader to derive diverse meanings in different states of his/her mind.

To conclude, let me return to the epigraphical excerpts. Cāṇakya's emphasis is on *nīra-kṣīra-viveka,* i.e. ability to discriminate between milk and water; not good and bad, for good and bad are binaries, whereas milk and water are not so. Water is as good as milk; may be even more for one who is dying for want of water in a desert. But between the two, milk is considered better most of the time by most of the people. Beautiful or otherwise, ethical or unethical, both of them rest on the notion of *viveka* which is needed in their discussion too. There can be certain principles or rules but they help us to an extent only. If subscribed rather rigidly, they become detrimental to creativity and human spirit. The systems of aesthetics and ethics are extraneous impositions and help to certain extent but they cannot be framed for commonsense.

Aesthetics and ethics are interrelated in Western tradition, as Kant saw it. Indian mind saw their inseparableness in the principle of *puruṣārtha catuṣṭaya*, which is the ultimate goal for all human pursuits. It has no copyright or signature of an individual, for it was enunciated and practised before the institution of author and individualism came into existence. The ultimate point is that human nature is varied and in a state of evolution. The inscrutability of what is called beautiful makes the task of construction of aesthetics 'difficult' for Plato and impossible to mortal beings like us. The beauty of human predicament is in endeavours to construct aesthetics because it is 'difficult' and inscrutable. Human fortitude lies in staring against the imminent failure, yet ceaselessly striving for what is impossible.

In discussion of aesthetics and ethics or in their comparative study in different traditions, the fact not to be glossed over is that aesthetic and ethical senses are more important than their systems; the former is for relishing whatever is worth relishing (*rasavanta* or *madhura*), and the latter is to be practised without causing any harm or unhappiness to others. That perhaps would ensure that we would be able to avoid the fate of the king Duṣyanta (read critics/scholars/aestheticians/ethicist in general and hairsplitters in particular) in Kālidāsa's *Abhijñānaśākuntalam.* The king, seeing a bee relishing a flower (I/24), while looking longingly at naturally beautiful Śakuntalā, states:

calapaṅga dr̥ṣṭispraśasi vahuśau vepathumatim ।
rahasyakhyiva svanasi mr̥dukarṇatikcaraḥ ॥
karo vyandhumatyaḥ pibaśi ratisarvasvadharam ।
vayamatatvanmesanamadhukar hatastvamkhalukr̥ti ॥

> You touch repeatedly her quivering eye the corners of which are tremulous; hovering near her ear. You sweetly hum, as though whisper a secret (of love); in spite of waving her hand you drink her lower lip, the very essence of enjoyment; (whilst) we, O bee! are undone through search for truth (regarding her); you indeed are blessed.

Let us learn from both Duṣyanta and bee alike and not be a mere critic but relish whatever is beautiful.

Moreover, discuss we must the issues like aesthetics and ethics by becoming fully aware of their traditions in the West and our own, and not be despondent if we did not have one. With respect we must try to understand other traditions of perceiving realities, for they enrich our existing perceptions. But that does not mean that in the process of appropriating other traditions we should get appropriated by them. We, as a culture, have not lost our paths meandering in the wilderness of words. We are, in fact, lost destinations in searching for their strayed, waylaid and distracted travellers. And that is what as the lost destinations we cannot afford for long.

Part II

Colonialism and After

4

India Self-(re)fashioning and Colonialism

Resistance and Polyvalence in the Nineteenth-Century Gujarati and Hindi Renaissance Prose Writings

INDIAN 'renaissance' is the Mona Lisa of Indian literature. However far-fetched this analogy may be, yet the statement is not without truth about the enigma that Indian 'renaissance' is or has been made out to be. The problem has not primarily been with the term or with its various counterparts in Indian languages like *navajāgaraṇa*, *punarjāgaraṇa*, *lokajāgaraṇa*, but with the designation of the period and the nature of its relationship with other preceding (European) and attendant (Irish) renaissances. One must, however, concede that there has been only one Mona Lisa and it has, to a good measure, been spared form overt political or non-artistic considerations. Indian renaissances, on the other hand, are multiple and their discussion is never politically innocent. Call it by whatever name we may, our compulsions and convenience persuade us, for the time being, to designate the nineteenth century particularly the post-1857 era as the period of Indian renaissance for our present purpose. Since our present endeavour is the first intervention from our side, the issue requires discussion of its various dimensions.

The use of the term Indian 'renaissance' for measuring our literature may sound imitative, pompous and out of place, with much justification, at least to those who see it as a pale patch on the Western, particularly English, renaissance. It may further appear to be an attempt to put on glory by using terms and categories of the former masters. Related to it is the point that the endeavour of seeing the period of colonization as the period of the 'renaissance' speaks of the success of the designs of the colonizers in projecting themselves as the catalytic agents of the 'renaissance,' as it took place during the period of colonization, thereby validating their presence in the colony. Fortunately, at least in the post-Independence period Indian scholarship unceasingly expressed its uneasiness with such givens as Indian 'renaissance' for the colonial period. The multiplicity of terms for the Indian 'renaissance' as *navajāgaraṇa, punarjāgaraṇa, lokajāgaraṇa sudhārayuga*, and *prabodhana* in our languages speaks of our dissatisfaction with the term Indian 'renaissance' and also with the terms used in Indian languages, for they fail to approximate what happened during the colonial encounter. In addition, it suggests that the phenomenon in different parts of the country during the nineteenth century was as diverse as the various regions of the country. Else, one term would have sufficed. However, our ceaseless engagement with the phenomenon called Indian 'renaissance' points to the magical effect that it has had on the Indian psyche. Of all these, the most significant is the realization of the fact that most of the present problems are bequeathed to us by the nineteenth century which was the period of transition between the pre-colonial and the post-colonial India. Therefore, to understand the present eco-socio-political and cultural problems, it is imperative for us to go to the nineteenth century, the cradle of the obtaining problems.

Regarding the usage of the term 'Indian renaissance,' it is possible to resolve it by following the way others responded to such a dilemma as this in the past. Lane Cooper, after being appointed as the Professor of Comparative Literature, was uncomfortable with the idea of chairing the department with whose nomenclature he was not satisfied. Rightly so, because comparative study of literature is possible but the entity such as comparative literature is inconceivable because literature in/by itself cannot be comparative. S.S. Prawer mentions Cooper's dilemma on the very first page of his book *Comparative Literary*

Studies: An Introduction (1973), but by the time he reaches the end of the paragraph he accepts the term comparative literature, and despite his disagreement with it uses it in the rest of the book for its brevity. On our part, it is convenience, not brevity, that inveigles upon us to use the term 'renaissance' despite our dissatisfaction with its usage.

It would not be incongruous to briefly discuss the phenomenon called 'Indian renaissance' because the moment the term is mentioned, it evokes the English Renaissance that was pedalled particularly with the establishment of English education system in the colonies that were either inveigled upon or compelled to use it as a model category to fashion themselves. It was, however, a period of glorious barbarism and inhuman 'sick' practices that began in the Elizabethan Renaissance England. It may be seen in penal, medical and colonial documents that are being brought out and increasingly studied by the New Historicists like Richard Wilson and Richard Dutton who wrote in their "Introduction" to *New Historicism and Renaissance Drama* (1992): "Read within archival continuum, what they represented was not harmony but the violence of Puritan attack on carnival, the imposition of slavery, the rise of patriarchy, the hounding of deviance, and the crashing of prison-gate during what Foucault called 'the Age of Confinement,' at the dawn of carceral society" (*carceral* comes from the Latin word *carcer*, meaning a prison — Wilson and Dutton, 8). Further, colonization, whose dark shadows still linger in human history, was a product of this 'glorious' period. It led to division of humanity in the vertical categories of race and colour and their domination, as is discernible in the words of the patent issued by Queen Elizabeth I to Sir Humphrey Gilbert to inhabit and possess at his choice all remote and heathen lands not in the actual possession of any Christian prince.

The project of colonization depended solely on appropriation of natural, economic, human and intellectual resources by legal and illegal means. Trade was used for legal acquisition of economic resources, as well as for theft by transgressing the law. Subsequent political domination led to exploitation of the human resources as slaves or cheap labour and of natural resources as cheap raw material for the industrial revolution. Translation was the means of appropriating intellectual resources that the colonizer could not either write off or domesticate otherwise. The project succeeded to such an extent that by the end of the second decade of the twentieth century almost 85 per cent surface of the earth, excluding the USA, was colonized.

The seeds of the project of colonization lay in the European Renaissance mind. In *The Tragical History of D. Faustus* (1588), Christopher Marlowe's Doctor Faustus wanted his spirits to perform many functions, including the following, "I'll have them fly to India for gold . . ." (I.i). Within twelve years on 31 December 1600, Queen Elizabeth I issued a Charter in factual terms to a group of merchants of London to trade in India and other South Asian countries. The first was fictitious, literary and dramatic; the second, a historical fact. Apart from being a mere co-incidence, it was a case of literature anticipating and pre-figuration of things to follow. Marlowe's words for necromantic spirits voiced the contemporary Elizabethan society's latent engagement with Indian 'gold' or prosperity resulting in its manifestation in Queen Elizabeth's Charter for traders. It paved the way for what happened after about a century and a half in the Battle of Plassey and the consequent colonization of India for exploiting economic, natural and human resources. The Renaissance England sent Sir Thomas Roe as the diplomatic cartographer to India paving the way for trade — legal and illegal — political domination and consequent exploitation of its human and natural resources. With their political victory in 1757, the Indian present was under their authority and so was the future. The past, different from Africa and even from that of the colonizer, was a ghost that needed to be exorcized. One way of achieving the end was its appropriation through translation. Translation was a means of appropriating the past and conditioning the present. The missionaries and Orientalists initiated the process. On the one hand, William Carey translated the Bible in as many as 56 Indian languages and dialects in the late seventies of eighteenth century, and on the other scholars like William Jones translated *Abhijñānaśākuntalam* not only to appropriate the Indian past, but also to romanticize and exoticize the Orient (India) with the purpose of making the colonies more attractive to the prospective subscribers who would be willing to go to the harsh and inclement climes and lands to sustain and further the project of colonization. Moreover, the aim was to intervene and condition the existing social structures. For instance, the main aim of William Jones' translation of *Manu-Smṛti*, as he had written in a letter to William Pitt Jr., was to erode the authority of the *paṇḍit*s in the court. Jones' omissions in his translation of *Śākuntalam* connoted impurity and amorality, if not immorality, of the Orient. By doing so, he eschewed what he considered Kālidāsa's eroticism, and imposed his own (Victorian) moral order. Max Müller's adulation for certain parts of Indian heritage notwithstanding, the fact remains that even Jones, his model, was not free from political overtones.[1]

There is no denying the fact that the colonizers drained Indian financial resources and sowed the seeds of linguistic, regional and religious discord among Indians. It has to be admitted here that they introduced trains, telegram, postal services, printing press and English education system with various attendant motives. The sympathetic or soft Oriental discourse was also a by-product of the process, though it was displaced unfortunately by arrogant Anglicist discourse in the nineteenth century. Even Indian Oriental

1. In 1785 Jones in a letter to Pitt the Younger bared his real motive of translating Hindu laws so as to keep "a check on the Pundits in the Court" (In Garland Cannon ed., *The Letters of Sir William Jones* vol. II, Oxford: Clarendon Press, 1970, p. 644). He further explained his motive to Pitt by mentioning that a "good system of laws, a just administration of them, and a long peace" will *render this country a source of infinite advantage of Great Britain*" (ibid.) italics mine. These letters, used as the co-texts, speak volumes about the way even the most enlightened colonial agents viewed the other, and undertook the project of translation.

discourse was not a uniform category or project, and within it the Indian Orientalists were of different shades and motives, and even a given Orientalist had multiple motives. William Jones, the translator of *Śākuntalam*, was different from Jones, the translator of *Manu-Smṛti*, and in sharp contrast to Jones's romantic valourization of India was Macaulay's dismissive denunciation of Indian knowledge. Moreover, Jones was different from James Cousins in his defence of India. Among all of them, Max Müller was a class apart in his sympathy and reverence for India. The above discussion makes it evident that not only Indian response to the Raj and other issues of the colonial period but the Orientalists' and the Anglicists' response to the colony was marked with polyvalence, not just ambivalence. The polyvalence was caused by multiplicity of motives and strategies of colonizers of different attitudinal and intellectual preferences and levels.

II

Before moving to Indian renaissance, particularly the issue pertaining to the language, it would be congruous to consider the phenomenon in the European context, for European/English renaissance keeps peeping into our discussion despite all my efforts to block its passages.[2] Also the colonial period being the period of transition from classical to modern languages (in case of the nineteenth-century India) can best be understood in the light of Mikhail Bakhtin's insight regarding the phenomenon in the European Renaissance period.

---

2. The fact quite often oversighted, even by Indian scholars, is that India, through its Sanskrit literature and thoughts contained therein had galvanized the European mind to such an extent that by the first quarter of the nineteenth century there was not even a single major university in Europe that did not have a Chair of Sanskrit, though there were a few like Fredrick Hegel and Karl Marx who were sceptical of considering the Vedas and Upaniṣads as philosophical texts. The knowledge systems pertaining to philosophy, grammar and language, and even polity, economy, medicine and sociology contained in Sanskrit, the language of composition, attracted European scholars, thinkers, historians and linguists to them. They included the French, Germans and British (particularly Irish) like Voltaire, Diderot, Jean Baptiste →

The Greek society was primarily monolingual and so was its literary consciousness. On the other hand, Roman literary consciousness was bilingual, as purely national Latin genres conceived under monologic conditions fell into decay and functioned against the background of the Greek language and

---

→ Gentil, Antequetil-Duperron, the translator of the Upaniṣad, Victor Hugo, Quinet, Michelet, Lamartine, and Andre Gide, the translator of *Gitañjalī* Andre Malraux and Sylvain Levi among many others in the twentieth century (all French), William Jones, Colebrooke, James Princep, Charles Wilkins, and James Cousins (all British), J.D. Herder, Goethe, Schiller, Schelling and Schlegel and above all Max Müller among the Germans. Victor Hugo along with dotting his corpus with Indian themes and motifs wrote *Suprematie* based on the episode pertaining to the contest between Agni and Vāyu to conquer a blade of grass in *Kaṭhopaniṣad.* Despite his ambivalence towards Asia he said, "Oriental studies have never been so intensive. In the century of Louis XIV one was Hellenist, today one is an Orientalist" (in Jeans Bies, 108). Edgar Quinet acknowledged India's contribution more than anyone else to what he called the "declaration of the rights of the being" (in Bies, 100). His historian friend Michelet in 1863 found the *Rāmāyaṇa* as "the Bible of kindness," "the sea of milk" and a bottomless shoreless ocean of love, pity and kindness, whereas he found everything in the Occident "narrow," in Greece "small" and in Judea "dray" (109-10). Lamartine found Indian philosophy as "the Ocean." "We are but its clouds. The key to everything is in India" (ix). The last but not the least is the case of Ferdinand de Saussure, who changed the West's perception of reality by changing their perception of language, the instrument of perception, by shifting the then study of language from diachronic to synchronic. The shift brought about a silent intellectual revolution and pioneered and impacted structuralism and post-structuralism in the twentieth century. The catalysis to this revolution came from de Saussure's reading of Indian grammarians and linguists. The works of Indologists particularly German and French reveal that Indian thoughts without clamouring for credit were responsible for intellectual renaissance in Europe in the nineteenth century. Even at the risk of courting immodesty it must be re-stated that in certain sense the nineteenth century was not an age of awakening for India only but also for the Europe, as it awakened itself to the world beyond it to the Orient and in particular to India and its knowledge systems that added to existing European perceptions.

Among the German Indologists the views of F. Max Müller need attention, for he considered the issue of India and Indian renaissance in greater detail. In his *India: What can it Teach Us?* he located Renaissance in India in Sanskrit literature, and stated:

→

forms. Moreover, the Latin literary world viewed itself in the light of the Greek world 'through the eyes of the Greek word.' From the point of polyglossia, Rome was in the concluding phase of Hellenism, a powerful and illuminating model of other languageness whose final gesture was to carry over into the world

---

→ I believe it will be found out that the fourth, fifth and sixth centuries were the age of the literary Renaissance in India. That Kālidāsa and Bhāravi were famous at that time, we know from the evidence of inscriptions. We know that in the sixth century the fame of Indian literature had reached Persia, and that the King of Persia, Khosru Noshirvan (reigned CE 531-79), sent his physician, Burzoi, to India, in order to translate the fables of *Pañcatantra* or rather their original, from Sanskrit into *Pahlavī*. The famous "Nine Gems," or "the nine classics," as we should say have been referred in part, to the same age, and I doubt whether we shall be able to assign a much earlier date to anything we possess of Sanskrit literature, excepting always the Vedic and Buddhistic writings (Max Müller, 1883: 67).

To support his points he incorporated the views of Professor Burnouf at *College de France* in Paris in the second quarter of the nineteenth century, for he was for him a man of "wide views and true historical instincts" and the last man to waste his life on "mere Nalas and Shakuntalas." Further, Max Müller sought the support of Burnouf's views in his recognition of Sanskrit literature particularly in Vedic and Buddhist literature because of his unerring grasp for studying history, human history and world history. He had seen in it commencement of a new chapter to Sanskrit scholarship, though Burnouf died at an early age. This is to be seen in the light of the English Orientalists and Anglicists. Among the Indologists, the French and Germans were more sympathetic to India and Indian literature (that was Sanskrit literature for them) than Anglicists who were gradually replacing the Orientalists whose model was Sir William Jones. However, if one accepts Max Müller's views, the Indian renaissance was directly related to the Vedic and Buddhist literature. Its derivative then would be that the Indian Reniassance took place much before, at least 2000 years before the European, Italian or English Renaissance.

Further, Max Müller used the term in a limited sense by confining it for an upsurge in literary activities in Sanskrit, as he referred to 'literary Renaissance.' That renaissance was, however, a thing of past that could be savaged and its significance could be measured only by William Jones and people of his ilk who had become rare species with the rise and predominance of the Anglicists, as he suggests in the "Dedication" of his book *India: What it Can Teach Us?*, and also later in the lectures. The significant thing is that

→

of Europe a radical polyglossia that facilitated the creation of the medieval polyglossia, rich in parodic travestying literature. Bakhtin opines that the inter-animation of languages that was working to destroy bilingualism reached its highest point. Further, he cites the question and the answer to it by the French historian

---

→ Max Müller was speaking of learning from India in 1882, almost five decades after T.B. Macaulay and his brother-in-law Charles Travelyn had rejected Indian knowledge; leave aside the question of learning from it. Without naming the Anglicists or Macaulay and others like Charles Travelyn and Thigaut he rejected them and called upon the prospective civil servants to take Jones as their model.

Max Müller was the high-priest of late German romanticism. And as a romantic he constructed India of his own and thereby interpreted the existing interpretations of India by the English Orientalists and later Anglicists. He saw the centre of true Indian creativity and thinking in the early Vedic literature. Only ancient India interested him that included the eternal countryside and unchanging peasants up to the year 1000 coinciding with the advent of the Muslims on the Indian soil. In Sanskrit literature, he considered only Vedic literature true to nature and authentic and the post-Vedic literature as modern and artificial. Remarking about the modern Sanskrit literature he averred that it "never was a living or national literature": "It here and there contained remnants of earlier times, adapted to the literary, religious and moral tastes of a later period. . . . But the great mass of that later literature is artificial and scholastic, full of interesting compositions, and by no means devoid of originality, and occasional beauty, yet with all that, curious only. . ." (Max Müller 1883: 88-89).

From the second quarter of the nineteenth century onwards, the Orientalists were on the wrong side of the colonial project in India of sustaining, stregthening and furthering it. Max Müller's speech was a true Orientalists'/ Indologists' lament on the waning species of the Jones. However, even for the Orientalists like Jones and Max Müller, India remained frozen and confined to classical period and to its classical Sanskrit literature only, as like the (literary) historians of the period like Maurice Winternitz, they did not discuss either contemporary India or its literatures of the nineteenth century in their works. Further, the Orientalist idea of unified past rightly gave precedence to Sanskrit literature, but overrode new Indian literatures, the descendents of Sanskrit, Prākṛt, and Apabhraṁśa, so their vision of literary history was not holistic. The Anglicists, on the other hand, were intervening in the present of India. The result was systematic de-systematization of native eco-socio-political, cultural, intellectual and educational structures and their replacement with their alien counterparts. The extension of the line of the Orientalists and Anglicists represented →

of language, Ferdinand Bruno to elaborate his point. Bruno posed the question: "Why was the task of transition to a national language accomplished precisely during the Renaissance, that period whose tendencies were otherwise overwhelmingly towards the classical?" He himself answered the question and said that the attempt of the Renaissance to establish the Latin language in all its classical purity inevitably transformed it into a dead language. It was impossible to sustain the classic Ciceronian purity of Latin while using it in the course of everyday life and in the world of objects of the sixteenth century, that is, while using it to express concepts and objects from the contemporary scenes (125-56).

In the light of the above observations, the Indian case becomes a meaningful site. Indian situation has always been multilingual with at least five Prākr̥ts, and Apabhraṁśa as the languages of common people and Sanskrit as the language of learned composition along with being the spoken language of a class of people who earned it with industry and intelligence. Linguistic pluralism is as old as India. Pluralism is a slogan in the West, but a reality in India. This was their Three Language Formula without any state intervention or commission. The poet, the Vedic, or later on Buddhist or Jaina, had the choice of expressing himself in any of the three languages — singly or in combination. The ninth-century poetician Rājaśekhara, the author of *Kāvyamīmāṁsā*, knew many languages, and composed his works in Sanskrit and Prākr̥t.

→ primarily by Jones and Macaulay respectively was Rudyard Kipling. There were friends and sympathisers among "sahibs," particularly some of those who came from Ireland and Scotland, like Henry Cotton, Verrier Elwin, A.O. Hume and James Cousins to add a few names. Jones and Max Müller knew their India, as they claimed, and admired it. Macaulay in his colonialist's arrogance that made him myopic rejected India without knowing it. Later representative of colonizer like Kipling was in between. He came to be perceived as a pro-India sympathizer, and like some of the Anglicists considered ruling the colonial societies as the 'white man's burden.' He did not find anything of much worth in India and in its art, music, literature and history. Further, as a sophisticated Macaulay with considerable creative talents, he was suspicious of his compatriots who claimed acquaintance or knowledge of India and considered their desire and efforts of knowing India as an instance of folly to be best avoided.

His concept of *Kāvyapuruṣa* bears evidence to linguistic plurality of the country:

śabdārthau te śarīraṁ, saṁskṛtaṁ mukhaṁ ।
prākṛtaṁ bāhu jaṅghanamapabhraṁśaḥ, paiśācaṁ pādau, uro miśram ॥
— *Kāvyamīmāṁsā*, ch. III

Words and meanings form your body, Sanskrit your mouth, Prākṛt dialect your arms, Apabhraṁśa your legs, Paiśācī your feet, and Miśra languages your bosom.

Apart from this ontological evidence of linguistic plurality at the ideal level of the *Kāvyapuruṣa*, the son of the goddess of learning, Sarasvatī, Rājaśekhara describes the then linguistic pluralism existing in the country in the following words:

gauḍādyāḥ saṁskṛtasthāḥ paricitarucayaḥ prākṛte lāṭadeśyāḥ ।
sāpabhraṁśaprayogāḥ sakalamarubhuvaṣṭakkabhādānakāśca ।
āvantyāḥ pāriyātrāḥ saha daśapurajairbhūtabhāṣāṁ bhajante ।
yo madhye madhyadeśaṁ nivasati sa kaviḥ sarvabhāṣāniṣaṇṇaḥ ॥
— *Kāvyamīmāṁsā*, ch. X

Poets from the reign of Gauḷīya (the region between Varanasi and the Bay of Bengal) exhibit special interest in Sanskrit. Poets from Lāṭadeśa (southern Gujarat including Khāndeśa lying between the river Māhī and the Narmadā love Prākṛt. Those belonging to Marubhūmi (Mārwāṛ or Mewāṛ of Rājapūtānā) and Punjab show special interest in Apabhraṁśa and make excessive use of *takāra, kakāra* and *jakāra*. Poets of Avantikā (Ujjain), Pariyātra (the north-western parts of the Vindhya Range), and Daśapura (the Mālwā region of Madhya Pradesh) are proficient in the use of Paiśācī or Bhūtabhāṣā, and the residents of Madhyadeśa (the region bounded by the river Sarasvatī and the Himalaya in the north and the Vindhyas) show a similar inclination.

The country divided into five regions in Rājaśekhara's time as "Uttara Patha," "Pūrva Deśa," "Dakṣiṇa Patha," "Madhya Deśa" and "Paścād Deśa" was known as the Cakravartīkṣetram. Rājaśekhara defines the Cakravartīkṣetram as:

dakṣiṇātsamudrādudīcīṁ diśaṁ prati yojanasahastraṁ ।
cakravartikṣetraṁ tatraiṣa nepathyavidhiḥ ॥

— *Kāvyamīmāṁsā*, ch. III

Cakravartīkṣetram is from the Southern Sea to the Himalayas in the north covering an area of one thousand *yojanas*, (one *yojana* = distance varying from 4, 4.5, 8, 9 to 16 miles).

The linguistic description of the country by Rājaśekhara is pluralistic, based on linguistic realities of the country that were later distorted and even forgotten. This pluralism was held together by federal concept of Cakravartīkṣetram, much before the cultural unity of the *bhakti-yuga*. It continued as late as the twelfth century. Hemcandrācārya, the twelfth-century Jaina poetician, wrote in *Kāvyamīmāṁsā* that the *mahākāvya* or epic could be written in three languages, i.e. Sanskrit, Prākṛt or Apabhraṁśa. The *Bṛhatkathā* was preserved in Sanskrit. Though in *kārikā* the name of *deśī bhāṣā* is written, yet in the *vṛtti* it is considered as a kind of Apabhraṁśa, and even Paiśācī is considered for literary purpose. Therefore, Indians have been living with linguistic pluralism for long and operating without being exposed to theories of translation. An average Indian is blessed with (or acquires) functional knowledge of more than one or two languages. In Gujarat, a *Kāṭhiāvāḍī* speaking person, for instance, who knows nothing about Sanskrit, translates and constructs a figure of Gaṇeśa or some other God when a priest in the course of solemnization of rituals recites a *śloka* that the person concerned cannot read in Devanāgarī script.

The nineteenth-century linguistic plurality with many modern languages and literatures in India was in direct continuity with the pluralist linguistic and cultural tradition that can be best described in terms of either *phūlagūnthanī* (a wreath of flowers) or *dīpaśikhā* that is made of different lamps. Different lamps have their specific positions and specificities, but once lit, the light that they give is one and the same. The 'inter-animation' of languages, if one feels tempted to use Bakhtin's term, continued for long till majority of people, led by the *bhakti* poets, in course of time moved towards *lokabhāṣās* and led to *lokajāgaraṇa*. These *lokabhāṣās*, along with composition in Sanskrit flourished in diverse ways. With the advent of Muslims, Persian language was added to the linguistic scenario, and a major part of its lexicon was assimilated in Indian languages. Yet another addition to it was in the colonial period in the form of English. In this period of *navajāgaraṇa* or *abhijñāna* during the nineteenth-century modern Indian languages flourished, and apart from their speakers, missionaries and some of sympathetic civil servants, like A.K. Forbes in case of Gujarati, contributed to it. It was a period of multilingualism in India and not a movement towards a destruction of bilingualism, as was in the European Renaissance.

III

Indian renaissance, whether we call it *navajāgaraṇa, punarjāgaraṇa, prabodhana* or *sudhāra yuga* or *abhijñānakāla*, was a period marked by all the characteristics of the terms that are used to describe India in the nineteenth century, particularly its later half. The phenomenon began in Bengal in the wake of the defeat of the Nawāb's forces in the Battle of Plassey in 1757, and then spread to different parts of the country with the extension of the colonial power and its subsequent transformation into imperial rule. Despite being a national phenomenon, it had its regional specificities because the progress, processes and strategies of colonization, to which the Indian mind responded in different ways, varied from region to region.

In the second half of the nineteenth century, the first struggle for India's Independence in 1857, whose centre was the northern India, re-defined the character of Indian society in different regions, as Indians tried to cope with their defeat and its lingering shadow on the psyche. The period was marked by a flux of thoughts from different Indian thinkers, writers and leaders who wanted to reshape, refashion and reform the society, so as to respond to the external 'other' and the internal 'others' and the malady arising out of such bi/trifurcations of the self.

The national issues were the core concerns of the then Indian thinkers and reformers, for they thought that the best way of throwing away the yoke of thraldom was reformation of their society from within, attaining larger national unity, and establishing a national identity, as Bharatendu said, *svatva nija bhārata gahe* (Let Bhārata attain its identity!). Multiple identities — religious, regional, linguistic and literary — were discussed in many diverse ways against the backdrop of the early (and motivated) endeavours of the alien colonizers regarding census on the caste, linguistic and religious lines so as to categorize and divide the subject for ruling it for long. Issues, locations and compulsions of these thinkers and writers and pressures on them were multiple, so were their responses regarding the concept of nation, its reformation, and emancipation from the exploitative rule. Amidst the diversity or polyvalence of their views, one can however clearly discern a thread of common concern for the country and its progress for which its unity was a precondition.

The nineteenth century was the age of polyvalence. The century witnessed the dawn of a new consciousness in its newly educated intellectuals. This new wave of consciousness swept the entire country eventually and was called differently as *punarjāgaraṇa, navajāgaraṇa, navajīvana, prabodhana* or *sudhāro* in Hindi, Gujarati, Marathi and Bengali among Indian languages. Historically it began in Bengal, the first to suffer the curse of colonization. There it was primarily an elitist movement emanating from the upper and upper-middle class with limited participation from the common people. From there, it moved horizontally in different parts of the country. The year 1857 and the struggle for India's Independence served as the line of demarcation. The preceding part of the century was marked by reformation and later by revival. Further, the northern India particularly its Hindi heartland being the centre of the 'Mutiny,' the focus shifted to it in the post-Mutiny period. The Hindi heartland suffered the most during the period, as the 'Mutiny' cast its lingering shadows on the psyche of the ruler and the ruled. The defeat led to self-appraisal, self-knowledge and self-fashioning as well. The entire tradition, and treatises —

the Vedas, Purāṇas, religious and sociological texts — had to pass through the crucible and its complex processes of appraisal — at times half-heartedly and on other times cruelly. The society began to discuss the questions of identity, status of women, widow remarriage, child marriage, and communal harmony. The debate between the Sanātanīs and the Āryasamājī, for instance in the northern India, left its impact on the region and its authors. Balakrishna Gupta's *Purāṇa samajhāne ko samajha cāhiye* (One needs sense to make sense out of the Purāṇas) is an intervention in the debate. The result was absence of unanimity on different issues of concern in the period, leading to polyvalence, though critics often see it terms of ambivalence of the native mind. The period, despite being the carnival of voices, was unanimous on the issue of unity that was achievable only through the construction of a national identity. By the beginning of the last quarter of the nineteenth century, it was realized by the nascent middle class, the product of the new education system, that self-knowledge, other-knowledge and political organization were indispensable for attaining emancipation from the colonial yoke. Consequently, what had begun in the form of *maṇḍalī*, *sabhā*, and *samāja* became fertile land for a political orgainzation like the Congress that despite having people from diverse regions and religions of the country became a rallying point. The emergence of the identity of nation, for which the colonizers took credit, and national consciousness was one of the greatest ironies of history of colonization aided by, ironically, the instrument of carving and embellishing the identities, i.e. English language and English education system that were imposed by the colonial power after systematically uprooting the native Indian systems of education.

"Know Thyself" was the *mantra* of *abhijñānakāla*, the term Namvar Singh uses for the nineteenth-century India. Knowing one's own self involves a few questions: Who is/are the other self/selves against which the self tries to define itself? What are the forces and motives, and instruments of recognition and redefinition? Since the self is conditioned and determined by the others, so all these questions are resolved by nature of relationship between the two. In case of the nineteenth-century India, the question of knowing one's self assumed the shape of the questions of identity — individual, caste, community, race/ethnicity gender region, religion and nation. As a consequence religious, regional, and linguistic identities were forwarded and asserted in different levels and periods from different quarters. In order to consolidate themselves the colonizers supported and even exploited the fissures caused by the assertion of various identities in the colony.

The other for the Indians was from within and from the outside. For the colonizer the other was a unified whole whose fragmentation into multiple identities was in the interest of the colonizer. Therefore, the makers of Indian *abhijñāna,* fully conscious of individual specificities, were always concerned with an overarching Indian identity. As a result the instrument of colonization like new education system, the language and literature of the colonizer, i.e. English, new judicial and bureaucratic systems were adroitly used to serve the native purpose of bringing about the unity and realizing the national identity in the political terms to resist colonization.

For the Indian psyche, the endeavour of knowing itself was multi-layered, as it had to know and carve itself in relation to multiple others within it, and also the one without.[3] All these — the selves and others — had their personal and public selves. The process of setting apart of a private self in opposition to public self, and also of defining one self in oppositon to others — from within and outside led to the shuffling of strategies leading to ironies, contradictions and inconsistencies. The colonized had to

3. The process of knowing the self and recognition, defining and constructing identities makes the entire act a site of power play in which the weak are often excluded or at least sidelined, so one finds no voice of women or dalits in the polyvalence of the Indian *abhijñānakāla* in its initial phase. Construction of identities by others acted as a catalysis and model for the weak, suppressed, women and dalits to strain for their identities and refashion themselves.

do it more often to survive against the master in order to resist its exploitative and tyrannical ways. These inconsistencies, ironies and contradictions constituted major subjects of the Western renaissance literature too, though there was no domineering other there from outside.

Since all periods of rebirth, renewal, revival and synthesis are turbulent, so those who lived through and responded to these historical processes and changes had to be the 'fittest,' i.e. willing to adapt themselves to the given situation in order to survive. As the Indian renaissance thinkers were defining their selves in terms of their own public and private selves, and the other too had its public and private selves, the compulsion to address to different constituencies made them fork-tongued and at times contradictory. However, the contradictions that their works contained were consequences of their dynamism with which they responded to multiple selves and the other in particular. They contradicted, for they were 'full of multitudes.' Hence, contradictions and inconsistencies in the authors and thinkers of the *abhijñānakāla* have to be seen not as the demerits but as the instances of polyvalence — multiple voices co-habiting the literary space of an individual author and different authors in different Indian languages as the constituents of the larger Indian polyvalence in the *abhijñāna* period.

Fashioning demands knowing. The British wanted to fashion India in the manner suitable to them, and the moment Warren Hastings had the map of India before him, he knew it and began the process of fashioning it. Against it, the Indians began to make disconcerted localized efforts of fashioning themselves against the colonial designs, and their manifestations can be seen in cases of not less than seventy small and major mutinies in different parts of India in the first half of the nineteenth century. So, to resist, it was necessary to self-fashion against the colonial endeavours of fashioning the colony. Since India had already been fashioned so many times in the past, so the nineteenth century was an age of self-refashioning and re-knowing.

In knowing the self, the knower and the object of knowledge are the same, though the others exert considerable influence in it. On the other hand, if one translates *abhijñāna* as recognition, the object of the recognition and recognizer are different. Moreover, the recognizer is more significant than the recongnized because the recognizer has the choice of choosing the instrument of recongnition and then passing the judgement. In the nineteenth-century Indian colonial period, the colonizer played subtly the role of recognizer and also of providing the instrument or catalyst of knowing to the colonized. However, by the third quarter of the nineteenth-century Indian thinkers like Bharatendu had come to realize the game. And the game of recognition was reversed on the colonizers, leading to the subsequent sustained political struggle for India's Independence to be led later by Gandhi who was much benefited from his readings of Gujarati writers particularly Narmad of the *abhijñānakāla*.

Language was the principal instrument of constructing the identity. There were, however, problems involved in it, as there was the question of redefining relationship between Sanskrit, and *lokabhāṣā*s and modern Indian languages. Linguistic pluralism of India was valourized to the extent of proposing different nationalities in India. As a consequence, linguistic diversity became a potential cause of division of the country, as one could see in the quarrel between supporters of Hindi and Urdu in northern India. On the other hand, was the intervention of English, the master's language and literature, and as the medium of instruction as well. Gujarat, however, presented a different picture in this case. While Dalpatram (1820-98) dealt with *Vidyābodha* (On Awareness of Knowledge), Narmad (1833-63) with *Deśābhīmāna* (National Pride), and *Svadeśābhimāna* (Pride of One's Own Nation) and Navalram Pandya (1836-88) with *Sachu Deśābhīmāna* (True National Pride), they spoke of progress of their own land, country and language, i.e. Gujarati, for they were acutely conscious of their identity. However, they were equally conscious of their larger Indian identity that needed one language. Keeping it in view Navalram with rare display of linguistic catholicity proposed Hindustānī as the language for the country. After discussing the unity of religion, caste and state that used to exist earlier in the country he focused on the question of linguistic unity, and said in his *Deśa ni eka Bhāṣā* (The Issue of One Language):

> Even if we do not call it *janabhāṣā* or the language of the people, even then, it was a language the people of most part of Hindustan could understand and speak as well, however incorrect it might have been. The truth is that the development of the language came to a halt with the establishment of the English rule, and gradually its influence was on the decline in almost all parts of northern India. Hindustānī is understood almost everywhere, and with reliable sources at my disposal, I can state that the Hindustānī is a language of travellers of southern India as well. Today if you wish to travel in Hindustan, it is necessary for you to know Hindustānī. This is the reason why all saints and *sādhus* speak this language and compose verses in it. In the modern context one cannot remain without saying that if Hindustānī cannot be called as the language of the people in our country, its state is like that of French in Europe now.
>
> — in Singh & Mehta, 59.

He remarked prophetically:

> It is difficult to say, if it would retain its place in the future. But a question worth consideration is, if in future this language loses its status, which language would occupy its place. If we do not think of our role in it and responsibilities and keep sitting thinking that time will find some or the other way, I think that every state would have its own language and the unity of our country would be fragmented. There is one more reason for this. Today the language of every linguistic region is becoming increasingly different from other languages along with its own development. That is why, as a consequence of the separatist process of development of languages in a few years the form of every language would be such as would multiply the difference among languages. At the moment it is easier to learn Marathi or Hindustānī but it would not be so after a few years. The people travelling from one province to another would not find a

> common language. Moreover, the scholars who would like to know about books being written in different languages of our country would have to learn all the languages. Needless to mention that such a work would be extremely arduous. Only a few people would be able to do it. It seems to me that despite belonging to one caste, one religion and being the Hindu subject of a state, we shall be separated from each other at the level of attaining knowledge. And if there is no unity at the level of knowledge which unity can sustain it? And even if we suppose that it would be able to sustain itself, will it be worth it? In that situation, Hindustan would lose its identity as a country and would be reduced to being a mere geographical region. — 60

Apart from their love for Gujarati at the state level and for Hindustānī at the national level, Gujarati thinkers and writers began to fashion their views regarding the place and status of English in the post-1857 period. It does not play down ambivalence and polyvalence in this regard until the advent of Mahatma Gandhi. By the first quarter of the nineteenth century, English came to be related with freedom, modernity, a sense of history and civilization, a sense of superiority and a purpose of civilizing the other. This divided the Indian society at a larger level, and split the psyche at the individual level. This ambivalence may be seen in case of a writer like Goverdhanram Tripathi (1855-1907) and Kant (Manishankar Ratnaji Bhatt). The *Scrap Books* of Tripathi are the sites of this ambivalence towards the colonizers and English, the instrument of colonial governance and Western cultural values. His English education was, to a good extent, responsible for this. If one examines his journey as a thinker of colonial presence, he seemed to submit to the foreign rule, expressing dismay at Indian situation, proposed pragmaticism or elasticity as a strategy or helpmate, and envisioned the class of Indians as the "loyal children of the government and patriotic children of the soil" (34).

Earlier in his notes, he has discussed different alternatives to the ways and strategies of colonizers in his *Scrap Book* III:

> India is invaded and subdued already. There is no question of Offensive or Defensive here, and Elasticity would be a nice

> helpmate in Constitutional warfare. The rulers are a clever set of people — an admixture of selfish aggressors and disinterested benevolent helpmates. India is worked by "push and pull" among these, and naturally the Home Interests generally carry the day. Yet even here we win morsel though often it is snatched away sometimes even from near the lips. — 51

There is a kind of incongruity in his perception of the colonizers. He knows them but nowhere questions their occupation and economic exploitation of India. He seems to have resigned to India's colonization and irrevocable necessity of the colonial rule. He proposes winning the "constitutional warfare" but does not question the constitutional validity of the colonial presence in India. His proposition of "elasticity" is based on his notion of their (colonizers') providential presence in the country, as he wrote in his *Scrap Book* II, dated 22 November 1892:

> India is under foreign control and the foreigner is the kindliest of all foreigners available. To get rid of the foreigner by force or fraud is an idea associated with all the incidents that remind us of his rule being foreign. The idea naturally haunts our uneducated instincts; to the educated instincts, the idea is both foolish and fallacious. It is foolish because it is not practicable, and because any experiments founded upon it would send the country from the frying pan into the fire. It is a fallacious idea because the distinction between the native and a foreigner is only transient, and the distinction is not a guarantee of the native being the better ruler than the foreign in such a mass of heterogeneous people as make up my country. The proper problem is not the absolute eviction of the foreigner but of his accommodation to the native element. — 145-50

Tripathi's *Scrap Books* reveal his acceptance of the superiority of the colonizer and submission to the British rule depending on his then assessment of the situation. He wrote in the second volume:

> The political sagacity and shrewdness, moral unity and strength, the practical art and energy and activity, the physical stamina and virtues, etc. make the rulers a giant to pigmy. . . . Yet, in the comparative conscience of British institutions and people, there

> is also a question of turning the pigmies into beings with higher statures. The smallest European is a very spark of fire; powerful for good and evil, more for the latter within the present generation in India. — 15 and 52

Ironical it is that the writer who seems to resist the colonial literary forms by asserting the native narrative techniques and thereafter employing them in his novel *Sarasvatīcandra*, as he stated in the "Introduction" of the novel, expressed his loyalty to the colonial master. His creative endeavours thus at times become sites of resisting and subverting the hegemonic and oppressive other at least in fiction, if not in fact. Submitting his creativity to his unflinching loyalty to the colonizer he wrote in the second *Scrap Book*:

> Was it a mistake to have written a book (*Sarasvatīcandra*) which has so disturbed the peace and happiness of my family? What is my duty? To boldly write such a book for my people or secure the peace of my family against such contingency? . . . My book is not only loyal, but my innermost soul feels that it is written for and must tend to the welfare of both the rulers and ruled.
>
> — 158-59

If Tripathi dithered and preferred pragmatics to patriotism, Kant (1867-1923) did not suffer from double-mindedness. However, if he found, after following a course of action, that he was wrong, he changed his views, and implemented them. His life and his writings appear to be tumultuous, as he received the influence of the colonizers, their religion, culture and language. He was his own critic, as may be seen in his criticism of Vedānta and Hinduism, his conversion to Christianity and then his return to the former fold. His *Siddhānta Sāra nu Avalokana* contains letters addressed to a widow Kāntā. Curiously enough the name is the feminine version of the author's name, hence emerges as the author's alter ego in debate with the creator. Kāntā, in one of her letters, criticizes Kant for his insufficient reading into Indian culture and yielding to English education. Let me quote a portion of the letter from *Siddhānta Sāra nu Avalokana*, as it pertinently comments on the majority of contemporary Kants, i.e. the Indian scholars:

> The truth is that you are blinded partly because of your affection for me and partly because of your English education. . . . I can say with confidence that you are neglecting a philosophy without understanding it. Can you really believe that a philosophy upheld for millions of years by millions of eminent scholars can be as dry as you make it out to be? . . . You know the other country more than your own and think there is not a single thing worth knowing in your own country. All this because the foreigners have taught you so. You know Christ, but you don't know Kabīr; you study Kant, but not Śaṅkara. . . . You all can fulfil the hopes of this country, if you wish, and without mistaking old superstitions for truth, do not mistake old truths for superstitions.
>
> — Kant, 1920: 92-93

Against Tripathi's long-lasting ambivalence, and Kant's dilemmas pertaining to colonizer's presence and their accoutrements Mahatma Gandhi did not suffer from any of his predecessor's problems. These three seen together form three stages of our response to the colonizer, and their cases help us in studying the impact of colonization, and its resistance. Gandhiji's crystal-clear views pertaining to English language, English literature, and English as the medium of instruction were pertinent as he saw them in relation to their impact on Indian family, society, and psyche by considering his own case. He spoke about the impact of English literature:

> A word about literature. We had to learn several books of English prose and poetry. No doubt all this was nice. But that knowledge has been of no use in serving or bringing me in touch with the masses.
>
> — *Young India*, 1.6.1921

The difference between colonial and post-colonial function of English is easily discernible here, as Gandhi laid emphasis on 'serving' the masses and bringing him in touch with them, whereas the Dispatch of Directors were concerned with 'utility' in their agenda. Gandhi was candid enough in suggesting, to much of embarrassment of the teachers of English, the irrelevance of teaching and learning of English literature,

> I am unable to say that if I had not learnt what I did of English prose and poetry, I should have missed a rare treasure.
>
> — *Harijan*, 9.7.1938

Gandhi had foreseen the consequences of the project of modernizing India through English, for it creates unbridgeable gulf between the English-equipped and English-unequipped impoverished people of the country. He stated, "We are traitors to our mother by remaining under such a system (of English education system) . . . a gulf has been created between the educated class and the uneducated masses." Seeing English as the cause of partitioning families, he remarked:

> The English medium created an impassable barrier between me and the members of my family, who had not gone through English schools. My father knew nothing of what I was learning. . . . I was fast becoming a stranger in my own home. I certainly became a superior person, even my dress began to undergo imperceptible changes. — *Harijan*, 9.7.1938

Further, he did not see English as the means of liberation. "Of all the superstitions that affect India, none is so great as that a knowledge of the English language is necessary for imbibing ideas of liberty, and developing accuracy of thought" (*Evil Wrought by the English Medium*, 10). Rather it was a sign of slavery for him.

> Is it not a painful thing that, if I go to a court of justice, I must employ English as the medium; that, when I became a Barrister, I may not speak my mother-tongue, and that someone else should have to translate to me from my own language? Is not this absolutely absurd? Is it not a sign of slavery?
>
> — *Hind Swaraj, Collected Works*, 5

This elongated discussion of language is necessary because language is the principal instrument of decolonization. As the sage Bhartṛhari remarked, *sarvam śabden bhāsate* (we take cognizance of the world with words), there arises the need for our own words for our own world. Language made of words constitutes reality, and also our consciousness with which we perceive the reality. These activities are best served by the languages that enter the child's ears with his/her mother's milk, not with other's language particularly the colonizer's. Gandhi perceived this in his Presidential Address to the Second Gujarat Educational Conference held on 20 October 1917:

> The correspondence that should exist between the school training and the character imbibed with the mother's milk . . . is absent when the school training is given through a foreign tongue. However pure may be his motives, he who thus snaps the cords that should bind the school life and the home life is an enemy of the nation.

With the colonizer's language the means and handmaid of colonization persist and prosper, for attitudes attached to it do not die. If the colonizer's language validates its necessity and presence in the post-colonial period and the post-colonial scholars and academics get convinced with their argument, there is everything wrong with this notion of decolonization.

IV

After the reformation in the first half of the nineteenth century, the later half was marked by revival of its traditions in order to re-establish itself against the other. Among others Dayanand Saraswati, Vivekananda and later Sri Aurobindo led this process with their arguments. Among creative writers Bankimchandra who initiated the process in Bangla, emphasized on the revival of the Hindu tradition, though his nationalist concerns were limited to his "Sonār Bāṅglā." In Gujarati writers like Narmad, Dalpat, and Navalram their Gujarati (regional) and national concerns co-existed simultaneously, and their attitudes towards religion and reforms underwent changes with time, making it difficult for critics to find logical explanation for being so. In Marathi, Vishnu Shastri Chipunkar was concerned with *Deśonnati* and *Amācya Deśaci Sthiti*. Despite the fire in his writing, he could not transcend caste and class consciousness leading to his non-acceptance of Mahatma Phule. Bharatendu in Hindi was conscious of his caste and religious identity, yet he could transcend them for the progress of the nation, as defining "Hindu" he said in his essay *Bhāratavarṣonnati Kaise Ho Sakatī Hai?* (How can India Progress?):

> Hindu Brothers! You too should give up your internal difference. Love each other. Follow this principle. Whoever lives in Hindustan, whatever be his/her colour, caste, is a Hindu. Help Hindus. All Bengalis, Marathis, Punjābīs, Madrāsīs, Vedics, Jains, Brāhmaṇas and Muslims should hold each other's hands.
>
> — Bharatendu, *Samagra*, 1013

This stress on unity and revival was a direct or indirect concern to all major and budding writers of the period. This strain is discernible in many writers of the period, even in a writer like Toru Dutt. After exploring the realm of French and English, Toru Dutt turned to Sanskrit in order to search for roots and cultural belonging, and explored them in The *Ancient Ballads and Legends of Hindustan*, fed from the *Rāmāyaṇa*, the *Mahābhārata*, the *Viṣṇu Purāṇa*, and the *Bhāgavata Purāṇa*. In the *Ancient Ballads* she responded to the heartbeats of the antique racial tradition. It seemed to answer her profound need for links with the living past of the country as well as serve her poetic purpose. Toru Dutt's was a unique case of revival, for there was no compulsion for her to revive or return to Sanskrit and Hindu traditions after conversion to Christianity. It indicates that even after conversion it becomes difficult to reject traditions that are part of the collective past.

V

Apart from the Orientalists and Indologists, quite a few Indian scholars have used the Renaissance as a trope of resurgence or re-awakening, and in the course of doing so they have seen many renaissances in India. For instance, Professor Dhurjati Prasad Mukherjee has spoken of different 'renaissances' in the long history of India in the Vedic-Aryan period, the Buddhist period, the Gupta period, the Harṣa and Vikramāditya period and the Muslim period. The saints and poets in different parts of the country wrote exquisite devotional poetry during the Muslim period. The nineteenth-century Renaissance, for him, was the last in this series. The problem with such a periodization, which often is a Waterloo of literary historians, is that it uses the term Renaissance rather simplistically because in its traditional sense the Renaissance takes place only once in history. Since the term means 'rebirth' or 're-awakening,' there is no possibility of renaissance at least in the Vedic period because that was one of the earliest efflorescence of human civilization. If it is a convolution in all aspects of life — in architecture, thought, painting, literature, culture, music, and sculpture — it took place only in the *bhakti* period not in others, which was revival and renewal and popularization of India's ancient intellectual and cultural heritage, enshrined as it was in Sanskrit, particularly through its rendition into *lokabhāṣā,* as Namvar Singh argues in his observations on the nomenclatural problem of Indian renaissance. Moreover, reformation is the key attribute of the renaissance, a consequence of the questioning of the existing institutions and traditions — social, political, cultural and intellectual. That did take place during the Buddhist and more so in the *bhakti* period. However, the Indian renaissance — whether in the *bhakti* or the colonial period, differed from its European or English counterpart, as it did question the existing institutions, but in majority of cases did not sever its links with its traditions particularly in the field of religion. The European renaissance had seen the disintegration of the power of the Church, followed by nihilism and secularism. These could never be the defining markers in India for various reasons because *nāstikavāda* (for which the term atheism is wrongly used as a synonym but it means any system of belief like the Buddhism or Jainism that does not subscribe to the authority of the Vedas and Upaniṣads) had not been a new thing in India. Moreover, the *bhakti* poets sought their *mukti* or emancipation, not in rejection of God but in their submission to the *bhakti* of God who was not a wrathful Old Testament God but a *nirguṇa* or *saguṇa,* or protector, even a friend, who takes birth as a human being whenever the Evil suppresses the Good beings. At the same time, not all Western Renaissance writers were atheists. Pico de Mirandola maintained in his *Oration on the Dignity of Man* that man, being dearest and greatest creation of God, keeps God in the centre. However, the Church was not always so benign.

Coming back to the discussion of Indian renaissance, Ram Vilas Sharma has seriously thought and extensively written on the issue with special reference to Hindi, and called the *bhakti* period as the period of *lokajāgaraṇa*. Further, he called the 1857 Mutiny as the period of *navajāgaraṇa* or *janajāgaraṇa* (in fact, Ram Chandra Shukla was the first critic to use the term *lokajāgaraṇa* for the *bhakti* period). Sharma separated *lokajāgaraṇa* from *navajāgaraṇa*. The former he attributed to the *bhakti* period and latter to the colonial period.

Ram Vilas Sharma spoke of the four phases of what he calls *Bhāratīya Navajāgaraṇa* of the nineteenth century that begins with the freedom struggle of 1857, followed by the Bharatendu, the Dwivedi and the Nirala Yuga. The problem with this periodization is that it uses a historical incident as a category to begin with and thereafter switches over to the periodization after the most prominent literary author of the period. Perhaps in the first phase he did not find anyone who could have stood in the league of the subsequent makers of Hindi literature. Sharma in *Bhāratīya Sāhitya kī Bhūmikā* (1996) did not consider the colonization as indispensable for India's *navajāgaraṇa* and proposed that a literary and political awakening or renaissance was possible without the British presence and the Raj. From his point of view, the colonial and cultural encounter was more of a disruption and less of an awakening. Nirmal Verma in his essay, "India and Europe: Some Rejection on the Self and the Other" (2000) expressed views supporting this position.

Namvar Singh who considered Ram Vilas Sharma as his *guru* in polemical discourse, as he stated in the Dedication of his book *Vāda Vivāda aur Saṁvāda* (1989), critiqued him in the context of complex mix of relations between the colonizer and colonized. He examined the processes of the colonial forces that wanted to shape Indian society and culture to suit their ends, and did succeed to a good measure, yet appropriated the credit of being the harbingers of this renaissance. He did not confine his critique to mere expression of his dissatisfaction with Sharma's terms but called the period as *abhijñānakāla*. The term may be a problem only for those who understand the Indian situation through translation in English of terms, because *abhijñāna,* if equated with 'recognition' is fraught with misunderstanding of the term, because *abhijñāna* at one level entails in it the question of identity and also what is 'above' knowledge.

In his discussion of Indian renaissance Namvar Singh considers the views of all significant critics but ignores Veer Bharat Talwar whose mis(chievous)reading of Indian 'renaissance' particularly Hindi renaissance has raised much dust. Namvar Singh's speech is purposive and silence more meaningful. His omissions are deliberate. Perhaps he considers Talwar's positions rather lopsided and sensational without much sense, and that the opposition to mischief to some extent validates it and breeds greater mischief. Therefore, he considers it better to leave it unattended. However, Talwar's intervention in the debate pertaining to the Indian 'renaissance' being rather radical and latest demands some response.

In his book *Rassākaśī* (2002) Talwar finds Hindi *navajāgaraṇa* based in Benares and Allahabad only. He reduces Hindi *navajāgaraṇa* to a movement for Hindi and sees it as a communal and fundamentalist movement. His well-researched endeavour sees Bharatendu and his compatriots as narrow-minded, the stooges of the British government. The ingenuity of his arguments notwithstanding, the charges levelled by him by foregrounding such facts as would help him in proving his preconceived opinions, demand re-reading of Bharatendu by seeing him in the historical context.

Against the 1857 Mutiny as the beginning of Indian *navajāgaraṇa* Talwar considers the submission of the "Memorandum Court Charter in the Upper Provinces of India" in 1868 as the starting point. The Memorandum demanded Nāgarī script in lieu of Persian in the courts. Foregrounding it as the core preoccupation of Hindi *navajāgaraṇa* Talwar sees designs everywhere even in publication and distribution of the Memorandum by Raja Shiv Prasad "Sitar-e-Hind" in the name of 'private circulation.' Talwar sees what he wants to see, and in the process of seeing narrowness in the Hindi *navajāgaraṇa*, he bestows narrowness upon the entire Hindi movement, and remarks:

> What is called Hindi *navjāgaraṇa*, its true name should have been Hindi movement because its central issue was only Hindi language and script and not religious or social reform.
>
> —157

Since the colonial period was marked by a process of defining and constructing identities, different identities were constructed on religious, regional, linguistic and cultural lines and often in terms of the other. Such a process suited colonial masters, for they initiated the process and controlled it. The ensuing melee or state of flux allowed the masters to wallow in and rule the divided folk. Moreover, the "Memorandum" was one of many symptoms of larger colonial designs. Various commissions were theatres of witnessing and orchestering interreligious, regional and linguistic feuds. The principal problem with Talwar is that he either does not understand the subtleties of colonization or deliberately ignores them to prove his positions pertaining to the Hindi *navajāgaraṇa* and its precursors. He accepts the presence of many voices against which Hindi was trying to emerge as the voice with the efforts of his so-called Hīndīwālās like "Sitar-e-Hind" and Bharatendu. He remembers Sitar-e-Hind's "Memorandum" but conveniently forgets that of Sir Saiyyad Ahmed Khan who had petitioned against the Devanāgarī script. The contents of the "Memorandum" of Bharatendu who followed Sir Saiyyad Ahmed do not earn his attention. In the very opening paragraph of his "Memorandum" Bharatendu calls himself "a Sanskrit, Hindi and Urdu poet." If he called Urdu as "the language of dancing girls and prostitutes," there should be reasons for it, for why would one like to compose in such a language and introduce himself as its poet? Its reason lies in the preceding paragraph of Bharatendu's

"Memorandum" (*Bharatendu Samagra*, 1054-60) that refers to the "evidence of Saiyyad Ahmed Khan before the Education Commission in which Khan had called Urdu as the "language of the gentry and Hindi that of the vulgar" (1057). The religious and communal anxieties notwithstanding, Bharatendu went on to suggest, "In spite of this though the Lala Sahib (*kāyastha*) will correspond with the Saiyyad Sahib Bahadur in Urdu yet when writing to his wife he must use the Hindi character" (1058). He considered both the *maulavī*s and *paṇḍit*s responsible for the then state of Hindi, as he said:

> The constant war in which *maulavī*s and *puṇḍit*s have engaged themselves has ruined the cause of true Hindi. Our vernacular is neither the language of the *maulavī*s or that of the *puṇḍit*s. It is something between; it is "the Golden mean". — 1058

Bharatendu, thus, spoke of saving Hindi from the clutches of the elite classes, and use it as an instrument of emancipating the masses that had to pay four *ānnā*s to learn the contents of a summons, or eight *ānnā*s to one rupee for writing out a small petition (1057).

In fact, Bharatendu's plea for Nāgarī script, despite all arguments against it, was a reformist gesture of empowering the common people, against 'landholders, cultivators and traders,' who did not know the Persian character particularly 'Śikasta' script, used by the officials such as *peśakāras*, *serśatadāra*s and *muharrir*s in the court.

> By the introduction of the Nāgarī character they would (*sic*) lose entirely the opportunity of plundering the world by reading one word for another and thereby misconstruing the real sense of the contents. . . . If Hindi is introduced who will pay (*sic*) four *ānnā*s to learn the contents of a summons, or eight *ānnā*s to one rupee for writing out a small petition? — 1057

There is no need to impose linguistic catholicity or religious secularism on Bharatendu, for he spoke for his language, religion and region. In the "Memorandum" he speaks against the 'deep-rooted prejudice' of the large majority of the Indo-Anglian officials against the natives of the then United Province. The un-stated reason was not far to find. Since the centre of the 'Mutiny' of

1857 was in the province, the colonial policy reflected its disapproval by marginalizing the people from favours like government jobs. "The natives of this country, at least of these provinces, have been under a strict impression for the last eight or nine years, that the government wishes to shut up the doors of education against them. . . ." (1058). So the core and circumference of Bharatendu in his writing have to be seen in the historical context. His region, his religion and his language were central to his concerns, but it did not mean that there was no space for others. Moreover, it would be wrong to term him a linguistic, regional and religious fundamentalist. His country precedes his mention of the problems of his province in the "Memorandum." Moreover, in his famous Baliya Lecture on Hindi he fervently pleaded the case of Hindi but at the same time he appreciated other languages including English, and called upon his people to learn from the experiences of others and progress in their own language (*Bharatendu Samagra*, 228-30). Also in a small piece entitled *Jātīya Saṅgīta* (Communal Music) he forwarded his inclusive model for such compositions as would be simple in the language of the people "in all languages of the people, i.e. Punjabi in Punjab, Bundelkhaṇḍī in Bundelkhaṇḍ, Bihārī in Bihar and in the language used by the people in a given part of the country" (*Bharatendu Samagra*, 1028). One can fault Bharatendu for his vision but wrong it would be to term his as communal or fundamentalist by citing "Hindi, Hindu, Hindustan." Such a selective, blinkered reading of the nineteenth-century social reformers, thinkers and savants on the basis of certain excerpts overrides the contribution that they made against social, political and their individual limitations.

True it is that Bharatendu came from the family of the royal supporters. It was further reinforced by his education to some extent. However, his fascination for English did not last long and it was followed by ambivalence and disillusionment, as the colonizers' claims to validate their presence in India proved to be hollow political pronouncements. He wrote in *Kavivacana-Sudhā* at the age of 24 on 8.2.1874:

> Some time earlier the Englishmen whenever they spoke of India,

> they apparently pronounced that they ruled the country for its welfare, and thought of its prosperity. They proposed to make us drink the elixir of knowledge, and that when the people would have knowledge and learn to manage themselves, we shall hand over the administration of Hindustan to its people and saying good bye to all, we shall go to our land.
>
> — *Bharatendu Samagra*, 1091

Then he went on to examine and compare the colonial and the Muslim rule in 'Badashah Darpan':

> The Muslims had hundreds of defects but had two good qualities. First, they made India their home so the wealth of this country remained here. . . . And the bravery of the Hindus remained intact. Someone has rightly stated that the Muslim rule is cholera and the English rule tuberculosis. In their (the English) rule our wealth and bravery are gradually eroding.
>
> — *Bharatendu Samagra*, 732

Further, he equated the English rule with the breaking of fire in the house and the relation between Hindu and Muslims to two sisters-in-law (*jeṭhānī* and *devarānī*). Speaking of the significance of the unity of the Hindu and Muslims he said, "If the fire breaks out in the house, the sisters-in-law should give up their mutual ill will and together try to extinguish the fire" (*Bharatendu Samagra*, 1013). These two instances are among many that disapprove of the charges of Bharatendu being a *rājabhakta* or *hinduvādī*. They further suggest Bharatendu's perspicacious understanding of strategies of colonization that include political domination primarily for economic exploitation, validation of its presence in the colony presenting itself as the catalyst of reformation and enlightenment. So he should not only be accredited with finding and defining term like *upaniveśa* to measure colonization in various issues of *Kavivacana-Sudhā* but also with indirectly suggesting the strategies of decolonization. Unfortunately, Vir Bharat Talwar fails to sight the issue of colonization, its forces, and ways of operation. In the darkness of night, despite having lamp in his hands he catches his own family member and thinks he has caught the thief, and lets the thief escape.

Among his contemporaries in Hindi, Bharatendu was the most conscious of his national identity and also inclusive, as he did not confine himself to either Hindus, as discussed earlier, or to his Hindi heartland. He called upon all the people of the country and said, "Bengali, Marāṭhā, Punjābī, Madrāsī, Vedic, Jain, Brahmo and Muslim, hold each other's hand." In his *Kāśī ke Chāyācitra* (1874) he saw Kāśī as the microcosm of India and also presents his concept of Indian Nation. "Here the people of different regions like Draviḍa, Magadha, Kānyakubja, Maharashtra, Bengal, Punjab, Gujarat, etc. are found doing their work in togetherness. And by going to localities where people of different castes live one would feel as if one has come to the land of these people, i.e. Dhaka in the Beṅgālī Ṭolā, Amritsar in the Lāhorī Ṭolā, and Pune in the Brahma Ghāṭ." By including woman and caste in the circumference of his concerns he enlarged the scope of the Hindi *navajāgaraṇa*, though it has to be admitted that these problems could not occupy so central a place in it as they were in the reformation movements in Gujarat or Maharashtra.

The denigrators of Bharatendu should realize the Bharatendu's appreciation of the British rule, if it was so, was either based on its merit or required as part of the strategy to communicate his message to his own countrymen as he did in the case of the famous Balia lecture. He appreciated the English collector, called upon his people to learn from the rulers and then criticized English rulers in front of the Collector. In *Kavivacana-Sudhā* (1874) he wrote:

> We do not deny the fact that the Englishmen have given knowledge to us and our brethren benefited considerably from it. Leave aside their claims that the days of Hindustan's prosperity are round the corner, the drought, famine and poverty are on rise every day. — *Bharatendu Samagra*, 1091

> When the British come from England, they are usually impoverished. And when they go back, they are Kuber, the god of wealth. . . . It proves that the main causes of disease and famine are Englishmen. — 1092

In fact, Bharatendu was among the first in Hindi to realize the true character of English education and civilization. He saw the American independence as the model and remarked in *Kavivacana-Sudhā*, 31.8.1874:

> The Muslims were hundred times more extravagant than the British. But they were the inhabitants of this country, so their wealth was spent in this country. . . . The way America became independent after being colonized, in the same way Bhāratvarṣa too can get independence. . . . Only twenty thousand Englishmen rule twenty crores of Indians of Bharata. These people are generally educated and civilized, but the citizens of India are tortured by the tyranny of these same people.
>
> — *Bharatendu Samagra*, 1092

The fact is that Bharatendu was not only providing us terms and idiom of knowing and naming the rulers in terms of colonization but exposed the true face of the project of colonization in the nineteenth century. The project was based on arrogance and superiority of the European and English civilization, which may be traced to the European renaissance that led to the Enlightenment project. And the colonization was nothing but an ugly extension of the Enlightenment project.

Keeping in view the lopsided reception of thinkers and writers of periods of crises, it is necessary to prepare strategies of reception. The problem is not with them, but with us, our motives, methodologies and instruments of speculation. Their overall assessment should be done by considering them in parts after separating and categorizing their roles, though the interrelationship of these parts and their mutual influence cannot be denied. Moreover, despite dismantling of existing hierarchies of literary forms and use of writing as an inclusive category including all literary and non-literary forms particularly in the the post-structuralist era, the reading of writing such as 'evidences' or 'testimonies' is inconceivable in cultural and historical vacuum. Bharatendu's 'Evidence' demands its reading in the light of its context and co-texts, i.e. other 'Evidence' by Sir Saiyyad Ahmad or "Sitar-e-Hind." In that case, Bharatendu, the creative writer has to be separated from Bharatendu, the critic (nascent), historian, social reformer and activist who was a subject of the Empress' empire. He played different roles under different circumstances with varying degrees of inclinations, qualifications and success. The failure or success of one role should neither influence nor determine the overall estimate of an author or thinker like Bharatendu.

The Indian writers and thinkers of the nineteenth century fought for the battered psyche of a disheartened Indian society. Their voices were stifled and steps monitored so it was necessary for them to package their voice or message for their countrymen by garbing it in a sugarcoated voice. Only fictional literature offered relatively free space, though that was not always free from the master's scrutiny. That accounted for ambivalence, nay, polyvalence. Therefore, the true voice of writers living in an age of crisis may often be found in fictional narratives or in works making use of literary device of fantasy. Bharatendu's speech *Bhāratavarṣonnati Kaise ho Sakatī Hai* contained many instances of polyvalence. He delivered the speech in the presence of D.T. Roberts, the English Collector of Balia, whom he eulogized and overestimated by comparing him to Akbar and his assistants Munshi Chaturbhuj Sahay and Munshi Biharilal to Abul Fazl and Toḍarmal in the very first paragraph. (In fact, mutual (over) appreciation is customary in public speeches, and it should never be taken literally.) Roberts who had presided over the lecture called Bharatendu a better dramatist than Shakespeare after seeing the performance of his plays "Satya Harishchandra" and "Neeldevi." But by the time the first paragraph ends, his use of analogy of three frogs to portray the Indian situation gives us a peep into his true estimate of all constituents of Indian social reality.

Fantasy along with fiction suits creative minds more than any other, for example, discursive prose of the essay form during the period of colonization and suppression. Bharatendu's fantasy, *Svarga meiṅ Vicāra Sabhā kā Adhiveśana,* created a separate world and subverted the existing social reality by relating to it (*Bharatendu Samagra*, 983-86). It offered greater freedom to the writer to express his views without courting displeasure of the objects of subversion. He divided the members of the Heaven into the Conservatives and Liberals. The former included Indra, the landlords of Bengal, Yājñavalkya, etc. The latter group included liberal Hindus, Muslims, Christians and some co-opted members from Africa. The question of space for Dayanand Saraswati and Keshav Chandra in the heaven was discussed by them and they allowed them with some remarks. Bharatendu's sympathies lay more with Keshava Sen for his efforts to bring out natural awakening and unity than with Dayanand, for he tried to cut a net with another, not with a knife. Through an undisguised fantasy Bharatendu could say what was otherwise not possible without incurring the wrath of subscribers of the group. Again, he used the mode of parody to satirize social and national evils and practices in *Stotra Pañcaratna* including *Śrī Vaiśyastavarāja, Strī Sevā Paddhati, Atha Madirāstavarāja,* and *Kaṅkar Stotra).* In the last piece he brought out the true character of colonizers:

> O kind-hearted! We crave to eat leftovers in your utensils. We desire to be respected with the mere touch of your hand. We wish to keep a letter or two, signed by you in our letter-box. O Englishman! Bless us. We salute you.
>
> ... ...
>
> O Placid and Sober One! We would do what pleases you. We would put on boot and pantaloon, spectacles on our nose, and eat with fork and knife on table. Be pleased. We salute you.
>
> ... ...
>
> O sweet-tongued! We would give up our mother tongue, and speak your language. . . .
>
> The Council is your mouth, respect your nose, regional partisan behaviour your way of emancipation, and taxation your eyes. O Englishman! We salute you, please protect us.

> Toll tax and police are your arms, officials your nails, tyranny of arbitrariness your back, income your heart. O Englishman! We salute you.
>
> Treasury is your stomach, greed your hunger, army your feet, titles your blessing. O Englishman! We salute you.
>
> — *Bharatendu Samagra*, 992-93

Keeping the context and compulsions in view in which the nineteenth-century writers operated it would be injudicious to call writers like Bharatendu as the flatterer of the Raj. He had the sword of governmental censor hanging over his head, and the danger of losing the government aid that was necessary for sustenance of his journal *Kavivacana-Sudhā*, the means of spreading their message to the people at large, as one can see in Bharatendu's editorial dated 8.6.1874. To seek the true voice we would have to penetrate underneath the cacophony of polyvalence and strategies of survival in all works particularly written in subversive mode and discursive prose, and see the evolution of the author like Bharatendu from "the Raj loyalty" to "the loyalty to nation."

The discursive prose writing, particularly the form of essays, was to good extent used by Narmad, Dalpat and Navalram in Gujarati, Vivekananda and Aurobindo in English, and apart from Bharatendu, by Balkrishna Bhatt, Pratap Narayan Mishra, Pandit Badrinarayan Chaudhary "Premghan" and Balmukund Gupta. Gupta's *Śivaśambhū ke Ciṭṭhe* subtly commented on the then economic, social and political problems plaguing the country. Prose, being a natural language of thought, this period witnessed the growth of prose in Indian languages. Also in prose, the literary form that these thinkers prolifically used was the essay. However, the essay was not a suitable medium to reach the maximum number of people who generally dislike instructive discourse, so the majority of writers of the period garbed their thoughts in a narrative and preferred the novel to the essay. In Gujarati, the case of Govardhanram Tripathi is before us, among others. He wanted to write an essay but he thought it better to write a novel, albeit, of his kind, to convey his thoughts through the narrative.

The consequence was his *magnum opus* novel *Sarasvatīcandra* in four volumes written between 1885-1901 (Tripathi, 1887: 7). Before him, Mahipatram Neelkanth wrote *Sāsu Vahūnī Laḍāī* in the sixth decade of the nineteenth century to "teach" people about social reforms through the "delightful" means of narration, as he dicussed it in detail in his "Preface" to that novel (Neelkanth, 33).

VI

The literature in Indian languages witnessed an unprecedented interest in experimentation in literary forms in the nineteenth century. Travelogues, biography, autobiography, letters, diary, drama, novel and later short story among others were introduced and made use of by creative writers for their purpose.[4] Of these the case of novel is much interesting.

Novel as a long narrative in prose (even in verse) was new to India; the narrative however was not, for India had been a cradle of narrative. So the advent of novel was marked with a tension between the form of the novel and native traditions of narration. In a way novel was return of the native narration that reached Europe through the translation of Indian narratives like *Pañcatantra* via Arab world, as noted by none other than Max Müller. But the

4. The fact is that periods of crisis such as the nineteenth century particularly its second half are the periods of imagining identity in which various factors play their roles. The introduction of the printing press and new literary forms like novel, biography, autobiography, travelogue, letter, and diary facilitated the process in India. The newspapers, magazines, journals like *Kavivacana-Sudhā* in Hindi, *Dandiyo* in Gujarati or *Keralapatrikā* in Malayalam played their pivotal roles in resisting colonization, reclaiming India's past, reforming the society and even imagining the community or country. For instance, the nineteenth-century Kerala was divided into Malabar, Cochin, and Travancore, yet there were newspapers, imagining a unified political space, called *Keralapatrikā*. The burgeoning press operated in living Indian languages, and it led to the formation of linguistic communities due to print technology. Bharatendu in Hindi published *Kavivacana-Sudhā* (1868-85), *Hariścandra Candrikā* (1873-85) and *Balbodhini* to disseminate culture, thought, cultivate taste and bring about reform. The last one deserves our special mention because Bharatendu invited women to participate in the debate on the contemporary issues by contributing to it.

subscription to the form of novel was more as an allegorical means of achieving the desired end (i.e. to portray society and thereby reform it), resisting colonization and of coalescing with the colonizer apart from articulating social and individual aspirations. Since the colonial encounter is a period of unsettled settlement and adjustment, so social behaviour and discourse particularly of the colonized is marked by not ambivalence but polyvalence, for the colonized has to keep changing his strategies to survive against and resist the hegemony of colonization.

Of all literary forms novel suits polyvalence. Its intrinsic formal elasticity and ability to accommodate diverse voices led to its popularity in the second half of the nineteenth century in Indian languages. Marathi opted for *Kādambarī* for the new term, Gujarati for *Navalakathā* after some initial hesitation regarding the choice between *Vārtā* (Mahipatram Neelkanth) and *Kādambarī* (Ichchharam Desai) and Bengali for *Upanyāsa* (Bhoodev Mukhopadhyaya). Hindi followed the Bengali term. But Gauri Dutt (*Devarānī Jeṭhānī kī Kahānī*, 1870), Ishwari Prasad (*Vāma Śikṣaka* 1872) and Shraddharam Phullori (*Bhāgyavati*, 1877) did not call their works as novel, and the historians put them in the category of treatises for the education of women. Bharatendu however serialised *Mālatī* in *Hariścandra Candrikā* through the term novel in 1875, though the term "novel" or *upanyāsa*, was not as popular by 1882, the year of publication of Lala Shrinivas Das's *Parīkṣāguru*. In his Preface, he called it a new "thing," a worldly narrative of education through experience (*anubhava dvārā upadeśa milane kī eka saṅsārī vārtā*). In the dedication, he termed his work as "my humble attempt at writing novel." After Bharatendu, Radhakrishna Das used the term *upanyāsa* in 1878. Later Radhacharan Goswami proposed a meaningful alternative term *navanyāsa* in *Saudāminī* (1890) but it failed to earn acceptance of writers or critics.

Since the colonial period was marked with the endeavours of imagining and constructing identities, so one finds ample evidences of Indian novelists' engagement with the past — historical and mythical — along with social novels aimed at reforming the evils plaguing the society as in *Sāsu Vahūnī Laḍāī* in Gujarati, *Devrānī Jeṭhānī kī Kahānī, Parikṣā Guru* in Hindi, *Alaler Ghare Dular* in Bangla, *Chaman Āṭha Ghūṇṭa* in Oriya among others. On the other hand, novels dealing with extra-natural and romance provided a refuge to the society that was trying to tide over the humiliation of defeat in the freedom struggle and was trying to come to terms with the existing harsh realities. The works like *Candrakāntā Santati* tried to synthesize *kissā* and *kathā* tradition with the form of the novel. With the generous proliferation of magic, witchcraft and ancillary supernatural elements one finds the works as an embodiment of magic realism. The redemption of the society from its evils and excelling in the art of fiction was the main concern of the novelists like Lala Sriniwas Das in Hindi and Mahipatram Neelkanth in Gujarati. Neelkanth, the author of *Sāsu Vahūnī Laḍāī* (1866), saw the society as constituted by units of communities and families. If family is peaceful, the communities made of families, and then the society made of communities would be peaceful, thus, paving way for the happiness and prosperity of all constituents. So the author made use of the *vārtā* as a vehicle for communicating the message for the readers at large. The work, as he stated in the sub-title of the novel, was aimed at becoming the *vārtārūpe kharī chhavi,* i.e. it was a 'just' or 'honest' image in the form of narrative. The image with fictitiousness gives pleasure, and its 'justness' teaches. Though the novel might not earn the approval of critics who would look for epical length, well-made plot construction, and art of characterization in it, however, the way he did not care for formal considerations, and made use of songs, *bhajanas*, story within the story and dramatic dialogue within it, the work deserves our appreciative attention for the author's audacity and commitment for the cause and not the form, the means nor the end of the work.

Sunder, the protagonist of *Sāsu Vahūnī Laḍāī,* is a metaphor of that part of weaker Indian society particularly women that suffers at the hands of its own people and sex (her husband, mother-in-law and sister-in-law). The ugly aspect of society as against the beautiful protagonist (Sunder) is exposed in the novel. Madanmohan in *Parikṣā Guru* is at one level microcosm of the Indian higher class that considered the sole aim of its life was to imitate the colonial masters by becoming the consumer of their external ways, behaviour and even goods. Consequently, he suffers. His education through experience, observation and timely help from his friend Brajkishor who becomes the author's mouthpiece articulate the agenda for the Indian society. These two novels amply demonstrate that the literary works, particularly fictional works of the period of *abhijñāna,* invite being studied as allegories. Moreover the fictional works of the period exhibit increasing centrality being given to women in the works of men, as one finds in the titles of works in Hindi, Gujarati and English, e.g. *Devarānī Jeṭhānī kī Kahānī, Śyāma Svapna, Vāma Śikṣaka, Candrakāntā Santati, Sāsu Vahūnī Laḍāī, Rājamohan's Wife* and *Bianca* among others. However, the centrality of women is superficial and ritualistic, restricted to the title only, not to the core of concerns on all occasions, as the women occupied only the marginal space in the matrix of power whatever its site was — family, community or society.

The main purpose of most of the novelists of the period was not to excel in the use of form of the novel but use it as an instrument of changing the society for better. For this purpose, the novelists took liberty with the form of the novel and made extensive use of songs, dialogues, story within story, quotations, at times making the work appear as a collage of quotations, hence artificial. In this admixture, one sees the glimpses of native narrative traditions prevalent in the society. The early practitioners of craft and art of novel writers like Neelkanth and Govardhanram Tripathi earn critical attention for playing with the form of novel and thereby moulding the formal space of the English/European form to their native realities and ends.

Apart from a social novel like *Sāsu Vahūnī Laḍāī* and historical novel like *Karanghelo,* the Gujarati novel made another experiment in the form of *Hind ane Brittania* in 1885 that the novelist called the "First Political Novel in Gujarati." Since the novel is not much discussed even in Gujarati, it would be congruous to introduce the novel by taking recourse to the "Summary" given by the novelist in English.

One day, about the close of the Lytton regime (1 January 1880) Indian Patriotism stood on the highest peak of the Vindhyan range in the heart of India, bewailing the great maladministration then prevailing in the country. . . . Patriotism laid the whole blame of the maladministration on the sons of Hind, when, all of a sudden, there appeared on the scene, bursting from the bowels of the mountain, Hind, seated on a tiger. . . . Entering into conversation with patriotism, Hind laid the whole blame of the maladministration on Britannia, while patriotism found fault with Hind, observing that her fallen condition and the supremacy of Britannia over her were mainly due to the cringing and mean habits of her sons, who had grown totally ignorant of all that constituted morality, politics, and maladministration.

Suddenly, in the nick of time, from the Narbadā, which flowed at the foot of the mountain sprang forth a lion, with Britannia on his back. Before Britannia and Hind had come face to face, signs became manifest of a fight between their lion and tiger carriers. But in obedience to the orders of Britannia, Hind called upon her tiger to desist and began to leave the place. She observed to her tiger that Britannia's star being then in the ascendant, it would do more harm than good to dispute with her the question of supremacy and subordination. On this the tiger and the lion stood apart, growling at each other. Britannia remarked to Hind that it was not for her to say that her star was in the ascendant, and her own in the decline, when, but for her (Britannia's) help in the hour of need, she (Hind) would have been nowhere. "Ah! I accept that," said Hind, "but only when my valiant sons are all dead and gone." So saying Hind, visibly affected, expressed her desire to leave the place. Britannia asked whether she meant by her valiant sons Tipu Sultan, Jasvantrao Holkar, Nana Saheb or Tantia Tope, of whom she ought more to be ashamed than proud. Hind requested Britannia not to speak anything ill of her departed sons as she did not mean to discuss the matter, being her slave and not on any footing of equality with her. Britannia, not admitting that Hind was enslaved to her, explained her position by citing instances and proofs as to what the different causes were that had conspired to put her in an enslaved condition. "These things," said Britannia, "have all happened through divine will; so let us bury the past and come to harmony and good terms." "Ah!," said Hind, "that is not possible until you do me Justice, where now injustice reigns rampant." Britannia observed that great were the straits to which she was reduced in the Black Hole affair and 1857 Mutinies. Hind then asked whether she should never desire for a change or relief from her present downtrodden condition. "Whatever that be," said Britannia, "before so doing thou shouldst bear in mind the various acts of kindness that I have done thee and the safety which I have afforded thee from incessant foreign invasions." "Oh!," replied Hind, "that was mostly for thy own selfish purpose, to gain the goodwill and affection of my people." Britannia, then, fired with indignation, observed whether hers was not a better government than that of Mohammad of Ghazni or the Ghoris or Aurangzeb, and whether hers was not a Rāma Rājya, with security and contentment reigning throughout the land from the Himalayas to Cape Comorin, and Jagannātha to Jacobabad. Hind cited various instances to disprove this, and showed how false was the position Britannia had taken up. This greatly incensed Britannia who exclaimed: "My sons are far nobler than thine; they are very willing to mix with thy sons, but it is thine who lack good manners and hate mine." Hind admitted this in part, but alleged as the cause of such hatred, the great tyranny of her sons on Indian soil, instances of which she cited from Burke, Bright, Le Grand Jacob, and other English and Anglo-Indian authorities and the cold look of disdain with which, with some honourable exceptions, she always treated her sons. To this Britannia replied by saying, and this very truthfully, "thou hast lost thy kingdom by the great poverty of thy military strength and the total want of system or method in thy civil and military administration, and resting thyself content with temporary strength and gain, when thou wast in need of permanent strength with a view to the permanent good and well-being of the country." Hind admitted this, and, worsted in her argument, she declared, with her eyes bathed in tears, that she would never return to the spot, until she had obtained real strength and power.

At this juncture, Liberty came down from heaven seated on a ball of cannon. Britannia grew greatly agitated on seeing her. But Liberty assured her that she had not come to trouble her but to bring about an amicable settlement between her and Hind. In reply to a question from Liberty as to what she wanted, Hind said that she wanted Britannia to leave her land and free her from her trammels. Liberty called her a fool and asked her, how she would administer her vast continent without any general and without any administrative Genius or Policy. "Times will take care of themselves," said Hind, "Were no Shivaji, Cromwell, Napolean and Washington but the products of the times they lived in?" Liberty asked where her vaunted heroes and warriors slept away during 1857 Mutinies. "No mighty spirit came forward at that time," said Liberty, "and if thou wouldst urge upon Britannia leaving thee, remember that the helms of power are sure not to remain with thee, but will pass into other hands." "That is exactly what I mean," interrupted Britannia, "Hind is not still able to rule herself." At this Liberty got much vexed and said, turning angrily to Britannia, "I know very well thy fitness for rule." She then spoke at length of the diplomatic way in which she had acquired territories in, and gradually spread her red colour over India, and consolidated her rule. "At first with view of establishing thy prestige, thou didst follow a noble and righteous policy, but latterly thou hast abandoned that policy of equality and justice, the policy of the tiger and the lamb drinking at the same fountain. (This part has much of administrative policy in it and is taken mainly from English historians and writers on India.) In conclusion, Liberty asked Britannia if she wished at all to do as the (Liberty) desired. "What wouldst thou do, Liberty," asked Britannia, "If I declined to do so." "I would make Hind free," answered Liberty. "If thou were to make Hind free," said Britannia, "she would fall into other hands." "That's true," said Liberty, "But what I desire to begin with is Reform." "I would accept that," said Britannia. Hind demanded a new rule, but this demand of hers was refused, and Liberty cited her native states as prominent instances of her own unfitness to rule. She therefore desired her to ask for reform under British rule, which she promised to obtain from Britannia. Hind accepted this and Liberty was greatly pleased at this settlement of a hot dispute. She said to Britannia and Hind that she thought of sending a great personage as her Indian viceroy, one who would rise above Bentinck, Canning and Mayo; one with whom the whole country would be enchanted; one endowed with wisdom of Rāma, the strength of character of Bhīma, the learning of Droṇa, the fortitude of Dharma, the forgiveness of earth, the beneficence of Mahādeva, the liberality of Karṇa, the veneration of *Gītā*, the holiness of Ganges, a God in human shape whose form (portrait) will be worshipped in every Indian home like one of her ten *avatāra*s. Just at this moment, as if to obey the commands of Liberty, two heavenly nymphs brought the personage spoken of by her, seated on a heavenly throne, and, at his very sight, both Hind and Britannia were satisfied. They thought that such was the great man each of them wanted. All at once flowers poured down in showers from the sky on this most noble personage, the Great Lord Ripon who brought about peace between Hind and Britannia, his greatest title to everlasting glory.

The work concludes with five very touching poems in connection with Lord Ripon's departure from India in five different languages, in English by Babu Ram Sharma of Calcutta; in Sanskrit by the great Bombay scholar, Pandit Gattulalji; in Hindustānī by the late eminent Benares Poet Harishchandra; and in Gujarati by two well-known poets of Gujarat, Narmadshanker and Savitanarayan.

Since I have ignored *Sarasvatīcandra,* a major fictional milestone in all Indian languages in the nineteenth century, and discussed *Hind ane Brittania* at length, the act demands some justification. *Hind ane Brittania* deserved space not because it is a superior work but because for the present purpose the work represented "third" stream of thought, i.e. reconciliation with the colonizers, against loyalty to the Raj, and resistance to the Raj. Using fictional form neither to resist colonizer nor support it outrightly he rather advocated reconciliation between Hind and Britain, and in a way asked both the colonizer and colonized to re-fashion themselves. Interestingly the novelist places Hind before Britain at least in the title of his work, though the latter is the master. Initially, the author had thought of the title as "On the Mountain Top" or "The Reconciliation of Hind and Britannia." The need for reconciliation emerged out of the demands for change in the years before the formation of Congress that marked the beginning of polarization of political forces for attaining Independence. Desai must have visualized the futility of such demands in the aftermath of the failure of the struggle for Indian Freedom. The novel was a rare case of seeking and forwarding reconciliation with the colonizer in fictional terms. Ironically, the novelist had to defend his work in the beginning of his work against prospective charges of writing against the British rule.

Significantly, the novelist called the work the "First Political Novel in Gujarati" and translated it as the *Rājakīya Kādambarī*. The use of word *Kādambarī* for novel in Gujarati is significant, for it seems that there was some tentativeness and hesitation in Desai's mind. What was *Vārtā* for Mahipatram Neelkanth becomes *Kādambarī* (in Gujarati), a term that Marathi has chosen from Sanskrit. The term *Navalakathā* that centred on the element of novelty or newness of novel was still not accepted by all. The Gujarati creative psyche was however coming to terms with the form of novel in *Sarasvatīcandra* regarding the term and its constituents. Goverdhanram Tripathi in the "Introduction to the First Edition" to his work spoke of the narrative in the novel as the *phūlagūnthanī* (a wreath of flowers) and also of the advent of co-hero before the hero, as against the English/European traditions of novel. He consciously established the distinctive identity of Gujarati novel against the European or English novel (11).

Not only novels but also the form of drama was employed for allegorizing the Indian society and its problems. Raja Laxman Singh translated Kālidāsa's *Śākuntalam* as *Śakuntalā* in 1868 in Hindi and Bharatendu translated *Vidyāsundara* from Bangla in the same year. The example in Hindi was Bharatendu's *Bhāratadurdaśā* (1875) in which the dramatist made use of native dramatic form and local dialectical words, i.e. *rūpaka* with frequent use of *gīta, lāvaṇī, dohā* and *caupāī*. The dramatist reminded the people of India of their glorious past, and pitiable present for which inertia, shamelessness of the natives and exploitation particularly economic exploitation by the colonizers are the main causes. The army of "Bhāratadurdaśā" has many warlords in it, i.e. inertia, religion, flood, drought, extravagance, internal quarrels. The army of Nadir Shah cannot face it. The intellectual characters include editor, poet, orator, Maharashtrian and Bengali intellectuals. But they are not persons of action. Mere revolutionary editorials and fiery poems would not serve the purpose of the nation. Bhārata Bhāgya commits suicide towards the end of the play. Once the fatalism is gone, the possibilities for India's awakening naturally increase. Equally significant was his *Andhera Nagarī*, as it commented on economic, social and political order. Money is supreme in *Andhera Nagarī*. No one cares for quality or value. Everything is subject to sale or purchase including caste, religion or justice. The rates of vegetables and milk cake are the same. *Ṭakā ser bhājī, ṭakā ser khājā*. Instead of criminals, honest people are punished. Unjust taxation, corruption, exploitation by moneylenders and bribery plague the society, making the common man's life miserable. His *Nīladevī* (1881) is a metaphor of straining listlessness of the Mother India expressed through the consciousness of its children suffering the tyranny of the indigo lords. These are, however, brief plays. The theme is treated in an elaborate manner in Gujarati in Dalpatram's

Mithyābhimāna in which the dramatist reinterprets the well-known story of a night-blind person who suffers psychologically and even physically for not recognizing his night blindness. Jeevram Bhatt, the protagonist is a symbol of Indian society in general and decadence of the learned brāhmaṇas in particular who are unwilling to accept their disease or decadence. In the absence of recognition, how can the disease or decadence be stemmed? False self-pride, conceit and hypocrisy lead to humiliation. In Act V of the play the dramatist introduced a significant text through the characters of Kutubmian and Vaghji. Kutubmian had run away from Delhi in search of job with 18 brothers because of 'famine' there. On the way they were attacked by a gang of Kolees. All brothers ran away in different directions, yet Kutubmian considered it as his victory and said that since he was not a miser so he gifted his turban and weapons to the Kolees. Adding to the display of vanity in words and trying to excel the others when he came to know that the name of the Rājpūt is Vaghji, he tells his name as 'five-seven snakes, ten-twelve elephants and ten-twenty *bāgh* (tigers) Khan.' Kutubmian brags of fighting against an army of thousands but the crocking of frog frightens him. In the ensuing wrestling duel, Mian fell down and Vaghji sat on him, yet he raised his leg and said that his leg was still up. It speaks of decadence of the Rājpūts and Muslims, the ruling classes of India, as they were nothing but braggarts who were proved powerless against the Englishmen, unmentioned in the play. The unstated other in the sub-text is significant because Gujarati writers including Dalpat had welcomed English rule as a respite against the tyranny of the Muslims and even the Marāṭhās. Thus, the perception of the colonizer was not the same in all regions and literature. Moreover, it was not too pragmatic to directly comment or criticize the colonial masters.[5] It was as difficult to write against

5. The vehemence of opposition and resistance that one discerns in Hindi was absent in Gujarati literature until the advent of Gandhi in the twentieth century. It was because people in Gujarat saw the English rule, English education and reforms as 'freedom' from the tyrannical oppression of the Muslim rule and misrule of native kings. Narmad, the herald of Gujarati →

the tyranny or exploitation during the English rule on the Indian soil, as it was for the *bhakti* poets, barring the case of Kabīr and to some extent Nānak, to write against the suppression of the less sophisticated Muslim rulers during the *bhakti* period.

To conclude, Indian creative response to the *abhijñānakāla, navajāgaraṇa* or renaissance, in its traditional or (post) modern sense as an ever-happening phenomenon, was as complex as were the processes, motives and forces of colonialism. This 'Mona Lisa' called Indian renaissance smiles for some and is otherwise for others. The beauty of the period and its literature lies in its complexity and even in temporal uncertainty to an extent that it allows space to its subscribers to go before and beyond the colonial period. The need is to receive this diversity, complexity and polyvalence affirmatively. It is expected that the scholars, particularly of comparative Indian literature, would be able to put the fragments of present endeavour of reconsidering questions of identity, and consequent polyvalence during the post-1857 period of the nineteenth-century Gujarati and Hindi literature together and see the 'whole' as the wise, using their imaginative faculty, see the full moon in the feeble curve on the 'second' day.

→ identity, in unambiguous terms stated in his essays like *Gujarātiyonī Sthiti* (The State of the Gujaratis) that the Gujaratis suffered the most after the advent of the Muslims in Gujarat. In his essays *Svadeśābhimān, svadeśa* stands for Hindudeśa. He spoke of the glory of Hindu *dharma*, Hindu *bhāṣā* and Hindu *jñāna*, and prays to God, "O God! Look at we Hindus who are wretched. Give us the understanding to walk on the right path" (in Singh & Mehta, 41). And he considered the English as lamps of the chandelier whose lamps give us light. (Also see the views expressed in an article of *Buddhivardhaka Grantha*, vol. 3, no. 1, January 1858 denouncing the "mutineers"). Narmad was associated with the journal as the editor, though it should not persuade us to believe that he subscribed to these views.

Navalram, Narmad's contemporary, considered English education as "the life force of reforms" (*Navalgranthāvalī*, 456-75). As late as 1996 *saṁvat* year, i.e. 1939) Mansukhlal Jhaveri noted in the journal *Prasthāna*, Magh, 1996: "After the advent of the British rule . . . the stagnant water of our life began to flow. . . . Sanskrit has been revived. . . . Our country has been revived after the advent of the English" (267-69).

5

Ornament or Blessing or Both

The Other in Colonial Paradigms with Reference to India

LET me indulge in generalization by stating a few resounding commonplaces to develop my argument pertaining to colonialism, the way I understand them, rather than taking recourse to jargon-laden critical opinions and definitions.[1]

Colonialism on the part of colonizers is realization of one's interests in colonization, its forces and processes, and their conscious use during the period of colonization for exploitation of the colonized.[2] It is the essence of processes of colonization that involves settlement of countrymen or communities of a country in another, with the former as the centre of their concerns and activities. The main motive behind colonization was

---

1. I am not the first one to use the term "other" in the sense I do. I am indebted to Fanon whose words I quote here:

   > In the colonies the economic structure is also a superstructure. The cause is the consequence; you are rich because you are white, you are white because you are rich. This is why Marxist analysis should always be slightly stretched every time we do have to do with the colonial problem. . . . It is neither the act of owning factories, nor estates, nor a bank balance, which distinguishes the governing classes. The governing race is first and foremost among those who come from elsewhere, those who are unlike the original inhabitants "the others" — 33

2. To problematize my argument further, the moment the colonized subject becomes conscious of these forces and processes and resists them through political and/or discursive practices, it becomes post-coloniality, or it at least co-exists with the latter.

exploitation of natural and human resources, particularly economic. No land will, however, allow itself to be exploited, until and unless its own people conspired against themselves. To achieve their end the alien communities dominated the new lands politically by defeating them in war and systematically destroying or destabilizing the native institutions — religious, social, educational, administrative, judicial and cultural. The colonial forces, in order to sustain and further their activities and validate their presence, constructed a body of knowledge to serve their purposes. This body of knowledge, known as Orientalism, oversighted, faulted, misrepresented and appropriated indigenous systems of knowledge and thereby helped colonizers consolidate their occupation so much so that the colonized themselves come to see amnesia in their own intellectual history and lack of will, confidence and the state of prostration at larger social or national levels. When colonization, with Orientalism as its handmaid, led to a large-scale appropriation and exploitation of alien, geographical terriory, it ended up in a large-scale occupation of the lands, known better as imperialism or imperial colonization.[3] In other words, Orientalism was a construct made of a body of discursive practices about the Orient by the people from the non-Orient who, to put it sympathetically, like the modern-day activists of the Green Peace, Human Rights and Environmental Movement, were at certain level seriously concerned with the preservation of knowledge, at least of India.

---

3. In fact, it is erroneous to use the term colonizer as a homogeneous category. The colonizers have one common interest but the people who go in the field and enact them are different beings of different temperaments and inclinations. With the consolidation of the rule or empire, these interests begin to leak or ooze out making the bottom of the colonial structure porous. However, only those interests are patronized that suit the colonial purpose. Those who do not subscribe to it are put in the category of rebels. Albert Memmi, in the not so frequently referred book, *The Colonizer and the Colonized*, distinguishes between the colonizers, who willingly adopt the role of usurper and one who reflects the colonial ideology. "If every colonial immediately accepts the role of colonizer, every colonizer does not necessarily become a colonialist" (19). The conscientious rejecter of colonial

→

Colonialism constructed itself on multiple subtle and sophisticated strategies depending upon circumstances. Colonial projects and their strategies were so subtle and sophisticated that the colonizers did not disturb such native institutions as served their purpose of sustatining their appropriation of wealth. Colonizers did not have one particular paradigm. Their strategies and discursive practices varied from continent to continent, from country to country and even within a country. For instance, within India they allowed *zamīndārs* (landlords), *nawābs* and kings to rule in different places till they were willing to be their agents. They used these as ornament-laden kings and *nawābs* as their mere ornaments. The Delhi Assemblage on 1 January 1877 and proclamation of the "Order of the Indian Empire" was a pronounced statement in this direction. The Delhi Darbar was a highly structured text arranged according to the number of guns for salute and title with the Queen as the epicentre, though not there. The gunsalute and titles were signifiers making and controlling the text. These kings and *nawābs* were not only ornaments but also blessings for the colonizers, for they did not mind being reduced to the position of tax collectors. They collected tax by all possible means for the colonizers. And by separating them from labour the colonizers made the entire upper, upper-middle and middle class of India impotent and parasitic. Ironically, this class of tax collectors thought of the colonizers as a blessing. It should be no surprise for any of us to see even the distinguished Indian minds like Raja Rammohun, Narmad, Dalpat, Bharatendu, Chiplunkar and Vivekananda in a state of ambivalence in their

→ practices refuses to conform to the given moulds of imperialistic value system, withdraws silently or remains to fight and change conditions around him. He alienates himself from his community and countrymen. He invites their antagonism by his open rebellion against their mode of life or implied criticism of code or values. He earns sympathy and tolerance of the colonized people but not love or complete emotional rapport. He becomes an outsider in both cultures. Colonizers are chased out of the country and the colonized do not make any exception. He thus leads a lonely existence — torn between personal loyalties and ideals.

response to colonizers in the nineteenth century. Ornaments or blessings, gunsalutes, and titles among others were the surreptitious instruments that colonizers used to validate, sustain and further their project.

One of the devices that colonizers used adroitly was that of "othering." Colonizers saw the natives as the other, and then examined, analysed and categorized them as (i) harmful, (ii) useful, and (iii) indifferent or useless others. The colonized were treated as the other on the lines of gender, race, region, religion and civilization. All the kings and *nawābs* in the Delhi Assemblage were useful others, jewels in the imperial crown, and they were further decorated with titles for being the useful other. In fact, their decoration was the ornamentation more of the decorator than that of the decoratee, for they were willing contributories to the crown.

Let us examine the game of "othering" played as it is in a few texts like *Othello, Seeta* and, *Things Fall Apart*, the texts separated from each other by centuries and continents. The reasons for choosing these texts would become evident during the course of their discussion. *Othello* represents the nascent stage of colonization, for if the play was written in 1604, then Sir Thomas Roe, Edward Terry, Ralph Fitch, Henry Lord and Thomas Coriate, the precursors of colonization in India, had not reached India by then, though Christopher Marlowe had speculated dispatch of his necromantic spirits to India in *Doctor Faustus* and the 'Scramble for Africa' was by now not a mere slogan but a reality so that Queen Elizabeth, a year before her death, had to proclaim a decree banning the entry of Negroes into England.

Othello studies colonization in terms of colour, country, continent and race. It is about Cyprus caught between the Venetians and Turks, or Christians and Muslims respectively. That Cyprus is a geographical reality, and was the core of the tug of war between the Turks and Venetians in the fifteenth and sixteenth centuries is a historical fact. Cyprus came to Venice when it defeated the Turks in 1487. The tussle for its acquisition continued between the two till 1570 when Mustapha, the military General of Salim II, attacked it in the month of May and took its possession. Either in his formative years or later on Shakespeare must have in his own way received these developments and then made use of them through a non-historical figure. The play presents Cyprus, the colony, as source of disorder, chaos, lawlessness and tragic wastage of the most exquisite human resources as against Venice, the epicentre of elegance of civilized behaviour, of law, order and harmony.

The game of othering is played at different levels in the play. Cyprus is Venice's other. Among *dramatis personae* Cassio is Iago's other, for he considers him an outsider in Venice, "Of here and everywhere" (Act I, Scene I, 1380) and thereby unfit for his promotion to the post of lieutenant. This is one of his motives for his malignant malice for him on the formula of the son of the soil, by which he treats Cassio as the other for his selfish interests that coincidently suit him.

The people of Cyprus find no elaborate or direct role in the play. Desdemona does mention them as "generous islanders" (Act III, Scene III), when she comes to remind Othello that they are waiting for him for dinner in the garden of the Castle. The nameless voices referred to in the form of the riotous noise in Cyprus are the other. But the play brings in the other in Venice in the form of Othello, the black, the thick-lipped chief of Moracco. He is a moor, African other in Venice, though a useful one. Even Iago, the prince of villains, comments on his military prowess.

For I know the state,
However this may gall him with some check,
Cannot with safety cast him.
Another of his fathom they have none.
To lead their business.

— Act I, Scene I, 148-50 and 153-54

Montano, the governor of Cyprus, also speaks of his ability:

> For I have served him, and the man commands like a full soldier.
> — Act II, Scene I, 133-34

His utility for the colonizers of Cyprus makes him indispensible for the state of Venice, and also for the continued occupation of Cyprus. The Duke acknowledges it, when he says:

> Othello, the fortitude of the place is best known to you; and though we have there a substitute of most allowed sufficiency, yet opinion, a more sovereign mistress of effect, throws a more safer voice on you. — Act I, Scene III, 220-24

His indispensability can be measured from the fact that the petition of Brabantio, a senior Senator, against Othello falls on the deaf ears of the Senate. The Duke instead of admonishing Othello rather asks the Senator to take the development in his stride.

Colonizers know their useful other, test them and then use the useful other, to appropriate another geopolitical territory. The harmful other in the play are the Turks. The Venetians use Othello as their useful other against the Turks. He too has proved his utility in sustaining the Venetian control over Cyprus in the face of challenge from the Turks. He did so in the past as well, as he himself speaks of it in the idiom that seems to contain vehemence of his master or user. He seems to have embraced his master's cause as his own, and staked his power for defending and furthering the cause of his masters. He is conscious of it when he says:

> . . . In Aleppo once
> *Where a* malignant and turbaned Turk
> Beat a Venetian and traduced the state,
> *I took by the' throat the* circumcised dog.
> And smote him thus.
> — Act V. Scene II, 351-55

The words (italicized by me) bring in the question of racial and civilizational divide between Islam and Christianity, the black and white, something on which colonizers capitalize. Though Othello is the indispensable, useful other for Venice, yet the general perception of the General refers to his being the other. Brabantio's parting remarks to Othello speak of the low esteem of the other, however useful it may be:

> Look to her Moor if thou has eyes to see:
> She has deceived her father and may thee.
> — Act I, Scene III, 290-91

Brabantio refers to his "moorness"[4] and also questions his ability to see. Ironically it is not the deceiver (Desdemona) but the deceived (Othello) other whose ability to see is questioned. It is further stressed in Lodovico who shockingly questions the Senate's faith reposed in Othello when he sees him abusing his wife in public.

> Is this the noble Moor, whom our full Senate call all in all.
> — Act IV, Scene I, 274-75

Even before his tragic end Othello himself is made to accept that he was 'a base Indian' who could not distinguish between a stone and a pearl and threw the pearl away. In fact, by saying so Othello himself approves what Brabantio had stated in Act I, Scene III, and stigmatizes his own race (of the other) as inferior subscribing to superstitions and beliefs. The play suggests it subtly through the handkerchief incident. That the handkerchief is the instrument of tragedy implies that Othello kills Desdemona whom he had addressed as the 'soul's joy' for the sake of a piece of cloth. Such a simplistic reading of the incident puts the other Othello in poor light, for he had only outer eyes, but not the inner eyes, to 'see' (only the masters have them), and so sacrified a pearl for a poor patch of cloth. The superior other would say so, and the other would consent to it.

Othello in the moment of distress becomes conscious of his

---

4. The Moor, as referred to in *Othello*, was a Muslim of the mixed Berber and Arab people inhabiting North-West Africa, particularly Morocco. These people attacked Spain in the eighth century CE. These were pagans originally and some of them were converted to Islam later on.

otherness, as he thinks of his 'blackness' associated with darkness, lack of knowledge and ultimately evil, as he ponders over his inadequacy, "Haply for I am black, . . ." His otherness, marked by blackness, the way it can be interpreted, has the answer to the question pertaining to the significance attached to the handkerchief by Othello. To him, the handkerchief is not just a piece of cloth but a cultural artefact, a cooked text whose meaning is accessible only to those who subscribe to it and have the knowledge of this textual system. Those who ridicule Othello for losing his mental equipoise and for murdering the 'divine' Desdemona that 'excels the quirky of blazoning pens,' neither understand his culture nor respect it. To appreciate his cultural system one has to go outside the play to the traces of Othello's pagan African culture against the dominant Christian Venetian culture that controls the hierarchy among cultures and their signification as well. The traces of this subtext are contained in the play in the references to the handkerchief that it was given to his mother by an Egyptian sorceress who made it different magical potions:

> That handkerchief
> Did an Egyptian to my mother give;
> She was a charmer . . .
>
> . . . there's magic in the use of it.
> A sibyl that had numbered in the world
> The sun to course two hundred compass
> In her prophetic fury sewed the work;
> The wombs were hallowed that did breed the silk;
> And it was dyed in mummy, which the skilful
> Conversed of maiden's hearts.
>
> — Act III, Scene IV, 69-79

His mother, while speaking of the potency of the handkerchief asked him to give that to his wife who will be faithful to him till she keeps, and the day she loses it, she would cease to be so. Desdemona lost the handkerchief under the circumstances known to us. But excepting Othello, everyone including Iago knows that she is honest and faithful. Othello murdered her for her alleged dishonesty, and that too in such a barbaric manner, as he did not pay heed to any of her pleas, even to her last wish of letting her pray. Between her honesty and the words of his mother, two things happen: Desdemona suffers, though she is truthful; and so does Othello, and his mother's words, his race and culture and his faith in them prove to be false. The words and conduct given to Othello prove that the essential nature of the black African race of Moors is barbaric, uncivilized and inferior to the white Christian European race.[5]

II

Chinua Achebe's novels contest the hegemonic given misrepresentation of the Ibo community that becomes a living metaphor of the Nigerian, African and all colonized societies in colonial or imperial discourses and their impact on social and cultural life. His *Things Fall Apart* deals with the falling apart of 'things' due to the advent of the 'other,' i.e. Christian missionaries in a traditional African rural society. The confrontation between the two, and the systematic marginalization of the indigenous things and thereby appropriation of the other dismantles pre-colonial social edifice of Africa. As the things fall apart, Okonkwo finds it difficult to exist in the 'other' structures, and he commits suicide, for he could not sustain himself. Like his protagonist Okonkwo, Achebe had found himself standing at the crossroads of culture, as he stated in an interview with Eleanor Watchel:

5. One can, in fact, go a step ahead, and state that colonizers used literary discourses to establish their cultural superiority, as may be discerned in the performances of, for instance, Shakespearean plays, the way they conditioned the taste of the subject and the media, controlled by the colonizers. Let me, to buttress my point, take the case of the performance of *Othello* that was staged by the Sans Souci on 21 August 1839. The cast had Mrs. Anderson, the daughter of the famous actress of the period Esther Leach, and one Bengali Indian named Baishnav Charan Adhya as Othello. It was considered, as reported then, "a memorable event in the history of Calcutta's theatre" in the nineteenth century, for "a Bengali Youth in an English Play in an English Theatre" catered "to a [large] English audience" (7). It was a revolutionary departure from the earlier practice in the sense that the natives →

> The image of crossroads is a good one, because crossroads are a place where there is a lot of traffic, not just human traffic but also spirit traffic. So it's a very powerful location. That's the idea I was trying to convey. Christianity was new, strange in many ways, but it was powerful, so was the traditional life of the people when I was growing up, we had already passed the initial encounter, which involved fighting at times literally, actual battles. Things had become more settled, and the advantage was that you saw a bit of the past and a bit of the future. That was where you stood. Of course, being of the Christian party, the missionary party, I was not really supposed to pay much attention to the traditional; what they did was thought to be heathenish, and I was not supposed to be interested in it, but I was. — Watchel 1955: 55

Achebe may have developed the ability to live between two opposite worlds and thereby giving the impression of the two being one, yet the fact is that the early colonizers constructed the binaries carefully and capitalized on them. Hence, it tantamounts to deliberate overlooking of a few historical processes that had impact on the colonized people, if one rejects the modern African as 'soul torn between two cultures,' as in the case of Achebe.

The British colonizers appropriated Nigeria in the late nineteenth century. They inferiorized the indigenous communities, and denied the suitability of their institutions. They validated their presence in the colony in the name of bringing knowledge and progress in the Nigerian communities. The Nigerians, according to them, were savages and barbarians without any sense of history. The British imposed their own administrative social-cultural structures on them. They did find some useful natives to collaborate with them, but the resistance continued in Nigeria leading to Lord Lugard's policy of its indirect rule in 1918 by

---

→ found no role for them in these exclusive play houses like the Sans Souci and the Chowringhee. But the role given to the native was that of Othello who was described as *real unpainted nigger Othello* (emphasis mine) in a letter published in the *Calcutta Star* (10).

ignoring the difference among the political and social structures of Hasua, Yoruba, Ibo and other communities among others. This system, with the intervening reorganization of 1930, lasted till the independence of Nigeria in 1960. The collaborators, or those who tried to be useful to the colonizers, were called by the natives as contemptible collaborators. The natives also played the game of the other but without the success of the colonizers, for they lacked in organized brutality and cunningness.

In *Things Fall Apart*, Chinua Achebe suggests different processes and paradigms of colonialism. The white men came as the missionaries to Africa. Once their religious structures set in, political, administrative and economic structures followed. Colonizers manifested themselves as priests, administrators, soldiers and traders. The interests of all of these converged at one point — appropriation and exploitation of the territory. The novelist informs us about these patterns much later in the novel while describing the visits of Obierika to his friend Okonkwo during the protagonist's exile. During his visit he casually mentions that Abame, one of the villages in the union of nine villages, is no more. Obierika narrates the tale of refugees from Abame.

> During the last planting season a white man had appeared in their clan.
> "An albino," suggested Okonkwo.
> He was not an Albino. He was quite different.

He sipped his wine.

> And he was riding an iron horse. And so they killed the white man and tied his iron horse to their sacred tree because it looked as if it would run away to call the man's friends . . . and they began to shoot. Everybody was killed except the old and the sick who were at home, and a handful of men and women whose *chi* were widely awake and brought them out of that market.
>
> — Achebe: 125-26

The "iron horse" brings forth the otherness in ideas and understanding which existed between the two systems. During his second visit to Okonkwo, Obierika refers to change in situation, for the missionaries had come to Umusfia. "They had built their church there, won a handful of converts and were already sending evangelists to the surrounding towns and villages" (Achebe 130).

It adds another dimension to the game of the other. The aliens try to dominate the natives politically. Those who try to resist are suppressed. One of the best ways to control them forever was to convert them. These converts did not become one with the "othering" other, and they come to exist as the new other, sandwiched between two hostile others like Nwoye, the son of Okonkwo.

The indigenous people led by Okonkwo also play this game of othering to their disadvantage. They play it more among themselves than with the colonizers thereby presenting themselves as a highly fragmented vulnerable other.

Initially, the Ibo treated the missionaries casually. Eventually, their evengelist reaches Mbanta, and Okonkwo pauses for a while to listen to them in the market square in the hope that it might come to chasing people out of the village or whipping them. It leads to the inevitable clash between Okonkwo symbolizing the traditional indigenous way of life, and the other way of life, from his perspective, represented by Christianity and its Church. The conversion of Nwoye, Okonkwo's son, symptomizes that the strategies of the more subtle and sophisticated dominant empire strikes against the very things that Okonkwo represents and lives for. It is a communal and emotional blow to him, for it creates another 'other' out of the existing harmful other. The othering empire uses the new other against the harmful other by splitting it.[6] In a situation such as this the colonizers exploit the primordial innocence of the pre-colonial pre-Christian Iboland in the name of the civilizing project.

---

6. Shakespeare's *The Tempest* also invites such a study. Ariel belongs to Caliban, the other, but Prospero, the colonizer, appropriates it and uses it against his adversary, i.e. Caliban. Please see the chapter "Towards an Indian Theory of Post-colonialism", in the present book.

Okonkwo's return to Umuofia in the third part of the novel after seven years of exile makes him see the drastic changes, brought in by colonization that had been reported to him. He has not only lost his place among the nine masked justices administering spirits in the clan but also the spirits for ever, for new colonial judicial structures have replaced them. Worse than this, he has lost the last opportunity to lead the war against the colonizers and regain what he had lost during the years of exile. But the changes are far more sweeping than what he could understand. When Okonkwo asks Obierika, "Does the white man understand our custom about land?," the answer of the latter sums up the change in the 'things.'

> How can he when he does not even speak our tongue? But he says our customs are bad, and our own brothers who have taken up his religion also say that our customs are bad. How do you think that we can fight when our own brothers have turned against us? The white man is very clever. He came quietly and peacefully with his religion. We were amused at his foolishness, and allowed him to stay. Now he has won our brothers, and our clan can no longer act like one. He has put a knife on the things that held us together and we have fallen apart. — Achebe 160

The passage is a study into colonial paradigms that reject indigenous systems, and divide the other and turn the useful other (contemptible collaborators) against the harmful other. Nwoye's conversion infuriates Okonkwo to such an extent that he hangs himself after he is set free by the court. His death is a suicide and murder as well that helps, if not his clan, at least the commissioner who had found the title for his book on the colonizer's benign civilizing mission in Africa, as *The Pacification of the Primitive Tribes of the Lower Niger* (198). This is how colonial paradigms operate and Orientalist discourses are constructed.

III

I think of no better way of starting the present section than by citing the excerpts from Colonel Meadows Taylor's *Seeta* (1872)[7] that contains the principal words of the title of this essay.

> I think if any Englishman married a Hindoo or a Mohammedan girl, after the customs and beliefs of her sect, in the good faith that such a marriage would be binding on him — why have not many of our old dignitaries done this and lived happily all their lives? — and many others — What a grand effect had the marriage of Akbar to a Rājpūt princess over the people at large! . . . I am putting the case hypothetically. I do not suppose it will ever be; but for all that there is many a Hindu girl like Seeta, who would be an ornament and blessing to any man . . . though perhaps it is best, after all, that it is not attainable — because of our social prejudices, which you and I can't overcome because our perceptions are narrowed with our isolated positions . . . and because if a man, one of us, married a native lady — married I say — he must exclude himself from society, which would require a strong mind.
>
> When the thing is impossible, Philip? — Taylor: 1882: 87

The conversation between Philip Mostyn and Cyril Brandon from the nineteenth-century novel by Colonel Taylor deals with Seetā, a "Hindu girl," a native widow standing as a witness at the trial of her husband's murder. Her 'beauty' and 'grace' attract the attention of Mostyn and Brandon, the judge and the magistrate. Like the author both these British officials busy themselves with the discussion of the colonial presence and also of validating it through the act of rescue.

Here, the thing that draws our attention immediately is the fact that Seeta is alive, very much. She should have been *satī* after her husband's death. All Seetas have to go through fire (*agniparīkṣā*) whether their husbands were alive or dead. The *satī* was also a test (*parīkṣā*), albeit the final one. If this Seeta of Taylor is alive,

---

7. For a better discussion of the novel *Seeta* from the perspective of the "gendering of the empire" please see Jyotsana G. Singh in *Colonial Narratives, Cultural Dialogues*, London and New York: Routledge, 1996, pp. 79-89.

then the credit for this should go to Lord William Bentinck, and a little to Raja Rammohun Roy as well. Seeta is the microcosm of all Indian women, and prospective *satīs*, as the text suggests. Before examining the rescue mission, that validates continued presence of colonizers in the colony, let me use Raja Rammohun Roy's works as the 'co-text' to examine the issue from a different perspective.

India was often portrayed as the land of *satī* and the colonizers as the rescuers of all Indian women from this evil. The fact, however, is that the *satī* was never a pan-Indian phenomenon. It was limited to a few parts of the country particularly Bengal and Rājpūtānā. By Raja Rammohun's time this practice had gained some momentum in Bengal and there were supporters of *satī*. His answer to a supporter of *satī* bears this out:

> It was never the case that the practice of fastening down widows on the pile was prevalent throughout Rajasthan, for it is but of late years that this move has been followed, and that only in Bengal, which is but a small part of Hindustan. — 330

Further, according to Roy, a widow had a right to inherit the property of her husband. He refers to the *Dāyabhāga* by Jīmūtavāhana, a text that had attained currency in matters of inheritance of property among the Hindus of Bengal. The book specifies that after the death of its owner the son inherits the property on "a ground which is applicable to the widow's case also" (398). It means that if a widow would inherit her husband's property, where was the question of her being compelled to commit *satī*? On the same page Roy mentions "The right of the widow to succeed in the first instance is declared" (ibid.).

Roy's writings reveal that in reality the colonizers were responsible for giving *impetus to the satī*. He quotes from Yājñavalkya, Kātyāyana, Nārada, Bhīṣma, Bṛhaspati, Vyāsa and Manu and suggests that even if the provisions for a widow were implemented in the right spirit, women in Bengal would have been saved from committing forced suicide.

He quotes Manu who permitted another wife in exceptional

circumstances, e.g. if the wife is a drunkard, wicked or barren and perpetually ill. Further if she is ill, yet loves her husband, she should never be insulted. He suggests that the rulers should appoint an authorized official who can accept applications for a second marriage. But the rulers never paid any attention to it. If they had, then they would have been deprived of their rescuing role. He writes:

> Had a Magistrate or other public officer been authorized by the rulers of the empire to receive applications for his sanction to a second marriage during the life of a first wife, and to grant his consent only on such accusations as the foregoing being substantiated, the above law might have been rendered effectual, and the distress of female sex in Bengal, and the number of suicides, would have been necessarily very much reduced.
>
> —380

Raja Rammohun Roy suggests that the rulers of the empire located in the far off centre are responsible for the distress of Indian women in the distant colony. If the provisions of the traditional text and rights of women were not deliberately ignored and the women were given rights to inherit the property, the number of women *satī* would have at least been less. The rulers, i.e. colonizers were not rescuers of the women of the colony but responsible for *satī*. However, the fact was that the women were Indian, so were logs and fire. Even the might of the colonizers as rescuers was our own.

Taylor's Seeta naturally evokes comparisons with her ultimate counterpart Seeta. Though the two are not comparable, the perusal in this direction brings forth some interesting points. Seeta of Vālmīki and Tulsīdās was abducted and remained in a state of confinement in Laṅkā. She would have been happier, if she had agreed to be an ornament of Rāvaṇa's harem. That would have been "blessing" for Seeta and Rāvaṇa as well. Rāvaṇa stops short of imposition of his wishes on her, and Seeta does not succumb to Rāvaṇa's temptations or pressures. Hence, she needs to be rescued. Rāma, her husband, rescues her with the help of his followers particularly Hanumān who in one sense may be called the real "rescuer" of Seeta, for his timely appearance in the Aśoka-Vāṭikā not only consoles Seeta in the moments of distress, but also saves her from taking any drastic step to end her misery.

Our study demands a scrutiny of the term and act of 'rescue.' In the act of rescuing, the rescuer is more privileged than the rescuee. In a patriarchal discourse, it has to be a male figure (one of the exceptional instances of a female figure rescuing a male figure is that of Sāvitrī). However, in the case of Seeta, the rescuer is on the mission of service to the rescuee and to the rescuer on whose behalf he goes on a mission. Since Rāma is Hanumān's object of devotion, and Seeta is dear to Rāma, hence Seeta is doubly dear to Hanumān and so the object of greater devotion. Neither Vālmīki's *Rāmāyaṇa* nor Tulsīdās's *Rāmacaritamānasa* betrays any element of either arrogance or self-aggrandizement on the part of the rescuer but of modesty or satisfaction for being the chosen one for the service of the object of devotion. Hanumān's motto and motive is that of *bhakti*, service and unflinching devotion to his lord, and things dear to him.

However, the fate of the nineteenth-century Seeta is altogether different from Seeta of Vālmīki, Bhavabhūti or Tulasidāsa. The rescuers of Taylor's Seeta have their masters or centre in a far off place. Theirs is a self-assigned civilizing mission, not an act of selfless service or devotion but of patronizing and of using her and the act of rescuing her as an ornament as well as blessing.

Taylor constructs his Seeta suitable for his purpose. She is a "Hindu girl" (87), a native widow of a goldsmith, and a witness at the trial of the murderer of her husband. Mostyn and Brandon, the self-proclaimed rescuers from the judicial and administrative services, find her presence to be irresistible.

> For a native woman, Cyril Brandon had never seen any one so fair or of so tender a tone of colour. Such he remembered, were many of the lovely women of Titian's pictures — a rich golden olive, with a bright carnation tint rising under the skin.
>
> — Taylor, 61

Further,

> It was impossible for the judge not to be struck by her beauty and grace. . . . He had never seen such an Indian woman before . . . and could fully understand Cyril's warm description of her after {his . . .} enquiries. — 84

Cyril Brandon sets out on his rescue mission of such an Indian woman in distress. He wears a disguise while joining a police party to protect her from the attack of Azrael Pandey, her husband's murderer having ostensible onomastic nomenclatural associations with Mangal Pandey, the leader of the 1857 Mutiny according to the colonial historians, whose sole aim is to capture and enslave her (96). Brandon here acts as an ideal servant or ambassador of the imperial empire. The novelist/ narrator speaks to his readers (the Victorian English (wo)men and English knowing Indians),

> If you gentle reader, wish to know (Brandon's) views of Indian policy, I must request you to read Her Majesty's Proclamation of 1858 in which he is a firm believer. He sees what has been done for the advancement of the people in education, and indeed in every other respect. — 439

Brandon's proposition of the philosophy of utilitarian reformation hanging around the ideals of justice, service and loyalty was a reflection on the post-Mutiny colonial period. Taylor, the novelist, believed that the Mutiny was a consequence of the Indian's resentment of 'new and powerful elements of Western civilization; and also of their desire to regain what had been lost.' Since Azrael Pandey becomes the microcosm of all native rebels, depicted, as in the villainous mould, as he said in his Introduction, ". . . in [her] I have endeavoured to depict the character of rebel and treasonable emissaries of the time" (ix). The fact, however, was that the Mutiny was a consequence of the colonizers' oppression of the native people, particularly farmers through their agents, and exploitation of the resources of the country whose consciousness had dawned on the people. The saviour-rescuer paradigm emanating from the utilitarian reformation of the 1820s and 1830s was the less abrasive way of validating and controlling the colony. In that sense Seeta contains in it a manual for the colonizers represented by Brandon, and the colonized, represented by Seeta, and culminating in their marriage.[8] Even in the ultimate synthesizing metaphor, the hierarchies, that are supposed to be diluted or at least toned down, not only exist but they are peddled. Since patriarchal/colonizing society prioritizes male to female figure, the novel does not show a native male's marriage with an English female. Further, to facilitate the marriage between the two, the novelist denativizes the native woman to a considerable extent.

Seeta is a different native woman in terms of her appearance and ideas. The novalist sets her apart from other native women, as he describes Brandon's response to her appearance in non-Indian European/English terms:

> One particular (image) came to his memory as a flash — the wife of the Duc d' Avalos in the Louvre picture, or Titian's daughter, carrying fruits and flowers, at Berlin. — Taylor, 61

The images that come to his mind are of a wife and a daughter, none of the mother, for the wife bears fruits in terms of becoming the mother of her husband's children and the daughter that carries

---

8. The institution of marriage was used as a strategic means of capturing, consolidating and controlling political power. Here it may be congruous to know the views of Bharatendu Harishchandra, the precursor of Indian renaissance in Hindi literature, expressed in the Preface of his *Badshah Darpana* (The Mirror of Kings) pertaining to the marriage of Akbar with the native princess, a historical fact that Taylor refers to in *Seeta* (87). Though scholars may consider Bharatendu's sense of history hazy, yet his words written around the period when the novel was written in the second half of the nineteenth century deserve our consideration for their upfront honesty: "My dear simple Hindu Brothers! Do not be surprised by hearing the name of Akbar. He was such an intelligent enemy that all of you still consider him to be your friend because of his power and intelligence. But that is not the fact. His policy was abstruse or sophisticated like that of the English. The foolish Aurangazeb did not understand him. Else the entire Hindustan would have been the Muslim India. What even the English did not understand, he had realized." Bharatendu, *Bharatendu Samagra*, Varanasi: Hindi Pracharak Sansthan, 1989, p. 732, (Translation mine.)

fruits and flowers — all that are willing to be his ornaments. Further, in her ideas, Seeta is a different native rebel suitable to colonizers, for the rebels prove to be the useful other:

> It is not a shaven head or a coarse garment that makes a virtuous widow . . . what I am I will remain. — Taylor, 79

Therefore, the novelist, finding her suitable for the colonizing project, charts a different course from the given one:

> Seeta might have settled down into a dull usual widowhood of Hindoo life; pious, absorbed in household cares . . . with no hope for the future. — Taylor, 50

Her hopeful future is her marriage with the rescuer. Cyril Brandon consents to his marriage with Seeta as a gesture of compassionate liberatism. He sets himself apart from the rest of the colonizers and prefers Seeta to Grace Mostyn, the English girl. The novelist with a deft stroke makes poor, 'little' Seeta, his wife, "by the Hindoo rites of her faith, which cannot be broken and which I respect" (241), says Brandon. However, English racism and native Hindoo religious bigotry haunt them.[9] The former considerations surge in Brandon, as he contemplates solemnization of the marriage

---

9. The native Indian woman was a subject of the discourse of the orientalists such as Sir William Jones who had written a poem on the Hindu wife called as a magical fruit. The poem deals with Indian women in different ages, *Satya, Dvāpara, Tretā* and *Kaliyuga*. The footnote to the poem contained a narrative from the *Mahābhārata* that a priest had mentioned to a Bishop. The narrative details Draupadī's honesty and truthfulness, as she confesses her desire that she had for a brāhmaṇa youth in her youth, in front of the Pāṇḍavas, her husbands. At the end, Jones writes the following words, aimed at the English ladies:

> Could you, Ye Fair, like this *black* wife,
> Restore us to primeval life,
> And bid that apple, pluck'd for Eve
> By him, who might all wives deceive,
> Hang from its parent bough once more
> Divine and perfect, as before.
> Would you confess your little faults?
> (Great ones were never in your thoughts.)
>
> — *The Works of Sir William Jones*, vol. XIII, pp. 230-31

in a Christian way, and her conversion in the end. Her death, while trying to save her rescuer Brandon from the attack of Pandey, depicts failure of another inter-racial marriage and consequently it is the non-white who suffers in the works of literary authors — be it Shakespeare or Taylor. It leads to Brandon's marriage with Grace, a suitable girl of his own race and class. The author tries to make Seeta a synthesizing symbol in her death, as she strains to chant Sanskrit prayers and Christian hymns before breathing her last. Seeta in a way emerges as a metaphor of helpless India who, despite her grace and heritage cannot help herself. She needs to be rescued by the representative of the colonizers who are depicted not only as able administrators but also embodiment of justice. They forward the model of reconciliation with the natives through marriage on the lines of Akbar. The space allowed to Seeta's religion after her marriage is projected as indicative of the catholicity of Christianity.

Othello, *Seeta* and *Things Fall Apart* reveal that the colonizers with their intentions, projects and paradigms played the game of othering at multiple levels in different ways by considering the colonies as blessing and mere ornaments. The need, therefore, is to go, beyond orientalism, to ornamentalism but without overlooking neo-orientalism.[10] To sum up, even at the risk of courting abruptness, it can be stated that *Othello, Seeta* and *Things Fall Apart* written in different centuries in three different countries, rather continents, reflect different attitudes to the processes and paradigms of the project of colonization. Here it should be remembered that Shakespeare unconsciously anticipated the game that his countrymen so adroitly played in the subsequent centuries. Taylor, on the other hand, offered himself as an instrument of the process of colonization. He lived the game, played it, reflected on it, and put forward his own model in fictional terms. Achebe fictionalizes the paradigms of colonization and the way colonizers played the game in Nigeria and used colonies for their purposes.

10. Please see the discussion of new-orientalism in "What a Fall Mr. Rushdie!", *The Literaray Criterion*, 1998, pp. 14-21.

6

Theorizing/Narrativizing Resistance and Colonization in India

> It is related that someone asked the late President Kruger whether there was gold in the moon. He replied that it was highly unlikely because, if there were, the English would have annexed it.
>
> — M.K. Gandhi

> There is nothing so bad or so good that you will not find Englishmen doing it; but you will never find an Englishman in the wrong. He does everything on principle. He fights you on patriotic principles; robs you on business principles; he enslaves you on imperial principles. — G.B. Shaw

CAVEATS should not precede pronouncements. In the present case, however, I will take recourse to them before discussing theorizing/narrating resistance in the colonial period.

The world of social reality is always uneven, though attempts at theorizing or evenizing it with either generalization or seeking paradigms implicit in it have been made frequently. Theorizing resistance is more complex, for (i) the resisted gets interwoven in the texture of the discourse of resistance, and (ii) the strategies of the resisted have been so subtle, sophisticated and chameleonic that its theorizing courts essentialisation of the colonized in particular. In such a situation, it is less risky to narrate the resistance, its practice and in the process seek paradigm in the discursive practices of the resister and the resisted. Further, theorization or narration of the colonial period is related to complex past and its memory. And there can be different attitudes to it, i.e. its rejection, indifference to it and even its celebration by digging archaeology of one's collective and individual past.

Memory here emerges as a mirror in which one sees one's own past in relation to the other that is the colonizer. The past often invites opposite views. Brian Friel represents one such view, "(I)t is not the literal past, the 'facts' of history, that shape us, but image of the past embodied in language . . . we must never cease renewing those images, because once we do, we fossilize" (Friel 66). Against it Frantz Fanon opined, "I do not have the right to allow myself to be mired in what the past has determined. I am not the slave of the slavery that dehumanized my ancestors. The body of history does not determine a single one of my actions. I am my own foundation . . ." (230-31). Both the attitudes have arguments in their favour and against. There can be a third attitude to past. The third attitude of indifference is a sign of individual or collective suicide because the colonized societies have to engage with decolonization, for which the past cannot be written off, though the process might be painful to both. The colonized society finds it difficult to erase the memory of the unpleasant past, for it contains the record of the endeavours of its preceding generation's resistance against the colonizers. The struggle of man against power or resistance is ultimately the struggle of memory against forgetting. The colonizing forces would like the other, i.e. the victim, to forget the past, for it is a record of their acts of atrocities. This struggle of man against power is for reclaiming, living and coming to terms with the past for which there might be different strategies. Walter Benjamin perceived historical memory as the fight for the oppressed past as a contest to disclose the moral claims of dead victims who must be included as partners in the emancipatory project of the present. It necessitates not forgetting but articulating the past, about which Benjamin stated,

> To articulate the past historically does not mean to recognize it "the way it really was." No man or men but the struggling, oppressed class itself is the repository of historical knowledge. . . . Historicism gives the "eternal" image of the past; historical materialism supplies a unique experience of the past. — 257–64

The notions of articulating the past and "coming to terms with the past" is related to "mastering the past" that Theodor Adorno criticized, while addressing the situation in the post-war Germany in 1977, for being tainted by the idea of some ultimate repression. (114-15). He considered the necessity of working through or reprocessing the past with the effort to commit the past to oblivion, and added:

> Coming to terms with the past does not imply a serious working through of the past, the breaking of its spell through an act of clear consciousness. It suggests, rather, wishing to turn the page and, if possible, wiping it from memory. The attitude that it would be proper for everything to be forgiven and forgotten by those who were *wronged* is expressed by the party that committed injustice. . . . One wants to get free from the past rightly so, since one cannot live in its shadow and since there is no end to terror if guilt and violence are only repaid, again and again, with guilt and violence. But wrongly so, since the past one wishes to evade is still intensely alive. . . . Should we consider it pathological to burden oneself with the past, while the healthy and realistic person is absorbed in the present and its practical concerns? That would be to appropriate the moral from "and it is as good as if it never happened," which is written by Goethe but uttered by the devil at a deceptive point in *Faust* to reveal his innermost principle; the destruction of memory. The murdered are to be cheated even out of the one thing that our powerlessness can grant them: remembrance. — Adorno, 115-17

Keeping these positions in mind, the present endeavour of theorizing/narrating the discourse of resistance in the colonial rule takes cognizance of the necessary risk involved in it but without overriding the words of Adorno that the effacement of memory is a sign that the consciousness of historical continuity has been atrophied. He averred, "Enlightenment about what happened in the past must work, above all, against a forgetfulness that too easily goes along with and justifies what is forgotten" (125). Edward Said has discussed an altogether different aspect of the phenomenon in his significant article entitled "Intellectuals in a post-Colonial World." While considering the question of history from post-Colonial perspective, he underlined the fact that ex-colonizer and colonized share a common history, yet each remembers it differently and asymmetrically. Said's objective, however, is not to monumentalize the asymmetry as a form of non-negotiable incommensurability. He worked through and beyond "the politics of blame and guilt." This task is the production of a relational post-colonial universal space. The question that emerges here is: from what perspective or political position is such a space to be imagined? Said's rhetorical strategies tend to downplay antagonistic and conflictual post-coloniality and focus on persuasion and understanding beyond and across boundaries. His own reading is an example of this strategy in his "contrapuntal reading" in *Culture and Imperialism* where the counter-point is the most useful and inclusive way of understanding the significance of any historical event or text. For him, on the one hand, the resistance and antagonism both are implied in the prefix "counter," and on the other, the aesthetic precontainment of antagonism within the figurality of the counter-point as a musical value. The point and counter-point, both despite their discrete trajectories are made part of an overarching structural synchronicity. The problem with the practice of counter-point is that it is unclear about whether it is representational or post-representational. Derivate to it is the question: which subject is speaking and who is being spoken for by the contrapuntal argument? This re/reading of the past — whether contrapuntal or traditional — through one's memory or re(-)visioning by studying the discourse of resistance becomes more complex when one thinks of theorizing about it. Since the resisters were witness to repression and strategies in different ways in different parts of the country, so their discourses contained polyvalence in them. Since narrating is easier than theorizing, so I would aim at playing both the roles depending on convenience, though that is not a virtue in a so-called academic critical discourse.

Resistance, whatever meaning is ascribed to it, manifests itself in three forms — its practice, its narration and theorization. It takes cognizance of the illegitimate presence of the oppressive other and consciousness of exploitation of native resource leading to resistance against these practices. Some practise resistance without being conscious of the other two. This includes those who fought against the external colonizers, and also social reformers who strove to emancipate the society from internal colonization. Some construct their discourse of resistance and narrate it, to use the words rather loosely, as did Narmad in general and Gandhi in particular in Gujarati, Vishnu Shastri Chiplunkar in Marathi and Bharatendu and Premchand in Hindi. The last category has people like Gandhi and Sri Aurobindo who not only theorized it but also played all three roles simultaneously.

Resistance is against the tyrannical and colonial forces that exploit the other for their ends. In the forthcoming sections I shall deal with colonization and two of its manifestations — external and internal colonization. Both of them perpetrate heinous crimes against the natives. However, the former is worse than the latter. Also, more often than not it is the internal colonization, in which certain hegemonic native forces exploit and oppress the other native forces by constructing discourses validating their ways that in the end invites external colonization.

II

The colonial period in the Indian history, as elsewhere, is one of the most complex legacies and therefore remains a contested terrain. Colonial encounter in India was not a 'tryst with destiny,' for that marks the end of the colonialism but a tryst with 'evil,' or if one is rather generous, at least tryst with 'mixed evil.' In India the colonial encounter was a part of the subtlest and fastest increasing European enterprise of exploitation between the nineteenth century and the middle of the twentieth century. Tracking the immensity of colonialist acquisition by the European powers, Edward Said has remarked in this regard:

> Consider that in 1800 the Western powers claimed 55 but actually held 35 per cent of the earth's surface, and that by 1878

> the proportion was 67 per cent, a rate of increase of 83,000 square miles per day. By 1914, the annual rate had risen to an astonishing 240,000 square miles, and Europe held a grand total of roughly 85 per cent of the earth as colonies, protectorates, dependencies, dominions and commonwealths. No other set of colonies in history was as large, none so totally dominated, none so unequal in power to the Western metropolis.
>
> — Said, 6

The enormity of the colonial expansion excluded United States of America that had attained its independence in the beginning of the last quarter of the eighteenth century, ironically within two decades of India's 'colonization.' I use the word colonization within single inverted commas, for colonization in India was a slow and steady process that took another hundred years till the 'Mutiny,' as the colonial historians would term it, the first major struggle for Indian Independence took place in 1857. The colonial project in India was as uneven as the country and the colonizers did not disturb the states that were willing to be the sources of revenue, without incurring financial and military expenses. So the entire India was not directly colonized, colonial purposes of exploiting natural, human, financial and intellectual resources were served in a better way by the indirect colonization. Moreover, it helped in ricocheting the wrath of common people that was directed at the native agents, who collected taxes ignoring the misery of the natives.

Here I must hasten to add that the Victorian historians used the term Indian "Mutiny" for the uprising of 1857-58. The basic purpose, according to Dennis Judd, was possibly to contain the struggle within the military framework and to deny the wider threatening ramifications, and the whole event could be dismissed as a work of groups of malcontent Indian mercenaries and their benighted religious prejudice enflamed by the agitation of barrack room lawyers (Judd 186). To malign the participants in the Uprising, the British forwarded a discourse stating that Mangal Pandey who first "mutinied" was stimulated to carry out his attack by the use of drugs, and the "unpleasantness" of 1857 was written off as the result of overindulgence in hashish (86). This bid to re-write the agenda for the rebellion succeeded as, stated Professor Judd, ". . . it is only recently that British historians and writers assessing the events have chosen words other than 'mutiny' to describe the uprising, or to have acknowledged the part played by civilian rebels" (86). Its seeds, however, lay in repressive politics of the British and 'their' Indian collaborators particularly landowners and arrogance born out of the instance in 1856. Dalhousie's revival of the controversial "doctrine of lapse" by which a native ruler having no legitimate heir was to forfeit his province to the Company, led to annexation of many provinces. And the only obstacle between two major centres of British provincial powers was Awadh between Bengal and Punjab, as they had to a good extent decimated the Marāṭhā and Sikh powers by then.

The rebellion of 1857-58 was not an isolated case. There were many others that took place in the first half of the nineteenth century, including those that were consequences of the Company's undermining the religions of the natives in 1806 and 1824 and also in 1852 when "a regiment had refused to serve in Burma, since crossing the sea could have involved its Hindu troops in a loss of caste" (73), and the tribal uprising of 1856 that Judd ignored in his accounts. In fact, Judd oversighted the role of Indian peasants in these rebellions.

So terrifying was the impact of the rebellion on British psyche that it damaged the British self-esteem and their assumption that the 'efficient' administration was enough to keep the subjects in a state of content. Further, it struck a ferocious blow to the British notion of security of their own people in India. True it is that the 'mutineers' of the Bengal army unleashed violence on the British civil and military population without sparing their women and children, the Kanpur massacre of captive British women and children being one such instance.

As the failure of the rebellion led to sadistic retaliation by the British, the captured 'mutineers' were shot down, bayoneted or hanged in pig's 'skin' to defile Muslims and in cow's skin to mortify Hindus. Brian Gardner described the British barbaric treatment of them including punishment as revenge by General Neill in Kanpur:

> I wish to show the Natives of India that the punishment inflicted by us for such deeds will be heaviest, the most revolting to these feelings and what they must ever remember. . . . The well [that had contained British bodies] will be filled up, and neatly and decently covered over to form their grave. The house in which they were butchered, and which is stained with their blood, will not be washed or cleaned by their countrymen but such of the miscreants as may hereafter be apprehended, who took an active part in the Mutiny, to be selected according to their rank, caste and degree of guilt. Each miscreant, after sentence of death is pronounced upon him, will be taken down to the house in question under a guard and will be forced into cleaning up a small portion of blood stains; the task will be made as revolting to his feelings as possible and the Provost Marshal will use the lash in forcing anyone objecting to complete his task. After properly cleaning upon his portion, the culprit is to be immediately hanged. — Gardner, 268

The blind indiscriminate suppression of the Mutiny continued unabated in all places particularly in northern India, the epicentre of the uprising. Jhansi, the town of the Rani of Jhansi, witnessed scenes of ruthlessness of the British army in treating the natives:

> Fire was blazing everywhere. . . . In the lanes and streets people were crying pitifully, hugging the corpses of their dear ones. . . . How cruel and ruthless were these White soldiers, I thought they were killing people for crimes they had not committed. . . .
>
> Not only did the English soldiers kill those who happened to come in their way, but they broke into houses and hunted out people in barns, rafters and obscure dark corners. They explored the inmost recesses of temples and filled them with dead bodies of priests and worshippers. . . . At the sight of white soldiers some people tried to hide in haystacks, in the courtyard, but the pitiless demons did not leave them there. They set the haystack on fire and hundreds were burnt alive. . . . If anybody jumped into a

> well the European soldiers hauled him out and then killed him, or they would shoot him through the head as soon as he bobbed out of the water for breath. —Gardner, 283

The elongated discussion of the great Indian uprising of 1857-58 was necessitated by the centrality of the event that acted as catalyst for constructing diverse discourses, not necessarily of resistance, in different Indian languages. However, it began the process of realization of colonizers' barbarism at least in the way they repressed the natives. The seeds sown by the uprising, despite the ameliorative gesture of the Queen's rule in the post-uprising era ultimately grew in the twentieth century in the form of resistance and rejection of the colonial rule.

III

The colonial encounter between India and the West in general and the British in particular was an encounter or clash between two civilizations and cultures, two religions — multi-religious predominantly Hindu and Islam on the one hand and Christianity on the other. After their political victory in the Battle of Plassey in 1757, some administrators of the East India Company were so beholden to Indian culture, its knowledge systems and religious texts that they began to translate them systematically. The establishment of the Asiatic Society was one such endeavour resulting in the translation of Kālidāsa's *Abhijñānaśākuntalam*, the *Śrīmad Bhagavad-Gītā* and later on the *Manu-Smṛti* among others, though the motives of translating them varied from one translator to another. For example, the translations of the Bible in 56 Indian languages by William Carey and his company were primarily aimed at spreading Christianity.[1]

1. The primary purpose of William Jones in translating *Abhijñānaśākuntalam* was exoticization of India. He sought erosion of the influence of the *puṇḍit*s in the courts by translating the *Manu-Smṛti*. The translation of the *Gītā* was an act of commissioned appropriation of a world of new knowledge in the guise of its presentation to the West. Surprisingly, the Vedas and the Upaniṣads remained untranslated for decades after the advent of the Company's rule.

The conversion of the colony to the religion of the colonizer was the primary desire, for religion was the easiest means of controlling the colony.[2] To legitimize conversion it was necessary to demean the religion(s) of the natives, as can be seen in the Motion brought to the House of Commons in 1793 for the propagation of Christianity in India. Since that was bypassed then, William Wilburforce continued his efforts by organizing a powerful evangelical movement in Britain and advocated again the Christianization of India in a parliamentary debate in June 1813. In this speech on 22 June 1813, he quoted the forms of Resolution of the company that "we are to enlighten and inform the minds of the subject of our East Indian empire," and proposed:

> By enlightening the minds of the natives, we should root out their errors, without provoking their prejudices; and it would be impossible that men of enlarged and instructed minds could continue enslaved by such a monstrous system of follies and superstitions as that under the yoke of which the natives of Hindustan now groan. They would, in short, become Christians, if I may express myself, without knowing it. —65

He lambasted all those who were appreciative of the Hindu religion in the following words:

> But our opponents encouraging one another in their error take still higher ground, and affirm, that if it were practicable to convert the Hindus to Christianity, it is not desirable. The principles of the Hindus are so good, their morals are so pure better than our own, as we are told by more than one gentleman: that to attempt to communicate to them our religion and our modality, is, to say the least, a superfluous, perhaps a mischievous attempt. —74

I must underline here that by the second decade of the nineteenth century, the influence of the Orientalists, sympathetic

---

2. Christianity dominated much superior Greek/Roman civilization and converted it, beginning with the conversion of the Roman emperor Constantine by early fourth century CE. However, only by the fifteenth century did the Europe become Christian.

to India, had begun to wane and Anglicists were on ascendance. The English Orientalists came under attack, as T.B. Macaulay stated, not in his infamous *Minutes of Education in India,* dated 02.02.1835, but in his *On India,* dated 09.03.1843.

> But we have, I am sorry to say, sometimes, deviated from the right path in the opposite direction. Some Englishmen, who have held high office in India, seem to have thought that the only religion which was not entitled to toleration and to respect was Christianity. They regarded every Christian missionary with extreme jealousy and disdain; and they suffered the most if enjoined by the Hindu superstition, to be perpetrated in open day. It is lamentable to think how long after our power was firmly established in Bengal, we, grossly neglecting the first and plainest duty of the civil magistrate, suffered the practices of infanticide and Suttee to continue unchecked. We decorated the temples of false gods. . . . We gilded and painted the images to which our ignorant subjects bowed down. We repaired and embellished the car under the wheels of which crazy devotees flung themselves at every festival to be crushed to death. We sent guards of honour to escort pilgrims to the places of worship. . . . All this was considered, and is still considered, by some prejudiced Anglo-Indians of the old school as profound policy. I believe that there never was so shallow, so senseless a policy.
>
> — 205-06

He was against all native religions — Hinduism and Islam but between the two, he preferred Islam to Hinduism, and condemned those, who favoured Hinduism:

> The duty of our government is, as I said, to take no part in the disputes between Mahomedans and idolaters. But, if our government does take a part, there cannot be doubt that Mahomedanism is entitled to the preference. Lord Ellenborough is of different opinion. He takes away the gates from a Mahomedan mosque, and solemnly offers them as a gift to a pagan temple. Morally, this is a crime. Politically, it is a blunder.
>
> — 209

To the credit of the British, it must be added here that there were quite a few who did not agree either with Wilberforce or Macaulay. Henry Montgomery said that the commitment of crime in London alone was 150 to 200 times more than those in the Deccan where he had served for 20 years (in Hansard, 22.6.1813, cols. 829-30). P. Moore stated that there was "no chaster or more meritorious set of men than inhabitants of India" (in Hansard, col. 872). Lushington countered the view that the literature in India was "destitute of morality" because he "had never found it so." On the contrary, the books which he had read in that country were perhaps "too much taken up with lesson of morality. Moral sentences intervened so often, even in their books of amusement" (in Hansard, 23.6.1813, col. 945). He went on to state that the moral sentiments of Indians with respect to the conduct of women were as good as ours, and their general practice better. And if they had vices, then they "are fault of their government, not of their religion" (ibid. cols. 946-47). Forbes considered the clause on "propagation of Christianity in India" fraught with danger as the Indians would take it as the interference with their religion and customs (22.06.1813, cols. 1017-18). T. Sutton believed that too open and avowed efforts to propagate Christianity would make the natives say, "you have taken from us our territories, you have seized upon our revenues; and not content with taking our country from us, you wish to deprive us of our religion. But religion you shall not take from us" (1.7.1813 cols. 1051-93)

Wilberforce had attacked the British officers who, as he thought, were in sympathy with Hinduism and were pursuing the propagation of Christianity, by using the authority of Robert Orme, Mr Holwell, Luke Scaraffton, Robert Clive, John Shore, John MacPherson, Lord Cornwallis, James Mackintosh and even Barnier and Tamerlane (in Hansard, cols. 842-50). He denigrated Hinduism of all conceivable degeneration for its followers' feeble sense of moral obligation and wretchedness, general corruption, governed by malevolent and licentious passions. Hindu divinities "are absolute monsters of lust, injustice, wickedness and cruelty. In short, their religious system is one grant abomination" (in

Hansard 22.6.1813, col. 864). Earlier he accused the natives in general and Hindus in particular of "the lower depth of moral and social wretchedness and degeneration." He called them "insolent and grossly sensual, cruel and cowardly, insolent and abject," "having all the vices of the savage life" without any of its virtues (ibid., col. 848).

Wilberforce's denigration of India's past and present, its people and Hinduism in particular was aimed at legitimizing the presence of the colonizers in India and at validating the Christianization of India, "But Sir, it is time to speak out, and to avow that I go much further than I have yet stated, and maintain, not only it is safe to attempt, by reasonable and prudent methods, to introduce into India the blessings of the Christian truth and moral improvement, but that true, aye and imperious and urgent policy, prescribe to us the same course" (in Dharmpal, 131). He pleaded with all members of one mind like him to support his views for the diffusion of Christianity in India. In the penultimate paragraph of his speech, he made it amply clear that the religion of the dominion should be the religion of the masters, i.e. Christianity:

> . . . the question is now put on its true basis, and it clearly appears to be no other than this, whether, as Christianity is the religion of the British empire in Europe, the religion of Brahmā and Viṣṇu is not to be acknowledged system of our Asiatic dominions.
>
> — 146

The enthusiasm of Wilberforce and supporters for Christianization of India was misplaced, for religion — for both Hindus and Muslims — was of vital consequence as it governed their lives. The Rebellion of 1857-58 and the earlier ones, as discussed by Dennis Judd, were caused primarily by religious sentiments. This was understood and in a way anticipated by English rulers in India and so they had considerably shifted focus from direct conversion to intellectual, cultural and thereby religious conversion through less abrasive means of education, English language and literature. The process began with Raja Rammohun Roy's letter to Lord Amherst in 1823, and also with the views in support of English education in Britain by Henry Derozio in a letter dated 3 August 1826 to his brother who was then studying in Scotland ("Education in India", 304-06). Macaulay and his brother-in-law Charles Travelyn were quite sure of conversion of the natives to Christianity through the English education system and English. However, they had to wait for a few years, as the 1857 rebellion in which the Hindus and Muslims fought together jolted the British psyche, and the colonizers got an opportunity to re-structure Indian education and the political and economic systems. Since they considered the unity between the Hindus and Muslims as an impediment to their designs, they tried, with considerable success, to create a schism between them in terms of religion and language and in terms of castes within Hinduism.

In spite of all these motives and methods of colonialism, designs of creating schisms in Indian society and compartmentalizing it for the sake of convenience, the fact remains that the resistance against it came to be constructed in the post-Indian Rebellion period. The multiple reasons that accounted for it included the rise of a new class of educated people from the universities (that were supposed to produce clerks), development and spread of ideas of national freedom, realization of colonialism as a mechanism of exploitation and oppressive purposes, construction of discourse of resistance by creative writers, religious and social leaders in different Indian languages, the formation of the Indian National Congress as an institution of resistance and the advent of Gandhi in India after his successful resistance through *Satyāgraha* in South Africa.

Before discussing Gandhi's strategies of resistance and locating his contribution in the regional (Gujarati) and national perspectives, it is imperative to note a view of colonization just opposite to Gandhi.

On the surface, colonialism is a consequence of political defeat of the native by an alien superior military, political and economic organization. But more than the military victory, to a good extent, it is a conquest of what Nicholas Dirk calls "cultural technologies of rule" (IX). Colonialism was a "cultural project of control." Colonial knowledge both enabled conquest and was produced by it; in certain important ways, "knowledge was what colonialism was all about" (Dirks, IX). In this sense, colonialism was a theatre of "knowledge" linked irrevocably to "power," in Michel Foucault's sense of knowledge and power, and experimentation. The entire project was organized around what Bernard S. Cohn calls "investigative modalities." "An investigative modality includes the definition of a body of knowledge that is needed, the procedures by which appropriate knowledge is gathered, its ordering and classification and then how it is transformed into workable forms such as published report, statistical returns, histories, gazetteers' legal codes, and encyclopaedias" (Cohn, 5). They included the Historiography Modality, the Observational/travel Modality, the Survey Modality, the Enumerative Modality, the Museological Modality and the Surveillance Modality. The First Modality had three strands as "inquiries" about knowledge of history and practices of Indian class/caste particularly the assessment and collection of revenue; ideological construction of the nature of Indian civilization; and histories of the British in India, i.e. the study of representations of specific events in England or India. The Second Modality was related to the creation of a repertoire of images and typification by following pre-determined schedules and seeing sights in predictable ways as found in the accounts of the European travellers in India and their travel routes. The Survey Modality involved exploration of the natural and social landscapes, through mapping, collecting botanical specimens, the recording of architectural and archaeological sites, and even the minutest measuring of a peasant's fields. Since India, as a colony, was a vast collection of numbers, the Enumerative Modality began in the seventeenth or the early eighteenth century with the arrival of British merchants and later in the post-Indian Uprising of 1857-58 in the form of a series of census, representing a model of the Victorian encyclopaedic quest for total knowledge with the purpose of creating social categories for administrative purposes. The Museological Modality was a product of the colonial view of India as 'a vast museum' of ruins, and a source of collectibles and curiosities to fill European museums, leading to excavations of archaeological cities and then the establishment of Archaeological Survey of India in 1859 for the generation and transmission of knowledge. The last modality was concerned with the surveillance of unsettled people or those who lived beyond settlements that the British were uncomfortable with like *saṁnyāsī*s, *sādhu*s, *fakīr*s, *guṇḍā*s, *ṭhug*s, herders and entertainers in a *bazaar*, in the narrow confines of a street or a *melā*.

"The conquest of India was a conquest of knowledge," observed Cohn (16). India created "complicated and complex forms of knowledge but codified and transmitted by Europeans." Indian scholarship was reduced to become instruments as translators, interpreters, compilers and informers in the colonial projects of constructing investigative modalities. For example, William Carey, as discussed by Sisir Kumar Das, compiled his work by "employing sensible natives" like Ram Raj Basu and Mrityunjay Vidyalamkar (Das, 74). Thus, the colonizers set the agenda of determining, processing and producing "useful knowledge, though they were not necessarily superior." The Indian scholar knew he was superior to his European Master in respect of Indian languages, (but) he was primarily "an informant, a mere tool in the exercise of language teaching to be handled by others" (ibid., 107). The desire of controlling the people needed the command over language that necessitated the spurt of linguistic projects by the British in the late years of the eighteenth century. This led to the production of a set of texts — grammars, dictionaries for the acquisition of working knowledge of languages and also competence so as to command people. In the process, grammar was converted from an Indian form of knowledge into a European/English object. William Jones's Persian grammar, Halhed's Bengali grammar and Gilchrist's endeavours of teaching the imperative forms and lexicons relevant to routine activities and discourse with servants and inferiors (Cohn 16–56), fall under these Orientalist projects.[3] This is what Raymond Schwab in his book, *Oriental Renaissance* (1984), called "Europe's magnificent appropriation of the Orient."

The entire project dehumanized and even reduced the colonized to objects that remained static and fossilized and needed the colonizers' intervention. This objectification is what Cesaire called 'thingification.' His remarks regarding the diametrically opposite discourses — of the colonizers and the colonized are worth quoting here:

> They (the colonizers) talk to me about progress, about "achievements," diseases cured, improved standards of living. I am talking about societies drained of their essence, culture trampled underfoot, institutions undermined, lands confiscated, religions smashed, magnificent artistic creations destroyed, extraordinary possibilities wiped out.
>
> — in Childs and Williams, 41

The preceding debate on Christianization should be seen in the light of conversion of the conquered, and the role that the church played in it. In her book, *Race and Racism,* Ruth Benedict used the word "racism" for racialism employed in the nineteenth century. The meaning of "racialism" was influenced by the war time experience of anti-Semitism. According to her, racism was not the first source of division during European expansion overseas, but took centuries to gain prominence. Religion had played its important role, as a land was not recognized as conquered until its inhabitants were converted to Christianity and for this reason missionaries travelled with them in all expeditions. Wilberforce's arguments need to be seen in the light of this project of colonization/Christianization

---

3. As against the prevailing notion of association of language with region, as had existed in India for centuries, the colonizers introduced the concept of *lingua franca,* thus dividing Hindus and Muslims in the Hindi and Urdu camps. As far as the caste in Hinduism is concerned, scholars are of the view that the British reinvented caste for their purposes. However, more than the British the natives were to be blamed, for they allowed themselves to be snared in the colonial designs.

of the natives of the colony including India, and should serve as a backdrop to our discussion of discourse of resistance in Indian writing in English, Gujarati, and Hindi in the colonial period.

IV

Henry Derozio, "the root of all evils and cause of public alarm," as the special meeting of the directors of the Hindu College called him before discharging him (329), was one of the earliest English writers to speak about colonization in India. In his poems like "To India — My Native Land," "The Harp of India," "To the Pupils of Hindu College," he identified himself with the Indian soil and its nationalist cause, though he was of Eurasian origin. He was among the first to make use of Indian myths and legends in the poems ("Highest Himalaya," "Ganga's Roll," "Chandra's Beams" and "Sweet Star"). For our present purposes we would consider his brief piece entitled "On the Colonization of India by Europeans" in which he discussed advantages and disadvantages of colonization by asking four questions: Will colonization endanger the British rule? Will it be beneficial or not to the natives in general? Will it affect the Indo-Britons, and in what manner? Will it prove the cause of the introduction of the arts and Sciences of Europe, throughout the empire? As early as 1829 he spoke of the general observation among the natives that India was maintained in subjection only by military force. He referred to the newspaper report, about the late Muharrum prayers at Lucknow in which the destruction of the Company's government was publicly wished. To counterpoise the natives it was proposed that a large number of Europeans be allowed to settle in the country.

In general terms, he found the opinion to be "founded on long, intimate, and accurate observation of the real state of things" (318). However, he had strong doubts whether Europeans could settle in the country without gradually dispossessing "the natives of their lands and causing incalculable misery and dissatisfaction" (318). He expressed the fear that the measure would reduce even the Europeans to the same, if not a worse condition than the Hindus or Mussalmans. However, he saw the advantage of colonization in the education among the natives and introduction of the arts and sciences of Europe. In the end he stated, ". . . colonization would not be beneficial, unless the British legislative interferes, and materially alters the present system of Indian policy, by admitting natives and Indo-Britons to a participation of privileges, on a similar footing, as far as practicable and expedient, with the Europeans. It is only by such a measure that "discontent can be prevented from broadening into rebellion. . . ." (319). One might not fully agree with all the views of Derozio on colonization but its historical importance cannot be discounted, for it was not obligatory on the part of a Eurasian to associate himself with the cause of the natives of, what he called, "our oppressed and neglected native country" (319). Though he did not show any consciousness of economic drain and material and psychological aspects, he left enough traces of the cause that might lead to discontent and subsequent rebellion(s) that preceded and followed Derozio's pronouncement ultimately leading to the 1857-58 Uprising. Derozio's words attain greater significance in the light of his contemporary Indian writers in English who leave aside the proposition of discussing, or resisting colonization, got themselves converted and longed for 'Albion's shore' as did Michael Madhusudan Dutt. Hurish Chunder Mukherji on the other hand, made a passionate plea in his *The Hindu Patriot* for reconciliation with the rulers after the 'mutiny,' as did I.S. Desai in Gujarati.

After Derozio, the colonial consciousness can be discerned in a thinly disguised manner in fictional endeavours that were more of fantasy than realistic novels, for fantasy is a relatively safer form of expression in the oppressive colonial rule. Kylash Chunder Dutt's *A Journal of 48 Hours of the Year 1945*, published in *The Calcutta Literary Gazette* on 6 June 1835, deals with the story of an imaginary unsuccessful revolt against the British colonial rule a hundred years later. In a way, the fantasy anticipated the Indian

Uprising within three decades. In a similar vein Soshee Chunder Dutt wrote *Republic of Orissa: Annals from the Pages of the Twentieth Century* that appeared on 25 May, 1845 in the *Saturday Evening Hurkaru*. The fictional fantasy dealt with the defeat of the British leading to the establishment of a democratic republic in Orissa. The works, set in the second decade of the twentieth century, saw the replacement of the colonial rule with democratic governance at a regional level almost 100 years before the actual independence. However, these were caricatures and bare narratives. In the following four decades Indian English writing remained unconcerned with colonial consciousness, let alone its resistance.

Toru Dutt, converted to Christianity along with her family at the age of six, betrayed her ambivalence towards the English in her works, yet she did not speak ostensibly on the issue of colonization, a tendency discernible in all Indian writers in English. However, she returned to Indian myths and legends in her works and thereby suggested her preference for Indian cultural associations to their English or Western counterparts. Only Dadabhai Naoroji in his *Poverty of India* (in two parts) (1873) and *Poverty and the British Rule in India* (1901) argued that the real Indian interest can be served by Indians and their fair share in the governance, for British administrative with economic policies, according to him, had undermined Indian interests. He was among the first Indians to note the economic aspect of colonization and drain of Indian economic resources and saw self-government as the only chief remedy of its plaguing India under the colonial rule.

Swami Vivekananda spoke eloquently about the ideals of country in his discourses in India and abroad and considered various causes of its degeneration in the present without oversighting its future that he saw safely ensconced in its women and youth. With his universalist approach and ideals of humanity, he preached a synthesis of all religions whereby one learns from another. He neither denigrated Western civilization nor ever hesitated to mention drawbacks of Indian society. His patriotism was the foundation of his universalism. And if his patriotism persuaded him to speak highly of his land, its cultural and civilizational attributes, he firmly believed that his land had a message for the world that the West needed Indian idealism and conquest of internal nature. However, he did not directly discuss the colonial situation in India and the way the colonizers exploited its resources, asserted their superiority to the natives and allowed its missionaries to denigrate the native religions.

Ananda Kentish Coomaraswamy, through his discourses on art, religion, metaphysics, language, poetics and culture, asserted the centrality of Indian achievements in these areas. He believed that the greatest art was entrenched in life and that ancient Indian civilization achieved the greatest height in art. Thus he resisted the views of the Raj scholars who denigrated Indian art. He considered Ceylon to be a part of India (by asking the question "Can we think of India as complete without Ceylon?") and wanted his countrymen to become Indians before (wanting to) hav(e)ing it. Moreover, he attributed the cause of India's degeneration to the divorce of art from life and also from its eternal and continuous traditions and conventions. Also he found the Indian scene of his time, despite its rich past, to be gloomy presenting the slow destruction of 'a living and magnificent organization.' The most tragic spectacle and the greatest danger for India, he saw in the loss of her spiritual integrity. He severely criticized industrialization and the colonial education system in which economic considerations became more central than educational, and emphasis shifted from the "personality" of the teacher to his "loyalty," leading to cleavage between the "ideals of the school" and the "ideals of the home." He found the missionary institutions caring more for "proselytizing" than real education that would aim at the development of character and integrated personality. (*The Dance of Śiva*, 154-71).

The fall from educational tradition, he equalled, to 'a descent from the Himalayas to the plains.' He found an "absence of cultivated and conscious taste in modern India and opined that the uneducated in India were better than those so-called educated, for the former were still familiar through oral tradition with an epic literature vast in amount and saturated with a great philosophy. He rejected modern education governed by the concept of quantity and mere accumulation of diverse facts and proposed education that should give rise to an integrated personality, capable of translating knowledge into experience (172-79). In his scheme of education, the teachers should be "dedicated" and should not be "officials of any kind," and they should be prepared to teach because they care so much for what they teach" (*Art and Svadeśī*, 143-50). The "rehabilitation of the past" in order to defend the "prolific" against the "devourer" was the first expression of national idealism. It did not imply for him a revival of the past and return to it, for the "prolific" have to make their home in the future but the future has to be built on the foundations of the past. Since the country then was ruled by the colonizers, they had little sympathy for the culture of natives and either tried to play the role of messiah or impose their own cultural values leading to the impoverishment of the arts and decay of traditional values. He remarked that the British occupation had always implied the discontinuance of patronage and the more rapid destruction of tradition. The arts cannot prosper as natural products of the native soil in the absence of a patron who understands the aspirations and forms of the artists. Western education, with its ideals of administrative efficacy, and industrial competition, has hastened the end of traditional culture throughout the east, nowhere more conspicuously than in India (*Rajput Painting* 25). Coomaraswamy's is not necessarily a discourse of the sort of Gandhi but he, in no secret terms, disapproved of the colonial presence in India and also rejected the myth of the beneficial consequences of the Raj, good governance, judiciary and a modern education system and the colonizer's contribution to the preservation of Indian arts and culture. Partha Chatterjee in his recent article has demolished all these myths. According to him, the form of government being introduced in colonial India was one that was being abandoned in Britain. Moreover, the myth of the benevolent colonial master as the inaugurator of the modern education system in higher education was also a false one, as he stated:

> Of the twenty universities of pre-Independence India, the majority were funded through endowments and donations by Indians. All post-graduate departments and science institutions were set up at the initiative of Indian educationists and against the vested interests of the colonial survey establishments. Modern education in India was a nationalist achievement, not a colonial gift. —12

After Coomaraswamy, Sri Aurobindo's discourse of resistance earns our attention. It can be seen at political, cultural, intellectual, literary, and spiritual levels. He began as a political activist and underwent imprisonment before moving to Pondicherry for his literary, intellectual and spiritual practices through which he resisted the Western paradigms and standards. His contributions to *Induprakash* (1893-94), the Bombay journal, contained his radical political ideas against the given political order. In his famous Uttarpara speech on 30 May 1909, he prayed to God, ". . . If Thou art, then Thou knowest my heart. Those knowest that I do not ask for *mukti* . . . I ask only for strength to uplift this nation, I ask only to be allowed to live and work for this people whom I love and to whom I pray that I may devote my life" (*India's Rebirth,* 43). He understood the malaise plaguing Indian society and the British ways, as he found Britain's civilizing mission in India as "the record success in history in the hypnosis of a nation" (ibid.). He realized the character of the colonizers like Gandhi did but criticized them and his own people more severely, "We were ruled by shopkeepers and consented enthusiastically to think of them as angels" (ibid., 43). He criticized the natives for following the European virtues, for if India followed in the footsteps of Europe and borrowed her political, social, economic principles, she would suffer from the malaise that Europe has. "If India becomes an intellectual province of Europe, she will never attain to her natural greatness or fulfil the possibilities within her. . . . India must remain India if she is to fulfil her destiny" (42). He resisted the native and colonial ways of Europeanizing India and opined that if the Indians would allow Europe to think for them, India would become "an ill-executed and foolish copy of Europe" (88). He rejected colonial institutions, particularly the education system, for it had divorced us from our own ideals. He remarked on 20 November 1919, "In India . . . we have been cut-off by a mercenary and soulless education from all our ancient roots of culture and tradition. . . ." (65). He was highly critical of the system, its method of the classroom and the way it "represses and destroys" the capacities that Indian students have (178). As an alternative to the given system, he proposed value-based education.

Sri Aurobindo's discourse of resistance differed from Gandhi's, particularly in his ideals of non-violence and *satyāgraha*; "Gandhi's position is that he does not care to remove violence from others; he wants to observe non-violence himself" (165). When Gandhi sent his son Devdas to see Sri Aurobindo in Pondicherry on 17 August 1924, he (Devdas) asked his views about non-violence. He told him, "Suppose there is an invasion of India by the Afghan, how are you going to meet it with non-violence?" (168). He not only questioned Gandhi's non-violence but went to the extent of calling him a European and "more Christian" than many Christians" (174), for he found all his preaching as derived from Christianity; though the "garb is Indian, the essential spirit is Christian" (173).

Sri Aurobindo's discourse is interesting for he constructed it on two planes — against the colonial rule and against the native resistance to the colonial rule, for instance, by Gandhi. On 23 June 1926, he wrote about Gandhi's movement,

> When Gandhi's movement was started, I said that this movement would lead either to a fiasco or to a great confusion. And I feel no reason to change my opinion. Only I would like to add that it has led to both. — 174

His discourse of meta-resistance did not spare Gandhi's *swadeśī*, though he accepted that the *satyāgraha* later gave some life to the country (178). Also, he expressed his disapproval of the *pūrṇa svarāja* if the people with dishonest financial practices were to run the country, as he remarked on 17 November 1938:

> All this promises a bad lookout when India gets *pūrṇa svarāja*. Mahatma Gandhi is having bad qualms about Congress corruption already. What will it be when *pūrṇa satyāgraha* reigns all over India. —208

As a literary critic, Sri Aurobindo resisted the use of Western standards in judging Indian works. Equipped with his perspicaciuous knowledge of Indian and European aesthetics and literature, he tried to reverse the paradigm which persuaded many of his contemporary Indians to use second-hand Western critical and theoretical tools. He resisted Western models of literary historiography, for their acceptance would lead to imposition of European perspective(s) on it. In the process, he asserted the value of different aesthetic and critical perspectives and questioned the hegemony of the Western critical paradigms that lead ultimately to devaluation and denigration of the native system by the colonial system that some of the colonized are more than willing to imitate and practise. Sri Aurobindo reversed the paradigm by proposing a hypothetical situation in which Indians would have evaluated the great European masterpieces if they (Indians) had colonized Europe/Britain. According to him, Indian readers would "dismiss the *Iliad* as a crude and empty semi-savaged and primitive epos, Dante's work as a nightmare of a cruel and superstitious religious fantasy, Shakespeare as a drunken barbarian of considerable genius with epileptic imagination, the whole drama of Greece and Spain and England as a mass of bad ethics and violent horrors, French poetry as a succession of bold and tawdry rhetorical exercises and French fiction as a tainted and immoral thing" (Sri Aurobindo: 1943, 83). His consideration of poetry in general and British poetry in particular, included in *The Future Poetry*, bears ample evidence of his resistance to alien cultural and aesthetic principles. Further, he left no occasion to defend Indian culture and tradition. He responded to William Archer's criticism of Indian culture in *India and the Future* (1917) with his *Foundations of Indian Culture.* Also he joined the issue pertaining to the nature of the Renaissance in India with Ramsay McDonald's (*The Indian Awakening*, 1910), C.F. Andrews' (*The Renaissance in India: Its Missionary Impact*, 1912) and James Cousins' (*Renaissance in India*, 1918) in his own *The Renaissance in India* (1920). He discussed the issue of India's contact with the West and examined different phases of Indian history in terms of its main tendencies including its rise and decline, the latter being characterized by a sinking of super-abundant vital energy, rapid cessation of the old free intellectual activity and spirituality without the large and clear flame of knowledge of the earlier times (*The Renaissance in India*, 16-17). He analysed the Renaissance in three steps — the reception of the European contact, the reaction of the Indian spirit and a process of new creation on the foundation of spirituality that "is not necessarily exclusive; it can be and in its fullness must be all inclusive" (45). In spirituality, he saw a greater reality than apparent not only behind man and the world, but within man and the world, and he considered the soul, the self a divine thing in man of the higher consciousness and in the process gives them a greater, diviner and more intimate sense. By following the law of her own nature, i.e. spirituality, India can develop herself and also serve humanity by being herself (51). Sri Aurobindo's discourse of resistance, thus, rested on the principles "Know Thyself" and "Be Thy Own Self," without trying to be poor imitators by being others, particularly Europeans. Indian English discourse in English can be read as a reception, even as a celebration and rejection through systematic resistance as in Coomaraswamy, Gandhi (since Gandhi wrote in English, he can be considered as Indian English writer as well), Sri Aurobindo, and B.R. Ambedkar's (counter) discourse.

The discourse of B.R. Ambedkar (1891-1956) resisting internal colonization in the form of oppression of dalits by high caste people gave an altogether different dimension to the discourse of resistance. Vivekananda and Gandhi were among the first to speak against untouchability. Earlier the Arya Samaj had pleaded for equal rights to the dalits with some success at least in northern India, followed by the founding of the Depressed Class Mission Society in Bombay in 1906. In 1932 Gandhi founded the All India Harijan Sevak Sangh that was primarily responsible for bringing out legislation by the Congress government that came to power in 1937 in certain provinces of the country, for ameliorating the injustice meted out to the dalits. These developments prepared the ground for B.R. Ambedkar's discourse that championed the cause of the scheduled caste dalits, though it differed from Gandhi. He founded the All India Depressed Classes Federation and All India Scheduled Caste Federation and launched the Mahad Satyagrah for dalits' rights of using water tanks that they were denied by the high caste people. Known more as an architect of the Indian Constitution, he constructed his discourse in opposition to Gandhi's approach to the issues of the scheduled caste and untouchables. Apart from his speeches and other writing in his *What Congress and Gandhi have done to the Untouchables* (1945), he wrote about the eco-socio-political and religious aspects of the problem and criticized him for his faulty approach towards dalits. He pitched the discourse of resistance against the internal colonization within external colonization and a counter discourse against Gandhi, for he (Gandhi) ultimately saw the problem from the perspective of a sympathetic high caste person. It made Ambedkar the unquestioned precursor of the dalit movement that ultimately led to the empowerment of dalits and later Bahujans. Besides, his discourses carried forward the movement for self-respect that was started by Periyar in southern India and Jotirao Phule in Maharashtra. This discourse presented yet another aspect of colonialism in India as a mixed evil, for it was during the colonial rule that the dalit movement could challenge the hegemony of high castes and sought assertion of self-respect, though they were not always pleased with the British colonialists for their callousness and insincerity in responding to their problems. Mahatma Phule's Memorandum before the Hunter Education Commission, Gopal Baba Walangakar's petition to the British in 1892 and Ambedkar's speech at Nagpur in 1930 are instances of their critique of the Raj's attitude towards them. Ambedkar's dissatisfaction with the Raj was valid to a good extent because after 1857, the British had become sceptical of the high caste particularly brāhmaṇas' loyalty to the Raj. Primarily high caste brāhmaṇas who dominated the Bengal army along with the Muslim sepoys, had refused to use the new cartridges for the new Enfield Rifle. The Bengal Army that fought the Battle of Plassey in 1757 was largely composed of Dushads. However, by the first quarter of the nineteenth century, the composition of the Army changed in favour of high caste people. The nature of caste composition changed between 1757 and 1825 after the British raised 74 regiments of native Bengal Infantry with high caste Hindus largely brāhmaṇas from Awadh, eastern United Province and Bihar. Consequently, William Bentinck in 1826 and Charles Napier lately in 1850 noted the inefficiency of the Army and the problem with high caste Hindus, for they preferred their caste to military discipline and refused to travel overseas or eat food cooked by low caste untouchables who, however, had no such problems so they increasingly found the favour of the Company and of the Queen later. Hence the British decided to recruit 24 regiments of Punjab Infantry between 1846 and 1857 comprising untouchable Mazahabi Sikhs from Punjab. These untouchable soldiers helped the British in lifting the siege of Delhi by Indian rebels on 15 September 1857. Earlier the British had won the Anglo-Marāṭhā wars in the western parts of India with the help of the Mahārs of Bombay Army. The Mahārs and the untouchables of the Madras Army, helped the British in defeating Tipu Sultan and thereby eliminating a major protagonist in southern India. Ambedkar's complaint against the Raj was that the British established their rule in India with the help of valour, discipline and loyalty of the untouchables in different parts of India but they did precious little for their emancipation and upliftment [Data taken from Raja Sekhar Vundru, *The Times of India*, 25 August 2005, 12]. The critical reception of the colonial rule was stimulated by the impression of the Raj as the facilitator of the process of empowering dalits. This accounts for their positive view of the Raj colonialists different from the other high caste discourse of resistance against colonialism.

Tentatively, the pattern of discourse of resistance in Indian English writing is — acceptance (reconciliation) to the extent of celebration, ambivalence and resistance leading to the rejection of colonialism in Gandhi and Sri Aurobindo, and construction of discourse counter to Gandhi's discourse in Sri Aurobindo and in Ambedkar, though on different grounds. Indian English writing in English, thus, contained in it discourse of resistance against external colonization and a critique of native discourse of resistance as well.

V

B.S. Cohn, as discussed earlier, strove to understand the true nature of colonization in India in terms of objectification of the colony and appropriation of its intellectual and cultural resources, and even intervention in its past and present through its representation. This view is contrary to what some "Englishmen state that they took and they hold India by the sword" (Gandhi, 35). Gandhi stated:

> The English have not taken India, we have given it to them. They are not in India because of their strength, but because we keep them. . . . They came to our country *originally* for purposes of trade. Recall the Company Bahadur. Who made it Bahadur? They had not the slightest intention at the time of establishing a kingdom. Who assisted the Company's officers? . . . Who bought their goods? . . . History testifies that we did all this. . . . We assisted them.
>
> — Gandhi 34

Gandhi understood India by seeing it with his own eyes; by travelling across the country. Prior to it, he had realized the true character of the colonial rule in India after seeing its real face in South Africa. He found Napoleon's description of the English as a nation of shopkeepers as "a fitting description" (35). He ascribed India's subjugation to its moral degradation and Indians becoming gullible consumers and imitators of Western imperialism. He stressed the Indian ideals of service and renunciation and used the symbol of *Carkhā* producing *khādī* and influencing individual and collective lives of the people and providing an alternative to the Western activity touching industrialization. He used his clothes and even body to identify with common and poor people. Moreover he confronted the strong on issues of common interest like salt that touched every person's life.

Gandhi devised his own way of *satyāgraha* whereby the dispossessed and oppressed could confront the powerful oppressor in a non-violent way through restraint and moral superiority. The British did not realize the potency of this simple weapon of Gandhi, with which he could awaken the hitherto unorganized and divided masses of India in a manner unprecedented in human history.

Before moving to the evolution of Gandhi as a strategist of resistance, it would be congruous to deal in brief with Gujarati literature, for Gandhi was one of its gifted readers and contributors.[4]

The colonization by the British evoked different responses in different parts of the country. In a good measure initially Gujarat did not perceive the colonial rule as an encroachment, exploitation and oppression associated with colonization. The same was the perception of the Gujarati writers almost by the end of the nineteenth century. Most of the writers saw in it freedom from tyranny, bad governance of the Muslim and native kings and also from the Marāṭhā who indulged in loot and arson in the areas adjacent to south Gujarat. Better law and order established by the British allowed business activities to take place, much to the satisfaction of the people in general. Moreover, the East India

---

4. Gandhi's Presidential Address to the Gujarati Sahitya Parishad in the year 1936 speaks of his understanding of Gujarati literature and its traditions in a historical perspective.

Company civil servants like Alexander Kinlock Forbes took an interest in archaeological and historical sites and remains of Gujarat, founded the Gujarat Vernacular Society at Ahmedabad in 1848 and wrote *Rāsa Mālā* in English containing historical sources of old and medieval Gujarat. These factors led to a better perception of colonial rule than elsewhere, particularly in northern India that was the main site of the 1857 Uprising against the colonial rulers and barbaric revenge by the colonizers, as discussed earlier. Gujarat remained more or less untouched by the mayhem associated with the Uprising. Gujarati writers like Dalpat, Narmad, Navalram Pandya and Govardhanram Tripathi, for instance, did not take even serious note of the event, though the second half of the nineteenth century was the period of their creative writing. The general perception was that English rule was providential and in overall welfare of India. The streak of this perception continued for long despite the intervention of Gandhi and his historical role in the struggle for India's Independence. For example in his *History of Gujarati Literature,* Mansukhlal Jhaveri as late as 1978 does not have more than one and half line for the "Sepoy Mutiny" (67). All these Gujarati writers did take their positions against social evils like child marriage, suttee, killing baby girls among others but not in favour of the 'Mutiny.' However, it does not mean that these writers approved of all the changes that had adversely affected native interests, and wrote about them allegorically and hid it in subtexts of their works.

Dalpatram Travadi (1820-98), one of the close associates of Forbes, and assistant secretary of the Gujarat Vernacular Society (1855-76), in his *Hunnarkhan ni Chadai* (Invasion of Industry) (1851) wrote allegorically about the adverse impact of foreign goods and industrialization under the colonial rule. The poem deals with the story of Hunnar (Industry), the king who has Yantrakhan (machinery) as his minister and Madarpat (a kind of cloth often used to cover bed-mattresses and quilts) as the commander-in-chief. The army includes different goods imported from foreign countries like China and England into India. The ensuing battles depict Indian cottage industries at the receiving end.[5] His contemporary Narmad in his voluminous corpus of writing, did not directly deal with foreign rule but discussed the decline of the Hindu society and need for reforms in it, though his views underwent a change in the later part of his career. His *Hinduo-ni Padatī*, that the author himself called the "Bible of Social Reforms," allegorized the war between the King Sudharāditya, and Vahemyavan symbolizing reform and superstition respectively with Narmad himself as commander-in-chief. It contrasted the present-day India infested by superstitions, casteism, conservatism, short-sightedness, and social inequality with its glorious past. This can be best put in the category of discourse of resistance against internal colonization primarily in the Hindu society that was India for him.

In his essay "Deśābhimāna," Narmad mentioned torture inflicted by Aurangzeb on the Hindus. As Narmad contradicted his views quite often, he mentioned the spirit of cooperation between the Hindus and Muslims particularly in business. The contradiction here is not as severe as it might appear. Narmad did not approve of the Muslim rulers and *nawābs*, as he did in case of the native kings, for they tortured common people, but spoke in better terms about the Muslim community. But he examined factors responsible for the division between the two that affected even his writing. He did not write in appreciation of the 1857 Uprising and mentioned it as a mere historical event on different occasions and then moved on. He rather appreciated British rule and its policy of concession to the natives as the grace of the Queen (208). However, he considered all hopes of Indians sitting in the British parliament like Canada and Ireland as futile

5. However, Dalpataram wove suggestive subtexts to his creative works particularly the play *Mitthyābhimāna*, for he critiqued the natives responsible for their downfall. For the discussions of the subtexts please see Avadhesh Kumar Singh, "Indian 'Renaissance' Self-(Re)fashioning and Colonialism: A Comparative Study of the 19th Century Gujarati and Hindi Renaissance Prose Writing", *South Asia Review*, vol. XXV, no. 1, 2004, 256-78.

(208). He later discussed "Swadeśābhimāna" in the eponymous essays but not even once considered it in opposition to the English rule (214-16). Surprising it is because how can the notion of pride of one's country come into existence without freeing it from the foreign rule? These were the contradictions of the age and not uncommon to Narmad, though his writings influenced Gandhi, as the latter mentioned in his autobiography, and thereby gave direction to Indian resistance against colonial rule.

In his comparative study of the history of "Hindustan" and "England" Britain, Narmad said that the Hindus and Muslims were happy as the subjects of the Company for 40 years (after 1818). The relationship between the English rulers and the native kings was friendly. Then the Mutiny (*Balvo*) took place in 1857 and thereafter the Queen reigned after taking over from the Company (Point no. 6, *Dharam Vicāra*, 55). After this fleeting mention, he moved on. Further, in his long essay "Aryo no Utkarsh" he remarked that the Rājpūts and Marāṭhās, the Muslims, Englishmen and French all caused havoc in the country that ended in the victory of the English company (ibid., 113). He asked the *Āryajana* (the Ārya people) to give up their pride of their country and consolidate and protect their own religion like the Musalmans who do not have a sense of pride of their country, but they are committed to their religion.[6]

After Narmad, Hargovinddas Kantawala (1849-1932) and Ichchharam S. Desai (1853-1912) need to be mentioned at least briefly for their concern with national or patriotic concerns, if not for their concerted construction of a discourse of resistance. Kantawala's poem "Panipat" or "Kurukshetra" dealt with battles that in the end weakened India. He further wrote on social reforms in *Saṁsāra Sudhāro*, and on the promotion and encouragement to

6. Navalram, a contemporary of Narmad, also avoided references to the Colonial rule or its critique. However, his *Itihas ni Arasi* deals with transitory character of the past. At one point he clearly mentions, *Aṅgrejo rāja kare, deśī rahe dabāi*" (The Englishmen rule and the natives remain suppressed).

indigenous crafts and skills in *Deśkārīgarī ne Uttejan.* Kantawala was concerned with the sad state of native industry in the colonial period that he did not resist as Dalpat did in *Hunnerkhan in Chadai.* Only I.S. Desai, for the first time demanded political freedom in Gujarati discourse in his article "Give Us Political Freedom" in the third issue of the monthly periodical *Svatantratā* (Independence) that he had started in 1878. The author was arrested and tried, but acquitted in the end. Later he ceased its publication in a year, and advocated reconciliation with the British in *Hind ane Britannia*[7] (1886). Govardhanram Tripathi, the author of the epic novel *Sarasvatīcandra*, recognized the 'selfish aggressors,' yet wanted his people to be 'loyal children of the government and patriotic children of the soil.' For him the question of being "offensive or defensive against the aggressors did not arise, so he wanted his people to follow the path of "elasticity"[8] (Scrap Book III, 510). Only in Gandhi did the disillusionment with the colonial rule take place after his stay in South Africa. The ambivalence and reconciliation that characterized Gujarati literature for almost five decades were replaced by resistance or *satyāgraha* that demands separate discussion.[9] Before doing that the discernible pattern in Gujarati literature's response to the colonial rule can be seen as marked by "reception," "ambivalence," "reconciliation," "resistance" and "rejection," the last two being associated with M.K. Gandhi.

---

7. See Avadhesh Kumar Singh: "Indian Renaissance Self-(Re)fashioning and Colonialism" for discussion of reconciliation in Ichharam Desai, 275-77.

8. For discussion of reception and ambivalence in the second half of the nineteenth-century Gujarati literature particularly Dalpat, Narmad, Navalram, Tripathi, and Gandhi, please see Avadhesh Kumar Singh, 263-66.

9. With their poetic discourses Zaverchand Meghani (1897-1947) and Dula Kag (1903-77), two contemporaries and followers of Gandhi contributed to the movement for India's struggle for Independence. In his collection of poems *Yugavandanā*, apart from folk literary works Meghani articulated the urge for freedom, sacrifice for the nation and sympathy for →

VI

Various words like *pratikāra, pratirodha* or even *virodha*[10] do not come close to the original sense of the resistance that Gandhi could capture in his term *satyāgraha*. The use of the word *āgraha* comes close to insistence, that has not only onomastic resemblance with resistance but also shares the same root *sistere*, i.e. stand. Resistance in this sense is insistence on one's own stand against the tyranny of essentializing, totalizing and homogenizing forces of exploitation. Gandhi gave it non-violent, positive connotations by bringing truth into it. Gandhi's odyssey to *satyāgraha*, his mode of resistance is no less interesting than his experiments with 'truth.'

Gandhi's narrative of resistance, i.e. *satyāgraha*, the means of India's Independence against the colonial force began outside India. His *Satyagraha in South Africa* (1-471) deals with it in detail. It begins with the entry of Indians in South Africa as indentured

→ underprivileged oppressed people of the society in the spirit of the Gandhian era. In his poem "Chhello Katoro" (The Last Cup of Poison) he tried to capture Gandhi's state of mind before he set out to attend the First Round Table Conference in 1931. For his unequalled popularity among the folk and elite alike and unflinching support to the freedom movement Gandhi had called him *rāṣṭrīya śāyara* (National Poet). On the other hand, Kag despite being a *cāraṇa kavi* (bardic poet) wrote extensively on Gandhi and strove to compose "Mohanayan" on Gandhi, the way the *Rāmāyaṇa* deals with Rāma. Both these poets presented a unique aspect of Gujarati literature by contributing to the discourse of resistance indirectly, though primarily their works belonged to the category of folk literature: For a study of Meghani see Avadhesh Kumar Singh, "Poetic Concerns of Jhaverchand Meghani", *Mīmāṁsā*, vol. V, October, 2003, 118-28. Also for Dula Kag see my article "Mohanayan: Dula Kag ek Purakalpan Sarjak", *Vāṇī to Amṛt Vādan*, ed. Ambadan Rohadiya, Gandhinagar: Gujarat Government Information Bureau, 2003, 71-77.

10. For that matter, the word *virodha* cannot stand for "resistance," for it is "opposition." The difference between resistance and opposition becomes evident when Edward Said used the conjunction "and," not "or" in the title of chapter three "Resistance and Opposition" of his book *Culture and Imperialism* (230-340). Discussing themes of resistance and culture, Said saw it in terms of periods preceded by decolonization. The period of "primary resistance," i.e. literally fighting against outside intrusion, is →

labour from 16 November 1860 onwards. They were deluded by Indian recruiting agents and their children being children of slaves, were put under stringent provision of colonial law. "The justification or excuse for sending labourers to such a far off land under indenture was that the labourers, after completing the indentures, would become free to develop their powers fully and consequently improve their economic condition" (37). The restrictions, stringent laws notwithstanding the suppression and discrimination reached a point beyond tolerance when the government of Natal decided to introduce a law into the legislative assembly of Natal in 1893 disenfranchising all Asiatic, barring those whose names were in the voters' list. The tale of resistance begins with "grievance" of what Gandhi called racial distinction; and "Indians resisted this measure" (39). For the first time the term "resist" appears in the volume.

The Europeans in South Africa, hungry for riches, resented Indians in Transvaal as elsewhere because of their trading skills and their acceptance by the native tribes and wanted to get them

---

→ followed by the period of secondary resistance, i.e. ideological resistance when efforts are made to reconstitute "a shattered community, to save or restore the sense and fact of community against the pressure of the colonial system" (Davidson 155). Later he saw resistance in terms of "great" related topics in decolonizing cultural resistance: (i) the insistence on the right to see the community's history whole, coherently, integrally marked by the endeavours to restore the imprisoned nation to itself; (ii) the resistance, far from being merely a reaction to imperialism, becomes an alternative way of conceiving human history; and (iii) a noticeable pull away from separatist nationalism towards a more integrative view of human community and human liberation (259-61). He recapitulated the main points of his argument. Since I cannot better his prose, I will quote him:

> The ideological and cultural war against imperialism occurs in the form of resistance in the colonies, and later, as resistance spills over into Europe and the United States, in the form of opposition or dissent in the metropolis. The first phase of this dynamic produces nationalist independence movements, the second, later, and more acute phase produces liberation struggles (333).

expelled through their petitions to the parliament, i.e. Volksraad, and they spread lies about them. "The Indians have no sense of human decency. They suffer from loathsome diseases. They consider every woman as their prey. They believe that women have no soul" (44). To Gandhi, these four sentences contained "four lies" and hence he protested against the discrimination. He enlarged the scope of resistance, undertook especially by the "Musalman" traders by enlisting the co-operation of "coolies," the term used for indentured labourers by the Europeans.

The realization of grievance is followed by insistence on one's rights and dignity denied by the colonial forces, struggle by violent and non-violent means, and then by the resolution with solemn determination not to submit to suppression (The Black Ordinance required finger prints and registering of women and children under 16). The resolution made by Gandhi and his companions was more than a resolution, it was a pledge, a vow on the suggestion of Sheth Haji Habib. This "pledge must not be taken with a view to produce an effect on outsiders. . . . Every one must search only his own heart, and if the inner voice assures him that he has the requisite strength to carry him through, only should he pledge himself and then only will his pledge bear fruit" (145). Gandhi warned the people present in the assembly of the hardship, risk and suffering, and declared, "But, I can boldly declare, and with certainty, that so long as there is even a handful of men true to their pledge, there can be only one end to the struggle and that is victory" (144).

Struggle against exploitation finds a way for itself. It is like a river that flows for years and then finds a name, the Ganges. The struggle of resistance is preceded by grievance and resolution to seek its redressal and needs a leader who fights for and with the victims of suppression. The struggle needs its own name, for foreign phrase could hardly serve the purpose of resistance. In the case of Gandhi, the theory of resistance finds a term after its practice and narration. The struggle for naming the struggle is no less unique in Gandhi. The borrowed terms do not serve the purpose of the struggle of resistance, nor do they do justice to its uniqueness, for every act of resistance is distinct in itself. Gandhi described the nomenclature of the first struggle of resistance, a successful one in the history:

> None of us knew what name to give to our movement. I then used the term "passive resistance" in describing it. I did not quite understand the implications of "passive resistance" as I called it. I only knew that some new principle had come into being. As the struggle advanced, the phrase "passive resistance" gave rise to confusion and it appeared shameful to permit this great struggle to be known only by an English name. Again, that foreign phrase could hardly pass as current coin among the community. A small prize was therefore announced in *Indian Opinion* to be awarded to the reader who invented the best designation for our struggle. We thus received a number of suggestions. The meaning of the struggle had been then fully discussed in *Indian Opinion* and the competitors for the prize had fairly sufficient material to serve as a basis for their exploration. Shri Maganlal Gandhi was one of the competitors and he suggested the word *sadāgraha*, meaning "firmness in a good cause." I liked the word, but it did not fully represent the whole idea I wished it to connote. I therefore corrected it to "Satyāgraha." Truth (*Satya*) implies truth, and firmness (*āgraha*) engenders and therefore serves as a synonym for force. I thus began to call the Indian movement "Satyāgraha," that is to say, the Force which is born of Truth and Love or non-violence, and gave up the use of the phrase "passive resistance," in connection with it, so much so that even in English writing we often avoided it and used instead the word "Satyāgraha" itself or some other equivalent English phrase. This then was the genesis of the movement which came to be known as Satyāgraha, and of the word used as a designation for it. — 151

The passive resistance was based on the premise that it was a weapon of the 'weak' or the 'voteless.' Some suffragists who had used the term did not eschew the use of physical violence when an opportunity occurred to make things hot for the oppressive state. Gandhi never wanted to accept being weak.

> If we continue to believe ourselves and let others believe that we are weak and helpless and therefore offer passive resistance, our resistance would never make us strong, and at the earliest opportunity we would give up passive resistance as a weapon of the weak. —156

The second difference between passive resistance and *satyāgraha* is regarding the use of violence or arms:

> Satyāgraha and brute force, being each a negation of the other, can never go together. Satyāgraha may be offered to one's nearest and dearest; passive resistance can never be offered to them unless of course they have ceased to be dear and become an object of hatred to us. In passive resistance there is always present an idea of harassing the other party and there is simultaneous readiness to undergo any hardships entailed upon us by such activity; while in Satyāgraha there is not the remotest idea of injuring the opponent. Satyāgraha postulates the conquest of the adversary by suffering in one's own person.
>
> —156-57

Gandhi had to invent a new term to denote the movement of the Indians in the Transvaal and prevent it from being confused with "passive resistance." However, he never italicised or underlined the word *satyāgraha* and spelt it with capital "S." The point worth noting here is that Gandhi added a new dimension to resistance by considering the other not as an enemy and harassing or injuring it. For him, it rather involved readiness to suffer in one's own.

Gandhi's resistance or 'insistence on Truth' stressed on truth leading towards reclaiming or recovering one's identity, dignity or self. But that can be realized only by truth. However, Gandhi did not ascribe any miraculous attribute to it. "There are no such miraculous properties in Satyāgraha, that a thing acquired by truth could be retained even when truth was given up" (459). It was a shield against the suppression of the British Empire. Had it not been for his great struggle and "for the untold suffering which Indians invited upon their devoted heads, the Indians today would have been hounded out of South Africa" (459). He further added,

". . . Satyāgraha is a priceless and matchless weapon, and those who wield it are strangers to disappointment and defeat" (460).

The British under-estimated Gandhi's *satyāgraha* initially, and the attendant scholarship misunderstood it for a considerable period. With his subscription to the ideals of renunciation and service, so dear to the Indian psyche for ages, he attracted the Indian masses, with his body clad in bare clothes like a *fakīr* and austerity of an ascetic. Harold Laski understood this when he remarked after seeing him:

> It was fascinating to see Gandhi at work and try and penetrate his secret. . . . But the drama of this wizard little man with the whole empire against him is a terrific spectacle. The basis of it all is, I think, the power of an ascetic over Eastern minds who resent the feeling of inferiority they have had for 150 years.
>
> — in Newman, 118

Why did Satyāgraha prove to be so powerful a weapon of resistance against the Raj? Different scholars have forwarded answers of all sorts. It would be interesting to know the response of a keen scholar of the British Imperial enterprise and Raj:

> To begin with, it offered no violent physical challenges to the Raj. This was prudent, for the British Raj, with its patient construction of alliances with local collaborationist's elite and groups, the playing off of one section of Indian society against another, and the sheer scale of its military organization and commitment, could simply not be defeated by unarmed, even if revolutionary civilians. Also *satyāgraha*, practised on a nationwide scale, promises to involve literally millions of ordinary Indian people in a series of peaceful demonstrations that could eventually undermine the Raj's authority and the British Administration's will to rule. Finally, owing mainly to the simplicity and quasi-religious qualities associated with *satyāgraha*, Indian resistance to British rule could become for the first time a mass movement, not the perverse of a Western-educated elite wearing suits, waistcoats and ties making speeches in English to audiences who could not always understand them.
>
> —Judd 128-29

Apart from these, Gandhi based his strategy of *satyāgraha* on his scathing critique of his own people and colonizers. He considered Indian colonization by the British as a consequence of the moral decadence of the natives who courted their own exploitation. But through his non-violent non-cooperation (*ahiṁsā* and *asahayoga*) he made *satyāgraha* attractive to India's masses — rural and urban, uneducated, rich and poor and men and women in a democratic self-disciplined manner that rejected the notion of the moral superiority of the colonizers, for they brutally repressed the unarmed non-violent participants in the movement.

Gandhi authored resistance as *satyāgraha* and led one of the most successful, disciplined and non-violent struggles in the history of human civilization against the most powerful empire equipped with sophisticated strategists, attended by an insatiable hunger for power and pelf. South Africa was Gandhi's laboratory of *satyāgraha* and also of its theorization. India was his major practising ground. He was born in India but made Mahatma by another land, i.e. South Africa where he saw the real face of colonization and its suppressive and exploitative practices. His motherland reaped the harvest of what South Africa had sown in him. Wherever and whenever there shall be suppression or exploitation, Gandhi's novel way of resistance would be the most viable alternative available to humanity, and his *Satyāgraha in South Africa* would remain the *Gītā* of resistance. Moreover, Gandhi as a theorizer, narrator and practitioner of resistance was free from what Said called 'the partial tragedy of resistance,' that it must to a certain degree work to recover forms already established or at least influenced or infiltrated by the culture" (253). That he could avoid the forms of the culture of empire is manifested in his *Hind Swarāj*, a text that charts out the blueprint of Home Rule unaffected by colonial institutions or their hangover, though one need not agree with all of his positions. I must add here that Gandhi did not require the crutches of the colonial system the way the Nehrus and the Gandhis needed them ironically in post-colonial India.

Thus Gandhi, the master strategist of the discourse of

resistance against the colonization, gave a purposeful direction to India's struggle for independence that later became a model for all resisters in the world. In the process he emerged as the most colossal figure impacting all aspects of social life including Gujarati language and literature. Moreover, Gujarati literary discourse that was marked with tacit support and reception, ambivalence and reconciliation in the last three quarters of the nineteenth century moved in the direction of resistance and rejection of the colonial rule through his intervention.

VII

Bharatendu Harishchandra was the precursor of the discourse of resistance in Hindi and one of the first in Indian languages.[11] For the first time he used the term *upniveśa* (colony) in relation to America's colonization by the British and its subsequent freedom from it, and thereby he suggested that the way America attained its Independence, India would also be free from colonization (*Kavivacana-Sudhā*, 31.8.1874). He missed no occasion to respond to all royal events and occasions through his poetic creations and praised the colonial rulers, thus giving the impression of being a *rājabhakta* (Raj loyalist), as he is often accused of.[12] However a closer examination of his discourse reveals that it was a kind of camouflage, and a part of his strategy to avoid the wrath of the colonial rule and its law of sedition for writing against it, yet he used his essays and journalistic writings particularly in *Kavivacana-Sudhā* for communicating his message to his countrymen. In his essay, for instance, "Bharatvarṣonnati Kaise Ho Sakati Hai?" (How

---

11. For detailed discussion of Bharatendu's role in Indian *Punarjāgaraṇa* (Renaissance) please see Avadhesh Kumar Singh,"Bhāratīya Punarjāgaraṇa aur Bharatendu" (Hindi) in Mahavir Singh Chauhan, ed., *Bhāratīya Navajāgaraṇa aur Bhāratendu tathā Narmad Yuga kā Sāhitya*, Ahmedabad: Parshva Prakashan, 1995, 68-94.

12. Also see Avadhesh Kumar Singh, "Indian 'Renaissance' Self-(Re) Fashioning and Colonialism", pp. 267-73 for polyvalence and subtleties in his discourse against colonialism.

can India Progress?) he, in the beginning, used hyperbolic terms to praise the colonial rule and its representative Mr Roberts, the Collector, who was on the stage, but then he went on to discuss ways of India's progress that in fact meant in the end its freedom from the colonial rule. Moreover, he was one of the first to point out the economic aspect of the colonial rule, as he said in the often quoted lines:

aṅgrejrāja sukhsaz sabai ati bhārī
par dhan videśa calī jāt ye hai duḥkha bhārī

This he explained in various issues of *Kavivacana-Sudhā.* He said in the 12.12.1873 issue of the journal:

> By whatever means the wealth is accumulated, it would go to England ultimately because all of our luxury items come from there. All our economic resources are drained and sent there. And what comes (from England) for us are mirror, toy, pen and pencil. — *Kavivacana-Sudhā,* 16.2.1873

Further,

> Foreign crafts and industry have invaded our country. Such a thing never happened (in the history of our country).
> — Ibid., 9.3.1874

> When the British come from England, how poor they are? And when they go back to England from India they are gods of wealth. . . . It proves that the English are the main cause of diseases and famine. — Ibid., 18.05.1874

Further, he countered the myths of colonial rule and their value of justice and freedom:

> The newspapers bark so much but no one listens to them. This is a benighted world. All claims of justice and freedom are false.
> — Ibid., 31.08.1874

All above quotations, translated from Hindi, exhibit Bharatendu's continuous engagement with the economic exploitation in the colonial rule. He went further in charting out his resistance of foreign goods by boycotting them, something that Gandhi practised in the twentieth century. But he was more pragmatic than Gandhi's idea of making bonfire of the foreign goods, when he said,

> By omniscient, omnipresent and omnipotent eternal God we take a vow and write that from this day onwards we shall not wear any foreign garments. However, whatever we have purchased and we have, we shall use them till they are reduced to rags. But we shall not put on any new English cloth. We would accept only Indian made clothes.
>
> — *Kavivacana-Sudhā*, 23.08.1874

So he had such an intense bitterness for the colonial rule and its exploitation of native resources that he systematically articulated it in his discourses, though the surface gives a different impression.

After Bharatendu in Hindi, the subtle and systematic construction of the discourse of resistance suffered in quantitative and qualitative terms. Only in works like *Śivaśambhū ke Cīṭṭhe*, Balmukund Gupta indirectly commented on economic, social and political issues faced by the country. In Hindi, one had to wait for the advent of Munshi Premchand whose works speak clearly about his social and political consciousness and the articulation of his resistance against internal and external colonization particularly in his novel *Karmabhūmi* that deserves detailed discussion.

In the intervening period between Bharatendu and Premchand, Balkrishna Bhatt, one of the members of the Bharatendu Mandal, considered Englishmen as the mine of cunningness and deceit. Apart from his essays, he edited *Hindi Pradeep* for 33 years since 1872. The cover of the journal used to be inscribed by *śubha sārā deśa sneha pūrit prakaṭa hue ānanda bhare.* It spoke of his love for his country that he wanted it to be filled with auspicious prosperity, love and happiness that was possible, according to him, by getting rid of the colonial rule and also by not mixing Raj loyalty with patriotism. Pandit Badrinarayan Chaudhary "Premghan" started two journals *Ānanda Kādambinī* and *Nāgarī Nīrada* with the purpose of expressing English policies and also articulating pain and suffering of the poor Indian peasants.

Mahavir Prasad Dwivedi (1864-1938) in the early part of the publication of *Sarasvati* did not publish anything that contained criticism of British rule. He nourished the streak of Raj loyalty that had been founded in the Bharatendu period without containing Bharatendu's criticism of English rule. In 1904 he wrote an article on Laxmibai who was praised because she had allegedly promised to help the British in the 1857 Uprising. In the same article Tatya Tope was called a cruel murderer. In 1905, the year of the partition of Bengal, he published eulogy of a king who had helped the British in the 1857 Uprising. Only in the later part of his career he changed his opinion regarding the colonial rule. This, however, does not discount his contribution to Hindi literary and critical discourse. Dwivedi's younger contemporary Maithilisharan Gupt's *Bhārata Bhāratī* (1913), written in response to *Mushas-Maddo-Jaje-Islam* or *Musaddase Hali* dealing with the past, present and future of the Muslims, brought about nationalist and cultural consciousness in Hindi land.

The discourse of resistance in the colonial period and its practices in Hindi found a new purpose and direction in Munshi Premchand, who in the early period of his career wrote in Urdu, and translated his works in Hindi. Then he moved to Hindi or Hindustānī, for his Hindi profusely used Urdu words in his works. After the confiscation of *Soẓ-e-Vatan* (1903), a collection of his short stories, it seems Premchand had given up political themes and moved towards resisting several social evils — feudalism, communalism, caste-system, exploitation of poor labourers and peasants in his works. It is possible to interpret this silence in two ways: (i) Premchand avoided such political themes as would annoy the then rulers, because creative writings critical of the government used to be either confiscated or prohibited, and he had already lost his job, and (ii) in the midst of all these developments he had perhaps realized that it was necessary to construct a discourse of resistance against internal colonization, i.e. exploitation and suppression by one privileged class, caste or race of the less-privileged and dispossessed poor people, low-caste and peasants in direct or even suggestive terms. The emancipation from internal colonization of natives by other natives would make the society fight against external colonization in a meaningful and sustained manner because a fragmented society cannot stand against more powerful and sophisticated forces of external colonization. He turned to political concerns of the age again in the 1920s when he foresaw hope of independence of the country, as Mahatma Gandhi led India's struggle of freedom, and remained concerned with major political incidents and movements of the period.[13] Since we shall foreground Premchand's discourse of resistance in his novel *Karmabhūmi*, written between 1929 and 1931, it is necessary for us to consider his letter written around the event of capital punishment meted out to Bhagat Singh and other comrades, though their path was different from Gandhi's, his model.

> I was waiting to attend the Karachi (session). Bhagat Singh's death by hanging has broken heart. With what hope could one go there now? People will hoot down Gandhi and the Congress

---

13. Premchand contributed his bit to the Indian's struggle of independence led by M.K. Gandhi. He dedicated his creative and critical and editorial endeavours to the great cause. It is evident in his editorial to the first issue of *Hans*, March 1930:

> It is a matter of extreme good fortune that *Hans* has been born at a time when a new epoch is being ushered in, in India and when the country is moving frantically to free herself from "the bonds of slavery.". . . How the memory of great victory will be celebrated is for the future, but the victory is such that there cannot be another instance of this type in the world history. Its memorial, therefore, would be an impressive one. To worship this new god to commemorate this great victory we stand here with the ceremonial earthen lamp. We are conscious that we are nobodies. And you may say it is strange that even before the start of the battle, we should think of victory and of erecting a memorial. But independence is only awareness of mind. To arouse this awareness is indeed independence. Our awareness has been so dulled into inanimation that it was beyond comprehension that this awareness could even take birth but India's oarsman (Gandhi) has given us this conception. It would grow and prosper. The way of liberation that we had thought of earlier proved in vain. Although, even at their inception,

→

> will pass into the hands of irresponsible extremists, and there will be no place for us. What path shall we pursue is not clear. I have lost heart. The future is bleak. The events in Banaras, Mirzapur and Agra, I fear, will encourage the government. But no government could ever commit a greater stupidity. How deep an impact could the government have created, if it had commuted the death sentence (of Bhagat Singh and his comrade) into transportation of life? Its attitude, however, betrays that there has been no change of heart, and that the government is determined to go its irresponsible way. — 290

The letter speaks of Premchand's keen observation and even participation in the decisive political events. He wrote the novel in the backdrop of these turbulent times — political and ideological. The main aim was independence. But what was the path? Bhagat Singh's or Gandhi's? He was with Gandhi but in full

---

→ there was stiff opposition from the conservatives, we shall be victorious in the struggle some day. Whether that day will dawn sooner or later depends on our efforts, the condition of our mind and heart. It is, of course, our duty to endeavour to usher in that day at the earliest. This then is the aim of *Hans.* And the policy of the journal shall be pursuance of that aim . . . whether it will be victory — crossing the expanse of water — or whether its life drama will end before the victory is achieved, is for an astrologer to say. But we are sure that its determination will not weaken. Such then will be its politics. In literature and society it would introduce qualities which have been left to it by tradition. (In Madan Gopal 307-08).

For Premchand the independence demanded Herculean effort like construction of *Setubandha* (bridge) that Rāma and his army did before achieving victory over Rāvaṇa's Laṅkā. In this endeavour, animals like monkeys, beers and squirrels, participated. He, not averse to the political role of the journal in bringing about awareness, i.e. independence, wanted *Hans* (swan) to contribute at least a few straws to the making of the new *setubandha.* Moreover, the note reveals Premchand's firm conviction or optimism about India's Independence in days to come that coincidentally India achieved within two decades under the leadership of Gandhi, its oarsman. His optimism and subscription to Gandhian mode of resistance through *ahiṁsā* and *satyāgraha* are discernible in *Karmabhūmi*. Without having sufficient reasons to disbelieve that Premchand did not have access to →

sympathy with Bhagat Singh and his comrades who had laid down their lives at the altar of the motherland. With his perspicacity he could foresee the reaction of the people against Gandhi and his fear was that if that happens, there was a possibility of Congress, being then led by Gandhi, falling 'in the hands of irresponsible extremists.' In the event of such a situation the movement for India's struggle would be fragmented and consequently unsuccessful because he cherished no hope from the government whose true repressive character was revealed to him as it did not condone Bhagat Singh and his comrade's death punishment. The novelist constructed a systematic treatise of revolution by combining revolutionary discourse and Gandhi's non-violence into one with an emphasis on Gandhi's *ahiṁsā* and *satyāgraha* with unflinching negation of compromise. Apart from this the reason behind foregrounding the novel *Karmabhūmi* is that this is one among the few novels that exquisitely constructs a discourse of resistance to external and internal colonization in one work in fictional terms. He had already dealt with internal colonization, exploitation of the poor particularly peasants, untouchability, sufferings of women, corruption in the high seats of religion and indifference among bureaucrats towards the common people and their indulgence in exhibitionism and the luxuries of life.[14]

→ Gandhi's writings particularly *Hind Svarāj* in the journal *Young India*, one can indulge in over-reading and find similarities between attributes of a *satyāgrahī* as proposed by Gandhi in *Hind Svarāj* and subscription to them in Amarkant in *Karmabhūmi*. As Gandhi mentioned, "After a great deal of experience it seems to me that those who want to become passive resisters for the service of the country have to observe perfect chastity, adopt poverty, follow truth and cultivate fearlessness" (73). Amar leaves his wife Sukhada and beloved Sakina, renounces his father, world of wealth and prefers poverty to prosperity by living in a village of poor and oppressed, and follows the path of truth and non-violence fearlessly. Amar in the novel thus is a Gandhian *satyāgrahī* of *Hind Svarāj*.

14. The novel could have easily been titled *Karmakṣetra*, instead of *Karmabhūmi*. If one can take liberties with the opening verse of the *Śrīmadbhagavad-Gītā*, then its philosophy or guiding words are, *dharmakṣetre kurukṣetre kṣtre kṣetre karman kurun*. If *dharma* is righteous conduct, *karma* is righteous action not →

Colonialism necessitates political defeat of the nations by a dominant, not necessarily superior, cluster of interests whose centre lies not in the colony but in a far off land, and involves systematic unsystematization of native material and psychological structures — religious, educational, bureaucratic, judiciary, economic — and their replacement by foreign institutions in the name of modernization. Thereby it justifies its presence in the colony. Its principal purpose is exploitation of native resources — economic through loot, natural resources as raw material, human through the use of natives as cheap labourers, and intellectual through its appropriation and translation. For this purpose they constructed discourses denigrating the native institutions and thereby justifying their presence in the colony and validating their intervention in the existing structures, e.g. the educational system. Premchand, in the very beginning, castigated educational structures imposed on India by exposing evils of the new education system and the higher education that issues degree certificates but not knowledge. The system had commodified knowledge and was being imparted by incompetent, indifferent and uncommitted teachers demeaning the noble profession of Indian culture. The novelist commented on education in the beginning:

> The earnest compulsion with which fees are collected in schools and colleges, surpasses the hardships even in the collection of revenues. On the fixed date of the month the fee is to be submitted. The inability to do so would lead either to cancellation of the name or pay the fine if delayed. In the Queen's College the rule was that the fee was paid on the 7th day, the fee was doubled by 21st or the name was cancelled. What can be the objective of such strict rules but to drive away the children of the poor from these schools? The same heartless bureaucracy which dominates

---

→ only in any undefined area of life but also for one's land, i.e. the motherland. It speaks of Premchand's immediate concern for the motherland but he discusses the discourses of resistance or strategies of resistance. At one level, they become principles of resistance of colonial suppression in any part of the world. Herein Premchand's work focuses on the immediate, yet transcends the specificities.

> government offices also dominates the working of our educational institutes. Bring fee from whatever source — borrow, mortgage your ornaments, sell off your utensils, steal but pay fees by all means. Else it would be either doubled or the name would be deleted. Some concession is given even in collection of taxes pertaining to land and property. The entry of kindness is disallowed in our educational institutes. The martial law is permanently imposed there. Money reigns supreme in our educational institutions as in the courts with greater rigidity and greater hardships. If you get delayed you are fined; if you are late, you are fined; if you do not remember your lesson you are fined; if you are unable to buy books you are fined; and if you commit a mistake, you are fined. Is it an educational institute or an institute to impose fines? That then is the purpose of Western education which is being praised in hyperbolic terms. Should it surprise us if these institutions produce children who are willing to sacrifice everything for money, cut throats of poor people and sell off their souls for money? —5

Education and other issues raised by the novelist in *Karmabhūmi* were not his new thematic preoccupations. He had dealt with them in one way or other in his short stories. For instance, the story "Baḍe Bhāī Sāheb" satirized the pitfalls in the education system. His attack became more vituperative in *Karmabhūmi,* for Western education had replaced native educational systems; thereby the colonizers committed one of the worst crimes of killing 'the beautiful tree' of Indian education, as Mahatma Gandhi had put it. The new system proved to be a cruel, heartless, money minting system. Further, he commented on the mindset of the colonized subject that sang paeans of the imposed education system without seeing its true character, for this changed the parameters of judging and defining success in higher education. For success it is not a degree but education that is necessary. "The real degree that we need is that of humility, service and simplicity. If we do not have them or if our consciousness is not awakened, the paper degree is useless" (71). This disapproval he articulated through his characters in the novel particularly Amarkant.

With his disregard for degrees, Amarkant, the protagonist, hates the education system and does not appear in the degree examination. His diatribe against the education system and incompetent teachers continues:

> When he used to see Professors as slaves to fashion, demeaning themselves for their petty selfish ends, doing the least amount of work and craving for maximum benefits, he used to suffer from immense anguish because those gentlemen were skippers of the country. They were the makers of the nation, yet not concerned with the fact that the people of India survive on two *ānnā*s a day. A common man does not get more than 50 rupees a year. Our teachers, however, need 50 rupees per day. Then he would remember about the past when our teachers used to live in cottages, away from selfishness and greed, practised ideals of pure life, as worshippers of service without caring for the result. They took the least from the nation and gave it maximum in return. They were real gods. And our present-day teachers are in no sense less than petty traders or state officials. What enlightenment shall they bring about when they themselves are in darkness? . . . It seems that all (the departments) are a herd of vultures gnawing at the corpses of the poor. The more and higher degrees one has, the more inflated his selfishness. It seems that greed and selfishness are the attributes of scholarship. Poor people do not get meals and clothes, but our educated people need motor car, bungalow and a platoon of servants. If this world is constructed by man, then he is unjust, and if by God, then what to say to him? —71-72

His vituperative criticism of the modern education associated with colonial rule continues even after his father's withdrawal of support for his education even in terms of fees. When Sukhada, his wife, proposes him to go to Lucknow and study there without any monetary worry with the prospects of going to England for acquiring a more respectable degree, he rejects it:

> For degree it is not so necessary that I become dependent on my in-laws. If I can earn some money on my own, I would study or enter some business. I was infatuated uselessly with education.

> A studious person can learn a lot outside the college. Without having any sense of pride let me state that the books of literature and history that I have read in these years, perhaps no one in the college would have read them. — 14

Apart from the education system, Premchand did not spare even Western civilization for its misplaced faith in its education system. Amarkant's friend Salim who helps him with his fee and other means asks Amarkant to help him with a few points for his speech on the topic of Western civilization:

> "Would you go to the meeting today?"
>
> "I do not remember even the topic."
>
> "The same old topic, the Western civilization."
>
> "Please tell me a few points. Else what shall I speak there?"
>
> "What is there to tell you? All of us know the evils of Western civilization. Just speak about them."
>
> "You would know, but I do not know even one."
>
> "One of the things is education. Wherever you see, it is nothing but business. The shop of court, shop of education and also of wealth. A lot can be spoken on just one point." — 7

Though a diversion, I must add here that it should not be construed here that Premchand was a blind denigrator of the Western civilization. He was against its selfish values and their uncritical imitations by the Indians. Through Sukhada's response to Seth Maniram's objectionable remarks the novelist stated:

> You consider yourself a great devotee of English civilization. Do you think English ways of dressing and making up are its main constituents? Its main constituents are respect and honour of women. — 168

Premchand's criticism of the colonial education system was not confined to mere words or idealism but to action as well. Along with Professor Shantikumar, Amar opened a *pāṭhaśālā* freed from fee, penalty and donations. This alternative education aimed at the natural development of tiny, innocent children who would be courageous, contented, and serving citizens of the society. Amar at a point of time goes to the extent of seeking his resignation from the post of Professor. It is a clash between pure idealism and practical/pragmatic idealism that demands some regular economic support for the institution. Hence, Premchand was not merely constructing discourses of resistance against the colonial system of education but providing an alternative as well, based on the pragmatic idealism of the people who have been a part of the system as a student or teacher as well. Salim, Amar's friend, is an example of those who make use of the education system to attain an administrative position so that they can rule by joining the tribe of the colonizers in one way or other.

The author's criticism of education continues in the second part of the novel, for a change this time from Salim, Amar's friend, who on the surface finds college-life dull and drab and monotonous in the absence of his friend, and sees the college campus as a theatre of shallow ritualism pertaining to the education system. The only change he saw in the convocation address by the vice-chancellor was his focus on simple life. However, his problem is that everybody preaches simple life but no one tries to practise it.

> Are all these unmemorable lecturers and professors models of simple life? They are raising their standard of living, why should the students not do so? I do not know why the vice-chancellor does not preach the lessons of simple life to his staff. Professor Bhatia has fifty pairs of shoes; some of them costing even Rs. 50 per pair. . . . Professor Chakravorty is a renowned miser. Neither wife nor God's prayer. But do you know the number of his servants? Only twelve. — 109

Thus, Premchand's criticism was not restricted mainly to the education system but to the main instruments of imparting knowledge/education, i.e. teachers who despite being Indians were not in touch with Indian realities particularly poor people. However, through his questioning of the system, its teachers and proposing an alternative system through younger generation he forwards his ideas and optimism as well.

Premchand, the novelist, snugly wove a few suggestive sub-texts to the fabric of the novel. As far as the sub-texts pertaining to untouchability, poor peasants and village life and Hindu-Muslim unity are concerned, he had dealt with them earlier. For instance, he had gone into the problem of untouchability in *Sevāsadana, Raṅgabhūmi* and *Kāyākalpa* in a different way. In *Karmabhūmi* the difference from its preceding counterparts is that the novel revolts against religious segregation and even suppression of the low caste people, as they were not allowed to listen to the *kathā* or enter the temple. In *Devasthāna Rahasya* the novelist had tried to depict corruption prevailing in the temples through the character of Mahant Trilokīnātha who had converted the temple into a seat of his personal luxuries and physical gratification, briefly comparing it with medieval English history and the privileges that the priestly class enjoyed then. Their crimes were heard in the court of the Pope, and they more often than not remained unpunished. The novelist indirectly sought intervention by the state somewhat along the lines of the Royal decree in England that brought the priestly class under the ambit of the law. However, he could not go beyond the portrayal of priestly misconduct and its criticism. It seems that Premchand's expectations from the state's intervention not only waned between his first novel and *Karmabhūmi* but he felt frustrated at it. The consequence was his discourse of resistance followed by action against Mahant Ashram Giri who seems to be the extension of Trilokīnātha of *Devasthāna Rahasya* with the difference that he combines religion with landlordship, and does not see anyone without receiving the present of one gold coin. The meeting between the Mahant and Amar for reducing the revenue tax of the farmers ends pleasantly on the surface, but in reality it had nothing but false promises. When he asks the sceptical people to be patient and not indulge in any sort of violence, it suggests Amar's Gandhian way of resistance (206). Further, the subsequent discourse speaks of resolution on the part of the hitherto voiceless minor characters to resist oppressive ways. Even bureaucracy has realized that the days of rich people are over. The words of Ghaznavi in conversation among Ghaznavi, Salim, the two officers, and Amar are Premchand's prophetic words,

> Dear, this was to happen some day or other. The rule of rich people would last for only a few days. This country is ruled by the Englishmen so even rich among us who naturally side with rich are now happy to side with poor because by being with them they would get honour. — 200

This change in perception of the poor and oppressed and the willingness of the haves to be with them speaks volumes about general change in the Indian psyche for freedom. Even Ghaznavi, the officer, realizes it and criticizes bureaucracy particularly the police department. This is an insider's criticism, for he was an officer with the colonial system. His observations about *swarāja* and Hindu-Muslim relationships and the fears of the Muslims are not only valid but anticipate what was to follow in the form of the Muslim League a few years after the publication of the novel:

> We too want *swarāja*, but except for revolution there is no other way. What is the need of such an army which eats up half of the revenue of the government? If the expenditure on army can be halved, the tax on farmers can easily be reduced to half. The only fear that I have from the *swarāja* is that the condition of the Muslims would become worse. By reading wrong histories both (Hindus and Muslims) have become enemies and what if the Hindus, given an opportunity, take revenge for false animosities. But I get consoled by the fact that an educated people like the Hindus would not be victims of religious gangsterism.
> — 212-13

Later in the conversation between Salim and Teg Muhammad, the leader of the butchers, reveals Premchand's establishment of high ideals of Islam, ". . . Islam has always helped the weak and you butcher them" (149). Again, "If to be a Muslim means that the poor should be butchered, then I am an infidel" (249).

Even earlier, the novelist had expressed his revolutionary views on religion through the protagonist, who tells his father:

> You consider bathing in the Gaṅgā, prayer and recitation as the

> *dharma*; whereas I consider truth, service and welfare of other (*paropkāra*) as my principal *dharma*. Bathing, meditation, prayer, fasting are mere means of *dharma* not *dharma* in itself. — 32

The Hindu religion contracted many ill practices and empty ritualism which the novelist resisted through its critical portrayal. One of the evil practices was untouchability. The high caste people deprived low caste people (the Harijans) from entering the temple and even sitting in the back-rows from a distance for listening to the *kathā*, for according to brāhmaṇas, they were unworthy of it. All appeals against it proved futile. So *satyāgraha* is launched by Naina, Shantikumar and Sukhada, as they want to settle the issue forever. Naina states, "The temple is nobody's property" (139). The Harijans are awakened and ready to resist the ways of *brahmacārī* by even staking their lives as well. Shantikumar's words inspire them:

> You serve others wholeheartedly, but you are slaves. . . . You are the foundation of the society. The society is based on you, but you are untouchables. You cannot go to temple. Where else can be such an unethical practice, except in our unfortunate country? Do you want to remain downtrodden and *dalit*s like this forever? — 139

Thus, the discourse of resistance against internal colonization is not limited to mere speculation but leads to execution in the form of *satyāgraha* that becomes a raging movement with the participation of Harijans under the leadership of Shantikumar. In the lathi-charge when Shantikumar is injured, Sukhada (who had come to know of her husband's sacrifice and ideals with which he served the people of a Harijan village) is so transformed that she leads the movement against the brāhmaṇas. The brāhmaṇas had to yield to the movement and the gates of the temple were opened to the Harijans.[15] The success of the movement is followed by

---

15. The movement against untouchability and for Harijans' entry in the temple should be seen in the context of the movement against untouchability that had begun in the 1930s and then Gandhi's disapproval of Ramsay McDonald's Communal Award relating to the depressed class (as the Harijans were called by the ruling class) in 1932. Since by that time the →

another movement for the construction of municipal quarters for workers. The municipality rejects the proposal and *satyāgraha* is again launched in which Samarkant, Amarkant's father, by now a transformed person, Sukhada and Naina participate and are arrested. Naina becomes a martyr of the *satyāgraha,* as she is shot dead by her husband. Naina's martyrdom compels the Board to succumb to the demands. The transformation of Sukhada and Samarkant expresses Premchand's faith in the possibility of human regeneration.

Premchand's discourse of resistance highlights the point that women in no way lagged behind their male counterparts. Sukhada and Naina are its examples. Sukhada questions the ideals of her husband initially but leaves the house with her husband. She, however, returns home to serve her ailing father-in-law, and then participates in the movement. She is clear about man's attitude towards woman. Even Amar thinks that women love ornaments. But Sukhada before leaving her in-law's house to accompany her husband gives up all ornaments. All arguments of Amar fail to persuade her, as she says:

> You would think that I would cry for ornaments and curse my fate. You do not know the kind of sacrifice that women can make? After the rebuke (of her husband Amar by Samarkant) I consider even looking at these ornaments as a sinful act; leave aside the question of wearing them. If you are afraid of the fact that I would clamour for them tomorrow, then I must assure you that even the word ornament would never come on my lips. If I ever do so, chop my tongue off. Also I must say that I would not be dependent on you. I'll earn for myself. One does not need

---

→ novel of Premchand was already printed, it speaks not only of Premchand's prophetic power as a writer but also his perception of the problems and strategies of resisting the high caste's repressive practices to justify their ways by interpreting the religious texts in their own ways. Also it suggests that (i) every movement of resisting colonization, internal and external, succeeds only with the participation of all men and women, and (ii) sacrifice of one's comforts, even of life, is another precondition of its success.

> much for meals, only show-off demands more money. If you give up the false world of rich people, then you can manage with a few annas. — 77

Premchand shattered the false image of woman as a weak, lover of luxuries, ornaments and dependent on men for financial security. When feminism as a critical category and its terms were not in usage in Hindi criticism, he depicted strong women characters like Sukhada, Naina and Sakina. Sukhada's transformation speaks about Premchand's concept of woman, her ideals and willingness to sacrifice if need be, as in the case of Naina among others. Earlier she tells Amar that she would accompany him when he wants to leave his father's house because of her principles: "Women have never been behind men either in suffering or in protecting principles" (371). Further, Premchand showed her as conscious of the difference between men and women and their world. In her discussion with Shantikumar who considers that marriage can never bring happiness, she retorts that for this perception he would have found women to be responsible for their failure. She ultimately makes Shantikumar agree to the following observation:

> But man has some animal instinct that he cannot give up even if he decides. This animalism makes him man. In the process of evolution he is behind woman. When he would attain the state of complete evolution, he too would become woman. Affection, love, tenderness, compassion are the foundation-stones of this creation. And these are attributes of women. If women understand it then the life of both would be replete with happiness. Woman becomes animal in her company with another animal. That's why both of them suffer. — 149

Sukhada considers it "a discovery" for all, for she for the first time heard words about women that did not depict her as a fool, worthy of admonitions by men and a fetter around man's legs.

Premchand changed the existing perception of women. He was not a feminist but was clear in his perception that without women's participation no society can ever progress. That is why he balanced man's subscription to ideals of sacrifice, renunciation and service of the poor and downtrodden and social equality by women as well in equal measure. Even Shantikumar acknowledges the fact that within a year Sukhada had done so much that even if Amarkant returns, he would find no space for him because what she had done was unimaginable. He sees in people like Sukhada a ray of hope for the future of a country infested with selfish people:

> At times I am worried about the selfishness of the civilized society. Everybody is concerned with one's own selfish interests. Selfishness of great people is equally great. This is the boon we have got after worshipping Europe for one hundred and fifty years. Despite this, our future is bright. I have no doubt about it. The soul of India is still alive and I have faith the time would come when we shall return to our old ideals of service and renunciation. Money shall not be the sole ideal of our life then, and our worth will not be measured in the scale of money.
>
> —143

Here Premchand expresses his optimism for future India in dark days of freedom and re-establishes the eternal Indian cultural values of service and renunciation that his women characters in *Karmabhūmi* demonstrate in ample measure. Conversely he forecasts that if India does not adhere to those ideals in future, it would not be India but a poor imitator of Europe.

The *karma* of *Karmabhūmi* is *krānti* (revolution) against social evils, false and oppressive religious practices, suppression of poor farmers and low caste people. Amarkant in the debate on *dharma* spoke on *krānti*. He considers the redemption of the country only through *krānti* that would be universal, and end false ideals, principles and those traditions that would be a precursor of a new era, break gods and goddesses made of clay into pieces, and emancipate mankind from the clutches of the government based on money and religion. Further, he has realized that mere speculation and lectures would not make any difference to the Hindu society, for it does not care for revolution preached even by the god of revolution. It gets disturbed only when one transcends the world of speeches and begins to practise revolution. It gets hold of the neck of the revolutionary when he translates his words into *karma*. The instrument of this revolution is the *dharma* of *karma* in practice and *satyāgraha*. When Salim and Amar meet in the jail, Salim's words fail to incite Amar to take recourse to violence against tax (*lagāna)* imposed on farmers. Salim considers violence to be the price of Independence and says, "You want freedom, but do not want to pay its price" (254). Amar responds, "What you consider as the price of freedom, do you know what is its price? Its price is ability to insist on rights and truth" (254). This insistence on the *karmadharma* and *satyāgraha* is the essence of resistance that Gandhi had practised in Africa.[16] Their resistance is based on truth, i.e. *satyāgraha*. However, it can succeed only if the resisters are united. Amar knows it well and says, "We are slaves because we have chained ourselves. The chain is that of difference among us" (255). Exploitation depends on difference and the alien forces exploit this difference and construct such discourses as would justify colonization. A little earlier Amar had considered the issue of non-violence against violence perpetrated by the rulers. And he had concluded that the world is dominated by sheer animal instinct. But even this instinct of colonizers has to take recourse to the discourse of justice, however contrived it might be. The colonial forces invent excuses to dominate or colonize other countries. So the way out is not in indulging in violence but understanding their strategies and resist them with equally sophisticated counter-strategies. He tells Salim:

> If you think that a nation could be free by indulging in murder and violence, then you are making a grave mistake. I do not call it freedom if a country passes from the dominance of a community to another that would rule with its sword. The true freedom dawns when a human being would be filled with values of

16. Please see M.K. Gandhi's *Satyāgraha in South Africa* for his understanding of colonization and strategies of resisting it (3-460). The chapters XII and XIII dealing with *Satyāgraha* are particularly relevant (141-58).

> humanity, and humanity is against dominance, injustice and selfishness. —255

Against the ideal of humanity or *insāniyat*, Premchand does not advocate meek tolerance of violence. At times violence is the only answer to violence. This he deals with the sub-text of the novel integrated into the early main part of the novel. The incidence pertaining to Munni, the wife of a Ṭhākur, being raped by a British solider in a crop field guarded by his two counterparts is a pointer here. The village people are silent spectators and no one comes to help her except Shantikumar, Salim and another student. Shantikumar is injured in his thigh by a bullet fired by a solider. All labourers also get infected by their courage and then they overpower the three soldiers and beat them. But the questions remain: Why did these people remain mute spectators of the rape of a woman of their own land? What would happen to the woman who had lost her honour? What is the course of action for her? And how dare these soldiers even think of committing such a crime? The answer to the last question is found by Amar who analyses the event and concludes that these white soldiers are men of the worst kind. They could think of doing so because India is enslaved by their country and their terror reigns in the minds of the native people. No one can even utter a single word against their sins. The answer to the first question is related to the above conclusion of Amar with the observation of Salim who thinks that the native people have lost their sense of self-respect and do not consider an act of crime against an Indian to be against them.

> So many of you kept staring yet did not do anything? . . . You can't protect the honour of your daughters and daughters-in-law. You would have thought that she is neither your daughter nor daughter-in-law. All daughters, daughters-in-law, and mothers in the country are yours. —23

The response to the second question: Munni does not go back to her home and wanders to take revenge by killing two English soldiers when they pass by the shop of Samarkant. She confesses to her crime but she professes not to be a murderer, for three white soldiers like them had spoiled her modesty six months before. Her act inspires Naina and Sukhada. Sukhada is even ready to worship Munni, for she has brightened the face of all her sisters. Amar considers her act as unjust because the English people whom she has killed did not rape her. Sukhada counters him angrily that all Englishmen are the same. She gives the example that some Frontier persons had kidnapped a white woman. The government then had planned to attack the entire Frontier. It did not even ask who the criminal was. For it, the entire province was criminal. This poor lady has not committed any crime; for she took recourse to such an action, because nobody was willing to stand by her, so she did so. She goes to the extent that she would do everything for her and even collect donations for pleading her case. In the court, "The concern that a woman would have for another can never be in a man's heart," (41) says she. Her case becomes a mission for all enlightened citizens particularly women. Though the judgement of the case is in her favour, she does not go back to her husband, for she considers herself too spoiled and defiled to return to him. Then passing a miserable life for a while she lands in a village where she devotes her time in the service of low caste people. Her case reveals Premchand's consent for violence, if needed, for self-respect against external colonization and oppression. Here Munni becomes a metaphor of enslaved India corrupted by the British colonizers. India rebels through Munni who takes revenge against her oppressors, suggesting aggressive revolution on the part of the colonized and its means of asserting self-respect and dignity. It is noteworthy that Premchand chooses a woman as the instrument of revenge against the British soldiers who are symbolic of oppressive and demeaning colonizers. Premchand's choice of a woman for revenge is deliberate and suggestive of Indian woman's might that if she chooses she can act for preserving her dignity in a way better than even her male counterparts.

Premchand in *Karmabhūmi* demonstrates that it is the duty of every being to perform one's *karma* for one's own motherland. This *karma* includes resisting oppression and colonization in all its manifestations, as he showed in the actions of his characters who not only resist but find out newer ways of resistance, i.e. insistence for one's own self-respect and honour for one's motherland against more powerful oppressors — be it more powerful native high caste people particularly brāhmaṇas and the priestly class, or the alien colonizers who consider India and Indian women as a commodity and an object of gratifying their lust. He finds new definition of *dharma* in its true sense and presents ways of practising *satyāgraha* and *krānti* or revolution that like charity begins at home with the individual who not only preaches but also practises it. Amar, with his example among many in the novel, further proves that it is the duty of high caste people to come forward and take part in the revolution and set the wrong right. Amar's work among low caste people in a far off village, Sukhada's, Naina's and Shantikumar's and Salim's work for low caste people's rights and Munni's revenge against the alien perpetrators of the heinous crime, support the view that the true service of the poor low caste people lies in making them conscious of their rights, and fighting for their rights with them is the only way to atone for the crimes of their ancestors. They are enlightened people belonging to high castes who succeed because the oppressed people have understood and recognized the cause and agents of their suppression and also ways of resisting them without caring for their lives. Without the participation of victims of suppression, no movement or *satyāgraha* can succeed. Upliftment of villages, low caste people, women and participation of the people belonging to all castes, locations, villages and cities, all religions — Hindus and Muslims — would ensure emancipation of land from slavery — physical and mental, native and alien. He further suggested that freedom from internal colonization, manifested in the form of oppression of women, low caste people and poor farmers is a precondition of its independence from external colonization.

Premchand's *Karmabhūmi* is, thus, unique not only in the entire corpus of Hindi literature but also in Premchand's fictional works, as it contains contours of a poetics of revolutions and of resistance not only through speculation but also execution. Ironically the upsurge in popularity of *Godāna* eclipsed *Karmabhūmi.* This is not an uncommon phenomenon in the world of "reception" that in different periods constitutes its own hierarchy. That is why the world of literary fortunes demands its own consideration, for every age needs its own reading of works and also its place in the corpus of the writer's work and in the world of words as well. Premchand's *Karmabhūmi* deserves being received by our generation as a text of discourse of resistance against colonization — internal and external.

The discourse of resistance against colonization in Hindi is characterized by ambivalence with a deep undertone of resistance, pragmatic indifference or acceptance and then resistance. Hence, a few points become clear: (i) the discourse of resistance attains its purpose and direction in the first half of the twentieth century when it is freed from indifference or ambivalence; (ii) the discourse of resistance is marked by polyvalence within one literary discourse and it varies from one literary discourse/writer to another; and (iii) Gandhi's discourse of resistance is the rallying point of all the three discourses, though there were a few discordant voices critiquing it in Indian writing in English in particular but not in Hindi that produced a rich corpus of writing under the influence of Gandhi in the first half of the preceding century.

VIII

Acknowledgement

I must express my sincere gratitude to Hans Breunig, University of Magdeburg, Germany for his astute reading of the first draft of the chapter and suggesting changes without which it would not have been what it is now. His comments were pertinent to the issue under discussion in the chapter. I cannot resist the temptation of sharing his views on a different yet untouched aspect in my chapter. The excerpts from Breunig's e-mail run thus:

You very plausibly argue how insensitive the English were (much like today's Americans in fact!) when they took over your country with its highly developed culture. That they learned how to pronounce imperatives in the respective languages bespeaks the quality of discourse they were interested in. Very striking is your quote how the English arrived poor and left as wealthy demi-gods.

Of course when you then look at, say, Schopenhauer, who wrote with great sympathy of the Upaniṣads, integrated the "veil of *māyā*" into his theory and tried to grasp what Indian philosophy was all about, you must be filled with a different emotion from that caused by what the occupying British did. But what would have happened to Schopenhauer if India had been a German colony? (Well, this is a very implausible hypothesis because the Germans, quite late, only wanted to have colonies because the British and almost every other European nation had them.) Would Indians understandably not rather turn their attention to the crimes committed by the occupiers instead of taking the philosophy of those who stayed at home seriously?

The people who are driven by monetary interests are usually not the greatest philosophers (actually, I dare say, on grounds a priori, that they cannot be; the first reported monopoly instigated by a philosopher in ancient Greece rather supports than disproves my point). But when I read the philosophy of John Locke — who is so badly materialized in handbooks, his spiritualism becomes indubitable once you go into his *Essay Concerning Human Understanding* (it is not true that he denies the existence of a priori principles and I can easily prove that he explicitly mentions the desire of happiness and the sympathy for others, in the shape of aversion to misery, as an inborn principle!). In the same way that people deny the thoughts which are subtle and make a system of what is blunt and distorted, they conduct their private and public lives. This is presumably why you did not see British philosophers in India in colonial days.

David Hume is another example of a great and benevolent mind — only those who went to India could reap greater profits by ignoring him. Rousseau's criticism of civilization is equally ignored.

> Your point concerning internal colonization is excellent. It is easy to deplore the tyranny of others if we can thus cover up our own — a phenomenon which holds everywhere in the world (look at how many governments use foreign arenas to keep the focus of public attention away from pressing internal affairs). At least there are people who can think their country free from all colonization. Perhaps we will not live to see more than that.
>
> — From Breunig's e-mail dated 8-9-2005

Further, he added his views on Western philosophers, particularly Schopenhauer who was sympathetic to India:

> Schopenhauer thinks that Immanuel Kant, the thinker he admires most, brought home to his readers, in a systematic and epistemological way, the central truth held by Plato and by Indian philosophers as an immediate conviction, namely the distinction between the Thing in Itself and mere Appearance. He writes (my own translation as I do not have an English version):
>
> "The same truth, presented in a different way, is the main dogma of the Vedas and the Purāṇas, the dogma of Māyā, under which name they understand nothing but what Kant calls Appearance, as opposed to the Thing in Itself: for the work of Māyā means the visible world in which we are, a charm conjured up, an ephemeral appearance without essence comparable to an optical illusion or a dream, a veil enveloping human consciousness, a Something of which it is equally false to say that it is or to say that it is not. Kant, however, not only expressed the same doctrine in an entirely new and original way, but he made it, through his most calm and sober presentation, a proven and indisputable truth; whilst Plato, like the Indians, had based their assertions merely on general intuition of the world, professed them as an immediate expression of their consciousness and presented them mythically and poetically rather than philosophically and clearly." (Arthur Schopenhauer, "Kritik der Kantischen Philosophie", in: Schopenhauer, *Die Welt als Wille und Vorstellung* (*The World as Will and Representation*), Zuercher Ausgabe. Werke in zehn Baenden, Band 2, 516) [about 3 pages into this text there is a major paragraph beginning "It was Kant's greatest merit . . .," then, in the same paragraph about 2 pages later.].

Schopenhauer thinks that European philosophers before Kant busied themselves with the veil of *māyā* (517). There can be no doubt, however true this may be that Schopenhauer is only a second-rate thinker in comparison with those he tends to criticize. I would not be surprised if his presentation of Indian philosophy was, in the last resort, as over-simplified as that of Kant, Leibniz and others.

7

Knowledge, Globalization and the Third World

An Indian Contextual Discourse

satya viśuddhistatrokta vidaivaikapadāgama ।
yukta praṇavarūpeṇa sarvavadavirodhinī ॥
— Bhartṛhari, *Vākyapadīya*, I, 9

Only that distinct intellect, free from all prejudices and predilections, expressible only through the word *praṇava* (*auṁ*), is true, for it is unifying without having any adversarial with other theses and views. And that is the prime principle of the Vedas.

On each occasion we should honour
Another man's sect, for by doing so
One increases the influence of one's own
Sect and benefits of the other man.
— Aśoka's inscription on a rock edict

. . . The only way the third world can transcend the sloganeering of its well-wishers is, first, by becoming a collective representation of the victims of man-made suffering everywhere in the world and in all times; second, by internalizing or owning up to the outside forces of oppression and then, coping with them as inner vectors; and third, by recognizing the oppressed or marginalized selves of the first and second worlds as civilizational allies in the battle against institutionalized suffering.
— Ashis Nandy, *Tradition, Tyranny and Utopias*

Jugrāfiyā mein sabase pahale yaha batāyā jātā hai ki duniyā gola hai । *ek ẓamāne mein beśaka, ye capaṭī hotī thī, phira gola karāra pāī gaī* । *gola hone kā fāyadā ye hai ki loga maśariqa kī tarafa se jāte haiṅ, magariba kī tarafa jā nikalate haiṅ* । *koī unako pakaḍa nahīṅ sakatā* । *smaglaroṅ, mujarimoṅ aura siyāsatadānoṅ ke liye baḍī āsānī ho gaī hai* ।

Hitler ne ẓamīna ko dobārā capaṭā karane kī kośiśa kī thī lekina vaha kāmayāba nahīṅ huā ।

purāne ẓamāne meiṅ ẓamīna Gula Muhammad kī taraha sakīna hotī thī । *sūraja aur āsamāna vagairah usake irda-girda ghūmā karate the* । *sāyara kahatā hai, "rāta-dina gardiśa meiṅ hai sāta āsamāna" phira ek Gaililyo nāmī sakhsa āyā aur usane ẓamīna ko sūraja ke irda-girda ghumānā śuru kara diyā, pādarī bahuta nārāẓa hue ki ye unko kisa cakkara meiṅ ḍāla diyā hai* । *Gaililyo ko to unhoṅne saẓā dekara āiṅdā isa kisma kī harakata ko karne se roka diyā, ẓamīna ko alabattā nahīṅ roka sake, harakata barābara kiye jā rahī thī* ।

Suru meiṅ duniyā me thoḍe hī mulka the । *loga khāsī amana-caina se ẓindagī basara karate the* । *pandrahavīṅ sadī meiṅ Columbus ne Amarīkā ko dariyāfta kiyā* । *usake bāre meiṅ do naẓariye haiṅ — kucha loga kahate haiṅ ki usakā kasūra nahīṅ, vaha Hindustāna ko, yāni hamako dariyāfta karane calā thā, magara galatī se Amarīkā ko dariyāfta kara baiṭhā* । *isa naẓariye se isa bāta ki tarabiyata milatī hai ki hama abhī taka dariyāfta nahīṅ ho pāye* ।

Dūsarā farīq kahatā hai ki nahīṅ, Columbus ne jāna-būjhakara ye harakata kī, yāni Amerīkā dariyāfta kiyā । *baharahāla agara yaha galatī thī bhī to bahuta saṅgīna galatī thī* । *Columbus to mara gayā, usakā khāmiyāẓā hama bhugata rahe haiṅ* ।

— Ibne Inśa

The very first lesson of geography informs us that the earth is round. No doubt, it used to be flat earlier but later it was found to be round. The benefit of its being round is that people go to the east but emerge in the west. No one can catch them. It has made things very easy for smugglers, criminals and politicians.

Hitler tried to flatten it again, but did not succeed.

In olden times, the earth used to be fixed like Gul Mohammed Shah (former Chief Minister of Kashmir). The sun and sky used to revolve around it. The poet says that the seven skies are in revolution days and nights. Then came a person named Galileo and he began to revolve the earth around the sun. Priests got very angry, and said they had been put in a big trouble. They punished him and thereby prevented him from indulging in this sort of mischief or misdemeanour in future. However, they could not stop the earth, and it keeps behaving in its own manner.

In the beginning, there were only a few countries in the world. People led their lives with much peace and ease. In the fifteenth century, Columbus discovered America. Regarding this there are two opinions — some people say that it was not his fault. He wanted to discover Hindustan, i.e. we people, but by mistake he discovered America. This view is supported by the fact that we are yet to be discovered.

The other group says that Columbus committed this mistake, i.e. of discovering America deliberately. Anyway if it was a mistake, it was a very grave one. Columbus died but we are paying for his mistake.

II

In Lieu of Script

KNOWLEDGE

A Chinese proverb says, "May you live in an interesting time!" Inscrutable that the Chinese are at least for me, I have not been able to decide if this proverb is a blessing or curse. Whatever its hidden meaning may be, we are perhaps living in an interesting, time, though every generation thinks of its time to be interesting, in its good mood. Ours is an interesting age because of rapid changes that have taken place in the last few decades and unprecedented gains made in advancing human development largely by technological breakthroughs. The rapid succession of these changes can be seen by examining various stages of human/societal transformation:

(i) Primitive society
(ii) Agrarian society
(iii) Industrial society
(iv) Post-Industrial society
(v) Information society
(vi) Knowledge society

The first stage can roughly be estimated from the beginning to fifth century BCE, the second from the fourth century BCE to eighteenth century CE, the third from the beginning of the nineteenth century to the middle of the twentieth century, the fourth from the middle of the twentieth century to the end of the century and the millennium, followed by the last phase primarily in the twenty-first century though its moorings might be seen in the last decade of the preceding century. The shift in terms of their principal engagement with products might be seen in terms of food materials, raw materials and agricultural products, industrial and post-industrial, i.e. post-managerial network products, information and knowledge products in all six societies respectively. One can easily discern that the duration of each succeeding phase has considerably decreased. The generation of knowledge has been at such a galloping pace that knowledge generated in the last quarter of the twentieth century, i.e. in roughly the last 20 years, has been more than the generation of knowledge in the preceding five thousand years. This explosion of knowledge makes our age 'interesting.' Even a cursory look at the history of knowledge informs us that between CE 00 and 1750, knowledge doubled in 1750 years; between 1750 and 1900 it doubled in 150 years, between 1900 to 1950 it doubled in 50 years, between 1950 and 2000 it doubled every 25 years. And now it is doubling every year because computing power is doubled in every 18 months and networking, i.e. bandwidth after every 12 months. On this basis one can roughly extrapolate that in 2020, and thereafter, it would double every month, and by 2050 almost everyday. The flipside of this interesting story is that the quantitative leap in generation of information and knowledge does not necessarily mean equal growth in wisdom. And secondly only a few nations and therein also only a few sections of the society control this pool of knowledge. Since knowledge flows through connectivity, those who wish to possess it should have connectivity. But this connectivity is limited to only a few privileged nations of the developed world. The UNDP 1999 Development Report noted that over the previous ten years, the number of people earning $1 a day or less had remained static at 1.2 billion, while the number of people earning less than $2 a day had increased from 2.55 billion to 2.8 billion. Further, by the late 1990s the fifth of the world's population living in the highest-income countries bottom had 86 per cent of world GDP, while 82 per cent of the bottom fifth just 1 per cent; 82 per cent of world export markets, the bottom fifth just 1 per cent; 74 per cent of the world telephone lines, the bottom fifth just 1.5 per cent. From the perspective of internet connectivity by seeing the world divided into developed and developing world, 15 per cent population of the world in the developed countries has 88 per cent connectivity with the internet, and 85 per cent population of the world living in developing countries has only 12 per cent connectivity. This asymmetrical generation and dissemination of knowledge suggests an alarming lack of uniformity and inequality in the distribution of knowledge economy in the society. In the present knowledge economy of society, the First World (and even the Second World) prospers, while the Third World suffers.[1]

---

1. Realizing the importance of knowledge, India established its Knowledge Commission. Dr Manmohan Singh, Prime Minister of India, launched the National Knowledge Commission on 2 August 2005 with the aim of "sharpening India's knowledge globally." According to the prime minister, India should be able to attract global investment in R&D activity. It is envisaged that the Commission would "come forward with creative ideas to promote the "knowledge base" of Indian economy and export its latent potential and leverage to make the country truly a "knowledge engine" of the world." According to the Chairman of the Commission, Sam Pitroda, the Commission would seek to bolster the knowledge base of the country including access to knowledge. It would also make proposals for the creation →

Knowledge, paths to it, its functions and ends vary from one culture and civilization to another. In the West and India they differed radically. The purpose of knowledge in the West was to exploit. This knowledge was based on intellect, logic, and rationality, whereas Indian tradition considered intuition or inspiration along with intellect as the means of knowledge. With the dominance of the West through colonization of the major part of the world, achieved through its scientific temper → rationality → enlightenment → industrialization → Industrial Revolution coinciding with expansion of colonization, the Western mode of knowledge was imposed on 'the wretched of the earth' in their bid to modernize the areas of darkness of the non-Western world. The ugly consequence of this phenomenon was that it suppressed the other non-Western modes of knowledge.

The other issue involved here is in the methodology of the Western knowledge system. It relies on difference as the mode of knowing. The philosophical disposition depends on difference to know a phenomenon, by seeing it in difference from other phenomena that are like it and unlike it. This theory of difference, relying on binaries, plays the game of othering and sees the world in terms of 'us' and 'them,' and focuses on studying and bringing out difference to divide and exploit them. This insistence on difference has been methodized by anthropology and social sciences in particular. Consequently, most studies, based on difference, in the non-Western parts of the world, supported or sponsored by Western institutions, aim at differences, leading to discord in these societies. The United States Educational Foundation in India (USEFI's) Campus Diversity Programme, for instance, promoted the study of diversity, not unity of the campus.

→ and application of knowledge and delivery of knowledge service.

The National Knowledge Commission of India submitted its Report in 2008 and 2009 in various parts. For a discussion of the Report please see Anadhesh Kumar Singh, "National Knowledge Commission Report to the Nation: Challanges and Opportunites", *University News*, November 2008, 2-8.

The difference is to be accepted, respected and recognized. The problem is when it is valorized beyond a point, when marginalization is fetishized, and made into a lucrative discourse. This problem crops up in humanities because literature is supposed to deal with literary values, and promote social harmony and values of life that suffer because of over-insistence on difference. The attitude is altogether different in Indian tradition as against the Western tradition. In the Indian tradition, *buddhi* or intellect is of two kinds: *nānātva buddhi,* i.e. differentiating intellect, and *anānātva buddhi,* i.e. unifying intellect. The unifying intellect sees the existence of different forms but does not fail to see the unifying element in all of them, which Bhartṛhari calls *sarvavādavirodhinī* in his *Vākyapadīya* (I.9). He said, *aprathaken śaktibhyaḥ prathaktven vartate.* [Though the *Brahman* (Infinite) is one, yet it appears different in different forms because of the strangeness of potency, though there is no genuine difference in the forms of *Brahman,* the Infinite.] (I.2). Forms are different in appearance, but underneath lies a common element that the differentiating intellect can/does not (want to) see. Further, he calls the differentiating intellect as inferior to the unifying intellect. It is so because the differentiating intellect does not lead to peace and harmony in society. It seeks difference but over-insistence on difference leads to discord. The question that arises here is: To what extent can we insist on difference? Or to what extent can we insist on assertion of marginalization? In an age of globalization, the entire world, particularly the "Third World," for its being more susceptible to fragmentation and exploitation by external and internal hegemonic forces, needs *ekatvabuddhi,* i.e. unifying intellect leading to wisdom for peace and harmony of humanity.

GLOBALIZATION

The term 'global village' was used by Marshal McLuhan in 1960 for a global network of communication. Globalization, related to it as a term, has a broad meaning but it has been reduced to a new market for earning maximum economic profit. The term market in the present world on the one hand includes an individual and on the other hand the whole world, particularly the 'developing' Third World. In simple terms, it is a camouflage for a new colonization. In the traditional sense the term 'market' used to be a visible place, but today it has become an invisible space with every individual as a market.[2]

Globalization has its ardent supporters and persistent enemies as well. People either love it or loathe it but cannot be indifferent to it. Let me take recourse to the views of one of the foremost Marxist theoreticians and critics and also to the Nobel Laureate and economist from India though based in the West and consider the issue from an Indian perspective. In his essay, "Notes on Globalization as a Philosophical Issue," Fredric Jameson deals with the phenomenon with a schematic account:

> Four positions on our topic seem logically available. The first affirms the opinion that there is no such thing as globalization. There are still two nation-states and the national situations; nothing is new under the sun. The second also affirms that

---

2. The term globalization stands for *bhūmaṇḍalīkaraṇa* and at times *vaiśvīkaraṇa*. However, the attitude to the term 'globe' and *viśva* differs in the Western and Indian cultures. Indian culture and civilization speak of *vasudhaiva kuṭumbakam* against the concept of the 'global village' that cares for the welfare of a few privileged, and of interest groups. In the concept of *vasudhaiva kuṭumbakam,* the buyer and seller relationship is replaced by equality of all; equality that marks the relationship among brothers and sisters, parents and children, each taking care of the other. One can contest the very practicality or existence of the concept in practice in history. But culture or civilization is not always known for what it practises but what it wishes to be and cherishes as ideals. Along with *vasudhaiva kuṭumbakam,* the other ideal *viśvagrāma* is worth mentioning here. Let me mention it here, for the sake of reference, as it appears in *Ṛgveda:*

   imāṁ rūdrāya tavase kapardine kṣayadvīrāya prabharāmahe matim,
   yathā naḥ śamasaddvipade catuṣpade viśvaṁ puṣṭam grāme asminnanāturam.
   — Maṇḍala 1, Sūkta 114

   This concept of *viśvagrāma* is free from greed, selfishness, discrimination or exploitation. It is based on sensitiveness, altruism, welfare of all, prosperity and happiness of all creatures and redemption of the entire world.

> globalization is nothing new; there has always been globalization and it suffices to leaf through a book like Eric Woolf's *Europe and the People Without History* to see that as far back as the Neolithic, trade routes have been global in their scope, with Polynesian artefacts deposited in Africa and Asian potsherds as far a field as the New World.
>
> Then, I supposed one should add two more: one that affirms the relationship between globalization and that world market which is the ultimate horizon of capitalism, only to add that the current world networks are only different in degree and not in kind; while a fourth affirmation (which I have found more interesting than the other three) posits some new or third multinational stage of capitalism, of which globalization is an intrinsic feature and which we now largely tend, whether we like it or not, to associate with that thing called post-modernity.
>
> — p. 54

All these positions might be found in existence or not in attendance in India. One can find in certain parts of India that there is nothing like globalization. At the same time some may say that it has been an ever-happening phenomenon in India in different periods. At least the present India does play its role, though ironically and marginally in the world market, if not as a leader then as a consumer of globalization. If consumption of weapons is an ironic and wrong criterion of being a participant in the market of globalization, in the year 2005 India came first in the arms purchase accounting for 15 per cent of global weapons sales or about $5.7 billion, though it was 127th on the Human Development Index of UNDP in 2004. To argue the case seriously, the multinational stage of capitalism can be seen in existence in some measure in the metros and also in emergence of a few Indian companies and arrival of a few multinational companies, though at the same time one sees a large part of India untouched by them. Moreover, in India one can see the co-existence of globalization and the nation state, something that globalization is supposed to transcend by proposing transnationalism or internationalism of the global village. In fact, in the 'Third World' societies like India, 'nation' has proved to be an important category to resist the evils of globalization by providing a rallying point to an already divided society. In the process, it aggravates uneven development existing between developed and developing nations, as has been pointed out by Noam Chomsky:

> Putting these details aside it seems fairly clear that one reason for the sharp divide between today's first and third world is that much of the latter was subjected to "experiments" that rammed free market down their throats whereas today's developed countries were able to resist such measures.
>
> That brings us to another feature of modern history that is hard to miss, in this case at the ideological level. Free market doctrine comes in two varieties. The first is the official doctrine that is taught to and by the educated classes and imposed on the defenceless. The second is what we might call "really existing free market doctrine": For thee but not for me: except for temporary advantage: I need the protection of the many States, but you must learn responsibility under the harsh regimen of "tough love." —p. 361

Against these views, Amartya Sen examines the issue in terms of its advantages and disadvantages and theory and practice. In "A World of Extremes: Ten Theses on Globalization," he considers globalization as the global economic order, thereby underscoring the significance of economics in it. He notes that the world has become incomparably richer than ever, but it presents abject misery and unprecedented prosperity simultaneously existing in it and in the process making it a world of extraordinary deprivation and staggering inequality. His ten theses in brief are:

1 Anti-globalization protests are not about globalization.
2. Globalization is not new, nor is it just Westernization.
3. Globalization is not in itself faulty.
4. The central issue, directly or indirectly, is inequality.
5. The primary concern is the level of inequality, not its marginal change.

6. The question is not just whether there exists some gain for all parties, but whether the distribution of gains is fair.
7. Many an economy is consistent with many different institutional conditions, and in conjunction with the latter, can produce different outcomes.
8. The world changed since the Bretton Woods agreement.
9. Both policy and institutional changes are needed.
10. Finally, we have reason enough to support globalization in the best sense of that idea.

Sen takes note of the changes in international economic, financial and political architecture of the world and institutions like the World Bank, and the International Monetary Fund among others. They were established in 1940s after the Bretton Woods Conference held in 1944. Much of Asia and Africa was still under the imperial rule that was about to melt within a decade. The power of NGO and the ideas of democracy, environment and human rights were still unrecognized in the world particularly after the Second World War. So he seeks changes at policy and institutional levels and also at the attitudinal level to it so that the inevitability of globalization is understood and its inherent advantages are not spilled on a spree of injudicious opposition to it. The basic question is inequality existing between two extremes — the rich and the poor societies, and also with a society like India. So the level of inequality is to be reduced and equal distribution of gains of globalization is to be ensured. Since human beings are the instruments of ensuring equality and fair distribution of gains, if globalization proves to be a folly or otherwise, we ought to be blamed more than the globalization itself.

It appears at least in India that globalization means Westernization, or Americanization to be precise, because of its unchallenged presence in the areas of economic activities and technological advancements, communication and warfare; and if globalization = Westernization = Europeanization = Americanization is an instrument of modernization, it is not to be discarded. As a society, and also as a participant in the process, we should be willing to stand and say no to Westernization or Americanization but accept modernization.

Let me consider globalization in an Indian context. Globalization, according to Amartya Sen, is not only inevitable but also an ever-happening phenomenon through its instruments or agencies like trade, travel, migration and consequent cultural reception and influence of the dissemination of knowledge — spiritual, scientific and technological, and a new economic order made possible by means of communication and transport. The movement of the process of globalization, i.e. coming together of different societies, countries and worlds, at the beginning of the preceding millennium (CE 1000) was 'from elsewhere to Europe', as it tried to absorb Chinese science and technology and Indian and Arab mathematics and knowledge systems. By the end of the millennium the paradigm shift had taken place in the movement and it came to be characterized by what can be termed largely 'from the West to elsewhere.' The donor civilizations became receivers and consumers. The rest of the world has been at the receiving end of this globalization of the West since then. It might be gauged from the fact that the five permanent members of the Security Council, the proponents and beneficiaries of globalization, are the top five exporters/traders of arms to the Third World, according to the Human Development Report, 1994.

India has been witness to globalization in its various forms and responded to them accordingly. There are five distinct stages of India's interaction and responses to globalization. The first stage began with the arrival of the tribes from the northern and western parts. The Indian response to this crude form of globalization was armed with political resistance, for they primarily aimed at exerting physical force and assimilation of those who stayed back. The second wave of globalization was in the form of its encounter with the Greeks from the West. The Indian response to it was in the form of King Porus's deeds and words to Alexander. Here I must add that Indians too went beyond their shores, as the records mention. Before Alexander's advent on India's western frontier, the tradition going back to the Aristotelian Aristoxenus (*c.* 300 BCE) related by Eusebius, the church father, mentions that an Indian visited Socrates in Athens and asked him the meaning of philosophizing, something in which he excelled incomparably. Socrates replied that he was studying the problems of human life. The Indian is said to have laughed at it and explained that it was impossible to do so without considering the divine. It was an idea of original wisdom, having religion and philosophy, metaphysics and ethics, Divine God and man undivided against the concept and project of philosophy as a rational and human enterprise.

Apart from King Porus's response, the response of the brāhmaṇas of India is worth noting here. In the encounter between Alexander and the Brāhmaṇas of India in the St. Ambrose version, the latter are said to have told the emperor in their highly suggestive response:

> If, then, you want to know the truth, come to India and lie naked in the wilderness, renouncing all the honours you love, all the marks of distinction you wear; only then shall we perceive you in our midst. You will then learn to love what you saw and wondered at a little while before. Nobody will fight any battle with you, nor will anyone have the power to carry away any other possessions. You will not live by the sweat and spoilation of others, for you will be rich in everything.
>
> — In Yaneswsky, p. 47

The next phase of globalization was in the form of the Islamic/ Muslim's arrival. The Indian response was the *bhakti* poetry of matchless literary and mystical significance in the world. It, on the one hand, redefined cultural unity and led to the synthesis of *sūfī* and *bhāṣā bhakti* poetry. The *sūfī*s were the earliest religious and philosophical interlocuters between Indian and Muslim worlds.

The phase that followed was the most sophisticated and subtle globalization in the form of the colonial encounter. The Indian response was in the form of Swami Vivekananda's spirituality, in terms of Sri Aurobindo's political and spiritual consciousness, and Mahatma Gandhi's strategy of resistance to the oppressive practices and attitudes of the colonizers. Gandhi ultimately led India to its Independence.[3]

The present phase of globalization is subtler than its preceding parts, for invisible institutions or interest groups, from abroad and native, come together and reap the consequent benefits. How India will respond to it remains to be seen. However, the preceding responses do suggest that Indian society would be able to find its own answer to the phenomenon. It might not produce individual messiahs to lead as in the preceding phases, but the collective social will with its contribution to the nation will succeed in receiving globalization critically and judiciously and thereby ensure fair and equal sharing of the benefits of the process.[4] Indian society has realized that to sustain itself and move ahead, it has to contribute to the welfare of the world and excel in three domains of *śastra, śāstra* and *arthaśāstra*. The document, "Vision India: 2020", forwarded by A.P.J. Abdul Kalam, Former President of India, is an evidence of this realization. Only by doing so will it succeed in eradicating inequality — eco-social-political — and make its voice heard at the national and international fora.

The Third World

It would be unwise to consider a term or category when it has been found to be irrelevant and has fallen out of usage, but in the history of knowledge it is quite fascinating to examine the ruins

---

3. For the discussion of resistance in Aurobindo and in particular in M.K. Gandhi, please see Avadhesh Kumar Singh, "Theorizing/Narrating Resistance and Colonization in India", in the present book.

4. For discussion of globalization, its impact and possible response to it from an Indian perspective please see "Decolonization and India", *Literary Discourse: Indian and Western,* ed. A.K Tripathi, P.K. Pandey and Sanjay Kumar, Delhi: Creative Book, 2005.

of a category because that helps us in understanding the forces that brought it into existence and also those that made it redundant.

The preceding century witnessed the redundancy of ideological movements and formulations with which humanity had lived for quite some time. The last quarter of the century saw the failure of the Left (Communism/Marxism) and the Right (Liberalism) as well. Communism, the god, failed the Left (symbolized to a good extent by the USSR and China) and the god of neo-liberalism, represented by the US, failed conservatism. Between the powerful Left and Right, the Third World tried to make space for itself. And if it failed, it should not surprise us, for many powerful ideologies and configurations more powerful than the given one failed in the preceding century.

The term Third World was coined by a French economist and demographer Alfred Sauvy in 1952 for the Third Estate of pre-revolutionary France. By this term he referred to social groups other than the most privileged groups of the day, the clergy and the nobility, the last two attending to the First and Second Estates respectively (Krieger, 908-09). In the common political parlance the term came to describe the emerging states other than the First World including Europe and North America in particular. The Socialist countries of Eastern and Central Europe were put in the category of the Second World. Mao Zedong of China gave an exclusive connotation to the term, as he considered the USA and the USSR as part of the First World, the other developed countries and satellites of the super powers as the Second World, and the rest of Asia (with the exception of Japan), Africa and Latin America as the Third World. Sauvy's phrase, used for some other purpose, replaced pejorative terms like 'backward areas,' 'underdeveloped countries,' 'societies in transition,' and 'peripheral countries.' In the 1940s the poor and marginalized countries of Africa, Asia and Latin America, were described as backward. In the 1950s it was replaced by 'underdeveloped.' The term 'Third World' was later rejected by the East because it implied a non-socialist alternative to capitalism, and by the West because it means that the countries of the Third World were poor because of the exploitation of the First World.

The term 'Third World' with its gradual acceptance began to have political and economic connotations. In the former sense it referred to countries on the margins of the bipolar world, and in the latter it referred to the low income countries. Put together it came to be associated with politically non-aligned and economically developing and less industrialized nations of the world. Along with its currency, some scholars questioned the terms on the grounds of disparate values, interests and objectives of the so-called Third World countries. C.R. Hensman stated, "The notion of an independent southern Third World is a romantic one at best. It can be studied only as an idea, as a dream, as a myth, or as political speculation, and not as a historical, sociological and moral reality"(36). There are others who consider the world in terms of three tiers of economy. For instance Immanuel Wallerstein opines that there is a single world economy and that is capitalist. The three tiers of the world economy are core, periphery and semi-periphery (Wallerstein 909). In the 1960s and 1970s, Third Worldism espoused the cause of the 'wretched' community of people and romanticized their struggle by proposing the developed countries as oppressors and exploiters. In the 1970s some other terms came in usage. To get rid of the sense of inferiority implicit in Third World, the term 'developing nations' came in use with distinction between 'oil producing' and 'non-oil-producing' nations. The terms such as 'newly industrializing,' 'less developed nations,' 'developing countries,' and 'Third World Countries' were used interchangeably during the period. The terms 'South' and 'North' came to be used as a geographic expression for two hemispheres. Willy Brandt in his Report, 'North-South: A Programme for Survival', and Julius Nyerere, the head of the South Commission, rejected the term 'Third World' and used the term 'South' for developing States and 'North' for industrialized countries. According to the Report of the South Commission, the

South exists on the periphery of the developed countries of the North. It stated,

> while most of the people of the North are affluent, most of the people of the South are poor; while the economies of the North are generally strong and resilient, those of the south are mostly weak and defenceless; while the countries in the North are, by and large, in control of their destinies, those of the South are vulnerable to external factors and lacking in functional sovereignty. —p. 1

After a while the term 'South' as against the North lost its appeal, and by the 1990s, scholars and analysts began to pronounce its death or end. N. Harris did it in 1987, followed by J.F. Bayart and M. Berger. According to Bayart, the validity of the category Third World was lost, for these countries were defined by their relations with the Super Powers during the Cold War. According to him, at a time when economies of the world have been integrated and a near universal market economy has come into existence, the Third World countries can no longer keep on harping as the victims of the bipolar world (Bayart, 51-71).

The term Third World may have lost the significance that it had in the 1960s and 1970s and it might be politically incorrect to use the term but it is still valid as a trope for a variety of reasons. The countries that form(ed) part of it may be as varied as they themselves are, yet all of them are post-colonial countries that attained their independence in the nineteenth century (the Latin American countries) and the twentieth century (Asia and Africa). They had and still have rich natural and human resources — oils, raw materials, knowledge systems as they were centres of major civilizations of the world. They have been victims of war caused by the fall-out of adversarial relationships between superpowers, and also the sites of political and social upheavals of different sorts. These countries accounted for three-fourths of the world population, and by the turn of the century it increased to four-fifths. Most of the two billion, each poor and desperately poor, of the six billion people on the planet by the end of the twentieth century were in the Third World (Woechlcke 28). Even after the redundancy of the term and also of the following term NAM (Non-Aligned Movement) that stood for the Third World, as a trope it stands for the dream of a new world order based on equity, equality, commonality of interests, inter-dependence and co-operation among different countries.

Now these countries — call them by whatever name as the Third World, South, NAM or developing countries — are at the receiving end in the process of globalization and in the attendent clash of knowledge systems in which their own systems have almost lost the battle. Evidently, it is the West's desire to study them in their institutions; for the West studies systems other than its own, either before or after controlling and fashioning them for their advantage.

What are then the emergent images of the new world order built on the ruins of various terms, categories, and movements like the Third World? In this, American analysts and theorists have proposed models or paradigms. Robert E. Harkavy, prominent among them, has visualized the post-Cold War era in seven models or theses; the three-block neo-merchantalist theses; the multipolar balance of the power model; the clash of civilization thesis; the unipolar dominance model; the zones of peace *versus* zone of turmoil; the global village model, and the bipolar redux model. All these models are self-explanatory, though not necessarily mutually exclusive. Yet none of them has the Third World in its scheme. These countries can at the most become the victims of neo-colonization. Since economic block would decide the future vision of the world, there are three possible blocks (as advocated by analysts like Lester Thurow, W.R. Mead, Edward Luttwak and Jeffrey Garten): (i) a German-centred European bloc; (ii) a USA-led Western Hemisphere bloc, centred on the North American Free Trade Agreement (NAFTA); and (iii) a Japan-led Pacific Rim region. In these schemes, the terms like 'global village' and globalization are empty, meaningless slogans, and in reality instruments of exploiting the weaker countries of the world.

Admittedly, geography has come to an end, distances have been abolished and terrains have been rendered irrelevant, and information technology has woven the world into a texture. But who controls the agents of this revolution caused by technology, means of communication and explosion of information? The Third World countries can claim their bit in the service sector, not in Research and Development or hardware. The technology and information that were supposed to be instruments of emancipation and freedom have become or are becoming weapons of neo-colonization, destabilization, international terrorism and instruments of Pepsification, Cocacolonization and McDonalization. The Third World societies are reduced to being mere consumers of these processes because they do not manufacture/produce knoweldge or *śāstra*, and without *śāstra* one cannot actively participate in the industry of *śāstra*, *śastra* or *arthaśāstra*, indispensable for survival in the present bipolar world divided into zones of peace and prosperity and turmoil and instability.

Moreover, the use of the term Third World as a trope is still meaningful for the othered, exploited, and oppressed societies, or such sections of society in all the three worlds. In this sense, the Three Worlds theory is also meaningful. There is a 'Third World' in the first and second worlds, and a 'First World' in the Third World countries with the difference in the percentage of people constituting the Third World. For instance, the percentage of people forming the 'Third World' in a Third World country may be the percentage of people of the 'First World' in a First World country, and the percentage of people forming the 'Third World' in a 'First' or 'Second World' country might be the percentage of the 'First World' in a 'Third World' country. This percentage would vary from country to country, but the fact remains that these worlds exist. If they do, they are not solely responsible for their sad state. The first world has also played its role, and it still does, in their conditions. Among the options available to the 'Third World' are included, what Ashis Nandy suggests in his *The Intimate Enemy* by trying to imagine, 'therapeutic spaces of reciprocal rehabilitation and healing,' in relation to the relationship between colonizer and colonized. The colonizer and colonized now are neo-colonizer (First World) and neo-colonized (Third World). More important than this is the option of trying the elimination of these Third Worlds wherever they exist which is possible only after the unity of all these Third Worlds has been established against their exploitation and for sharing the benefits of globalization.

The 'Third World' as an eco-political category or 'Third Worldism' as an 'ism' might be obsolete, but in literature 'Third World' literature still makes sense, for it makes us aware of pressures — literary, cultural, political and (literary) theoretical, exerted by the First/Second World literature, as Indian academia to a good extent gives the impression of being dependent, even subordinate to them, particularly to its American and British counterparts in the university system, as has been discussed by Aizaz Ahmad[5] (43-45). The major problem with the category, despite its relevance, tends to be hegemonic as the 'Third World' literature places literature in English at a pedestal higher than indigenous non-English literature, for instance, *bhāṣā* literature in India.

III

Postscript

IN LIEU OF CONCLUSION

I began the piece with an extract from Ibne Insha in order to respond to globalization in literary terms in a way different from economists. Literature and economics respond to it differently.

---

5. For more incisive and comprehensive discussion of the "Three World Theory" and "Third World Literature" please see Aizaz Ahmad, "Literary Theory and 'Third World Literature' : Some Contexts" and "Three Worlds Theory: End of a Debate", in his *In Theory, Classes, Nations, Lteratures,* Delhi: Oxford University Press, 1994, pp. 43-72 and 287-318, respectively.

The latter, despite all criticism of globalization, ultimately submit to its charm with the hope of reaching its benefits (read 'at the most fringe benefits') to the poor in underdeveloped or developing Third World societies. Economists cannot write it off altogether, for that would put a question mark before the very existence of their subject and discipline, and in the process to the validity of their own existence. Literature, on the other hand, considers it as a game of hegemony of the privileged against the unprivileged that are marginalized, exploited and suppressed. By its very nature, literature sides with the marginalized and speaks through the language of minimization or maximization to elicit certain emotive state of mind. It works through various literary techniques and devices such as 'defamiliarization,' 'tension,' 'gesture,' 'myth,' 'metaphor' or 'images.' An image or word picture is primarily a reductionist device, for it reduces the entire phenomenon to something, but that is the way literature operates as a system and criticizes the phenomenon. The concept or image of globalization used to be understood as Westernization that was reduced later to Europeanization and scholars like Edmund Husserl and Martin Heidegger had advocated the Europeanization of the world.[6] This trend found subscribers even among non-Western scholars like Dipesh Chakravorty and Deepak Lal who support Europeanization, empire or globalization in an indirect

---

6. Edmund Husserl, on the basis of his notions of the exclusive spirit of 'philosophy,' 'science,' and 'pure theory' that he considered as the European phenomena, proposed that only Europe could provide other traditions with a universal framework of meaning and understanding as well. "Hence, the other traditions (including Indian) will have to 'Europeanize' themselves, whereas we, if we understand ourselves properly, will never Indianize, ourselves". According to him, the "Europeanization of all foreign parts of mankind is the destiny of the earth."

   (E. Husserl, *Die krisis ger europaeischen Wissenschaften und die transcendental Phaenomenologie,* ed. W. Biemel, The Hague, 1954, 320.)

   Like Husserl, Martin Heidegger proposed the 'complete Europeanization of the earth and mankind' in a less arrogant and unambiguous manner. Like Husserl he credits only the Greek European tradition with the genuine concept of philosophy. But he shares only a little of Husserl's enthusiasm

→

manner in *Provincializing Europe* and *In Praise of Empires: Globalization and Order* respectively. In literary discourse, globalization is used as a synonym of Americanization. That's why I took recourse to Ibne Insha's views on America from a literary perspective. But globalization has changed character of American society, as a good number of Indians, Pakistanis and Chinese and others are in

---

→ regarding the global mission. The domains of knowledge like philosophy, science and technology might have dominance with the expansion of European forms of knowledge, but the very desire of dominance on the earth speaks of their being parochial. Moreover, despite dominating them, they have failed in providing a medium in which these traditions could realize their full potential, meaning and purpose. The way out then is in trying to transcend, what he calls, "What is European," and reach beyond "Occident and Orient." But he sees no way to circumvent the means of technology and conceptual framework provided by the European tradition. (M. Heideggar, *Unterwegs Zur Sparche,* Pfullingen, 1959, 103, II rpt. 1960.)

Ironically, Husserl proclaimed the inevitability of the global mission of Europe a few years before the beginning of Second World War, by which time the European Empire had begun to melt. The end of Second World War witnessed the hastening of the process. Husserl in a way proposed the intellectual colonization of the 'Rest' of the world by the 'West.' What a great irony it has been that thinkers and scholars from other than European traditions, including Indians like J.L. Mehta, Dipesh Chakrabarty and Deepak Lal, among others, have not only accepted their dominance, but also genuflect before them! For instance, Mehta accepts the irretrievable and inescapable global presence of Western science and technology. He avers that there is no other way open, to us in the East, but to go along with this Europeanization and go *through* it. Only through this voyage into the foreign and the strange can we win back our own selfhood; here as elsewhere, the way to do what is closest to us is the longest way back (Mehta 1967: 466). If this is what Mehta believes and if he thinks the Europeanization of the earth as irreversible, there is no need for him to think. The Europeans would do it better than others including Mehta and his ilk that think like him. If he is right, all non-European traditions including Indian have become redundant. The fact, however, is because of the Husserls, Heideggers in Europe and the Mehtas in India, that the traditions like Indian thought are more meaningful today and do not suffer at all from obsolescence. Moreover, if the 'voyage' into Europeanization is the only way of winning back *one's own selfhood*, it is not the longest way back but the worst way. Has any tradition or society ever regained its self-hood through others? Will the 'selfhood' regained thereafter be worth it? Will it not be 'other-hood' →

America. America as a trope now stands for prosperity at the expense of others, power and dominance. If he were given a chance now in the first decade of the twenty-first century, Ibne Insha would consider the phenomenon called America and Americanization not in a lesson of geography but in a chapter or treatise in economics. However, the problems of economics have much to do with geography, because geography and cartography

---

→ camouflaged and called 'selfhood'? Mutual interaction leading to mutual enrichment of different traditions is always desirable, but not submission of one to the other.

Dipesh Chakrabarty reads the Enlightenment as symptomatic of a Eurocentricism that will not allow reciprocity of influence between the West and the Rest. In his *Provincializing Europe* he has no problem in acknowledging the benefits of the Enlightenment. Please see Dipesh Chakrabarty, *Provincializing Europe: Postcolonial Thought and Historical Difference,* N.J. Princeton University Press, 2000.

Deepak Lal in his *In Praise of Empires: Globalization and Order* (2005) favours empire(s) intellectually and considers them essential for peace and prosperity in the world, for they ensure stability, disseminate knowledge, provide a framework for beneficial trade and awaken people on the path of progress. The question which then arises is: what kind of empire(s) is/are needed? The answer he gives is that the kind of empire needed is an empire that promotes gentlemanly capitalism and secures an international liberal economic order. Will the US abdicate from the responsibilities self-imposed or thrust upon it ? Against these worries he proposes two moralist positions: (i) the Americans will refuse to recognize themselves as an imperial power, for they would not accept to bear the cost of being called an empire; (ii) the neo-cons Americans will accept their country's imperial destiny and thereby promote the wrong kind of empire. They would seek deep moral justification of their act with their bid to promote democracy and Westernization. He, in his defence of empire, forgets that democracy cannot be trasplanted, and that America has no mandate either from God or even from its own people to democratize the societies/states, for it is an undemocratic consideration to impose. Moreover, the very claim of the author that empire is beneficial for the colonies is counterfactual. Against his argument that the British liberal Empire was an engine of economic growth, it must be said that the Empire was neither liberal nor beneficial. Can the Empire that imposed all kinds of differential tariffs and exploitative taxes on salt be called liberal in the sense of the term? Or is the plea for empire in the name of order an excuse for validating globalization?

were the instruments of colonization and of appropriating and controlling geophysical resources in order to exploit them to enrich one's own economy.

For the postscript I take recourse to a Hindi work by Kashinath Singh who in his *Kāśī kā Assī* unveils the ugly impact of Americanization or globalization with a discussion on the presence of Americans in Varanasi and later on the decadence of the city. Catherine, an American, working on the city with the support of data collected by her about the *rāṇḍa*s, *sāṇḍa*s and *saṁnyāsī*s (widows, bulls and *sādhu*s), speaks about the demographic changes in the last five years and conclude, *Banārasa Mar Rahā Hai* (Varanasi is dying) (p. 110). Gaya Singh, a character, is critical of those inhabitants of Varanasi who accept such pronouncements about their city by foreigners particularly Americans uncritically, for they are beholden to everything American. Targeting Deenbandhu Tiwari, Singh who supports the American view, says that Tiwaris among brāhmaṇas, riding a camel, cholera among the diseases, and *paṭwārī* among the kāyasthas are the most unreliable. Gaya Singh globalizes Indian folk common sense as he rewrites this popular saying by adding 'American Woman' to the list. Here comes the crux of discussion between the two, proposing Americanization, i.e. globalization as the real cause of the death of Varanasi. I'll transcribe the discussion in Hindi to preserve the punch and feel of Hindi, and then translate it, though loosely, into English. The postscript is not in lieu of a conclusion, but is a conclusion itself of a beginning showing the way literary creativity in *bhāṣā*s has begun to respond to globalization in their societies without being awed by its theorists, supporters and opponents:

> *Banārasa to mara rahā hai lekin vahāṅ se nahīṅ jahāṅ ke āṅkaḍe devījī de gaī haiṅ* । *devījī, tumhāre pāsa to pūre nagara ke haiṅ, lekin mere pāsa to sirf assī ke haiṅ* । *aur unhīṅ ke binā para maiṅ batā sakatā hūṅ ki sīḍhiyoṅ para kitne kilo heroin, kitne kilo brown śugara, kitne kilo carasa aur kitne ḍibbe morphine kī khapata huī hai isa bīca* । *ghāṭoṅ para viyāgarā, penāgarā, niyāgarā aur kina-kina cījoṅ ke powder bika rahe haiṅ puḍiyoṅ maiṅ do-do sau rupaye ki-eka puḍiyā aur kharīda kauna rahe haiṅ — būḍhe* । *corī-chipe* । *pension kī rakama roṭī-dāla*

meiṅ nahīṅ puṣte mein jā rahī hai । aur suno, gubbāre aur gullī-ḍaṅḍā kī umara vāle bacce ghāṭa, chhata aur khiḍakiyāṅ dekhakara, jawāna ho gae haiṅ samaya se pahle hī । kisa taraha ghūrate haiṅ isī umara meiṅ sayānī laḍakiyoṅ ko । kabhī dekhā hai?

"yaha to T.V. kā kamāla hai! dīnabandhu ne asahamati zāhira kī ।"

"nahīṅ, T.V. to nirodha aur condom bāṅṭa rahī hai, yah to vaha sīkha rahe haiṅ jo dekha raheṅ haiṅ ।"

"lekin āpa khāmakhvāha nārāẓa haiṅ amarikā se? jo ḍhāī-tīna haẓāra videśī haiṅ galiyoṅ meiṅ, unameṅ se sabase kama amarīkī haiṅ ।"

"galiyoṅ meiṅ aur sabase kama," Gaṅgā Singh haṁse । "kyā ho rahā hai galiyoṅ meiṅ, dekhā hai kabhī? "dollar kā dhandhā ।" dīnabandhu, dollar amarikā kī jībha hai । vaha suru meiṅ mulka ko aise cāṭaṅā śuru karatā hai । jaise gāya apane bachaḍe ko pyāra ke sātha cāṭatī hai । bāda meiṅ jaba camaṛī chilane lagatī hai, khāla utarane lagatī hai । darda śuru ho jātā hai, jībha para kāṅṭe ubharane lagate haiṅ, jabaṛe calane kī āwāẓ sunāī paṛatī hai । tab patā calatā hai kī yaha jībha gāya kī nahīṅ, kisī aura jānavara kī hai । aur kyā samajhate ho, jo dekhate-dekhate deśa kā deśa cabā gayā ho aur usa meiṅ bhī soviyat rūsa ke jaisā deśa — usake liye nagara kā mohallā kyā cīẓa hai?

"ab yahī dekho । āpa laṅkā se hara śāma āte ho, bhāṅga khāte ho, cāya pīte ho, gapa-śapa karate ho aur lauṭa jāte ho । magana rahate ho, ki vāha re hama । liṅga para globe uṭhākara tāna diyā hamane aur duniyā dekhatī raha gayī । kabhī jānane kī kośiśa ki, kyā ho rahā hai yahāṅ? patā hai āpako ki mohalle meiṅ kitane makāna kharīde haiṅ inhoṅe lokala ādamiyoṅ ke nāma se? makāna lokala ādamī ke nāma aur raha ye rahe haiṅ । kitane aise makāna haiṅ jinakī marammata ke liye inhoṅne paise lagāye haiṅ khuda rahane ke liye? pharẓī śādiyāṅ kī haiṅ vīẓā ke extension ke liye । bīsoṅ cyber caffe khulavāye haiṅ, gharoṅ meiṅ apane janasamparka aur suvidhāoṅ ke liye । ise hī hum samajhate haiṅ globalization? unheṇ jitanī bāra ānā-jānā ho — āyeṅ-jāyeṅ, jaba taka rahnā ho taba taka raheṅ, lekina hama? hai hamārī haisīyata, eka bāra bhī amarīkā jāne kī? hamārā ghara unakā ghara hai, lekina unakā ghara unhīṅ kā ghara hai, hamārā-tumhārā nahīṅ । abhī kyā dekha rahe ho, thoṛe dina bāda bhī ye boleṅge — assī jarjara ho rahā hai, ḍhaha rahā hai, mara rahā hai, hameṅ de do to nayā kara deṅ —

ekadama camacama । *kala banārasa camakāyeṅge, parsoṅ dillī ko ṭhīka kareṅge, narsoṅ pūre deśa ko hī goda le leṅge aur jhulāyeṅge, khilāyeṅge apanī goda meiṅ* । *yaha bāda mein patā calegā ki hama kisakī goda meiṅ haiṅ* । — *jasodā maiyā kī yā pūtanā ki?"*

— 112-13

Banāras is dying but not for those whose data have been given by Madam. Madam! You do have data about the whole city but I have only about Assī. And on their basis I can say how many kilogrammes of heroin, brown sugar, charas and how many packets of morphine have been consumed in the intervening period? Packets of Viagra, Penagra, Niagra and powders of many other things are being sold on the *ghāṭ*s. One packet for rupees two hundred each. And who are the buyers — old people purchase it clandestinely. The pension money is being spent not for *roṭī-dāl* (simple food consisting of bread and lentils) but for making the body strong and sturdy. And listen to me! Children who are supposed to play with balloons and *gullī-ḍaṅḍā* have attained puberty prematurely by staring at the *ghāṭ*s, roofs and windows. Have you ever seen the way they stare at grown up girls at this very age?

"This is the miracle of TV." Deenbandhu expressed his disagreement.

"No, TV is distributing Nirodh and Condoms. These children learn what they see."

"But you are unnecessarily angry with America. Among the two or three thousand foreigners that you see in the streets, the number of Americans is the smallest."

"So small in the streets?" Gaya Singh laughed.

"Have you ever seen what is going on in the streets? Business of dollars. Deenbandhu! Dollar is the tongue of America. In the beginning it licks just like that. Like a cow licks a calf with affection. Later on when the skin begins to be peeled and flayed, and it pains, thorns appear on its tongue, and the sound of jaws is heard, then one comes to realize that it is not the tongue of a cow but of some other animal. And what do you understand?

The country that had swallowed a country in its entirety — well before our eyes — that too a country like Soviet Russia, a locality of a city is of no consequence to it."

"Now you see, you come from Lanka every evening, to have *bhāṅga* (hemp), take tea, gossip and then return. Happily and haughtily you compliment yourself and think, "We are great." Lifting the globe on our phallus we pulled it all over, and the world stood aghast. Have you ever tried to know about what is happening here? Do you know how many houses they have purchased here in your localtiy in the name of local residents? The houses are in the name of the local people and the foreigners live in them. How many houses have been repaired with their money for them to stay in? They have registered fake marriages for the extension of their visas. They have got scores of cyber cafes opened in the houses for their communication and comforts. This we consider as globalization. They can come and go as they wish, stay as long as they want. But what about us? Do we have resources to go to America even once? Our house is theirs, but their house is only theirs, not ours. This is just a beginning. After some time they would say, "Assī is in a decadent state, it is eroding, and dying. Hand it over to us (Americans), and we would make it absolutely new, and make it glitter." They would make Banāras shine tomorrow, repair Delhi day after tomorrow, and two days later, they would change the entire country, and rock and dandle in their lap. Only later on, we shall come to know if the lap is of Yaśodā or Pūtanā.

The extract shows difference between two knowledges — data-based knowledge of social sciences and language of metaphors of literary discourse. It further informs that knowledge may be manipulated, depending upon attitude and agenda of the user. The 'Third World' countries like India have to be increasing conscious of it and by using different kinds of knowledges discriminate between Yaśodā and Pūtanā and expose subtle ways of neo-colonization — external and internal as well.

8

Towards a New Framework of Literary Studies in Post-Colonial India

I BEGAN the present piece with the hope of preparing a horoscope of literary studies in India. By the time it came to its end, I realized that my endeavour has turned out to be nothing but the horror-scope of English studies in India. Though English is the source of my livelihood, yet my concern lies neither with English nor with comparative literature, but with such literary studies in India as would help me know and understand the languages and literatures of our country, respect their differences and foreground the commonalities, a process that could play a role in integrating the country, without ignoring or neglecting languages and literatures beyond our national frontiers. Unfortunately, language and literary studies and research even in post-Independence India have increasingly based themselves on the paradigms of Western ethnography that aggressively seek and paddle difference in the so-called post-colonial societies so that with the valorization of difference, the possibilities of their disintegration can be gauged and then exploited so as to colonize these societies anew.

The 'Crisis' of Comparative Literature and India

The statement that comparative literature is dead may fail to disturb the students of literature any more, for in the last quarter of the preceding century the 'end' or 'death' of things familiar and fundamental to us, like God (Nietzsche), history (Francis Fukuyama), geography (Arvind N. Das), politics (Martin Jacques), literature (Alvin Kernan) and the author (Roland

Barthes), among several other things, has been pronounced. At least these prophets of doom would have liked us to believe these prophecies. Susan Bassnett added her mite to these by making her pronouncement regarding comparative literature.[1] In one sense, however, comparative literature was always already 'dead,' in 'crisis,' with 'no substance in it,' 'a non-subject,' without meaningful methodology or nomenclature, as Benedetto Croce, Lane Cooper or Rene Wellek, among others, informed us, long ago. Questions and pronouncements such as these have, however, only given new purpose and direction to comparative literature.

A crisis is a decisive point in the history of a discipline. As in the case of a patient, the crisis in comparative literature was a question of concern for Rene Wellek. However, the present crisis in the opening decade of the twenty-first century is a decisive point not only in the history of comparative literature but also for literary studies in India. Changes in the form and reception of literature from the 'solid' written work to the fast-melting visual text notwithstanding, literature still survives, and so do literary studies or comparative literature. Comparative literature, thrives in its transformed state as cultural and post-colonial, and translation studies, though the last had been hitherto denigrated as 'marginalized,' 'subsidiary,' 'derivative,' 'subservient,' 'parasitic,' and even 'juvenilia.' In the light of these doomsday pronouncements about the present state of comparative literature, it may seem ironical to several to think of envisioning the future of literary studies in India in terms of comparative literature.[2] The so-called crises notwithstanding comparative literature, it is of interest to us, for it suits the Indian linguistic pluralistic situation. In fact, the 'crisis' in comparative literature is nothing but a consequence of the challenges and examinations of mainstream

1. Susan Bassnett, *Comparative Literature: An Introduction*, London: Routledge, 1994.

2. Structuralists had rejected the idea of synonymy and with their emphasis on binary oppositions refused to admit translation studies as a serious sphere of academic operations, which affected the place →

European and particularly American versions of the discipline. On the contrary, in a true and natural linguistic pluralism such as one finds in India, the question of a crisis in comparative literature does not arise, because all Indian languges and literatures would have to move sooner or later to the methodology of comparative literature, as it comes to us. In India, literary studies are in a state of crisis because we ignored linguistic and literary realities for so long and did not take recourse to the methodology of comparative literature, either as it existed, or in modified form to suit us, as Sisir Kumar Das and Amiya Dev among others have long been suggesting.[3]

Indian Linguistic and Cultural Realities

Before appraising the state of literary studies in India, it would be appropriate to examine Indian linguistic and cultural realities. Linguistic pluralism is as old as India, as a result of which the Indian consciousness is fundamentally a translational consciousness, though the word 'translation' may not have been used in its traditional sense. The question of how so many literary trends, traditions and movements have been thriving in India, which has been a multilingual country for centuries, without there having been any theories and methodologies of translation demands an answer. Those who live in linguistic and cultural pluralism do not need either the term 'translation' or its

→ of translation in literature studies and comparative literary studies adversely. Only in the last quarter of the century have translation studies been taken up seriously with the interventions of scholars like I.A. Richards, S.S. Prawer, Eugene Nida, Andre Lefevre and Susan Bassnett among others.

3. The credit for using the term Indian comparative literature should go to Professor Amiya Dev who uses the term in 'Towards Comparative Indian Literature' in K.A. Koshi (1987). Credit for arguments in its favour should go to S.K. Das's 'Why Comparative Literature in India?' in Amiya Dev and S.K. Das (1989). Professor Das's words regarding Indian comparative literature are worth quoting: 'Our comparative literature must be comparative Indian literature because nothing else can be the basis for our literary study' (100).

methodologies, for these are part of their cerebral systems. Translation is generally a solution that is developed by a monolingual society confronted with other languages. If monolingualism is a curse, translation is ironically a happy by-product of this curse. And monolingualism has ever been unthinkable and unaffordable in India.

Pluralism is a slogan in the West, but a reality in India.[4] The Indian linguistic and literary scenario has always been pluralistic with the co-existence of Sanskrit (as the compositional language). Prākṛts (as many as five) and Apabhraṁśa in the ancient period: a three-language formula that had existed without the need for any state intervention or commission. The poet, whether Vedic, or later on, Buddhist or Jain, had the choice of expressing himself in any of these three languages — singly or in combination, a state that continued till as late as the twelfth century, when the Jain poetician Hemcandrācārya wrote in *Kāvyānuśāsana* that the *mahākāvya* or epic could be written in three languages, i.e. Sanskrit, Prākṛt or Apabhraṁśa. The *Bṛhatkathā* was preserved in Sanskrit.

---

4. The pluralism pervades all spheres of Indian life, even its perception of reality and time. The pluralistic perception of time was noted by the official Calendar Committee appointed five years after the independence under the chairpersonship of Meghnad Saha who had said that the calendar was an indispensable requisite for modern civilized life. Saha had identified more then thirty well-developed calendars in systematic use in the country. The authoritative *Whitakar's Almanac* reduced the long list of seven principal Indian eras by translating the Georgian year 2000 into these selected major calendars: (i) Year 6001 in the *Kaliyug* calendar; (ii) Year 2544 in the Buddha Nirvāṇa calender; (iii) Year 2057 in the Vikram Saṁvat calendar; (iv) Year 1922 in the Śaka calendar; (v) Year 1927 (shown in terms of five-yearly cycles in the Vedāṅga's Jyotiṣa calendar); (vi) Year 1407 in the Bengali San calendar; and (vii) Year 1176 in the Kollam calendar. These perceptions of time in distinct calendars pertain to diverse yet interrelated histories of the communities, localities, traditions and religions.

   Amartya Sen has discussed this issue at length in his piece in *The Little Magazine* (www.littlemag.com). The immense variety of systematic →

Though in the *Kārikā*, the name of *deśī bhāṣā* is written, in the *Vṛtti* it is treated as a kind of Apabhraṁśa, and even Paiśācī is considered for literary purpose. An average Indian is blessed with (or acquires) functional knowledge of more than one or two languages other than his 'mother-tongue.' In Gujarat, a Kāṭhiāvāḍī-speaking person, for instance, who knows no Sanskrit, 'translates' and constructs a figure of Gaṇeśa or some other god when a priest in the course of the solemnization of rituals recites a *śloka* that the person concerned cannot read in Devanāgarī script. Despite this multilinguality, we seem to function without a conscious theory of translation. This linguistic 'plurality' caused by unconscious processes of 'translation' is an integral part of the Indian consciousness, and needs to be taken into consideration when constructing a model of literary studies in India. So while there may be more than 1550 languages in existence in the country, as linguists like Professor K.V. Subbarao inform us, these can nevertheless be grouped in five or eight clusters in terms of linguistic and regional contiguities. This linguistic plurality, characteristic of many modern languages and literatures in India, is in direct continuity with the pluralist cultural tradition that can be best described in terms of either the metaphor of the *phūlagūnthanī* (a wreath of flowers) or that of the *dīpaśikhā*, which

→ calendars corresponding with cultural and regional variety and variations notwithstanding, Sen does not overlook the basic unity underlying the diversity, as he states that since despite this high variance, there is a concept of the country as a unit that has survived through history. To be sure the presence of this concept is exactly what is denied in the oft-repeated claim that India was no more than a large territory of small to medium fragments, united later on by the controlling powers of British rule. According to Sen the variety of calendars, divided not only by religious connections but also by regional diversity, seems to be deeply hostile to any view of Indian unity. However, he adds that it must be noted in its context that many of these calendars have strange similarities in terms of months and also beginning of the year. For elaborate discussion please see Amartya Sen, "India Through Its Calenders", *The Argumentative Indian*, 2005, pp. 317-333.

is made of different lamps. Different lamps have their specific positions and specificities, but once lit, the light that they give is one and the same.

Ironies of Histories of Literary Studies in India

In stark contrast to Indian linguistic and literary pluralistic realities, the departments of literature that came into existence during the colonial period and even after Independence were single-language departments that strove hard to maintain their different identity and created a false image of superiority of English literature over literatures in Indian languages. Further, literary studies, which were to have served the purpose of understanding societies they were located in, and their constituents, unfortunately alienated one from the other.

Another instance of irony was the fact that, in the first quarter of the nineteenth century, when Europe raved with encomiums for Sanskrit, we in India craved for the replacement of Sanskrit by English. By 1825, there was not even a single major university in Europe that did not have a chair or centre for the study of Sanskrit. Voltaire, Victor Hugo, Quinet, Eugene Burnouf, Michelet, Duperon, Diderot, J.D. Herder, Goethe, Schiller, Schelling, William Jones, Charles Wilkins, Schopenhauer, Thoreau, Emerson and F. Max Müller, to name but a few, sang paeans in the praise of Sanskrit and the knowledge available in it. At least two names deserve special mention here.

The first is that of Max Müller because he had gone beyond the romantic phase of Europe's engagement with India. And without being misled by Macaulay's dismissive rejection of India and its literatures almost five decades earlier, he lectured to prospective ICS officers in Cambridge in 1882 about India and what it could teach them. Indirectly, he questioned the Anglicists' rejection and denunciation of India, and went to the extent of telling them that as the colonial masters they should resist being teachers, and rather learn from the culture and civilization of their subjects. So, while Europe revolutionized or at least enriched itself with knowledge from India, we abandoned it either under the persuasion or the coercion of the colonizers who had by that time very systematically cut down what Gandhiji termed 'the beautiful tree' that was Indian education. The situation did not change much in independent India, as the Sanskrit language came to be associated with a class or caste, and along with the language, the unique body of knowledge it enfolded was denigrated. In the entire history of human civilization, ours may well be an unprecedented case in which people abandoned their own intellectual traditions without trying to know them. There can be no worse instance of intellectual suicide than ours.

The second name is Ferdinand de Saussure's, who did his doctoral dissertation on the Vedas, and who taught Sanskrit all his life, and revolutionized the European perception of language, which had for centuries remained diachronic. Saussure's study of Pānini's *Aṣṭādhyāyī* and Bhartṛhari's *Vākyapadīya*, in particular, changed Europe's perception of the word, by which we take cognizance of the world. After learning from Bhartṛhari that the world is construct of (word) language (*bhāṣā vikalpa*), Saussure shifted the study of language in Europe to a synchronic model that provided paradigms for the structuralist and post-structuralist movements of the second half of the twentieth century. Indian literary critics use indiscreetly the paradigms, the positions and the jargon of structuralist and post-structuralist critics like Claude Lévi-Strauss, Roland Barthes, Michel Foucault, and Jacques Derrida, and ironically enough, continue to study the works of these and other Anglo-European theorists in 'Literary Criticism,' to the exclusion, in their own country, of Pāṇini and Bhartṛhari, leave alone any question of room for other important critics like Bharata, Bhāmaha, Daṇḍin, Ānandavardhana, Abhinavagupta, and Jagannātha, to name but a few.

One finds that the Anglo-Eurocentric core of departments of English in India has dissolved, despite the best efforts of academic status quoists in the last quarter of the preceding century. The syllabi of English studies in India, in the process of decanonization, began to accommodate non-English studies oriented towards Indian writing in English and Indian literatures in translation. Though the nomenclature of these departments and their areas of operation remained more or less the same, besides continuing to remain monolinguistic in the majority of these instances, in most of these departments at least some of the faculty had in their own way begun to pursue comparative literary studies steadfastly focusing their attention on writing in Indian languages, though not systematically all the time. Though some departments did try to incorporate comparative literature as part of their syllabi, their number, as also that of departments of comparative literature, remains not very large in our country.

Despite its suitability, given the Indian situation, comparative literary studies, both as a discipline and as a model, failed to gain currency, leave alone supremacy, in India for various reasons, e.g. the centrality ascribed to English, and the establishment of one-language departments out of the anxiety of influence or fear of submergence, ignoring the multilingual reality of the country, and the failure of the 'school' or subsidiary system, and the absence of job-opportunities for the students of comparative literary studies.

However, two positive trends related to both literary studies and particularly to comparative literature are discernible in our academic scenario. Firstly, the University Grants Commission's reports on *The Curriculum Development Committees in English*, published in 1989 and 2002, laid emphasis upon the viability of offering translation studies either as part of degree courses or independently. Secondly, Indian scholarship in academic institutions and outside have increasingly begun to understand that it has for long been at the receiving end of the theory-data paradigm in which the West — the erstwhile colonizer — is the donor or initiator, and the rest — the so-called others or post-colonial societies — are the imitators or receivers of this theory, the guinea pigs upon whom the former's theories are tested.[5] It

5. See the 'Introduction' to Kapil Kapoor's *Literary Theory: Indian Conceptual Frameworks*, Delhi: East-West Press, 1998.

has been all the more intensely realized than ever before that this paradigm has to be reversed by receiving the Western theories and pronouncements proactively, by going back to our own literary and critical traditions and reviving whatever has the possibility of life, in the manner of the West, which revived the rhetoric of Greek antiquity in the twentieth century for its critical and interpretative purposes, alongside understanding, accepting, digesting and assimilating into our critical traditions whatever is good in the Western critical tradition. Equipped with a newly acquired self-confidence and lack of self-consciousness, Indian scholarship has begun to question 'given' theories and categories, including, among others, post-modernism and post-colonialism. On the one hand, the tendency to measure Indian literary texts, trends and movements in terms of these 'isms' and categories has became rife in our academic and critical discourses to the extent that the majority of contemporary Indian literatures in the last quarter of the last century became 'post-modern,' even as, on the other hand, the consciousness dawned that these are neither our categories nor our agenda.

However, the predominant tendency in English academia still under the spell of the colonial hangover was an indifference to creativity in modern Indian languages in particular, alongside an effort to enter and to remain in dialogue with 'foreign' texts and their interpreters from abroad, i.e. England and now America, and on their 'foreign' terms. However, as global and local converged in different ways, there was an impending danger of the local getting submerged economically, culturally, intellectually and in the end politically in the context of globalization. In the face of this danger, insecure and fearful, the local began to assert its specificity in linguistic, literary and cultural terms. The 'Home' and 'Abroad' dialogue continued as earlier, but was now marked by a changed tone and nature, characterized by if not equal terms, then at least a demand for equal terms; if not in practice, at least in ideas. The need for living dialogue between the languages and literatures of the country has been increasingly felt in these last few decades, and the realization has also dawned that the dialogue between 'Home' and 'Abroad' should ideally be preceded by this dialogue between 'Home' and 'Home.' While a 'Home'and 'Abroad' dialogue can take place alongside of the dialogue between 'Home' and 'Home,' never should it be allowed to flourish at the cost of the dialogue between 'Home' and 'Home.'[6] This dialogue will become more meaningful when Indian scholars attempt to forge a methodology for comparative literary study of Indian texts in their source language versions without waiting for or taking recourse to their translations, and thus become the centre of activities in our 'English' departments. A healthy initiation of a dialogue between Indian literati has been made already, though in a small way, mediated by some distinguished scholars particularly of English in India, rooted in their own literatures, and willingness to learn about other Indian literatures.

My suggestion that we adopt a 'Home and Home' first and 'Home and Abroad' later strategy for literary studies may seem idealistic to some, but it is achievable in practice in the context of Indian linguistic and literary pluralism, unless one thinks in singular terms. Multilingualism is neither a problem nor a disadvantage, though we must admit that we have failed to convert it into and project it to our advantage. Further, Indian English and literature in it are no longer 'issues,' as a result of which literary production in English has to be treated as part of the output of Indian languages/literatures without, however, privileging it in our consideration of literary studies. The place of English in India should be that of the handmaid, not that of master, midwife or mother. It needs to function as a window to the world to appropriate the knowledge available outside. However, we should not get so enamoured by the window that we ignore or close other doors, particularly ours.

Here, I must hasten to add that the linguistic situation of India

6. I use these terms in the sense Harish Trivedi employed them in the seminar on translation called 'Home and Abroad,' organized by him in Delhi University in 1996.

does not warrant any helplessness and dependence on English. The Indian languages are capable of carrying their burden.[7] They have the requisite vibrancy and cultural strength to survive on their own. They can manage without English, or with a selective and functional complementary role for English. In fact, the worst thing to have happened in post-Independent India, apart form the Partition, was the organization of Indian states on linguistic lines, the second partition of the country.

Fortunately, the people of India have always, in their own way, set right political blunders. If one were to walk along the borders of the western Indian states, one would find the inhabitants there speaking a mixed language or multiple languages like Rajasthani, Hindi, Gujarati, Marathi and many dialects. The people on the border areas of Rajasthan, Gujarat, Madhya Pradesh and Maharashtra speak a wonderful 'mix' of languages. There are many such linguistic twilight zones in our country where many languages collapse, collide and merge into one. As between the borders of Gujarat and Maharashtra, between Gujarati and Marathi, the unnamed and unacknowledged, yet spoken language by the people is neither Gujarati nor Marathi but a mixture of the two, i.e. 'Gujarathi.' Similarly there exists what may be called 'Tamilyālam' between/on the borders of Tamil Nadu and Kerala around Pālghāṭ. India offers a situation in which many clusters of languages operate, though they do not appear so visible. It is possible to visualize a solution to the problem of creating a viable model for literary studies anchored in comparative and translational operations in our country through examining these language/literature clusters: I see eight already in existence in our country, though 'colonized' minds under the influence of English do not recognize these. The figure of 'eight' is also special because of its auspiciousness, as the *aṣṭadhātu* is considered suitable

7. For an extended discussion of literary studies in the context of English, please refer to my article 'Decolonizing English Studies in India' in Adesh Pal et al., eds., *Decolonization: A Search for Alternatives*, Delhi: Creative, 2001, pp. 122-48.

for making the idols of gods and goddesses, though the *pañcadhātu* is equally well-known for its strength and auspiciousness. In fact, the geophysical, though not the political, map of India, answers the oft-repeated question: "In absence of English, which Indian language can replace it as a pan-Indian language?" Demographical cosiderations do not answer such a question; every language, though from the same culture-group, exists with its unique specificities. These clusters will replace English in the end, provided we recognize them, read and teach their literatures in our classrooms. For instance, the departments of English in Gujarat, Maharashtra and the western Madhya Pradesh and Rajasthan should prescribe and teach Hindi, Marathi, Gujarati and English (Indian English writing) texts at least in the optional space, to begin with, something that the Department of English Comparative Literary Studies, Saurashtra University, Rajkot (Gujarat) has attempted by prescribing two Gujarati, two Hindi and two Indian English texts. It will in due course of time orient our one-language departments, e.g., Assamese, Bengali, English, Gujarati, Hindi, Malayalam, or Tamil, into departments of comparative literary studies, thereby bringing our languages and literatures to the centre. The problem is that we have never considered our languages capable of shouldering their burden. We have either sought pride in their pasts, or in the glories of Sanskrit, without the passion or the commitment of Max Müller or Michelet,[8] or condemned and strove to run down their sister languages, if we compared them at all, and at the same time genuflected before other non-Indian languages, particularly English.

Literary Studies and Comparative Literature in India

If comparative literature is to serve as the fulcrum of our model of literary studies in India, it would be incongruous to examine questions pertaining to comparative literature, literary studies,

8. See F. Max Müller's *India: What can it teach us?*, 1883, Delhi: Rupa, 2002, pp. 57-81 and Michelet's *'La Bible de l'humanite'*, *Oeuvres*, vol. 5, Paris: Bibliotheque Larousse, 1930 pp. 103-10.

and India in their so-called 'post-nation' context. Literature strives to delineate society — a specific society that may be a region, community or country. In the course of doing so, it tries to chart out the blueprint of society, to imagine a community, country or nation. Thereby it acts as both the mirror and the lamp of the society. The notion of the nation, at least of the Western sort, at times becomes an alienating category or agency fraught with the dangers of insulation, of alienating one literature from the other, and of confining literatures within narrow linguistic, cultural and regional lines — something that literature is supposed to resist. It was a danger perceived by the progenitors of the idea of comparative literature, like Goethe, for as a branch of literary study, comparative literature endeavoured to de-alienate literatures. In the West, comparative literature began as a reaction to aggressive and insulating nationalism. The West reaped the fruits of nationalism whose ugly consequence was colonization, which increased to such an extent that by the second decade of the twentieth century not less than 85 per cent surface of the earth was under its hold. Goethe in Germany and a few decades later Matthew Arnold in England cautioned against narrow nationalism in literature in their own ways.[9] Goethe used the term *weltliteratur*, for 'world literature' in 1827, though the word 'world' meant Europe for him, albeit provisionally. Arnold, in the second half of the nineteenth century, warned his fellow critics against the dangers of isolationist subscription to their own national literatures only, suggesting instead that every critic should try to possess at least one great literature besides his own, and the more unlike his own the better. Ironically, his world was narrower than Goethe's. Goethe went beyond Germany and Europe in his quest for a 'world literature,' but Arnold's catholicity, despite his quest for 'ideas,' which happened much after Goethe's time, did not look outside Europe for the 'one great literature.'

9. See Matthew Arnold's 'The Function of Criticism at the Present Time' in S. Ramaswami and V.S. Sethuraman, eds., *English Critical Tradition*, rev. edn., vol. 2, Madras: Macmillan, 1986, pp. 17-43.

Paradoxically, in India, comparative literature, which is not so distinctly related to nationalism at least of the West, arose with the rise of nationalism. It may have well been a coincidence that the first universities in India came to be established in 1858, a year after the first struggle for Independence. They came to be established in coastal towns like Bombay, Madras and Calcutta, which incidentally were not the centres of traditional Indian learning. Departments of English came into existence in the second half of the nineteenth century, and unfortunately, remained single-literature departments for long. It was also around this time that modern Indian literatures all over India strained to attain maturity through the creation of a corpus of writings in different forms and genres. In addition, these literatures tried to appropriate in their own ways the literary and non-literary forms that they did not already have. With the rise of modern Indian literatures, various local specificities, which may be termed sub-nationalities within a pan-Indian nationality, came into existence. They, however, did not raise their heads in the sway of *swadeśa, swadeśī* and *swatantratā* during the freedom struggle. These specificities — Assamese, Bengali, Gujarati, Marathi, Malayalam, Punjabi, Tamil and Telugu among others — along with presenting themselves in a harmonious chorus with the national spirit did try to carve out a place for their specificity in linguistic and literary terms.

Departments of comparative literature came to be established in and around these new places of learning, like at the Jadavpur University in Calcutta, and the Gurudev Tagore Chair of comparative literature at Bombay University, and at University of Delhi, among others. These were followed by the introduction of comparative literature either as part of the syllabi or as a separate course, or as compulsory or optional component. Such opportunities for comparative study helped Indian literatures accept the existence of the other literatures and languages of India, in resisting the possibilities of hegemony by dominant groups, and also in broadening the perspectives for prospective assessment and interpretation of our own literatures, for the true measure of a literary work is another work of that sort.

The relevance of comparative literary studies in the current period coincides with the rise of neo-nationalism in India, which itself is a consequence of certain changes in ideological positions. In the heydays of the Nehruvian era, to be a nationalist and a person of faith was to be anti-internationalist, narrow-minded, bigoted and non-progressive. Internationalism was neither something new for people who believed in *vasudhaiva kuṭumbakam*, nor impracticable as a principle, provided other 'nations' too subscribed to it, and national interests were not frittered away, as unfortunately happened in 1948 when India lost almost one-third of Kashmir, and again in 1962, when China occupied Akshai-Chin. Such was the disillusionment of the people with politics and its practitioners in the intervening period that by the end of the 1980s and the early 1990s, earlier notions had became suspect in the eyes of the people. The idealistic internationalism of Nehru, the last revered pan-Indian politician, was now found to be a parasitic concept, at least for India, even as religious fanaticism was unacceptable to the culture and spirit of the country. In the economic field, the Left and the Right both shifted away from their traditional positions so much so that the new off-Left and the new off-Right do not appear to be very different from one another, at least in practice. Globalization, the new *avatāra* of internationalism, and in reality a seductive mask of neocolonialism, has, on the one hand, exposed the bankruptcy of the slogans of the Right, Left and those in between, and has, on the other, made the 'local' (little specificities) more conscious of its identity and of the dangers imminent to it, particularly of its submergence into the global. In a situation such as this, the nation becomes a sort of strategy to preserve and further the interests of this 'local,' and sustain it against the homogenizing forces of the global. The nation may now be a luxury for the Western nations that have reaped the harvest of the crop called the nation, but for countries like India, the nation is still an entity that is essential if we are to protect our identity, even as we prevent our nationhood from attaining proportions dangerous to others, whether these be others from within or without. These considerations have persuaded even the liberals and floaters to rethink their positions, pushing them in the direction of what can broadly be termed nationalist secularism or liberal nationalism, which has led to an amalgamation or synthesis of faith and national pride in national identity and in one's own religious, regional, cultural, communal or racial and linguistic identities. However, the pitfalls of valorizing religious identifications over those of the nation have also come to the fore. Unfortunately, the alarmists in our country have raised a lot of clamour whenever there was a call to state or discuss these long existing realities — be they in the field of religion, culture and literature. Various 'little specificities' are not dangers in themselves. But they may well assume menacing proportions if they are suppressed, and are not allowed to grow or denied the place due to them in the entire scheme of things. These voices or identities always wait to be heard and accepted. They do not seek opportunities for insulation or isolation, but for dialogue, and nothing can be more dangerous than thwarting this yearning. A comparative framework for literary studies in India can facilitate this process by accepting the existence of all others (languages/literatures) and initiate the process of dialogue as often as possible and with as many as possible. The comparative structure best suits Indian linguistic and literary realities, for we have more than two score recognized literatures, and many more written and oral languages and dialects. But what is more important is that we examine existing paradigms of literary studies and prepare our own models, keeping in mind our realities and experiences, and the literatures that contain in them these experiences.

Literary studies in India, because of their single-language *avatāra*s, have for long been marred by utter disregard for the literatures in the languages of Indian origin. Departments of modern Indian languages have been ignoring, and continue to ignore, other languages and literatures, contemporary and classical. England, France and Germany can afford to do so but not India. Even something like the system of a 'school of languages' becomes another cluster of language departments that are absolutely isolated from one another, without any provision for an honest implementation of courses in other Indian languages, at least as 'subsidiary' subjects (with at least 20-25 per cent weightage, i.e. at least two papers from other languages per course or programme). Initially, comparative literature as a discipline, except where it had its own departments, were Euro- or Anglo-centric at heart and in content and character, as colonialism would have it; the comparative literary operations, paradoxically, overlooked Indian languages and literatures. The Indian languages were not thought of as worthy of comparative consideration while English literary works or authors were compared, if possible, with their counterparts in select world literatures (SWL) like the French, German, or Russian. Select Indian literature(s) (SIL), designating usually literature in the local language of the region where the department was located, entered into comparative literary dialogue with SWL without a thought for sister languages/ literatures. For instance, the prestigious department of comparative literature at Jadavpur did not, at least initially, invest in comparative pursuits in Assamese or Oriya, as they did, of course naturally, in Bengali and in European languages, particularly English. In the Hindi heartland, Sūrdās and Premchand were compared with Milton and Gorky respectively but nearer home, the dialogue between Hindi and other Indian literatures was not as vigorous as it should have been. In addition, translations among Indian languages were few and far between. The flow of translational operations was from world literatures into Indian literatures, not among and from the literatures in language of Indian origin (LLIO). Moreover, the absence of translations made comparative literary studies a difficult proposition.

A different model is necessary to set right this imbalance in literary studies in India. Since Indian writing in English (IWE) has become part of our Indian Literatures, it is possible to replace English literature with IWE, which owes a lot to Indian languages and has considerably affected LLIO. Here, what is to be borne in mind is that literary studies are to be founded on the principle of *ādāna pradāna* (exchange or give and take), or *saṁvāda* (dialogue), which should take place first among literatures in languages of Indian origin, then between IWE and LLIO, and thereafter between Indian literatures and world literatures, not merely with English, but with as many world literatures as possible.

But even this model of literary studies in India limits the scope of literary studies in that it confines itself to contemporary literature. Literary studies in India, alongside retaining its emphasis on the notion of 'Home and Home, and then Abroad,' must take proper cognizance of its rich literary traditions in ancient and medieval literature in Sanskrit, Prākr̥t, Pāli, Apabhraṁśa, and beyond them, its oral and folk literary traditions. To realize this aim, we must move to a paradigm in which Sanskrit and the other Indian languages (SOIL), inclusive of ancient literatures and other literary traditions, form the core. IWE will thus move from the centre on to being one amongst the Indian literatures. In the first stage, thus, there should be dialogue between Home and Home — amongst contemporary Indian literatures with an awareness of SOIL, which should be the foundation of both literary studies and comparative literary studies in India. The LLIO should interact with SOIL, exploring possibilities of comparative literary studies thus, with both LLIO, and with ancient and contemporary world literature, and pursue them accordingly. This could take place in different ways, but in no situation should it happen by bypassing either LLIO or SOIL.

Here I must touch upon, however briefly, the state of dialogue between two or all literatures in languages of Indian origin, for this is of great importance to us, as it may determine the nature and future of cultural and (sub)national identities. It may not be incongruous to take recourse to a term from Indian music, *jugalabandī*, to suggest a model for dialogue between 'Home' and 'Home' in literary studies and comparative literary studies. The *jugalabandī* between native literatures and between native and alien literatures should take place on equal terms. In the past, we squandered quite a bit of our energy in trying to adjust our native notes to Western musical instruments. Indian scholarship has, in general, committed the heinous crime of ignoring LLIO for long, longing instead for a dialogue with non-LLIO at the cost of LLIO. At least now, though quite belatedly, with the critique of our preceding literary practices the need is being felt for the use of our own instruments, for sounding our own 'notes,' and for bringing our literatures into the fold of our literary pursuits. And for those who cannot do without theory, once Indian literary studies, enriched by this *jugalabandī*, are systematically instituted and thrive vigourously, the theory of Indian literary studies and comparative Indian literary studies will proceed from this practice.

Here I must sound a caveat regarding the proposed paradigms: I make no claims to the finality of any of the models I have outlined above; rather, I must foreground their provisional nature. I have offered time and place specific alternatives that nevertheless lay no claim to universality. Keeping this in view, I would submit that, in the present age, scholars of comparative Indian literary studies have to focus more on understanding various Indian literatures as sympathetic outsiders and cautious insiders, and less on comparison merely for the sake of passing judgements and preparing a hierarchy of languages and literatures. Comparative studies can often be odious and the attendant judgements may ignite ominously dangerous controversies and passions, particularly in case of the nascent CILS framework. At a time when terms like nation, nationality, sub-nationalities, nationalism and neo-nationalism are being (re)considered, and different specificities strain to assert themselves and seek their re-definition and reconstruction, it is preferable that Indian comparatists eschew hierarchical value judgements, though it is difficult to divorce comparison from judgement. The relative worth of works has to be suggested, and not pronounced explicitly. In the control of lesser minds, the common comparative pursuit may degenerate into articulation of personal predilections that will ruin the conditions for dialogue, even alienating literatures, whereas the true end of literary studies, comparative and otherwise, is to aim for de-alienating literatures.

Agenda for Literary Studies in India

The pursuit of literary studies in India, attempted without concern for its linguistic and literary pluralities, is, as we have noted above, unrealistic, parasitic and dangerously divisive in its nature. Languages and literatures in India, instead of uniting the people, have been (ab)used, for far too long, and are still being used, to divide the country. If literary studies in India, or for that matter in any part of the world, cannot bring people together, unite them in resisting the nefarious processes of the forces of exploitation and tyranny that succeed by dividing their subject, do not help in understanding and respecting each other, and provide the vision (against the 'provision' that is primarily the concern of sciences) of a world order based on values, these literary studies are not worth having at all. Literary studies in India and elsewhere must celebrate these values and create room for the possibility of human values of life based on happiness, love, peace, dignity, and harmony, rather than inventing and glorifying difference, and creating a world of unending discords. I offer the following agenda for literary studies in India.

- Keeping the Indian cultural, linguistic and literary ground realities in view, literary studies in India must move towards a comparative Indian literary studies famework. This would help us in studying and understanding our literatures and other literatures as well, leading to mutual illumination and enrichment. The Indian school of comparative literature, like the French and German schools, would be a happy by-product of the process. For this, comparative Indian literary studies should not be mediated only through English departments, as this would not serve our purpose if the practice leads to reversion to the single language department. No single language department should be allowed in a cluster for specialised study. The focus should be on the study of interliterariness.

- Single-language departments should not be opened, and existing single-language deparments should be encouraged to switch over to the 'school of languages' system, or to literary studies, but with the provision for subsidiary study of other languages in it. At least one-fourth of the total course contents should go to literature(s) of the other languages from the cluster-group, as discussed earlier.
- Departments of English should be re-christened departments of literary studies in English, with at least 25 per cent of the course content coming from the literature of the cluster-group. In the process of becoming relevant, these departments have appropriated bits of everything from European Classics, Commonwealth, Canadian, Australian, Third World, Post-colonial, Feminist, and Indian English literatures to diaspora and translation studies, but have ignored literature(s) of the land or cluster.
- The teaching and learning of languages, particularly English for specific purposes, should be facilitated separately through centres of language study. The main problem with language teaching in our country is that Indian languages are 'under-taught', and if they are taught at all, that takes place in an unsystematic manner. On the other hand, English is 'over-taught,' with at least eight to thirteen years being devoted to it, and that too in so many diverse ways that the grammatical structures of the mother-tongues, for instance, are disturbed and replaced before being entrenched in students' minds. This haphazard acquisition of language gives the learners neither confidence nor constructive opportunities for bettering their language skills. The focus should shift from horizontal to vertical communication in the study of language.
- Teaching faculty appointed in language and literature departments should be allowed and asked to teach certain portions of their choice in other language and literature departments.

- Philosophical thoughts forms the foundation of education. Unfortunately, philosophical studies have suffered in direct proportion to the prosperity of economics, commerce and management in our education system. To set it right and base literary studies on solid foundations, it is necessary to introduce a foundation course in Indian philosophical thought at the undergraduate level, so that ideas of an author operating within or under the influence of certain school(s) manifested through his/her creative writings can be understood in the proper perspective.
- Indian poetics should be made an integral part of the literary criticism paper. To begin with, one unit, i.e. at least 20 per cent of the paper or course-work, can be devoted to it by dividing the entire paper or course contents in five units, namely Indian poetics, Western classical poetics, English criticism from its beginning up to 1900, Anglo-American criticism in the first half of the twentieth century, and contemporary criticism, including structuralist, post-structuralist, and post-colonial criticism. A literary studies course, with the first year earmarked to an Indian language like Sanskrit, Tamil or Hindi, should have one unit on Western criticism. This unit-wise compartmentalization is best introduced at the undergraduate level, from which point the student can move towards the comparative study of various non-Indian and Indian schools, including criticism in contemporary Indian languages and others like Tamil poetics.
- There should be (a) compulsory course(s) for acquiring and upgrading skills like proofreading, editing, writing or translation for media — print and electronic — with provision for internship and hands on experience.

I will end with a skeletal outline of a model curriculum for postgraduate programmes language departments in the country:

MA Curriculum for Language and Literature Departments

Duration: 2 years

Papers: 8 or 10 (16 or 20 courses)

MA Part I: Papers 1 to 4/5 on the literature of particular language, arranged either chronologically or form-wise with 12.5/10 per cent weightage for each paper.

MA Part II: Papers 5/6 to 8 or 10 with 12.5/10 per cent weightage for each paper, depending on the choice of the school or department. The papers can be arranged in the following manner:

- Literary criticism, as discussed above;
- Sister language literatures from the linguistic cluster;
- Hindi or literature of any other Indian language, the more different, the better;
- English or European literature for a department whose single-language emphasis was on one language of Indian origin; European or world literature for those who opted for an MA course with English as major language; and,
- Advanced study paper on an author, form, movement, comparative study of critical approaches or schools; or folk literature or media studies.
- Skills acquisition/upgradation courses with internship.

Part III

Literature and Theorizing in India

9

In Their Own Words and Worlds
Women Saint Poets and their Poetry

aham rāṣṭrī saṅgamanī vasūnām cikitusī prathamā yajñīyānām ।
tān mā devā vydadhuḥ purutrā bhurystāntrā bhuryāvesayantīm ॥

— *Vāk*

I have *māyā* for mother-in-law;
the world for father-in-law;
three brothers-in-law like tigers;
and the husband's thoughts
careful of laughing women:

No god, this man.
And I cannot cross the sister-in-law.
But I will
Give this wench the slip
and go cuckold my husband with Horā, my Lord.

My mind is my maid:
by her kindness, I join
my Lord,
my utterly beautiful Lord from the mountain-peaks
my lord as white as jasmine
And I will make Him
my good husband.

— *Mahādeviyakka*

SINCE poetry of women saint-poets falls under the category of *bhakti*, it would not be inappropriate to contextualize it by discussing *bhakti,* the movement and the contribution of women to the corpus of *bhakti* poetry.

There are different views regarding the origin of *bhakti,* in Indian culture and religious practices. Its development can be traced to the Vedic literature where it can be discerned in the verb *bhajāmahe* in the *mantra*: *tamu stotāḥ*: *viṣṇu sumatim bhajāmahe.* (1.156.3).[1] There are other *mantra*s as well. *Yajña*s are an earliest form of *bhakti.* The *upāsanā* (worship) of the "Upāsanā Kāṇḍa" of the *Khaṇḍa Traya* is nothing but another form of *bhakti.* The worship of the Supreme Being (that we can term for the present purpose as *bhakti*) is suggested in the Vedas, as it is the only path to reach the Supreme Being's abode.[2] The seeker should go to His/Her shelter, *tvamagne vratapā asi deva ā martyeṣvā* । *tvaṁ yajñeṣvīḍyaḥ* । (*Ṛgveda,* 8.11.1). Further, the seeker considers Him/Her everything, i.e. mother, father, brother and nourisher (*Yajurveda,* 32.10.) and protector. *Tvaṁ hi naḥ pitāvaso tvaṁ mātā śatakrato babhūvitha* । *adhā te sumnmīmahe* । (*Ṛgveda,* 8.98.11).

The study of the Vedic discourse reveals that the Vedas are the source of origin of spirit of *bhakti,* though the term is nowhere used. The attributes of *bhakti* can be seen in the relationship sought or to be established between the seeker and the Supreme Being known by different names in the Vedas. Even the shelter of the Supreme Being (Lord), the coveted destination of the seeker (*bhakta*) here, is mentioned in the *Ṛgveda*:

---

1. In the *mantra, bhajāmahe* has *bhaja* as its root from which *bhakti* is derived. Please see the entry *bhaja* in M. Monier-Williams, *Sanskrit-English Dictionary,* Oxford, 1956, p. 743.

2. *vedāhametām puruṣam mahāntamāditya varṇam tamasaparastāt* ।
tamevam viditvā 'timṛtyumeti nānyaḥ panthā vidyatayanāya ॥
— *Śuklayajurveda* 31.18

   Also the *Ṛgveda* (1.164.20) says that all services and rewards are contained in the infinite word. All gods reside in it. One who does not know imperishable *Brahman,* what does he know? Those who have known this eternal *Brahman,* need not know anything.

   ṛco akṣare parame vyoman yasmin devā adhiviśve niṣeduḥ ।
   yastann veda kimṛcā kariṣyati yaittadvidusta ime samāsate ॥

uruṁ no lokamanu neṣi vidvāntsvarva jjyotirabhayaṁ svasti ।
ṛṣvā ta indra sthavirasya bāhū upastheyām śaraṇā bṛhantā ॥
— 6.47.8

The Upaniṣads, e.g. *Muṇḍakopaniṣad* (2.2.4), *Śvetāśvatara Upaniṣad* (6.11), and *Chāndogyopaniṣad* (3.18.1) consider the attributes of *bhakti* in various ways. The term *bhakti* appears for the first time in the *Śvetāśvatara Upaniṣad* (6.23.4). The *Śvetāśvatara Upaniṣad* further mentions the shelter of the Lord as the basic tenet of the *bhakti*.[3]

The Upaniṣadic discourse suggested the states of devotional being (*Muṇḍakopaniṣad*, 3.1.1), primacy of faith of the knower/ seeker (the *Muṇḍakopaniṣad*, 1.2.11) and even the significance of the role of *guru* (teacher) in the odyssey of seeker (*Kaṭhopaniṣad*, 1.2.7). However, only that person becomes a devotee (*bhakta*) upon whom God bestows *bhakti* or devotion (*Kaṭhopaniṣad*, 1.2.24). But the *bhakti* referred to in the Upaniṣads is mere "dry" devotion or worship or a ritual. It lacks in living love in its various forms — an essential attribute of *bhakti*. In the Upaniṣadic discourse, it was a way of thinking from a way of living in Vedas, marking shift to *jñāna* (knowledge) from *karma* (action) and into abstract from concrete. It left no space for delicate devotional feelings as found much later in the *bhakti* discourse.

The *Gītā*, after the Upaniṣads, discusses *jñāna*, *karma* and *bhakti*, though it lays greater emphasis on *jñāna*. Each human being is born to act. But it (action) should be without *āsakti* (attachment) and dedicated to Lord. The *jñāna* (knowledge) acts as a raft, as Kṛṣṇa says to Arjuna:

api cedasi pāpebhyaḥ sarvebhyaḥ pāpakṛttamaḥ ।
sarvaṁ jñāna-plavenaiva vṛjinaṁ santariṣyasi ॥
— 4.36

---

3. The Vaiṣṇavas particularly consider *prapatti* (surrender to the Lord) as higher than even *bhakti*.

yo brahmāṇām vidadhāti pūrvaṁ yo vai vedāṁśca prahinoti tasme ।
tathā dsevamātmabuddhi prakāśaṁ mumukṣuvai śaraṇamahaṁ prapadye ॥
— 6.18

> Even if you were the faultiest of all sinners, this *jñāna* (knowledge) alone would carry you like a raft across all your sins.

He further says:

> *yathaidhāṁsi samiddho 'agnirbhasmasāt kurute 'rjuna* ।
> *jñānāgniḥ sarva-karmāṇi bhasmasāt kurute tathā* ॥
>
> — 4.37

> As the blazing fire turns the fuel to ashes, Arjuna, even so the fire of knowledge turns all actions to ashes.

The Lord in *Gītā* says, *mayy arpita mano buddhir yo mad bhaktaḥ sa me priyaḥ* (12.14). He who has dedicated his *mana* (mind) and *buddhi* (intellect) is a *bhakta* (devotee) dear to me. Kṛṣṇa says that He is *jñāna* (knowledge). "The man of knowledge is My Own Self. He is identical with Me and, therefore, he is dear to Me and I am dear to Myself" (*Gītā*, 7.17-18). It means that the *jñānī* (one who has attained knowledge) is at the highest rung. Devotion is the means not the end. The *Gītā* sees devotees in four categories:

> *caturvidhā bhajante māṁ janāḥ sukṛtino 'rjuna* ।
> *ārto jijñāsur arthārthī jñānī ca bharatarṣabha* ॥
>
> — 7.16

In the first category is the devotee, who is in some trouble and wishes to be saved from that (*ārta*). The second type is *jijñāsu* or inquisitive, who prays to God to know the secret of creation and universe because he cannot know them. The third type is *arthārthī* who prays to attain material prosperity or fulfil some need. And the last is *jñānī* who knows that God is worth knowing.

Of these devotees, God likes the *jñānī,* the man of knowledge and wisdom the most, for s/he has established an identity with Him, and is possessed of exclusive devotion. He is extremely dear to the wise man because s/he knows Him in reality (7.17). Moreover, one who has closed all the doors of the senses, holds the mind in the cavity of heart, fixes the life breath in the head, remains steadfast in yogic concentration on God and leaves the body uttering the one Indestructible Brahmā and dwelling on Him in absoluteness reaches the supreme destination (*parama gati*).

The *Gītā,* further, says that even those devotees who, endowed with faith, worship other gods worship Him alone (9.25). The Lord, further, speaks about His own attributive presence before His devotees. Whosoever offers Him a leaf, flower, fruit or even water with love, He appears in person before that disinterested devotee of sinless mind and partakes of that article delightfully offered to Him (9.26). Lord Kr̥ṣṇa adds that His devotees who seek Him, even so does He approach them because all men follow His path in every way:

ye yathā māṁ prapadyante taṁs tathaiva bhajāmy aham ।
mama vartmānuvartante manuṣyāḥ pārtha sarvaśaḥ ॥

—4.11

Kr̥ṣṇa assures all His devotees represented by Arjuna that His devotee, who performs all his/her duties for His sake, depends on Him, without any attachment, free from malice towards all beings, reaches Him (9.55). The *Gītā,* though concerned with *jñāna* and *karma* in particular, deals with different aspects of *bhakti,* and thereby furthers the suggestion of *bhakti* in the Vedas and its literal appearance in the Upaniṣads.

The *Nārada-Bhakti-Sūtra* is an extension and rejoinder to the *Gītā* as well. In the *Gītā, bhakti* or love of God is based on intellect, reasoning, knowledge or wisdom. The *Nārada-Bhakti-Sūtra* counters this view without mentioning the title of the *Gītā* that according to some, devotion or *bhakti* can be generated only through knowledge (*tasyāḥ jñānameva sādhanamityeke,* 28). Some others posit that knowledge and devotion depend upon one another. But according to Nārada, *bhakti* is itself the fruit or effect of the practice of devotion, not the result of something else. It means that it is self-sufficient. Knowledge of *bhakti* is not enough, for the mere look of the royal palace or dainty food (or its knowledge) does not satisfy the beholder (31.32). It can be attained only through the grace of God by a worthy seeker (53). The constant and unfailing love and service to God matter the most in *bhakti.*

Nārada takes note of his predecessors like Parāśara or Vyāsa. Parāśara defines *bhakti* rather simplistically in terms of attraction to worship among others as prescribed by the scriptures. *Pūjādiṣvānurāga iti pārāśarīya* (in the *Nārada-Bhakti-Sūtra,* 16). According to Garga, it (*bhakti*) is the attraction for stories of God's play as incarnations (*kathādaihviti gargaḥ,* 17). To Nārada, devotion is surrender of all activities to God and extreme anguish if He is forgotten [*nāradastu tadarpitākhilācāratā* I *tadvismarṇe parama–vyākulateti* (*ca*) (*Nārada-Bhakti-Sūtra,* 19)]. However the greatness of God is never to be forgotten. For instance, in the devotion of the *gopī*s of Vraja there was no blemish of forgetfulness of the greatness of the object of love (*Nārạda-Bhakti-Sūtra,* 22). Without this knowledge of greatness of the object of love, the love will be of baser form like that of paramours.

The *Nārada-Bhakti-Sūtra* is realistic enough regarding the fact that devotees despite being absorbed in love or devotion need not ignore their health or public opinion or avoid daily activities (*Nārada-Bhakti-Sūtra,* 14). Despite having one-pointedness of devotion to God, the devotee's conduct should be in conformity with views of common people and Vedic scriptures and indifferent to views opposite to it (*lokavedeṣu tadanukulācaraṇam tadvirodhiśī–pudāsenta,* 11). Moreover, it (*bhakti*) should be in conformity with *śāstra* (scripture) until one's faith is firmly founded (*bhavatu niścayādādaryādurdhvam śāstrarakṣaṇam,* 12). Else there is fear of falling from the ideal (*anyathā pātityāśaṅkā, Nārada-Bhakti-Sūtra,* 13). Here, Nārada's *bhakti* subscribes to *loka* and Veda but a little earlier while speaking of *nirodha* or complete cessation or control of the senses in *bhakti,* he explains it (*nirodha*) as discarding public opinion (*nirodhastu lokavedavyāpāraṇyāsaḥ,* 8). It can be inferred here that the *Nārada-Bhakti-Sūtra* takes note of *loka* and Veda but there is no complete rejection of them, as one finds in later *bhakti* poets. The seeds of rejection of *śāstra* are sown along with social revolution in terms of social distinctions which do not exist because they are God's very own (*yatastadiyāḥ,* 73). With one stroke, distinctions such as those of caste, learning, beauty, family, wealth, and profession among others that had plagued Hindu society for long, are removed (*nāsti teṣu jātividyārūpa kuladhanakriyādi bhedaḥ,* 72).

The main impediment to *bhakti* is bad company (*kusaṅgati*) which is the source of *kāma* (desire), anger, *moha* and *māyā*. In fact, he goes on to say that by rising above the Vedas, i.e. *sannyasti*, one can have access to love (of *bhakti*). To the question, who can ward off *māyā*?, the sage responds: *yo vedanāmapi sannyasasti, kevalamavicchinā anurāgam labhate* (*Nārada-Bhakti-Sūtra*, 49).

The Sūtra texts like the *Śāṇḍilya-Bhakti-Sūtra* and the *Nārada-Bhakti-Sūtra* dealt with theoretical aspects of *bhakti*. Its practical aspect was developed in Purāṇas that dealt with *saguṇa* form of god which was opposite of what Śaṅkarācārya said in a prayer, attributed to him:

> O lord, forgive me my three sins:
> You are everywhere, yet I worship you here;
> You are without form, yet I worship you
> In these, and these other forms;
> You need no praise, yet I offer you
> This prayer.
> Lord, forgive me my three human sins.

The Purāṇas transformed the advaitic vice into virtue, for love needs not an attributeless (*nirguṇa*) and formless god but a god having human form and attributes, for without form, mind finds it difficult to concentrate. So the cycle of incarnations or *avatāravāda* came into existence. The incarnations were portrayed in their supreme beauty and power leading to love and reverence respectively. Hence there was a shift in portrayal of characters. For instance, Kṛṣṇa of the *Mahābhārata* is *laukika* (a mortal being of this world) but in the Purāṇas he attains *alaukika*, divine, status. Thus, the Sūtra texts and Purāṇas prepared theoretical and practical background of *bhakti*. The Gupta emperors gave it, i.e. the *Bhāgavata Purāṇa*, royal patronage, and their flag had Garuḍa, the vehicle of Lord Viṣṇu, on it which speaks of acceptance of the *Bhāgavata* by that period.

II

The *bhakti* in the *Gītā* is *jñāna-bhakti* (intellectual devotion). The

Nārada-Bhakti-Sūtra interpreted the *jñāna-bhakti* of the *Gītā* in formulaic form without losing sight of its various aspects. The *Śrīmad Bhāgavata* established it in illustrative mode in the ninth century. It dealt with the origin of *bhakti* in its very beginning:

> *utpannā draviḍe sāham vṛddhim karnāṭake gatā* ।
> *kvacit kvacinmahārāṣṭre gurjare jīrṇatām gatā* ॥
> — *Padma Purāṇa,* Uttarakhaṇḍa, pp. 50, 51

> Born in the Draviḍa, I grew up in Karnataka. I earned respect here and there in Maharashtra and waned in Gujarat.

This pronouncement regarding the development of *bhakti* was made in the *Bhāgavata* period written in the ninth century. It would have been re-written in fifteenth or sixteenth century in the history of *bhakti,* for it went up to Kashmir and attained its eternal youth in Vṛndāvana and Mathurā. Another tradition later than the *Bhāgavata* speaks of the origin of *bhakti* in southern India but mentions its development beyond Gujarat and the role of Kabīr in northern India.

> *bhaktī dravīṇa upajī laye rāmānanda* ।
> *pargaṭa kiyā kabīra ne saptadvīpa navakhaṇḍa* ॥
> — Hazariprasad Dwivedi, p. 54

> Born in the Draviḍa, i.e. the southern India it was brought to the northern India by Rāmānanda where it was manifested by Kabīr all over India.

The *Bhāgavata* not only articulated Purāṇic, if not epical, dimension of *bhakti* but also considered its kinds, and celebration.

Moreover, the *Nārada-Bhakti-Sūtra* is an interpretation and elaboration of *bhakti* in the *Gītā*. The *Gītā* not only deals with *bhakti-yoga* among other but puts knowledge above all. The *Nārada-Bhakti-Sūtra* interprets the *Gītā*'s *yoga* and replaces knowledge with *bhakti.* The *Bhāgavata* takes a step ahead and ends ambivalence of the *Nārada-Bhakti-Sūtra* towards Vedas and scriptures, and explains elimination of caste and other social distinction in terms of mythological narratives about the sports of Lord. The shift in emphasis on passionate devotion from the *Gītā*'s knowledge —

centric and speculative *bhakti* — may be seen in many aspects, including *dharma*. The *dharma* that was determined by the Vedic commands, by the time of Smṛtis became what is followed by the learned without attachment and antipathy to which the heart assents. The *Bhāgavata* proposed a new aspect of the notion of *dharma*, which is the core of Hinduism and crucial to the understanding of Hinduism. S.N. Dasgupta rightly remarked regarding it:

> *Dharma* according to the *Bhāgavata* consists of the worship of God without any ulterior motive — a worship performed with a perfect sincerity of heart by men who are kindly disposed towards all, and who have freed themselves from all feelings of jealousy. . . . Thus *dharma* as supreme devotion to God is superior to the Vedic definition of *dharma*, which can produce only sense-gratification of various kinds. — Dasgupta, pp. 10-11

The *Bhāgavata* is an elaboration of a new mode of worship and subscription to the Kṛṣṇa's *saumya-mānuṣarūpam* (11.51), sought by Arjuna overawed by the *viśvarūpa* (cosmic vision) of Kṛṣṇa. The familiar human form of Kṛṣṇa is the subject of the *Bhāgavata Purāṇa*: from the chaos in which Kṛṣṇa is born and then passes through various vicissitudes of life as an incarnation of God in human form who is a God Himself, and then restores order in the society or world.

Moreover, the *Bhāgavata* is a compendium of devotion. The *navadhā bhakti* which found its expression in different ways in *bhakti* poets is discussed in it. The *Bhāgavata* categorizes *bhakti* on the lines of three kinds of human nature as *sāttvika bhakti* (devotion with no worldly motivation), *rājasika bhakti* (devotion motivated by the desire of power, i.e. power and wealth); and *tāmasika bhakti* (devotion marked by the forces of *tamas*, i.e. darkness, arrogance and jealousy). The *Bhāgavata* furthers categories of devotees into four kinds, in the *Gītā*, as discussed earlier, and proposes nine ways of *bhakti*:

> *śravaṇam kīrtanam viṣṇoḥ smaraṇam pādasevanam* ।
> *arcanam vandanam dāsyam sākhyamātma nivedanam* ॥
> — *Bhāgavata*, 7.5.23

> Hearing about Him, reciting, remembering and serving at the feet of Viṣṇu, worshipping, saluting and serving Him, becoming a friend to Him and entreating Him (are nine folds of *bhakti*).

In a way it is a simplification of the eleven kinds of *bhakti* mentioned in the *Nārada-Bhakti-Sūtra:*

> *guṇamāhātmyaśakti-rūpaśakti-pūjyāśakti-smaraṇaśakti-dāsyaśakti-sakhyaśakti-vātsalyaśakti-kāntaśakti-ātmanivedanaśakti-tanmaya-śakti-paramavirahaśakti-rūpā ekadhā api ekādaśadhā bhavati,* — 82

> *Bhakti*, though one, manifests itself in eleven forms, i.e. (i) love of God's blessed qualities, (ii) love of beautiful form, (iii) love of worshipping Him, (iv) love of remembering Him incontinently, (v) love of serving Him, (vi) loving Him like a friend, (vii) loving Him as a son, (viii) loving Him as the husband, (ix) love in submission to him, (x) love of complete absorption or being drowned in Him, and (xi) love of experiencing anguish of separation from Him.

The *Bhāgavata* goes a step beyond the *Gītā* and the *Nārada-Bhakti-Sūtra.* Despite being God, Kṛṣṇa is dependent on His devotees who do not "know anything other than Me, nor do I know anything else but them" (*Bhāgavata* 9.4.60-68).

Apart from the new relationship between God and devotees, the *Bhāgavata* revolutionized social relations. The society, plagued with decadent and static caste system, needed a text that would not only speak for the lost and lowliest but also placed them, if not higher, then at least at par with others in social hierarchy. The *bhakti* in the *Bhāgavata* is the means, as it stated in III.33.7, that a *cāṇḍāla,* a low caste with sincere faith and devotion was dearer to God than a brāhmaṇa without it. It rejects the notion of superiority of brāhmaṇas. Poverty was not a burden or curse but an essential qualification of a true *bhakta.* God favours the poor, for He himself is so (10.60.4). Thus it offers some solace to the distressed of all sorts. The *Bhāgavata* however does not represent the viewpoint of the established orthodox social and economic groups. On the contrary, the wealthy, learned and influential supporters of the *status quo* appear as the prime opponents of devotional religion in the *Bhāgavata*. Praise of poverty and compassion for the distressed characterize the social teachings of the *Bhāgavata* (Hopkins, 9-15).

The *Bhāgavata* presents a new cosmology, psychology, and geography through the biography of Kṛṣṇa. It is a biography of Kṛṣṇa from his birth to his sports as a human being. It makes forays into the psyche of possessed souls of human, animals and natural beings. On the surface it is questioning of the institution of marriage, and on the other it is sublimation of unsanctioned relationship. Another important feature of the *Bhāgavata* is its transitional status between the *Gītā* and Jayadeva's *Gītagovinda*. Kṛṣṇa, the gracious being, becomes the God, an incarnation of Viṣṇu, who conducts himself through predicaments of life as a human being. Kṛṣṇa had *gopīs* as friends but none as one would adorn the central place. A mere mention of a nameless *gopī* in the *Bhāgavata* is fully developed as a full character in subsequent literature by Kavi Līlāsukha (eleventh-twelfth centuries) in *Kṛṣṇa-Karṇāmṛta* and Śrī Vallabhācārya in the fifteenth century. Between the two emerged an unprecedented combination of music and rhythm, love and devotion in Jayadeva's *Gītagovinda* (twelfth century) which develops Rādhā as an embodiment of amorous devotion (*prema-bhakti*).[4]

Rādhā adds a new dimension to the *bhakti* tradition. The early reference to Rādhā can be traced to *Gāthāsaptaśatī* and in the *Padma Purāṇa, Matsya Purāṇa* and *Brahmavaivartta Purāṇa*. The *Bhāgavata Purāṇa* has no character like Rādhā excepting a feeble reference to a *gopī* in 10.30.24. The acceptance of unsanctioned love indicates the possibility of her existence in folk tradition before the poets like Jayadeva (Sanskrit), Vidyāpati (Maithilī), Caṇḍīdāsa (Bengali) and Sūrdās (Hindi) among others immortalized her in Indian psyche and literature. In Jayadeva, Kṛṣṇa and Rādhā, as a beautiful woman, share passionate love for each other. It deals with three stages of mutation of the two into passionate love and longing, the separation and the reunion. *The*

4. For detailed discussion of Rādhā see Sisir Kumar Das, *Rādhā, The Mad Lover: Essays on Medieval Indian Religious Poetry*, Calcutta: Papyrus, 1984.

Indian Song of Love, as Edwin Arnold translated it into English in 1881, existed, as it does even now, at multiple levels — as a devotional poem, for it deals with fourth mode of *bhakti* of the *Bhāgavata,* i.e. *smaraṇam* (remembering) and a poem of love 'physical and spiritual' dealing with *vilāsa līlā* (amatory sports) of the two, making us agree to the view that there is nothing sacred or profane in Indian tradition. It is this multiplicity of existence of the *Gītagovinda* that makes it the most commented upon text apart from the *Gītā* and the *Bhāgavata.* The Indian mind's acceptance of Rādhā-Kr̥ṣṇa relationship can be seen in its sanctity to a socially unsanctified relationship to such an extent that it is considered more sacred than even Sūkta texts.

III

The above endeavours at defining *bhakti* focus on the role of heart and head (intellect). The former leads to submission and the latter to intellect. The latter adds worship of the Supreme Being or deity along with love for it/him or her. In a way it is a synthesis of love and unflinching *śraddhā* (devotion).[5] The Vedic texts/discourse by sixth to seventh century BCE in its various ways focused on *karma-*

5. There is another way of looking at it from the perspective of love and relationship. The *Atharvaveda* stressed the significance of *kāma* (love). It says, "*Kāma* (love) is the first born, loftier than the gods, ancestors and men. You, O love, are the eldest of all, altogether mighty. To you we pay homage" (9.2.19). When a higher self loves a lower self it is *vātsalya* (affection). When two equal selves love each other, it is *prema* (love). If a lower self loves a higher self, it is *bhakti* (devotion). It can be seen in terms of submission as well. When two equal selves meet and submit to each other, it is *prema.* When a lower self submits itself to a higher self, it is *bhakti.* And when a higher self submits itself to a lower self, it is *vātsalya.* The nature of relationship and submission determines the nature of relationship and *bhakti.* In all three of them there is "love" as the permeating element. But the nature of relationship between two selves depending on their status determines the kind of *bhakti.* There is combination of all three in *bhakti,* so it is the highest form of love.

   This relationship is reflected in different kinds of *bhakti* in the *Gītā,* the *Nārada-Bhakti-Sūtra* and the *Bhāgavata.* Later, Tulasīdāsa discussed it as the *navadhā bhakti* in "Āraṇyakāṇḍa" of *Rāmacaritamānasa, dohā* 4-35, *caupāī* 3-4 and *dohā* 16, *caupāī* 3-6.

kāṇḍa (ritualistic) worship. In the Upaniṣads it became intellectual meditation despite its unprecedented metaphysical perspicacity. The dreariness of Vedic ritualism and *Nirguṇa Brahman* of Upaniṣads were incapable of satisfying religious desires and aspirations of common people. To meet the demands of common people, new religious modes came into existence which can be divided into two parts: *nāstika* (atheistic) and *āstika* (theistic). The first branched out into Buddhism and Jainism propounded by Buddha and Mahāvīra and the latter into Purāṇic discourse which gave pre-eminence to *bhakti* revolving around Viṣṇu and his incarnations of Rāma and Kṛṣṇa. Accordingly new discourses were constructed like the *Nārada-Bhakti-Sūtra* and the *Śāṇḍilya-Bhakti-Sūtra* that stressed the significance of *bhakti* and preferred it to *jñāna* and *karma-yoga.* These texts extend the interpretation of *bhakti* in the *Gītā* that considers righteous conduct and observation of rules necessary. Nārada and Śāṇḍilya consider them otherwise. In the *Gītā, bhakti-yoga* was equal to *jñāna-yoga* and *karma-yoga* which became subordinate to the *bhakti-yoga* in the Sūtra discourse. The seed of *bhakti* in the Vedic discourse became a sprout in the Upaniṣadic literature. It grew into a plant in the *Mahābhārata* and the *Gītā,* and in the *Bhāgavata* it became a tree laden with flowers.

The Purāṇic discourse and its forms of worship found its acceptance in southern India. There were, however, two major impediments: one was re-establishment of Vedic *karma-kāṇḍa* or ritualism and the second was enunciation of non-dualism by Śaṅkarācārya. The non-duality of *Brahman* and *ātman* (soul) rejected the very idea of *bhakti.* However, the Vaiṣṇavites of southern India particularly the Āḻvār saints did not bother about the scholastic tenets of monism and the towering personality of Śaṅkara and his philosophy. Nāthamuni and the *ācārya*s of the tenth and eleventh centuries extended the tradition of Āḻvārs.

In the northern parts of India there was a general decline of Buddhism. *Tantra sādhanā* and *vāmācāra* plagued the society in which love degenerated to lust and sexual delinquency. To fill this vacuum the *gopī*'s love for Kṛṣṇa was a projection of its sublimation.

The new wave of *bhakti* began with the Āḻvār saints of Tamil Nadu in the southern India. In the southern India, Buddhism and Jainism were prevalent up to sixth century but Vaiṣṇavism surged afterwards and resulted in creation of *bhakti* literature in Tamil. The Vaiṣṇava *ācārya*s spread it in different parts of northern India. The movement simplified *bhakti* of the Upaniṣads and the *Gītā* for its devotees.[6] The Vaiṣṇava *ācārya*s were called Āḻvārs in the southern India. They sang, spoke and wrote in Tamil. Their oral compositions were transcribed and written by Nāthamuni in the ninth century. Though many of them were lost over a period of time, yet there are still about 4000 compositions in the collection called *Divya-Prabandham*. The Āḻvārs and *ācārya*s shared many similarities but differed in terms of emphasis, as the former focused on *bhakti* alone whereas the latter synthesized *karma* and *bhakti*. The former were not scholars like their counterparts who were scholars of eminence. In brief, heart dominated the Āḻvārs but it was head in the case of *ācārya*s. The Āḻvārs stressed the superiority of *bhakti* marked by recitation of *nāma* (*nāma smaraṇam),* and total surrender to Lord. They considered the threefold path of *karma, jñāna* and *bhakti* as the means for reaching God but the best way to achieve the desired goal was in seeking God's shelter and being entirely dependent on the grace of God. Their new and simplified version of *bhakti* opened its door to all men and women, rich and poor, high and low in the language of people.

Of different Āḻvārs (*āzh* or *āl* meaning drowned or immersed and *ar* is the honorific suffix) twelve are considered significant, though there is no unanimity about their number. The commonly accepted Āḻvārs with their Sanskrit name include

	Sanskrit Name
1. Periyāḻvār	Viṣṇucitta
2. Āṇḍāl	Godā (female saint)
3. Kulaśekhara Āḻvār	Kulaśekhara

6. For detailed discussion of the Nāyanmārs, the Āḻvārs and related schools, see Sisir Kumar Das, *A History of Indian Literature 500-1399*, pp. 27-51.

4. Tirumaḷiśai Āḻvār	Bhaktisāra
5. Tiruppaṇ Āḻvār	Yogivāhana
6. Madhura Kavi Āḻvār	Madhura Kavi
7. Tirumaṅgai Āḻvār	Parkāl
8. Nammāḻvār	Ṣaṭakopa
9. Bhūdattāḻvār	Bhūtayogin
10. Pey Āḻvār	Mahāyogin (Bhrāntayogin)
11. Toṇḍaraḍippoḍi Āḻvār	Bhaktāndhrireṇu
12. Poigai Āḻvār	Saroyogin

The Āḻvārs were paralleled by the sixty-three Nāyanmārs who interestingly for our purpose were preceded by Punītādevī, a woman devotional poet, known as Kāraikkāl Ammaiyar, who lived in the sixth century. After her marriage into a rich family, she became an ascetic in the shrine of Tiruvālaṅgāḍu near Chennai. She called herself a *pey* or ghost in her compositions and sought refuge at the feet of God for her release from all agonies of life. As one of the early voices of woman devotional poets she sought solace in her God from sufferings of her life, as she says:

> Some say He is in heaven. Let them say so.
> Some say He lives in the kingdom of Indra.
> Let them say so. But I will say, the god,
> whose throat became dark as He drank
> the poison in the ancient times, yet so
> radiant is He, lives in my heart.
>
> — V. Bhattācārya p. 69

Apart from Āḻvārs and Nāyanmārs, Raṅganātha Muni is considered as the first *ācārya*, followed by Yāmunācārya, Rāmānujācārya, Nimbārkācārya, Madhvācārya and Viṣṇu Swāmi among others. They founded four principal schools of *bhakti*: Śrī Sampradāya (Rāmānujācārya), Madhva Sampradāya (Madhvācārya), Nimbārka Sampradāya (Nimbārkācārya), and Rudra Sampradāya (Viṣṇu Swāmi). Rāmānujācārya proposed the principle of Viśiṣṭādvaita which is a philosophy of religion, neither pure philosophy nor religion, and that of *bhakti*. The object of *bhakti*, i.e. the Lord, can be attained through knowledge (*jñāna*) and devotion (*bhakti*) but *prapatti*, i.e. complete surrender to God is indispensible.

Madhvācārya did not accept Viśiṣṭādvaita (qualified monism) and proposed his Dvaitavāda (dualism). According to him, Viṣṇu is the Infinite Being (*Brahman*) who has infinite attributes with absolute control on *sṛṣṭi, sthiti, saṁhāra, niyama, āvaraṇa, bodhana, bandhana* and *mokṣa*. He has power to appear in different forms and incarnations. In his view, the cause of suffering of a being is *māyā* and the way of redemption from it is *bhakti*, for it removes the screen of *māyā* and frees a being from its clutches.

Nimbārkācārya founded the Nimbārka School around the principle of Dvaitādvaita. According to it, God, being and world are separate entities. Despite it, God and human being are inseparable because a being is dependent on *Brahman* (God) which is the cause of the world. Hence, the existence and relationship between the being and world rest on God's desire. In this school, Rādhā and Kṛṣṇa are the Supreme Infinite Beings. Rādhā is equal to Kṛṣṇa, as she is the Supreme Goddess who fulfils all desires.[7] The school sees Kṛṣṇa *bhakti* in five states of *śānta, dāsya, sakhya, vātsalya* and *mādhurya*.

Not much is known about Viṣṇu Svāmi, the person and his period. The text ascribed to him is *Sarvajñasūkta*. He considered God as Saccidananda and proposed that Kṛṣṇa is God incarnate with Nṛsiṁha as the main incarnation. Hence, the *Nṛsiṁhāvatāra* is the God for him and his object of devotion.

The *bhakti* movement became a pan-Indian movement around fourteenth century, as it took northern India in its sweep. It became a movement of masses, as it branched out in *nirguṇa* and *saguṇa* forms of worship. The former developed into *Jñānāśrayī* and

7. *autuvāme vṛṣbhānujāṁ mudā, virājamānāmanurūpasaubhagām* ǀ
śakhī sahastreḥ parisevitaṁ sadā, smarem devīm sakaleṣṭakāmdām ǁ
— *Daśaślokī, śloka* 5, in Baldev Upadhyaya, *Bhagavat-Sampradāya*, 344

Premāśrayī (knowledge-centric and love-centric respectively) and the latter into Rāma-centric (*Rāmāśrayī*) and Kṛṣṇa-centric (*Kṛṣṇāśrayī*). Rāmānanda played a very pivotal role in it. In the tradition of Rāmānujācārya he freed *bhakti* from the clutches of language and caste, as his disciples like Anantadāsa, Sureśvarānanda, Sukhānanda, Narahariyānanda, Yogānanda, Bhāvānanda, Pīṭa, Sen, Dhana, Raidāsa, Kabīr among others came from different castes. The *bhakti* poets in northern India included Kabīr, Raidāsa, Guru Nānak, Dādu Dayāl, Santa Sundaradāsa, and Malūkadāsas all from knowledge-centric *bhakti* traditions, and Kutuban, and Malik Mohammad Jāyasī in love-centric *nirguṇa bhakti* tradition. Tulsīdās, Swāmī Agradāsa, Nābhādāsa, and Hṛdayarāma wrote in the Rāma-centric *saguṇa bhakti* tradition, and the Kṛṣṇa-centric *saguṇa bhakti* tradition included Vallabhācārya and his disciples like Sūrdās, Kumbhana Dāsa and Kṛṣṇadāsa. Vallabhācārya's son Viṭṭhaladāsa also had four disciples namely Govinda Swāmī, Cittaswāmi, Caturbhuja Dāsa and Nandadāsa. All of them put together were called *aṣṭachāpa kavi* (Eight Poets).[8] Others included Mīrā, Hita Harivaṁśa, Swāmī Haridāsa (of Haridāsī or Sakhī Sampradāya), Vaiṣṇava Dāsa and last but not least Rasakhāna. The demarcating line between *nirguṇa* and *saguṇa*, *Rāmāśrayī* and *Kṛṣṇāśrayī* is very thin, i.e. a poet like Narsinh Mehta belongs to *saguṇa* and *nirguṇa* as well.

IV

Bhakti marks an unprecedented change in the history of Hindu culture in particular and Indian culture and literature in general. A.K. Ramanujan termed it a 'shift' and stated:

> A great many-sided shift occurred in Hindu culture and sensibility between the sixth and ninth century — or so it seems to that hindsight we sometimes call a sense of history. Bhakti is one name for that shift. — Ramanujan, p. 103

He used the term 'shift' in terms of linguistics and elaborated it thus:

8. For their detailed discussion, see Dhirendra Verma, *Aṣṭachāpa,* Allahabad: Ramanarayan Bookseller, 1950.

> . . . the shift is systematic, begins in a small way, in a particular locality or even community, and slowly spreads from there in waves, depending on a variety of conditions; the innovation does not universally replace the older forms, but develops a parallel existence that may come to dominate, cross, and transform the relevant, older linguistic or cultural forms — in this case, religious conceptions, practices, and patterns of feeling expressed by them. It is this complex of concepts, practices, patterns of feeling coupled with their artistic expression in texts, temples, etc. that I call "sensibility" here.
>
> — Ramanujan, p. 103

Rāmānujan's word captured the impact of the *bhakti* movement on the psyche of millions of Indians for about 900 years between the ninth and seventeenth century in particular. It varied in terms of its causes and intensity in different regions of the country. Its causes were different in the northern and southern India. But it was such a massive phenomenon that it attracted the attention of the native and foreign scholars. The European scholars could not digest the fact that such a movement of great consequence could be of native origin. How could the colonial masters concede the fact that the enslaved people even before their advent could have such a phenomenon? How could something so strong happen without their intervention? So Weber interpreted *śvetadvīpa* (the white island) described in the *Mahābhārata* as Europe, the birthplace of white races. Sir Grierson equalled it to the flash of lightning against the darkness of old religious sects. These views were contested by Bal Gangadhar Tilak and Krishnaswamy Iyengar among others. Acharya Ramchandra Shukla, while introducing the "Bhaktikāla" in *Hindī Sāhitya kā Itihāsa* (History of Hindi Literature) remarked that with the establishment of the Muslim rule there was no space for pride and enthusiasm in Hindus. Their temples were being destroyed in front of them and idols broken and revered persons insulted. But they could do nothing. They could neither sing songs of their glory nor could they hear about their past without feeling ashamed. The Hindus remained clouded with despair for a long time. Such a defeated community had no other way open to it other than seeking the power and mercy of God (Shukla 61). On the religious front there was decline all around. The combination of *karma, jñāna* and *bhakti* that keeps *dharma* alive had been disturbed by the perversion of the Siddha, Kāpālika, Vajrayāna, Nātha and Vāmācārī Buddhist traditions. The Hindu *dharma* had considerably declined by the time the Muslims came to India. Their invasion was a big 'shock' to it. There was a vacuum created by inaccessibility to the common people of the scholastic tradition of commentators of the *Brahmasūtra*, Upaniṣads, the *Gītā* among others particularly in the common people. The *bhakti* movement came forward to fill the gap and engage and sustain them as it democratized esoteric knowledge contained in scriptures and sacred texts in Sanskrit by singing and composing in languages of people. Hazari Prasad Dwivedi rejected the proposition of his predecessors and thereby contributed with his interpretations to our understanding of *bhakti.* Disagreeing with Grierson he remarked that the flash of lightning was not such as Grierson thought about it. For this to happen, clouds had been gathering for centuries. But the question of its sudden emergence deserves attention. According to him, its main cause was in the confluence of the Vaiṣṇavite *ācāryā*s of the southern India and concrete imagination of the Purāṇas (Dwivedi 53). However, for those who consider *bhakti* as an offshoot of the influence of Islam particularly Sufism would well remember the words of Hazariprasad Dwivedi who remarked regarding the influence of Islam on Hindi literature:

> I do not forget the influence of Islam but wish to state with emphasis that even if Islam had not come (to India), even the twelve *ānā*s of Hindi literature would have been the same, as it is now.
>
> — Dwivedi, p. 16

Moreover, he did not subscribe to Acharya Shukla's propositions of *bhakti* as a reaction of defeated people against the Muslim invasion and affliction. Had it been so, the *bhakti*, according to him, would have come into existence first in northern India particularly around Sindh region and not in the southern India?

The plausibility of Dwivedi's arguments notwithstanding, the fact is that the movement was so pervasive and intense in its consequences that settled interpretations elude us still.

The *bhakti* along with bringing about a major shift in existing social hierarchies and distinctions put forward a new definition of poet, poetry and poetics. A *bhakta* or saint did not need education, learning, or a family of high caste people or royal patronage to be a poet. There was no need for him/her to renounce the world. False renunciation, it seems, had become a common profession for those who had no other path left to them. In fact, such people courted severe criticism for their renunciation as Tulasīdāsa said, *mui nārī ghara sampati nāsī* । *muḍ muḍāi bhaye saṁnyāsī* (When wife was no more, and all property or home was gone, then people became a *saṁnyāsin*).

The *bhakta* poets did not care much for worldly power and pelf; rather some of them spurned it. Rejecting royal patronage, Kumbhana Dāsa spoke:

mokon kahā sīkarī son kāma ।
āvatajāta panhijyān tūtain bisur gayo harināma ॥
jinako mukha dekhe dukha upajat tinako karana pari parṇāma ।
kumbhanadāsa lāla giridhara binu aur sabai bekāma ॥

What have I to do with Sīkarī, the capital of Akbar? While going and returning I break my footwear and forget the name of Lord. The faces whose mere glance produces sorrow I had to salute them. Excepting Giridhara Kṛṣṇa all else is useless.

Nammāḻvār, the celebrated ninth century Tamil devotional poet, too voiced similar feeling much before Tulsī or Kumbhana Dāsa:

My lord of a thousand names
gives and gives
the fame of his giving
crosses all boundaries
I cannot praise anyone else
Cannot say to some paltry thing of this world.
"Your hand is bounteous as the rain
Your shoulders are strong as the mountains"

I cannot tell such barefaced lies.
— No More Kings, 3.9.7 in A.K. Ramanujan, p. 58

The *bhakta* poets spurned power not only political but also one associated with knowledge and poetry. Most of the *bhakta* poets became poets without any conscious desire to be poets. Poetry flowed from them as it was a consequence of their devotional experience. They did not compose with the sole aim of becoming poets. Most of them were not well-read but they were certainly "much heard" (*bahuśruta*) and learnt much from the company of the good souls and their teachers. The mainstream literary discourse took its time in accepting them in their fold. Despite it, their ability to delve deep into human hearts led to their acceptance by *loka* without which perhaps much of their compositions would have been lost for us. So even against the resistance of the learned, their voices could not be suppressed for long. They challenged the existing idioms and principles of poetics. However, such was their currency that poetics in Sanskrit and *bhāṣā* languages had to re-define their canons by recognizing *bhakti* as a *rasa* after dilly dallying for centuries. Ironically when Sanskrit poetry waned and Sanskrit poetics became apologetic about itself due to increasing inability of the younger generation to either appreciate it or modify it in accordance with the obtaining experience, the *bhakti rasa* came to be established finally with the work of Brahmanand Sharma and Karpatriji Maharaj on *bhakti rasa*.

V

Bhakti was a consequence of not an induced but natural innocence, "an ecstasy; it was this frenzy that nourished a new genre of poetry" (Sisir Kumar Das, pp. 1-8). In the process of doing so it produced a rich body of poetry. This new genre of poetry was enriched by the Nāyanmārs, the Āḻvārs, the Vīraśaivas and the *bhāṣā* poets from different castes, regions, religions, and genders. This element of ecstasy expressed in different literary and metrical forms was unique because at a certain level it was related to mysticism as well. Betty Heimann saw this connection between ecstasy and mysticism by seeing their proximity in terms of meaning:

> Ecstasy, in the literal sense of the Greek term *ekstasis*, means to escape from one's own rational and definite position; in this sense it has the same aim as mysticism, although each approaches it from a different angle. — p. 95

Like their male counterparts, women devotional poets resorted to poetry to escape from the ungodly world given to them. The ecstasy of their experience might have been more than what their words could capture because they spoke or sang in a state or language over which they might not have had any conscious control. The *bhakti* writing put together, marked "the triumphs of emotion over intellect, of the concrete over the abstract, of the acceptance over its ascetic denial" (Zvelebil, p. 194).

Bhakti was an unfathomable ocean of love fed by inexhaustible springs of mystical experiences. This relationship between *bhakti* and mysticism demands discussion. *Bhakti* and mysticism are related, as they are concerned with God and experience of bliss. *Bhakti*, it can be said is a state of being or experience which might be of different kinds. For the sake of convenience, it can be put under the umbrella term mystical experience that might change from culture to culture and from civilization to civilization particularly between pagan[9] and non-pagan or monotheistic civilizations. It would be pertinent here to examine/consider experience in the Indian and Western traditions. Mysticism has been considered from ontological perspective,[10] i.e. from content or goal of mystical experience but not so much from epistemological experience with primary focus on mental processes involved in the experience. Moreover, there are opposite views regarding the nature of experience, though there is a near unanimity

9. I use the term "pagan" knowing full well its pejorative connotations, for the Latin root for it *paganus* stands for a rustic heathen because more country people were later on becoming Christians than the people of towns. Since there is no term for describing Hindu civilization in English, I use the word "pagan" which for me stands for *prakṛti pūjaka* (nature worshipping), and *ūrjā pūjaka* (energy worshipping) people.

10. See Rudolph Otto, *Mysticism: East and West*, New York: Collier Books, 1962, pp. 10-18.

about transcendental unity of mystical experience. Swami Vivekananda, a great mystic himself, remarked, "Mystics in every religion speak the same tongue and teach the same truth."[11] R. Otto also supported the view when he stated:

> . . . mysticism is the same in all ages and in all places, timeless and independent of history, it has always been identical in East and West and other differences vanish here. Whether the flower of mysticism blooms in India or in China, in Persia or on the Rhine, its fruit is one. —Otto, p. 81

Mystical experience unites all devotees, for all of them are concerned with transcendental experience that can be or has been experienced but has found no words to articulate it. It is inexplicable and unheard because it is inarticulatable. However, if compositions and words are denominators, one can say that despite having similarities every experience was unique. Kabīr, Sūrdās, Tulsī were all *bhakta*s and mystics; Sūra, Mīrā and Narsī Mehtā were devotees of Lord Kṛṣṇa, but it is difficult to say that all of them had equal intensity and identical experience of their devotion. Similarly, Āṇḍāḷ, Mīrā, Mahādevī Akkā, Lal Dêd and Gaṅgāsatī were all women devotional poets and mystics with the same end in view but their experiences on their way were not identical. All of them wrote in different languages using not only different signifiers but also the signified, i.e. God or the object of devotion. Similarly, Āṇḍāḷ, Mīrābāī, St. Teresa, St. John of the Cross and Meister Eckhart from different religions and sects would have had different experiences because if devotees of the same religion or sect betray irreducible differences, there would be differences in the experiences of devotees and mystics from different civilizations, cultures and religions.

Mysticism[12] is an experience and all experiences are sources of knowledge whether they can be worded or not. The West has

11. See Swami Vivekananda, *The Complete Works of Swami Vivekananda*, vol. VI, Calcutta Advaita Ashram, 1973, p. 81.

12. The word "mystic" is derived from the Greek *mystikos* meaning "of the mysteries." The term *mystikos* is derived from *mystos* (keeping silence) →

two views. One view accepts the validity and cognitive import of religious experience. The other views like Logical Positivism and Marxism do not accept it. The first group can further be considered in two subgroups. The first of these opines that the appreciation of the divine is a consequence of inference or interpretation from/ of religious experience. In it the validity or religious experience is accepted but whether or not it can be understood as wholly immediate and self-evident is a subject of analysis and interpretation. The other sub-group proposes religious experience to be immediate and a self-authenticating encounter with the Divine. This immediacy is of two sorts, i.e. revelational and mystical. Revelational immediacy is achieved when human mind's certain character/property apprehends God in the form of an insight or certitude. This is also known as the divine-human encounter that can be understood in terms of "I-Thou" relationship of Martin Buber. The second kind of immediacy is about the direct experience of God achieved by transcending the senses through contemplation. This is termed mysticism.

On the other hand, the Vedānta of Hinduism, in its different schools recognizes three valid means (*pramāṇas*) of knowledge: *pratyakṣa* (perception), *anumāna* (inference) and *śabda* (verbal testimony). The Upaniṣadic statement like *tattvamasi* (That thou art) can, however, accept direct initiative knowledge. These are means of knowledge for empirical knowledge. Mystical knowledge of the ultimate reality is not a means of knowledge but its supreme end.

Mysticism is the transcendent, life-transforming experience of the ultimate reality. It is often of three types: Nature Mysticism, God Mysticism and Soul Mysticism. All three of them are

→ which is close to Sanskrit word *maun*. On the other hand, according to Betty Heimann, *mueo* in its original Greek was a technical medical term meaning "to unite," i.e. to join together the edges of wound and was subsequently used in the general sense of "rejoining whatever has broken apart"; thus, *mueo* may mean either to close the lips or to shut the eyes. She defines mysticism literally as "combining things which had been separated, so as to restore their primal unity" (95).

discernible in Hindu culture, whereas Christian Mysticism has primarily been God Mysticism. Nature Mysticism is primarily seen in pagan cultures, particularly in hymns of the *Ṛgveda*. It was followed, if not completely taken over, by Soul Mysticism of the Upaniṣads and God Mysticism of *bhakti* schools which found its expression in the *mārga* or paths of knowledge and the path of love, known as the *mārga* of *jñāna* (knowledge) and *bhakti* (devotion). Also, Christian mysticism grew around the path of love and divine Grace. The similarities between the two notwithstanding, the basic differences between Hindu[13] and Christian religions that form the basis of mystical experience need discussion.

Both of them have different views regarding the nature of man. Human personality in Christian theology is regarded dichotomous (consisting of the body and mind, the latter itself being called soul and spirit). The Pauline doctrine of Original Sin is transmitted to mankind and it has tainted human soul to such an extent that man cannot save himself. On the other hand, in the Hindu view, human being is not dichotomous but trichotomous and consists of body, mind, and spirit, known as the *ātman* or self. One's actions determine one's state of being. Evil tendencies derived from one's own actions taint the mind. However, they do not impact *ātman* or real self.

The Judeo-Christian and Hindu traditions differ in the nature of soul's relationship with God. In the former, God is the self-existent creator, and the other who has created things. God and soul can come closer by mystical experience but they can never be one because they are altogether different in nature. But according to Vedānta schools, God is the Supreme Self and the individual selves that are self-sufficient and share the nature, are only reflections or parts of Him. Mystical experience does not remain trapped with the forms and realizes the integral relationship

13. I avoid the term Hinduism and Hindu religion, for Hinduism is neither limited as an "ism" is, nor is it a religion in the sense of organized religion like Christianity or Islam. It is a culture based on *dharma* marked by righteous way of living.

between God and souls. This view does not see man as a sinner but allows him to say, *aham brahmāsmi* (I am the Infinite Self). First of all, the Infinite Self is not wrathful and does not punish the individual self for claiming to be Him or a part of Him. Also there is no adversarial relationship between "I" and other individual self/selves because it accepts that *tattavamasi* (That Thou art). So how is the dialogue between I and you possible? The response to it is in *saṅgacchadhvam, samavādadhvam sambomanasi jānatam* (Let us walk together, let us speak together and know together).

Further, regarding the salvic value of mystical experience Christianity considers incapability of penance or sacrifice in getting rid of the Original Sin. It can be wiped off by Divine Grace achieved by Christ through his crucifixation and the Cross. This grace is communicated through baptism and sacraments. Thus freed from Original Sin, a soul will attain salvation after death by being in God's presence in heaven. Thus, salvation does not need mystical experience as a prerequisite (Poulain, XVII). On the other hand, the concept did not prosper in Hindu philosophy, though the *Gītā* mentions possibility of *mokṣa* or mystical experience through Divine Grace. It considers mystical Reality as a *sine qua non* for *mukti* or *mokṣa* (salvation or liberation). *Mokṣa,* in fact, is one of the main ends of life along with *dharma* (righteousness), *artha* (material well-being), and *kāma* (righteous gratification of desires) and thus it is not a metaphysical but a physical category.

Moreover, Hindu and Christian mystical traditions differ in terms of nature and fate of mystical experience. The Judeo-Christian tradition relies on the belief that the real essence of God can never be seen by a living being.[14] God told Moses in the *Old Testament*, "Thou canst not see My Face, for man shall not see Me and live" (Exodus XXXIII, p. 20).

Even according to Greek Orthodox Church, God's essence (*ouisia*) cannot be perceived; so what mystics see in the form of

---

14. The concept of grace did not prosper in Hindu civilization though the *Gītā* mentions *mokṣa* or mystic experience through divine Grace.

vision is the *energeia* or *enercia* of God. Against it, Hindu view holds that a human being is a part of Supreme Reality, or *Brahman* and so God's actual essence can be experienced. The Upaniṣadic discourse approves it and the subsequent development of *bhakti* schools proposed that God does not only have personal attributes but also a real anthropomorphic form in the form of non-attributive *nirguṇa* and *saguṇa* (as Rāma, and Kṛṣṇa among others) which can be experienced.[15] The Advaita Vedānta accepts that the attainment of the total identity of the individual self with *Brahman* is possible in this very life, though they do not accept that the impersonal Absolute can be the object of knowledge.

Bhakti was an expression of experience of ecstasy that did not take cognizance of existing shibboleths and broke off all banks, like a deluge. It celebrated victory of heart over head, of the concrete over the abstract, of acceptance over rejection, and of celebration over denial. The sweep and shift brought out by it can be discussed and interpreted but without success on most occasions, as it resists exercises of system building and abstraction, for it was a reaction against them. This can be better understood in term of *kathā*s or narratives, as they are a proven mode of explaining even the abstract into concrete to humanity at large.

VI

Since the preceding discussion traced early manifestations of *bhakti* to Vedic and Upaniṣadic texts, a small consideration of voice of women in that discourse will not be inappropriate here. Like many *mantra*-seeing *ṛṣi*s there were *ṛṣikā*s (women seers), who composed

15. The *Gītā* too on occasions more than one proposes that it is possible to perceive and know the true essence of God and attain oneness with it (11. 54 & 18. 55). Lord Kṛṣṇa in chapter XI tells Arjuna that he would give him "divine eyes" to see the transcendental "cosmic form." The "divine eye" is the higher faculty or intuition of the Vedic *mantra*s particularly *dhi* of the *Gāyatrī mantra*. It becomes *buddhi* in the Upaniṣads. The *Kaṭhopaniṣad* mentions, "The *ātman* is seen through a subtle, one pointed *buddhi*" (3.12). The *Muṇḍaka Upaniṣad* states, "The luminous inner self is seen when the mind is purified and knowledge becomes clear" (3.1.8).

hymns in worship of gods. Vāk, one of the Vedic women *ṛṣis*,[16] speaks about herself being the god of *rāṣṭra* (nation), bestower of property, knower of the Supreme Being, and subject of worship in the *yajñas* in *Ṛgveda* (10.125.1). She claims that *Gods pervading everywhere had seen her in many forms.* She is one of many voices of women in the earliest Vedic writing. *Bṛhaddevatā* (2.82-84) mentions about 27 women seers in the Vedic period. All of them were *mantra*-seeing *ṛṣis*. Reciting *mantra* and invoking gods was not the sole privilege of men; the Ṛgvedic society allowed its women to recite *mantra*, and some erudite ones could see or experience the Infinite.

Of these Viśvavarā was born in the family of sage Atri who was the father of Dattātreya, Durvāsā and Soma and married to Satī Anasūyā. He was a priest of the dynasties of Puru, Anu, Duhyu and Yadu. Viśvavarā's compositions are found in the 28th *sūkta* of the 5th Maṇḍala of the *Ṛgveda* in the form of prayer and appreciation to the God Agni (Fire). Invoking the god she offers *āhuti* to the god and says that early in the morning the light of the god of fire spreads itself in the high sky, so Viśvavarā prays to him.[17] Further, one who welcomes and adores Agni receives prosperity and never becomes a pauper.[18] Later she invokes Agni to annihilate her enemies and pray to the god for further strengthening the bond

---

16. Yāska in his *Nirukta* has explained the term *ṛṣi* as one who has seen *dharma*. "*Sākṣātkṛtdharmanaḥ ṛṣyo babhūvuḥ*" (1.6). Moreover, it meant that *ṛṣi* was one before whom the self-generated Supreme Being presented Itself. She practised penance and had seen (understood), the Vedic *mantra*:

    yad yad enān tapasyāvān brahma svayamabhūḥ
    abhiyānarṣat yad ṛṣinām ṛṣitvam iti vijñāyate
    — 3.3

17. *samiddho agnidivir śocirśreta*
    pratyaṅgkuśasamurviya vibhāti ।
    ati prāci viśvavara namobhiḥ
    devān etanā haviṣā ghṛtāci ॥
    — 5.28-1

18. *viśvam sa dhatte draviṇam yaminva* ।
    syātithyamagne ni ca dhattitpuraḥ ॥
    — 2

of mutual love between husband and wife for social, familial security and stability.[19]

Apālā, like Viśvavarā, came from the family of Atri. She was an unlucky woman, for she had skin diseases and did not have fully grown body. As a consequence her husband expelled her from his house. It was something that she could not digest even in the fold of her father's house. So she prayed to god Indra for a happy married life with her husband's affection. By the time Apālā wrote, Indra was established as the most powerful god and purveyor of victory. The largest number of *sūkta*s in the *R̥gveda* (about 250) are dedicated to the worship of Indra. *Somarasa* was the dearest drink to him, as it infused immense power into him. Apālā knew it well so she offers it to him in *R̥gveda.*

kanyāru vārvāyatī somamapi srutāvidat ।
astaṁ bharantya bravīdindrāya sunvai tvā śakrāya sunvai tvā ॥
— 8.91.1

In her unique way, she further seeks from Indra:

kuvicchakat kuvit karat kuvinno vasyasaskarat ।
kuvit patidviṣo yatīrindreṇa saṅgamāmahai ॥
— 8.91.4

Humiliated and forsaken by her husband, she seeks Indra's shelter and prays to him to make her free from diseases and distresses of her family members, ensuring their prosperity and happiness.

After Apālā, Ghoṣā has two *sūkta*s (39 and 40) in the tenth Maṇḍala of the *R̥gveda.* She was born in the family of the sage Kakṣivan, mentioned in 1st Maṇḍala (116.126) of the *R̥gveda* and in 9th Maṇḍala (74). Despite being born in the family of sages she did not get a suitable bridegroom for her so she lived in her father's house but got fed up. She prays to Aśvins who possessed limitless knowledge and power. *Yo vāṁ parijmā suvr̥daśvinā* (10.39.1) (I pray day and night to Aśvins moving in their beautiful and strong chariot (10.40.11-12).

19. *sam jāspatyā suyamamā krunuśacara*
—3

It should not be construed that all women Vedic poets wrote to shed off or for emancipation from their physical diseases in their compositions. There were quite a few women sages who composed highly mystical hymns. Aditi is a *sūkta darśinī* sage. She is highly inquisitive, learned, possessed with mystical faculty and experience. Her inquisition into origin of universe and gods leads her to succinctly express her mode of constructing knowledge about them:

> *brahmaṇaspatiretā saṁ karmāra ivādhamat* ।
> *devānāṁ pūrvye yuge 'staḥ sadjāyata* ॥
> — 10.72.2

Aditi illustrates it by stating that the way a blacksmith ignites fire through air from air-sheaths, similarly god Bṛhaspati fused life into universe. Thereafter truth was born in the universe. From this primitive water element, various beings were created. Aditi says regarding it:

> *yaddevā adaḥ salile susaṁrabdhā atiṣṭhata* ।
> *atrā vo nṛtyatāmiva tīvro reṇurapāyata* ॥
> — 10.72.6

Earlier all gods lived together in water. Later the most brilliant of them, i.e. the Sun came out and settled itself in the sky. In the next *ṛcā* she mentions her twelve sons namely Mitra, Varuṇa, Dhātā, Aryamā, Aṁsa, Bhaga, Vivasvān, Śakra, Pūṣā, Savitā, Tvaṣṭā and Viṣṇu (*Manu-Smṛti,* 1.8).

From these verses it becomes evident that she is not only a *mantra*-seer but also a metaphysician. Like her is Vāk, the daughter of the sage Ambhrana. She seems to have seen and experienced the ultimate Supreme Being. She through her compositions makes us realize the true form of God and His/Her divine power. She says:

> *ahaṁ rudrebhirvasubhiścarāmyahamādityairuta viśvadevaiḥ* ।
> — 10.125.1

Commenting on the omniscient and splendid form of God she further remarks that she is the god of the nation, giver of property and wealth, and knower of the supreme element, worthy of worship in the *yajñas*. The omnipresent gods have put her in many places and seen her as well (10.125.3).

Later she pronounced herself beyond worldly concerns, creator of all beings and pervading the heaven and the earth with her greatness. Her pronouncements speak volumes about her faith in her intellectual and spiritual achievements.

After the Vedic *ṛṣikās*, the voice of women finds its expression in the Upaniṣads in a different way. Two narratives centring around Yājñavalkya bring women like Gārgī and Maitreyī (who are neither poets nor even narrators in the given narratives) in centre of concerns indirectly because of their intellectual prowess, nobility and willingness to sacrifice material gain for knowledge. Gārgī disturbs Yājñavalkya with her serious spiritual questions and Maitreyī with her renunciation of her share in the property for spiritual quest(ion)s.

The sixth Brāhmaṇa of the *Bṛhadāraṇyaka Upaniṣad* opens with the questions of Gārgī, the daughter of Vacaknu (III.6.1). In the court of Janaka, Gārgī came to Yājñavalkya and questioned him about the nature of *Brahman*. She came there merely to know from Yājñavalkya about the supreme reality and not to vanquish him or to examine his knowledge, as is indicated by some lines of the eighth Brāhmaṇa (III.8.2). Gārgī Vācaknavi asks Yājñavalkya:

> O Yājñavalkya, the whole earth is said to be pervaded by
> (a layer of) water; where is that layer?
> Yājñavalkya replied: It is in the (layer of) air.
> Well, where is this (layer of) air?
> Gārgī, it is in ether.
> Where is this ether pervading?
> Gārgī, it is in the region of the *gandharvas*.
> Where is that region located?
> It is in the realm of the sun.
> Where again is that (situated)?
> Gārgī, it is in the region of the moon.

> Where is that again?
>
> It is in the region of the stars.
>
> Where is that region located?
>
> Gārgī, it is in the region of the gods.
>
> Where is that region of the gods?
>
> It is in the worlds of Indra.
>
> Where is that world of Indra situated?
>
> It is in the world of Prajāpati.
>
> Where is that region of Prajāpati situated?
>
> It is the world of *Brahman*, O Gārgī.
>
> Where is that world of *Brahman*?
>
> O Gārgī, ask me not any more, thou art asking that which is not to be asked. Cease thy queries, lest thy head drops down dead on the floor!

Vācaknavi Gārgī stopped at this threat of Yājñavalkya.

The eighth Brāhmaṇa opens again with the dialogue of Gārgī. She prays before the assembled brāhmaṇas to give her permission for asking Yājñavalkya two questions. The brāhmaṇas granted her the permission, and she addressed Yājñavalkya thus:

> O Yājñavalkya, as a hero from Kāśī and Videha with his bow and fatal arrows, I have come with two questions before you. Answer me my two questions.

Yājñavalkya consented, on which Gārgī asked:

> The layer that is above the sky and below the earth which is described as being situated between the earth and the sky and which is indicated as the symbol of the past, present and future, where is that situated?
>
> It is the layer of air situated in the ether.

Gārgī replied:

> Salutations unto thee, O Yājñavalkya. Thou hast answered well my question. Now prepare for the other. Where is that ether pervading?

Yājñavalkya replied:

> O Gārgī, what you are asking, the Brāhmaṇas designate as *akṣara*. It is neither big nor small; neither short nor long; nor red, nor wet nor shaded, nor covered with darkness; neither air nor sky; neither attached (to anything), nor (does it) consist of juices, smell, eyes, ears, speech, mind, prowess, life and mouth; nor can it be measured, nor has it the inner (cavity) nor the outer; neither can it be eaten nor does anybody eat it. The sun and moon are regulated by the order of that *Akṣara Brahman;* the earth and sky are transfixed by Him; the moments, days and nights, half months and months, seasons and years are regulated by the layer of this *akṣara*; rivers from the white mountains flowing to the east and those flowing to the west are following their courses by the order of this *akṣara*; it is in accordance with the Law of this *akṣara* that men praise the bounteous, gods follow the sacrificer and *pitṛ*s and *darvi* offering. O Gārgī, in this world one who offers oblations without knowing this *akṣara*, or sacrifices, or meditates for several years, destructive are the fruits of his deeds. He who departs from the world without knowing this *akṣara* is to be pitied; on the other hand one who departs from this world knowing this *akṣara* is a *Brahman*.

> O Gārgī! the *akṣara* is imperceptible, but perceives all; hears himself though not heard by others; thinks of all though himself is beyond the realization of others; himself knows all but is unknowable to others as he is beyond the intellect of any person. Besides this *akṣara*, there is none that sees, none that hears, none that thinks, none that knows. It is this imperishable *Brahman* who is pervading this sky.

Gārgī, satisfied with the answer, returns after duly saluting Yājñavalkya and the assembly.

The persistent enquiry of a woman brought forth the finest definition of the Supreme Reality. The motive of her enquiry was not to test Yājñavalkya but to learn from him about the nature of *Brahman*. Yājñavalkya, reluctant to impart the knowledge of *Brahman* to her, threatens her with dealth, and tries to stop her. But the inquisitive Gārgī is not to be vanquished; she proceeds again, and the sage had to give way to her resolution. He imparts knowledge of the Supreme Reality to her in spite of himself.

The second important narrative is that of Maitreyī and Yājñavalkya. It appears in two places (*Bṛhadāraṇyaka Upaniṣad,* II.IV and IV.V). In the earlier account the entire chapter is devoted to this dialogue and the latter is named after Maitreyī with slight alterations.

Yājñavalkya had two wives Maitreyī and Kātyāyanī. The former was a *brahmavādinī,* i.e. desirous of knowledge of *Brahman* and the latter a woman of worldly pursuits.

One fine day Yājñavalkya sought his wife's (Maitreyī's) consent to rise above the household stage of his life to *pravrajiṣyām* or *vānaprastha,* i.e. departure to forest. Before that he wanted to divide his property between Kātyāyanī and Maitreyī. Maitreyī, on hearing of the resolutions of Yājñavalkya to divide his property, uttered one of the noblest expressions ever made by a woman: "Lord, if this whole earth with its treasure were mine, can I attain immortality through them?"

Yājñavalkya replied:

> No; your life will be happy like that of the rich who are possessed of things of enjoyment, but there is no hope of attaining immortality by riches or by deeds that are done by riches.

Hearing this, Maitreyī said:

> What should I do with that which cannot raise me above death? Tell me what thou knowest as beyond death.

Then Yājñavalkya began his discourse on the way to immortality:

> A husband is dear not for the love of a husband, a wife is dear not for the love of a wife, sons are dear not for the love of the sons, wealth is dear not for the love of all, but for the love of the self. Verily it is this Self that should be realized. As a lump of salt when thrown into water, becomes dissolved and wherever we test the water it is salt, so does this great soul endless, unlimited, consisting of nothing but knowledge rise out of these elements and vanish again in them. When he has departed, there is no more knowledge.

Hearing this Maitreyī was slightly bewildered. At this Yājñavalkya replied:

> There is nothing to bewilder: for when there is duality, one sees the other, one smells the other, one knows the other, but when the self only is all this, how should he smell another, how should he see, hear or salute another?
>
> The Self is to be described by "Not not." He is incomprehensible, imperishable, unattached, unaffected, so how should he know the Knower? Thus far goes immortality.
>
> — *Bṛhadāraṇyaka Upaniṣad*, II.I.1

At the end of the discourse, Yājñavalkya went away into the forest and disappeared, but Maitreyī's noble words still resonate in the infinite space of time.

It becomes evident here that the Ṛgvedic women sages/poets were not concerned with metaphysical issues only. Rather they wished for a happy social and familial life. Despite being plagued with physical or other problems, they did not lose faith in their gods. In other words, they were early ancestors of women devotional poets with unflinching faith in their gods. Some of them were *brahmavādinī*s, a tradition that continued in the Upaniṣads.

The importance of the discussion between Gārgī and Yājñavalkya lies in the fact that women capable of carrying on religious discussions were admitted into these assemblies. Their voices attained intellectual maturity, confidence and mystical depth in the Upaniṣadic period. Though numerically they might be small, their voices prepared a backdrop for discussion of *bhakti* and kinds of its devotees in the texts titled the *Gītā*, the *Śāṇḍilya-Bhakti-Sūtra*, the *Nārada-Bhakti-Sūtra* and the *Bhāgavata*. Regarding their association with the *bhakti* movement, we need not overlook the fact that many of the *bhakta* poets, men and women, did not have any access to the sacred texts either because of their gender, castes or linguistic inaccessibility.

VII

Against the voices of women in the Vedic, Upaniṣadic discourse, i.e. in the written Śāstra tradition, and *bhakti* literature, the often ignored folk voice and its reception of the voice of women need consideration however small in measure it might be. Moreover, it demands response to a few positions regarding women icons of Indian culture like Sītā or Rādhā who have come under critical scrutiny in the obtaining time. Sītā is an ideal of Indian women, an ideal devoted dutiful wife following her husband unquestioningly in the learned tradition as in Vālmīki's *Rāmāyaṇa* and Tulsīdās's *Rāmacaritamānasa* and many other versions in different Indian languages. However, all of them are *ayana*s of Rāma. They, in the learned tradition, are Rāma's epics but Sītā's tragedies from her birth to death. Not that Rāma did not suffer but he did so for upholding his *maryādā* or standards and values but Sītā suffered more than her husband for following him. The *loka* or folk tradition has done more justice to her than its learned counterpart by proposing her superiority to Rāma with justification. The following Gujarati folk song, sung by professional singers even now, would help me in proving my point:

dayā nā sāgar tame rūpa nidhān thai
bhale bhagavān kahedāvo
pana rāma tame sītājī na tole nā 'vo
rāma tame sītājī na tole nā 'vo.

sole śaṅgār sajī mandir ne dvāre
phūl ne candan thi re pujāvo
pana rāma tame sītājī na tole nā 'vo
rāma tame sītājī na tole nā 'vo.

kāchāy kān tame, ṣenā bhagavān tame?
agni-parīkṣā konī kīdhī
tamare pāchaḍ jene bhagdoy vethyo
ene lokoni vāte tyāgī dīdhī.

pati thai patnī ne parakhtā nā 'vdī
ghaṭ-ghaṭ na jñātā thai bulāvo

pana rāma tame sītājī na tole nā 'vo
rāma tame sītājī na tole nā 'vo.

tāmarā pahelā aśok vana mā
sītājī-e rāvaṇa ne saṁharyo
daityo ni vachamā nirādhār nāri chaṭā
daś-māthā valo jotā bhāgyo.

marelā ne maryo emā karyūn śūn parākrama
amtho vijay no lyo co lhāvo
pana rāma tame sītājī na tole nā 'vo
rāma tame sītājī na tole na 'vo.

dayā nā sāgar tame rūpa nidhān thai
bhale ne bhagavān kahedāvo
pana rāma tame sītājī na tole nā 'vo
rāma tame sītājī na tole nā 'vo.

The folk song may thus be loosely translated thus:

An ocean of human-kindness and beauty incarnate
May you be called a Lord!
But O Rāma, You don't equal Sītājī
No Rāma, You don't equal Sītājī.

All decked out in the temple
With flowers, and with sandal you are worshipped
But O Rāma, You don't equal Sītājī
No Rāma, You don't equal Sītājī.

Gullible as You are, how can You be a God?
And who did You set to test!
One who endured all her life for You,
You forsook her for people's rumours.

A husband so You are,
but failed in knowing your other half,
You, who is omniscient
and yet You misunderstood her.
O Rāma, You don't equal Sītājī
No Rāma, You don't equal Sītājī.

In the Aśoka-Vāṭikā, before you did
Sītājī had already trounced Rāvaṇa
Amidst the demons, one helpless woman and yet
The ten-headed one took flight.

What valour in killing the already killed?
For no good you enjoy Your victory.
But O Rāma, You don't equal Sītājī
No Rāma, You don't equal Sītājī.

An Ocean of human kindness and beauty incarnate
We call you our God too
But O Rāma, You don't equal Sītājī
No Rāma, You don't equal Sītājī.

The learned tradition hinges around Rāma but the folk voice questions and subverts it by passing judgement substantiated by unassailable arguments that Rāma does not equal Sītā. It means that Sītā is superior to Rāma in the folk version, for she vanquished Rāvaṇa before Rāma did. The folk voice here speaks for Sītā, the woman who is an iconic figure in folk discourse for reasons different from its learned counterparts.

If Sītā is an embodiment of an ideal wife subscribing to the *maryādā* of her husband in the *loka* (folk) tradition, Rādhā is diametrically opposite to her in the sense that she is a celebration of the socially unsanctified yet existent love of two already married individuals. She is a post-*Bhāgavata* creation, yet she received such recognition of Indian psyche, particularly folk, that many do not know about Rādhā's husband or Kr̥ṣṇa's wife Rukmiṇī. Rādhā's name is associated to Kr̥ṣṇa or Śyāma as Sītā's is to Rāma. Their unison has symbolically been eternalized in wedding of their names. Both of them, however, precede their male counterparts, and their acceptance might be discerned in the use of their names in daily greetings. In many religious sects, Kr̥ṣṇa's significance springs from the interest that Rādhā takes in him or from his association to Rādhā. In a folk narrative in Braja, a dialect of Hindi, a devotee is shown repeatedly reciting "Rādheśyāma, Rādheśyāma." Pleased with his prayers, Kr̥ṣṇa appeared before him. Opening his eyes he found Śyāma standing before him. Seeing Him, the devotee asked the cause of His presence because he had sought the grace of Rādhā not Śyāma. He asked Him to go away and come, if at all, with Rādhā. He said that he was not reciting Śyāma's name but that of Rādhā. His name is a tail of Rādhā and so Śyāma mistook his prayer. He further said that without Rādhā, Śyāma was a non-entity for him. To prove his point he said that if from his name the sound *ra* of Rādhā was taken away, Rādheśyāma would have become "Ādheśyāma" (Half Śyāma):

hotī na rādheśyāma mein rakār merī rādhā kī ।
merī saun rādheśyāma ādheśyāma hote ॥

Many examples of celebration of woman-power, even her superiority might be seen in Indian folk tradition. Moving away from the pan-Indian icons like Sītā and Rādhā, there are many women protagonists that have caught the folk imagination for their transforming influence on their male counterparts. The Toral-Jesal narrative from Kutch in Gujarat is one such example. Toral, an extremely beautiful and spiritually oriented young lady from Kutch, was abducted by Jesal Jadeja, a bandit rebel who was bewitched by her beauty. While he was taking her forcibly away in a boat, all of a sudden there was lightning and thunderstorm from nowhere in the sky. This unsettled the otherwise high spirited Jesal, a bravado, and he wanted to save his life. He who had taken so many lives scampered for his own and begged for life to Toral who spoke to him thus in a much celebrated Gujarati folk song:

pāpa tāru parakāśa jaḍejā,
dharam tāru sambhar ।
tāri bedaline budavā nahī daūn
em toral kahe che ॥

Make your sin manifest,
Hold on to your *dharma,* Jadeja.
I will not let your boat sink.
Thus spake Toral.

Thereafter, Jesal confessed all his sins in the subsequent five stanzas of the folk song and pleaded to Toral with the phrase *tame re taryā re amne tarjo* (Do salvage me, as you have yourself achieved). It is a rare instance in the world, in which a woman promises salvation to her abductor, but she has no malice towards him. For her, even a cruel bandit and murderer has all possibilities of spiritual regeneration. The way Kṛṣṇa tells Arjuna, his friend, relative, disciple, and devotee, *yogakṣemam vahāmyaham*[20] (I assure merciful protection to my devotees), she, like Kṛṣṇa, promises full security and protection to Jesal. The enlightenment comes to them who rid themselves of the burden of one's sins. The being, body, and boat are alike in the sense that they float and do not sink if they are light. Hence, *knesis* (bucketing out) is imperative for mortals seeking redemption. Hers is a rare instance of expression of woman power that promises redemption to a man like a god that she is not, and thereby she replaces God with her conviction in the power of confession of sins and faith in righteousness (*dharma*). Her unflinching faith in her commitment makes her a symbol of spiritual power whose words have been immortalized by *loka*, (folk) tradition. The revolutionary folk voice earns our attention for the way nameless members of folk communities vouchsafe for silence and voice of women.

VIII

Bhakti is an experience and not a suitable subject for explanation or interpretation. Those who have experienced it do not explain or interpret it, and those who speak about it have neither understood nor experienced it. Against the absurdity of such endeavour human mind still essays to capture it like one's shadow. The desire of such a noble destination and endeavour for it

---

20. The *śloka* in the *Gītā* (9.22) runs thus:

ananyāścintayanto māṁ ye janāḥ paryupāsate ।
teṣāṁ nityābhiyuktānāṁ yogakṣemaṁ vahāmy aham ॥

The devotees who love no one else and think of me only and worships me with a disinterested spirit and are united in thought with me, to them I bring full security and attend to their needs.

deserves appreciation. Reaching or not reaching there does not matter much. Let us try to understand the nature of *bhakti* in terms of a narrative from *Caitanya Caritāmṛta*, for Indian mind constructed knowledge in the form of narratives as *dṛṣṭānta* (illustrative mode).

When Caitanya Mahāprabhu met Rāmānanda Ray, an equally distinguished mystic, he asked Ray about the nature (*svarūpa*) of *bhakti.* Rāmānanda replied that when the heart gets filled with *ānanda* (bliss) by singing, thinking and contemplating about God, His attributes, name, form and *līlā* (sports), it is *bhakti.* Caitanya Mahāprabhu said that that was fine but asked about an extraordinary definition, for human heart achieves happiness not in hearing and thinking about God only but also from other things like seeing the moon. Rāmānanda Ray said that it is true that many things give pleasure. Explaining *bhakti* he added that besides pleasure or happiness or bliss when one experiences that a living relationship has been established with the object of devotion, i.e. God, its name, form and *līlā* (sport or miracle) in its manifestation, it is *bhakti.* It is a state in which a devotee establishes relationships with God in numerous ways.

Caitanya Mahāprabhu said, "Whatsoever you say is fine but we have relationships with many, i.e. husband, wife, brother, mother, father and friends. Should we then consider it *bhakti*?"

Rāmānanda Ray replied, "Mahāprabhu! all these relationships mentioned by you have desires in them. All relationships are desireless in *bhakti.*"

Caitanya Mahāprabhu agreed but asked Rāmānandajī to explain further. At this Rāmānanda said, "To do so, I can give the example of the *gopī*s of Braja who were *bhakti* incarnate." Caitanya Mahāprabhu agreed to a good extent but still implored Rāmānanda Ray to add to his explanation.

> Mahāprabhu! Beyond it I can say only this that as a wave rises in the ocean and ebbs later, in my experience in the ocean of universe, various waves of *bhakti* emerge and disperse. Nothing but only love remains and thrives. Kṛṣṇa becomes one wave and Rādhā another, they rise and then meet. The wave of Rādhā

> rises, and so does the wave called Kṛṣṇa. Both of them disperse and get merged in the ocean. In the most exalted state of *bhakti*, it goes on incontinently in the mind and heart of a *bhakta*.

Mahāprabhu agreed with Rāmānanda Ray and was so pleased with the answer that his eyes were flooded with tears of inexplicable bliss.

Returning to prosaic discussion after the ease of the narrative it can be said that *bhakti* is devotion. But is devotion possible without love? Certainly not. Love is epicentral in *bhakti*. But what kind of love? Inordinate love which is like the Pole star. It does not move like others, and remains steadfast and unflinching. It knows no ego that imposes limitations on the object and subject of *ahaṁkāra* and ultimate merging of the self with the other unconditionally. Second, it knows no fear because fear is a consequence of desire and its prospective unfulfilment. Third, love does not desire exclusive possession of the object of love. So many *gopīs* were in love with Kṛṣṇa but none of them was jealous of others. 'Love and exclusion,' to paraphrase Mahatma Gandhi, can never go together because perfect love is possible only in a state of perfect non-possession. Fourth, love brooks no bargain. It desires nothing so there is no question of seeking anything in return. It is not a means to some end but an end in itself. Fifth, the uniqueness of love lies in the uniqueness of the subject and object of love. No other object or idea or ideal is higher than it. The object of love or beloved is the highest. Sixth, true love does not subscribe to any pedantry as it does not rationalize or believe in reasoning as a Gujarati phrase goes, *prema paṇḍitāī na jāne* (Love knows no scholastic and pedantic discourse). Knowledge, in fact, is hindrance to love and devotion. Knowledge is a result of loss of innocence which (innocence) is a precondition of unconditional submission in love and devotion. Uddhava's knowledge of *śāstra* or intellectuality was torn to pieces by simplicity of love of *gopīs* of Braja. Intellectuality is the cause of ego which is a hindrance to love, as it leads to argumentation. It is a lived experience not just inference and so beyond reasoning. Last but not least, true love should lead to liberation. It is dedication and devotion to one that is all. It frees the devotee from bondages of choice. On the surface, one seems to be in a state of choicelessness by choosing one, but the entire dilemma of exercising choice from existing multiplicity of choices is written off. The liberation is caused by naturalness that breaks off all bondages and thereby frees the devotee from the labyrinth of attachments. The love of *bhakti* thus is unattached love (*anāsakta prema*), based on sacrifice and renunciation with no desire, practised as it was by the *gopī*s who received adulation from learned and folk traditions that still pay obeisance to the women of Braja. *Bande Brajastrīnāma.* Like their Braja counterparts, the love of women *bhakti* poets was, to use Sri Ramakrishna's words, like a huge tidal wave that submerged not only their selves but filled all the little brooks and ditches around them to the brim in such a way that every pore of existence was drenched and every drop became an ocean. This love was not only spiritual but physical also. Āṇḍāḷ and Mīrā considered themselves married to Viṣṇu and Kṛṣṇa respectively. Āṇḍāḷ voices her love for her lord in the following words, marked with sensuousness:

> So great is my desire
> To unite with the Lord
> Who rests upon the milky ocean
> That emotion chokes my breath,
> My breasts rise and fall
> And quiver in joy.
>
> — Dehejia 93

But it would be wrong to consider only physicality of love in such compositions by women devotional poets. Physicality was a prop for spirituality. In other words, both of them existed simultaneously in their writing. Like physicality and spirituality, possession (of Lord) and renunciation (of world) existed simultaneously, in women devotional poets, for renunciation and service were natural cultural ideals of women devotional poets. Love demands renunciation of everything that one owns and is owned by, and service of God remains the sole purpose of life for which they renounced all physical and worldly pleasures.

The voices of women devotional poets are rich in form and content, and have survived till now because of their acceptance in the *loka* (folk) tradition. Going by signifiers in their compositions the choice of their Lord with whom they sought or achieved union was determined by their cultural and civilizational forces. The contents of their voices had their origin in their ecstatic experience and formal aspects in the company of their fellow noble souls and exposure to various traditions. Hence, their voices exist simultaneously in the learned and unlearned and oral and written traditions. Moreover, their ecstasy had a method, achieved through the harmony that they had established with their lord. When this harmony recurred through words, it took the form of poetry. But they were not always content with voicing their harmony or lack of it caused by separation from the lord; they expressed their feelings through their body by discarding its covers of clothes, or dance. (In the recent history only Mahatma Gandhi made such a strategic use of body, as women devotional poets did, for the dual purposes of associating with his weak and poor countrymen and resisting the might of the colonial forces.) Like true *bhakta*s of A.K. Ramanujan, they were not content to worship a god in word and ritual, nor were they content to grasp them in theology; they needed to possess them and be possessed by them. They needed also to sing, to make poetry, paint shrines, sculpture; to embody them in every possible way. "In *bhakti*, all the arts become also "techniques of ecstasy," "incitement to possession" (116). In other words, women devotional poets made contribution to different art forms — poetry, dance and music — that cannot be studied simply as poetry, though for the sake of convenience it can be used as a metaphor for all arts. Meandering in the woods of ecstasy whose articulation came to be known as their art or poetry was their harmless artistic response to the tyranny of their tormentors.

The women devotional poets were rebels and social

revolutionaries, as they rebelled against familial and social prescriptions for which they suffered before and even after becoming the devotees, physically and mentally. They questioned institutions of family, marriage, and religion for their inadequacies to satisfy their spiritual quest. Mīrā, the trope of *bhakti*, is a measured study in this role of her counterparts in and outside the country. Nābhādāsa, a *bhakta* poet, summed it up thus:

loka lāja kula śṛṅkhalā tajī mīrān giridhara bhajī
sadraśa gopikā prema pragaṭa kaliyugahīn dikhāyo
nira aṅkuśa ati nidara rasika jasa rasana gāyo
duṣṭanī doṣa vicārī mṛtyu ko udhyam kiyo
bāra na bāṅko bhayo, garala amṛta jyon piyo
bhakti niśāna bajāya kain, kahun te nahit laji
loka lāja kula śṛṅkhalā taji mīrān giridhara bhajī
— Nābhādāsa's *Bhaktamāla Saṭīkā*, p. 694

Mīrā discarded prohibitions of society, family and clan fearlessly, and by singing about her lord she showed, rather practised the path of devotion in the Kaliyuga, and faced all enterprises of killing her by her family members. She was betrothed to Rāṇā of Chittoṛ by her family but she chose to marry Kṛṣṇa by breaking all bondages.

Like Mīrā, most of the women devotional poets did not harbour any ill-will or malice for their tormentors even at verbal levels. Mīrā, for instance, followed the path of *bhakti* against all prohibitions:

rājā barjai rānan barjai, sab barjai parivārī ।
kunvar patavi so bhi barjai, aur sehalya sārī ॥
— *Mīrā Bṛhat-Pada-Saṁgraha*, no. 14

No surprise that she had to pay the price for trespassing prohibitions. She showed courage in facing the wrath of Sisodiyā Rāṇā by saying, *Sisodyo ruṭhyo maharo kāin kar lesī* (*Mīrā Bṛhat-Pada-Saṁgraha*, no. 181) (What can Sisodiyā do if he is displeased with me?) The only thing he could do was to torture her physically. She detailed all tortures inflicted on her but without any malice towards her tormenters:

jahar kā pyālā rāṇājī bhejyā koi dhyo mirān ke hātha ।
kara caraṇāmṛta mīrā pī gaī, koi āpa jāno raghunātha ॥
sānpa piṭārā rāṇājī bhejyā, koi dhyo mīrā ne jāya ।
kara khag vali pahiryo, koi āpa jāno dīnānātha ॥
rāṇājī dāsī bhejyan koi jāvo ne mīrān pāsa ।
mar gayā hoi to jala dijyo natar nadi men bahāy ॥
ho ji ho sisidiyā rājā manādi vairāgī dhan ro kyā karūn ॥
— *Mīrā Bṛhat-Pada-Saṁgraha,* no. 196

She narrated sufferings of all sorts but there is no trace of hatred in her heart. On the contrary she used the respectful suffix *jī* for Rāṇā. Rather she pitied him and his family, and said:

rāṭhauḍ dhiyādi sisodyān re ke sātha ।
le jātī baikuṇṭha kun nek na mānī bāta ॥
— *Mirā Bṛhat-Pada-Saṁgraha,* no. 264

She remarked that she would have taken all of them, i.e. all her kins in the Rāṭhores and the Sisodiyās to heaven if they had followed her advice. Rare are the examples of tolerance and forgiveness, excepting Mīrā in women devotional poetry and Toral in folk literature, such as this.

Bhakti was a river in which various women poets were immersed and thereby transformed into new beings. At one level it was a metaphysical suicide and at another a new incarnation in the same life. Thus, they carried two selves with them — the remains of the old self that they had left behind and the new self that was merged in the higher self, i.e. God. The Therīs, Āṇḍāḷ, Mahādevī Akkā, Janābāī, Ratnābāī, Mīrā, Candrabatī, Bahinābāī, Terigoṇḍa Veṅkamma, Lal Dêd, and Gaṅgāsatī among others stood out of their selves and became oblivious of their old selves and unreceptive ambience.

The voices of devotional women poets are rivers of love and devotion surging to meet their ocean of *bhakti*. They breathed Upaniṣads in their own tongues, lived *Gītā*'s precepts of *karma, jñāna* and *bhakti,* and experiencing torrents of divine deluge they became immortal temples of *bhakti*. They came from different regions and religions, castes and creeds, and had mystical visions and experience, though they were as varied as they themselves. Their lives were vortexes of voices that they heard and sang without any desire of recognition. The folk or *loka* traditions still cherish them and celebrate their singing silences in the yawning gaps of their voices.

The basic intent of discussion of *bhakti* and women devotional poets was to perspectivise *bhakti,* contribution of women devotional poets and issues related to them without laying any claim to their comprehensiveness or completeness, for its facets are so diverse and inexplicable that only *neti* (*na idam brahma iti*), i.e. "That this is not *Brahman*" can sum up the fate of all who strive to capture it. But even *neti, neti* at a point of time persuades exhausted spirits to ignore all inadequacies of discussion and conclude not with *neti, neti,* but *iti* (*idam brahma iti,* i.e. This is *Brahman*). Provisionally, of course.

10

Self or Motherhood
Feminist Discourse in India

. . . I call with the firm tone of humanity, for my arguments, Sir, are dictated by a disinterested spirit — I plead for my sex — not for myself. Independence I have long considered as the grand blessing of life, the basis of every virtue and independence I will ever square by contracting my wants, though I were to live on a barren health.
— Mary Woolstonecraft

If observed, we are brought up in a way that we think in one particular way and live in another. What is the meaning of those great writers and their books in the context of our lives? We read about those people who are not part of our geography. After reading them, it is quite natural that they become part of our thinking. We read Simon de Beauvoir, and live in a society in which a woman, despite her husband's insistence cannot get rid of her *purdah*. When it comes to the husband and wife, we show them as if they are lover and beloved, knowing it full well that the truth is hidden from none. The husband knows his wife and the wife her husband. And the people around know each other. All of us are actors of a play who with right sort of dialogues and acting are successful in playing our roles and hiding our real selves. What is seen or heard exists. This is the rule of life. This is a game. Then I thought what is wrong in saying what I feel as true, if I have not to play this game.
— Rashida in Manzoor Ehtesham's *Sookha Bargad*

"What should I carry for the newly-born girl?"
A few flowers
from some garden
a few sentences

from some poem
and the belief
that after growing up she shall see the world
with her own eyes
that she shall break shackles
shackles within the shackles
ask for freedom
and nothing less than freedom.

— Nirmala Garg

ON 18 January 1900, when questioned about women of India at the Shakespeare Club in Pasadena, California, Vivekananda referred to his inadequate knowledge of women of India — of their relations, of different languages and dialects that Indian women speak, of their gender and castes and also of their manners and customs. Keeping the hazardous nature of his task in view he spoke of the ideal of Indian women. As I mull over the feminist discourse with reference to the Indian situation, I find myself in a situation worse than Vivekananda's, for he was a wise observer of human nature and a keen thinker. However, he found his knowledge of Indian women "not to be so complete" (54). He was, fortunately, unconcerned with the exclusivists' question so often raised by feminists who might have deprived him of the right of speaking about women on biological grounds. Admittedly, only she, not he, knows what she experiences, so only she can speak of it. If insisted a little too far, each one of us, from monkeys or gorillas to men or women in the last millions of years, has lived his or her life independently. Pain differs from person to person. The other can neither speak of nor share it. In a situation such as this, my endeavour becomes an encroachment, making me aware of the Stephen Heathean dilemma of (his) man's space in the feminist discourse. Fortunately, at least for me the dilemma did not last for long, as that of Hamlet, as he could carve some space for men in it. There has to be some space for men for they are the cause of the cause. They were the subject and women, the object in the patriarchal discourse. By subverting the structures, women strive to become the subject of their feminist discourse. The displacement impacts not only man-woman relationship but also man's perception of woman and his own. The present space, if at all, for a man in the feminist discourse is a consequence of his preceding roles. I too earn this space because of this strange/natural relationship. To take recourse to Ghalib:

> *kābe ke in butoṅ se riṣtā hai dūr kā,*
> *goyā hum yahān ke nahīn, nikāle hue to hain,*

> We, the stones, are distantly related to the Kābā. We may not be from there, we are at least thrown out from there.

It may be a subtle way of becoming an insider and then sabotaging the feminist discourse. Shouldn't this be the concern of the feminists?

The truth, however, speaks differently on the other end. Difficult it is for me to be either a feminist or femenist whatever way one may spell it, for a woman's is a natural and authentic experience that she earns by/with her body, something that I cannot have. The authenticity and naturalness are integral parts of feminism. That is why their voice shall be theirs and not mine, however honest and sympathetic I may try to be. It is not possible for a man to read or participate in the discourse like a woman, but he can know the feminist discourse. It is here that Vivekananda's discussion of the ideals of Indian women get problematized, for by doing so the man prescribes, and fixes roles. If they violate these 'given' roles, they become subversive rebels, 'unwomanly' or 'unIndian' for the prescribers of these roles, and revolutionaries for the feminists. All these rhetorical arguments notwithstanding, I consider my arguments as the claim of the ink in the pen.

II

"What do 'they' ultimately want?," asked a perplexed friend after a presentation on feminist writing.

The tone of my friend in pronouncing 'they' disturbed me,

though I too was trying to cope with the same question. Perhaps men are victims of an unnecessary anxiety at the loss of space, at being deprived of their ability to deprive or suppress. They suffer from the fear of impotence that they feel at the impending loss of their power of suppressing or even oppressing women. What they (women) seek is their own space, independence, and equality, denied to them for long. Referring to it towards the end of her book, *A Vindication of the Rights of Women,* Mary Woolstonecroft pleads for a fair treatment of women:

> Be just then, O ye men of understanding! and mark not more severely what women do amiss, than the vicious tricks of the horse or the ass for whom ye provide provender — and allow her the privilege of to whom ye deny the rights of reason, or ye will be worse than Egyptian task masters, expecting virtue where nature has not given understanding. (283)

Nowhere in the book does she betray even an iota of arrogance or immodesty. On the contrary, she speaks of women's emancipation for the sake of men, for if they (men) wanted suitable companions for them, they have to spare space for them — for full development of their faculties and the realization of their own selves. Yet Horace Walpole called her "a hyena in petticoat." (cited in the "Introduction" to *A Vindication of the Rights of Women*). The history of humankind is witness to it that whenever a woman questioned the given social and cultural structures and sought independence for herself, her nascent longings were suppressed or made fun of with such pronouncements. The questions of Gārgī teased Yājñavalkya so much that he silenced her by chiding her with the words: *Gārgī mātiprakṣi ma te mūrdha vyapapatdanāt praṣanya* (Do not overquestion, Gārgī. Else your head will fall off.) (*Bṛhadāraṇyakopaniṣad,* chapter III, Gārgībrāhamaṇam, VI). In the *Abhijñānaśākuntalam,* the disciples of Kaṇva abandon pregnant Śakuntalā in the court of Duṣyanta after the king refused to recognize her. Left to herself, she begins to cry and begins to leave. Ironically, Śaradvata, one of the disciples, reads it as her act of becoming "free," and says, *"kim purobhāge svatantrayam-avlambase"* (*Abhijñānaśākuntalam,* Act V.26.8) (O wanton woman!

Do you resort to freedom?). In fact, there is no way out for her, for both the palace and the hermitage as well have rejected her. The patriarchal structures that reign in both the places demand mute acceptance of the rejection. She cannot even cry. Her crying is construed as her rebellion. Even her tears are intolerable, for they scare man.

Fear leads to torture and suppression. Man begins to torture what scares him. That is how he has behaved with Nature, and woman and tried to condition her nature by imposing on her structures suitable to his purposes. An emancipated woman ceases to be his colony, for she charts out her paths and follows them, thereby annihilating all possibilities of her physical and emotional exploitation. Her defiance of the given roles that perpetuate her exploitation makes her a rebel — a man-made category. This is the price she has to pay for her freedom. Quite a few literary works by men and women have dealt with this issue. Yashpal's *Divya* in the eponymous novel becomes "Dara", a slave, as Bhoodhar Sharma has purchased her from Pratul, the slave trader. She (her milk in particular) becomes a commodity. Bhoodhar sells her to Chakradhar, a priest, as a foster-mother, for his wife did not have enough milk to feed her child. In the ensuing conflict between her duty as a foster-mother and her motherhood, her son remains hungry if she feeds the son of Chakradhar; and if she fails to do so, then she fails in her duty. The priest and his wife scold and reprimand her for doing so. The wife of the priest sees the only convenient way of getting rid of Dara's child. On knowing the plan, she runs away from the priest's house and somehow reaches a Buddhist monastery on the outskirts of the town. She seeks shelter there. The monk does not accept her, for she asked for the shelter as a mother. When she expresses her willingness to be a woman servant there, the monk asks her if she had the permission of father, husband or son. She tells him that her father was no more, she had no husband, and the son was in her lap. The monk still scorns her requests and begins to leave the seat. At this, she falls at his feet and pleads with the arguments that the monk had sheltered Āmrapālī, the prostitute, and here he leaves her as a destitute — without food or shelter. The monk responds indifferently that a prostitute is a 'free' woman.

A woman does not have many options to exercise. She can accept the patriarchal structures and play her roles as daughter, sister, and mother. Her acceptance of patriarchal tyranny helps her in taking care of her body or belly, to be precise. In the process, her womb further complicates her dilemma. Her glorification as a dutiful wife may lead to her murder in private or as *satī* in public, and as a mother (a woman with a belly and a womb) to her real and symbolical suicides, as the roles on more occasions than one hinder her self-realization, for she does not live but exists on the terms of others. These terms become thick layers on her self.

A woman could be 'free', if at all, only as Āmrapālī or Mīrā. She has to either sell off her body in instalments for her belly or negate her body and womb as a spiritual devotee as Mīrā did. This spirituality is a sublimated form of self-courted *satī*. The rejection of an individual by family and society precedes rejection of familial and social givens and negation of the physical self. In one sense, it is an act of rebellion. Ironically, the result of this 'metaphysical suicide,' *a la* Albert Camus, is the most precious possession of humanity, as in the case of Mīrā, in the form of devotional poetry.

A woman can be Sītā or Rādhā or Mīrā or Āmrapālī. The crucible of patriarchal yardsticks determines her fate. She is made Sītā or Āmrapālī. Āmrapālī is the freest of all, for she has to prove nothing. Sītā has to prove herself that she is Sītā. It is Sītā, not Rāma or Lakṣmaṇa — not even Rāvaṇa — who has to go through fire. She becomes a Rādhā. That is her choice. Rādhā's is an exceptional case. She is a rebel against social ethos, yet the Indian society did not condemn her. Rather her social acceptance clouds the character of Rukmiṇī, the legitimate wife of Kṛṣṇa. Mīrā is to an extent compelled to be a rebel and becomes Mīrā by choosing the path of metaphysical suicide instead of committing physical suicide. The lesser sisters of Mīrā find it difficult to either accept the givens or revolt against them. It is the predicament of the educated women of middle-class in the fictional world of Shashi Deshpande. They are trapped between two worlds — of their father or husband. They are either so used to little comforts provided by the middle-class life that they find the world beyond too insecure and difficult to live, or they develop an ability of endurance. They cannot slam the door and leave the house of their father or husband. If they do so, they have to lead a life of emotional vacuum. Rādhikā in Usha Priyamvada's *Rukogī Nahīn Rādhikā* (Wouldn't You Stop Rādhikā?) intends to pursue a course in Arts in the USA against the wishes of her father. She supports herself in the USA and completes her study. On return she finds herself in an emotional and cultural vacuum. She suffers for her decision of being herself on her return, as he refuses to support her emotionally or financially expecting her to come to him, kneel and beseech his help. She does go to him as a daughter but finds that her father has not forgiven her for defying him. As an arrogant patriarch, he is too engrossed with his artistic pursuits and the second wife to receive his daughter on her return from abroad after years. She leaves her father's place and tries to establish herself without counting on either her father or rich brother. The more she tries to come to terms with her own self in the process of establishing amidst aliens in Delhi, the more she is trapped in it.

Since feminism as a movement saw its rise in the West, it was expected to find its expression in Indian writing in English among Indian literatures. However, one finds that there are, fortunately or unfortunately, not many subscribers to it at least in Indian English novel. On the one hand, there is a virtual scramble for categories like post-modernism and post-colonialism, on the other hand the Indian women novelists betray no hasty willingness for the label or category of feminism that they can legitimately claim. Shashi Deshpande, for instance, invested much of her energy in rejecting the label of feminism in the initial days that her critics were so willing to paste on her and her works. Later on she changed her position, and called herself a feminist. "In my life, I mean. But not consciously as a novelist." ("Shashi Deshpande Talks to Lakshmi Holmstrom," *Wasafiri*, 17, Spring 1993). The central issues of her concern remain the degradation, the subordination and the inequality that women experience and continue to live in these conditions. She rejects the category of the feminist writing or writer, for writing can be good or bad but not man's or woman's, according to her.

Anit Desai's *Cry, the Peacock* is a 'strange' exception to it. Strange I say because the novelist is not deliberately expressing feministic concerns, and her neurotic protagonist is not fully conscious of her preference for herself over her husband against the traditional Indian wife's willingness to sacrifice her life for her husband. With the character of Māyā, the female protagonist, who is a young and sensitive girl obsessed by a childhood prophecy of a non-avertable disaster, the novelist seems to dabble with feminist concerns. Māyā's dilemma is not so concerned with either her belly or womb, for the patriarchal social order (her father and husband) has resolved these questions, of course, in its own way. But a woman that she is, she is not, as her male counterparts often mistake her to be, a mere belly or womb. A woman is above all intellect too. She has a heart (with feelings and emotions) and head (intellect). The questions of her belly and womb are resolved in such a way for her that she is emotionally and even intellectually impaired. Haunted by the obsession with the prophecy, she leads a life of marital discord with a streak of neurotic fantasy, aggravated by her husband's inability to respond to her emotional needs. Gautam, her husband, unlike his mythical counterpart, lives not for living Māyā but for material form of Māyā, i.e. money. In the end, she has to choose between her husband and herself. Since she sees her husband's lack of interest in life and its shades, she pushes him off, his figure "an ugly, crooked gray shadow that transgressed its sorrowing chastity — caught between her and the worshipped moon" (208), "down to the very bottom through an intensity of air." Māyā's act of self-assertion and rejection of her husband's life invites feminist reading, though male chauvinists may always run her choice down by saying, 'that's what mad women do.' The counter questions crop up here: Who made her mad? Who impaired her psyche?

Arundhati Roy's *The God of Small Things* begins with the promise of examining the feminist concerns in the Indian context by portraying "small things" — dalits, women and children. Their "gods" — Marx, Men and God — have failed them. Women and *dalit*s share a similar fate, for by their very birth they are stigmatized for none of their faults. The moment their sex or caste is determined, they are cast away and forced to live with the given stigmas. They cannot lead their lives according to their desires. This similarity of fate brings Vellutha and Ammu together. Vellutha, the untouchable, struggles against the high-caste dominated society. He is crushed to death by the police for allegedly molesting Ammu, a high-caste woman who, in fact, had taken the initiative in the affair. Ammu is locked in a tragic struggle with her family, society and its morality. She sought freedom from these shackles and paid the penalty ultimately. When she went to the police station to help Vellutha who is in the custody because of her, the police inspector calls her a *veśya* (prostitute). With her broken marriage and condemnation by her family members — brother, even mother and grand aunt — she is left with no option but to leave the walls of her home and seek a job for herself. Even the novelist conveniently gets rid of her by showing her dead in a room of a lodge.

The novelist portrays the double standards of social behaviour and morality through the characters of Chacko and Mamachi. Mamachi is a victim of the partiachal familial and social order in which the husband can be as cruel and brutal as he wishes, and the women have to tolerate it. Ironically, some of the women become handmaids of suppression of their own. Mamachi's husband is a polite, generous, loving husband and an affectionate father to the world but a tyrannical, cruel father and husband who humiliates, even beats, his wife and children for flimsy things. "He worked hard on his public profile as a sophisticated, generous, moral man. But alone with his wife and children he turned into a monstrous, suspicious bully with a streak of vicious cunning." (180). Like Papachi, his son Chacko too has a two-sided personality. In the house, his room has a secret separate entrance that facilitates satisfaction of his "man's needs." Mamachi knew of her husband's libertine relationship with the women working in the factory, so did Baby Kochamma. The women in the Ayemenem house give implicit sanction to Chacko's "man's needs," but not Ammu's desire for Vellutha. It shows that a woman at times subscribes to the double standards that support suppression of other women by the patriarchal order. These women are the victims of patriarchy and become the perpetrators of torture, inequality and injustice against women unconsciously. Futher, in India untouchability cuts across religious and regional lines. Even the Syrian Christians who swear by the Western culture at the drop of a hat subscribe to it. Baby Kochamma does not allow Ammu to help Vellutha, for he is a low caste. She goes to the extent of making Esthan condemn Vellutha on the pretext that by doing so he would save his mother. It is injudicious to impose terms on the creativity, yet one feels that Arundhati Roy missed an opportunity by not including a *dalit* woman in the compass of concerns for "small" things because she is doubly suppressed or, to use the more fashionable term, "doubly colonized." For one she is a *dalit*, and then as a woman she has to carry the burden of the generation of suppressed Velluthas and of their suppression on her. The Velluthas suppress her. She is the smallest thing. Arundhati Roy, the new Goddess, also failed her.

III

Indian English poetry is frailer in terms of poetic quality and scantier in quantity than Indian English novel and the participation of women in it is even less. However, some of the poets such as Kamala Das, Gauri Deshpande, Mamta Kalia, Eunice de Souza and Sujata Bhatt among others, write about women and themselves with greater loyalty to their cause, spiky bite and resilience than their much famous fictionalizing sisters. They express their angst freely against the conventional concept of Indian women and define the roles that they had to play until now. Mamata Kalia comments slyly and ironically on the non-happening predicament of women, when she says: "But nothing ever happened to me/ except two children/and two miscarriages . . . (*"Sheer Good Luck"*). She outrightly rejects man's perception of things and man-centred discourses on which women are fed:

> I can't bear to read Robert Frost.
> Why should he talk of apple picking . . .
>
> I haven't even seen an apple for months . . .
> Whatever we save we keep for beer
> And contraceptives. ("Against Robert Frost")

Without being apologetic for being a woman, she happily accepts her belly and womb. They are not fetters for her, but an essential part of being, so she celebrates them with all the resources at her disposal. Further, she has a free will and intellect that do not yield to the standards and norms of behaviour and conduct fixed by men, as she says: "I want to pay Sunday visits/totally undressed . . . ("Compulsions"). Concerned with the types of Indian women that silently endure, it is the role of wife that has earned the attention of their poetic faculty. In the poem, "The Old Playhouse", Kamala Das writes about it:

> It was not to gather knowledge
> Of yet another man that I came to you but to learn
> What I was, and by learning, to learn to grow, but every
> Lesson you gave me about yourself . . . .
>
> You called me wife,
> I was taught to break saccharine into your tea and
> To offer at the right moment the vitamins. Cowering
> Beneath your monstrous ego I ate the magic loaf and
> Became a dwarf. (87)

Gauri Deshpande draws a clear line of distinction between female and male species and tries to define feminine, if not feminist, sensibility. Let me withdraw myself and allow the poetess to speak for herself and her counterparts.

> Sometimes you want to talk
> about love and despair
> and the ungratefulness of children.
> A man is no use whatever then.
> You want then your mother
> or sister
> or the girl with you went through school,
> and your first love, and her
> first child — a girl —
> and your second. (89)

These extracts from randomly selected poems contain in them all the phases — female, feminine, and feminist. Yet they do not show radical departure of the kind of the Western feminism which proposed insulation of the world of women from that of the men before entering the post-feminist era. The reason for this may be that family still exists in India despite many blows to it, and if it exists, though in its changed form, the credit for it should go to women. The radical individualism of the West does not find favour with Indian mind that by its nature thinks holistically, though the whole may mean family, community, society, nature, or whole universe. Further, layers of familial, social relationships are multiple to the extent of complexity, definite to the extent of science, and strong to the extent of extremely caring and even encroachment. In the West, the only effective relationship is that of husband and wife. That too, till it lasts. The transitory nature of husband-wife makes light of mother-father relationship causing a free-play of other relationships like brother-sister relationship that are concrete and strong in India, leave aside the grandfather and grandmother who are bound to old age homes.

Vrinda Nabar has listed various factors — caste, class, economic deprivation, sectarian fragmentation, size and numbers, overpopulation, the growing power of fundamental forces, the sway of superstitions, female foeticide and above all the essential nature of what she terms as Hinduism that create "vastly different scenario in India encompassing contradictions of a kind undreamed of in mainstream [Western] feminist philosophy" (26). It should, however, not mean that the Western feminist theoretical insights, for instance, Elaine Showalter's observations regarding the three phases in the Western women writing as "feminine," "feminist" and "female" (13), are of no use to us. These factors, singly or combined, account for different literary responses by Indian women writers. An Indian poetess, though she may be utterly disgusted with her father, does not call him 'a bastard,' as does Sylvia Plath in "Daddy", "Daddy, daddy, you bastard, I'm through" (478). However intense or intolerable may have been her hurt, all of our ingenious racial, biological or psychological interpretations of the poem fail to find the suitability of calling her father a 'bastard.' It is not a question of mere cultural shock but of the poetess's inability to find a suitable 'objective co-relative' for her legitimate wrath against patriarchy. Her failure compels her to bastardize her poetic art. As against this famous poem stands the not so famous poem of Mamta Kalia, "Tribute to Papa". The tribute becomes a pregnant site of generational difference with regard to values, ideals and ways of looking at each other and the world around. The poetess rejects her father's life of "limited dreams." In her ironic mood, she terms her father to be "an unsuccessful man." That's what a "Lower Division Clerk, Accounts Section" can be.

> You want me to be like you, Papa,
> Or like Rani Lakshmibai.
> You're not sure what greatness is,
> But you want me to be great.
>
> I give two donkey-claps for your greatness,
> And three for Rani Lakshmibai . . .
>
> Everything about you clashes with nearly
> Everything about me. (90)

She intends to choose her own course, follow her own ideals, so she rejects her father's notions of greatness and the Indian model of a woman as Lakshmibai who fought and died in one sense for the sake of women but her son — something that patriarchy would not mind. She even thinks of disowning her father and calling him by his surname. The 'new' woman shows utter disregard for her father's otiose notions of morality by which he lives. She does respond to her desires but carefully, without even making her cowardly father think of suicide. That makes one think of a different model of Indian feminism from the Western feminism, for Indian women have a different history, different ethos, and forms of social stratification and patriarchal domination. They live in different social and cultural realities, and respond to them in varied ways. Keeping this in view, K. Satchidanandan rightly speaks of developing a feminist literary theory specific to our own creative and critical situation, without abandoning shared patterns of reading and writing (5). He further observes that it would be simplistic to assume that the White middle class feminist theories can ever explain Janabai's appeal to Viṭhobā, Sumaṅgalmātā's Buddhist serenity purged of all lust and hate, Mahasweta Devi's account of the tribal Jasodā or Draupadī or Sugathakumari's Devakī dreaming in her prison of Kr̥ṣṇa, the liberator (8). Indian feminist literary theory because of the pluralistic Indian situation will be pluralistic and provisional, though at the core the vision will be 'fixed.' It will be Indian — inclusive therefore ever progressive. My participation in this process demands another occasion. I have, however, to keep in mind what Shashi Deshpande in the afore-mentioned interview observed regarding feminism. "But to me, feminism isn't a matter of theory: it is difficult to apply Kate Millet or Simon de Beauvoir or whoever to the reality of our daily lives in India. And there are such terrible miconceptions about feminism by people here. They often think it is about burning bras and walking out on your husband, children, or about not being married, not having children, etc. I always try to make the point now about what feminism is not and to say that we have to discover what it is in our lives, our experiences. And

I actually feel that a lot of women in India are feminists without knowing it. . . . So for me feminism is translating what is used up in endurance into something positive." Shashi Deshpande's caveat against injudicious acceptance, application of the Western feminist theories and construction of our own theory has another side. Whatever may be the theory of feminism, it should be constructed without ignoring the other India (the two Indias being India and Bhārat) — the women of Bhārat, the unlucky non-middle-class, non-upper-class, the uneducated rural, particularly *dalit* multitude of Indian women, though that can be used to divide the women. Here it is worth remembering that the *dalit*s — men and women — are subject of suppression by age-old economic and social deprivation at the hands of the high-class. That way the *dalit* women are freer than their other middle class high caste women, for they do not remain confined to the four walls and participate in economic activities.

For my present purpose, I can think of no better way of concluding this endeavour of mine, though abruptly, than end it with a poem entitled "Even the other Foot out of the Threshold." by Saroop Dhruva, an Indian poetess in Gujarati, who charts out a new course for the Indian Cinderallas, by re-writing the fairy tale of Cinderella.

Cinderella
What is this?
Why have you stopped?
See, one of your feet is still
inside the threshold.
How much time left in going out?
Let both hands of the clock meet at 12.
Let you be left outside the door,
and the doors be shut completely.
Lose you will, if at all, then these golden shoes,
and these garments of yours.
So what.
That way, these tangled tufts and the tattered rags

the naked feet and hollowed slackened eye
are your reality.
Within the four walls
before the stove in a corner of the house, or
on the other side of seven layers
your reality was the same . . .
That is your past.

However . . .
People had given you
Rosy flower-printed frocks
to save their prestige
and retain their control on you.
That too
On one condition . . .
Learn only that these people would teach,
Speak what they want you to speak.
Only theirs is the right choice,
not what you like,
You may exist . . .
If . . ., then . . .
If . . ., then . . .
If . . ., then . . .
Only then, you shall get the promise of safety.
Within the Lakṣmaṇrekha drawn by them,
With the sound of the clock kept by them,
And by their winding up,
You have to live . . .

Now the time has come.
Say, which side you have to go?
But do remember that you were alone inside,
Alone you are, so shall you always remain . . .
But outside . . .
Outside there shall be many Cinderellas of the past . . .
Some gathering papers, and some selling vegetables.
Some sowing, some harvesting,
Some with axes and some empty-handed . . .

Reading, teaching, gleaning and gathering wood or
Giving birth to children, rearing them, marrying, and getting married,
Getting something or other done,
Cooking, sewing, or making pavements,
Barefooted, in tatters, Cinderellas, Cinderellas . . .

Moreover . . .
Do remember this too
That neither for them nor for you,
A golden fairy is now to come;
No magical band will touch you.
Yes, it may happen that one day
Even these rags would not be available for them.
Then that shall be your disrobing ceremony.
Then it may happen that you have to then
Cover yourselves with your breaths
And wander around by covering yourselves with each other's sighs . . .

Come what may . . .
You have to pluck the feathers of the fairy tale
so popular after your name . . .
And then,
You have to weave
your dress
after removing the threads
one by one
from the cocoon wrapped around you.
And that would never be
A camouflage to escape
To hide or be hidden!!!

Then . . .?
Set out,
See, can you hear?
One, two, three, four, five, six, seven, eight,
nine, ten, eleven

And . . .
Do withdraw at least now
Even the other foot out of the threshold." (64-55)

It seems that Swarnalata, the Indian ancestor of Cindrella, has decided to withdraw the other foot out of the threshold and respond to her brain, belley and womb simultaneousely.

11

Constructing an Indian Theory of Feminism
Problems and Potentialities

> Those who eat (food grains), eat with my *śakti* (power/energy); those who see, see with my *śakti*; those who breathe, hear whatever is said, do with my help only. Those who do not know me in this form, attain the low status because of their ignorance.
>
> — *Śakti-Sūkta*

> Am I a woman, am I a widow, that you are asking me about the problems of women? — Swami Vivekananda

> . . . men should take feminism seriously, but they should not appropriate it, women may welcome men to feminism but they need to remain cautious both about motives and possible consequences. — Mary Eagleton

These epigraphical excerpts serve different purposes for me. They celebrate the power of woman as *śakti*; provide a recognition of the fact that she knows it; voice the dilemma of a male participant in feminist discourse; and resolve the dilemma with the words of caution for men and women both. All these statements notwithstanding, the fact is that I for sure do not know if my present endeavour will fall in the category of defection or encroachment. Between the two, i.e. my limitations and uncertainty, rests the fate of my endeavour.

I must borrow a little honesty and sincerity from Swami Vivekananda and pay heed to the words of Mary Eagleton and take feminism seriously, for along with the *dalit* discourse, it is the most resilient of obtaining Indian discourses, and so unignorable for a student of literature like me. I can, however, shake off the burden of anxiety by considering the entire discourse in the categories of (i) feminist consciousness, that is a consequence of experiences as a woman, leading to feminist discursive practice out of the experience; and (ii) feminist discourse, a larger category including all discursive practices by men and women but with sincere concern for women. I rest content with the second, and do my bit with my 'intervention,' a word that was so dear to the Marxist critics, in the present feminist discourse, for one can love it or loathe it, but cannot be indifferent to it.

Since I am a student of literature, I, for my purpose, will rely heavily on literary works, in languages of Indian origin, for Indian creativity in languages of Indian origin is more authentic than say, Indian English writings because its scope and depth of experience of the addresser, his/her addressivity, and the class of the addressee are limited, though so very visible that the children of writers writing in Indian languages ask their parents as to why they do not write in English.

Let me begin with a not so impersonal note. As a student of literature I found the world of literature infested with different categories and sub-categories. The next moment, after the word *literature* was pronounced, saw the world being divided as poetry, drama, fiction, non-fiction, followed by their futher division, for instance, of poetry as 'classical,' 'romantic,' 'modern' and 'post-modern.' None of them disturbed anyone. However, a category like 'feminist literature' disturbed most of us at the very mention of it. For these disturbed souls, literature was literature; it could not be feminist or menist or femenist, without acknowledging the fact that it has always been menist, excepting a few pleasant patches of feminist discourse here and there. The question that used to be over-sighted in the process was that if literature can be modern or post-modern, high or low, why couldn't it be feminist?

Whether one is disturbed by feminist consciousness and its

articulation or not, the fact is that it exists as a category. However, much of our feminist discourse takes the Western formulations or paradigms as its model. In the process, it leads to an uncritical acceptance of the Western agenda of feminism as our own, and in the end to a complete disjunction with our own traditions. As an ironical consequence, those who advocate feminism and invest their resources in establishing its acceptance, become uneasy even at the prospect of discussing, leave aside the question of proposing and constructing an Indian theory of feminism.

On the surface, the scepticism against the proposition of such a theory would convince all. One would say that theory is a theory; it cannot be Indian, non-Indian or a–Indian. Further, if there is or can be an Indian theory of feminism, will I accept the proposition of Pakistani theory of feminism?

These questions demand their critical assessment whose want leads to mis/underestimation and further erosion of confidence in our traditions and culture. If there can be an English, American or French school of feminism, or Black feminism, why can there not be an Indian school of feminism? There is a rich corpus of literary and sociological writing in our languages — classical and modern as well — that can be put in the category of feminist consciousness or discourse and considered for constructing such a theory, though theory need not necessarily bank on this corpus, for in one sense theory is a speculation as against practice.

Further, the need for an Indian theory emanates from the fact that the Indian situation and Indian ways of looking at the world are different from others. The Indian society differs from others, particularly from the Western society in the sense that it is a service-oriented society or duty-oriented, not a right-oriented society. The duty-oriented society manages itself not by fighting for rights but by excelling in performing duties, i.e. *dharma* (righteous way of doing for a given individual in given situations. This is one of the reasons that persuades me to suggest that alongwith of National Human Rights Commission (NHRC), we should have instituted National Human Duties Commission also.

If fathers, sons, brothers and husbands perform their duties — and mothers, daughters, sisters and wives follow suit — the question of oppression of women will just not arise. Ananda Coomaraswamy had seen this duty-orientedness of Indian society in terms of service, and had rightly pointed out with an implicit warning:

> Indian women do not deform their bodies in the interest of fashion: they are more concerned about service than rights: they consider barrenness the greatest possible misfortune, after widowhood. In a word, it has never happened in India that women have been judged or have accepted purely male standards. What possible service then, except in a few externals, can the Western world render to Eastern women? Though it may be able to teach us much of the means of life, it has everything yet to relearn about life itself. And what we still remember there, we would not forget before we must. (139)

However, it should not be construed that I intend to suggest that women in India suffer from no suppression, and that the ideal of service-orientedness or duty-orientedness takes care that all is or is not well with them. True it is that I am an Indian, and proud to be so; but I am not such a chauvinist as would consciously gloss over whatever ugly or disgusting the Indian picture may have in it. However, neither my modesty nor self-effacement prevents me from stating that the uniqueness of Indian situation, experience and viewpoint demands specific attention.

Theory is seeing; theorizing is an act of seeing, through a state of impasse created by a thick wall of words replete with multiple layers of meanings in a work whose different counterparts form a piece of literature. The act of seeing demands totality of perception, or at least of perspective, something more easily said than done as in the case of Indian woman and situation. The obtaining feminist discourse in India offers a situation in which the Western paradigms dominate, and they use the Indian situation as their data. Since the process of "epidermalization," in which the slave behaves with his/her compatriots the way the master used to behave with him/her, operates more in societies and minds that are haunted with colonial hangover, the Western theory-fed/ intoxicated miniscule minority of English educated upper class *Femina-* or *Society*-reading, Western theory wielding Indian women may hijack the feminist agenda and discourse. A small minority of well-placed women, ensconed in secure luxuries of life, speaks for the rest of their oppressed and dispossessed counterparts whose emancipation should in fact be the core of the feminist agenda. However, the fact is that the minority excludes the majority. An Indian feminist theory cannot afford to be exclusive. As an attitude, exclusiveness is un-Indian. In accordance with the Indian situation it has to be pluralistic, un-homogenizing and inclusive of position and problems of women of all regions, religions, castes, classes and communities, be they bureaucrats or workers, scientists or social workers, farm-workers or factory-workers, and particularly the *dalit* women.

The case of *dalit* women offers a complex situation. Women and *dalit*s share a common fate; it is worse in the case of *dalit* women, for they are stigmatized for no fault of theirs the moment their sex or caste is discovered at the time of their birth. The similarity of their fate brings them together. Women in India are about 50 per cent of the total population, and the *dalit*s (or *bahujan samāj*, to use a more politically correct and comprehensive term) form about half of the Indian population. Hence, almost one fourth of the total Indian population offers itself for a far more complex feminist consideration than the other one-fourth; for this class of women carries the burden of their oppressed men. With no intent of dividing the feminist discourse, it has to be admitted that the case of *dalit* women deserves separate and special consideration within feminist discourse. They offer a rich site for feminist discourse and its theory, for they have been associated with labour, and hence are a happening space. In fact, they enjoyed greater freedom in their familial affairs because of their participation in the labour, and were never confined to the four walls of their house, like their upper caste counterparts. Here, if I am allowed to speculate, the *dalit* feminism or feminist discourse has greater vibrancy and possibilities of study than that of the upper class or city or metro based discourse, for if feminism has anything to do with empowerment of women, it is this class that needs it the most. And a true indigenous Indian version of feminism will have to bring them into the core of the discussion. Sunny Singh, the Indian English novelist, reflects on this point, though not necessarily in relation to the problem of the *dalit* women:

> . . . I feel that there is a need for empowering women in India to reach the same levels as the role models from history. Unfortunately, the leaders of the women's movement in the country (politically, ideologicaly, socially) have simply tried to use Western feminism in Indian situation. What we really need is a homegrown version of feminism — call it *Kāli*-ism if you wish — to be radical and extremist, or simply *nārī*-ism. But it must take into account our conditions, ideas, and historical developments. (134)

For my purpose let me cite Sunny Singh again to transcend my individual limitations and attain authenticity in the process. Addressing the issue of the indigenous theory of feminism she states:

> The homegrown version should address our issues, in our context. This means realizing that rural farm worker in India has very different concerns than a woman in a similar profession in the USA or Africa. There are some basic commonalities of experience within the different socio-cultural, economic layers in India. So an educated middle class woman in a major metro still has concerns in common with an illiterate dairy co-operative member in Gujarat. The point is to find a common platform to air these concerns and do something practical about them. We need to empower women in our own cultural context. Without an essentially Indian component, feminism will make no impact in the streets or in a village in the country. And like other things in India, this brand of feminism must be inclusive of ideologies and practices, even to the point of being mutually contradictory. That is the essence of India, after all. (134-35)

These words lend support to my insistence upon an Indian theory of feminism, and chart out the path as well. An Indian theory of feminism has to be inclusive, even though it becomes contradictory in the process. The problem, however, is that when one thinks of being inclusive in the case of Indian situation and women, then one finds even at the end of a sincere endeavour that what is excluded is more than what is included. For a better view I can at least clean my lenses, if not the entire scene.

Let me therefore turn to the point pertaining to theory and theorizing. To theorize is to speculate. In relation to speculation, theory is an instrument — speculum — of bringing into view what remains otherwise hidden. This speculation is a multi-dimensional activity. In it, one speculates on some phenomenon, and others see this speculation, which is simultaneously being seen by the first speculator. In other words, 'I see. My act of seeing is seen by you. And I see my seeing being seen by you.' It is a multi-dimensional, at least three-faceted activity. In its loose sense, everyone, including a creative writer, is a theorist, for she/he is nothing but a seer, a speculator or a theorist. Hence, this seeing is a construct, and like all constructs, it is not a politically innocent activity. I, on my part, need not be apologetic, if this endeavour of theorizing has some political connotations in it. The quantum of political connotation would, however, depend on, and be determined by the position and participation of the community of seers. The community of seers/speculators minimizes and controls the political connotations by not allowing them to get established as the final statements on truths, though this community cannot stop them from being speculated about. With all its political connotations and limits (the latter I need not discuss here, for that would throw a spanner in my present purpose), theorizing, the act of seeing, viewing or speculating is by its very nature a positive act, for it enriches all those who are involved in the process either as constructors or as speculators of these constructs by making them aware of the very process by which theories about them were constructed, and the way we (women) received different formulations about ourselves (themselves). It makes us aware of others' positions and situations, and more so of our positions and situations. Hence, societies like ours should pariticipate vigorously in it. Here, let me state that the terms and phrases like the end or limits of theory are misnomers. They are traps laid for us by those who think that we shall naïvely walk into them, stop thinking in terms of theories, and give in to discussion of their politics and economics and also their construction, while they busy themselves with constructing, processing, fine tuning and packaging and pedalling theories in the rest of the world for consumption.

To a good extent the West is successful in its project, as it skilfully uses the Śāstra of theory as Śastra and successfully persuades or compels us to be either their buyers or victims. Theorizing is the need of the time for us, though it is fascinatingly fatal, and wise scholars among us advise against it, for those who attempt it find it a risky act of eye-searing drudgery, and those who have to read it find it extremely boring.[1] However, it is a risk worth taking because if the West can take this risk and reap the harvest in the process, why should we not rear our crop? As regards the question if there can be a Pakistani or Sri Lankan theory of feminism, one may say, *why not*, provided those who press for such theories — namely, the scholars of Sri Lanka and Pakistan — can really produce a theory of feminism, which is distinctively relevant to their individual condition. Let the sceptics among us know that the Gresham's Law does not operate for long in literary criticism. In the end, only good critical pieces survive, though bad ones may drive the good ones out of circulation initially. An Indian or Afghanistani theory of feminism will survive only if it has some substance in it, and if it would offer a new way of looking at different phenomena pertaining to Indian and Afghanistani women and possibly for women all over.

As stated earlier, the proposition of constructing an Indian

---

1. Please see Rene Girard, "Theory and Its Terror," *The Limits of Theory* edited with Introduction, by Thomas M. Kavanagh, California: Stanford University Press, 1989, pp. 225-54.

theory of feminism is fraught with multiple problems and limitations. The limitations, however, are solely mine.

Since I am a student of literature, literary texts will be my sole source of collecting and processing data pertaining to women in India, though Indian tradition does not sanction the use of literary texts for determining or commenting on social situations, for this task is better served by sociological texts or Dharmaśāstras. My problem is further aggravated by my limited exposure to a few texts from a few Indian languages like Sanskrit, Hindi, Gujarati and English. Further, the Indian situation is extremely diverse. In the vast Indian landscape, women of diverse castes, classes and backgrounds live and flourish in their individual ways. They live in modern, medieval and ancient periods simultaneously. Further, their roles and network of relationships are multiple, yet relatively stable in comparison to relationships in the West, and so varied and complex that they may baffle anyone unexposed to them. On the other hand, in the West the relations are the few, and among them the only stable one is that of the mother, because of instability of the marital relation and frequency of divorce. India offers a vast range of relationships with a definite name to each one of them. Every relationship is named and thereby known, for naming is necessarily knowing. Every relationship is a unique world with its *dharma*, making our society a vibrant one — a bouquet of sub-cultures in which they contribute to its conception and enrichment. This very strength of the Indian situation, however, heightens my limitations.

Further, against this complex and varied situation, a problem that hinders the attempt to construct an Indian theory of feminism is the unfortunate tendency in Indian academia to ignore the Indian tradition, situation and the roles that Indian women play, to misrepresent Indian texts, and to pick from them only a few lines and *śloka*s for attention. We, in our attempt to be called modern, participate consciously or unconsciously in India-bashing. Let me strive to substantiate these points.

The Indian treatment of women is confined to the Smṛtis,

particulary to the *Manu-Smṛti* and *Parāśara-Smṛti* among others. The generalized allegations include the protest that these are all Brāhmanical texts. This emphasis, in turn, antagonizes all non-brāhmaṇas who are allergic to the word brāhmaṇa, little realizing that, in its original sense, the word does not mean one who is born in a brāhmaṇa family, but one who knows *Brahman* (*brahmam jānati yaḥ saḥ iti brāhmanaḥ*); and that such a person may be born in any family. Further, it is argued that the *Manu-Smṛti* lionizes women in the *śloka*:

> *yatra nāryastu pūjyante ramante tatra devataḥ* ।
> *yatraitāstu na pūjyante saravāstatrāphalaḥ kriyāḥ* ॥
> — *Manu-Smṛti,* chap. III, 56

but condemns women in other *śloka*s. This is an instance of gross injustice to the text and to the whole tradition, for the text is subjected to vituperative condemnation without reading it as a whole. Whatever is discriminatory in the text, should of course be condemned, resisted and rejected, but only after reading it carefully, and preferably in the historical context. I feel tempted to add here, "Burn it if you wish but only after reading it." In fact, the worse part of the whole story is that even our scholars contribute to this process in many ways. They read the Western feminist texts from Mary Wollstonecraft to Naomi Woolf, but they do not read Indian texts, though they revile them and thereby the entire Indian tradition, for these texts make the tradition.[2] The *Parāśara-Smṛti* is another text subjected to this condemnation without being read with due care. The remarks which smack of discrimination against women may well be criticized but those

2. See and compare the views of Kanta, the alter ego of Kant. . . . I can say with confidence that you are neglecting a philosophy without understanding it. Can you really believe that a philosophy upheld for millions of years by millions of eminent scholars can be as dry as you make it out to be? . . . You know the other country more than your own and think there is not a single thing worth knowing in your own country. . . . You all can fulfil the hopes of this country, if you wish, and without mistaking old superstitions for truth, do not mistake old truths for superstitions." K.J. Cheetaliya, *Siddhānta Sarnu Avlokana*, Mumbai: Hind Sevak Samaj, 1920, pp. 92-93.

that valourize the position and role of women should also be acknowledged. For instance:

vyālgrahi yathā vyālam balādudharate bilāt ।
evem strī patimudhratya tenaiva saḥ modate ॥
— *Parāśara-Smr̥ti,* chap. IV, 33

As a snake catcher pulls out a snake from its hole, similarly a pious woman redeems her husband lying in a low state.

Here a wife is a redeemer of her husband, not his mere subordinate, nor an object of his exploitation and oppression. Further, the Smr̥ti allows a woman her right to remarry in five conditions, a fact which takes the sting out of the oft repeated allegation that women had no right to remarry in the Smr̥ti period:

naṣṭe mr̥te pravrajite klīve ca patile patau ।
pañcsvapatsū nārīnan patiranyo vidheyate ॥
— chap. IV, 30

A wife, whose husband's whereabouts are not known (e.g. he is lost in a foreign land), if he is dead, has become ascetic, is impotent, or has fallen, can have another husband.

Much of what is speculated regarding the ill-treatment of women particularly in the post-saṁhitā period may well be true, yet it is undeniable that in the Vedic Saṁhitā period women's position was better than what is often painted to be, though the society may have been patriarchal in that period.[3] The word *nārī* was connected to its root *nara*, rather combined with it, like *Vāgartha* in which meaning is merged with a word or speech.[4] A woman (*nārī*) was *ardhāṅginī* (one half of the being of man) but in no way subordinate to man. She was *sahadharmiṇī* (co-traveller on the path

3. Please see the discussion of the Vedic women seers in "In Their Own Words and Worlds." in the book.

4. The Indian concept of Ardhanārīśvara with *nārī* (woman) and *nara* (man), Śiva or Śakti, *Puruṣa* and *Prakr̥ti* merged in one is unique in itself, as it serves as an ideal for Nārīsm. In it *nārī* is life force, and *nara* is latent. The former, i.e. Śiva is a *śava* (a corpse) without *Śakti*, i.e. the life force. In Nārīsm, the *nārī* plays an active energising role, leave aside the question of being subordinate to man.

of *dharma*), fully capable of taking her own decisions. Of different women mentioned in the Vedic Saṁhitā texts, Maitreyī is a symbol of freedom of expression. When Maharṣi Yājñavalkya wants to embrace *saṅnyāsa* (the fourth stage of life as a wandering ascetic after renunciation of the world), he says to his wife Maitreyī, "Maitreyi, I want to embrace the life of a wandering ascetic. *I seek your permission,* and I want to divide whatever I have between Kātyāyanī (Yājñavalkya's second wife) and you." (Italics mine). Here Yājñavalkya is obviously not an arrogant man who decides to renounce the world without caring for the sentiments of his wives. He does not sneak into the ascetic's world of renunciation like Buddha who perhaps did not have confidence in either himself or in his wife. Yājñavalkya knows his wife, and her answer befits the confidence of her husband in her strength, as we know that she asked for knowledge, the imperishable wealth rather than her rightful share in her husband's (perishable) property. Vedic women had rights for education and knowledge, as exemplified in Maitreyī's case. Moreover, her case was not an isolated one. Along with Maitreyī, there were a host of such women like R̥ṣikā Ghośa, who had earned her name for proclaiming the importance of the Vedas everywhere, *Dakṣiṇā* who had underlined the significance of *dāna* (gift, offering or endowment), Romaś; Lopāmudra; and Vagabhurana had excelled herself in comments on *sr̥ṣṭi* (creation), and Juhū who was known for her sharp intellect. These women of the Saṁhitā period enriched the Vedic discourse and in the process earned various honours for their counterparts.

The Saṁhitā discourse refers to women as *Kulpa* (family fosterer), *Dhruva* (steadfast), *Puraṇdhriḥ* (framework or platform of the society), *Prataran* (the rudder of life), *Śivā* and *Kalyāṇī* among others. In the society of this period the family was paramount and its foundation was the institution of marriage. Sūrya blessed the bride with *samrājñī bhava* after solemnizing the Vedic marriage. At the time of marriage the would-be bride, after hearing *saptapadī bhava*, tells her prospective husband 'If you promise to consider me as an associate (*sahayogī*) in *yajña*, *dāna* (offering) in business and other social obligations, and respect my opinion, then I am willing to be your *vāmāṅgī*' (a wife or one who sits at her husband's left). Then the man would respond *grahaṇāmī te saubhāgatvye* (I accept thee for my good fortune). Romaśā tells Rājā Bhavyavyā, 'O King! Accept my advice and act on it. Never consider any work as trival. Like the sheep of the Gandhāra region, each pore of my body is full of hair. I am endowed with a mature mind. The Vedas and *vedāṅgas* (works auxiliary to the Veda) are like hairs in the pores of my body. That is why I am Romaśā.'

Continuing with this elongated diversion, it may be re-stated that the Indian situation resists generalization, and thereby further problematizes the issue of theorizing, for theories and theorizing cannot do without generalization. For instance, the general impression that the position of Indian women worsened at the pan-Indian level after the advent of the Muslims demands re-examination. The Muslim advent in India can be traced to eighth century. However, it was only in the eleventh to thirteenth centuries that the Muslims made their presence felt through their invasions and subsequent domination of the major parts of the country, particularly the north and north–western part of the country. With the establishment, terms like *pardā, dīvān-e-khairāt* and *harem* became social intitutions. Not restricted to the Muslim families, they became an integral part of the upper Hindu society as well. The *pardā*, with its Persian origin, was an ornament but also an armour against invasion, and the *harem* was a prohibited, safe, exclusive place, though the king, the centre of power, could encroach upon this space. The *Dīvan-e-Khairāt* was instituted by Feroz Shah Tughlaq to alleviate the problems of poor parents of girls. Then began a period of intense darkness for Indian women; as practices like *pardā* were introduced in India. Female voices of dissent, like that of Mīrābāī, were isolated and rare. Yet it cannot be said that in the whole of India, women did not participate in expressing disagreement during the period. In certain parts of the country, women were conscious of their state, and articulated their thoughts at a larger scale. If we take the case of Karnataka, there were a number of Vīraśaiva women writing the *Vacanas*. These Vīra-Śaiva women writers played their pivotal role in the socio-religious revolution in the twelfth-century Karnataka. Of the fourteen authorized volumes of *Vacana*s (each volume containing about 1300 to 1400 *Vacana*s), one is exclusively by thirty-three women writers, and it speaks volumes about the freedom that the twelfth-century Kannaḍa women enjoyed in social, religious, cultural and literary fields, when the West did not allow its women to write. Though these women wrote under the influence of their male counterparts, yet their works bear the stamp of individuality, as they raise their voice against the double exploitation, like the untouchables, besides exhibiting typically feminine sensibility in the expression of intense feelings with lyrical gaiety. An example may be taken to illustrate the point. The high caste brāhmaṇas regarded woman as essentially impure, an embodiment of excretion. But the Vīraśaiva women writers openly questioned the prevalent notions of purity and impurity. They argued in their *Vacana*s that impurity was a matter of mind and not of the body. They suggested the remedy:

> If the impurity of the mind is mitigated,
> Will there be room for the impurity of body?
> — Akkāmahādevī, *Samagra Vacana Samputa, SVS*, vol. 5, V.349

They vented their ire against those scriptural texts which had branded them impure:

> Vedas, Śāstras, Āgamas and Purāṇas
> All are broken rice and chaff of pounded paddy.
> Why pound them, again?
> Why thrash them, again?
> If the head of the mercuric mind is chopped off
> It is all sheer void,
> Cenamallikārjuna!
> — Akkāmahādevī, *SVS*, vol. 5, V.305

With the co-operation of their male counterparts and maintaining importance of righteousness in words and actions by attaching importance to the present, as in *Vacana*s of Akkamma and Kalavve, these Vīraśaiva women strove to remove the slur of inability and impurity from womankind and in the process strove to prove that women are as strong and pure as men, and equally efficient in all fields.

The case of the Vīraśaiva women writers underscores the fact that the position of women, their endeavours to resist repression and articulate their grievances varied from region to region and period to period in India, making it difficult for one to either generalize or theorize.

Equally important to mention here is that Indian society, even today, views things in an integrative and holistic way. Hence, the changes that take place in society do not appear as radical and revolutionary as may appear in an unintegrated or disintegrated society. The units of society, such as relations, communities and even castes among others, absorb the shock of misfortune through sheer togetherness. The negative aspect of this collective endurance is that it does not allow community members to develop individual resilience. Its positive aspect is that the individuals, women in this case, run a lesser risk of becoming neurotic, as against what happens in the West. This accounts for scarcity of neurotic characters in Indian literature as against their profusion in Western literature.

Further, societies like ours, with a complex web of familial and social relationships and a long tradition of inclusive, cummulative, integrative, and holistic thought patterns, tend to develop and even operate not in ponds of thought, so to say, as streams of thought flowing like a river, meandering through the forest of growth, with many tributaries joining it and distributive streams going out of it. This is the reason behind the continuous engagement of Indian mind with the problems of women in one form or the other in different periods, though the treatment meted out to them may not have always been either even or positive, for even here men authored these discourses. That is why India or Indian writers have not, in general, proved a very fertile ground for feminist activism. Sunny Singh has rightly remarked in this regard:

> When I lived in the West, I could not fully understand their feminist ideas and aspirations. Women I knew at home were far

> too empowered to need liberation. And there were always female role models from history and mythology for every field of life. Indian women had been conquerors, military leaders, artists, poets, and rebels. The Western concerns therefore made very little impact. — 134

Even today not many Indian women intellectuals and writers — be it Madhu Kishwar, Shashi Deshpande or Mridula Garg among others — relish the label of feminism. If some of them do associate themselves with it (and if they do not, then critics try to bracket them), they redefine the category. As late as 2001, for Kishwar's and Deshpande's may be an old story, Sunny Singh, an Indian English novelist, and Mridula Garg, a bilingual Indian writer in Hindi and English, spoke of their discomfort with the tag of feminism. In an interview with Anastasia Guha, Mridula Garg speaks of her uneasiness with the label:

> Feminism needs to be redefined if we want to apply the term to literature. A work of fiction is complex and evocative of human foibles, it cannot follow given ideology or toe a politically correct line all the time. If feminism means that I speak for everyone with equal honesty, then I am a feminist writer.

On the other hand, Shashi Deshpande seems ambivalent in her attitude towards feminism, though she rightly accepts the fact of oppression of women. She says:

> Women have been quite suppressed, quite oppressed. We, the middle-class people with education, are quite lucky. But a large section of Indian women are suffering even today. We have women going about with the *ghūṅghaṭa* on their faces. And women who have no chance even to decide about having children. We have many people who still advocate *satī*, who consider dowry a necessity, who count it a loss when a girl is born and profit when a boy is born. It is this abysmal difference that I want to do away with, as a feminist. . . . You have to take the history of women into consideration when you judge women's writing as a whole. When you deal with just my work, then take me as an individual writer and deal accordingly. Do not call it women's writing as a whole. Do not call it women's

> writing or feminist writing. . . . Today we have women writing about women [and] for women. These works are being published by women, curtsied by women, read by women, and studied in the Women's Studies Departments and so on. I had this "women lib" separating women's writing. It is just self-defeating.
>
> — 254-55

Earlier she lamented the prevalence of "terrible misconceptions about feminism, by people here" (248). She considers feminism not a matter of theory, and finds it difficult to apply the Western theories to the reality of our daily lives in India. She redefines feminism as "translating what is used up in endurance into something positive: a real strength" (249). In this sense she feels that a lot of women in India are feminists without realizing it (249).

Shashi Deshpande's engagement with women's concerns in her fictional works and interviews, if viewed in totality, can help us in forming an idea about her notion of feminism. Her positions marks the following stages: consciousness of the suppression and oppression of women, its articulation with full consciousness of the limiting impact of this choice of the subject matter; and recognition of the possibility of extravagance and exaggeration in the articulation, leading to rejection of negative attitude of her women characters towards either society or their strength. Her rejection of the tag of feminism in the Western sense and thereafter its redefinition by stressing the 'positive' aspect stems from her cognizance of the Indian reality and Indian women as they are, though her canvas, i.e. the middle and upper middle class, in her novels is quite limited.

Moving a step further towards an Indian theory of feminism, *reaction* is the first stage of every movement either preceded, paralelled, and succeeded by the *speculation* of the ideals, to be followed by their *realization*. These three stages are difficult to skip in a movement. Indian feminist theoretical formulations have also to concern themselves with these stages and also with the question: What after emancipation or empowerment? After all, Indian women have to think of themselves as beings with not merely belly and womb, but with intellect or *prajñā*. This faculty should make them think of their reaction against exploration, emancipation from oppression or suppression, rejection of the givens and then realization of their fullest potentialities. As human beings, they are not to be content with mere reaction by slamming the door but have to contribute to their environs wherever they are. This is the reason why most of the works in Indian languages in different periods, even the contemporary ones like Surendra Verma's *Mujhe Cānda Cāhiye* in Hindi and Kundarika Kapadiya's *Sāta Paglā Ākāśa Mān* in Gujarati offer a more positive model of feminism.

Further, Indian theory of feminism has to receive and respond to theoretical positions very carefully. Let us take, for instance, the case of the much abused slogan, the 'death of the author.' The subscription to this seductive formulation leads to the negation of the role of patriarchal inscribers which is a hopeless proposition. Moreover, it persuades women not to participate in the act of authoring or rewriting. Even at the risk of repetition I must state that both reading and writing are political acts, and are subject to manipulation. Indian women must accept the true nature of these acts, and participate vigorously in the acts of reading and writing, which would include examination of the given discourses, and constructing new ones as well.

Further, it is to be admitted that the language, tone and tenor of women's writings are different because they are by women. Further, women are not merely women but a class having their own identity, and located in some definite time and space. They belong to a class, community, race, religion and region. Hence, their articulation demands, if not separate all the time, 'competent' or 'responsible' discussion, i.e. with care and sensitivity. However, a creative work cannot choose its readers. Its virtuosity lies in its ability to earn readership from all genders, classes, ages and regions. The comparing and contrasting of responses would decide as to which response(s) is/are competent.

Moreover, the construction of an Indian theory of feminism is a means of knowing others, and thereby oneself. It is one of the ways of resisting oppression and suppression, of emancipation and empowerment. However, the real concern before a theory of feminism, particularly Indian, is to be aware of the neo-colonial and neo-capitalist forces in the contemporary world, for the weaker class or sex suffers more than the rest at the hands of these forces. The invisible neo-colonial forces and neo-capitalists that thrive on consumerism by stimulating desire and thereafter obliterating the notion of propriety use women to further their interests. Consequently, women are at the receiving end of these forces and their agencies. Their discourses and even their bodies are used to sell off cosmetics and even things like truck-tyres that have nothing directly to do with them. A theory that does not help women in becoming aware of these phenomena, and in sustaining them against the suppressive patriarchal or cruel seductive market forces that does not empower the weaker ones, or does not allow them to grow and realize their potentialities, and be true women in harmony with themselves and also with others in the society, is not worth its name; for it would 'see' or 'speculate' but partially. An Indian theory of feminism has to be inclusive of all traditions — folk and elite, oral and written — regions, religions, castes and classes, positive, proactive, provisional (that is why 'an' not 'the' Indian theory of feminism); and, above all, constructive with central space for women. If allowed to choose from many terms in usage for feminism, I would go for *nārīvāda* for it has *nari* in its fold, and it allows women to look beyond the prevalent, merely reactionary forms of feminism — victim feminism, victimizer feminism or power feminism.

I have for my purpose chosen two works, from my brief exposure to Indian literature, to support the paradigms for an Indian theory of feminism. The choice excludes so many. I have not chosen any from Indian English writing in general and the novelists like Anita Desai or Shashi Deshpande in particular, primarily because their principal female characters come from educated middle, upper middle class, and their reaction does not go beyond verbal or non-verbal forms. They cannot act, as they are to some extent used to some comforts attendant to the middle and upper middle class. Some of them I have discussed in the chapter, "Self and Motherhood: Is that the Question?" Here I choose *Mujhe Cānda Cāhiye* because it offers a different male perspective and has positive connotations as against quite a few novels by men and women novelists like Usha Priyamvada's *Rukogī Nahīṅ Rādhikā*, Prabha Khaitan's *Chinnamastā* or *Iddanāmam* among others. I choose *Sāt Paglā Ākāśa Mān* for slightly different reasons, because its author Kundarika Kapadiya, a woman novelist in Gujarati, is committed to feminism, and above all is positive and proactive in its outlook.

Surendra Verma's *Mujhe Cānda Cāhiye* shows a discernible feminist pattern in the tranformation of Silbil into Varsha Vashistha. At the very outset, this young daughter of a school teacher of Shahjahanpur is concerned with a few stinging existential questions, "Why is she born? What is the purpose of her life? Will she have to exist the way her mother, brother and elder sister do?" (4). Her initiation begins with rejection of her name and surname like 'Yashoda' and 'Sharma' respectively. She not only rejects the name given to her but herself chooses her name and becomes 'Varsha Vashistha'. Her father, who swears by Kavi Kulguru Kālidāsa at every pretext, does not allow her to participate in a school play, for he considers, ironically, these performances as *nauṭaṅkī*. The typical middle class mentality prevents her father to accept her proposal to contribute to financial resources of the family by doing tuitions arranged by a lady teacher, even though he is incapable of managing fee for her. She questions her father's rigid middle-class mentality and her sister's narrow understanding of *strī-dharma* that asks daughters to get married, as and when the family arranges it, and then breed children. Against these familial prohibitions, she gives tuitions, participates in the play, goes through admission test of National School of Drama (NSD), becomes an established theatre personality, and a successful commercial film actress. All through she remains utterly honest in her relationships. She tells truth to her father, even about her personal life. She supports her younger brother's education, and the family on all occasions. She is candid in her dealing with her boy friend whose child she mothers but whom she could not marry for he died prematurely.

Silbil longs for the 'moon,' and to a good measure succeeds in getting it. For this, she questions the given, rejects whatever hinders her journey, carves her own path, and contributes in her own way to the growth of all around her. In a certain sense, she is extremely fortunate. Her path to stardom is not strewn with thorns. She achieves without suffering much in comparison to other characters in the novel. However, her success does not obfuscate her sense of duty, if not service. Moreover, she does not either reject her body, or embrace perversion. Her *nārīvāda*, more pronounced in the first half of the novel, is not merely reactionist or rejectionist, but proactivist. She slams no door, burns no clothes, small or big, but keeps returning to her old address in the crucial moments when her family needs her support. She does not disturb or destroy any family, but rather builds families. By the end of the novel, she comes to know the realities of life (what is real?), and once she is sure about her destination (ideals/goals), she achieves them (realization of her goals).

On the other hand, Kundarika Kapadiya in *Sāta Paglā Ākāśa Mān* (*Seven Steps in the Sky*), written almost a decade before *Mujhe Cānd Cāhiye* spells her views in her preface to the novel. She considers women's emancipation necessary for men's growth. If women are not emancipated, then even men will remain fastened. It is in our interest that our companion grows fully (42). But in her project, women will have to play an active role. According to her, the exploiters never bring about revolution. Only exploited people have to strive for it. It is not a destructive, blood-smeared revolution, but one of values (39). Vasudhā, a beautiful sensitive woman, does not meander through different cities and metros like Varsha Vashistha of Surendra Verma. She leads her married life in Mumbai before leaving for Anandgram, and thereafter finally for the Himalayas. As an ideal housewife, she has fulfilled almost all familial and social obligations. Vyomesh, her husband, is a typical patriarchal mindset. He has inherited the obtaining economic, social and cultural order that he worships blindly. Vasudha would have continued to be in the usual manner amidst patriarchal social order, had she not, in a given moment, decided to be a 'true woman,' a proposition that no one in her family understands. For the family members, particularly her husband, a woman can be a *satī*, warrior, or scholar but not a true woman. That moment is a party hosted by Vyomesh to celebrate the marriage of a young officer of his company. He gets a telegram informing him of the death of his Faiba (paternal aunt) who had ruled Vasudha like a mother-in-law, though for Vyomesh she has been a mother. He keeps the telegram in his pocket and continues with the party, something that disturbs Vasudha.

By the age of 25, she mothers three sons. At the time of the birth of her second son she was in a critical condition. When she was out of danger, Vyomesh felt relieved. With the doctor's permission, he meets Vasudha for a while. This incident gives another jolt to her.

Vyomesh went in hurriedly.

"Vasudha . . . Vasudha . . ." his voice was choked. "Thank God. Are you alright now? I was so disturbed!" He took Vasudha's hand in his, and caressed: "With God's grace you are out of danger. If something had happened to you . . . then what would have happened to me? How could I have taken care of the children?"

A faint smile flashed on Vasudha's pale face. She pulled her hand out of the hands of Vyomesh. Lying half asleep in the state of anaesthesia, a line of question spread in her consciousness. "Was there no problem, if there were no children? Is it so?" (81).

She further feels discriminated and even humiliated when her husband does not give her Rs.500 that she wants to give to Ranjanben so that she could help a young lady who committed suicide afterwards. Vyomesh's insensitivity and indifference disturbs Vasudha so much that she begins to re-examine her existence and role in the family.

Her life takes a turn at the age of 50. The layers of experience marked with the scars of suppression and oppression ultimately show their effect. The turn in a life is in the race of women as such. She can now resist the oppression with a fearless and healthy state of mind. She thinks that the husband's behaviour towards her may be because of his ignorance. Since her children are properly settled in different fields, she decides to leave home. However, she does not run away from life. She leaves her home which is neither an act of escapism nor that of a negative, destructive soul. She leaves her family but gains a larger family in Anandgram where she will serve other women and society at large. She wants to realize her independent personality. Even the notice of divorce served by Vyomesh does not unsettle her. She played the role of an activist fighting for the cause of women suffering at the hands of different patriarchal institutions like politics and police. She finds an alternative world in the form of Anandagram. That is her acceptance of new responsibilities for all women. Now she does not fight for herself but for her entire sex. Her transcendence of individual self marks her positive transformation.

There comes a moment in the novel when Vasudha begins to think in terms of her awareness of these little acts of suppression of women. She thinks of confronting and waging a struggle against agencies of oppression. This fire of her struggle becomes light on her path of emancipation. Whenever an exploited or suppressed class struggles against exploitation, it has to pass through these stages. The novel's protagonist goes through the three stages, as discussed earlier, namely, of reality, ideal, and realization.

The novel questions women's oppression, considers various options for their emancipation, and even puts to rest a few doubts that may arise in our minds. In the words of the novelist:

> Women's equality means rejection of the dominance of man, not of man as such. The relationship between men and women, and women and men is the fountainhead of the bliss of love. With their relationship of love both of them attain a lot, and they can come out of narrow boundaries of their egocentricism. The project

> of women's emancipation does not envisage life insulated from men. It is a concept of life being enriched by mutual dialogue. But such a relationship can come in existence only on the foundation of equality. (39)

Nārīvāda, an Indian version of feminism, proposes proactive, inclusive, constructive speculation based on the principle of equality and harmony. The two novels from two different Indian languages, in their different ways, share similarity of positive feminism. Kapadia's commitment to feminism flows from her pain, and feelings for her counterparts. The strain continues in the same vein in Kapadiya's introduction *"Sāt Paglā Sāthe Chalavano Ānanda"* (The Pleasure of Taking the Seven Steps Together) and again in Meera Bhatt's *Sāt Paglā Sāthe* (With the Seven Steps), suitably subtitled *Ek Cintana Kathā* (An Ideational Novel):

> When she is born, you get angry.
> When she goes for work, you oppose her.
> When she is at home, you call her idle.
> When she gets married, you burn her.
> But can you live without her?
> Your mother? wife? sister? (iii)

The novel explores the questions pertaining to married life, that is, the crucible of human civilization and culture. Those who have mastered the art of leading and celebrating life will do justice to it. It adds sincerity to positive and constructive Indian *nārīvāda*, and in the process takes Kapadia's *nārīvāda* a step further, though some people surmised that Bhatt's novel was a rejoinder to Kapadia's, on the basis of similarity in the titles of both the novels.

Let me conclude with a poem *'Merī Bahne'* (My sisters) by Nirmala Garg:

> My sisters remain concerned for me
> I for that matter do not worship or read holy texts
> About God I am of the opinion that
> He is not a living object like us
> He is not like a sparrow
> Or like grass

He cannot think .
He does not know what's justice
What is injustice and whom it is concerned with
He has no eyes
He cannot distinguish between a tyrant and an innocent
He cannot go from one place to the next
He cannot purchase grocery
Knows no price or rates of market
What is the smell of perspiration
He does not know.
The smell arising out of *rotī*
Does not make him joyous.
He has never heard songs of cloud
Humming of the earth
He does not know what is heaving?
He is in fact made of our weaknesses
Our ignorance
Our endless temptations
Our getting frightened at every pretext
All these have boosted his morale
My sisters kneel before him
And pray
May God forgive them
For they do not know what do they say.

The God in the poem I have translated as 'He.' It could have been 'She' or even 'It,' keeping the attributes, described in the poem, in view. The God of the poem may be an idea, a tyrannical patriarch or in our context negative, rejectionist feminism of the Western sort. The way out is suggested by Varshas and Vasudhas to choose and practise *nārīvāda*, Indian versions of feminism or womanism, suitable for our climes. The true character of Indian feminism, thus, would emerge in its pluralistic inclusive discursive practices, particularly by sparing space for dalit, rural and exploited women of India.[5]

5. Also please see my paper "Bhārat mein Strī Vimarśa Siddhānta aur Sandarbha" *Strī Lekhana — Sṛjana aur Sandarbha*, Ahmedabad: Parshva Prakashan, 2011, pp. 56-77 in Hindi.

12

Towards an Indian Theory of Post-colonialism

Post-colonialism is one of the most 'wanted' (Paranjape 1998: 48) 'isms' in the obtaining academic discourses, so much so that there is "a veritable scramble for post-colonialism" (Slemon 15). The unprecedented scramble for it and its 'wantedness' (wantonness) make it one of the greatest swindles in the history of contemporary criticism, to be matched only by post-modernism. The reasons for this are not far to find. Like other 'isms,' it comes to us by post or *poste* as part of the grand Western project that treats the rest of the world as the data or guinea pigs supplying the terms and criteria of measurement or evaluation of others. It is neither our category nor our agenda. It is given to us. It is our naïvety that has persuaded us to accept it and, barring a few distinguished reputations, most of us seem to wallow in it without questioning it.

To begin with, the referent of post-colonialism is not fixed. Not necessary that it should ever be firmly fixed, for it is an 'ism' or *vāda* not a *śāstra*. Even then an 'ism,' if suffixed to a term, demands that term to be surer or, more definite, less open-ended and anarchic than what post-colonialism is. That is why it means different things to different critics. They write it differently. For instance Vijay Mishra and Bob Hodge write it with hyphen with the justification for retaining it that if the hyphen is dropped, the term post-colonialism is used as "an always present tendency in any literature of subjugation marked by a systematic process of cultural domination through the imposition of imperial structures of power . . ." (Mishra & Hodge 1991: 284). So do Peter Childs and R.J. Patrick Williams (1997). Others write it without a hyphen. Before the discussion pertaining to the hyphen in post-colonialism becomes a bramble in one's throat, one feels tempted to write it as 'Post(?) - (?) colonial(ism)?' A question pops up here: is this exhibition of scepticism of some use to us or just another instance of our subscription to the still fashionable deconstructive methodology?

Bill Ashcroft, Gareth Griffiths and Helen Tiffin use the term post-colonial to cover all the culture affected by the imperial process from the moment of colonization to the present day. This is because there is a continuity by European imperial aggression.[1] Stephen Slemon problematizes the definition of post-colonial, as forwarded in *The Empire Writes Back*, the so called Bible of post-colonialism, as he writes:

> Definitions of the "post-colonial" of course vary widely, but for me the concept proves most useful not when it is used synonymously with a post-independence historical period in once-colonized nations, but rather when it locates a specifically anti- or post-colonial *discursive* purchase in culture, one which begins in the moment that colonial power inscribes itself body and space of its Others and which continues as an often occulted tradition into the modern theatre of neo-colonialist international relations.(3)

This formulation disentangles post-colonialism from political independence. In this case India becomes a post-colonial country not on 15 August 1947 when it attained its Independence but the day it started conceiving and constructing its various sets of discursive practices to resist colonialism, its ways, its ideologies and legacies. Then it becomes difficult to pin it to historical point,

1. The economic aspect of post colonial criticism has not earned much critical attention due to it. Terry Eagleton has rightly remarked that within "post-colonial thought" one is allowed to talk about cultural differences, but not or not much about economic exploitation (Eagleton, "Goodbye to the Enlightenment", *The Guardian*, 5 May 1994).

for Indian post-colonialism may be traced as far back as the discursive practices of different Indian writers like Bharatendu Harishchandra in Hindi, Narmad and Dalpat in Gujarati, Vishnu Shastri Chiplunkar in Marathi and Bankim Chandra in Bengali among the different Indian writers who played multiple roles in the nineteenth century, and in the twentieth century the freedom fighters like Gandhiji whose *Hind Swaraj* may be called a poetics or manifesto of Indian Post-colonialism.

Gayatri Chakravorty Spivak adds another dimension when she calls the term post-colonialism "just totally bogus" (Spivak 1991: 224) and she prefers the term post-coloniality to it, though she does not draw the demarcating line between the two terms. Later on she does throw some light on it as she says, "In post-coloniality, every metropolitical definition is dislodged. The general mode for the post-colonial is citation, reinscription, rerouting the historical" (Spivak 1993: 217). Anthony Appiah ungenerously calls it 'a *comprador* intelligentsia' which stands for "a relatively small, Western-style, Western trained group of writers and thinkers who mediate the trade in cultural commodities of world capitalism at the periphery. . . ." (348).

Whether post-colonialism is written with a hyphen or without one, whether it is fluid or fixed, bogus or genuine, and whatever it may be, it is to be accepted that it has attained an unsurpassable currency in our academic world whose questionings lend it greater strength. In reality, it is continuation of colonialism, an *avatāra* of colonialism and another name for neo-colonialism whose culture is hyper-consumerism, and philosophy, post-modernism, if the term philosophy is used a little loosely.[2] It is in currency and has come to stay in our critical and literary discourses. The cardinal question is: how should we respond to it? And before that, Can we?

In a fast changing and shrunken world, it is neither possible nor advisable to insulate ourselves from what is happening

2. Please see my "Editorial Note," *Critical Practice*, vol. IV, no. 1, January 1997, v-x.

around and also being done to us. Post-colonialism is still happening to us. Rather than regretting it what is needed is to understand it and its condition(s), its strategies and ways of operation. It cannot be wished away. We can respond to it and resist whatever is inimical to our interests with our own counter-strategies. We can do so in some of the following ways: (i) we can reject it and without taking note of it we can allow it to thrive around us, and get throttled in the end; (ii) we can accept its currency and supremacy, and surrender ourselves to it; (iii) we can celebrate it and commit intellectural and cultural suicide; and (iv) we can receive it pro-actively — understand it and resist and reject whatever is negative in it and accept pragmatically whatever may be of use to us in it, or redefine it or construct our theory or model from our own texts, though that may amount to complicit participation in it.[3] In fact, all post-colonial societies should do it though that may have political overlays in it, for by doing so they can resist the *singularity* of the term that "effects a re-centring of global history around the single rubric of European time" (McClintock 1992: 293), and also resist the homogenizing project of the West or the "globalizing gesture of "the post-colonial condition" or "post-coloniality" which "down-plays multiplicities of location and temporality as well as the possible discursive and political linkages between "post-colonial" theories and contemporary anti-colonial, or anti-colonial struggles and discourse" (Shohat 1992: 104).

The construction of a theory of post-colonialism is more easily said than done. Keeping my own prescription in mind, my present endeavour is directed at nailing this term on the anvil of an Indian text and beat it along with the nail till it is turned to thin air so that it attains some Indian tinge by reading into Kālidāsa's *Abhijñānaśākuntalam* vis-à-vis William Shakespeare's *The Tempest* with focus on hitherto neglected psychological aspect of post-colonialism in particular, for political, sociological and

3. Please see Harish Trivedi for his responses to "post-colonialism," pp. 231-47.

economic aspects have in comparison been discussed in greater detail.

II

Abhijñānaśākuntalam is Kālidāsa's crowning artistic achievement. This statement, though a resounding commonplace, seems less dangerous than the oft-quoted pronouncements sounding over praise "I name thee, O Śakuntalā; and all at once is said," (Goethe) or patronizing statements ['Our illustrious poet, the Shakespeare of India' (Sir William Jones), 'the Shakespeare of India' (Sir Monier-Williams)]. Such proclamations as these still trickle us to such a measure that we oversight their not so innocent implications. Such distinguished reputations as Jones and Monier-Williams compared the uncomparables and after doing that they did not specify the points of dissimilarities between the two. Kālidāsa and Shakespeare between them do not share many similarities except for the terms drama, dramatic and dramatist. The comparison, however, is yet another instance of measuring the colonized from the standard of colonizer, however unconscious it may be. In the process they did injustice to Shakespeare as well. Further, it is interesting to note that if both of them have been equated, what has prevented all the Western critics in all these years and ages from calling Shakespeare, as the Kālīdāsa of England?

Kālidāsa's achievement lies in breathing life, love and poetry into a bare lifeless unromantic epic tale. With his keen eyes of a genius 'in fine frenzy rolling,' the poet-dramatist sublimated the story of sordid passion to the very quintessence of ideals of love and poetry. He picked up a rough stone and by chiselling it, he transformed it into a pure gem. It is no surprise then that Kālidāsa's poetry, characterization, plot construction, his diction, his treatment of nature and vision have attracted attention and adulation of critics in India and abroad. I would concentrate on a few hitherto oversighted or marginalized aspects of the play.

Abhijñānaśākuntalam is a rich reservoir of multiple meanings fed by springs — large and small — flowing from every pore of the play. If examined beneath the surface of the play, the armature of the play, as furnished by the dramatist, seems to rest on various binary oppositions like nature-culture, rich-poor, folk-elite, village-city, man-woman, hunter-hunted, hermitage-palace of *grāmya* and *āraṇyaka* among others. The moment these binary oppositions are discovered, the play becomes a pregnant site hiding in it immense possibilities of interpretation from different perspectives.

III

Abhijñānaśākuntalam bears in it enough ruptures which become evident when the play is viewed in the light of its source text. Kālidāsa transformed the epic-tale into his play after appropriating the source text which represents the crude, simple and sordid realities as they were, except for a few instances like the one in which the epic-poet strives to oversight the fatal flaw of Duṣyanta in the original tale. The king rejects Śakuntalā for the reasons far from convincing. His proposal of love, consummation and then his rejection give him the character of a lecher who would feign to hide his debauchery.

Kālidāsa on more occasions than one represents Duṣyanta as a bee that ever seeks fresh honey (Act V, *śloka*s, 1 & 19). His unwillingness to accept Śakuntalā knowingly degrades his love into disgusting gross lust. Difficult it is to surmise the fate of the Śakuntalās who might have been exploited and then abandoned by this 'rake' who could afford this and remained uncensured, for he was the king, the centre of power. It suggests that there is something wrong with Duṣyanta, the man. If he can afford to forget or pretend to do so in case of the celestial beauty like Śakuntalā, how many Śakuntalās might have been seduced and then rejected by him?

Kālidāsa made greater and effective use of the supernatural in the form of Durvāsā's curse and its resolution through the fisherman's tale than the epic poet did to cloak the sins of the king. Ved Vyāsa was a poet historian, related to Duṣyanta however distant that relationship may be, and belonged to the family whose history he was narrating. So the compulsions of the centre of power and his association demanded that the narrator should either exclude the instances of royal omissions which was not possible in this case, and if retained, then their gravity should be lessened through the introduction of supernatural like the celestial voice (*Mahābhārata*) or the curse (*Abhijñānaśākuntalam*). The compulsions and situation of Kālidāsa were different from Veda Vyāsa. He assumed the role of a poet-dramatist and that provided him more space to shuffle around and bring about the changes in the original story. Further, in Duṣyanta he did not see the origin of the Kuru dynasty but a *dhīrodātta nāyaka* (a worthy or sublime hero) suitable as Śakuntalā's paramour, her husband, her *svāmī* (master), and her son Bharata's father. Kālidāsa did achieve some measure of success in this, for in comparison the conduct of Kālidāsa's Duṣyanta is more acceptable than that of his counterpart in the epic. In Kālidāsa, Śakuntalā suffers, and Duṣyanta prospers at Śakuntalā's expense, however exquisite her portrayal in the play may be. It had much to do with his age from whose octopusean tentacles he could not extricate himself on a few occasions, particularly in treating his women on terms equal to men. In spite of this, Kālidāsa (un)knowingly leaves enough 'blind' spots suggesting the real face of Duṣyanta (man). For this we have to go a little close to both the texts and look at their margins.

IV

Let us stand at the threshold of the play and enjoy the pleasure of looking into the text. Our bid to centralize something marginal like the title may take us at least a few inches closer to the authorial intentions and compulsions, and sources and forces, however elusive they may be, which a literary work is made of.

Śakuntalā goes through considerable transformation in *Abhijñānaśākuntalam*. Kālidāsa's Śakuntalā is of a different age, smeared as she is in the environs, dust and soil of Kālidāsa's age. In the epic, if the title of the work can be a criterion to judge the centrality of a character, Śakuntalā is the central character. Just as Section 1 (7b) 62-69 (B 68-74; C 2799-3125) of the "Ādi Parva" (The Origins) is sub-titled after her as "Śakuntalopākhyāna," similarly Kālidāsa titles the play after her. But in fact it is not Śakuntalā but her recognition which is central in Kālīdāsa. And in this recognition it is the recognizer, not the recognizee, who is central. The recognizee is at the receiving end. That Kālidāsa wanted to centralize Duṣyanta, for which he changed Duṣyanta for the better, becomes evident from the title of the play.

Śakuntalā in the epic is "Śrī incarnate," "black-eyed girl" (65.1), "the sweet-spoken girl" with "a flawless body" (65.5). Vaiśampāyana further appreciated her for her "beautiful hips, a lustrous appearance, and charming smile. She was radiant with beauty, with the sheen of austerities and the calm of self-restraint." The king also addresses her "as perfect of shape as of age," "fair-waisted girl," "such perfection of beauty" (65.10).

Ved Vyāsa's Śakuntalā is the quintessence of the beauty of the *Mahābhārata* age. She is simple, straightforward, and innocent though initially fearful but fearless and assertive when the king does not accept her. Sentimentality and emotional indulgence are foreign to her. With no qualms in her heart she calmly tells Duṣyanta the story of her birth, and like a pragmatic mother she bargains the destiny of her offspring with the king for offering herself in the *gāndharva* marriage (67.15). She yields to Duṣyanta's importunities but does not commit the mistake that Mīr did:

> *mīr sāhib hi cūke, ai bad-ahd,*
> *varnā denā thā dil kasam lekar* (147)

> He gave his heart, but got no pledge,
> A mistake, surely, Mīr did make.

In the king's court when Duṣyanta refuses to recognize her, she faces him quite courageously without being nervous. Her eyes turned copper red with indignant fury, her pursed lips began to tremble and from the corner of her eyes she looked at the king with the glances that seemed to burn him (1.7, 68.20). She lectures to the king in the open court demanding justice for her son, and scolds him for 'lying like a commoner.' She says, "Why do you slight me in your assembly as though I were a commoner? I am surely not baying in a desert — why don't you hear me?" (1.7, 68.30). "My birth is higher than yours, Duṣyanta!" (1.7, 69.1). She is confidence incarnate. Even after her rejection, she is sure of her son's future which is her prime concern. She tells Duṣyanta:

> There is no consorting with one like you. Even without you, Duṣyanta, my son shall reign over four-cornered earth crowned by the king of mountains. — 1.7, 69.29

Kālidāsa's Śakuntalā appears as an obedient daughter, beautiful beloved with bashfulness of a courtesan modelled after one from the court of the King Vikramāditya or the one in whose court he may have lived. She is a devoted wife and loving mother. She is a modest, shy or coy, and submissive woman lacking in confidence of her counterpart in the *Mahābhārata* suggesting change in the position and status of women in the age of Kālidāsa.

Ved Vyāsa's Śakuntalā is a product of the society that subscribed to the spirit of matriarchal society. Kālidāsa's Śakuntalā, on the other hand, is a product of a patriarchal society in which women are subservient to men. The tradition enunciated by patriarchy naturally found Kālidāsa's Śakuntalā more convenient to itself than Veda Vyāsa's. The acceptance of this tradition signalled prospective decline in the status and position of women in Indian society.

Kālidāsa leaves quite a few evidences in the play regarding the position of women in the play. The imagery of the play reveals the subordinate position of the woman. The wife is referred to as creeper and husband its supporting tree (Act 1:20: 15-6). In the conversation between Anasūyā and Priyaṁvadā, woman (wife) is compared to creeper, the *Viśākhā* star, and river; and a man (husband) is a tree, the Moon, and the sea (Act 3:1 1-18). Further, a wife was not supposed to go against her husband, even if ill-treated by him, says Kaśyapa in his piece of advice to Śakuntalā (Act IV, *śloka* 18). Moreover, in the court of the king (Act V) when Duṣyanta does not accept Śakuntalā, Śaradvata leaves Śakuntalā at Duṣyanta's mercy:

> *tadeṣā bhavataḥ patnī tyaja vainā gṛhāṇa vā* ।
> *upyanturhi dāreṣu prabhuta sarvatomukhī* ॥
>
> — Act V, *śloka* 29

> Here then is your wife. Abandon her or accept her. For husbands have all-extending authority over wives.

Thereafter, Śaradvata and Śāraṅgrava forsake pregnant Śakuntalā. Gautamī, seeing Śakuntalā weeping piteously and following them, says to Śāraṅgrava, "What possibly can a poor daughter do when her husband is harsh in repudiation?" Hearing this Śāraṅgrava turns to her, and says angrily, *kim purobhae, svatantryamavalembse.* (Wanton girl, do you resort to independence?). (Act V, 2, 6, 8).

He futher says,

> *yadi yathā vadati kṣitipastathā tvamasi kiṁ punrutkalayā tvayā* ।
> *atha tu vetsi śuci vratamātmanaḥ patigṛhe tava dāsyamapi kṣamam* ॥
>
> — Act V, *śloka* 30

> If you are as the king says, what has your father to do with you who have transgressed the family? If, on the other hand, you know your own vow to be pure, even slavery in the family of your husband is sufficient for you.

This scene in a way comments on the subservient position of a wife in comparison to her husband in the age of Kālidāsa. She was the husband's property to be mastered and abandoned if convenient for him. And in such a situation even her own people would not shelter her. The husband's (man's) was the ultimate verdict. But the conduct of Kaṇva's disciples is deplorably unworthy of them — worse than Duṣyanta's, as they leave poor Śakuntalā quickly with a child to her fate in a condition in which even an unknown woman should not be left unattended.

Duṣyanta, the king and *gṛhastha* may be excused but not Śārañgrava and Śaradvata, for these *saṁnyāsīs* were in the best position to defy the laws of the culture. Kālidāsa misses an opportunity to express at least his dissatisfaction with the then insultingly inhuman treatment of women. It should however not be construed that the dramatist on his part subscribed to such an inhuman treatment of woman in his age. Moreover, the man-woman binary set informs us that polygamy, a barometer to measure the nature of women's position in a society because it indicates woman's economic and social dependence on man, was not uncommon in Kālidāsa's days. Duṣyanta has many wives in his palace breeding intrigues and rivalry among them to win the king's affections. Haṁsapadikā cleverly censures the king through her song, for after enjoying her he has forgotten her, as his affection found new resort in the new queen Vasumatī (Act V, *śloka* 1). Duṣyanta himself accepts that he had many wives (Act III, *śloka* 19).

Further, Kaśyapa's piece of advice to Śakuntalā is, "Act the part of a dear friend to co-wives" (Act IV, *śloka* 18) suggesting the existence of polygamous practices where it was affordable. In the next act Kālidāsa introduces a minor story of Dhanamitra with the purpose of ennobling the character of the king. A leading merchant named Dhanamitra carrying on business by sea died in a ship disaster. 'And childless, they say, is a poor man. His riches go to the king's treasure,' is what has been written by the minister. The king comments on the report that since he had great riches, he must have had several wives. He was told that one of his wives, the daughter of a merchant of Sāketa, was soon to have a child. The king passed the judgement that the child would have inheritance rights (Act VI, 23-34-42). It means that the unborn child was entitled to the father's property but not the living widow suggesting once again the subordinate position of women. It would have been ideal if Kālidāsa had provided some respectability to women by making his hero pass judgement at least in favour of the widow. Kālidāsa contemporized his characters and made them behave accordingly and in the process he could not rise above the prejudices of the age against women. His treatment of Śakuntalā and of women in general is that of the Manu or the post-Manu period. Manu did not recognize women's right to inherit. Nārada made provisions for her maintenance; and Bṛhaspati (First century CE?) and Yājñavalkya admitted her rights. Manu lip-serviced women in principle but treated them disgracefully. Kālidāsa depicted women in his play as he saw them around him. Though he does not express his dissatisfaction against their exploitation, and the poor and unequal treatment meted out to them in the course of the play, he provides a few small rents in the thick veil of the play through which we get an idea of their subjugation and subordination.

V

Kālidāsa thinks in terms of pairs. He conceives and constructs his play accordingly by comparing and contrasting different genders, classes, worlds and views. He pairs Duṣyanta and Śakuntalā, two worlds within them, and compares them with another pair from another world of Kaṇva (the loving hermit) and Gautamī (the motherly figure), further compared with the divine pair Mārīca and Aditi. Śakuntalā is further compared with Haṁsapadikā and Vasumatī in the palace and in the hermitage with her two companions of almost contrasting nature, Anusūyā (grave and sensible) and Priyaṁvadā (playful and vivacious). These female pupils of Kaṇva are balanced by another set of male pupils Śāraṅgrava (proud, fearless and haughty) and Śaradvata (reserved and calm). Duṣyanta is given another companion in the form of Mādhavyar, his *vidūṣaka* or jester.

Apart from the man and woman binary opposition, the play presents other prominent binary sets such as nature and culture, *grāmya* and *āraṇyaka*, forest and city, palace and hermitage and the hunter and the hunted. In the play the *grāmya* and *āraṇyaka* represent the two opposite poles of the settlement — the wilderness and ordered peacefulness, of order and disorder, of nature and culture. The play contrasts the two diverse backgrounds — of nature (forest) and culture (court). The forest knows no law or rule of cultured court. The moods of nature — with teeth and claws red in blood on the one hand and on the other with helpful nature overbrimming with its bounties — rule the forest with no clear structures. The court on the other hand is a structured model after the patterns of manufactured culture with almost no intervention of the nature. The intervening laws of culture are alien to the forest.

The plot construction of the play presents this dichotomy quite clearly. Acts I to IV depict the natural world. Even Duṣyanta after seeing Śakuntalā draws a demarcating line between the two worlds — between garden-creepers and forest-creepers, between the beauties of his *harem* and the beauty of the forest. The subsequent acts unfold a different cultural world of the court marked with artificialities and crookedness — an altogether different world swarmed with men lapped in the flames of love, lust, moral obliquities and intrigues as opposed to the world of beautiful bounties of nature and living in harmony with them (Act IV, *śloka*s 10 & 11). In the last act, Act VII, the dramatist again takes us away from the gross and stifling world of the court and the capital to a divine world of bliss different from Kaṇva's hermitage also. The consideration of the play on the lines of the binary oppositions of nature and culture becomes problematic because of Kaṇva's hermitage. The hermitage defies being clearly categorized in any of the two. It is closer to nature but not absolutely unconnected with the life of the city. It is related to the culture, city and court in the way the *saṁnyāsa* is to *gṛhastha*. Further, there is the divine Immortal World of Heaven that stands above all the three worlds — the nature and city (cultural), hermitage (life in harmony with nature) and heaven (spiritual). The binary structures of nature and culture are suggested, spelt and scandalized simultaneously by Kālidāsa in his play.

Lying otherwise separately, it is the hunt that connects the binary oppositions — nature and culture together. Culture, a cooked product of nature (raw), attacks its progenitor in the play and in the epic. The description of the hunt in the epic is more graphic and detailed than in the play. It is a war against nature (represented by the forest) animals, women (Śakuntalā), led by Duṣyanta representing culture, the court, city, and man. Its catastrophic consequence is the dirty dance of death, destruction and havoc, all around. The hunt knows only two parties — the hunter and the hunted.

The hunting expedition led by Duṣyanta, the master hunter, disturbed the atmosphere of the forest with its tumultuous noise. Not being content with it the king "stalked about killing wild game and fowl with javelin, sword, mace, bludgeon, halberd" (1.63.15). "Many families of tigers he laid low" (1.63.10). And a large number of deers were killed in the massive hunt. Kālidāsa also describes the hunting in the play. Duṣyanta is in fact "addicted to the chase," informs the *vidūṣaka* (Act 11, 13). The *senāpati* also considers the hunting a vice and wants the *vidūṣaka* to persuade the king against hunting.

Kālidāsa voices his disapproval of hunting through his marginal characters like the *vidūṣaka* and the *senāpati* which is not the case with the epic suggesting change in the then society's attitude towards nature and animals — not to be merely mastered even if by the killing, but to be with them in harmony.

Notwithstanding this change in attitude towards nature, Duṣyanta's hunting expedition is in no way less calamitous. He comes to the forest as a hunter of animals. But his deeper approach in the forest leads him to the hermitage of Kaṇva adding a new dimension to his hunting. The animals of the forest, and the inhabitants of the hermitage — animals and human beings, all are vulnerable to alien (hunting) ways of the city and its people represented by Duṣyanta and his people. The city, its palace, its court, its culture and people leave their dark disturbing shadows on forest, hermitage and its inhabitants. Śakuntalā (means 'bird,' named so because she was protected by birds when she was abandoned in the desolate wilderness by Menakā after her birth) symbolically represents the scar of that onslaught of the city. Vaikhanas, a pupil of Kaṇva's hermitage, who prevents the deer being killed by Duṣyanta, says, "King, this is a deer of the hermitage. He should not be killed" (Act 1, 9, 7). He futher says:

> *na khalu na khalu bāṇaḥ sannipātyo 'yamasmin*
> *mr̥duna mr̥gaśarīre tūlarāśivivāgniḥ* ।
> *kr̥bata hariṇakānāṁ jīvitam cātilolama kva ca*
> *niśitanipātā vajrasārā śarāste* ॥ 10 ॥
>
> *tadāśu kr̥tasaṁdhānaṁ pratisaṁhara sāyakama* ।
> *ārttatrāṇāya vaḥ śastra na praharttumanāgasī* ॥ 11 ॥

> Not indeed, not indeed, should this arrow be shot at the *delicate* body of a deer, like fire upon a heap of flowers. Where alas is the extremely frail life of a poor deer and where your arrows of sharp descent and adamantine strength? Therefore, withhold your arrow which has been well aimed. Your weapon is for the protection of the distressed, not to strike at the innocent.
>
> — Act I, *śloka*s 10-11, emphasis added

This statement covers not only the deer but also Śakuntalā and all other innocent ones including societies. Ironically, in the play, the deer is spared but Śakuntalā is not. The delicate innocent Śakuntalā could not protect herself from the sharp and shrewd seductive ways of the man and the city, although hers is not a fully uncourted calamity. Here, Śakuntalā in a way becomes a symbol of a colonized society.

VI

Imperialism means the practice, the theory, and the attitudes of a dominating metropolitan centre ruling a distant territory; "colonialism," which is always a consequence of imperialism, is the implanting of settlement on distant territory" (Said 1993: 9). If we accept Edward Said's definition of imperialism and colonialism, the play opens itself up to colonized and colonizer binary sets and also to its reading from that perspective. Duṣyanta's hunting expedition is the city's invasion on nature and its societies for the sport of the former. Śakuntalā's story contains in it the story of the city (the capital or metro) trying to control and rule over the distant territories. There may not be a clear-cut instance of accumulation and acquisition in the play but it suggests that colonialism in his larger sense existed in one form or the other in all societies before they took it upon themselves either to colonize or be colonized.

Colonialism entails in it a loss of innocence on the parts of both the colonizer and the colonized as well. Duṣyanta had already lost his innocence, and his advent into the hermitage spells Śakuntalā's loss of innocence. Though the opposition between nature and culture, man and woman and colonizer and colonized seems to have been, to a good measure, diluted by Kālidāsa, yet Śakuntalā at a level becomes a microcosom of the colonized societies. Śakuntalā in a sense becomes a colony and Duṣyanta a colonizer. Duṣyanta exploits her, her innocence, her resources and her world like a colonizer (He is referred to as the *bhoktāra* (the enjoyer) in the play" (Act II, *śloka* 10). Her colonization, exploitation and then rejection are legitimized and sustained by diverse discourses of polygamy, social sanction or the supernatural produced by the culture. Colonization leads to *abulia* — lack of will, social prostration, loss of confidence and amnesia.

With the last point of amnesia, the consideration of Śakuntalā gets problematized. If the colonized society suffers from amnesia, Śakuntalā too should. But it is Duṣyanta who does. In the epic the amnesia is a feigned one — and in the play it is caused by the curse. Śakuntalā escapes amnesia, for she is rooted in nature and in her heritage and values. Her roots help her in sustaining herself and her confidence with which she challenges and even rebukes the king in the epic. Her roots have become a little weaker by the time she reappears in the play. In the play she does not lose her memory but she fails to assert herself like her counterpart of the epic even in the face of her imminent rejection. She says only this, *kathamanen kitven vr̥pralabhdhāsmi* (Act V, 263). (How have I been deceived by this villain?).

Taking this point a little further it can be said that societies like the Indian, that unfortunately suffered colonization, could withstand the colonial ways and operations, for they were rooted in their past, heritage, values and culture. If Indian society has survived colonization, it was because India did not lose her memory. The African societies could not sustain themselves, for they were either not so rooted as to withstand colonial pressures or so pragmatic as to turn around the ways of colonizers after understanding or assimilating them, as can be seen in the texts like *Things Fall Apart* or *A Grain of Wheat* among others. From the preceding discussion it can also be inferred that no singular or homogenizing theory of colonialism or post-colonialism can speak for colonized or post-colonial societies, for the strategies and operations of colonial forces varied from country to country and continent to continent, and so did the resisting discursive practices.

Abhijñānaśākuntalam contains in it not only the possibilities of seeking contours of colonial but also the post-colonial paradigm. At the end of the play Duṣyanta repents and seeks Śakuntalā's forgiveness. And she too obliges him gracefully. The reconciliation between Duṣyanta and Śakuntalā is the post-colonial period not in its traditional but in a new positive sense in which the erstwhile colonizer and colonized societies forgive each other for the way they treated each other — an otherwise explosive reality which they think they are condemned to remember — and work together closely for the betterment of their worlds leading to a new world for a new generation, not of reactionists, of the *Bharatas* (*bha* means 'light,' and *rat* means 'engaged') — of those engaged in the pursuit of light. This condition of post-coloniality would be in consonance with the Indian spirit.

VII

William Shakespeare's *The Tempest* also offers itself to its consideration according to the colonizer and colonized paradigm. Even at the risk of repetition I must put it briefly that Prospero stands for the colonizer and Caliban for the colonized. To put it baldly, Prospero, the Providence of the play, is in a state of prosperity and of 'happy making' as the beneficent character of his allegorical name may suggest. But in reality he makes only his daughter, his own self and his people 'happy,' not Caliban for he had tried to un/outdo Prospero and thereby earned the colonizer's condemnation as "a devil, a born devil" (*The Tempest* IV, 162). In the last scene, the scene of reconciliation that marks the end of the colonial period at least for Caliban, the "rarer action of virtue" is for Prospero's people and not for the colonized. Prospero's noble conscience feels no prick or repentance for whatever he did to Caliban, the colonized. On the contrary, arrogance and condescension characterize his behaviour towards Caliban. Instead of repenting or seeking forgiveness from the colonized, Prospero admonishingly says:

> He is as disproportioned in his manners
> As in his shape. — Act V, sc I, 200-201

Caliban calls himself "a thrice-double ass" (295), promises to be "wise hereafter" and seeks Prospero's grace. Prospero responds with the words, "Go to; away!" (237).

Can this be a suitable paradigm for the post-colonial condition? If we compare this with the scene in *Abhijñānaśākuntalam*, we find that Kālidāsa's text offers a more pro-active paradigm for post-coloniality. In *The Tempest*, the seeds of that colonial arrogance failed to inveigle upon the sensitive and creative souls like T.S. Eliot and many of his ilk to say even a few words for the inglorious crimes committed by their colonizing brethren. The virus still survives in the bones of the colonizers, as was discernible during the visit of Queen Elizabeth II in the golden jubilee year of India's Independence when she declined either to feel sorry or to apologize for the Jallianwala Bagh massacre.

Part IV

Criticism and India

13

Continuity and Change in Indian Critical Tradition

When human thought assumes systematic, scientific and formulaic-mantric form, it becomes Śāstra. The Śāstric thinking lays the foundation for further consideration, interpretation, expostulation and re-formulation of different Śāstric discourses on poetry, philosophy, polity, economics, music, arts and architecture among others. This tradition in India, a cradle of diverse domains of knowledge since the dawn of human civilization, led to the construction of various knowledge systems and helped it in earning the place of eminence among the civilizations of the world. The range — scope and depth — of Indian knowledge systems is immense, as it includes the Vedas, Vedāṅgas, Purāṇas, and the six Darśanas in it without excluding *nāstika darśana*s. All systems earn our attention for their comprehensiveness, catholicity of mind and many-sidedness. They do not keep their subscribers in any space of ignorance of others. These schools posit their positions only after their proposition and critique (*maṇḍana* and *khaṇḍana*) of the *pūrva-pakṣa*. Such an instance of intellectual honesty and methodology is not only unique but also rare in the entire history of human thought.[1]

1. It would not be incongruous for me to discuss a category like *siddhānta* to give an idea about the Indian tradition here. The term is used loosely as a synonym or equivalent for English term "principle," though the Sanskrit poetical tradition has its definite meaning. The *Mahābhārata* proposes that the proposition of a subject before others is called *sthāpanā*, but when we establish our view (*mata*) after removing the counter-arguments, related to it and born out of the concerned subject and when the consequent view or meaning is acceptable to others as well, it is called *siddhānta* (*sthāpanākṣepa* →

The term Sāhitya -Śāstra, Kāvya-Śāstra and Alaṁkāra-Śāstra are used synonymously for different reasons. The last term earns

---

→ *siddhānta paramārthajñātam gatai — The Mahābhārata,* 1.70.44). Bharatamuni states that minute consideration of the opposite views and different ideas pertaining to a topic or subject in the proposition of conclusion received after their logical disputation is called *siddhānta — (pūrvapakṣam nirasya siddhapakṣa sthāpanam — Śabdakalpadruma,* part VI). Another view is that when we prove our view with certainty regarding a subject, it is called *siddhānta* (*sidhhānto niścayo yasmin — Amarakośa Ṭīkā,* 73). On the other hand, the *Nyāyakośa* states that *siddhānta* involves articulation of doubts regarding the subject that we wish to propose, consideration of the opposite view, its disputation and establishment of one's view with desired evidences (*pramāṇa dypanyasen pūrvapakṣa nirasake siddhapakṣaya sthāpanā rūpe — Nyāyakośa,* Bhīmācārya Jhalakikar edition). According to the *Nyāyakośa,* the observation of this process is desirable by all in all the places. The *Vācaspatyamakośa* (part V) defines *siddhānta* as the establishment of one's view with the help of different evidences of the knowledge like perception after disputing the opposite view — (*siddha niścintanto yacat. Pramāṇa ghupanyasen pūrvapakṣa nirasya siddhapakṣya sthāpanā rūpe*). Following the same line *Tarkabhāṣā,* a treatise of *darśana,* states that when there is an acceptable view or conclusion after logical disputation and necessary evidences, it is *siddhānta* (*pramāṇīkatva namyupagatarthaḥ siddhāntaḥ — Keśavamitra Tarkabhāṣā Ṭīkā*).

Apart from the poetical and philosophical traditions, the Āyurveda, the science of life, too has defined *siddhānta* as the *nirṇaya* or judgement acceptable after being examined by arguments and evidences of various souls [*atha siddhāntaḥ. siddhānto nam yaḥ parikṣakai bahurvidhām parokṣya hetubhi sādhiyatva sthāpayet nirṇaḥ sa siddhānta* (*Caraka Saṁhitā,* Vimānasthānam Adhyāya 8/337)]. The above definition makes the following elements or stages clear:

(i) Indication of the *pūrva-pakṣa* or the former opposite view.

(ii) Explication of impropriety in the view through arguments and evidences.

(iii) Systematic establishment of one's view.

(iv) Acceptance of the view by others.

The schematization is different from the dialectical paradigm of thesis, anti-thesis and synthesis. Here thesis is preceded by anti-thesis (*pratipakṣa*) of an already existing thesis (*pūrva-pakṣa*). The thesis (*uttara-pakṣa*) after its acceptance by others is called *siddhānta.* The above discussion speaks volumes about the methodology of philosophical, theoretical and poetical enunciation in the Indian tradition.

→

its name due to centrality of *alaṁkāra* in the literary discourse. The criticism of literary discourse is termed as literary criticism (*sāhitya ālocana* or *samīkṣā*), and criticism of literary criticism is known as *mīmāṁsā* in Indian tradition. The terms of literary discussion in their germinal state may be seen as early as in the Vedic discourse. However, their first systematic formulation appears in Bharatamuni's *Nāṭyaśāstra* (fourth century BCE?). The *Nāṭyaśāstra*, apart from being a treatise of *nāṭya* and exposition of *rasa* in the sixth chapter, contains discussion of the terms such as *alaṁkāra*, *chanda*, *guṇa* and *pravṛtti*. In the process of doing so, it emerges as an encyclopaedia of arts, particularly theatre arts, and a patronymic text from where different streams trickle and become rivers in the course of time in which different *ācārya*s coursed and contributed to it as well.

Bharatamuni's *Nāṭyaśāstra* is to Indian critical tradition, what Aristotle's *Poetics* is to the Greek or Western mind. A statement such as this is a resounding commonplace with much truth in it. The fact, however, is that the *Nāṭyaśāstra* is even more than that in many senses, for the text in itself is an exquisite study into the process of Indian minds' construction of knowledge and its texts.

The *Nāṭyaśāstra* is a systematic study of *nāṭaka*,[2] the most exquisite of all *kāvya*s (poetic discourse), which is the finest of all

→ For the sake of enlarging the perspective, let me add it here that the term became part of common usage in Hindi and other languages in such a way that the critics like Mahāvīra Prasād Dwivedī, Rām Candra Śukla, and Śyāmsundar Dās used it but did not define or explicate it. In Hindi *Śabdasāgara* (part VII, 3542) edited by Śiva Sundara Dās the term has been loosely defined as a well-thought-out view, accepted as truth by a certain group or school. Jainendra Kumar too considers it as a "faith" or *viśvāsa* that attains its definite role after passing through argument and counter-argument. One can see that the term lost its definite character and meaning in contemporary Hindi criticism, as the mainstream academic world moved away from the traditional critical rigour with the proliferation of the Western/English critical terms.

2. The term *nāṭaka* is often translated as drama. However, *nāṭaka* is more comprehensive than drama, as it involves dance, action, sculpture and music as well. A better corresponding equivalent term for the word *nāṭaka*, would be "performance."

forms of arts. In its study of *nāṭaka* and its ancillaries like poetry, music, dance, sculpture and other fine arts the author follows the traditional mode of invocation, something that one does not see in the Greek poetical texts, though the Greeks too were pagans like the Indians and had many gods to appease. When the Indian mind, in the form of its manifestors Bharata, Kuntaka, Abhinavagupta and Kṣemendra among others, invokes his god(s) or goddess(es), he does not indulge in mere ritualism. He, in the process of invoking the god, goddess or both submits himself to a larger self. The creation demands submission of the self to the superior being, for by doing so one becomes integrated to that being. Without being so or having at least a fragment of it, it is not possible to construct texts of lasting significance. Writing a text or constructing a system of knowledge has never been an exercise in ego pandering in Indian critical tradition. It excelled in self-effacement and also in its annihilation of self for the larger good.[3] In fact, exorcizing the ego was/is a precondition for creation of something of larger good in our tradition in which the doer is merely an instrument, for the larger cosmic forces operate through him/her to achieve their ends.

The invocation in the *Nāṭyaśāstra* to Pitāmaha Brahmā, the creator, and Maheśvara Śiva, the destroyer, is followed by the statement of *prayojana*. Chapter I of the *Nāṭyaśāstra* is primarily concerned with the origin of the *nāṭya*, the purpose behind writing it, and its functions. The *Nāṭyaśāstra* is so inclusive that it leaves no subject pertaining to theatre, stage and performing arts out of its compass. Bharatamuni defines *nāṭaka* thus:

3. In the *Nāṭyaśāstra* the self-effacement is discernible at the level of narrativization of the origin of *nāṭya* in the first chapter. Instead of claiming credit for him/itself, Bharatamuni or the tradition constructs a narrative that gives the credit to Brahmā for the origin of *nāṭya*. Moreover, the philosophical tradition speaks of another way of self-effacement in Indian tradition apart from the annihilation of the self, i.e. to enlarge the self in such a way that it permeates all. The *Īśopaniṣad* says:

   yastu sarvāṇi bhūtāni ātmanyevānupaśyati ।
   sarvabhūteṣu cātmānaṁ tato na vijugupsate ॥ 6 ॥
   yasmin sarvāṇi bhūtāni ātmaivābhyudvijānataḥ ।
   tatra ko mohāḥ kaḥ śokaḥ ektvamanupaśyataḥ ॥ 7 ॥

yo 'yaṁ svabhāvo lokasya sukhaduḥkhasamanvitaḥ ।
so 'ṅgādyabhinayopeto nāṭyamityabhidhīyate ।।
— *NŚ* I.121

When the imitation of different natures of common people, happiness and unhappiness combined in one, appear on the stage in the form of acting, it is called *nāṭya*.

In order to understand *nāṭya* in its completeness, one must understand the creative process that begins with imitation of the world and results in its manifestation in an audio-visual form of the *nāṭya*. Bharatamuni says, *bhaviṣyataśca lokasya sarvakarmaṇadarśakam.* Thus, the role of probability has also been included here for the audience. The process of *nāṭya* is complete when it comes on stage in the audio-visual form. Recognizing the role of audience, the *Nāṭyaśāstra* considers it as one of the important components of theatre, for the success or failure of a *nāṭya* depends on the audience.

The *nāṭya,* made of *pātha,* i.e. recitative elements from the *Ṛgveda,* the song from the *Sāmaveda, abhinaya* or enactment from the *Yajurveda, rasa* or emotive states of being from the *Atharvaveda,* is an imitation of three worlds: an actual world, the writer's world, and an actor's world by the spectators. Further, *nāṭya* combines in it three levels: first at the poetic level a dramatic piece is created by an author, which is subsequently taken up for production by the stage-performing artistes. Visualization of this stage production by audience forms the ultimate stage of *nāṭya*. From the poet's point of view, *nāṭya* is basically *anukīrtana.*[4] It is *anukaraṇa* (redoing or imitation) for the actor, and *anudarśana* or *anubhavana* for the audience.

Here the word *sarvasya,* as used by Bharatamuni means all

4. Here it is worth mentioning that the *nāṭya* is one of ten types of *rūpaka,* as they are mentioned in the *Nāṭyaśāstra* and later elaborated by Dhanañjaya in the *Daśarūpaka.* The terms *anukṛti* and *anukīrtana* are different in the sense that the former is an imitation of individual being or situation, and the latter of universal, "as it ought to be" of Aristotle. All citations from *Natyashāstra* (*NS*) are from *Natyashastra of Bharatamuni: Critically edited with Pradip Hindi Commentary, Various Readings, Introduction, Preface, Index and Critical Notes,* ed. Babulal Shukla Shastri, Varanasi: Chaukhamba Prakashan, 1984.

kinds of people, i.e. good and bad. And finally by the word *bhāvānukīrtana*, Bharatamuni means the representation of the natures and actions of the people along with the same emotions and feelings that they have in real. Moreover, drama is *saptadvīpānukaraṇam*, i.e. representing all kinds of emotions, natures, situations and good and evil deeds of all kinds of peoples of all the places of all seven continents. Here, three worlds mean the world of past, of present and of future.[5] Dramatist imitates the actions of all the people in the past, present and future. *Nāṭya* is not an imitation of either gods or demons but of all the feelings or emotions of all the people of all kinds.[6] Further, it would cover all people of all ages, of all places of all the seven worlds, *saptadvīpānukaraṇaṁ nāṭyametad bhaviṣyati* (*NŚ*, I.119). Bharatamuni further says that righteous conduct, sports, politics, economics, labour, hard work, comic situations, wars, desires and death are found in different parts of drama as various themes.[7] Thus, Bharatamuni's *nāṭya* has something for all kinds of people, of all the places and in all the places. In other words, the *nāṭya* is like the *kalpavṛkṣa* and one can get whatever one desires from it. It teaches *dharma* or righteous conduct to those who are against it, love to those who desire gratification of physical services, chastizes

---

5. *naikāntato 'tra bhavatāṁ devānāṁ vā 'nubhāvanam* ।
trailokyasyā 'sya sarvasya nāṭyaṁ bhāvānukīrttanam ॥
— *NŚ*, I.107

6. *devānāmasurānāñca rājñāmathakuṭumbinām* ।
brahmarṣiṇañca vijñeyaṁnāṭyaṁ vṛttāntadarśakam ॥
— *NŚ*, I.120

nānābhāvopasampannaṁ nānāvasthāntarātmakam ।
lokavṛttānukaraṇaṁ nāṭyametanmayākṛtam ॥
— *NŚ*, I.112

uttamādhamamadhyānāṁ narāṇāṁ karmasaṁśrayam ।
hitopadeśajananaṁ dhṛti krīḍāsukhādikṛtam ॥
— *NŚ*, I.113

etadraśeṣu bhaveṣu sarvakāmkriyāsvatḥ ।
sarvopadeśajananam nāṭyam loke bhaviṣyati ॥
— *NŚ*, I.114

7. *kvaciddharmaḥ kvacitkrīḍā kvacidarthaḥ kvacicchamaḥ* ।
kvaciddhāsyaṁ kvacidyuddhaṁ kvacitkāmaḥ kvacidvadhaḥ ॥
— *NŚ*, I.108

the ill-bred and unruly, promotes self-restraint in the disciplined, bestows courage upon cowards, enthusiasm upon heroic persons, enlightenment upon people of poor intellect, wisdom upon the learned, entertainment upon kings, and stability of mind upon people afflicted with sorrow. Moreover, it educates persons longing for material prosperity about the ways of earning, and brings composure to persons with agitated minds.[8]

Along with these educative purposes, the *nāṭya* helps in achieving the *puruṣārtha catuṣṭaya,* though in the chapter IV, applicable to *smāvakāra,* Bharatamuni drops *mokṣa* from the list. Further, the *nāṭya* provides delight to its audience or spectators through *rasa,* the soul of the *nāṭya.* The *rasa* theory is one of the greatest contributions of Indian aesthetics through Bharatamuni, and no subsequent poetician could be indifferent to it. It is so comprehensive that it covers all forms of literary discourse, not just for instance tragedy in case of Aristotle's *Catharsis.* Further, it includes total effect of a text, and also of its parts that provide the same effect of relish, as the whole would.

The *Nāṭyaśāstra* is in the sphere of its existence a multi-media text. It is not concerned merely with *nāṭaka* but with other forms of art like music, dance, sculpture and poetry. Further, in *nāṭaka* it is concerned with its different aspects, i.e. theatre, stage, acting among others. And all these aspects are dealt with in detail in it. Since no knowledge statement is restricted either to one kind of tradition, or form, the *Nāṭyaśāstra* as a text of knowledge does not confine itself to one form of drama, art, or domain of knowledge. Forms as such are external manifestations of the creative energy, they are not so significant as the seat of creative energy, i.e. mind or idea, the motion of the mind. The *Nāṭyaśāstra* focuses on the principal artistic form, i.e. *nāṭaka* and its ancillary forms but not

8. *dharmo dharmapravr̥ttānāṁ kāmaḥ kāmopasevinām* ।
nigraho durvinītānāṁ mattānāṁ damanakriyā ॥
klībānāṁ dhārṣṭyajananamutsāhaḥ śūrmāninām ।
abudhānāṁ vibodhaśca vaidagdhyam viduṣāmapi ॥
īśvarāṇāṁ vilāsaśca sthairyaṁ duḥkhāradditasya ca ।
arthopajīvināmartho dhr̥tirudvignacetasām ॥
— *NŚ,* I.109-111

on the sub-forms of the form like tragedy, comedy, tragic comedy, and dramatic romances. So the consideration of a problem in the Indian critical tradition is neither narrow nor exclusive. Rather it is interformal and interdisciplinary.

The *Nāṭyaśāstra* is a comprehensive, systematic, unambiguous and holistic knowledge text. As a comprehensive Śāstra, it includes both *loka* and Śāstra in it. As a Śāstra, its point of reference should primarily be *śiṣṭa*. The *Nāṭyaśāstra*, however, includes *loka* (folk) and its traditions whose point of reference is not the Śāstra but *anubhava* (experience) and *vyavahāra* (behaviour) of the common people. The sage poetician departs from the tradition of Śāstric abstract and formulaic writing by taking recourse to the descriptive-narrative mode of *kāvya* for that makes it accessible to a larger audience — *loka* and *śiṣṭa* (popular and elite). Against the general impression that Sanskrit poetics and its poeticians excluded *loka* from the ambit of theoretical considerations, the facts, evident as they are from the texts, speak otherwise. The *nāṭya* as an artistic form was for that matter evolved for the folk. He calls it *Vinodajanandamaloke* (I.123). Apart from the *Nāṭyaśāstra* in the Indian poetics, Bhāmaha of the *alaṁkāra* school in his *Kāvyālaṁkāra* stressed the significance of the knowledge of *loka* and its behaviour. Without its essential knowledge, he considered it inconceivable to be a poet, particularly a *satkavi* or good poet (*Kāvyālaṁkāra*, I.19).

A critical text like an edifice rests on the frame, wings and bricks of critical terms and categories. In a competent critical text these terms and categories are precise, unambiguous without any play or overlapping. This ability of Bharatamuni is discernible all over the *Nāṭyaśāstra* particularly in the description of *karaṇa* (combined movements of the hands and feet in dance) and *aṅgahāras* (movements of the body). Bharata enumerates all thirty-two *aṅgahāras* and 108 *karaṇas*. He enlists them precisely in terms of numbers and then describes them so graphically and minutely that they can be painted, postured and also sculpted.

Further, he does not oversight any aspect of imitation after proposing his theory of imitation in Chapter I. He discusses physical representations, vocal representations, costumes and make-up, patterns, and prosody. Further, the author structures the treatise in Chapters XXXVI-XXXVII. Each chapter is numbered and, though untitled, deals with certain principal issue in detail. It can be summed up in the following manner:

I *Nāṭyotpatti* (Origin of Drama)

II *Prekṣāgṛhalakṣaṇam* (Description of the Playhouse)

III *Raṅgadaivatapūjana* (Salutation or *pūjana* to the Gods of the Stage)

IV *Tāṇḍavalakṣaṇa* (Description of the Class-dance)

V *Parśvaraṅgavidhāna* (Preliminaries of a Play)

VI *Rasa* (Emotive States of Being)

VII *Bhāva* (Emotions and Other States of Being)

VIII *Upāṅgābhinaya* (Gestures of Minor Limbs)

IX *Hastābhinaya* (Gestures of Hands)

X *Śarīrābhinaya* (Gestures of Other Limbs of the Body)

XI *Carividhāna* or Movements

XII *Maṇḍala vidhāna* or Movements

XIII *Gatipracāra* (Different Gaits)

XIV *Kakṣyapravṛtti* (Different Zones and Local Styles or Usages)

XV *Chandovidhāna* (Rules of Prosody)

XVI *Chandoviraciti* (Metrical Patterns)

XVII *Kāvyalakṣaṇa* in *Vāgābhinaya* (Attributes of Poetic Discourse or Diction of Play)

XVIII *Bhāṣābhidhāna* (Rules of the Usage of Language)

XIX *Svaravyañjana sambodhana* (Modes of Address and Intonation)

XX *Daśarūpavidhāna* (Ten Kinds of Play)

XXI *Sandhyāṅgavikalpa* (Limbs of Segments)

XXII *Vṛttividhāna* (Styles)

XXIII *Āhāryābhinaya* (Costumes and Make-up)

XXIV *Sāmānyābhinaya* (Harmonious Representation of different Natures)

XXV *Vaiśikopacāra* (Dealings with Courtesans)

XXVI *Citrābhinaya* (Varied Representation through Acting)

XXVII *Siddhivyañjaka* (Success in Dramatic Representation)

(***N.B.*** : The Chapters from XXVIII to XXXIII deal with music, songs, melody and musical instruments.)

XXVIII *Jāti-svara-lakṣaṇa*

XXIX *Tatatodhyavidhāna*

XXX *Suṣiratodhyavidhāna*

XXXI *Tālavyañjaka*

XXXII *Dhruvavidhāna*

XXXIII *Atodhyavidhāna*

XXXIV *Prakṛtividhāna* (Three Natures of Men and Women)

XXXV *Bhūmikāvikalpa* (Division of Members of Theatre Group and their attributes)

XXXVI *Nāṭyāvatāra* (Narratives of the Curse of the Sons of Bharatamuni and of the King Nahuṣa)

The editions that have XXXVII chapters have the narrative of Nahuṣa separately in it.

The principal thematic pre-occupation is stated succinctly in one word in the last line at the end of each chapter. It could easily serve as the title of the concerned chapter. This sums up the entire chapter in one word speaking volumes about thematic structuring of the text whose 36/37 chapters can be reduced to 36/37 words, if one intends to do so. Its use at the end acts as the defamiliarizing device, as it does not condition our reading of the contents of the chapter. By unfolding the title at the end of the chapter, the author provides the answer to the puzzled minds for which the chapter may be a riddle, and makes the reader rethink the entire discussion in the chapter in the light of the title. Also, it allows readers to verify their tentative positions and understanding at the end of the chapter. Moreover, the chapterization is structured on philosophical and thematic grounds. The *nāṭya* has eleven constituents (*nāṭyāṅga*) — *rasa, bhāva, abhinaya, dharmī, vṛtti, pravṛtti, siddhi, svara, atodhya, gaṇa,* and *raṅga,* and they are discussed in the subsequent chapters.[9] Further, the number of chapters in the *Nāṭyaśāstra* is 36/37, as discussed above. The number corresponds to 36/37 ontological categories of Kashmir Śaivism.[10]

The *Nāṭyaśāstra* is a mega patronymic text of poetics because it contains seeds of some major subsequent schools. And all subsequent theories of *dhvani, vakrokti, aucitya, alaṁkāra* and *rīti* interact with it in one way or the other. The *ācārya*s and commentators intervened in it from within and in the process of doing so they modernized it in different ages. For instance, the theoreticians of *dhvani* critiqued *rasa* in order to establish centrality of *dhvani* in poetic discourse, as all proponents of different schools did. Their interventions led to new interpretations of *rasa* in the light of *dhvani,* and as an instance of synthesis, *rasa dhvani* came into existence. These interventions from the *rasa* theorists and non-*rasa* theorists enriched the tradition that continues till now in different forms.

Apart from the *Nāṭyaśāstra* there are numerous critical and

---

9. Abhinavagupta mentions that Bharatamuni quotes Ācārya Kohala's opinion that accords the number of constituents of *nāṭya* to be eleven:

rasa bhāva abhinaya dharmī vṛtti ।
pravṛtti siddhi, svara adhyodhya gan raṅga ॥
— *Abhinavabhāratī,* 6.10

Like Bharatamuni, Abhinavagupta considers the number to be five, *abhinayatrayam* (*āṅgika, vācika tathā āhārya gītaḥ ātodyam*) *ceti pañcāṅga nāṭyam* ॥ — *Abhinavabhāratī,* 6.10

10. Please see the beginning of opening chapter of Abhinavagupta, *Abhinavabhāratī* for the discussion of these 36/37 categories.

theoretical texts in different schools in Indian poetics that can serve as case studies in constitution of knowledge. Bhāmaha's *Kāvyālaṁkāra* is an exquisite instance of systematically constructing a poetical treatise in the Indian tradition. The reason behind singling it out is that it deals with basic assumptions of literary theory.[11] If one considers just the first *pariccheda,* one sees the way the text has been structured. After the brief invocation, the critic deals with the *prayojana* (objectives) of composing *kāvya* or literary discourse, its *hetus* (means), *yogyatā* (competence or qualifications) of the prospective composer, and *doṣa* (faults). Then he defines *kāvya* (*śabdārtho sahitau kāvyam*), its division as aural and visual, its consideration on the basis of subject matter, of stature of the *nāyaka*, of different literary forms, style, of embellishment of speech (*vāṇī*), of faults of speech and of use of words. The ideas and paradigms in the text are so systematically, precisely and densely written that the author mentions, for instance, the faults of speech in a *śloka* (I *Pariccheda*, 47) and then explains them in the remaining twelve *ślokas* of the *pariccheda*. Such a precise, systematic and methodical constitution of knowledge in different schools and texts of Indian poetical tradition is rare, and not found, if I am permitted to state it with utmost modesty, even in the Bible of the Western criticism, Aristotle's *Poetics*, as it exists.

II

Indian poetical tradition and constitution of knowledge in it, as discussed in the preceding paragraphs, has been received differently — either glorified or vilified without knowing or understanding it. Both saw it as fossilized and static, and in the process ignored its existence and manifestation in new forms. The questions pertaining to 'break' or 'rupture,' 'amnesia' or 'aphasia' in Indian critical tradition, though initially they hurt, have served it more than as mere emotional glorification, for they have

---

11. For detailed discussion of the assumptions of literary theory please see Kapil Kapoor, "Assumptions of Literary Theory", *Literary Theory: Indian Conceptual Framework*, New Delhi: East-West Press, 1998, 64-83.

compelled us to re-read the tradition.[12] Let me re-read Indian critical tradition in the light of these questions.

Since Indian critical tradition forms an integral part of Indian intellectual tradition, it would be congruous to consider the nature of Indian intellectual tradition itself. In the words of Pandit Bhagavat Shastri, Indian intellectual tradition is *bhāratīya jñānaparamparā sanātana gaṅgāpravāha* (the Indian intellectual tradition is like an eternal ever-flowing Gaṅgā). Kapil Kapoor describes it as "a continuous and cumulative tradition of thinkers, texts and conceptual structures in different areas of human thought"[13] (Kapoor 17). He further states, "In each case, there is a source text, primary texts, *saṁgraha* texts, recensions and a long line of commentators" (Kapoor 8). Since Indian poetical/critical tradition is integral to Indian intellectual tradition, so the metaphor of the Gaṅgā is applicable to it. The Indian critical tradition flows like the sacred river Gaṅgā after its origin (*āvirbhāva*), and many tributaries join it on its way. The tributaries get merged into it (*antarbhāva*). This *antarbhāva* leads to *lopa* (disappearance). The river, if there comes a mountain or any intervention on its way, halts and goes ahead after deflection. Some distributaries go out of it as the branches of the main river that may appear as the re-emergence (*prādurbhāva*) of what was submerged. This process of submergence of some and re-emergence of some other goes on continuously in the critical tradition.

The last statement regarding the continuity of the Indian critical tradition with special reference to the *Nāṭyaśāstra* needs

12. Bill Ashcroft, Gareth Griffith & Helen Tiffin, *The Empire Writes Back*, London & New York: Routledge, 1981; Ganesh Devy, *After Amnesia: Tradition and Change in Indian Literary Criticism*, Hyderabad: Orient Longman, 1992.

13. For elucidation and illustration to support the point, please see the entire discussion under the sub-head "Indian Intellectual Tradition" in *Literary Theory: Indian Conceptual Framework*, pp. 7-13.

Here let me add that Indian critical tradition, like the Indian intellectual tradition, is neither singular nor exclusive. However, poetical traditions, assumptions and methodology in Sanskrit, the language of knowledge composition, form the core and foundation of Indian poetics.

substantiation. Even the sceptics of Indian critical tradition accept the continuity of the Indian critical tradition till Pandit Jagannatha. Since the questions of 'break,' 'rupture,' 'end,' or 'amnesia' in Indian critical tradition pertain to the post-Jagannatha period, my endeavour would be directed at examining Indian critical tradition and its continuity or otherwise in the post-Jagannatha period.

The sceptics commit gross injustice against the Indian critical traditions either deliberately or out of their ignorance when they speak of amnesia or rupture in Indian critical tradition because none of these happened. The facts regarding the Indian critical tradition, however, speak for themselves. If one goes by the quantity of works, though it is always not a valid criterion, the number of works written in Sanskrit on various Indian schools of poetics in general and on the *rasa* theory in particular during the post-Jagannatha period was more than what happened during the pre-Jagannatha period,[14] though some may still claim that many of these were in the forms of commentaries — *ṭīkā* or *bhāṣya*. But these sceptics forget that the *ṭīkā* and *bhāṣya* form the core of all Indian critical traditions. The subsequent thinkers and critics contribute to tradition in the form of their *bhāṣya* and *ṭīkā*. Ādi Śaṅkarācārya, to take an example from the philosophical discourse, did not compose a new philosophical treatise. Rather he wrote a *bhāṣya* on the *Gītā*, and by doing so he enriched the tradition and lent a new continuity to it with his interpretation.

Apart from various *ṭīkā*s and *bhāṣya*s in Sanskrit, the new tendency of *lokabhāṣīkaraṇa* that had set in during the *bhakti* period impacted Indian critical tradition in a positive manner.[15] It happened first with the philosophical knowledge and then with Indian critical traditions. The *bhakti* poets like Kabīr, Sūrdās, Tulsī

14. Please see the appendices to prove my point, prepared from different sources and texts. The Appendices lay no claim to their completeness. There may be many more books and manuscripts available in different non-mainstream libraries. I have on my part mentioned the bibliographical details of whatever were available to me. For helping me in preparing the Appendices I am thankful to Sri Rajendra Chotaliyaji.

15. I use the word *lokabhāṣīkaraṇa* for the process of transferring of knowledge or tradition into *lokabhāṣā*s, for which at times the term used is →

in Hindi and Jñāneśvara in Marathi, Narsī Mehtā in Gujarati, Nānak in Punjabi among others, rendered dense, mystical and abstract philosophical knowledge into *lokabhāṣās*. The critical works followed the works of *bhakti* poets. The important works of criticism written during the period included Kupārāma's *Hitarañjanī* (1541) that analysed the *rasas* on the basis of the *Nāṭyaśāstra* and the types of heroines, and Bhānudutta's *Rasamañjarī*. Sūrdās wrote *Sāhityalaharī* (1550) on poetics and rhetorics. Mohanlāl Miśra and Gopa authored *Śṛṅgārasāgara* (1559) and *Alaṁkāracandrikā* respectively. The later Mogul period saw efflorescence of Braja Bhāṣā that in reality was watered and nourished by the Sanskrit literary discourse. During the period some of the poets wrote both in Sanskrit and Braja, while others were influenced by it. Bihārī's *Satasaī*, for instance, bears distinct influence of the works of Kālidāsa, *Amarūśataka*, *Gāthāsaptaśatī*, and *Āryasaptaśatī*. Mahākavi Dev composed his poetical/critical works in Braja/Hindi, and also *Śṛṅgāravilāsinī* in Sanskrit. Bhikhārīdās wrote *Kāvyanirṇaya* in Braja, a language of the people of the western part of present Uttar Pradesh, which is also an endeavour of *lokabhāṣīkaraṇa* of Indian poetics, as it rendered the Indian critical tradition in the language of the people without laying any claim to the originality of contribution. In the process, the tradition assumed a new garb, though the principal ideas remain the same. And the continuity of ideas is more significant than the language, the bearer of ideas. Unfortunately, the subsequent Rīti period of Hindi literature (1650-

→ "vernacularization," a politically incorrect word, because "vernaculars" were the languages of the slaves.

Here I must add that in Indian tradition *loka* and *śiṣṭa* are not binary opposites, as the West-trained minds have made it out to be. For example, in the "Introductory Chapter" entitled *Paspasahnika* of *Mahābhāṣya*, Patañjali clearly pronounces, *prayukto lokārthaḥ*. In this tradition, *loka* is prestiged over the *śiṣṭa*. Author belonging to *śiṣṭa* has no authority. The *loka* is the authority of word, meaning and the relationship between them. Elaborating it, he further says that we do not approach a grammarian (at the top rung of the hierarchy of *śiṣṭa* in the world of words) for words in the manner we approach a potter for pots. For words and meaning one has to go to *loka*. Thus, in Indian tradition, *loka* and *śiṣṭa* are complementary, and not adversaries in binary mode.

1850) is "more sinned against than sinning" primarily by the moralist tone of the Dwivedi period of Hindi literature, led by Mahavir Prasad Dwivedi. This led to oversighting of critical activities during the period. Following Keśavadāsa's *Kavipriya* and *Rasikapriya* that at times appear to be a bland re-statement of Sanskrit poeticians like Bhāmaha and Daṇḍin, models for Keśava, the works like Matirām's *Rasarāja,* Dev's *Rasavilāsa, Sukhasāgara-taraṅga,* Toṣanidhi's *Sudhānidhi,* Padmākar's *Jagavinoda,* and Venipravīṇa's *Navarasa-taraṅga* were composed. The other group of poeticians of the period took Mammaṭa's *Kāvyaprakāśa* and Viśvanātha Kavirāj's *Sāhityadarpaṇa* as its model, and critics like Cintāmaṇi Tripāṭhī (*Kavikulakalpataru),* Deva (*Śabdadarśana*), Śruti Miśra (*Kāvyasiddhānta*), Kulapati Miśra (*Rasarahasya*), Śripati (*Kāvyasaroja*), Somnātha Miśra (*Rasapiyūṣanidhi*), Bhikhārīdāsa (*Kāvyanirṇaya*), Pratāp Sāhī (*Kāvyavilāsa*) commented on the *guṇa*s as the proper forms of excellence. Cintāmaṇi, a critic of the period, proposed *dhvanikāvya* as great poetry. These poeticians, however imitative they might appear to be, sustained the unbroken continuity of the Indian critical tradition.

The following period after the Rīti period in Hindi, i.e. the Bhāratendu Period (1850-1900) witnessed the emergence of modern Indian languages from the *lokabhāṣā* of the preceding periods in the nineteenth century. The period marked the development of prose in these languages particularly in the second half of the nineteenth century. Prose, being more suitable for articulation of ideas, was used for critical writings as well. Consequently, the mode of composition of critical discourse shifted from verse to prose. The process of interaction of Indian critical tradition in Sanskrit with new daughter languages began in this period. A new thing that happened during the period was the encounter of Indian critical traditions with the Western, particularly English, critical traditions as a consequence of colonization. This added a new problematic dimension to the development of the Indian critical tradition because while the

Orientalists and Indologists raved in the praise of the so-called 'classical' Sanskrit,[16] the Anglicists with the new education system expelled the knowledge in Sanskrit in the new educational institutions, as they very systematically de-systematized the indigenous systems. The adversarial mode of relationship between Sanskrit and its daughter and sister languages so subtly pedalled during the period became an unmitigated curse, as Sanskrit for various reasons came to be associated later with a caste, and not only poetical and critical traditions but the entire knowledge in Sanskrit came to be abandoned. The seeds of adversarial relationship among the Indian languages sown during the colonial period ultimately led to linguistic division of the country in the post-Independence period, that was the Second Partition of the country, and worse than its first counterpart. The point not to be missed here is that English emerged as the master language. All these divergences notwithstanding, Indian critical tradition continued in different Indian languages at multiple levels that I would like to discuss by focusing on Hindi criticism, as a case.

It was a period of re-emergence of Indian critical tradition in modern Hindi prose. Though the critical output during the period in Hindi was not so profuse in quantity because Hindi criticism was in a nascent state, yet it is significant from the viewpoint of purpose and direction, as in certain ways it questioned the Rīti poeticians' obsession with prosodic artificiality, categorization and description of heroines (*nāyikābheda*). In his brief life Bharatendu, after whom the period is named in Hindi literature, contributed immensely to the tradition with his intervention in the form of his essays and other forms of his writing. His essay "Nāṭaka" (1883) studied the rules and processes of ancient Indian dramaturgy, and proposed harmonization of the Eastern and Western principles of dramatic criticism. The sole purpose of the work was not the analysis of the rules laid down in the *Nāṭyaśāstra*

16. Please see Fredrick Max Müller, *India: What can it Teach Us?* Delhi: Rupa, 2002. First published 1883. (Lecture III, "Human Interest of Sanskrit Literature", 57-81).

but consideration of literature in the light of these principles for recognizing the dynamism of literature.

With his brief and sketchy contribution Bharatendu lent continuity to Indian critical tradition, with his exposition of critical principles bequeathed to Hindi criticism by Sanskrit poetics and the Western-English critical traditions, received as part of the unfortunate colonial encounter. His essay "Nāṭaka" is an illustration of this continuity and synthesis, as it confluences both indigenous and alien traditions, and initiates the process of establishing critical sense. While discussing the *rasa* he expressed his dissatisfaction with their number, as they did not, according to him, accommodate the new experience. He had the critical audacity to question the sacredness of the *Nāṭyaśāstra* as the fifth Veda and also the rigidity of the traditionalists who did not distinguish between subtle shades of emotions, and confused the *bhakti rasa* with the *śānta* and the Sāṁkhya with the *śṛṅgāra rasa:*

> *Bhakti* — tell me the *rasa* under which you would include it, for this *rasa* has a permanent (*sthāyin*) validity with the devotee and adored deity as its *ālaṁbana* (fulcrum), and scriptural references and pious gatherings as its *uddīpana* (exciting element). How can you include it under the *śānta rasa,* for its permanent mood is *vairāgya*?[17]

However, he did not limit his dissatisfaction to mere questioning,

---

17. Please see Bhārtendu Hariścandra, *Bhārtendu Samagra,* ed. Hemant Sharma, Varanasi: Hindi Pracharak Publications, 2000.

    In his letter Bhārtendu refused to accept sacredness of classical poetic doctrines, as he stated, "It is really fantastic that the belief about the *rasa*s is supposed to be identical with the faith in the religion of the Vedas, a faith which enjoins an uncritical acceptance of whatever is written therein and regards anything contrary as a fall from grace. The validity of a *rasa* or a sentiment is to be sought in the experience and does not require any sanction of tradition. If you have it in the experience, accept; if not, do not." *Kavivacanasudhā,* no. 22, 5 July 1872.

    By stating this, Bhārtendu was performing his duty as a critic who, by questioning whatever is questionable in the tradition, strove to renew and contemporarize it in the light of new situations and experiences.

and proposed four additional *rasas*, i.e. *bhakti* (devotion), *vātsalya* (parental bliss), *sakhya* (friendly feeling), and *ānanda* (bliss).

The tradition of interaction between Sanskrit and other Indian languages like Hindi continues uninterrupted during the period and after. In this chain of continuity in Hindi, apart from the critical works of creative writers like Jaishankar Prasad, Suryakant Tripathi "Nirala" (*Prabandha Pratimā* and "Preface" to *Parīmala*) and Acarya Janakivallabha Shastri (*Sāhitya Darśana* and *Cintādhārā*) one must mention Ramchandra Shukla's *Rasamīmāṁsā*. The treatise critiques the *rasa* theory in Hindi and examines it in the light of new psychological theories and critical positions of New Critics, in particular I.A. Richards. After Shukla one can see it in operation in the works of Nandadulare Vajpayee, Hazari Prasad Dwivedi, Sachchidananda Hirananda "Agyeya," Nagendra, Rama Murti Tripathi, Baldev Upadhyaya, Gulabrai, Bhagirath Misra, Tarakanath Bali, Desraj Singh Bhatti, Sachchidananda Choudhary, Nirmala Jain and Kumar Vimal among others.[18] In other modern Indian languages the engagement with Indian critical tradition continues through the critical endeavours of Anand Shankar Dhruv and Ramprasad Baxi (Gujarati), Mohitlal Majumdar and Surendranath Gupta (Bengali), R.S. Jog and V.N. Watve in Marathi, V. Raghavan (English-Kannada), T.N. Srikanthaiya (Kannada), and Joseph Mundeshwari (Malayalam) among others.

III

It has to be admitted that with its *lokabhāṣīkaraṇa* in the *bhakti* and later in the Rīti period from (1100-1850), its interaction with new traditions from the other half of the nineteenth century and afterwards, Indian critical tradition grew horizontally, not so much vertically, as the increased width of the river in the rainy season does not necessarily correspond with increase in its depth. Unfortunately, the new education system and its institutions did not have place of true honour for indigenous critical traditions. If Indian knowledge systems like philosophy, for instance, that form

18. Please see the Appendix "Select List of Works in Hindi on Indian Poetics."

the backbone of critical and literary studies had not been vanished from the Departments of Philosophy, it was at least subordinated to the Western philosophy. In Departments of Literary Studies, foreign, particularly English, critical traditions were coronated, and Indian critical traditions with longer history and richer paradigms were subtly expelled from their own land. The example may be seen in the paper entitled "Literary Criticism" in the English syllabus in most of Indian universities. The paper is often decked with the Greek and Roman (Plato, Aristotle, Longinus, Horace), the English (from Sir Philip Sidney, to Raymond Williams), the German (Goethe, Schelling, Schiller to Althusser via Hegel, Marx and Nietzsche), the Russian (Victor Sklovsky), the American (American New Critics to Stephen Greenblatt) and the French (Ferdinand de Saussure to Jacques Derrida via Claude Lévi-Strauss and Roland Barthes) critics. However, in this scheme of literary criticism one is shocked at the absence of Indian literary critics in Indian educational institutions even after more than sixty years of Independence. It is nothing but an instance of self-inflicted and cultural inferiority complex, an unprecedented instance of intellectual suicide in human history. The fact, however, is that Ferdinand de Saussure, who brought about the revolution in the Western perception of language and reality by shifting its study from diachronic to synchronic among others, was primarily a scholar and teacher of Sanskrit.[19] Pāṇini and Bhartṛhari whose texts acted as catalysis for his insights were relegated to marginal

19. With his reading of the Indian poeticians Ferdinand de Saussure brought a chain of shifts in the Western perception of language, and all Indians as the descendants and inheritors of Pāṇini and Bhartṛhari can rightly be proud of it. The question here arises is: Why couldn't the Indians who knew these thinkers and their works for long think of these insights? One of the reasons might be that interface between two opposite traditions — the polemical tradition of the West and the Indian reverential metaphysical tradition fructified in such insights as of de Saussure. The question that arises is: why didn't Indian mind, that inherited these traditions, come to such insights? The answer to it is that there is essential difference between the reception of alien influence by the free mind and the colonized mind. The former receives influence as catalysis, and the latter are either persuaded to swallow whatever is selectively given or inundated by influence and swept off their feet.

positions in the Indian mainstream education system. English literature, English criticism and teachers of English because of colonization, became central for non-academic reasons. On the other hand, in the Departments of Indian languages like Gujarati, Hindi and Sanskrit among others, the Western poetics went on to occupy a place of eminence, though the interaction between the Indian poetics and Western poetics did not take place in the absence of a level playing ground. Ironical it is that when the critics in the West, in America, were either craving for Sanskrit or reviving their classical traditions (of rhetoric particularly as New Criticism), Indians were dumping our rich critical traditions into the dustbin of insignificance out of their ignorance and cultural and intellectual inferiority complex perpetuated by the processes and forces of colonization.

IV

After the diversion in the preceding section, let me return to the question of continuity and change in Indian critical tradition. Notwithstanding all questions and misunderstandings regarding Indian critical tradition, the facts reveal that poetical and critical works continued to be written in Sanskrit in the post-Jagannatha period and in modern Indian languages as well. True it is that in the post-Jagannatha period the scholars almost seem to have granted the fact that the core structure (*svarūpa*) of different elements of literary discourse was more or less fixed after their discussion for more than 2000 years. So the need for being entangled in debate over these elements was abandoned. Further, there was pressure from the emergence and currency of *bhāṣā*s. As the tendency towards simplification and description of idiom and contents proliferated, a new trend came to the fore. The new scholars in the post-Jagannatha period seemed to subscribe to Pandit Jagannatha's pronouncement *nirmaya-nūtanamudāhāranurūpam*, and they began to mention self-composed examples. Therefore, a new breed of critics came into existence and they began to use the term *kavi* as their surname, as in the case of Narasimha Kavi, Vidyaram Kavi, and Krishna Kavi. This tendency took another turn in Acharya Vidyanath who had initiated the tradition of "Yaśobhūṣaṇa" in poetics. The *ācārya*s now began to compose panegyrics partly or fully in the honour of their patrons in the treatises of poetics. Bhatta Dev wrote *Alaṁkāramañjūṣā*, and *Alaṁkārakaustubha*, while others entitled their works after their patrons like *Nañjarājayaśobhūṣaṇa*, *Rāmavarśobhūṣaṇa*, *Yaśvantyaśobhūṣaṇa*, and *Rāmacandrayaśobhūṣaṇa*. There were a few *saṁnyāsin* scholars and *ācārya*s like Sri Krishna Pārabrahmatantra who sang of their deity.

I should better concentrate just on the *rasa* theory and see the continuity of tradition of interaction, interpretation, discussion and extension of the Indian poetics in the post-Jagannatha period. Chitradhar in *Śṛngārasāriṇī*, Acyutarai in *Sāhityasāra*, Chhajjuram Shastri in *Sāhityabindu*, Haridutta Wagish in *Kāvyakaumudī*, Narasimha Kavi in *Nañjarājayaśobhūṣaṇa*, Sri Krishna Kavi in *Maṇḍaramaṇḍacampū*, Venudutta in *Rasakaustubha*, Gangaram Jadi in *Rasamīmāṁsā*, Visvesvar Pande in *Rasacandrikā*, Bhudev Shukla in *Rasavilāsa*, and Rājacūḍāmaṇi Dixit in *Kāvyadarpaṇa* interpreted the given interpretation and thereby continued and extended the tradition. Some of them went to the extent of questioning Bharatamuni, against the general perception that the sacredness of the *Nāṭyaśāstra* as the fifth Veda disallowed sceptical reading of the *rasa* theory. The critics like Sri Krishna Kavi mentioned only eight *rasa*s, something commonly acceptable to many of his contemporaries, but later on he added the *śānta rasa* to it. The *ācārya*s like Sri Krishna Kavi, and Haridutta Wagish considered the *vātsalya rasa* as well, something that was attempted by Bharatendu in Hindi in the nineteenth century. Vidyaram and Acyutarai included the *bhakti rasa* and Shivaram Tripathi added *śraddhā rasa*. Some of them departed from Bharata's hierarchy of *rasa* (*Bharatakārikākrama*). Venidutta gave no reason for that; Acyutrai however did. He considered *rasa* on the lines of *sāttvika*, *rajas* and *tamas* and categorized them accordingly. To him the *śānta*, *śṛṅgāra* and *karuṇa* were *sāttvika*; *hāsya*, *adbhuta* and *bhayānaka* were *rajas*; and *vīra*, *bībhatsa* and *raudra* were *tamas* in their nature. The question then arises, if *śānta, śṛṅgāra* and *karuṇa* all three are *sāttvika*, then how do they differ? The solution comes from *Siddhāntabindu* of Shri Madhusudan Sarasvati. Acarya Sarasvati divided the *jāgrita, svapna* and *suṣupti* into three each as *jāgrita-jāgrita, jāgrita-svapna* and *jāgrita-suṣupti, svapna-jāgrita, svapna-svapna, svapna-suṣupti, suṣupti-jāgrita, suṣupti-svapna* and *suṣupti-suṣupti*. On these lines, the poetician divided *sāttvika-sāttvika* as the *śānta, sāttvika-rajas* as the *śṛṅgāra, sāttvika-tamas* as the *karuṇa, rajas-sāttvika* as the *hāsya, rajas-rajas* as the *adbhuta, rajas-tamas* as the *bhayānaka, tamas-sāttvika* as the *vīra, tamas-rajas* as the *bībhatsa*, and *tamas-tamas* as the *raudra* (*Sāhityasāra*, 102).[20] Contributing to the tradition Acarya Shivaram Tripathi considered the nine *rasa*s from nine different points of view as *snigdha, dṛṣṭa, dīna, kruddha, drapta, bhayānvita, jugupṣita, vismita* and *śānta*.[21] The study of the *rasa* theory proves continuity of Indian critical tradition despite obstructions that it had to face, and deflections and transformations that it underwent in different periods. What needs to be remembered here is that a tradition spanning more than 2500 years cannot remain the same in any case. Like a river it changes its course, width and depth in different seasons and terrains. These changes or transformations are what

20. The study of Sanskrit poetical texts written during the post-Jagannatha period reveals facts about the continuity of the tradition, as contrary to the wrong impression created by various scholars. Please see the Appendix.

    Also please see Nagendra & Tarkanath Bali (eds.), *Bhāratīya Kāvyasiddhānta*, Delhi: Hindi Madhyam Kriyanvayan Nideshalaya, University of Delhi, 1969 for understanding the continuity and manifestations of the Indian poetics in different Indian languages by the twentieth-century critics.

21. *snigdha, dṛṣṭa tathā dīna kruddha drapta bhayānvitā* ।
    jugupṣita vismitaśca hanteti rasādraṣṭhayaḥ ॥
    — *Rasaratnākara*, 100

    The continuity of Indian poetical tradition is discernible in the discussion of individual *rasa*s of the *rasa* theory and of various schools of Sanskrit poetics. For example, in case of the Alaṁkāra school, the works of Pandit Rewa Prasada Dwivedi [*Alaṁkārsarvasva of Ruyyaka and Maṅkha* (ed. & tr. in Hindi) Varanasi: Chaukhamba Sanskrit Sansthan, 1979 and *Vyaktiviveka of Rājānaka Śrī Mahimabhaṭṭa* (ed. & tr.) Varanasi: Chaukhamba Sanskrit Sansthan, 1982] are living embodiments of the composition of poetical knowledge and its continuity in the twentieth century.

we have termed earlier as deflections, and not 'end,' 'break' or 'amnesia' that in fact took place in the Western classical critical tradition, as the classical texts were unknown for hundreds of years to a larger part of Europe before they were found out and translated in English and other modern European languages from the fifteenth century onwards. The Indian critical tradition, despite all interventions from outside, survived, as it was used to interventions from within. It suffered its desecration at different levels and stages — in the form of destruction of its manuscripts and texts,[22] its expulsion from the mainstream education system, absence of not so perspicuous and polemical minds in the later periods, indifference and incompetence of native scholarship, politicalization of everything in English and projection of everything in Sanskrit as inimical to its daughter/sister languages. It, however, survived in individual endeavours and in non-mainstream educational institutions beyond the gaze of the 'educated Indians,' whom Anand Coomaraswamy called the 'victims of Indian education.' Therefore, the majority of modern scholars know (and find it easier to pronounce their names) — T.S. Eliot, Victor Sklovsky, Ferdinand de Saussure, Claude Lévi-Strauss, Roland Barthes, Mikhail Bakhtin and Jacques Derrida but not Bharatamuni, Bhāmaha, Kuntaka, Kṣemendra, Ānandavardhana or Abhinavagupta among others.

Ironically, quite a few of the post-Independence and so-called post-colonial scholars fail to see this continuity. They fail to understand the nature of Indian intellectual and critical traditions, as referred to above, and see deflection as 'rupture,' 'break,' 'end,' and 'amnesia,' as the easily available alien terms are flaunted and used to measure the Indian situation. Equipped with

---

22. Despite some loss of certain knowledge treatises and manuscripts, as is natural to oral compositions of knowledge systems in Indian tradition, and the destruction of manuscripts, what has survived in Sanskrit is one of richest reservoir of knowledge in the entire world. Peter Scharf states, "The manuscripts in Sanskrit number 100 times more than those in Greek and Latin put together." Peter Scharf, "Preface" to *Rāmopākhyāna*: *The Story of Rāma in the Mahābhārata*, London: Routeledge Curzon, 2003, IX.

ethnographical methodology that sees all phenomena in terms of difference and working merely on a couple of Indian languages — Gujarati or Marathi — without acquiring knowledge of Sanskrit poetics and that too with a blinkered vision, it is not impossible to indulge in negative generalization about Indian critical tradition. In addition, even in Sanskrit, Gujarati and Marathi the critical texts and facts are not fully researched, though the judgements are pronounced. The fashionable trend to sensationalize the issue is to condemn the main constituent of the knowledge system, and side with another constituent in order to locate and validate one's own positions.

Among the proposers of the thesis of discontinuity one can do nothing but sympathize with Ashcroft et al. for their inability to comprehend Indian poetics in Sanskrit, Tamil or in modern Indian languages, as they could have had access to Indian poetics only through translation. One is surprised when a nativist like Professor Devy, pitches one native language (Sanskrit) against other native counterparts, and sees 'amnesia' in the Indian critical tradition with the help of some generalizations on the basis of his limited exposure to Marathi, Gujarati and even briefer to Sanskrit. It surprises me to note the way a thinking mind like Professor Devy comes to the conclusion about 'amnesia' in Indian criticism without considering other constituents of the tradition like Hindi, Bengali or Tamil among others. Though the significance of his insightful study of Indian criticism during the colonization, and its impact on Indian creativity is beyond doubt, one cannot resist from stating that in the process of critiquing the colonial enterprise, he not only buys the 'amnesia' of the colonizers but also furthers it. The colonizers used the thesis to validate their presence in the colony, so that they could teach the natives how to save, preserve and restore the cultural memory. Undeniably, much was forgotten in terms of historical evidences, and psychologically also the colonization had depleted the morale of the country, but what happened in history does not necessarily correspond with other domains, for instance creativity, criticism and culture, particularly music. The term 'amnesia' is forgetfulness — partial or complete, leading to disjunction or disorientation. It is related to, as understood by experimental psychology, violent unconsciousness of memory. If one accepts the psychological dimension of cultural amnesia, one finds that Professor Devy in the process of furthering his thesis uses psychology selectively and abandons it afterwards. For example, in Freud, whom he quotes extensively, repression should lead to displacement, sublimation and symbolic representation. If repression implies amnesia, as Professor Devy alleged, then when, how and in what forms the sublimation or symbolic manifestation takes place?

The implications of amnesia thesis in Indian critical tradition, by ignoring hard evidence against it, are more serious than they appear on the surface. Amnesia leads to a pathological condition that is characterized by the loss of faculty of using or understanding spoken or written language. If long continued, it heads for 'aphasia,' a term from psychiatry that denotes a form of mental disorder in which volition is either impaired or lost. It leads to prostration of an individual, community or entire society, a condition not desired even in animals. If accepted uncritically, the thesis insults the sacrifices of martyrs in the history of struggle for India's Independence, and also the critical works of all great Indian minds before and after Pandit Jagannatha, though the number might be small, including Professor Devy's.

In a way Professor Devy does much service to Indian critical scene by giving it a psychological jolt. Leave aside the Sahitya Akademi Award that the book earned for its author, for awards are often not true measurements of a work, the fact is that Devy's book is one of the three significant contributions to Indian criticism in English in the last decade, or in the last quarter of the twentieth century, the other two being Aijaz Ahmad's *In Theory: Classes, Nations, Literatures* (1994) and Kapil Kapoor's *Literary Theory: Indian Conceptual Framework* (1998) — the last one is discussed earlier in the main body of the chapter. Ahmad's book meaningfully analyzes and critiques key concepts, propositions and developments like literature (among the signs of our time), literary theory and "Third World Literature," Orientalism and Indian literature among others in the second half of the twentieth century from the Marxist perspective without overriding India.

Let me wind up the present endeavour with the discussion of the critical turns or *deflections*, that the Indian tradition took in various periods. The first *deflection* took place in the *bhakti* period, second in the Rīti period, the third in the nineteenth century, and the fourth in the twentieth century. The first *deflection* saw *lokabhāṣīkaraṇa* of Indian poetics and the beginning of the process of branching out of Indian critical tradition into *lokabhāṣā*s along with consideration of new experience, creativity in the form of *bhakti* literature; the second *deflection* was marked by its stylistic and prosodic rendition of the tradition or *śiṣṭīkaraṇa* of the tradition in the *lokabhāṣā*s, and Piṅgala-Śāstra in many Indian languages (e.g. by Dalpat in Gujarati) were composed. In its third *deflection* in the nineteenth century, the tradition in its manifestation emerged in the form of modern Indian languages that have a continuous tradition of engagement with Indian poetics, as we saw in the case of Hindi among other Indian languages. In its yet another *deflection*, it assumed the garb of English through translation of its texts into English beginning with the endeavours of the Orientalists (as the translation of Bharatamuni's *Nāṭyaśāstra* by Manmohan Ghosh) and through endeavours aimed at historiography and commentaries (in the works of scholars like P.V. Kane, S.K. De, Ganganath Jha, Bishnupada Bhattacarya, A. Sankaran, Subramania Iyer, V. Raghavan, Krishna Chaitanya, K. Krishnamoorthy, Kunjunni Raja, M. Hiriyanna, V.K. Chari, Krishna Rayan, Adi Rangachari, Tatachariji among others in English). These endeavours were directed at transferring the knowledge of Indian poetical tradition into English for the academicians in the higher education system in India that did not have or did not want to have access to it directly. In the meantime, some scholars examined the Western English literary texts in the light of various theories of Sanskrit poetics, and thereby tried to change the prevailing theory (from the West) and data (texts for application from the non-West) paradigm. This stream has been given a purposeful direction by Kapil Kapoor's *Literary Theory: Indian Conceptual Framework* (1998), for it sees Indian critical tradition in the light of Indian intellectual tradition and also in its present context, covering all cardinal concerns of literary and theoretical discourse in a precise, systematic and methodical manner. In the process, it provides Indian conceptual framework to literary theory based on Indian poetics in the obtaining West — (theory) — intoxicated Indian academic world without being complexed. (It does mention about a dozen Western critics and authors including Aristotle thrice.) The fact worth mentioning here is that while Indian critical tradition branched out in different modern Indian languages, the composition of treatises and commentaries on various schools of poetics continued ceaselessly in Sanskrit, though they remain, unfortunately for us, unnoticed by mainstream scholars of English barring a few distinguished exceptions some of whom have been mentioned above.

In a situation such as this, two points deserve our consideration. The first pertains to the absence of dialogue among various streams of Indian critical traditions existing in Sanskrit, *lokabhāṣās*, modern Indian languages and English. The dialogue among these streams is necessary for the future of Indian critical tradition whose foundation rests on various schools of Sanskrit poetics in particular and others as well including Tamil poetics, and in various schools of contemporary criticism in Indian languages. The need is to study concepts, categories, paradigms and theories propounded in Sanskrit poetics, and also to modify and adapt them, if needed, to suit the demands of modern experience, its articulation in literature and its assessment. The second point is related to the question of revival of Sanskrit poetics. One view holds that the question of revival of Sanskrit poetics does not arise, for it is very much alive. Those who do not know it, should go to it and enrich themselves by knowing it. The other view is: if there is an absence of dialogue among various streams of Indian critical tradition, and if we are not aware of our critical tradition and of its continuity in various forms, we genuflect before the Western theories, the situation demands corrective measures including revival of what is of lasting significance in our critical traditions in the form of theoretical terms, categories and conceptual framework. Revival is not evil, indiscreet revivalism is. Revival and renewal are natural processes. In fact, revival is one of the renewal mechanisms common to all great traditions and civilizations for maintaining continuity. For instance, much of the New Criticism, the most significant school of the Western criticism in the first half of the twentieth century, was discreet revival of the rhetoric that did not belong to the twentieth century but to the classical Greek and Roman period. Fortunate are we that there is so much available to us that can be revived. Revive we must whatever deserves to be, and modernize it and be modernized in terms of our critical traditions.[23] Renewal and revival, if attempted with discretion, are virtues. We must take a cue from the history of criticism and remember: No civilization as yet ever became great by imitation, but no civilization would ever become great by giving up its own traditions and by embracing others.

Postscript

It is easy to reject and difficult to defend, for those who defend

---

23. Our thinkers, being aware of the significance of revival, and also of its dangers if attempted injudiciously, have suggested strategies of revival. For instance, Kālidāsa states:

purāṇamityev na khalu sādhu sarvam na cāpi kāvya navmityavādham ।
santaḥ parīkṣyanatarabhajante mūḍaḥ paraḥ pratyayney buddhi ॥
— *Mālavikāgnimitra* I.2

(All is not good merely because it is old; nor is a poem to be despised because it is new. Wise accept one or the other after scrutinizing it carefully. Only a fool has his judgement guided by the opinions of others.)

The *bhakti* poet Goswāmī Tulasīdās wrote in *The Rāmcaritamānasa*:

saṁgraha tyāgu na binu pahcāne.

(Neither acceptance nor rejection should be attempted without recognizing the object.)

are vulnerable for carrying the burden of their responsibility. But to reject or defend without taking cognizance of the evidence, for or against, is an intellectual crime. Equally criminal is not to defend the tradition against the contrived perceptions constructed by over-sighting the facts inadvertently or otherwise. The Postscript continues with the principal concern of the Chapter pertaining to the continuity of the Indian critical tradition in the twenty-first century with evidences about it.

Acharya Revaprasad Dwivedi's book *Sanskrit-Kāvyaśāstra kā Ālocanātmaka Itihāsa* (2007) substantiates some of my positions in terms of facts, as he studied Sanskrit poetics in the following four categories or terms of (a) *siddhānta* (principles), *kalpa*, and *sampradāya;* (b) of *dhāma*s, i.e. Kañcīdhāma (Bharata and Daṇḍin), Śraddhādhāma (Bhāmaha, Vāmana, Udbhaṭa, Ānandvardhana, Abhinavagupta, Kṣemendra, Kuntaka, Mahimabhaṭṭa, Mammaṭa; Mahākāleśvaradhāma (Dhanañjaya, Dhanik, Bhojarāja; and Viśveśvaradhāma Kāśī) (Appayya Dixit, Madhusudan Saraswati, Panditraj Jagannatha, Karpatriji, and Sanatana; (c) *sahasrāvadhi* (millennium), i.e. First Millennium (Bharata and Bhāmaha), Second Millennium (Vāmana, Acyutrai), Third Millennium (from Vishweshwar Pandit onwards; (d) the *ācārya*s of Sanskrit poetics from Bharatamuni to Swami Karpatriji. In the last section *Tṛtīya Sahasrābdi,* i.e. the Third Millennium (1701 to 2005) he discusses the contemporary poeticians. Vishweshwar Pundit and Narsingh Kavi serve as links between the generation of Pandit Jagannatha and twentieth-century poeticians. *Alaṁkāra-kaustubham* of Vishweshwar Pundit, written some time in the middle of eighteenth century, extends the tradition of *alaṁkāra* without saying anything new. In *Rasacandrikā* and *Alaṁkāramuktāvalī* he deals with *rasa* but it remained a metaphysical thing and could not become a thing of this world. So the alienation of *rasa* that began with Ānandavardhana continued. Neither Appayya Dixit nor Pundit Jagannatha and Vishweshwar Dixit could halt the process or give it a new direction. The chapter "Adhunātana Sanskrit Kāvyaśāstra" (423-52) considers the issue of continuity in compositions of poetical texts/treatises in Sanskrit up to 2005. It discusses works like Swami Karpatriji's *Bhaktirasārṇava* (1940), *Bhaktirasavimarśa* (1980), Rewa Prasad Dwivedi's, *Kāvyālaṁkārakārikā* (1976), *Nāṭyānuśāsanam*, and *Alaṁbrahma.*

The second half of the twentieth century witnessed emergence of a few significant texts and departures therein, for instance Brahmananda Sharma gave social orientation to the tradition by bringing *śrama* (labour) into its fold. In his *Vāstavālaṁkāradarśanam* (1969) and *Kāvyasatyaloka* (1980) he proposed the significance of Truth and Labour, as he stated '*satyam hi śaraṇam mamaḥ.*' In the beginning of *Kāvyasatyaloka* he, along with being a critic, assumes the role of a mythopoeist, and prays to a new god named as Śrama:

śramam tu vande śramik ca tataḥ param ।
śrama śramikrūpen pratiṣṭhā jagato mātā ॥

The new god is a consequence of the realization and shift brought about the centrality of labour in the existence of humanity. In fact, the existence of world rests on labour and his/her labourer. It was a major shift from metaphysical to realistic consideration of issues of life, literature and poetics. Shivaji Upadhyaya's *Satyasandarbhaḥ* (1990), Jagannātha Pathak's *Saundaryakārikā* (1991), G.C. Pandey's *Saundaryavimarśaṇa* (1995) and *Bhaktirasavimarśaḥ* (1991) among others discuss poetical principles in the light of truth, beauty and devotion. Radhavallabh Tripathi related it to *loka* and Gyanchandra Pandey discussed it in modern terms and experience. It brought in some fresh whiff of air under the influence of contemporary movements in literary and related disciplines.

Sanskrit critical tradition has found its expression in English as well. Illustrious critics who contributed to the new corpus of Sanskrit criticism by writing about it in English include Hiriyanna, S.K. De, P.V. Kane, V. Raghavan, K. Krishnamoorthy, Krishna Chaitanya, K.K. Chari, Ayappa and Panikkar among others. Though most of their writings are introductory, informative and descriptive in nature, they serve the main function of making

Sanskrit poetics and its importance known to non-Sanskrit-knowing Indian and foreign scholars. Also the cases of their application and study to/of these schools or approaches in terms of contemporary texts led to mutual illumination and interpretation. Without discounting the contribution of the works like *History of Sanskrit Poetics,* and *Comparative Study of Indian and Western Poetics*, it can be said that since the last quarter of the preceding century, despite the charges against the Sanskrit texts as mouthpieces for 'syndicated Hinduism,' there has been a greater acceptance of Sanskrit poetics in the mainstream Indian English studies in the country. The names of critics like Bharatamuni, Bhāmaha, Vāmana, Bhaṭṭa Lollaṭa, Kuntaka, Ānandavardhana, Abhinavagupta, Kṣemendra, Rājaśekhara and poetical writings like the *Nāṭyaśāstra, Kāvyālaṁkāra, Vakroktijīvitam, Abhinavabhāratī, Locana,* and *Kāvyaprakāśa* among others are no longer foreign to Indian students of English literature. Yet another instance of irony in case of Sanskrit studies is that it is gaining some ground in the land of its origin at a time when in Europe and U.S.A. the Departments and Chairs of Indology are being closed and replaced by the Departments of South Asian Studies.

14

Rethinking Literary Theory in India

It is not the answer that enlightens but the question.
— Eugene Ionesco

All we can do is to search for the falsity content of our best theory.
— Karl Popper

Nothing can overcome the resistance to theory since theory is itself this resistance, the loftier the aims and better the methods of literary theory, the less possible it becomes. Yet, literary theory is not in danger of going under; it cannot help but flourish, and the more it is resisted, the more it flourishes, since the language it speaks is the language of self-resistance. What remains impossible to decide is whether this flourishing is a triumph or a fall.
— Paul de Man

If theory means a reasonably systematic reflection on our guiding assumptions, it remains as indispensable as ever.
— Terry Eagleton

THE discussion of the title "Rethinking Literary Theory in India" demands contextualization, as it might appear rather belated and misplaced to think of theory at the beginning of the second decade of the twenty-first century when the heydays of theory are over. Even the discussion about the 'End' or 'Death' of theory, 'After', 'Post' theory courts the risk of suffering from obsolescence, as volumes one after the another, have already heralded the end of the centrality of theory.

The twentieth century witnessed an unprecedented ascendance in the fortunes of theory particularly in its second half. Though most of the literary theorists — Jacques Derrida, Michel Foucault, Paul de Man, Hillis Miller and Terry Eagleton to name a few among others — were close and competent readers of literature, theory prospered at the expense of literary studies and theory became a discipline in itself. However, in the ascendance of theory lay the seeds of its fall, as overindulgence in theory by its subscribers and the attendant self-reflexivity of theory severed its links with literary practices. Consequently, a few shrill notes about the end of theory, paralleled by the pronouncements like the 'post-theory', the 'end' of theory and 'after theory' were heard by the end of the preceding century in the form of the publication of Thomas Docherty's *After Theory* (1997), *Post-Theory: New Directions in Criticism* (1999) by Martin McQuillan et al. (eds.), *What's Left of Theory?* (2000) by Judith Butler, John Guillory and Thomas Kendall (eds.), Valentine Cunningham's *Reading After Theory* (2002); Jean-Michael Rabate's *The Future of Theory* (2002); Terry Eagleton's *After Theory* (2003); Michael Payne and John Shad's edited *Life.After.Theory* (2003). The 'end' or 'death' of theory did not literally mean the 'end' or 'death' of theory, for they are used as trope for 'disorientation' towards theory. It referred to the theory fatigue, caused by the surfeit of theory in the second half of the twentieth century. The end of theory suggested erosion in its status of centrality, as it came to be realized that literary theory is not indispensable for literary studies.[1] The Indian academia experienced the hegemony of theory belatedly in the last quarter of the century and still finds subscribers for theory.

---

1. The proposal 'post-theory' is problematic because it presupposes that it is preceded by the period of theory which in turn means that there was a pre-theory period, free from the knowledge or pursuit of theory.

   Moreover, the term 'post-theory' does not mean anti-theory necessarily. It suggests that the theory *per se* or theory as an independent and separate discipline has failed to sustain interest, and cannot survive on its own. Theory, it seemed, had abandoned literature, but theorists did not, as all competent literary theorists were competent readers of literature. Moreover, literary theory was to a good extent shaped by perceptions from philosophy and social sciences like psychology, sociology, feminism, political sciences, economics, post-colonialism, and cultural studies. Hence, it moved towards interdisciplinarity. Please see Avadhesh Kumar Singh, *Towards Interdisciplinarity: (the) University, Humanities and Social Sciences in the 21st Century*, Delhi: Creative Books, 2010.

One of chief reasons for disorientation with and the 'end' of theory, apart from the above-mentioned, is the bankruptcy of criticism and its inability (more of critics and less of criticism) to add to the existing centres or issues of criticism. Perhaps major issues of literary theory or criticism have been explored and exhausted. The principal concerns of art/literary criticism or theory revolve around the hinges — art/text, artist/author, ambience/context, audience/reader and co-text. Though they are intertwined, different periods of critical history have foregrounded one of the hinges of criticism.[2]

Before rethinking theory in India, let me take a brief view of the Western critical tradition in terms of the critical and theoretical hinges, for approaches that came into existence around them shaped Indian critical perceptions in the twentieth century in particular.

Generalization is a fascinating yet fatal enterprise, because it is based on totalization. Nevertheless, at times conscious indulgence in it helps in understanding a phenomenon, as it provides certain angularity for vertical probing in the issue which is otherwise not possible. With this sense or license, it may be generalized that critical enterprise in the twentieth century may be measured in two terms — textuality and neo-textuality, the first dominated the first half and the latter the second half.

The New Critics brought text in the centre in an unprecedented manner, and relegated context and author to subordinate positions. Roland Barthes questioned the author(ity) and dislodged the author from a high pedestal centrality and enunciated the death of the author in his article "The Death of the Author", and had earlier pronounced that 'I' that writes the text is never; itself, anything more than paper 'I'. As language refers to itself, so it is disconnected from reality and "Linguistically the author is never more than the instance saying I: Language knows a subject not a person". (Barthes: 169) The moment writing commences, the

2. For discussion of the issue and study please see "Compoetics in India: Alternative Frameworks in India" in the present book.

disjunction between the author as a person and the text occurs, and the author enters into his 'death'. It is the death of the empirical author who employs language to express himself. It is the 'language' which speaks, not the 'author', because the author fails in mastering the language. In the process of mastering language, s/he surrenders her/himself to language and becomes its servant. Barthes here moves a step ahead of Eliot in announcing the death of the historical and implied author as well. In non-existence of the implied reader, the text fails in attaining a fixed meaning but a 'plurality of meaning, an irreducible plurality'. The text, for Barthes, is not 'co-existence of meaning but passage, traversed, thus it answers not to an interpretation . . . but to an explosion, a dissemination'. The meaning of the text exists in the system of roles and conventions not in the text, as believed for long. Thus, the meaning of the text is diffused and dissipated, not centralized. He, however, admits that the author can enter through the back door as a guest, like "one of his characters, as another figure sewn into the rug; his significance is no longer privileged and parental, the locus of genuine truth rather ludic. He becomes a *paper author*" (italics added). Michel Foucault, however, countered Barthes's argument and sought to re-establish the author when he remarked that a certain number of notions that are intended to replace the privileged position of the author seem to preserve that privilege. In this essay 'What is an Author?' he suggested that the author still lives in spite of numerous endeavours to kill him as his name is associated with a set of works which make it difficult to reject the author. But Jacques Derrida in his very attitude to language, posits that language is disconnected from reality, so reality inclusive of the author's physical reality remains outside verbal universe of the text. It expelled the empirical author and denied the implied author too. The author, however, entered by the retroscena in deconstruction because the very idea of decentring presumes presence of centre before it was decentred, and thus re-centring follows it. And the moment we are in view of the centre, the author creeps in.

In an age of radical change there has been a good deal about criticism verging at times on complacent self-admiration, albeit critical narcissism, and on other occasions on polemic and summary rejection. An unprecedented interest in criticism led to the growth of a sprawling jungle of critical/literary theories of which some have definitely added to our understanding of literature and criticism. Marching a step ahead, the rejectionists of theory declared the futility of criticism with annoying aplomb, without studying or understanding them. But what gets oversighted in the process is that if literature is a human creation and compels human response to it in the form of various critical formulations; it is possible only through assertion of criticism.

There is, however, no denying the fact that critical theories were stretched to a point where they tend to be means of subverting texts, or thus get subverted in the process. Barring some jarring notes in this chorus or chaos of critical theories warning us not to make cult of critical theories or turn its progenitor into a totem, the prevailing enthusiasm for critical theories has almost touched the lunatic fringe. The theory-dominated world of criticism was paralleled by, what Umberto Eco calls, the activities of 'the followers of the Veil' in *Interpretation and Overinterpretation* who might be anyone who is dissatisfied with obvious, apparent explanations, believing that there is a deeper, more profound truth to be dis/uncovered behind the surface of appearances. This mistrust of perpetual reality motivates much of our ongoing scientific, religious, philosophical and critical discourse. It became the bane of literary/critical theory prompting more outrageous textual interpretations.

The crisis in theory was no longer a debate if certain approach is superior or inferior. Or whether criticism helped or hampered our appreciation of literature. The crisis in criticism emanated from disquieting questions posed from within as to what criticism is and what it has to do in different periods. To ask whether or not it has a future is a non-question. The issue is in what way it is to be re-constituted as a discipline. The question may be answered only by critical practice.

History of criticism has been the history of critic's response towards the creative work, for criticism has been concerned with writer's response to a certain experience or reality (fictive or factual) as manifested in the work concerned, and with its context that shaped that experience or text, and also with examination of this (reader's/critic's) attitude to the text. The text exists somewhere in this relationship between the text and the reader/critic. It is shaped particularly by his choice of tools with which s/he receives it and reconstructs its meaning after entering into its entrails, its interiority and forces that shaped it. This process of receiving a text, interpreting it and evaluating it directly or indirectly has been characterized by frequent shuffling and reshuffling and displacement of various centres of criticism. Close examination of the history of criticism reveals that it has revolved around a few shifting centres, i.e. artist (author), art (text), ambience (context) and audience (reader) in different eras. In other words, almost entire critical discourse has centred on a few questions: who says it? (Author), What/Where/How is it said? (Text), For whom is it said? (Reader), When/Why is it said? (Context), though this generalization may lay itself bare to charges of reductionism and crude dismissiveness which to an extent is caused by the fact that critical approaches tend to share or overlap each other.

After its preoccupation with moral and then aesthetic concerns to a good measure, initially, critical discourse revolved around artist (author) and context in their traditional sense. The New Criticism reacted against biographical or historical criticism and questioned the authority of the author and displaced him by emphasizing the close reading and the explication of a text which according to the critics of this school is autonomous, and autotelic, and so it should be examined on its terms and not as something else. This distrust of author's centrality resulted in his displacement and centred the text, though the death of author was formally announced not by the New Critics but by (post)-structuralist Roland Barthes whose position in this regard has been discussed in brief earlier. Nevertheless, criticism journeyed to one of its destinations in the form of textual criticism.

The text's autonomy was challenged by proto/quasi-structuralism of Northrop Frye and subsequent structuralists who employed linguistic analysis to disclose how structures are formed and how they operate in 'texts' which, from the structuralist point of view, may include anything from a wrestling match to traffic lights. The hierarchical displacement of text as a self-contained object brought audience/reader in the centre of critical exercise in the 1970s through Hans Robert Jauss's theories, according to which the text is largely defined by our act of perception and reader's response which are essential for determining meaning and value in a literary text. Edmund Husserl and Martin Heidegger provided philosophical foundation to this view through phenomenology that involves a merging with the objects that are perceived by us through our consciousness. That is why a text has multiple meanings and possibilities and not just singular meaning. However, gross mis-reading is prevented by controlling the text or the informed reader, opine Wolfgang Iser in *The Act of Reading: A Theory of Aesthetic Response* (1978), and Stanley Fish in *Self-Consuming Artifact* (1972) and *Is there a Text in This Class?* (1980), though in Harold Bloom's *A Map of Misreading* (1975), misreading is not pejorative but individual creative and valuable. The point that I intended to put forward is that criticism returned to audience/reader in an exceptional manner, and thus, reader also, one of the milestones of criticism, came to be reckoned with in the process.

As structuralism gave way to post-structuralism, through its gradual evolution, its ahistorical and anti-humanistic approach to literature came under severe criticism for its subversive nature, and revival of interest in contextual (social, cultural and political) aspects led to another displacement in the arena of criticism. This centring of context (ambience) was different from old historicism and though essentially political rather than historical in its critical pursuit, it came to be practised as New Marxism and maintains that literature is always political in the sense that it brings forth social and economic circumstances that produce a work of art, contained in it. Transcending the limitations of party-line, propagandistic discourse and a particular methodology such a critic may accept deconstructionist differential view of language and that history cannot be coherent rendering of known events. Yet literary history for him/her is likely to be seen as the record of producing, distributing and consuming certain cultural artistic product, and the literary historian can surmise and suggest the flow of historical forces that condition literary discourse. While the declining years of the century witnessed the end of political history, geography and politics in a way but political criticism flourishes in the form of New Historicism or New Marxism by leaning heavily on context (ambience) in its own way.

Criticism has, thus, passed through the four stations, i.e. artist, art, audience and ambience, and has arrived its full circle. The New Historicists, led by Stephen Greenblatt, proposed parallel reading with the concepts of textuality of history and historicity of text, and thereby added a new centre of co-text, with the proposal of parallel reading; a literary text and non-literary text. That criticism banks on repetition of these centres is further suggested by the frequent shuffling and reshuffling of prefixes like 'pre', 'post' and 'anti' and 'new' or 'neo' in critical discourse, paralleling our social consumerist discourse in which commodities like toothpaste and soap among others are paraded (without much newness) after adding 'new' or 'super' before their names. This is symptomatic of emptiness and lack of fertility, and that criticism is fast becoming a wasteland of critical theories. It is also worth mentioning here that the quest for alternative aesthetics and efforts to rediscover critical traditions in the so called Third World on the one hand speaks of potentialities and possibilities of their native critical traditions and aesthetics that remained ignored (even by their own people) in the colonial period, and on the other hand purposeful silence of the First World indirectly suggests bankruptcy of the Western criticism. Otherwise what prompted the scholars, critics and writers of the First World to take upon themselves the role of saviours of culture, literature, art, critical and aesthetic traditions of the Third World?

II

Theory, as a generic term, came into use in the second half of the twentieth century with the works of scholars like Roland Barthes, Jacques Derrida, Deluze and Michel Foucault in particular for combination of philosophy, sociology, economics, history, literature and criticism. Since post-structuralist perceptions influenced the basic positions of various domains/subjects with interdisciplinary orientations, at times (literary) theory and other domains of knowledge like philosophy or social sciences appeared to occupy the same space or seemed to overlap each other. However, it was not sociology because it mistrusted generalizations, under the post-structuralist incredulity against generalization and totalization, and its (sociology's) basic position that human behaviour is quantifiable. Since it did not concede to the proposition that a philosophical system is capable of explaining all phenomena, it was not philosophy.

Literary criticism criticizes literature, its analysis, evaluation and appreciation; literary theory theorizes about literature by asking question about literature as to what is 'literary' in literature. Literary theory and critical theory share their common premises with the difference of domain that the former deals with literary and the latter with the critical domain which has larger domain. There are two common definitions of critical theory. Departments of English at universities across the world use it for 'the criticism of literature', almost making no distinction between critical theory and literary criticism in general usage. Its other definition is derived from this 'Frankfurt School' group with Max Horkheimer, the head of the Institute for Social Research in Frankfurt, in Germany, and Theodor Adorno as a primary representative. The later 'Frankfurt School' tradition, with Jurgen Habermas, adopted a somewhat modified and rather compromised Marxism, married for the most part with communication theory and with structural-functionalism in sociology. It was sought in the twentieth century as an alternative to capitalist 'social science' and also to Leninist forms of 'dialectical materialism'. It recognized the persistent longevity of the capitalist system but at the same time pondered over ways and issues of its injustices, and proposed to consider the world in terms of history, philosophy, and science, criticizing 'mainstream' social science as plagued with ideological attitudes.

The ascendance of post-modernistic (margin/al/ized vs. centre/al/ized) discourse and Jacques Derridean deconstructionist mode of reading attained its currency in India with its convenient critical minds, as it tried to subsume *dalit*, feminist and post-colonial discourses in it. While the last discourse had its moorings in the erstwhile colonial power locations, the languages of Indian discourses remained superficially involved with it, excepting fashion mongering critics who would drop these terms at the slightest pretext.

III

Before rethinking theory in India, it is imperative to consider a few questions pertaining to the Indian critical tradition, distractions, diversions and distortions in it.

Rethinking critical theory in India is not possible without addressing the issue of disjunction in Indian academia that showed increasing inability to handle the intellectual traditions bequeathed to it. Indian mind constructed the Śāstras in all possible human activities. That was possible because they were preceded by a period of creativity, fuelled by focus on grammatical, dārśanic (philosophical) particularly *nyāya* (logic) school,[3] and dialogical

3. Take the case of tradition of logic in India in the words of B.K. Matilal, which was preceded by long dialogic tradition beginning in the Upaniṣads and in the debates between orthodox and heterodox schools:

> Logic developed in ancient India from the tradition of *vādavidyā*, a discipline dealing with the categories of debate over various religious, philosophical, moral and doctrinal issues. There were various *vāda* manuals available around the beginning of the Christian era. They were for students who wanted to learn how to conduct debates successfully, what tricks to learn, how to find loopholes in the opponent's position, and what pitfalls to be wary of. . . . Of these manuals, the one found in the *Nyāyasūtras* of

→

traditions. The tradition of logic went into the making of 'argumentative' Indian, and there was interaction among different systems of knowledge that took particular care of the counterview or *pratipakṣa* before countering it. In Sanskrit poetics, for instance, Bhāmaha devoted almost one entire chapter to *nyāya* (logic) towards the end of his *Kāvyālaṁkāra* (Rhetorics in Poetic Discourse); for logic is integral for the construction of arguments in poetics too. Moreover, there are ample evidences in the work to prove that he knew Buddhism so well that he gives the impression of being a Buddhist. Similarly, Ānandavardhana and Abhinavagupta were leading exponents in the Śaivism. Indian intellectual traditions, including philosophy which was the foundation of

---

→ Akṣapāda Gautama (*c.* CE 150) is comparatively systematic than others:

> Debates, in Akṣapāda's views, can be of three types: (i) an honest debate (called *vāda*) where both sides, proponent and opponent, are seeking the truth, that is, wanting to establish the right view; (ii) a tricky debate (called *jalpa*) where the goal is to win by means fair or foul; and (iii) a destructive debate (called *vitaṇḍa*) where the goal is to defeat or demolish the opponent, no matter how. . . . The first kind signals the employment of logical arguments, and use of rational means and proper evidence to establish a thesis. It is said that the participants in this kind of debate were the teacher and the student, or the students themselves belonging to the same school.
>
> The second was, in fact, a winner-takes-all situation. . . . Tricks, false moves, and unfair means were allowed according to the rules of the game. . . .
>
> The third type was a variety of the second type, where the winner was not supposed to establish his own position . . . but only to defeat the opponent using logical arguments, or as the case was, tricks or clever devices. — Matilal 2-3

Moreover, for a discussion of Indian dialectics from a systematic perspective but in a not so known book, please see Esther A. Solomon, *Indian Dialectics: Methods of Philosophical Discussion*, vols. I & II, Ahmedabad: B.J. Institute of Learning & Research, 1978. In the book she discussed dialectic in the pre-dārśanic literature, and considered Indian preponsity for argumentation in the Vedic literature Nirukta, Buddhist Piṭakas, Jaina Āgamas, episodes in the *Mahābhārata*, dialectic in the *Caraka Saṁhitā*, and discourses on law and polity like Dharmaśāstras and *Arthaśāstra*.

Indian critical tradition, suffered with the intervention of colonization. When the foundation suffered, the building did not remain unimpacted.

Many parallels may be drawn between the present debate in Indian philosophy and the discussion of gaps, absences, distractions, distortions or even the 'so-called' disjunction ('so called' because there was no complete disjunction in India, as in case of the West) in Indian critical traditions. And it is possible for contemporary Indian criticism to learn from the case of Indian philosophy. Regarding 'gaps' or 'death' in Indian philosophy, one group of scholars opines that there existed philosophical systems in India which were destroyed during the colonial period. Sudipta Kaviraj proposed the thesis of the sudden death of Sanskrit (2005: 119-142), and Michael Dummett (13-17) saw it in terms of blanketing of Indian philosophy. Daya Krishna (1996) and Kalidas Bhattacharya (1982) considered in terms of death of philosophy in India. Sheldon Pollock had earlier viewed it in terms of 'The Death of Sanskrit' (2001) and rejected the Oxford and Orientalist scholars who had advocated that before the advent of colonialism there was 'stagnation' in India (2001: 393-94). He posited that there existed 'a rich, varied and vibrant culture of intellectual activity' around 1750 CE in Indian sub-continent as one of the 'most innovative epoch of Sanskrit systematic thought (in language analysis, logic, hermeneutics, moral-legal philosophy, and the rest)'. During the period, many thinkers came up with 'new formulations' though of old problems, but in 'entirely new discursive idioms'. They often employed 'a new historicist framework; some even called themselves (or, more often enemies) 'the new' scholars (*navya*)' (2001: 393-94). His subsequent piece on Appayya Dixit during the period, i.e. sixteenth and seventeenth centuries, Appayya Dixit reconsidered the difference between Pūrva- and Uttara-Mīmāṁsā, and the *navya* came to 'signify not just a different relationship with the past but a different way of thinking' (2004: 770 & 2001a: 5).

To consider the split in Indian philosophical tradition after the colonial intervention, A. Raghuramraju (2006) employed the trope of Jarāsandha's body[4] from the epic *Mahābhārata*. In the duel

---

4. In the story, abridged from C. Rajagopalachari's version of the *Mahābhārata*, Bṛhadratha, the king of Magadha, married the twin daughters of the *rājā* of Kāśī with the vow of impartiality to either. Since the king remained unblessed with a child, in his old age he went to the Sage Kauśika of the Gautama family, and requested him to bless him with children. While the sage, out of compassion, was thinking of helping the king, a mango fruit fell into his lap. He gave it to the king with his blessings.

   Keeping his vow of impartiality, the king cut the fruit into two halves and gave one to each wife. Consequently, the wives became pregnant but they each gave birth to half a child — 'each half a monstrous birth which seemed a revolting lump'. They were indeed two equal and complementary portions of one baby, consisting of one eye, one leg, half a face, one ear. Seized with grief, they commanded their attendants to tie the gruesome pieces in a cloth and cast them away. The attendants threw the child bundle on a heap of refuse in the street.

   A cannibal *rākṣasī* happened to pass that way. Elated at seeing the two pieces of flesh, she gathered them up both at once. The halves came together the right way and they at once adhered together and changed into a whole living child, perfect in every detail. The surprised *rākṣasī* who did not wish to kill the child took on the guise of a beautiful woman and, going to the king, presented the child to him. The delighted king handed him over to his two wives.

   The child became known as Jarāsandha. He grew up into a man of immense physical strength, but his body had one weakness, namely the being made up by the fusion of two separate parts, it could be split again into two, if sufficient force were used. It became the cause of Jarāsandha's death. In the duel, Jarāsandha and Bhīma were so equally matched in strength that they fought with each other continuously for 13 days without taking rest. On the fourteenth day, Jarāsandha showed signs of exhaustion, and Kṛṣṇa prompted Bhīma that the time had come to make an end of him. At once Bhīma lifted him and whirling him round and round 100 times, dashed him to the earth and seizing his legs tore his body asunder into two halves. As Bhīma roared in exultation, the two halves at once joined and Jarāsandha, thus made whole, leapt up into vigorous life and again attacked Bhīma.

   To help Bhīma, Kṛṣṇa picked up a straw, tore it into two pieces, and cast the bits in opposite directions. Bhīma at once took the hint, and tearing Jarāsandha into two pieces he threw the two portions in opposite directions. Since the pieces could not come together and join, Jarāsandha thus met his end. *Ḥrākṣasī — Mahābhārata*, 1976: 79, pp. 24-25.

between Bhīma and Jarāsandha, each time Bhīma severed the limbs of Jarāsandha, they magically came together again. On Kṛṣṇa's indication, Bhīma tore him into two and threw the two parts of the body in the opposite directions, which, however much these tried to come together, failed to become one. Like Jarāsandha's torn body, the various parts of dialogic tradition in India, following the colonial intervention, have never been able to come together again. At the best they could only touch each other. In retrospect, perhaps what Indian thought needs today is the compassion of the *rākṣasī* who brought the two parts of Jarāsandha's body to the king. Here, the distance is not physical; it is an instance of physical nearness and visual distance (7-8). "This interesting story embodies the important truth that two sundered parts joined together will still remain weak, with a tendency to split" (C. Rajagopalachari, *Mahābhārata*, 1976: 77-78). Not only Indian philosophical tradition, but also the Indian critical tradition is like the Jarāsandha's body — made of the yoking of two distinct traditions — the Indian and the Western.

The analogy is not misplaced here. In fact, it can serve the purpose to understand the cause of major shift and decline in Indian critical tradition, for I would, however, not term it as 'amnesia' or 'break' for it. There was no absolute disjunction from the entire tradition, though it was attempted in the mainstream higher education. The analogy and need for a compassionate *rākṣasī* for redeeming Indian philosophical tradition is equally applicable to Indian critical tradition which needs a synthesizing mind, capable of energizing the tradition and defending itself aggressively. Moreover, the critical tradition declined because Indian philosophical tradition suffered during the colonial period in particular. Since the Indian intellectual psyche was complexed, the interaction with the Western critical tradition could not be used as a positive catalyst the way the West used its interaction with the Indian grammatical tradition.[5] The fact is that Indian

5. Ferdinand de Saussure's reception of the Sanskrit linguistic and its use as catalyst lent a new and purposeful direction to the Western philology and linguistics and made it synchronic from diachronic.

critical tradition was absenced from the education system, and the Orientalists like Friedrich Max Müller who raved about the greatness of India through his translation of Sanskrit scriptures like the Vedas and Upaniṣads restricted themselves to the fossilised ancient India. His lectures in *India: What Can it Teach Us,* that he had delivered in 1880s to the members of the ICS, who were to go to India, was in fact a deep lament over the diminishing tribe of the Indologists like William Jones. The nineteenth century was a period of culmination of India's political, cultural and intellectual decline. Moreover, it was also a period of cultural regeneration as well from the last quarter of the nineteenth century onwards, for it could not go further low. At least in the space outside the mainstream education system, the tradition survived but did not either flourish or get modified or modernized. It was left to new scholarship to come out later in the twentieth century, to examine and analyze the phenomenon, question the tradition and the causes of its decline and modernize it. The two parts of the same body representing two traditions are fated to meet the fate of Jarāsandha, sooner or later. However, the Western and Indian traditions are not homogeneous traditions. Moreover, the colonial perceptions that the East and the West cannot meet have been shattered long ago. The fast means of transport and exponential change brought about by the ICT and computational ability have shrunk the world, and proved that if the fire rages in the East, the West will not be spared for long. In this coming together, only 'fit' traditions will survive.

Moreover, the Vetāl narrative in Kṣemendra's *Vetālapañcaviṁśati* (with its versions in Somadeva's *Kathāsaritsāgara,* Jambhaladatta and Śuvadāsa) may serve the purpose of understanding change and distortion in Indian critical tradition that took place in the colonial period. It (the story) was creativly reworked by Thomas Mann in his novelette *Die Vertauschten Kopfe* (The Transposed Heads) on the basis of his reading of Heinrich Zimmer's last book *The King and the Corpse* edited from the working notes by Joseph Campbell. Zimmer to whom Mann dedicated the novel with ironic connotations 'To Heinrich Zimmer, the Great Indian Scholar: Returned with thanks' narrates the tale of two lifelong friends and a girl. The maid married one of the two but the marriage was not particularly happy. Shortly following the wedding, the couple together with their bachelor friend, set out on a visit to the parents of the bride. On the way, they come to a sanctuary of the blood-thirsty Goddess Kālī, and the husband excused himself for a moment to go to the temple alone. There in a sudden excess of emotions, he decided to offer himself to the image as a sacrifice; and with a keen-edged sacrificial sword that was there, he lopped his head from his shoulders, and collapsed in a pool of blood. The friend, having waited with the bride, went into the temple to see what had happened, and when he beheld the sight was himself inspired to follow suit. At last the bride came in only to take flight again, intent on hanging herself from the limb of a tree. The voice of the goddess commanded her to halt however, and sent her back to restore the lives of the two young men by replacing the heads. But because of her distraction, the young woman made the interesting mistake of putting the friend's head on the husband's body, and the husband's on the friend's.

The ghost inhabiting the corpse now asks the king who should be regarded as the rightful husband of the girl.

In the original tale, the head being the highest of limbs, the rightful husband should be the body where the head of her husband was. Departing from the answer of the source narrative, Mann makes Śrīdāman to represent the spirit and Nanda the nature. Sītā, of the partridge eyes, the glorious colour, the divine hips, the furrow, the recreative Principle of life, of Māyā Incarnate is first depicted to be happy at the 'accidental' transposition of heads. She was married to the fair youth Śrīdāman, the intellectual brāhmaṇa merchant whose refinement had reduced the importance of his body, to no better than mere appendage to his fine head. Secretly she longed for Nanda, the smith and cowherd, Kṛṣṇa manifestation, dark of skin and hair with Śrīdāman's head and Nanda's body. Sītā gets her ideal husband. It is like the best of Shakespeare's *Hamlet* and *Othello* in one, with the combination of brain and brawn. Mann's narrative does not draw to a close here, and deals with the sole surviving descendant of Śrīdāman and Sītā, named Andhaka (meaning near blind), or Samādhi (concentration or heightened consciousness), a perfect combination of the separate qualities of his parents and uncle. Andhaka is not a perfect synthesis of his father Śrīdāman (the spirit), Nanda (the body) and Sītā (the female principle) because Andhaka with his poor eyesight is not a synthesis but an unexpected phenomenon. For Mann, Andhaka's poor eyesight far from being a handicap, kept him away from living too much in the body's concerns, as he developed an artistic temperament towards the things of the mind. His original name Samādhi, i.e. putting together or concentration, or heightened consciousness was forgotten and he came to be known by the new name. Since he had mastered the art of cultured speech, grammar, astronomy and the art of thought, he became the reader to the king of Banaras at the age of twenty. Though he could see only three paces before him, he sat on a splendid palace terrace in fine garment under a while silk umbrella and read aloud to the prince in a pleasing voice, from all the sacred and profane writings.

The narrative serves the purpose of understanding the distraction, distortion and disjunction in the Indian critical tradition. Whether it was a natural or accidental phenomenon in the long history of India, may be a matter of debate but it was a reality. Śrīdāman stands for Indian critical tradition, and Nanda for the Western critical tradition. Sītā, the colonized Indian psyche, is attracted to both the traditions of spirit and nature. Kālī represents the Śakti principle that is thirsty for intellectual energy with the capacity to revive the dead tradition, if they surrender to it. In the critical moment, the colonized India psyche gets distracted and places the head on the wrong body. So Indian tradition loses its character and the true synthesis of the best of the two traditions did not take place in terms of the subsequent post-colonial generation. As the colonized psyche, s/he imitated the master and his ways, the imbalanced and strange hybrid was naturally expected. The new generation or tradition represented by Andhaka is 'near blind' at its worst, and at the best is Samādhi, representing the act of putting together, though the positive connotations are lost upon people who go by his external disability. But his industry helps him find space in the king's court. Like Andhaka, the Indian critical tradition became near blind, not fully blind. Andhaka, however, is no Tiresius who despite his blindness had the insight and ability to see and foretell future. The tradition in the colonial period suffered because of the Andhaka generation that did learn a few tricks in sophistry and stylistics that would help him in gaining place in centres of power because the centre cannot 'read' for itself. Hence, the Andhakas rule the roost. Thus, Andhaka becomes a trope for the post-colonial Indian critical tradition and its participants.

Indulgence in analysis of factors responsible for the decline or distortion, however good an academic exercise it may be, would lead to paralysis, if unattended by rectifying action. The question 'What is theory doing in India?' is to an extent similar to the question 'What is English doing in India?'[6] Theory is an industry in the West, and terror in the rest, particularly in India. In the West, its economics and politics govern processes of its production and supply through aggressive marketing and consumption. Its consumers in India use it to terrorize others by fusillades of various terms, critical clichés and jargons as bullets and shrapnels. At best its adherents add to existing perception and at the worst act as terrorists and make an extra endeavour to become theoretical *fidāyins* (suicide bombers). At an earliest possible opportunity and given space they explode themselves amid/before their own people and kill them — bystanders and passersby indiscriminately by committing suicide in public. Indian criticism, barring a few distinguished exceptions, is parasitic, derivative and imitative. They are happy to be weather cocks. Languages of Indian origin have certainly produced critics of eminence who have given new

6. Please see Avadhesh Kumar Singh, "What is English Doing in India: Responses to an Awkward Question", in *English and Vernaculars in India*, ed. Makarand Paranjape and G.J.V. Prasad, Pearson Publications, 2010.

meaning to existing critical idiom. But they either remain limited to their languages or out of their anxiety of appropriating publicity join acolytes or practioners of Western criticism.

All visible faces of Indian criticism notwithstanding, the fact is that only a few critical discourses have sustained their interest in them. The major discourses in India include: *dalit* discourse, feminist discourse, diaspora discourse, regional [*kṣetriya* or *jamini* (land)] discourse in the form of Telaṅgānā, Vidarbha, Gorkhaland, Singur and rural or village-centric discourse, called as *grāmīṇa vimarśa* pertaining to disintegration of villages and the end of villageness. These are primarily perceptions of creative concerns but they, particularly the first two, have lent their intensity to critical discourses related to them. In a way they share similarity in their origin and end as well. A *dalit*, a woman or a rural person are not born so, but they are attached with a label when they are born for no fault of theirs. They have to live with and suffer the stigma attached to them. Being rural is no stigma but the way metro encroaches upon the rural and exploits, it has become a metaphor of exploitation. Fortunately, these discourses lack uniformity and vary in intensity from one to another language. For instance, *dalit* discourse in Marathi is different from its counterparts in Hindi or Gujarati. Moreover, they share the fate but not the same dais. Consequently, they have embraced the risk of being cumulatively weak in terms of their presence or widening the base of theoretical formulations.

Nativist discourse had all literary ingredients and arguments to support it and emerged as a major critical discourse in India because no critical discourse can have either depth or scope and relevance in absence of its moorings in certain traditions particularly native or local. Despite all claims of universality and 'flattening' of the earth, the fact is that no discourse is created in a value-free zone. Moreover, there can be no universal critical standards excepting comparison with the similar or opposite kind, or standards emerged or validated from/by one's (of an individual, group or community) own experience(s). In fact, one of the alternatives of writing postmodernism and post-colonialism can be nativistic, i.e. by re-contextualizing them or relating them to native experience, situation or reality. Wedding postmodernist and post-colonial perception with nativist moorings can be one of the best ways of writing them in Indian ways, but its opponents or modernistic and postmodernistic internationalists raised the phantom of ghettoization to such an extent that it was rendered untouchable even by those for whom it stood. In addition to it, all nativists in due course of time, barring a few exceptions like Bhalchandra Nemade, became internationalists or they sought and found locations in metros. As a consequence, the overarching discourse of post-structuralism/postmodernism, simplified as centre *vs*. margin seems to have subsumed *dalit*/rural/feminist discourse. The possibilities of post-colonialism as a serious discourse — particularly as a perception and a way of reading remain to be seriously exploited in India. Will Indian critics begin to receive literary and critical categories critically or at least relate them to Indian experience and explore new possibilities?

IV

India contributed to theory by constructing theories or Śāstra in almost all domains of knowledge. India was a donor of knowledge to the world till the end of the first millennium, but the situation reversed by the beginning of the second millennium, and subsequently India became a recipient from the eleventh century onwards. The second half of the nineteenth century witnessed resurgence of interest in Indian knowledge systems but that benefitted Europe more than the Indian counterparts which were fossilized. Raymond Schwab in the chapter 'There is an Oriental Renaissance' of his book *The Oriental Renaissance: Europe's Discovery of India and the East 1680-1880* rightly called it 'An Oriental Renaissance — a Second Renaissance, in contrast to the first" (Schwab 11). This myth of Indian renaissance in the nineteenth century was pedalled primarily with the purpose of justifying the presence of the colonizers on the Indian land, as they were the instrument of it. The Indian scholarship also felt gratified, for they could show to the world that they also had what their masters had had in their history.[7]

For us in India, there is a hard lesson to learn in the theory business. Since the West has forsaken theory, so should we in India too discard it, and throw the gems like the proverbial monkey. Theorization comes naturally to us, and with the long tradition of constructing theory or Śāstra in different domains of human life, we should be able to receive theoretical traditions and formulate new ones. However, we have neither handled theory properly nor contributed to it in any significant measure. We neither resisted the Western theory, nor did we prepare the inventory of alternatives so as to exercise the most suitable alternative to the situation. Rather, we accepted to be either passive consumers or weather-cocks. Barring a few exceptions, the state of theory in India is marked by being derivative, parasitic and irrelevant. Nothing serious or systematic was done to rectify the situation that would have been possible by bringing in philosophical and grammatical traditions as integral parts of literary and critical studies in the post-Independence period. Consequently, the literary theoretical scenario is marked by indiscriminate indulgence in symptomatic criticism. Academic sessions in seminars and conferences at least in English would immediately betray the prevalence of criticism of convenience, as papers on Rohinton Mistry would figure in seminars on diaspora, Canadian literature, Indian English literature, and minority discourse among others. Moreover, everything has become postmodernist and post-colonial, as they are coveted categories for the writers and also for academic critics who consider their ultimate achievement in seeing a text as a postmodernist text on the basis of symptoms of postmodernism like open-endedness, multiplicity of meanings, self-reflexivity of meaning among others.[8]

7. Please see Avadhesh Kumar Singh, "Reconsidering Indian Renaissance" in *Indian Renaissance,* ed. Avadhesh Kumar Singh, Delhi: Creative Books, 2003. ed. pp. 6-54.

8. For discussion of postmodernism in India and its indiscreet use please see the chapter 'Postmodernism in India" in this book.

Like physicians of allopathic medical system that is based on symptoms, who prescribe antibiotic drugs for symptoms of fevers and cold indiscriminately, Indian academic critics pronounce a text postmodern or post-colonial on the basis of symptoms without caring for their philosophical connotations and conditions that produced them and discourses that they critiqued.

V

Instead of responding to the given problems, let us constitute the problem in order to have some freedom. Barring a few exceptions, the contemporary critical discourse is lop-sided, as it is not in touch with three essential ingredients: classical tradition in Sanskrit, Western critical particularly English critical tradition, contemporary creative and critical traditions in modern Indian languages. All good critics of substance in Indian languages operated not in just their own but among traditions existing in their time, space and traditions (in the Indian sense of the term *paramparā*) — Sanskrit, their own language and languages contiguous to it or of interest and English, thereby making them in touch with creative and critical practices — classical and modern — in Indian languages. Moreover, the best of Indian critics in the most of modern Indian languages would compare fairly well with the best in other critical traditions. The only issue is their non-availability in English, thereby, they are invisible and absent from the mainstream intellectual and critical/theoretical f(r)ameworks. Let me reconsider the existing situation and propose a few frameworks.

Literary theory reached India in the 1980s through its Departments of English. Prior to it, literary criticism used to confine itself in selections from Aristotle to T. S. Eliot with excerpts from their critical writings prescribed in the syllabi. It expanded its hold to other languages/literature departments from departments of English that made an extra effort to insulate themselves from other indigenous critical traditions. English criticism had non-English critical texts — Greek, Latin, German, Russian, American and French but had no space for critical traditions in Sanskrit and Tamil. Only towards the second half of the last quarter of the twentieth-century, Sanskrit poetics and its schools came to be accommodated to some extent in the Indian academia, though the close study of the Sanskrit texts and their critique with a bid to modernize remains a distant dream. The names of even obscure French and German critics, their works and tongue twisting terms and categories were at least known, though least understood. Ironically many texts like *Tolkappiyam* remained unprescribed, unmentioned and undiscussed in Indian academic circles.

Literary theory as a discipline established itself in the third quarter of the twentieth century in Europe. The practitioners of theory in India forgot that dynamism of theory as a discipline is conditioned to a large extent by the connections and linkages that exist or are established between knowledge production and knowledge transmission in the domain of interpretation, the main act of critical pursuit. The connections and linkages between native and the Western traditions were neither established nor explored. However, knowledge flowing out of research should find its place in the syllabi, and teaching should keep pace with developments in the discipline anywhere in the world and in the ancillary disciplines, extending the frontiers of the disciplines and addressing the contemporary issues too. The ideas and proposition and paradigms that permeated classrooms in India remained unchanged in India, barring a few places and classrooms. Teaching of critical theory is 'about' it by glossing over the source texts. Even committed teachers are either constrained or persuaded by new generation or convenient learners to simplify the concepts beyond their recognition or give/dictate notes. Therefore, two opposite situations — valorization of theory and vulgarization of the discipline come in existence simultaneously. This has made the enterprise 'soft' and woefully low in terms of standards. To enliven the critical and the discipline of critical theory in India, it is necessary to modernize, rather than mourn the loss of the golden age, the classical tradition beyond the limitations of ritualistic nationalism and colonial complex(iti)es. Moreover, only a comparative approach — comparing Indian and the Western (without forgetting the northern, the western, the eastern, and between the Indian and the Western) critical traditions and comparing and juxtaposing Indian experience with that of other societies is the way of redeeming Indian critical tradition.

Apart from the above, Indian critical tradition has to learn from the best of the Indian and the Western critical minds, the way they constructed their discourses. In the seventh century, a poetician like Bhāmaha in Sanskrit poetics in his *Kāvyālaṁkāra* prepared his framework and constructed his discourse accordingly, as he dealt with poetry, its *hetu* (means), *prayojana* (objectives), definition, kinds and its life-force in *alaṁkāra*. Then he went on to discuss kinds of *alaṁkāra*s (figures of speech), with his own illustrations which gave him rare distinction of being a poetician poet or critic who composed examples to support his definitions. Towards the end of his discourse, he discussed Nyāya for construction of discourse. Similarly, S.T. Coleridge, the nineteenth-century English critic, metaphysician and romantic poet, shared his framework and methodology in a subtle manner in Chapter XIV of *Biographia Literaria* in the form of his discussion of 'philosophical inquisition' after initial paragraphs before he defined poem, poetry and poetic genius. In the twentieth century, Ramchandra Shukla, a renowned Hindi critic, gave a new direction to literary historiography in his *Hindī Sāhitya kā Itihāsa* (History of Hindi Literature), with his historical sense and literary sensibility with which he could see the core of a writer in his/her oeuvre in a few lines that he cited to interpret the poet or author and unveil the author in the process. To reach that stage, he prepared a framework and methodology of his operation, as may be discerned in the introduction of *Hindī Sāhitya kā Itihāsa*. He shared his framework and methodology with his readers and scholars so that they could learn from his mistakes at least. If Hindi still waits for another history equal or close to Shukla's history, the reason is that his introduction remains seriously unread, interpreted and the framework undeciphered and methodology misunderstood and unfollowed. Those who could, like Hazari Prasad Dwivedi, Ram Vilas Sharma and Namvar Singh contributed significantly to Hindi critical tradition with their critique of Shukla's frameworks and interpretations.

In such a situation the question: 'what is theory doing in India?' is to be replaced with 'how to do theory in India?' For it we have to equip our critical tool kit and prepare frameworks in different languages so as to facilitate their comparative study. Some of the frameworks — framework of argumentation, of interpretation, of concerns and of values — are discussed below.

Framework of Argumentation

Theory is all about system-building. It is about methodology of system-building which demands construction of frameworks. It requires understanding and reading of/into the predecessor's framework, its critique and construction of a new one proposing new/different structure and interpretation. Even the rejection (read counter-construction) of the old framework is marked by a sense of responsibility on the part of the theorist.

The construction of a framework involves a mode of argumentation which rests largely on the ability of an individual or of a tradition to philosophically speculate and formulate theoretically. Various traditions of philosophical speculation and theoretical formulations flourished in India. However, philosophy and grammar suffered in India from the nineteenth century onwards in particular. In Indian taxonomy of knowledge systems, grammar was accorded a place of eminence because the grammarian was supposed to know the true nature of word and its power to make meanings. Word is a brick and mortar of constructing world and its meanings, and thereafter critiquing them. Without word there would be no world. That is why word has been elevated to the status of *Brahman* (the Infinite) without any beginning and beyond the realm of death. '*Ānandī anidhanam śabdabrahmam*' (Bhartṛhari, *Vākyapadīya*).

Unfortunately, the study of grammatical traditions found no space in higher education, and the departments of Darśanaśāstra (philosophy) and Sanskrit restricted themselves to ritualistic retention and recitation of information and did not create knowledge by questioning them in the light of Indian and Western traditions of *darśana* and philosophy. Ironically, along with philosophy, grammar and linguistics suffered in India. Wherever departments of Linguistics were in existence in India, they were closed down gradually in the last few decades of the twentieth century. With a shift in focus from subjects like grammar, linguistics, *darśana* to professional courses, science and technology, the very ability to speculate and formulate theoretically suffered in the country. Academic community and society did not feel disturbed with the de-stabilization of the foundation of the humanities in general and theory in particular. Linguistics suffered due to language teaching with borrowed models supplied with financial support from agencies like the USEFI and the British Council. Native language teaching, thus, suffered at the hands of ELT that had to give way to amateur literature teaching. Literature teaching did not remain unspared by the fashion of theory borrowed and imitated mindlessly from the West. Theory and its market (read fashion) prospered, and linguistics, literature teaching and reading in particular suffered in India. Philosophy, logic in particular, and linguistics, particularly grammar, have to be made an integral part of humanities for constructing frameworks of argumentation and redoing theory.

Framework of Interpretation

In principle, theory is important but in reality interpretation is more than theory and its knowledge. Knowledge of theory at best produces parrots and weather cocks. Knowledge is tested when the knower applies it to a text or texts to primarily understand it, and that s/he becomes the instrument of unveiling and even creating a new layer of the text(s). The framework of argumentation does not ensure interpretation. Interpretation that already exists is to be understood in terms of its framework, and its ability to carry the meaning through words as the vehicle. A new framework is to be prepared accordingly so as to realize new interpretations. Ānandavardhana and Abhinavagupta with their *Dhvani Siddhānta* (Theory of Suggestion) provided a new framework of interpretation in Sanskrit which was different from the schools of *rasa* and *alaṁkāra*, though later on they synthesized the theory of *rasa* school with their own, proving thereby that the framework does not come in the way accepting what is good in the other school, and thus contributing a new *rasa*, i.e. *śānta rasa* to the *rasa* theory, and new interpretation of the *Mahābhārata* in the light of the *śānta rasa*.

The quest for the study and preparation of new framework leads to the construction of new and alternative works. For instance, Hegel prepared an alternative framework of looking at history. He did not create an alternative system to the knowledge system of history which was in existence but he changed the way of looking at history. He advocated that phenomena — objects, events, people and nations may be understood only within their specific historical contexts that constitute an integral element in the constitution of these phenomena. He saw the phenomena in terms of his philosophy that was based on the notion of dialectic which operates at the levels — logical, phenomenological (manifested in terms of the form taken by consciousness) and historical. What alternative did he propose? He proposed an alternative mode of looking at phenomena and with an alternative engagement with them from a different perspective of history. Before him there were alternative modes of looking at the world. Rene Descartes had focused on reason. John Locke and David Hume questioned him and proposed an alternative framework of seeing/understanding the world in terms of experience. Thomas Hobbes joined them with his alternative framework and stressed on matter. Hegel considered and questioned all of them, and proposed his alternative methodology by seeing all of these systems in historical perspective, and saw the dialectic as operating through history. Karl Marx adapted Hegelian dialectic and his methodology and related it to practical life in the form of class conflict. Marxism is not only political, economic and social theory but also a form of practice in the spheres of human existence.

Hegelian dialectic was a way of thinking about any object or circumstance in a series of extremely complicated, yet comprehensive stages. Each stage supersedes the earlier but retains what was indispensable in the previous stage. The first stage views the object as a simple datum or fact about the world. The second stage with a broader perspective sees the object as 'externalized', as having no independent identity but constituted by its relations with other objects. The third stage sees the object as a 'mediated' unity, its true and principal unity. The importance of dialectic to Marx emerges from his understanding that the freedom Hegel speaks is the freedom of the bourgeois class to demolish the economic and political structure of feudalism and absolutism whose social hierarchy is based on either superstitions or irrational theology. With it, at least in fiction, there was a possibility of organizing society on rational principles, a free market economy, and a human subject who saw his individual interests enshrined in general law. Here was an alternative and possibility of revolution for the humanity. Hegelian dialectic became a powerful instrument through which it was possible to negate an obtained state of affairs. It provided Marx a model of history not only as driven by political and ideological conflicts but also preserved and transcended in their negation by the subsequent phases.

Closer home, *bhakti* and its interpretation may be considered an illustration, as discussed in Chapter 9 of the book. Acharya Ramchandra Shukla had seen it as an asylum of the defeated Indian society, as he discussed in the *History of Hindi Literature*. Hazari Prasad Dwivedi saw the origin of the *bhakti* in the Natha and Siddha sects and posited that even withont the Islamic contribution, 75 per cent character of *bhakti* would have been the same. Namvar Singh added to it with his interpretion of the existing interpretation that the shift was in terms of new orientation towards *lok* in *bhakti* in his book *Dūsari Paramparā kī khoj* (Quest for the other Tradition). Shukla, Dwivedi and Singh critiqued their preceding interpretations and posited their own frameworks.

Framework of Concerns

In order to rethink theory in India, it is necessary to think of theory beyond theory, and theorize about the framework of concerns in a literary work/s. They may be understood as concerns in literary work and metaliterary concerns articulated in a work. They are best understood in terms of *vyāpakatā* (scope of a work), and *gaharāī* (depth of a work), as they have been discussed by Namvar Singh in his first essay '*Vyāpakatā aur Gaharāī*" (Scope and Depth of a Work) in his book *Itihāsa aur Ālocanā*. Namvar Singh uses them to discuss the fictional works of Hindi writer Munshi Premchand. The two terms may be seen as the criteria to measure the worth of a work of art. A good work of art/literature is marked by both of them. They are the terms and tools of investigation into an artist's or a writer's ability to sustain her/his creativity, and to explore the minuteness and interiority of experience of moments, and see them in relation to eternity. For instance, Vālmīki's *Rāmāyaṇa*, Veda Vyāsa's *Mahābhārata*, Tulsīdās's *Rāmacaritamānasa* possess both these attributes. To have an obverse instance at this point, if one examines Vikram Seth's *The Golden Gate* and *A Suitable Boy*, one finds that his *The Golden Gate* has depth, but very limited scope of concerns, and his *A Suitable Boy* has scope but only stray occasions of depth. They are present but in disproportionate measure. It means that a work of literature, or art for that matter, appears static the way it exists. But in reality, it is always in a state of motion — horizontal and vertical. That is why it creates a sphere of energy. The vortex of simultaneity of horizontal and vertical motion of a work of art makes it lasting, as different generations see them differently by separating the horizontality and verticality of motion at times, and by displacing the locus of the simultaneity of the motion through interpretation. It is this framework of concerns that makes Munshi Premchand an eminent critic. His concerns shifted from his predecessors who were occupied with exploitative feudal class and rich businessmen to poor hardworking peasants and labourers who suffered at the hands of the rich and the privileged. Consequently, he pronounced that standard (*mayār*) of beauty (*husna*) has changed. He did not see beauty in courtesans and in description of their feminine beauty from tips to toes (*nakhaśikha varṇana*), but in a woman who is working in the field after feeding her child and making him asleep on the boundary of the field. Indian *dalit* discourse, and to some extent feminist discourse, brought a paradigm shift in it when it rejected the Śāstra, its standards of a work of art, and brought anger, struggle against suppression at the centre of concerns. The framework of values is to be revisited in terms of new realities, and their discourses.

Framework of Values

Literary theory is not about literariness but also about theory of frameworks. Indian cultural history and situation demands consideration of literary and theoretical frameworks in terms of framework of values, articulated not just in literary works but values implicit in the very act of theorization and objectives behind it and their realization in the process. True worth of a work of art in a society that despite its rich cultural ideals and long history is mired in large scale poverty, discrimination and inequality, will be measured in terms of the principal literary value in its ability to stand with/by the poor, suppressed and voiceless. Post-structuralists theoretical framework, for instance, displaced the centre-hegemonic framework of values, as it spoke for the voiceless, and thus suggested articulation of new values in discourses.

Mere literariness unattended by interliterariness or inter-literary consciousness is a highly insulating concept. The literariness of literature lies in 'defamiliarization', 'estrangement' or in its ability to attract attention towards itself through *vakrokti* (marked statement or obliquity) or *camatkāra* (miraculous property). The miraculous property or obliquity is the highest value of literature or art, for it arrests the attention of the reader and sustains it later. It becomes a scaffolding for supporting a framework of literary values. But it would be wrong to limit literary values to rhetorical devices, obliquity of discourse or William Empsons's ambiguity as a verbal nuisance. The core of literary values lies in values of life, life in terms of all beings and forms, celebration of its weals and woes, of dance and death. The values of human life in entirety are the crowns of all. Literature that values the life of the weak and suffering souls in distress earns the attention of all generations. The New Critics' preoccupation with literariness or poetic in poetry led to their skewed vision. The centrality of literariness in analyzing or appreciating a literary discourse is a literary fact but establishing and celebrating interrelatedness or interliterariness among species — similar or otherwise — is a part of human existence and nature. Hence, inter-literariness is inevitable, and it illuminates literariness and its study through comparisons inherent in the process.

The framework of values of art or literature needs to be acutely conscious of the fact that art and literature remain what they are and are valued for the way they exist. The critique of framework demands that they (artistic and literary works) are not vulgarized through either commodification or fetishization of objects through their worship as art objects. Both of them deny literature its existence, and condition its reception in a certain way. Both the processes and institutions of commodification or fetishization or worship are equal enemies of literature, for objectification and idolization are unending processes, as they move to extreme forms of de-humanization and ritualism by market. It is equally applicable to the world of advertisements and gender/feminist and *dalit* discourse in India and elsewhere. On the one hand woman is reduced to the level of a prostitute, and on the other elevated to the level of a goddess by the same institutions of market and patriarchy. In between the market uses her in advertisements to create and multiply demand by using her body.

Frameworks are fated to be dated, their fundamentals however remain the same. The conclusions arrived at through a framework often earn attention of other critics, whilst framework and the process of constructing them are often neglected. Conclusions are often proved wrong in the course of time. The frameworks and processes undertaken are more interesting than the conclusions, for they are like pathways that may be of no consequence to the traveller but of enormous import to the successors who may see what went right or wrong with them. For example, in the *Poetics* Aristotle compares epic with tragedy and concludes that tragedy is superior to epic on different grounds. *Prima facie*, one might say that Aristotle made the mistake of comparing the incomparable. But the argument cannot be sustained because the point of comparison between them is one of similarity that both of them imitate action of men better than what they are. Despite many reasons, Aristotle forwarded arguments to prove the superiority of tragedy. The conclusion is flawed and erroneous on the premise that tragedy has two additional parts, i.e. song and spectacle, than epic. Irony is that while discussing constitutive parts of tragedy, he called song and spectacle least important of all. Notwithstanding this, the fact is that his framework and methodology of comparative study are not to be faulted. They have to be deciphered. It includes proposition of problem: comparison of tragedy with epic, similarities between the two, their dissimilarities and conclusion on the basis of the preceding discussion with arguments substantiating the ultimate position. Although Aristotle might have erred in his conclusion, as in case of his judgement regarding the superiority of tragedy to epic, for his comparative thesis was governed by the logic of quantitative determination of the constitutive parts whose functionality or importance was not considered superior in dramaturgy. Aristotle's methodology, however, serves as a model for comparative study.

It is equally important to remember that the best frameworks demand being transcended. All critics of substance recognized and understood it before preparing their own. Also they did not allow themselves to be imprisoned by either their preceding or even own frameworks. However, more important than scholarship, argumentative ability or theoretical formulation is a critic's catholicity or inclusiveness that needs refined yet inclusive sensibility. Moreover, in criticism the process and objective of making a framework is as important, if not more than, as the validity of framework.

The framework of argumentation equipped with logic and devices is of no significance if it is bereft of framework of values. For instance, however significant is the framework of structuralism and its interpretation, the fact is that mere subversion cannot help it in the long run. Mere subversion cannot serve the purpose.

Presentism, apart from the absence of frameworks, is the new malady plaguing contemporary Indian criticism. The obsession with contemporaneity is a consequence of demands of publishing market that needs and supports promotion of their product. Present authors are also pleased, as they come into discussion through their works, and a critic assumes the role of a journalist, police, and judge in one. S/he reports, files First Information Report (FIR), prepares chargesheet and passes judgement on new writers and new works of old writers. Like the TRP of TV serials and 'circulation' of newspapers, the prospective coveted tags like 'Best Seller' and awards are to a good extent dependent upon such media management. Most of the critics like to be seen either on TV screens or in newspaper columns, for it provides instant visibility and good remuneration. No one can fault critics for making use of new media but the fact is that the compulsions of media condition critical and theoretical articulations. Consequently, the critic's ability to prepare theoretical framework and to posit sustained argument are neither developed nor tested. It has given rise to journalistic criticism. As a result, the main function of critical and theoretical enterprize is to re-evaluate. But, barring a few critics, there are not many who have acquired tradition with industry, and have the capability to receive the tradition or contemporary works in the light of tradition, leave aside the question of evaluation or contribution to the tradition. Tradition is almost forgotten. In Indian critical tradition, 'the past presences' despite pastness of past and 'present absences' despite presence of the present, presents a curious case of tradition whose antithesis is the West, i.e. the modern is seen with no survivors from the past. The uniqueness of India lies in retaining several significant aspects from the past, thereby maintaining certain amount of continuity.

Indian creativity has not failed as much as the ability to theorize and critique the creativity has, to a good measure. The healthy sign of criticism in Indian languages, however, is dissatisfaction with the present state of criticism and awareness of its limitations about its historical role. Speak to any competent critic in India, such as Namvar Singh in Hindi or Sitanshu Yashaschandra in Gujarati, s/he would not be content with the present health of criticism because of its deviation, disintegration or disengagement with tradition. They are equally concerned about tradition and about the fact that its re-evaluation is not taking place without ovesighting the present creativity. All competent Indian critics still get entrenched in their critical battlements against mediocrity, lest its charlatanism gets established as truth.

Postscript before 'Lead Out'

Despite proliferation of theory, critical approaches and their rejection, literary text remains the central concern. New textual criticism dominated more than any other critical movement; the first half of the twentieth century was dominated by New Criticism, and the second half by neo-textuality of deconstruction which is post-structuralism put to practice. Deconstruction is based on the premise that text is not to be deconstructed, for it has already deconstructed itself. Only thing to be done is to find out where the text has done so. But to find out the sites of deconstruction, i.e. gaps, breaks, ruptures in the text, one has to go *close* to the text. This close reading was the basic tenet of New Criticism. Hence, New Criticism and Deconstruction shared textuality in their own ways in the twentieth century. Despite this, with the rise of fortunes of ICT, science, technology, management and professional courses, literary studies suffered due to lack of interest in reading by the end of the twentieth century.

The early years of the twenty-first century brought text in centre of concerns in humanities and literature departments for different reasons, as humanities shifted from canonical (classical) to non-canonical (marginal) texts. Text came into discussion, albeit indirectly, with focus on reading — either through cultural studies, interdisciplinary approach or through reinstatement of aesthetic value of the experience of reading. Earlier, the debate pertained to de-canonizing the canon by transcending and even ignoring the tradition and canon by bringing non-canonical marginal texts in focus. The classical/canonical studies did not take to marginal discourses, and the marginal discourse is so concerned with the difference that it tends to be limited. The new problem that cropped up is: a lack of passion among students for reading literature. Richard Ohmann noted with dismay that the number of English majors shrank at least 50 per cent in the past twenty years (Ohmann: 2002: 92) Harold Bloom lamented in his 'Elegiac Conclusion", 'only a handful of students now enter Yale with an authentic passion for reading" (Bloom 2000: 226), and saw in the lack of passion for reading among the students the implicit prediction for the fall of 'Departments of English" (read all departments of literature in Indian context), for it is impossible to teach someone to love great poetry, if one does not love poetry [in *Falling Into Theory*, ed. David Richter, 225-234]. However, there are many voices on the other side of the elegy. Reading is an event that happens to different people at different times. Gerard Graff, for example, had to wait for the advent of a knowledgeable professor who introduced him to close reading after his initial dislike for books at an early age. In his "Disliking Books at an Early Age" (in *Falling into Theory*, 40-48) he narrated his early struggles with literature but 'through exposure to such critical reading and discussion over a period of time that I came to catch the literary bug' (Graff: 2000: 45).

There are other aspects related to the issue. The skills acquired upon having education in English lend a different dimension to the job market with specific purpose. Ohmann has noted them

> English teachers have helped train the kind of workforce capitalists need in a productive system that relies less and less on purely manual labour. Moreover, we have helped to inculcate the discipline — punctuality, good verbal manners, submission to authority, attention to problem-solving assignments set by somebody else, long hours spent in one place — that is necessary to perform the alienated labour that will be the lot of most.
>
> — Ohmann 92

The question of literary or critical theory becomes redundant, for reading is the precondition for the survival of literary and critical pursuits and for the inference of theoretical principles and approaches. The situation is no better in India.

I have termed the remarks here as 'Postscript before 'Lead Out' because they constitute the postscript to the present chapter. Since they transact with the concern for bringing text and its reading in the centre of concerns in literature departments, they serve as the living and justifiable link with the 'Lead Out' of the book that deals with the issue of interliterariness and contactuality.

15

Postmodernism in India

OURS is an age of 'isms' in which we are fated to define and measure our pre-suffixed and hyphenated existence in terms of these 'isms'. However, in the obtaining 'three minute's culture', nothing lasts, leave alone a particular 'ism'. With every new morning some or the other 'ism' becomes old and falls, as it heralds the advent of 'neo'/'new,' 'pre' or 'post' either by post-speed or ordinary post or by *poste* that in French stands for a T.V. station and can serve a befitting metaphor for media — print and electronic.

Of all these 'isms,' in the later half of our century, 'one of the meanest, cruellest, bloodiest in human history,' as Peter Drucker called it, postmodernism and post-colonialism have had more enduring life than their other counterparts. So much so that by the end of the century the subscribers of the postmodernism and post-colonialism have come to be known as the 'po-mo' and 'po-co' generations.

Postmodernism has been, and still remains, the most fashionable word in the world outside the First World for reasons whose explanations may lie in post-colonialism making our yoking together of postmodernism with post-colonialism in our context considerably legitimate. The fervid interest in postmodernism and its uncritical reception in the so-called post-colonial Third World (I use the term for the sake of convenience and brevity. Given a choice I would prefer the 'Pre-First World' to it) and in the countries like ours in particular, as the West with all its media gives us these 'isms,' a la Shakespeare, 'in the throat, as deep as to the lungs,' should surprise all sensible people and attract their critical attention also. Coming as I do from a 'Third World' country,

I find it difficult to pronounce altogether so favourable a sentence upon postmodernism, as do the greater mortals from the First or even the so-called Third World, not entirely without susceptible formulations.

Postmodernism is a consequence of change in the West's understanding of man and the world. The West understands man and the world with its three discourses: the metaphysical discourse of the ancient world, the theological discourse of the medieval world, and the scientific positivistic view of man. These three ways of perception or discourses went through the states of disintegration leading to an unprecedented state in which the West seems to have no clear way of understanding the nature of man, his position in the universe or the purpose of his life. Consequently, the West is 'really' lost for the first time — a fluid and extravagantly chaotic state that Alasdair MacIntyre referred to in his book *After Virtue.* He further remarked that in the West we have not only lost our morality but even the notion of morality is completely lost. Confusion is all, nay, greater confusion is all, as postmodernism celebrates, and also wants us to do so, the carnival of confusion and uncertainty.

Ours is no flattering state — rather worse, for we are consumers of this postmodernism without going through the stages and states that the West went through. In India we have had modernism without modernization. Modernism is an essence or pickle of modernization. It is fragrance of the dough called modernization that is a consequence of industrialization that leads to modernism and the way it affected the West. Industrialization in India, however, has been slow and very uneven, and so it remains even in its post-colonial era, say nothing of it in the colonial era that witnessed systematic unsetting of indigenous industries and institutions. And the leftovers of the so-called industrialization thrown at us were more aimed at exploitation of native natural resources, consolidation and preservation of colonialism thereby, serving colonial interests rather than our development.

If postmodernism has anything to do with modernism, with

post-scientific positivism or post-industrial society, it is almost inconceivable to think of postmodernism in our country. Only our naivety would have persuaded us to believe and accept that we have had modernism, and are in the postmodern era now. But, the ground reality has a different story to tell, if we are willing to listen to it. Postmodernism neither grows in our climes, nor does it even sit well on us, if we put it on us to appear fashionable. 'Isms' like postmodernism and post-colonialism are not products of hot houses but of certain eco-socio-political order and culture that forge condition, mood or perception called postmodernism. Ironical it is that postmodernism is being used as category, label or brand at least in our literary and critical discourses. This happens to be a fashionable trend, as it comes from the West, and a convenient category for our critical reputations to measure our literary and critical endeavours. A considerable number of our literary writers and literatures seem to be vying with each other to earn this label or category. In Hindi, for instance, Sudheesh Pachouri is the wholesale dealer of postmodernism. It is discernible in a few articles such as 'Postmodern Gujarati Story' by Ajit Thakore (with no ostensible reference or discussion to post-modern phenomenon in it or discussion of Gujarati Short Stories in the Postmodern mode) or 'Games of Fiction: Search for Postmodernist Mode in the Malayalam Fiction of 1990s' by E.V. Ramakrishnan (the redeeming feature of this enabling endeavour of the critic is that it focuses on a 'search' for the postmodernist mode without being obsessed with it) (99-106). Ironically, these two are not mere critics but writer-critics. And if our writer-critics do not resist the invasion of alien 'isms' and 'post,' there is something wrong with our 'post-colonial' condition. One of the notable exceptions among Indian critics is Namvar Singh who has questioned and resisted postmodernism in his article 'Śatābdi kā Avasān aur Uttarādhunikatā' (1995: 7-12). However, a successful Hindi novelist like Manohar Shyam Joshi listlessly longed to place his novel *Hariyā Hercules kī Hairānī* in the postmodern category, as the dust-jacket of the novel states. The temptation of postmodernism as a category is so irresistible for the author that he suggested that his novel is postmodern in its craft and narration. By doing so he prescribed consideration of his novel as a postmodern novel to be received with postmodernist tools. In the process he inversely suggested lack of faith in prospective critical intentions and abilities to locate the text properly. The novelist, thus, strove to condition and control the role of reader critic. With his author/ity, he smothered the critic; whereas, postmodernism is supposed to accept the 'other.' Is it the spirit of postmodernism? Is the Author dead? Long live the Author! Is it not the anxiety of being postmodern? Isn't it the anxiety of earning a label like 'postmodern' or 'post-colonial' that comes from the First World? Is it post-colonialism? And, if this is post-colonalism, what is colonialism then?

Imperialism, as addressed by Edward Said, is the practice, the theory and the attitudes of a dominating metropolitan centre ruling a distant territory; colonialism is almost always a consequence of imperialism of the implanting of settlements on distant territories. To him, imperialism and colonialism are not merely acts of accumulation and acquisitions. They are sustained by and gain impetus from impressive ideological formulations that include ideas that people of certain territories require and beseech domination and also forms of knowledge related to it. The civilizing project of the West led to colonization of 'a grand total of roughly 85 per cent of the earth' by 1914 from 55 per cent earlier but actually . . . 35 per cent of the earth's surface' (Said 1993: 6). The cultures of these colonies were impacted by the imperial and colonial processes in different measures in different parts of the world. Colonizing forces are still active, though their ways and methods of operation have become subtler, sharper and more dangerous. These forces have co-opted postmodernism as a tool to serve their purposes. Postmodernism is the philosophy of neocolonialism, and consumerism is its culture. Ironical it is that the first post-colonial nation, if political independence is the criterion, is the foremost neo-colonizer today.

Admittedly, postmodernism is the only philosophy or

discourse from the West that at least in principle proclaims that there are others. It valorizes heterogeneity of con/texts and interest groups. So far so good. Acceptance of existence of others should, however, rest on modesty and piety not in their Christian sense but in their Indian sense of *vinamratā* or *bhakti* towards others. Postmodernism was supposed to wage war against totalization in principle, but the way it is (being) peddled by the West with arrogance in the non-Western world, has made it a totalizing concept. In practice postmodernism is nothing but an empty slogan used as camouflage by the neo-capitalist culture which, equipped with its means, methods and modes of consumption and media, imposes a homogenizing super voice, language and culture over others proposing neo-universalism of its kind.

Postmodernism is one of the outward teeth of the elephant called neo-capitalism. This elephant tramples others, though it remains invisible. That makes neo-capitalism more dangerous than capitalism. It reaches the nooks and corners of hearts and houses with air and waves. It seduces others with its tempting 'little revolutions' that happen so often with 'extra,' 'new' or 'super' added to everything that it is almost impossible to sustain oneself. Postmodernism acts as a handmaid of neo-capitalism, for it provides theoretical and philosophical framework to neo-capitalism and to its consumerist culture.

The neo-capitalist consumerist culture sees everything in terms of resources, productivity and commodity and profit to the detriment of the consumers. It has led to commodification of art and literature and their consideration by non-literary non-artistic criteria. Fredric Jameson had tried to locate the postmodern as a condition arising out of the development in the sixties of the consumerist capitalism (53-92). Within a decade and half after Fredric Jameson's critique of postmodern and late capitalism, the neo-capitalism, keeping its pernicious consequences in the rear, rages ahead, accentuated by the highly sophisticated interaction through technological means. The subtle hyper mercantile ways of neo-capitalism have proved hollowness of postmodernism and also of post-colonialism. Neo-capitalism is the reigning reality of the so-called post-colonial societies. These societies remain consumers of postmodern and post-colonial discourses of neo-colonial countries and their East Indian Companies. Neo-colonialism of neo-capitalist countries, fuelled and fawned by flamboyant consumerist culture, survives and thrives on its ability to transform itself and hide its colonial colours and tantalizing telos. 'Others' can exist, and do so too, but on the terms of arrogant neo-colonizers as the neo-colonies and consumers. Resistance to neo-colonial ways, if any, is anticipated, appropriated and hijacked by neo-colonizers and their agencies.

In this context, I am reminded of Udai Prakash's story about a dog. On a Dīwālī night, a few children tied a string of crackers to its tail and set fire to its end. The dog barked, cried, ran and fell. Vinayak Dattatrey threw a few pieces of bones towards the dog that chewed the bones and yelped out of fright of bursting crackers. Vinayak laughed at this bizarre tragicomic sight. When asked by people he said about the cause of his laughter, "See this dog. It is a true consumerist of the Third World. A horrible instance of postmodern consumerism!" (*Hans*, February 1997). In the context of our endeavours to understand ourselves, this story becomes a pertinent comment on our so-called post-Independence post-colonial situation in the Third World in general and ours in particular. Post-colonialist liberty unattended by intellectual independence does not mean much. Even at the risk of being called a pessimist I must state that the post-colonial state is a mirage, colonialism is always present. Only its colour, external appearance, or demeanour change. Its nature remains the same. Colonialism yields place to neo, new or newer colonialism.

Neo-capitalist forces, accompanied by the philosophy of postmodernism, culture of neo-consumerism operate in ways subtler than ever before facilitating replacement of visible capitalist colonialism with neocolonialism. Colonialism was like a mountain but neo-colonialism is an iceberg whose tip only is visible; that too, to a few. It deceives the best of our perceiving reputations making the task of our writers and critics more difficult and complex. It cannot be ignored or rejected. It can be understood, gnawed at, and resisted.

Postmodernism has no fixed referent. "We begin our definition with Postmodernism is . . . and are already in trouble" (Marshall 1992: 3). It is written differently by different people with hyphen and without it (as I do to disentangle it from modernism and stress the changed perception), in past or present tense, in singular and plural. "What is/are/was/were/postmodernism(s)?" (Woods 1999: 1). What this term refers to is not specifically clear, as it is "stretched in all directions across different debates, different disciplinary and discursive boundaries, as different factions seek to make it their own, using it to designate a plethora of incommensurable objects, tendencies, emergencies" (Hebdige 1988: 181). In this free play of postmodernism "you get the postmodernism you deserve" (David Antin, "Modernism and Postmodernism", *Boundary*, 2, 1, 1972). The only place where it is fixed is the dictionary where it is sandwiched between postmaster and post-mortem. Coming as it does, it is posted to us by the West. In fact, the West is the writer, processor; pack(ag)er, postmaster and distributor of postmodernism. Its uncritical acceptance or celebration will tantamount to the post-mortem of our own living bodies.

Whatever postmodernism is — in whatever manner our society, our critical and literary faculties are responding to it — it has to be admitted that we can love it or loathe it but cannot be indifferent to it, for it is inconceivable to escape it. It has attained so much currency that it cannot be wished away. It is still happening to us. Rather than regretting it what is needed is to understand it and its condition(s), its strategies and the ways of operations. The societies like India have to prepare their strategies, receive and respond to it. Our literatures and criticism can play their own roles in baring its ugly hidden face by penetrating under the skin of its connivance and thereby, resisting whatever is inimical to our national and social interests with our counter-strategies.

We can respond to it in some of the following ways: (i) we can reject it and without taking note of it, we can allow it to thrive around us, and get throttled in the process; (ii) we can accept its currency and supremacy, and surrender ourselves to it; (iii) we can celebrate it and thus commit intellectual and cultural suicide; (iv) we can receive it pro-actively — understand it and resist and reject whatever is negative in it, and accept pragmatically whatever is of use to us in it; and (v) we can think of alternatives to it, and redefine it or re/construct our theory or model from our texts, though that may be a sort of complicit participation in it.[1]

Of all the alternatives to postmodernism, *deśīvāda* (nativism) is the most potent. Before discussing *deśīvāda* in the Indian context, it shall not be incongruous to consider some of its aspects.

Let us unhesitantly accept that nativism is not a politically innocent construct. It shares its etymological root *nosci* or *natus* with nation — a loaded term relating nativism to birth in its narrow sense. (Incidentally indigenism and *deśīvāda* are also related to "gen" or "gene" (birth).) At times *deśīvāda,* the Indian counterpart of nativism, lays emphasis on language so excessively that the notion appears to be a linguistic construct. This reliance on language is justifiable because language is related to *racanā-cetanā* (consciousness of creation), *racanā* (creativity) and *racanā-āsvāda/svīkaraṇa* (reception). Whatever may be the limitations of language, it is the only medium by which we can express our experiences — fictive or factual — reposed in our conscious, subconscious and unconscious mind. Moving a little further, it is language through which we take cognizance of the world. The language gets mixed with our consciousness and like paint becomes the integral part of canvas. The moment we try to pull and tug the paint from the canvas, a few shreds of the canvas also come out. Hence, *deśīvāda* insists on language for the sake of fidelity and sincerity of expression of experience.

---

1. Please see Chapter 12 "Towards an Indian Theory of Post-colonialism" in the present book as an endeavour that may fall in the last category.

Deśīvāda and nativism share quite a bit of premises, yet the synonymity of the two would amount to mortgaging our specificity, though Professor Bhalchandra Nemade, one of the precursors of this movement, and the subsequent subscribers like Ganesh Devy and Makarand Paranjape do not mind using the term as it is in English. *Deśīvāda* is not celebration of ghetto culture. Nemade is against those pseudo-claims of catholicity and universalism as against narrowness. He is unopposed to cosmopolitanism or universalism with full cognizance of its limitations. But, he is aware of inherent contradictions of internationalism, even theoretically, internationalism without nativism as its basis is impossible, because, nativism is a multi-centred, descriptive and real concept, whereas internationalism is an artificial and parasitic concept.

Although *deśīvāda* relies heavily on language, there is no reason at least for us in India to seek divorce between *deśīvāda* and nation. In the so-called post-nation society, a term accepted by some of us to measure our post-Independence state, we must note that in the West the nation was an organization of interest groups. With these organized interest groups the West saw the other races and societies as its adversaries and either annihilated them or colonized them. They reaped the harvest by exploiting non-Western societies and communities economically, culturally and intellectually. The nemesis did await them in the form of the World Wars. The West then pronounced it as an evil — a position subscribed to by quite a few non-Western scholars like Rabindranath Tagore. He could not transcend the then historical pressures that led to the formation of the organized modern nation, as his lectures on nationalism reveal.[2]

To me, *deśīvāda* is not disengaged with nation — not the rigid exclusive notion of the West and of Tagore but of Gandhi — that is an inclusive one leading to happy internationalism. The Western

2. Please see Rabindranath Tagore, *Nationalism*, Delhi: Rupa, 1992, 1st edn. 1917. For discussion and critique of Tagore's views please see Avadhesh Kumar Singh's "The 'Crisis' in Nationlism and India," 2006:265:284.

society may have reached the post-nation state that need not mean that we too have also touched that state and so reject the notion of nation altogether. Reject we must the modern Western notion of nation but not Gandhi's. For us the nation is the unit with which we can resist the onslaught of the postmodernist, neo-colonizer, neo-capitalists and the mindless Westernization. This relationship between *deśīvāda* and nation proposes *deśīvāda* as a strategy that with its insistence on identity, specificity and authenticity resists direct or indirect cultural or intellectual invasion or encroachment by 'other' or alien homogenizing forces and disallows its use as data. Moreover, our *deśīvāda* is more inclusive than nativism in the way Gandhi's concept of nationalism is from the Western nationalism. *Deśīvāda* for us cannot afford to exclude the *dalit*, feminist/womanist, labourers' and farmers' discourses, much in the same way it cannot exclude Gandhi's nation.

Deśīvāda encompasses all aspects of economic, political, intellectual, cultural and social life; but if I focus on literature only, then it is more for critics than for writers, for no true writer of substance would like to write under any 'ism' or *vāda*. If s/he does, s/he will be faithful not to the experience but to the *vāda*. What is of interest to me as a member of the Indian pluralistic society is that the *deśīvāda* does not allow me to accept those standards, criteria and categories that are not approved of by my own experience. Therefore, it is the duty of the critics, and of the critical faculty of the creative writers, to keep reminding the creative faculty about the role of the consciousness, experience, culture and medium of creative writing.

Deśīvāda needs not my advocacy when history supports it. Let me take a few instances from the Western history. In the sixteenth century, with the rise of English nation the British society was faced with the question: What should be the course of the developing British drama and poetry? On the one hand were native forms of drama like the mystery, miracle, morality and interlude; and on the other hand was the rich tradition of the Greek and

Roman plays, prescribed then in schools and colleges. Sir Philip Sidney, Gabriel Harvey, Spenser, Ben Jonson and their Areopagus Group favoured the rich classical yet foreign tradition of antiquity. On the other hand, the Cambridge School of Thomas Wilson, John Cheke and Roger Ascham supported the native literary forms. They admired Rome but loved London. The conflict was between the native and the foreign literary forms. All students of English literature know it well that it progressed by exquisitely balancing its native traditions with their alien counterparts in the sixteenth century, as William Shakespeare resisted and even assimilated the systematic foreign modes with his native wild wood notes.

The Americans also found themselves on the crossroads of history where they had to encounter their moment of choice. R.W. Emerson delivered his famous lecture 'American Scholar" on 31 October 1837, more than six decades after the political independence. The lecture was hailed as a declaration of independence from cultural colonialism (Lewison, 1939: 122). His quest for the American Scholar was a part of the debate between the subscribers of the nascent American and the established Greek-Roman European traditions. Regarding myth, his friend Margaret Fuller opined that they (the Americans) were the direct descendants of the Europeans so the Greek and Roman myths were their own. Hence, they can be used for their literary creativity. But, mythology needs past that America did not have then. And the past cannot be manufactured, else the Americans would have. Emerson constructed a new definition of myth, as he wrote in his journal that myth is what is believed in by most of the people on most of the occasions in most of the places. It was in perusal of this project that the myth of the Frontier, the Road, the American Dream, the American Adam, and the Success were constructed and made use of by the novelists and later dramatists in such a way that American literature not only carved a particular niche for itself in the world literature by the advent of the twentieth century but also shaped its identity distinct from English literature.

There are two principal fears of provincialism and revivalism often raised against nativism. The fears of suppression of 'little voices' by dominant hegemonic power groups trying to impose homogeneity and of the rise of 'little nationalities' due to insistence on specificities are not absolutely baseless. They can bring the pluralist India on the brink of disintegration — particularly, when these little nationalities begin to clash against each other. As far as the charge of parochialism against nativism is concerned, it has to be admitted that even Shakespeare would have been a parochial writer if, by the standards of sceptics of nativism, English language and literature unattended by their traders, pirates and army and consequent colonization of a large part of the world, were not to become an international language.

The critics of nativism see the seeds of revivalism in it. Quite natural. Narrow rigid nativism may lead towards revivalism. But, it has to be borne in mind that 'revival' *per se* is not as bad as revivalism is. Revival attempted after considering the questions — what should be revived and what should not be? — is not always either unwarranted or unwanted. Unwise it would be, to consider the past traditions as a useless lump and discard them altogether. It may prove fatal for new creativity, for the fears of revivalism inveigle upon them to sever links with the tradition. For instance, most of our twentieth-century problems are descendants of their nineteenth-century counterparts. Hence, it is imperative for us to go to the reformers, thinkers and writers and the model that they had constructed to examine them in their complexities in order to eradicate them. To take whatever suits our purpose of preparing our strategy, to respond to our specific problems, is neither retrogression nor revivalism. Is return to the Indian literary and critical traditions to seek and revive whatever has possibility of regeneration? If it is so, then this revivalism is better than the slavish imitation of the Western theories, a rampant practice. Did the Western criticism not revive rhetoric for its own development? The rhetoric belonged to the ancient Greece and Rome, not to the twentieth century. Almost a century ago Vivekananda, after his return from the West, was concerned with the question pertaining to revival in religion in particular. In his 'Reply to the Address of Welcome at Madurai' he spoke on different aspects of revivalism:

> There is danger ahead as well as glory; for revival sometimes breeds fanaticism, sometimes goes to the extreme, so that often it is not even in the power of those who start the revival to control it when it has gone beyond a certain length. It is better, therefore, to be forewarned. We have to find our way between the Scylla of old superstitious orthodoxy and the Charybdis of materialism — of Europeanism, of soullessness, of the so-called reform — which has penetrated to the foundation of Western progress. These two have to be taken care of. In the first place, we cannot become Westerners, therefore, imitating the Westerners is useless . . . in the second place, it is impossible.
>
> — Vol III, 1994: 172

In his 'Reply to the Address of Welcome at Ramnad" on 25 January 1897, he spoke to the then generation caught in the warp of the Westernization and native Indian tradition. It was a question that haunted him and he responded to it again almost in the same idiom by probing further into the issue every time with his arguments. The question, like one of *yakṣa*'s, still haunts the Indian society:

> There are two great obstacles on our path in India, the Scylla of old orthodoxy and the Charybdis of modern European civilization. Of these two, I vote for the old orthodoxy, and not for the Europeanized system; for the old orthodox man may be ignorant, he may be crude, but he has a faith, he has strength, he stands on his feet, while the Europeanized man has no backbone, he is a mass of heterogeneous ideas picked up at random from every source — and these ideas are unassimilated, undigested, unharmonized. He does not stand on his feet and his head is turning round and round. — Vol III, 1994: 151

Vivekananda may be accused of advocating 'old orthodoxy' and of willingness to be co-opted by the revivalist fanatics. But, he needs no one, at least not me, to support him against the sceptics. He was fully aware of the dangers implicit in revivalism, as he forewarned us against consequent fanaticism. But, he preferred orthodoxy to Europeanism. We need not subscribe to his views or be an alarmist or a rejectionist. But we have to bear in mind that the obtaining Westernizing conditions control the other by determining its choice. What we need is to prepare a strategy of revival for survival. Everything is not to be revived. The important question is: What should be revived? And what should not be revived? Some of our sage writers have left a few pieces of advice for us in this regard. 'In Conversation' with me Namvar Singh, the noted Hindi critic, referred to Tulsīdās who said in the sixteenth century, *saṁgraha tyāgu nā binu pahacāne* (acquisition or rejection without recognition — both are dangerous). Tulsīdās forewarned us against 'unrecognized" indiscreet accumulation or rejection of our past and condition. In the twentieth century Suryakanta Tripathi Nirala, a Hindi poet, also said:

> *bhrama meṅ jo liyā, jñāna meṅ lo tum gin gin* ।
> *bhrama meṅ jo diyā, jñāna meṅ do tum gin gin* ॥

> Whatever you accept in ignorance, you should accept in the state of knowledge; whatever you reject in ignorance, you must do so in full knowledge.

Acquisition of something new or alien or abandonment of one's own without recognition or consideration — both are equally dangerous. Whatever is rotten should be forsaken as surgeons remove the malignant from the body. But, what harm is there in accepting what has the possibility of life and regeneration? Instead of wailing over the fear of revivalism what is needed is pragmatic, progressive and positive revival of our traditions. So, we will have to understand the difference between ignorance and knowledge. Like the proverbial blindman who threw away valuable gold and diamonds and kept stones with him, we have almost thrown away our ancient poetics and Alaṁkāraśāstra. The Westerners, on the other hand, have been taking out gold from their patchwork and developing theories for long. We must also do the same. In this sense revival is not bad, if it is done with discretion, discrimination and wisdom, observed Namvar Singh (1999: 165-77).

To conclude, let me go back to *deśīvāda*. Postmodernism and post-colonialism can be suitably written as *deśīvāda* or should be written with full consciousness of *deśīvāda*. Concerned as it is with roots, but it should not be forgotten that even the birds do not make their nests in roots. Human beings also do not make their home 'in' the foundation but 'on' it to look beyond into the sky above. Our love for our roots should not inveigle upon us to keep holding on to our roots or tie them around our necks. That would prove suicidal. Despite this, there are some legitimate reservations against *deśīvāda*. K. Satchidanandan has referred to some of the legitimate fears like parochialism, revivalism and dangers of disintegration in his article 'Nativism and its Ambivalences" (1996: 1-10). And, if our fears and anxieties pertaining to *deśīvāda* persist, it becomes imperative for us to reconsider and redefine the term keeping our obtaining context and situation in mind. We can look back and go beyond Nemade — if not as far as Bharatendu, Chiplunkar, Narmad, or Bankim in the nineteenth century — for a new dimension that Gandhi gave to *deśīvāda*, which to some critics has always ever been present in the twentieth century with his *svadeśī*. His *svadeśī* was a strategy or an alternative against *videśī* or *paradeśī*. As of now, politically the problem of *paradeśī* or *videśī* is over, though indirectly it challenges other voices, cultures, literatures and societies. There is no denying the fact that we have to take even from *videśī*, whatever is useful to us in it. And, if our *deśīvāda* has failed to remove our fears and anxieties of our own people, it should be redefined. Gandhi had to make a choice between *svadeśī* and *paradeśī/videśī*; we have to make a choice between *kudeśīvāda* and *sudeśīvāda*. And our choice should fall on *sudeśīvāda* — positive progressive, pragmatic, inclusive, and *svastha* (*sva* + *stha* = located in one's self). The alternative to postmodernism is *sudeśīvāda* whose alternative there seems to be none.

16

Towards Compoetics in India

Alternative Frameworks of Comparative Study of Poetics

INDIA, in its long and attested intellectual tradition, has contributed to different domains of knowledge. In the process of doing so, Indian thinkers have sounded caveats against insulation of knowledge systems and traditions. Suśruta, for instance, in *Suśruta Saṁhitā*, a text pertaining to the science of life, not mere medicine, stated, *ek śāstram adhiyāno na vidyā śāstra niścayam* (do not arrive at any conclusion by studying just one discipline). (*Suśruta Saṁhitā*, Sūtrasthāna, "Prabhāṣnīya Adhyāya", Chapter IV, *śloka* 7) Bhartṛhari, a grammarian and philosopher king of Ujjayinī, in the *Vākyapadīya* 2.484, emphasized the importance of knowing one's own as well as the alien traditions:

> The intellect acquires critical acumen by familiarity with different traditions. How much does one really understand by merely following one's own reasoning only?

Statements such as the preceding ones supporting diversity and multiplicity of systems and traditions and the necessity to accept and understand them abound in all major Indian texts and traditions. The statement may be read thus: what does s/he know who does not know his/her tradition, and what does s/he know who knows only his/her own tradition.

With its rich history of co-existence marked by inclusiveness and tolerance, India emerges as one of the most suitable sites for comparative study of literature in general and poetics in particular. The other side of this argument is that with its large number of living belief systems or speculative thoughts, India lived its diversities for so long and naturally that these became a part of its psychic and cultural systems, and so did not seriously consider devising a methodology for comparative studies. This may be because comparative study is generally understood as being built around reactions against the definite other, which is evil in the Western tradition, while in the Indian tradition, the other is not evil; it is, in fact, a part of me. In case it is not me, the problem is not with the other but with me who is intoxicated with the differentiating intellect (*nānātva buddhi*) that is inferior to the non-differentiating intellect (*anānātva buddhi*), for the latter sees no duality or difference. However, the *anānātva buddhi* is difficult to attain. Even gods have to seek the help of higher selves to achieve it. In the "Laṅkā-Kāṇḍa" of Tulsīdās's *Rāmacaritamānasa*, after the victory of Rāma over Rāvaṇa, gods celebrate by showering flowers on him and singing paeans in praise of Rāma. Brahmā (the Creator of the universe) also joins the galaxy of gods. In the end he seeks Rāma's blessings thus in "Laṅkā-Kaṇḍa" of *Rāmacaritamānasa* (110/10):

> *ab dīndayāl kr̥pā kariye*
> *mati mori bhedakari hariye.*
>
> With folded hands I beseech you,
>
> O Lord! Please make me free from *bhedakari mati* (differentiating intellect).

India has a unique convergence of its indigenous critical traditions, i.e. Sanskrit, Tamil and modern Indian languages — *bhāṣā*s and *bolī*s. The Western critical traditions, i.e. Greek, Roman, English, French, German and Russian joined it as tributaries and became an integral part of the tradition. It is natural to explore the possibilities of comparative study of different poetic traditions in India for their mutual illumination. The present endeavour considers the existing state of Indian poetics and explores the possibilities of a comparative study of poetics without oversighting the issues pertaining to practice and pedagogy.

Aesthetics

Aesthetics is not an Indian but a Western category. Aesthetics is a science of perception of beauty through senses. Senses have their own limitations and are to a good extent unreliable means of knowledge or experience. Moreover, they remain restricted to the external aspects of the objects which are subject to change. Indian mind was primarily concerned with the unchanging spiritual and eternal interiority. This orientation to exteriority and interiority may be discerned in the fact that the Western world of art portrays Jesus Christ with eyes open, whilst in the Indian art Gautama Buddha is portrayed with eyes closed.

Poetics and aesthetics are often used synonymously, erroneously of course. They converge at a point of experience — *rasa* experience in the Sanskrit and aesthetic experience (catharsis) in Aristotle's *Poetics*. In that sense, aesthetics may be translated as *rasānubhūtiśāstra*. No Sanskrit poetician could remain indifferent to the experience of *rasa* that came to be associated with *brahmānanda* (bliss of the Infinite). After expostulating the principle of *dhvani*, Abhinavagupta had to recognize the importance of *rasa*, and go back to *rasa* as the ultimate of all artistic endeavours. He synthesized *rasa* and *dhvani* in one, and proposed *rasadhvani*.

Poetics

With a change in the concept of poetry, the world of poetics also underwent a change. When Aristotle used the word 'poetics' in relation to the theory of poetry, he was referring to all prevalent literary forms by the term 'poetry'. It was equivalent to the Sanskrit term *kāvya*. Poetics as the theory of poetry corresponded with Kāvyaśāstra as the theory (*śāstra*) of *kāvya* (poetry). Sanskrit used different terms like Lakṣaṇaśāstra, Kriyākalpa, Alaṁkāraśāstra, Kāvyaśāstra, Sāhityavidyā and Mīmāṁsā among others in various contexts before Kāvyaśāstra came to be accepted as equivalent to poetics. This inclusive term 'poetry' was later replaced by literature (*sāhitya* in Hindi and many other languages), writing (*vāṅgmaya*) and then discourse (*vimarśa*). (It is also possible to consider the term *vācana* in place of *vimarśa*, as it includes written as well as oral traditions). Poetics then becomes the theory of different kinds of discursive practices. The scope and nature of poetics has become considerably inclusive. It is now not just Kāvyaśāstra but Vimarśaśāstra, Vācanaśāstra or Vāṅgmayaśāstra. I see no reason for not accepting Sāhityaśāstra, for *sāhitya* is an inclusive category, for it is more than literature which is concerned primarily with 'letters' and later with 'literature' and 'high literature' before being disinterred by the Structuralists and post-Structuralists. The term *sāhitya* is rooted in 'togetherness' or 'with welfare' and is not fettered by any binary of 'writing' or 'speech', 'high' or 'low', 'margin' or 'centre'. Hence, the term Sāhityaśāstra serves the purpose with its inclusivity.

Let me refer to the anarchy in the world of aesthetics/poetics, in that the terms 'aesthetics' and 'poetics' are used synonymously. One may come cross titles like Indian Poetics, Indian Aesthetics or Sanskrit poetics in India, but even a brief scrutiny or peep inside would reveal that the discussion hovers around the schools of Sanskrit poetics — *rasa, dhvani, alaṁkāra, aucitya, vakrokti* and *rīti*. The disciplinary *maryādā*s or compulsions disallow indiscipline, hence aesthetics and poetics are not to be confused or considered identical. Yet, the relationship between poetics and aesthetics is not too far-fetched, as they converge at the point of experience and they involve the *rasa* experience in the Sanskrit and aesthetic experience (catharsis) in Aristotle's *Poetics*. The *Poetics*, for that matter against the title, is more about aesthetics and less about poetics. It

> is neither principally a defence of poetry, nor a treatise on how to write it, nor an enunciation of principles of literary criticism, though it has elements of all of these: it is first and foremost a work of aesthetic theory, the questions it poses are: 'What is poetry? and 'What is the nature of pleasure in it?'[1]

1. Please see the discussion "Aristotle's Theory of Aesthetic Pleasure" in Russell & Winterbottom 1972: 220-21.

The Scope of Comparative Poetics

The title of the chapter privileges "Comparative Poetics in India" over 'Comparative Indian Poetics', for there is nothing like Indian poetics, as there is no language like Indian. Sanskrit or Tamil language may lay claim to it. Indian is a denominative term having regional, cultural and political/constitutional connotations. Comparative poetics, like comparative literature, is more about methodology and less about literature and poetics. 'Indian comparative poetics' has neither sense nor syntax. It is merely a term of convenience. For that matter, poetics has been abandoned by the practitioners of comparative literature in the West, as the Western scholarship abandoned theory and poetics in the declining years of the twentieth century; the century of unprecedented growth of history. However, in the ascendance of theory lay the seeds of its fall, as a shrill note about the end of theory, paralleled by the pronouncements like the 'post-theory' and 'after theory', in the form of post-theory was heard by the end of the preceding century in the form of the publication of Thomas Docherty's *After Theory* (1997), *Post-Theory: New Directions in Criticism* (1999) ed. by Martin McQuillan et al., *What's Left of Theory*? (2000) ed. by Judith Butler, John Guillory and Thomas Kendall, Valentine Cunningham's *Reading After Theory* (2002), Jean-Michael Rabate's *The Future of Theory*, Terry Eagleton's *After Theory* (2003), Michael Payne and John Shad's *Life.After.Theory*, ed. (2003). The end of theory did not literally mean the death of theory. It speaks about the theory fatigue caused by the surfeit of theory. The end of theory is symptomatic of disorientation with theory which means that it is possible to receive and appreciate a literary or an artistic work without knowing theory. It meant disorientation towards theory due to surfeit of it and suggested erosion in its status of centrality, as it came to be realized that literary theory is not indispensable for literary studies.

So when theory suffered, its fate was shared by its sister poetics. Even in the heydays of theory, poetics did not prosper. Comparative poetics was to suffer more, ironically at the hands of practitioners of comparative literature. The reports of American Comparative Literature Association (ACLA) in the last decade of the twentieth century and the first decade of the twenty-first century are indicative of the decline in the fortune of theory and poetics in general and comparative poetics in particular. The ACLA reports by Charles Bernheimer, entitled *Comparative Literature in the Age of Multiculturalism* in the 1990s and the ACLA's last report, *Comparative Literature in an Age of Globalization* (2006), edited by Haun Saussey, do not even consider comparative poetics worth the discussion. Only literary theory earns some obituary like space in Richard Rorty's "Looking Back at Literary Theory" in little less than five pages in the Report by Haun Saussey. However, it should not mean that we ape the West (read Europe in general and America in particular) blindly and abandon the comparative study of poetics because we have a rich heritage of construction of Śāstra in almost all areas of human activity, and have plurality of as many poetics in India (Sanskrit, Tamil, and all modern languages) as are languages and literatures in the country. It means there is enough scope to practise comparative study of poetics in India, their similarities, dissimilarities, resemblances and interrelatedness among them. The possibility of their comparative study with their non-Indian counterparts — European, American, Arabic-Persian, Chinese or Japanese — opens up new vistas of comparative study.

The oft-cited binary to Indian poetics is Western poetics, which in turn stands for European poetics. It is high time the Indian academe reconsidered the scope of the study of Western poetics, as 'Western' should include our immediate West — the Arabic-Persian poetics too. The Arab world is India's real West in terms of geographical contiguity and cultural transactions. This extended 'Western poetics' should be studied along with the many critical traditions in India.

Constituents of the Study of Comparative Poetics in India

The discussion of poetics veers more around history and theory of poetics, and less around its practice and frameworks. The forthcoming discussion pertains to alternative frameworks of comparative study in India.

I

Poetics as the Theory of Poetry

Poetics, in the traditional sense as the theory of poetry and in the contemporary sense as the theory of discourses, deals with the following preoccupations in different languages:

1. *Kāvya*, its definition, nature and classification (poetry)
2. *Śabda-śakti* (word-power): Here the focus would be on the comparative study of *śabda-śakti*. For instance, Sanskrit has four kinds of *śabda-śakti*, i.e. *abhidhā, vyañjaśā, lakṣaṇā*, and *tātparya* whereas English has two, i.e. literal/referential/abstract/denotative and metaphorical/emotive/paradoxical/connotative.
3. *Artha* (meaning in poetry)
4. *Hetu* (poetry and its means)
5. *Prayojana* (poetry and its objectives)
6. *Guṇa* and *doṣa* (meritorious attributes and blemishes)

These may be the principal preoccupations of comparative study of poetics in different languages. Put together, as they are given here, or in any other combination, they may be used to build a framework for close study of literary texts. To some extent this may help in responding to the charge that Sanskrit poetics does not have textual analysis or theory of creative process in it.[2]

2. For a study of a theory of creative process in Indian epics and their comparative study within one language, i.e. Sanskrit, please see Avadhesh Kumar Singh, "Mythical Narrative as a Mode of Constituting Knowledge: Theory of Creative Process in the Narratives about the *Ramayana* and the *Mahabharata*" in the present book.

II

Poetics and its Departures

From the viewpoint of various 'departures' in Indian poetics in Sanskrit, the following may be considered: I must add it here that I prefer the term 'departure' to 'School' because proponents and subscribers of various schools refer to others while addressing the issue of the core, principle preoccupation or life of the *kāvya*. In the process, they found different cores — in *rasa, alaṁkāra, rīti, aucitya, vakrokti,* and *dhvani* or *rasadhvani*):

1. A comparative study of *rasa* with the prospect of its comparison with the contemplation on the aesthetic experience in the West.
2. *Alaṁkāra* for prospect of comparison with rhetoric.
3. *Rīti* for the prospect of comparison with stylistics.
4. *Dhvani* for the prospect of comparison with the theory of suggestion/symbolic meaning.
5. *Vakrokti* for the prospect of comparison with 'the artistic'/ 'literary'/ 'poetic' in art/literature/poetry and Russian Formalism in particular. Textuality of New Criticism or Practical Criticism may also be a part of such a comparative study with the principles of *vakrokti.*
6. *Aucitya* for the prospect of comparison with decorum and propriety in the West.[3]

Along with the study of the departures like *rasa, alaṁkāra, rīti, dhvani, vakrokti,* and *aucitya,* as they are dealt in Sanskrit poetics and their counterparts in the Western poetics and Tamil poetics (*Tolkappiyam*), here, one could also consider a study of the main concerns of the Western poetics in terms of art/text, artist/author, audience/reader, ambience/context, and co-text and various schools in comparison with their counterparts in the Indian traditions.

---

3. Please see Mohit K. Ray, *A Comparative Study of the Indian and the Western Poetics*, Delhi: Sarup & Sons, 2008 for a recent study on the lines suggested here.

Here, I propose to respond to the often asked question about the possibility or reality of an Indian School of Comparative Literature (ISCL) based on Sanskrit poetics or on poetics in the Indian languages. In terms of practice and its acceptance as a discipline in academic institutions, it does exist in India, though in frail and fragmented forms. It might be worthwhile here to consider some suggestions that have been made to make this a greater reality. I would like to mention here one of the suggestions that came from Professor Namvar Singh, the noted Hindi critic. He remarked in the course of his Valedictory Address on 30 March 2010, to the International Conference on Comparative Literature, organized by the Department of English & Comparative Literary Studies, Saurashtra University, Rajkot (28-30 March 2010), that the Indian School of Comparative Literature can derive its principles and methodology from the Alaṁkāra School of Sanskrit with its long history from Bharatamuni's *Nāṭyaśāstra* to Pandit Reva Prasad Dwivedi's *Ālambrahma* (2005). It is more easily pronounced by distinguished minds than realized by others, for only the former are the most qualified to do so. However, there is ostensible design and purpose in the position. Since the basic premise of *alaṁkāra* is comparison between the two objects, it is possible to see and elaborate purpose in this proposition, as the figure of speech *upamā* (simile) may be the basis of all comparative studies of literature or poetics. The Sanskrit *alaṁkār*-ists (rhetoricians) from Bhāmaha to Reva Prasad Dwivedi, discussed the principles and kinds of *alaṁkāra*s at length in greater detail than the Western rhetoricians. Moreover, one can get further support from the other Sanskrit Schools as well, particularly in case of propriety of comparisons which is the bane of comparitists. For example, while discussing the issue of propriety of *upamā*, Kṣemendra, the principal proponent of the *aucitya* (propriety or decorum) School, mentions *hṛdayasādṛśī upamā*. It means the simile should have similitude of the core of comparison. This may be taken as the first principle of comparative literary study and may be appropriated and phrased as *hṛdayasādṛśī tulanā*. These principles need to be developed further, which, however, demands another occasion.

III

Comparative Study of Poetical/Critical Approaches

Various principles of theory of poetry or literary discourses that go into the making of poetics in different languages may also be compared and studied. Comparative poetical endeavours may focus on the principal hinges of art/literary discourse:

(i) Art/Text — Textual Approach and *kṛti-niṣṭha abhigama.*

(ii) Artist/Author — Author-centric approach and *kaviniṣṭha abhigama.*

(iii) Audience/Reader — Reader response and *sahṛdaya abhigama.*

(iv) Ambience/Contex — Biographical/sociological approach and *aucitya abhigama.*

(v) Attendant/(Non-literary) Text/Co-Text — New historicism and *parapamaparāniṣṭha* or *sahakṛtiniṣṭha abhigama.*

In the preceding part, the comparative study is proposed on the lines of the comparison of the Western critical approaches and approaches in Sanskrit and other Indian languages. A study such as this would include study of similarities, dissimilarities and resemblances. There would be quite a few issues like the critical approaches and literary theories in the twentieth century that would demand study in the causes of presence and absence of the given approach(es) in a tradition. In imaginative and speculative minds it would become a creatively fascinating instance of culture studies.[4]

---

4. For comparative study of poetics, particularly Indian and the Western, the following indicative areas may be considered:

Rasa:

(a) **Locus of *rasa*:**

In the author (an expressionist view).
In the composition (an autotelic view).
In the spectator (Reader Response view).

→

IV

Comparative Literary Methodology for Comparative Study of Poetics

Comparative literature is no literature; it is methodology. Comparative poetics, similarly, is no poetics, but a methodology. In this case, the methodology of comparative literature and its

---

→ (b) ***Rasasūtra***: configuration of *rasa* and Eliot's "Objective Correlative" and A.K. Ramanujan's *Correlative Object*. (*Vide* Krishna Rayan's "Translating Sanskrit Critical Terms" in his *The Lamp and the Jar*.)

(c) **Sublime** and ***adbhuta*** *rasa*.

(d) **Aesthetic perception** (Kant) and ***Rasa Mīmāṁsā***.

Bhāṣā: Language — Bhartṛhari and Wittgenstein

Śabda Śakti: *Abhidhā, lakṣaṇā, vyañjanā* (*dhvani*) with I.A. Richards's 'referential' and 'emotive' meanings.

Poetry: Poetic process and function of poetry (Dryden; Arnold; Eliot) and *prayojana* in Indian poetics.

Poet - (in Coleridge; Rainer Maria Rilke) and Rājaśekhara; Paradigms of creation: Potter (the Indian) and Carpenter (the Western).

Mimesis (Plato; Aristotle); Bharata's *anukṛti*; Śaṅkuka's *anukaraṇa* and *anumiti*; Bhaṭṭa Tauta's *anuvyavasāya* and *anubhavana*.

Origin of Drama/Poetry: Nietzsche (Birth of Tragedy) and Bharata (*nāṭyotpatti*); Rājaśekhara (*kāvyapuruṣotpatti*).

Discursive devices (*yukti*s) and **Poetic Conventions** (*kavi samaya*) in the West and in India.

Taxonomy of Literary Discourses: Rājaśekhara and Northrop Frye

Croce's 'Poetic Genius' and *Pratibhā* in Indian poetics (specially Abhinava & Rājaśekhara)

Charges against and defence of poetry in the West (Plato-Aristotle; Stephen Gosson-Philip Sidney; John Dryden; Samuel Johnson; Thomas Love Peacock – P.B. Shelley; Matthew Arnold, C.S. Snow – F.R. Leavis) and in India, particularly Rājaśekhara; Ācārya Mammaṭa.

"White Mythology" by Derrida and use of myths in Indian Poetics by Bharata and Rājaśekhara.

Simile and Metaphor: Aristotle, *Rule of Metaphor* (Paul Ricoeur) and *upamā* and *rūpaka* in Alaṁkāraśāstra.

Influence of philosophy on poetics in the West and in India.

main concerns can be of much help to comparative poetics. The following methodology/approaches of comparative literary study may be used for comparative study of poetics as well:

1. *Placing*: Placing one poetics or critical approach by / along with another, leading to 'mutual illumination'.
2. *Thematology*: Comparative study of major poetical/critical themes of concern.
3. *Genology*: Comparative study of a school from one poetics with another in different poetics.
4. *Influence*: Influence of one poetics or critical tradition on another.
5. *Reception*: Reception of one poetics or critical tradition in another.
6. *Historiography*:
   (i) Comparative study of history of critical tradition.
   (ii) *History of poetical ideas*: Comparative study of evolution and history of poetical/critical ideas (it may be synchronic, as here, and also diachronic study, as in the last IV category, of critical terms).
   (iii) *Movements*: Comparative study of critical movements.
   (iv) *Periodization*: Comparative study of critical periods.

V

Poetics as Critical Tradition

Poetics, as a scientific or systematic study of theory of discourses, includes study of literary criticism and critical traditions in India. Hence, it would be interesting to see comparative poetics as a comparative study of various critical traditions. Indian critical tradition could be seen as a stream that begins as a trickle, and then becomes a river in the plains where it is joined by many tributaries. In the course of its flow, certain distributaries move away from it and become either a full river or dry out after some time. The whole process can be understood in terms of *āvirbhāva* (emergence), *pravāha* (flow), *antarabhāva* (disappearance), *punarbhāva* (re-emergence) and *antarlīna* (submergence).[5] These five stages have their parallels in the occult Kāśmīra Śaivism: *sṛṣṭi* (emanation or projection), *sthiti* (maintenance), *saṁhāra* (withdrawal), *vilaya* (concealment of the real nature), and *anugraha* (grace).[6]

---

5. For detailed discussion of various stages in Indian critical tradition, please see, "Continuity and Change in Indian Critical Tradition", in the book.

6. The five stages are discussed in the following *sūtra* and its *ṭīkā* in Kṣemarāja. *Pratyabhijñahṛdayam: The Secret of Self-Recognition*, tr. Jaideva Singh, Delhi: Motilal Banarsidass, 1982, p. 73.

   1. *Tathāpi tadvat paṭca kṛtyāni karoti.* (*sūtra* 10)

   Commentary

   iha īśvarādvayadarśanasya brahmavādibhyaḥ ayameva viśesaḥ, yat

   sṛṣṭisaṁhārkartāram vilayasthitikārakam ।

   anugrahkaram devam praṇatārtivināśanam?

   — *Svacchanda Tantra* 1.3

   Translation

   Even in this condition (of the empirical self), he (the individual) does the five *kriyā*s (deeds) like Him (i.e. like Śiva). (Sūtra 10)

   Commentary

   Here, the distinction between the Īśvarādvaya philosophy from (that of) the Brahmavādins lies in this — that the divine whose essence is consciousness always retains his authorship of the five-fold act which is in accordance with what has been stated by the grand *svacchanda* and other disciplines (of Śaiva philosophy), viz.

   (I bow to the) Divine who brings about (1) emanation (*sṛṣṭi*), (2) re-absorption (*saṁhāra*), (3) concealment (*vilaya*), (4) maintenance (*sthiti*), who dispenses, (5) grace (*anugraha*) and who destroys the affliction of those who have bowed down (to Him). — *Svacchanda Tantra* 1.3

   Explanation of the *pañcakriyā* (the five acts) brought about by Śiva is as *Īśvaradvya-darśana* means the system of philosophy which does not believe in any other principle (*advaya*) than *Īśvara*, the Lord. This is the characterization of the Śaiva philosophy of Kashmir which maintains that Śiva is the whole and the sole reality.

   Brahmavādins refers to those Vedāntins who believe that a principle, called *māyā*, other than the *Brahman* is responsible for *sṛṣṭi*, *sthiti*, and *saṁhāra*. Literally, it means advocates of this doctrine.

→

Indian critical traditions were preceded by an elongated period of sustained creativity. The consideration of principles of poetry and its theory was a natural consequence. It began with Sanskrit poetics in the northern India, and Tamil poetics in the southern India. The former flourished in different schools and debates for centuries. With the emergence of *bhāṣā* literatures in Braja, Awadhi and Bhojpuri, Sanskrit poetics, particularly *alaṁkāra, rīti* and *guṇa-doṣa* was adapted by them. The *rasa* theory was tested in terms of new creativity and

---

→ It follows:

1. *Sṛṣṭi*: 'Letting go'; casting out of oneself. The usual translation 'creation' is misleading. Creation implies that the creator acts upon an external material, and thus brings about the world-process. This translation does not do the justice to the Indian point of view. *Sṛṣṭi* is derived from the root *sṛj* which means to 'let go', 'to pour forth', 'to project'. This implies that the world-process is already implicitly contained in Śiva. He only lets it go or projects it out of himself. He has not to work on an external material in order to bring about the world-process. According to Śaiva philosophy, the world is not a creation, but an emanation; it is theophany.
2. *Sthiti*: 'maintenance' of the world process.
3. *Saṁhāra* or *saṁhṛti*: 'Withdrawal or re-absorption'. It does not mean destruction of the world. It is only re-absorption by Śiva for a time. Destruction is only a metaphorical and secondary sense of *saṁhāra*, not its primary sense.
4. *Vilaya*: concealment of the real nature of the Self.
5. *Anugraha*: grace.

The five *kriyās* imply that Śiva lets go the universe out of himself, imparts existence to it and finally withdraws it into himself only to let it appear again. This makes a cycle which is called a *kalpa*. There is no final end to the world-process. The cosmic process is repeated from eternity to eternity.

Anugraha is the act of grace by which Śiva brings about the liberation of man. The first four *kriyās* are cosmological, the last is soteriological. The five *kriyās* are not artificial mixture of two standpoints — one cosmological and the other soteriological. Rather *anugraha* is the *raison d'être* of the first four *kriyās*, it is that for the sake of which the first four *kriyās*, come into play. It expresses the abounding love of Śiva. The Śiva performs this five-fold act even when he is in the form of an empirical ego (*jīva*). In this philosophy, like Śaṅkara's Vedānta, the Absolute is not without activity (*niṣkriya*). Vedāntins' principle of inactive *Brahman* is ridiculed in this system.

new *rasas*, such as *bhakti rasa*, were added by people such as Rūpagoswāmī. In this context, the poetical traditions in the modern Indian languages with reference to Sanskrit, Hindi and Gujarati could be included in the study of comparative poetics in India.

In the second half of the nineteenth century, the Western criticism joined the river of Indian critical tradition as tributaries, resulting in interesting developments in the already existing critical theories. Bharatendu Harishchandra (1850-85) is a prime example of this convergence in "Nāṭaka" (Drama), with his critique of the *rasa* theory and his insistence on *bhakti* and *vātsalya* as new *rasas*. Ramchandra Shukla's *Rasamīmāṁsā*, is an instance of reinterpretation of the *rasa* theory in the light of the psychoanalytical theory.[7]

The question, whether or not this metaphoric consideration of the Indian critical tradition as a river is true about any other tradition. If so, then how does it help us in comparative study of poetics in India? The answer lies in the fact that India has as many critical traditions as are languages and discourses — oral and written. The study of such critical traditions will give us insights into how two critical traditions, simultaneously, manage their flow as well as the inflow of many tributaries, and the way one tradition copes when a distributory moves away from the mainstream, and dries out in the course of time. Moreover, it would bring to surface the interrelatedness of different critical traditions in India. This will be a major lesson for comparative literature and comparative poetics as disciplines of study.

VI

Comparative Poetics and Alternative Aesthetics/Poetics

Indian critical tradition, apart from its rich past, and reception of other critical traditions suffers from being parasitic, derivative

7. Please see Bhartendu Harischandra, "Nāṭak" translated as "*Nāṭak*" (Drama), from Hindi to English by Prabhat Kumar Pandeya, in *Critical Discourse and Colonialism*, Delhi: Creative Books, 2005, pp. 19-60.

and unimaginatively imitative. There have been some exceptions in almost every Indian language, in the twentieth century, like M. Hiriyanna and G.C. Pandey in English and Sanskrit respectively, Ramchandra Shukla, Gajanan Madhav Muktibodh, Hazari Prasad Dwivedi, Hirananda Sachchidananda Agyeya, Nagendra, Ram vilas Sharma and Namvar Singh in Hindi, R.V. Pathak, Umashankar Joshi and Suresh Joshi in Gujarati, B.S. Mardhekar, R.B. Patankar, Bhalchandra Nemade and Sharan Kumar Limbale in Marathi among others, who have to a good extent, contributed to criticism and critical traditions in their languages through the reception of indigenous/Indian and the non-Indian critical approaches and traditions, creating new critical idiom and interpretations of literary texts. However, they are confined to their own languages that respect things only in English.

The quest for new or alternative aesthetics and poetics has its source in the new literary discourses in India — oral, *dalit*, and feminist, as they bring in different experience with them which cannot be understood, experienced or appreciated with the traditional poetic or aesthetic standards. Oral discourse can not be measured by the poetics constructed on the basis of written discourse. The same is the case with *dalit* and feminist discourses. Their ability to challenge and scandalize the formal categories and to resist discrimination and suppression brings feminist discourse close to *dalit* discourse, and offers the possibilities of a comparative study of their poetics as well. The consideration of feminism along with the *dalit* discourse t/eases each other. As a new category, the case of the '*dalit* feminism' would, it might seem on the surface, weaken both of them. *Dalit* men have for centuries borne the burden of the suppression and exploitation at the hands of high caste men. But within the *dalit* society/ community, patriarchy operates in almost the same manner as it does in the high caste society. The only difference may be that *dalit* women perhaps have earned their space and freedom because they are the agents of labour and contributory, at times the sole, source of resource generation in the family. It does not discount the fact that some *dalit* men, like other workers, are given to a few vices like drinking on which they spend their hard-earned wages, and in an inebriated condition they become a burden on their spouses or family members, as they drain limited financial resources and expose themselves to health and financial hazards. Hence, a *dalit* woman has to carry a *dalit* man as one burden more than their men. Their men had to carry the mountain of foreign colonization, internal colonization by the high caste, whereas *dalit* woman had to carry her inter-colonized male as well. Despite it the voice of *dalit* women is almost absent in the Indian *dalit* discourse. The *dalit* intelligentsia might find the category [*dalit* woman (feminist) discourse] as a means of dividing and thereby weakening the discourse, but the contribution of *dalit* women in the *dalit* discourse would lend a new direction to *dalit* discourse, as it would bring new fire and intensity in it. At the same time, Indian feminist discourse without *dalit* women discourse would be partial, limited in its scope and parasitic in nature; though such a category to Indian feminist activists might appear unwanted and as a ploy to weaken the movement. Notwithstanding the anxieties and concerns of *dalit* activists and their movement, *dalit* feminist discourse would carve a niche for itself in the global feminist discourse with its intensity and authenticity. Some might find that the term *dalit* feminist discourse makes no sense because women are *dalit*s by birth. Feminist and *dalit* aesthetics/poetics received and used the Western feminist and black aesthetics, respectively, to their advantage, and so may be comparatively studied. Moreover, the diversity of *dalit* experience/discourse and poetics in different Indian languages, e.g. Gujarati and Marathi may also be explored through their comparative study.

In Lieu of Conclusion

I have tried my best to inflate the balloon of comparative poetics in India. Let me puncture it too lest its acolytes overinterpret its import, and privilege poetics over poetry. Between poetry and poetics, the former is more valuable than the latter. The history of poetics' historiography reveals that poetics comes into existence when poetic/literary creativity reaches its culmination. For instance, Sanskrit poetics came into existence, after Bharatamuni's *Nāṭyaśāstra* in fourth century BCE, in the form of Bhāmaha's *Kāvyālaṁkāra* in the seventh century, by which time the best of Sanskrit creativity in the form of the Vedas, Upaniṣads, Vālmīki's *Rāmāyaṇa*, Veda Vyāsa's *Mahābhārata* and Kālidāsa's writings had come into existence, and so was the case with the Greek poetics, which saw its realization with Aristotle's *Poetics* in the third century BCE by which time the best period of Greek literary creativity was over. Natural it is, because principles of poetics demand being inferred from able literary practices. So poetics is often taught at the cost of poetry in the academic world. The main objective of teaching and practising comparative poetics should be to see the way knowledge is constituted in literary discourses, and the way the principles of their theory are inferred and applied, as different from the political and theoretical ideologies of contemporary discourses.

Comparative poetics, however, is a liberating category, as it accepts the existence of other poetics, and considers them worth studying and learning from each other. The Śāstra like poetics is associated with disciplinary arrogance and often tends to be prescriptive. The comparative poetics brings in an element of modesty by positing that no Śāstra is complete in itself and so different poetics complement and supplement each other. Moreover, it accepts the fact that poetics is subservient to creativity.

After a rather elongated and abstract discussion of comparative poetics, it would not be discordant to wrap up with pleasant poetic composition by resorting to a poem from Ramesh Parekh, a distinguished Gujarati poet, about the obligations of poetry:

Kavitae Shu Karvanu Hoy!

Kavitā
Shiyalu ratrie taapnu petave,
Zaadne galmadhu chhayadi padta shikhave unalama,
Chomasama kahe varsaadne — khaabki pad!

Shu shu banvanu hoy kavitae
Kaach sandhvanu ren?
Bhukhyanu ann?
Anindrana dardini ungh?
Sainikna ghav par pato?
Ha !

Shishuna kalshorno utsav ujavvano hoy,
Chumban tarsaya phulo mate patangiyu banvanu hoy,
Matana stanma dudh banvanu hoy,
Aapghat mate janarna pagma sakal banvanu hoy,
Shayankhandna shushk ekantma
Madhur aekya rachvanu hoy kavitae.
Jya ishwarna hath na pahoche
Tya pahochvanu hoy kavitae.

E badhu to kharu j,
Pan sauthi motu kaam e ke
Tene aakhun gaam unghtu hoy tyare
Jagadvano hoy kavine."
— Ramesh Parekh, 33

The poem in its English translation would run thus:

What Has Poetry to Do?

Poetry becomes a fireplace in the shivering night;
it teaches the trees to be the sweet shade in summer
and tells the rain in the monsoon, "Unleash yourself."
Poetry has to play multiple roles:
Glue for joining the fragments of glass,
food for the hungry,
sleep for the insomniac,
dressing for the wound of a soldier?
Yes, Indeed!

It has to celebrate the festival of a child's prattle,
become the firefly for the flowers starving from want of a kiss,
milk in the breasts of a mother,
fetters around the feet of a person setting out to commit suicide;
it has to create a sweet unison in the dreary solitariness
of the bedchamber.

Poetry has to reach
where gods have no access.
All this is true indeed,
But the most important one is,

When the entire village is fast asleep,
It has to awaken the poet.

Compoetics has to perform the same functions that poetry does for society. Poetry and poetics are interrelated and interdependent, though they are independent disciplines. This interrelatedness exists at the level of their functions, as they try to awaken the creator/ artist/poet and society. Poetics infers principles or theories of literary discourse on the basis of discursive practices, and without being prescriptive sees to it that false theories do not get established as poetical truths. Comparative poetics unveils the patterns of human critical faculty in different countries and cultures; it broods over various discursive manifestations and practices. In case of India which offers a rich complex of *sāmasik sanskṛti* (compound culture), the comparative study of poetics becomes a study in 'interpoetics' or 'compoetics', the latter standing both for compound poetics and comparative poetics. Compoetics, thus, with its various frameworks becomes an even more exciting enterprise, as India emerges as a veritable United Nations of Poetics.[8]

---

8. The author is thankful to Sri Maulik Vyasa, Department of English, Christ College, Rajkot, for reading the paper and helping in different ways, particularly in translation of Ramesh Parekh's Gujarati poem into English.)

Lead Out
Interliterariness and Contactuality in India

"We are going, first, to bring Greece to its knees," Pyrrhus said.
"And then?" asked Cineas.
"Then we'll annex Africa."
"After Africa?"
"We will move on to Asia to conquer Asia Minor and Arabia."
"And then?"
"We'll go all the way to Indies"
"And after the Indies"
"Ah!" said Pyrrhus, "then I am going to rest."
"Then why," asked Cineas, "don't you just rest right now?"
— Simone de Beauvoir

bhrama meṅ jo liyā, jñāna meṅ lo tum gin gin।
bhrama meṅ jo diyā, jñāna meṅ do tum gin gin॥
— Suryakanta Tripathi 'Nirala'

THE brief narrative in the epigraph of the "Lead Out" might seem to suffer from ambivalence towards the choice between endless aggression and ultimate end. The judgement in the end is unambiguous. Between the end of literary and critical exercises there may be ambiguity among their acolytes, but the fact is that be it literature, literary and critical theoriest, literariness is the sun around which all these interrelated planets and stars revolve.

In the "Lead Out" I propose to discuss the issue of contactuality in interliterariness, before considering the case of intersystemic literary reception, as studied ably by Ipshita Chanda in her *Reception of the Received: European Romanticism, Rabindranath and Suryakant Tripathi 'Nirala'— A Case Study in Inter-Systemic Literary Reception* (2006) which is the interliterariness 'still' and (instead of 'but' of Alexander Pope) interliterariness 'methodized', as it recognizes and celebrates interliterariness in India in the light of comparative framework.

Reception presupposes contact. Contactuality, as the dynamic of power and consequence of institutional and individual movement with their ideas at small and large scale, generates ideational relations, based on the change that both undergo in different measure, of course. Change is inevitable and so is its consideration. In Plato, it becomes 'drift'. "Plato's sense of drift had expressed itself in his theory that all change, at least in certain cosmic periods, must be for worse; all change is degeneration." (Popper 1945: 7) Plato had taught that all development starts from the original, the perfect Form or Idea so that the developing thing must lose its perfection in the degree in which it changes and in which its similarity to the original decreases. Aristotle, "the inventor of logic" (Popper: 3), "not a man of striking originality of thought", "in spite of his stupendous learning and his astonishing scope" (Popper: 3), admitted changes but termed them as improvement, thus, change may be progress.[1]

This brief Platonic intervention is essential because the journey of European romanticism with its travel from Europe to India, Bengal to be precise, and then from Bengali to Hindi through literary intermediaries like Gurudev Tagore (Bengali) and 'Nirala' (one of the precursors and practitioners of Chāyāvāda movement in Hindi poetry that was influenced by Bengali romantic movement

1. Plato had proposed 'mythical and semi-ironical presentation' of the theory of descent by degeneration in *Timaeus*, which Popper calls 'a general theory of the *origin of species by way of degeneration*, down from the Gods and the first man. Man first degenerates into a woman, then further to the higher and lower animals and to the plants'. (Popper 1945: 316) Gomperz calls it "a theory of descent in the literal sense or a theory of devolution, as opposed to the modern theory of evolution, which since it assumes an ascending sequence, might be called a theory of ascent." (Gomperz in Popper: 482, German edition. Cited in Popper: 316)

that in turn was impacted by the English romanticism) is seen in terms of 'drift', 'degeneration' and 'progress' too. The measure of 'drift' and 'progress' ('degeneration' for Plato) depended on the creative intensity of the individual, the generation or the culture that received it. The 'drift' of creative ideas and movements from one artist/writer and culture/country to another is at the best put in category of poetic license and at the worst 'stealing' and 'theft' that are prerogatives of genius and mediocre respectively. From this perspective, 'Nirala' would not fall either in the category of thief or borrower. To comparatists, he would be in the category of 'intermediary' between Hindi and Bengali through Tagore.

Comparisons are odious but natural. The human instincts involved in the act and processes of comparisons are instincts of jealousy and power. There lies the strength of all comparative studies, as they would be practised as long as human species survive. The desire for methodology is their biggest burden, for human beings as the most variable data for study and research can at the best be seen in terms of patterns, not as 'science' in the technical sense of the term but at the best in the sense of 'knowledge systematized'. The insistence on systematization demands methodology. Comparative literature as the discipline of study is no exception to it, more so in case of comparative study of Indian literature with a long, continuous and attested tradition in which ancient and modern, oral and written, *loka* (folk) and *śloka* (elite) not only co-exist side by side but within each other.[2]

Before comparative literature came into existence in the West in the declining decades of the eighteenth century, and in the 1950s in India (to be precise in 1956 at the Jadavpur University), comparisons were made in Indian literatures but with varied motives, usually without subscription to any methodology.[3]

---

2. Needless for me to mention it here that I use 'Indian literature' as a generic term for 'literatures — written and oral — available in Indian languages.'

3. In the Sanskrit tradition and later on in Hindi too, like many Indian languages, there have survived many instances of comparisons, without specific authorship. At best such pronouncements may be termed as →

However, the comparisons were consequences of literary contacts within one literature and with contiguous literatures that witnessed many literary and cultural movements like Indian *bhakti* discourse which is a unique phenomenon in terms of contactuality. Sisir Kumar Das's insightful study pays critical tribute to it in his study of the idea and practice of Indian literature.[4]

Needless to state the commonplace that literature is communication, but seeing it as communication makes us see its components that go into its multi-layered making and its reception. Literary reception or inter-literary contactuality presumes cultural sharing of, to rephrase Roman Jacobson's terms from his theory of communication, 'addresser', 'addressee', 'address', 'contact' 'context' and 'code'. Contact is one of the six components in it but assumes the place of significance in reception as the order of components of communication involving various causes and

---

→ impressionistic judgements, perhaps by over-enthusiastic admirers of a given poet, as they did not even care to substantiate their claims. Comparing Kālidāsa, Bhāravi, Daṇḍin and Māgha, the couplet reads thus:

upamā kālidāsāya bhāraverathagauravam ।
daṇḍinapadalālityam māghesanti trayoguṇaḥ ।।

(Kālidāsa is unparalleled for the use of similes, Bhāravi for the majesty of meaning, Daṇḍin for the beauty of phrasal arrangement, Māgha has all three attributes.)

It must have been stated by one of the acolytes of Māgha, as the following must been inspired with the sole motive of establishing the superiority of Sūrdās, the seventeenth century Hindi *bhakti* poet over Tulsīdās, the author of *Rāmacaritamānasa*, and Keśavdāsa, the author of *Rāmacandrikā* in the Rīti-kāla of the Hindi literature.

sūr sūr tulasī śaśi udagan keśavadāsa
ab ke kavi khadyot sam jahāṅ tahṅ karat prakāśa.

(Sūrdās is the Sun (of the sky of Hindi poetry), Tulsīdās, the moon, and Keśavadāsa is a bird. The present poets are like fireflies who flash light here and there.)

4. Please see S.K. Das, "Prologue" (1-23) & Appendix I "Integrated History of Indian Literature" & Appendix II (341-370). *A History of Indian Literature* vol. VIII: 1800-1910; *Western Impact: Indian Response*, New Delhi: Sahitya Akademi, 1991.

consequences of highly porous space of contact(uality). Contact ends with coming together of diverse or similar elements; whereas contactuality, to me, refers not only to a set of processes that facilitate the coming together of the elements (individuals and institutions with or without any motive) but also, and more importantly, to the dynamics that set off the creation of a new world out of integration. It does not entail either one swallowing the other wholly or explosion of influence. It is best captured in the original sense of the term which means 'touch wholly' which can best be described a beautiful contradiction on the surface, as the touch cannot be 'whole'. It has to be gentle, partial and local. But, the gentle touch acts as a catalyst of change that stirs and inspires a string of feelings and thoughts which in the process envelops the whole system.[5]

India, having a rich and long continued tradition of cultural transaction within and with the world outside offers itself as a pregnant site for contactual comparative study. Ipshita Chanda's work explores the world of contactuality, and studies individuals and institutions that acted as intermediaries between the West and India (European, English in particular and Indian languages, Bengali in particular) and between Bengali (Tagore) and Hindi (Nirala), and with a framework (and that is the big difference it makes in relation to anarchic comparative studies in Hindi and other Indian languages without any framework) that can serve a potent case study for comparative literary study between/among highly porous boundaries of Indian languages. Tagore received the Western romanticism directly, whereas Nirala through Tagore and directly as well for the community of his contemporary creative and critical minds, readers and his own creativity. In view of the observations in the preceding paragraph, I must state that Tagore's was the gentle touch on the creativity of those who came in contact with him.

5. In its Latin root of the word 'contact' *conting-ere, contactium,* to touch — *con,* wholly, *tangere,* to touch. Touch rests on ability to 'draw' or 'move', deliberately or by a configuration of circumstances.

In terms of literary contactuality in India, Gurudev Rabindranath Tagore is among the few to have influenced, and still does so, cultural and literary space with his discreet reception of other influences and his reception in India and beyond, in the last century. He influenced many an author of Indian languages during his life and even after. He could do so, as he was the receptacle of various cultural movements of his period. The range of his reception and ability to cast soothing influence may be measured from the fact that on the western Indian peninsula he influenced Zaverchand Meghani (1897-1947), his contemporary Saurashtrian Gujarati folk writer whom Mahatma Gandhi had hailed as the *rāṣṭrīya śāyara* (the National Poet). Meghani acknowledged Tagore's influence on his creativity to the extent that at the end of his poems he mentioned the title of Gurudeva's work that catalyzed his creativity, as might be discerned from his writings in *Saurashtra ni Rasadhar* (5 volumes).[6]

Tagore belonged to the rare category of philosopher artist. It made him concerned with the basic issues of the universe, man, the relation between the two that determined the place of man in the universe, creativity and the role of various cultural institutions without glossing over the major events of his period and seeing the relevance of cultural tradition bequeathed to him in terms of the events around him and the world. This made him *svastha* (literally 'healthy' but for me *sva+stha=* located in self, so culturally healthy) and *viśvastha* (located in the world) simultaneously; and so, despite being entrenched in his tradition, he could be the most comprehensive soul. These attributes attracted to him critical and creative minds from different languages like Nirala, who may be put in the category poet critic, a premise that both Tagore and Nirala shared, like John Dryden, William Wordsworth, S.T. Coleridge, Matthew Arnold and T.S. Eliot in the English critical

6. For discussion of Zaverchand Meghani, please see K.D. Kurkoti *Saurashtra ni Rasadhar*: A Critique", *Mīmāṁsā*, vol. 5, October, 2003 119-28; & Avadhesh Kumar Singh, "Megahani and His Poetic Concerns", *Mīmāṁsā*, vol. 5, October, 2003, pp. 106-18.

tradition. Apart from these, both of them were anchored in Indian intellectual and philosophical tradition enshrined in the Upaniṣads.

Nirala's reception of Tagore and Tagore's reception of the Western ideas is a meaningful study of reception in Indian literature. In the tradition of the Ṛgvedic hymn *ā no bhadrāḥ kratu yantu viśvataḥ*, Tagore interacted with the noble thoughts of his cultural and the other European traditions without being blown off his feet. His reception of the European Romantic movement that Ipshita Chanda has carefully delineated in her book, is a case in view. He did not receive it as a lump but with discrimination.

Reception is based on the basic premise that the world of ideas needs foreign element as a catalyst for its enhanced poetic creativity. Nirala had realized the significance of 'foreign elements for reform' and of intermingling of diverse thoughts and feelings to strengthen process of creation.

> We are aware that those areas of our land in which the languages are deemed to be relatively rich and strong have become thus only because foreign elements have mingled with them. The influence of those elements have irradiated the native elements and multiplied the native forms a thousandfold, just as the rays of a single sun contain all the brilliant colours of the rainbow.
>
> — *Nirālā Racanāvalī* 1999: V.5: 449

As an evidence, he had been a witness to the interface between Kabīr, the *bhakti* poet whose *pada*s he had translated and Tagore, the European Romanticists and Tagore, and Tagore and W.B. Yeats and its fruitful consequences. He realized it against the linguistic jingoism preached by ghettoized nativists, particularly in Hindi, who swaggered around the linguistic realities as if they 'owned' Hindi, and equated Hindi to Uttar Pradesh, i.e. UP. Against such linguistic nationalism, he wrote:

> In some periodicals the verses of unknown poets dating from four to five hundred years in the past are printed on the cover in order to protect "UPness" and the editor does not even hesitate to actively spread such "UPness," as if he wants to preserve the UP of 400 years ago for another 400 years in the future, and

> thus, do Hindi a great service. —Ibid.: 461

Equipped with this realization of the importance of mutual illumination in the world of ideas and creativity, Nirala was qualified to receive the best from others (Bengali and Tagore) for strengthening his creativity in particular, and of Hindi in general. Having been born and brought up in Mahishadal in Bengal before his advent to the Hindi world in Lucknow in the 1920s, he was well exposed to the inner rhythm, musicality and power of Bengali. His admiration for Tagore was based on his worthiness (*yogyatā*) as he has studied Tagore the poet and found him "the foremost practitioner of the art of poetic composition in the whole world" (ibid.: 29), as he substantiated his statement:

> His rhythm is replete with endless variations and awash with innumerable sweet waves of musicality that lap against the craggy cliffs of the west and cause them to erode and crumble — in place of high and low, there prevailed harmony. — Idem

His *Ravīndra-Kavita-Kānan* (The Garden of Ravindra's Poetry), having transl(iter)ation of Tagore's poems with a biographical introduction, is Nirala's tribute to his understanding of the poet.

Reception is a history of odyssey of ideas — literary and non-literary, from one land to another. Neither *ādāna* nor *pradāna* is stigmatic, if it is practised with discretion, as Nirala had stated in poetic terms, as stated in the epigraph, to be transacted in a state of *jñāna* (knowledge). To achieve it, *viveka* (discretion) is needed whose process, not definition is metaphorically articulated in the term *nīra-kṣīra-viveka* (the ability to distinguish between *nīra*, i.e. water and *kṣīra*, i.e. milk). It is said that the swan, when offered milk and water, drinks only milk and leaves behind water. The metaphor needs to be read a little carefully. It seems to propose a hierarchy in which milk is superior to water. It is against the fact, for water is equally important, may be more so in certain circumstances, as a thirsty person may even lose his/her life. Water, not milk or victuals made of milk, would really quench his/her thirst. The swan does not devour the mixture of milk or water as a lump but takes only what suits it. A competent comparatist is a swan who has to become a reality rather than remaining a myth.

Let me broaden the scope of reception by taking recourse to the views of Munshi Premchand, the celebrated Hindi novelist and a contemporary of Tagore and Nirala, who had his views on reception (*ādāna-pradāna*) between Bengali-Hindi. Discussing the influences that impacted the Hindi novel in the second half of the nineteenth century in his article "Upanayas" (published in *Samalochak*, January 1925), he deals with the popularity of translation of European detective novels and their publication in Hindi. It was expected that original novels would be written in Hindi but:

> . . . the tide of Bengali novels intervened and is still on. Whatever novels — good or bad — were available in Bangla were translated without proper consideration. I have no objection against enriching the treasure of one's own with the jewels of some other language because rich languages keep translating works of other languages into them. However, is a language worth it if it has nothing that is its own but only translations? From this perspective, *Candrakāntā Santati* emerges as a work of much significance. At least it is our own work. Our objective is to make Hindi a national language, but can the seat of the national language be attained by mere translations? . . .
>
> Moreover, when we see that a Hindi knowing person can pick up so much knowledge of Bangla that he can understand general books of Bangla, then there is no point in translating Bangla works in Hindi. If we have to translate, why not translate from languages richer than Bangla? . . . It is imperative for our young minds who want to serve literature that they learn European languages and pack the treasure of Hindi with their jewels. They would be able to give us a few things that are otherwise unattainable through other means.
>
> — Premchand in Singh & Mukherjee, 2005: 79-80

Though these views pertain to the interaction between Hindi and Bengali novel in the last quarter of the ninteenth century and onwards, it is possible to infer some insights that might be useful for reception studies in India. Premchand was fairly exposed to Bengali literature in Varanasi that has had a strong presence of Bengali cultural community for long. His principal intent is to enrich and establish his Hindi language and literature, and is willing to receive Bangla and other languages, not through just translation but through inborn richness of his own language. Sounding as a linguistic nationalist, he considers *Candrakāntā Santati* 'a work of much significance', for it is 'our own work'. (Incidentally, he had in the preceding part of the same essay, not thought very high about *Candrakāntā Santati*, for it was to him a 'mere imitation of *Tilism Hoshuruba*' of Urdu.) He was intent upon enriching Hindi with the best in the world, without sacrificing its specificity as well. Indiscriminate reception and explosion of influence are equally dangerous. Tagore interacted with other native and alien traditions and received the European influence without being blown off his own cultural foundations, and thus, cast his soothing influence on writers of his and subsequent generations.

Ipshita Chanda has discussed the interaction between Tagore and the West, Tagore and Nirala who, in the light of his reception of Tagore, lent a new direction to Chāyāvāda with his critical and creative interventions. She has, in the course of her case study, outlined the contours of Hindi literature from medieval times to the first decade of the twentieth century, as witnessed by him. She successfully brings out the contribution of Nirala to the Chāyāvāda movement in particular and Hindi literary tradition in general. She has discussed the development of Chāyāvāda in Hindi from Muktadhar Pandey (*Hindī meṅ Chāyāvāda* 1920) to Namvar Singh (*Chāyāvāda* 1955) via Ramchandra Shukla (Kavitā meṅ Chāyāvāda 1929), innovations by Chāyāvādī poets, and the acrimonious debate between Sumitra Nandan Pant, a leading practitioner of the Chāyāvāda School in Hindi and Nirala. Along with her critical consideration of development of Chāyāvāda as a movement, she has succinctly put together the interpretations of Hindi in English. She recognized not only the import of interliterary contactuality in India with reference to Bengali (Gurudeva Tagore) and Hindi ('Nirala'), but also for methodically studying its practice in India without over-sighting the intricacies of the Indian literary scenario. The study would help those who have been searching for a framework for intersystemic comparative literary study. However, Chanda's study of Tagore's criticism by Ramchandra Shukla needs to be explored, as she does not approve of it. Shukla is no sacrosanct, so is not Tagore. The influence of Bengali literature on Hindi or *ādāna-pradāna* between the two did not earn unequivocal approval from many Hindi scholars and creative writers. It was not merely out of anxiety of influence but due to the negative impact that it had at crucial junctures on Hindi literature, particularly in the first half of the twentieth century. Examined closely, there is no accusation against Tagore by Ram Chandra Shukla but against the practitioners of Chāyāvāda, who indiscreetly swore by and swallowed Tagore without understanding his vision and spirit. Shukla was not anti-Tagore but anti-Chāyāvādī who did not follow Nirala's guidelines for acceptance of influence in the illusion-free state of mind. By doing so, he tried to expose the inconsistencies and contradictions of the Chāyāvāda and exaggerated treatment given to the Bengali influence on the movement. He was in line with Premchand who, as discussed briefly in the present piece, censured the tendency of his Hindīwālās, who rather than capitalizing on the opportunity to experiment and carve a new Hindi novel in the last decades of the nineteenth century and the early part of twentieth century, followed Bengali novel as their model mindlessly.

Let me take the opportunity, caused by my meta/reading about/of interliterary relation between Tagore and Nirala, occasioned by the pre/text, to propose some response to the often-asked question about the possibility or reality of Indian School of Comparative Literature (ISCL). In terms of practice and its acceptance in the form of the discipline in academic institutions, at least now it exists in India, however frail and fragmented in the efforts it might appear to be. As the school and framework, there are many suggestions that have to become a reality. As one of the suggestions came from Professor Namvar Singh, the noted Hindi critic, who remarked in the course of his Valedictory Address on 30 March 2010, to the International Conference on Comaparative Literature, organized by Department of English & Comparative Literary Studies, Saurashtra University, Rajkot (28-30 March 2010) that ISCL can derive principles or methodology of comparison from the Alaṁkāra School of Sanskrit with a long tradition from Bharatamuni's *Nāṭyaśāstra* to Pandit Rewa Prasad Dwivedi's *Ālambrahma* (2005). Since the basic premise of *alaṁkāra* is comparison between the two objects, it is possible to see the validity of the proposition which gets further support from the proponents of other schools as well. For example, while discussing *upamā* (simile), Kṣemendra, the principal proponent of the *aucitya* (propriety or decorum) school, mentions *hṛdayasādṛśī upamā*. It means that the simile should have similitude of the core of comparison. It may be the first principle of comparative study. Else, it leads to comparative literary torture. These principles need to be inferred and developed which demand another occasion.

In the present context, another way of realizing and developing the principles of ISCL is to infer them from the writings of the competent ['careful' (responsible) and 'sensible' (empathizing and responsive)] practitioners of comparative study of literature, particularly poet critics or critic poets from different Indian languages like Tagore in Bengali, Nirala, Hazari Prasad Dwivedi in Hindi among others who might not have been fully aware of the discipline. Nirala compared poets and authors in Hindi, and Hindi authors with others from Indian and foreign languages. Keeping his Tagore-centric comparative study in view, it should be noted that he compared Tagore with P.B. Shelley in two of his essays,[7] Tagore with Tulsīdās, the *bhakti*, Tagore with Bihari, the

7. Nirala shared Tagore's admiration for Shelley who, for Tagore was "the creative mind which could only approach Truth through its joy in creative effort. For true creation is the realization of truth through the translation of it into your own symbols". (Cited in S.K. Das, *A History of Indian Literature* vol. IX, 1910-56, New Delhi: Sahitya Akademi, 1994, 501-02)

Rītikāla Hindi poet with full cognizance of similarity and dissimilarity in their time, location and tradition. He anticipated the questions pertaining to the justification of the comparative analysis of the two poets (Tulsīdās and Tagore) from two different periods in time, and responded to them. He admitted the fact that the external form of the poetry changes with changing times. He illustrated the case with the example of change from Sanskrit of the Vedic times to Brajabhāṣa via Pāli and concluded that the soul of poetry remained unchanged. So he concluded, "In this respect, we have every right to compare poets from different periods, in my opinion." (Nirala v.5: 287) Nirala's ability to see the similarity and difference, changing and unchanging elements, lent an insightful direction to his study in which he did not gloss over the subtleties of the compared individuals, works and issues, and saw them in terms of their traditions. Before comparing the philosophy of Shelley and Tagore, he saw the difference of definition and their meanings in their respective traditions:

> The definitions of philosophy extant in India and in Europe are very different. In India, the meaning of philosophy or *darśana* is to meet face to face, to behold the truth, not only to believe in it; but in Europe the quest of knowledge is called philosophy. Where there is a quest for knowledge there is no meeting, no *darśana*, and where there is a meeting, there is no quest.
>
> — Nirala v.5: 464

Like Tagore, Nirala is a model for comparative study marked by his radical rejection of singularity of literature through appreciation of 'good qualities' of other literature(s),[8] acknowledgement of inter-literariness between/among literary systems for mutual enrichment, recognition, with the exercise of discrimination, of catalytic elements/ideas to be accepted or renounced, comparative analysis of changing literary externalities and unchanging spirit

8. Nirala, as he himself noted, "had heartfelt devotion for the good qualities of European poetry; I acknowledge the power in their descriptions, but that from their descriptions, but that from their perspective, through comparative analysis". (*Racanāvalī* v.5: 202)

and their celebration. The ISCL, inferred from the practices from Tagore and Nirala among others, would rest on the *dīpaśikhā* model, a lamp with many lamps all around in all directions at different degrees and locations which, after being lighted give one light in all directions. It leads to synthesis of lights. The ISCL would believe in unconditional *sāmasikatā* (compoundness), and subscribe to the fact that nature has endowed human beings with two eyes, so that they should be used for seeing more than one literary system. The *sāmasikatā* or integration of the two or more, characterizing Indian culture and literature, leads to the generation of new thoughts and gives a new lease of life to the systems. It opens up, like the *trinetra* of Śiva, the 'third eye', the inclusive integrating vision.[9]

9. The third eye of Śiva is a combination of the two and even going beyond, the sixth sense, with an ability to see through by burning the gross and dross. Moreover, the *jñāna* (knowledge) is termed as the third eye of human beings in *Subhaṣita-Ratna-Sandoha* (p. 194), *gyānam tratiyam manujasya netram samasta tatvartha vilokadakṣam*.

APPENDIX A

Select List of Compositions in Sanskrit in the Post-Jagannatha Period

Name of the Author	*Father's/Teacher's Name*	*Place of Birth/Work*	*Period with Year*	*Works (including creative)*
Group (A)				
1. Rājacūḍāmaṇī Dīkṣit (Alaṁkāra)	Satyamangal Ratnakhet Shri Nivasadhavan (Father)	Tondira-Sursamudra	Later half of sixteenth century or First half of seventeenth century (1636)	1. *Yajuḥśākhāvyākhyā;* 2. *Daśopaniṣad Vyākhyā;* 3. *Śāstradīpikā Vyākhyā Karpūrvārttikā;* 4. *Dvādaśalakṣaṇī Vyākhyā Tantracintāmaṇi;* 5. *Saṁkarśa Muktāvalī;* 6. *Rucidattavṛttirnyāyacūḍāmaṇī;* 7. *Cintāmaṇidarpaṇam;* 8. *Śṛṅgāra Sarvasvanam Bhūnā Bhujacampu-purakoyyuddhakandaḥ;* 9. *Bhāratacampū;* 10. *Vṛttitārāvalī;* 11. *Ratnakhetvijayam;* 12. *Mañjubhūṣiṇī;* 13. *Rāmakṛṣṇadharmabhuvam Kathātrayī;* 14. *Śaṅkarācārya Tārāvalī;* 15. *Śaṅkarābhyudayam;* 16. *Kaṁsavadham;* 17. *Rukmiṇīpariṇayam;* 18. *Alaṁkāracūḍāmaṇi;* 19. *Citramañjarī;*

				20. *Kāvyadarpaṇam;* 21. *Raghunāthabhūpavijaya;* 22. *Kāntinatipariṇayam;* 23. *Sāhityasāmrājyam;* 24. *Advaitacintāmaṇī.* (inclusive of creative works)
2. Bhūdev Śukla (Alaṁkāra)	Shukdev/Sukdev (Father) Śrīkanṭh Dixit (Teacher) Ram/Rama (Teacher)	Jambusar (Gujarat)	Later half of seventeenth century	1. *Rasavilāsa;* 2. *Rukmiṇīvilāsa;* 3. *Rāmacarit;* 4. *Dharmavijaya;* 5. *Ātmatattva Pradīpa;* 6. *Īśvaravitasdīpikā;* 7. *Taraṅgiṇī.*
3. Rāmdeva Ciranjīva Bhaṭṭācārya	Rāghvendra Satavhan (Father) Raghudev Nyāyālaṁkāra (Teacher)	Gauḍ Region	Around CE 1731	1. *Kāvyavilāsa;* 2. *Mādhavacampu;* 3. *Śṛṅgāratatinī;* 4. *Vṛtratnāvalī;* 5. *Kalpalatā;* 6. *Śivastotra;* 7. *Vidvānmodataraṅgiṇī.*
4. Viśveśvara Bhaṭṭa Paṇḍit (Alaṁkāra School)	Laxmidhara (Teacher & Father) Yaśodhara (Teacher)	Patia, Almora (Uttar Pradesh)	First half of eighteenth century or 1675-1715 (Jagannath Joshi)	1. *Alaṁkārakaustubha;* 2. *Kāvyāratnam;* 3. *Ātmakaramuktāvalī;* 4. *Ātmakarapradīpa;* 5. *Rasacandrikā;* 6. *Kavīndrakarṇābharaṇam* (with commentary); 7. *Samañjasa Rasamañjarī* (commentary);

Name of the Author	*Father's/Teacher's Name*	*Place of Birth/Work*	*Period with Year*	*Works (including creative)*
				8. *Lakṣmīvilāsakāvyam;* 9. *Romāvalīśatakam;* 10. *Vakṣojasaṣṭakam;* 11. *Holikāśatakam;* 12. *Rītivarṇanam;* 13. *Navamālikā* (play); 14. *Śṛṅgāramañjarī* (commentary); 15. *Siddhāntasudhānidhi Darśana;* 16. *Tattvacintāmaṇi-Didhītipraveśa;* 17. *Tarkakutūhalam;* 18. *Āryasaptaśatī;* 19. *Kāvyatilakam* (commentary); 20. *Naiṣadha-kāvya Ṭīkā;* 21. *Mandāramañjara Gadyakāvya* (commentary); 22. *Āryaśatakam;* 23. *Mandāramañjarī Kathā;* 24. *Abhirāmarāghava;* 25. *Bhāvapradīpa.*
5. Narasiṁha Kavi "Abhinava Kālidāsa" (Nāṭyaśāstra)	Śivarāma (Father & Teacher) Yogānanda (Teacher)	Mysore (Alur) (Charmrey-Mahisur)	Later half of of eighteenth century	1. *Nañjarājayaṣobhūṣaṇa;* 2. *Candrakalākalyāṇa.*
6. Vidyārāma (Alaṁkāra Nāṭyaśāstra)	Veṇīrāma Vajrapati	Pasuñja (Ahmedabad)/ Udayapur, Koṭā	Around-1706	1. *Rasadīrghikā* (1906).

7. Āśādhara Bhaṭṭa II (Alaṁkāra)	Rāmjī Bhaṭṭa (Teacher & Father) Dharaṇīdhara (Teacher)	Pija Vaso-Patapatan, Badodara (South Gujarat)	Mid seventeenth century (1674-1754) Nāgeśa Bhaṭṭa first half of eighteenth century	1. *Alaṁkāradīpikā;* 2. *Kavidānanda* (commentary); 3. *Triveṇikā;* 4. *Prabhāpaṭala;* 5. *Advaita Viveka;* 6. *Āśādharī* (Nyāya); 7. *Rasikāmanda* (Alaṁkāra-Śāstra); 8. *Vṛtti* of Mallinātha's Commentary on *Kirātārjunīya;* 9. *Kuvalayānandakārikāṭīkā;* 10. *Vyākaraṇakārikā;* 11. *Punarāvṛttivivecana.*
8. Bhaṭṭa Deva "Purohit" (Alaṁkāra)	Nahanabhai (Teacher) Bāla Kṛṣṇānanda Sarasvatī (Teacher)	Raner (Rander-Surat) Wrah Pattan (Olpad)	Around 1765-66	1. *Alaṁkārmañjūṣā;* 2. *Viśvasrai Yuddhavarṇana;* 3. *Amaruśataka Vyākhyā.*
9. Venīdutt Śarman (Alaṁkāra/Rasa)	Jagannatha Sharma	Tribhukti (Tirhuti)	Later half of eighteenth century	1. *Rasakaustubha* (Rasa); 2. *Alaṁkāramañjarī;* 3. *Virudāvalī.*
10. Acyut Rai Śarman "Modak" (Kāvya-Śāstra)	Śrī Nārāyaṇa Śāstrī (Teacher) Nārāyaṇa (Father)	Pañcavaṭī, Nasik	Nineteenth century	1. *Sāhityasāra* (1831); 2. *Bhagīrathacampū;* 3. *Kṛṣṇalīlāmṛta;* 4. *Nirañjanamañjarī;* 5. *Advaitāmṛtamañjarī;* 6. *Nītiśotpatra;* 7. *Praṇaya Prakāśa* (commentary); 8. *Pañcadaśī* (commentary); 9. *Advaitarājyalakṣmī;*

Name of the Author	Father's/Teacher's Name	Place of Birth/Work	Period with Year	Works (including creative)
				10. *Advaitavidyāvinoda;* 11. *Avaidikamatatiraskāra;* 12. *Īśadeśakavivivecanamañjarī;* 13. *Gītaśataśatī;* 14. *Gauḍalaharī;* 15. *Jīvanamuktivivekavyākhyā;* 16. *Mahāvākyārthamañjarī;* 17. *Viṣṇupadalakṣaṇam;* 18. *Kaṇṭhastavaḥ;* 19. *Saudhayagyakalpadruma.*
11. Śrīkṛṣṇa Kavi (Kṛṣṇa Sharman or Kṛṣṇavadhūta)	Vasudevyogeśvar (Teacher)	Guhapur	Later half of nineteenth century (1835-1909)	1. *Mandāramarandacampū;* 2. *Kāvyālakṣaṇa;* 3. *Rasaprakāśa-Kāvyaprakāśa* (commentary); 4. *Sārasvatālaṁkāra Sūtra & Kāvyaprakāśa Bhāṣya* (commentary).
12. Śrīkṛṣṇa Brahmatantra Parakala (Kṛṣṇa-mācārya Vakīl) (Alaṁkāra)	Tatacārya (Father)	Mahisur (Parakal Vaishnavanath Amidela)	1839-1916	1. *Alaṁkāramaṇihāra;* 2. *Alaṁkārikā;* 3. *Tattavanirṇayavidhi* (1890); 4. *Raṅgarājavilāsacampū;* 5. *Kārttikotsavadīpikācampū;* 6. *Śrīnivāsavilāsacampū;* 7. *Uttarāṅgamāhātmya;* 8. *Rāmeśvarābhijaya;* 9. *Nṛsiṁhavilāsa;*

				10. *Madanagopālamāhātmya;* 11. *Piyūṣalaharī;* 12. *Haṁsasandeśa* and other compositions.
Group (B) 1. Sundaramiśra Añjagiri			Later half of fifteenth century and the first half of the sixteenth century	1. *Nāṭyapradīpa* (CE 1613); 2. *Abhirāmamaṇi Nāṭaka* (1599).
2. Viśvanātha Dev (Śarmā)	Trimaldev (Father)	Dharasur (S. India), Later came to Varanasi	Sixteenth century	1. *Citra Mīmāṁsā;* 2. *Mṛgāṅkalekha*
3. Narahari (Rasa Theory/ Alaṁkāra)	Jagadamūrti Nādamūrti (Teacher)	Vijapur	1580-1627	1. *Navarasamañjarī.*
4. Aruṇa Giri (Alaṁkāra/ Kāvya-Śāstra)	Śeśādri (Father) Veṅkaṭdri (Teacher)	Koladeśa, Uttar Bimbali (Vatakkunkur)	Later half of sixteenth century and first half of seventeenth century	1. *Godavarmayaśobhūṣaṇa.*
5. Sudhindrayogin (Yati)	Vijayendra Yati (Teacher)	Tanjore	First half of seventeenth century	1. *Alaṁkāranikāśa;* 2. *Alaṁkāramañjarī* (commentary); 3. *Śubhadrāpariṇaya* (Nāṭaka).

Name of the Author	Father's/Teacher's Name	Place of Birth/Work	Period with Year	Works (including creative)
6. Kṛṣṇa Dīkṣita or Kṛṣṇa Yajvan		Tanjore	Seventeenth century	1. *Raghunātha Bhūpālaniya;* 2. *Alaṁkāramuktāvalī.*
7. Yogyanārāyaṇa Dīkṣita	Govind Dīkṣita (Father)	Tanjore	Seventeenth century	1. *Alaṁkāra Ratnākara;* 2. *Sāhityaratnākara;* 3. *Raghunātha-Bhūpavijaya;* 4. *Raghunāthvilāsa Nāṭaka.*
8. Viśvanātha Nyāya (Siddhānta) Pañcavan	Kāśīnātha Vidyā-Nivās Bhaṭṭācārya (Father) Raghunātha Śiromaṇi (Teacher)	Navadīp (Bengali)		1. *Alaṁkārapariskāra;* 2. *Bhāṣāpariccheda* (1634); 3. *Piṅgala Prakāśikā;* 4. *Nyāyasūtravṛtti;* 5. *Padārtha-Tattvaloka;* 6. *Nyāsatantrabodhinī;* 7. *Subartattavaloka.*
9. Bālakṛṣṇa Bhaṭṭa (Alaṁkāra)	Govardhan Bhaṭṭa (Father)		1625-1700	1. *Alaṁkārasāra* (1702).
10. Kṛṣṇabhaṭṭa (Kāvya-Śāstra)			Seventeenth century	1. *Praśnamālā.*
11. Kavicandra (Alaṁkāra)	Kavi Karnapur (Father)	Dirgakgram	Sixteenth or seventeenth century	1. *Kāvyacandrikā;* 2. *Cikitsāratnāvalī;* 3. *Sāralaharī;* 4. *Dhātucandrikā.*
12. Mauni Kṛṣṇa Bhaṭṭa	Raghunāth Bhaṭṭa (Father)			1. *Vṛttidīpikā.*

13. Akabashah "Bade Saheb" (Nāyaka-Nāyikā)	Shahraj (Father)		1646-1672/75	1. *Śṛṅgāramañjarī* (tr. *Akbarasāhiśṛṅgāramañjarī*).
14. Śonthimar Bhaṭṭāraka (Alaṁkāra)			Seventeenth century	1. *Rasasudhānidhi*.
15. Mathurā Prasād (Kāvya-Śāstra)	Badarīnāth	Distt. Hardoi (UP)	1878?	1. *Kavitārahasyam*.
16. Lakṣmīdhara (Laxman Sūri) Dakṣiṇāmūrti Kiṅkar (Kāvya-Śāstra)	Yogeśwar (Father) Koṇḍubhaṭṭa (Teacher)	Cherikuri (Krishna river Andhra Pradesh)	Mid-seventeenth century	1. *Alaṁkāramuktāvalī*; 2. *Rasamañjarī*; 3. *Bharataśāstragrantha*; 4. *Ṣaḍbhāṣācandrikā* (Prākṛt Vyākaraṇa); 5. *Anaṅgarāghavaṭīkā*; 6. *Prasannarāghava Ṭīkā*; 7. *Gītagovinda* (commentary).
17. Raghunātha		Tanjore	1675-1792	1. *Sāhitya Kutūhala* (Citrakāvya).
18. Samrāja Dikṣita (Śyāmarāja)	Narahari Bindu Purandar (Father)	Mathura	Later half of seventeenth century	1. *Śṛṅgārāmṛtalaharī*; 2. *Sudāmācarita* (Nāṭaka 1681); 3. *Ratikallolinī* (1719); 4. *Akṣaragumphā*; 5. *Āryatriśati*; 6. *Dhūrtanartaka Prahasana*.
19. Gokulnath Maithil (Alaṁkāra)	Pitambar "Vidyānidhi" (Father)	Magarauni (Madhuvani)	After 1650	1. *Raśmicakrama*; 2. *Ālokavivaraṇam*; 3. *Nyāyasiddhāntatattva*; 4. *Devakālanirūpaṇam*;

Name of the Author	Father's/Teacher's Name	Place of Birth/Work	Period with Year	Works (including creative)
				5. *Lāghavagauravarahasyam;* 6. *Kusumāñjalivivaraṇam;* 7. *Padavākyaratnākara;* 8. *Khaṇḍanakuṭhara;* 9. *Kundakādambarī;* 10. *Kādambarīpradīpa;* 11. *Kādambarīkīrtiślokaḥ;* 12. *Kādambarīpraśnottaramālā;* 13. *Kāvyaprakāśavivaraṇam;* 14. *Rasamahārṇava;* 15. *Śivastuti;* 16. *Vṛttataraṅgiṇī;* 17. *Śuddha-vivekaḥ;* 18. *Masamīmāṁsā* (1709); 19. *Sūktimuktāvalī;* 20. *Madālasā Nāṭakam;* 21. *Amṛtodayanāṭakam;* 22. *Viśiṣṭavaiśiṣyabodhaḥ.*
20. Caturbhuja (Kāvyaśāstra)				1. *Rasakalpadruma* (1689).
21. Veṅkat Kṛṣṇa		Tanjore	Seventeenth century	1. *Śabdabhedanirūpaṇam.*
22. Narsinh (Alaṁkāra)		Tanjore	1684-1710	1. *Guṇaratnākara;* 2. *Śivanārāyaṇabhañjamahodaya.*

23. Nārāyaṇa		Tanjore	Later half of seventeenth century	1. *Śabdabhedanirūpaṇa.*
24. Rāmabhadra Dixit		Tanjore	Later half of seventeenth century	1. *Śabdaśaktinirūpaṇa.*
25. Vīreśwar Paṇḍit Bhaṭṭacārya "Śrivar"	Lakṣmana		Seventeenth century	1. *Rasaratnāvalī.*
26. Indrajīt (Alaṁkāra)				1. *Rāmacandracandrikā* (1712); 2. *Rasikapriya* (Hindi).
27. Sukhadeva			Seventeenth century	1. *Śṛṅgāralatā.*
28. Bhāva Miśra (Alaṁkāra)	Miśra Bhaṭak		Seventeenth century	1. *Śṛṅgārasārasī.*
29. Śrīkara Miśra			Later half of eighteenth century	1. *Alaṁkāratilaka.*
30. Bhāskar Miśra			Later half of eighteenth century	1. *Sāhityadīpikā.*
31. Subuddhi Miśra			Later half of seventeenth century	1. *Tattva Parīkṣā;* 2. *Kāvyālaṁkārasūtravṛtti* (Vyākhyā).

Name of the Author	*Father's/Teacher's Name*	*Place of Birth/Work*	*Period with Year*	*Works (including creative)*
32. Kāmarāja Dīkṣita	Swarāj Dīkṣita (Father)	Varanasi	Later half of seventeenth century	1. *Kāvyenduprakāśa* (Nāṭyaśāstra); 2. *Rasanirṇaya* (Alaṁkāra).
33. Rāmānandapati "Vividhardhya Tripāṭhī (Camatkāra) Parangam"	Madhukar Tripāṭhī (Father)	Varanasi	Later half of the seventeenth century	1. *Caturbhūjāṣṭaka Stotra* (1666); 2. *Vedārthamantrasaṁgraha;* 3. *Tattvadīpikā;* 4. *Tarkagumphana;* 5. *Liṅgānuśāsanam;* 6. *Śyāmastavarājaḥ;* 7. *Kālaprātrividhāṇam;* 8. *Guhyasodhavivaraṇam;* 9. *Rasikajīvanam;* 10. *Padyapiyūṣam;* 11. *Rāmacaritram;* 12. *Dhanyāṣṭakam;* 13. *Śaśāṅkaśatakam;* 14. *Hāsyasāgaraḥ;* 15. *Kāśīkutūhalam;* 16. *Kīrātabhāvadīpikāḥ;* 17. *Kāvyaprakāśaprakṛtārtha.*
34. Kṛṣṇa Sūrī	Gopālācārya	Tanuku (Dist.)		1. *Alaṁkāramīmāṁsā;* 2. *Sāhityakalpalatīkā.*
35. Gadādhara Bhaṭṭa	Gauripati (Girīśa)	Mithilā	Between fifteen and	1. *Rasīka Jīvana* (1670).

			seventeenth centuries	
36. Kāśī or Kāśīkarkavi Lakṣmaṇakavi		Tanjore	End of seventeenth or beginning of eighteenth century	1. *Alaṁkāragrantha.*
37. Sudhākara Mahāśabde			1699-1743	1. *Sāhityasārasaṁgraha.*
38. Rāmacandra Vāgīśa	Vidyānidhi	Bengali	Eighteenth century	1. *Kāvyacandrikā.*
39. Venidatta Śarman Tarkavāgīśa Bhaṭṭācārya "Śrīvar"	Viśveśvar "Śrīvar"		1583 (Kane) eighteenth century (Davasthalī)	1. *Alaṁkāracandrodaya;* 2. *Rasikarañjanī* (Commentary).
40. Bhīmasena Dīkṣita	Śivānanda			1. *Alaṁkārasāroddhāra;* 2. *Ratnāvalī Ṭīkā;* 3. *Sudhāsāgara;* 4. *Alaṁkārasthiti;* 5. *Kāvyaprakāśa* (Commentary 1723).
41. Hari Prashad Māthur	Mathur Mishra Gangesh or Gangeshwar			1. *Kāvyārthagumphā* (vs 1775); 2. *Kāvyāloka* (1728).
42. Jagannāth Miśra			Later half of eighteenth century	1. *Rasakalpadruma.*

Name of the Author	*Father's/Teacher's Name*	*Place of Birth/Work*	*Period with Year*	*Works (including creative)*
43. Shambhūnath				1. *Alaṁkāralakṣaṇānī.*
44. Citradhara	Mahamahopadhyay Vaṁśadhara	Mithilā Mangoroni (Darbhaṅgā)	Later half of eighteenth century	1. *Śṛṅgārasāriṇī;* 2. *Vīrataraṅgiṇī.*
45. Gaṅgārāma Jadi	Nārāyaṇa Jadi (Father) Śrīlakaṇṭha (Teacher)	Vārāṇasī	1775-1850	1. *Maṇimālā* (unavailable); 2. *Naukā-Rasataraṅgiṇīṭīkā;* 3. *Rasamīmāṁsā* (vs 1808); 4. *Tātparyaṭīkā* (vs 1830); 5. *Gaurīkasūtrāṇī.*
46. Sadāśiva Makhin (Dīkṣit)	Chokkanath	Kerala	1724-1798	1. *Bālarāmāyaṇava-Rāmavarmayaśobhūṣaṇam;* 2. *Vasulakṣmī* (Nāṭaka).
47. Kalyāṇa Subrahmaṇya Suri (Kotyayana)	Subrahmaṇya	Pirungal-Ponnali-South Malabar	1724-1798 around	1. *Alaṁkārakaustubha* (with commentary).
48. Yaśasvī Kavi	Gopala			1. *Sāhitya Kautūhala* (1730); 2. *Ujjvalapada* (Commentary).
49. Sukhalā Miśra (Father) Gaṅgeśa Miśra, Hari Prasād Māthur (Teacher)	Bābūrām/Bābūrāī			1. *Śṛṅgāramālā* (1801).

APPENDIX B

Select List of Texts in Sanskrit in the Post-Jagannatha Period

Title of Work	Author/Editor	Publisher/Year
1. *Nāñjārjuna Yaśobhūsaṇa*	Narsiṁha Kavi Abhinavakālidāsa ed. E. Krishnamacarya	Orient Institute, Baroda, 1930
2. *Rāmavarmayaśobhūṣaṇa*	Sadasiva	Travancore Archaeological Series, vol. 18
3. *Kāvyakalānidhi*	Krishnasudhi	Shri Ramvilas Press, Madras, 1893
4. *Apparāya Yaśaścandrodaya*	Aaanivilla Vekatashastri	Shri Bhairav Press, Madras, 1915
5. *Sāhityakalpadruma*	Narayana	- - -
6. *Kāvyakaustubha Sāhitya Kaumudī*	Baldeva Vidyabhusana	Kavyamala Bombay 63, Commentary, 1897
7. *Kāvyakaustubha*	Baldeva Vidyabhusana tr. Haridas	Navdeep, Bengal, 1957
8. *Kāvyenduprakāśa*	Kamraj tr. Babulal Shukla	Chowkhambha Series 1966
9. *Sāhityasāra*	Acyutacarya Modak tr. Vasudev Laxmana Pansikar	Nirnaya Sagar Press, Bombay
10. *Alaṁkārakaustubha*	Visveswara Pandita	Kavyamala 166, 1898
11. *Alaṁkāramuktāvalī*	Visveswara Pandita	Chaukhamba Sanskrit Series, 1927
12. *Alaṁkāra Pradīpa*	Visveswara Pandita	Chaukhamba Sanskrit Series
13. *Alaṁkāra Mañjūṣā*	Deva Sankara ed. S.L. Kotie	Scindia Oriental Series 1, Ujjain 1940
14. *Alaṁkāra Muktāvalī*	Kṛṣṇācārya	Satyadhyana Vidyapitha, Belgaum
15. *Alaṁkāra Muktāvalī*	Hamsasudhi	Arsa Press, Visakhapattnam, 1897
16. *Kṛṣṇabhūpālīya*	. . . . .	Govt. Press, Mysore 1931
17. *Alaṁkāramaṇihāra*	Sri Krishna Parkalyati	Oriental Research Institute, Mysore (Govt. Library Series Mysore)

Title of Work	Author/Editor	Publisher
18. *Kāvyavilāsa*	Ramdev; eds. Batuknath Sharma and Jagannatha Shastri	Saraswati Bhavan Banaras no. 16, 1925. (Govt. Sanskrit Library, Banaras)
19. *Śṛṅgāramañjarī*	Akbar Shah "Bade Sahab" ed. V. Raghavan	Archaeology Department, Hyderabad State, 1951
20. *Rasacandrikā*	Madhusudan Kavindra ed. S.N.G. Shastri	Vishva Bharati, 1969
21. *Rasacandrikā*	Visveswara Pandita	Chaukhamba, Banaras, 1962
22. *Rasaratnākara*	Shivarama Tripathi	Kavyamala, 6, Bombay
23. *Rasavilāsa*	ed. Premlata Sharma	Poona Oriental Book House Poona, 1952
24. *Rasamahārṇava*	Gokulanatha Maithila; tr. Dharmanatha Jha and Kumudanatha Mishra	Kavyamala, Bombay
25. *Śṛṅgārāmṛtalaharī*	Kamraja Dixita	Kavyamala Guchchhaka 14, Bombay
26. *Rasamīmāṁsā*	Gangaram Jadiv	Kashi Sanskrit Series Banaras, 1885 Lalbahadur Shastri Kendriya Sanskrit Vidyapeeth, New Delhi
27. *Kovidānanda*	Asadhara Awasthi	Pub. in Dr. Brahmamitra second Gucchaka
28. *Triveṇika* [Summarised *Kovidānanda*]	Asadhara	Saraswati Bhavan Series, form of Banaras 1925; Bharatiya Sahitya Vidyalaya, Varanasi
29. *Kavinda Karṇābharaṇa*	Visveswara Pandita	Kavyamala Part VIII, 1891
30. *Kāvyacandrikā*	Nyayavagisa	Venkateshwar Press, Bombay, 1912
31. *Kāvyadarpaṇa* (vols. I, II)	Rajacudamani Dixit tr. T.K. Bala-subramaniam	Vani Vilas Publishing House, Srirangam
32. *Kāvyavilāsa*	Ciranjiva Bhattacharya tr. Pandita Batuknatha Sharma and Jagannatha Shastri	Govt. Sanskrit Library, Saraswati Bhavan, Banaras
33. *Rasadīpikā*	Vidyarama	Rajasthan, Puratattwan-

Title of Work	Author/Editor	Publisher
	tr. Pandit Behura	veshan Mandir, Jodhpur Gopalanarayana (Rajasthan)
34. *Rasakaustubha*	Venidatta Sarman tr. Lekhnatha Sharma	. . . .
35. *Alaṁkāra Mañjarī*	Venidatta Sharma tr. Badrinatha Jha	Mithila Sanskrit Vidyapeeth
36. *Sāhityasudhāsindhu*	Vishwanatha Deva tr. Pandit Ramapratap	Bharatiya Vidya Bhavan, Delhi, 1968
37. *Navarasamañjarī*	Narahari; tr. P.G. Lalye	Hyderabad
38. *Godavarmayaśobhūṣana*	Arunagiri Kavi	The University Manuscripts Library, Trivandrum
39. *Vṛttidīpikā*	Maunikrishna Bhatta tr. Purushottama Sharma Caturvedi	Rajasthan Puratattwan-veshan Mandir, Jodhpur
40. *Rasika Jīvanam*	Ramananda Tripathi tr. Prof. Karunapati Tripathi	Sampurnanand Sanskrit Vishwavidyalaya, Varanasi, 1978
41. *Rasika Jīvanam*	Gadadhara Bhatta tr. Dr. Jatindra Vimala Choudhary	Sanskrit Kosh Kavya Sangrah Series 4
42. *Rasa Kalpadruma*	Jagannatha Mishra	Orissa Sahitya Akademi
43. *Śṛṅgārasāraṇī*	Citradhara	Triloknath Jha, Darbhanga 1965
44. *Kavikaustubha*	Raghunatha Manohar tr. Fateh Singh	Rajasthan Prachyavidya Pratishthana, Jodhpur, 1968
45. *Kāvya Kaumudī*	Haridasa Siddhanta Vagisa; tr. Bhavescandra Bhattacarya	Calcutta
46. *Sāhitya Bindu*	Chajjurama Shastri	Meherchanda Lachmandas, Delhi 1969
47. *Sāhitya Vimarśa*	Kautsa Uppala	Someswara Shri Venkateshwar Oriental Sharma Institute, 1951
48. *Jaipur ki Sanskrit Sāhitya ki Den*	Prabhashankar Shastri (in Hindi) (Bibliography)	. . . .

Title of Work	Author/Editor	Publisher
49. *Ādhunik Sanskrit Sāhitya*	Hiralal Shukla	. . . . .
50. *Alaṁkārarasamañjarī*	Kriste Narayana Shastri	Chaukhamba, Varanasi
51. *Alaṁkārarasamañjarī*	Gopala Shastri (with Hindi tr.)	Chaukhamba, Varanasi
52. *Kāvyālaṁkāra Koṭikā*	Revaprasada Dwivedi	Chaukhamba Surbharati, Varanasi, 1977
53. *Sāhityaratnākara*	Dharmayuti	Sanskrit Parishad, Hyderabad
54. *Abhinava Rasamīmāṁsā*	Brahmananda Sharma	Archana Prakashan, Ajmer 1975
55. *Śṛṅgārṇavacandrikā* (*Alaṁkāracandrikā*)	Vijayvarni, tr. Vaman Mahodaya Kulkarni	Bharatiya Gyanpeetha, Varanasi, 1969
56. *Rasa Ratnapradīpikā*	Allaraj; ed. R.N. Dandekar	Bharatiya Vidya Bhavan, 1945
57. *Alaṁkāra Saṁgraha*	Amritananda Yogi ed. P. Balakrishna Murti	Venkateshwara Oriental Series, Tirupati
58. *Akbarśāhi Śṛṅgāradarpaṇa*	Sundar Jain	Anoop Sanskrit Library, Bikaner
59. *Alaṁkāraśekhara*	Keshav Mishra	Chaukhamba Sanskrit Sahitya Series, Banaras
60. *Sāhitya Sāra*	Sarvesacarya	University of Travancore, 1948 (Trivandrum Sanskrit Series)
61. *Alaṁkāraratnākara*	Sobhakara Mishra; ed. C.R. Devadhara	Oriental Book Agency, Poona
62. *Alaṁkāramuktāvalī*	Visveswar Pandit; tr. Vishnuprasada Bhandari	Chaukhamba Sanskrit Book Depot
63. *Rasacandrikā*	Vishnuprasad Bhandari	Banaras

APPENDIX C

List of the Texts on Indian Poetics in the Post-Jagannatha Period

(A) PUBLISHED WORKS

1. Bhatta Devsankara Purohit, *Alaṁkāra Mañjūṣā.*
2. Narsiṁhakavi (Abhinava Kālidāsa), *Nāgārjunayaśobhūṣaṇam.*
3. Acyut Rai Sarman "Modak," *Sāhityasāra.*
4. Bhudeva Shukla, *Rasavilāsa.*
5. Rajacudamani Dikshit, *Kāvyadarpaṇa.*
6. Ramdeva Ciranjiva Bhattacarya, *Kāvyavilāsa.*
7. Visveswar Pandit "Bhatt," *Alaṁkārakaustubha.*
   ———, *Alaṁkāra Muktāvalī.*
   ———, *Rasacandrikā.*
8. Vidyarama, *Rasadīrghaka.*
9. Asadhara Bhatta, *Kovidānanda.*
   ———, *Triveṇikā.*
   ———, *Alaṁkāra Dīpikā.*
10. Venidutta Sarman, *Rasakaustubha.*
    ———, *Alaṁkāramañjarī.*
11. Srikrishna Kavi, *Maṇḍaramendacampū.*
12. Krishna Sarman, *Rasaprakāśa.*
13. Sivarama Tripathi, *Rasaramaṇī.*
14. Gangadhara Pandit, *Rasamīmāṁsā.*
15. Viswanath Deva, *Sāhityasudhāsindhu.*
16. Akbarshah, *Śṛṅgāra Mañjarī.*
17. Sanrama Dikshit, *Śṛṅgārāmṛta Laharī.*
18. Ramananda Yati Tripathi, *Rasikajīvana.*
19. Kamraja Dikshit, *Kāvyendu Prakāśa.*
20. Jagannatha Mishra, *Rasakalpadruma.*

21. Citradhara, *Śṛṅgāra Sāriṇī.*
22. Gangarama Jadi, *Rasamīmāṁsā.*
23. Baladeva Vidyabhushana, *Sāhitya Kaumudī.*

 ———, *Kāvyakaustubha.*

24. Venkatacarya Dixit, *Alaṁkāra Kaustubha.*
25. Raghunatha Manohara, *Kavi Kaustubha.*
26. Krishna "Sudhi," *Kāvyakalānidhi.*
27. Haridasa Siddhanta Vagisa, *Kāvyakaumudī.*
28. Sitarama Sastri, *Sāhityopadeśa.*
29. Chajjurama Sastri Vidyasagar, *Sāhitya Bindu.*
30. Kautsa Apala Someswara Sarma, *Sāhitya Vimarśa.*
31. Caturbhuja, *Rasakalpadruma.*
32. Amritananda Yogi, *Alaṁkārasaṁgraha.*

(B) UNPUBLISHED TEXTS

1. Rajacudamani Dixit, *Alaṁkāracūḍāmaṇī.*

 ———, *Kāvyadarpaṇa.*

2. Bhaskaracarya, *Sāhitya Kallolinī.*
3. Venkatanarayana, *Śṛṅgārasārāvalī.*
4. Sudhindra Yogini "Yati," *Alaṁkāranikāśa.*
5. Krishna Dikshit (Krishna Kavi), *Raghunātha Bhūpālīyā.*
6. Balakrishna Bhatta, *Alaṁkārasāra.*
7. Kavicandra, *Kāvyacandrikā.*
8. Laxmidhara Dikshit, *Alaṁkāramuktāvalī.*

 ———, *Rasamañjarī.*

9. Ghasirama Pandita, *Rasakaumudī.*
10. Anantaraya (Anantacarya), *Kavisamayakallola.*
11. Kollori Rajasekhara, *Alaṁkāramakaranda.*
12. Kanticandra Mukhopadhyaya, *Kāvyadīpikā.*
13. Ramasubramanyam Sastri, *Alaṁkāraśāstravilāsa.*

14. Kalyana Subramanya Suri, *Alaṁkārakaustubha.*
15. Narasimha, *Alaṁkārasāra.*
16. Ananta, *Sāhityavicāra.*
17. Tirumel Venkatacarya, *Rasamañjarī.*

(C) PUBLISHED TEXTS

Kavivar Venidatta, *Alaṁkāramañjarī*, ed. Kavisvar Badrinath Jha, Darbhanga: Mahila Institute of P.G. Studies and Research in Sanskrit.

Sri Krishna Bhatta, *Vṛttidīpikā*, Jaipur: Rajasthan Puratananveshan Mandir, 1956., 1st edn.

Sri Krishna Kavi, *Maṇḍaramandacampū*, 2nd edn., Mumbai: Nirnayasagar Press, 1924.

Sri Kamraj Dikshit, *Kāvya Suprakāśa* (seventeenth century), ed. Shri Bābulāl Sukla, Varanasi: Chaukhamba, 1966.

Sri Rupagoswamin, *Nāṭakacandrikā*, ed. with Hindi tr. and comm. Babulal Sukla, Varanasi: Chaukhamha Prakashana, 1964.

Sri Visveswar Pandey, *Alaṁkāramuktāvalī*, ed. Vishnuprasad Bhandari, Kashi: Chaukhambha Grantha Mala, Vidya Vilas Press, 1984.

Visvesvar Panday, *Rasacandrikā*, ed. Pandit Vishnuprasad Bhandari, Varanasi: Chaukhamba Series, Vidya Vilas Press, 1983.

(D) LIST OF SELECT WORKS ON ALAṀKĀRA SCHOOL OF INDIAN POETICS COMPOSED IN THE POST-JAGANNATHA PERIOD

(i) Sadasiva Mukhin, *Rāmavarmayaśobhūṣaṇa.*
(ii) Unknown author, *Alaṁkāramañjarī.*
(iii) Narayana, *Sāhitya Kalpasumana.*
(iv) Krishnadhi, *Kāvya Kalānidhi.*
(v) Cavali Ramsudhi, *Sāhityacintāmaṇī.*
(vi) Bhaskaracarya, *Sāhitya Kallolinī.*
(vii) Narasimhakavi, *Nāñjuayaśobhūṣaṇam.*
(viii) Rājaśekhara, *Sāhityakaumudī.*
(ix) Narsiṁhācārya, *Alaṁkārenduśekhare.*

(x) Balakrishna Bhatta, *Alaṁkārasāra.*

(xi) Baldeva Vidyabhushana, *Sāhityakaumudī.*

(xii) Hariprasada, *Kāvyāloka.*

(xiii) Venkamatya, *Alaṁkāramaṇidarpaṇa.*

(xiv) Kamraja Dikshit, *Kāvyenduprakāśa.*

(xv) Srinivasacarya, *Śabdālaṁkārasaṁgraha.*

(xvi) Devsukar Purohita, *Alaṁkāramañjūṣā.*

(xvii) Varadaraya, *Utprekṣāmañjarī.*

(xviii) Narasimha, *Guṇaratnākara.*

(xix) Indrajit, *Rasikapriya.*

(xx) Krishna Dikshit, *Raghunāthabhūpālīya.*

(xxi) Gangaram Jodi, *Rasataraṅgiṇī.*

(xxii) Gokulanatha Maithil, *Rūpamahārṇava.*

(xxiii) Candrakant Tarkalamkara, *Alaṁkārasūtramaṇi.*

(E) SELECT LIST OF INDIAN CRITICS WITH WORKS ON OR RELATED TO INDIAN POETICS IN INDIAN LANGUAGES IN THE TWENTIETH CENTURY

Laxminatha Bejbarua (Assamese).

Trailokyanatha Goswami (Assamese).

Mohit Majumdar (Bengali).

S.N. Dasgupta (Bengali).

Atulcandragupta (Bengali).

Ram Candra Shukla (Hindi).

Hazari Prasad Dwivedi (Hindi).

Nagendra (Hindi).

Nandadulare Vajpayee (Hindi).

Rewa Prasad Dwivedi (Hindi).

Ram Murti Tripathi (Hindi).

Anand Sankar Dikshit (Hindi).

Ramprasad Baxi (Gujarati).

Anandasankara Dhruva (Gujarati).

T. Venkataiyah (Kannada).

K.V. Puttappa (Kannada).

T.N. Srikanthaiya (Kannada).

Joseph Mundeshwari (Malayalam).

A.R. Rajraj Verma (Malayalam).

K. Murar (Malayalam).

K.N. Vatve (Marathi).

R.S. Josh (Marathi).

Upendra Bhanj (Oriya).

Nilkanthadas (Oriya).

Tolkappiyam (Tamil).

S. Kesavraja Mudaliyar (Tamil).

Pudumaippittan (Tamil).

M. Varadrajama (Tamil).

C. Raghunathan (Tamil).

K. Ramalinga Reddy (Telugu).

Viswanatha Narayana (Telugu).

G.V. Subramanyam (Telugu).

APPENDIX D

Select List of Works in Hindi on Indian Poetics in the Twentieth Century

Ramacandra Sukla, *Rasa Mīmāṁsā*, 1949.

Lakshminarayana Singh "Sudhansu," *Jīvan Ke Tattva aur Kāvya ke Siddhānta*, 1942.

Ramadehin Mishra, *Kāvya Mein Aprastuta Yojanā*, 1948.

Baldeva Upadhyaya, *Bhāratiya Sāhitya Śāstra*, Part II, 1948.

———, *Bhāratīya Sāhitya Śāstra*, Part I, 1950.

Gulabarai, *Siddhānta aur Adhyayana*, 1951.

Ramalal Singh, *Samīkṣā Darśana*, 1952.

Sitarama Caturvedi, *Samīkṣā-śāstra*, 1954.

S.P. Khatri, *Ālocanā, Itihāsa Tathā Siddhānta*, 1955.

Nagendra, *Bhāratīya Kāvyaśāstra kī Bhūmikā*, 1955.

Sri Vatakrishna, *Vīrarasa ke Śāstrīya Vivecana*, 1956.

Ramamurti Tripathi, *Vyañjanā aur Navīna Kavitā*, 1957.

Nagendra, *Rasa Siddhānta*, 1964.

Ramamurti Tripathi, *Aucityadarśana*.

Krishnadeva Jhari, *Rasa-Śāstra aur Sāhityasamīkṣā*, 1965.

Indra Pal Singh, *Śṛṅgāra Rasa kā Sāhitya Vivecana*, 1967.

Acarya Parasurama Caturvedi, *Śāntarasa*, 1967.

Siva Balak Roy, *Kāvya Mein Saundarya aur Udātta Tattva*, 1968.

Bhagiratha Misra, *Kāvya Mañjūṣā*, 1965.

Ramanaresa Verma, *Vakrokti aur Abhivyañjanā*, 1951.

Om Prakash, *Hindi Alaṁkāra Sāhitya*, 1956.

Bholasankara Vyasa, *Dhvani Sampradāya aur Uske Siddhānta*, 1956.

Suresacandra Gupta, *Hindi Kāvya Meiṅ Anyokti*, 1960.

Ananda Prakasa Dikshit, *Rasa Siddhānta Svarup Viśleṣaṇa*, 1960.

Manohar Kale, *Ādhunik Hindi Marathi meiṅ Kāvyaśāstra Adhyayan*, 1963.

Tarakanatha Bali, *Rasa Siddhānta ki Dārśanika aur Naitika Vyākhyā*, 1964.

Saccidananda Caudhary, *Hindi Kāvyaśāstra meiṅ Rasa Siddhānta*, 1965.

Krishnadeva Jhari, *Vibhatsa Rasa aur Hindi Sāhitya*, 1966.

Ramlakhana Shukla, *Sādhāraṇikaraṇa: Ek Śāstrīya Adhyayan*, 1967.

Nirmala Jain, *Rasa Siddhānta aur Saundarya Śāstra*, 1967.

Kumar Vimal, *Saundaryaśāstra ke Tattva*, 1967.

Ramswarth Caudhary, *Madhur Rasa Svarūpa aur Vikāsa*, 1968.

Desrajsingh Bhati, *Hindi mein Śabdālaṁkāra Vivecana*, 1961.

Gayaprasad Upadhyaya Sastri, *Dhvani Siddhānta aur Vyañjanāvṛtti*, 1970.

Ramvilas Sharma, *Saṁskṛti aur Sāhitya*, 1941.

Nagendra, *Kāvya Cintan*, 2nd edn., 1951.

Nagendra, *Vicāra aur Vivecana*, 2nd edn., 1956.

Babu Gulabrai, *Adhyayan aur Āsvād*, 1957.

Bibliography

Abhinavagupta, *Abhinavabhāratī*, ed. & tr. Acharya Vishveshvar, Delhi: University of Delhi, 1965 (Hindi).

———, *Lochana*, Delhi: Meharchand Lachhmandas, 1988.

Achebe, Chinua, *Things Fall Apart*, New Delhi: Allied Publishers, 1993.

Ādi, Śaṅkara, *Vivekacūḍāmaṇi*, Gorakhpur: Gita Press, 1932 (Sanskrit text with Hindi paraphrase).

Adorno, Theodor, "What Does Coming to Terms with the Past Mean?", in *Bitburg in Moral and Political Perspective*, ed. Geoffrey Hartman, Bloomington: Indiana University Press, 1986.

Agnimahāpurāṇam, English tr. M.N. Dutt, ed. & rev. Joshi K.L. Shastri, Delhi: Parimal Publications, 2 vols., 2005.

Ahmad, Aizaz, *In Theory: Classes, Nations, Literatures*, Delhi: Oxford University Press, 1994.

Albright, Daniel, ed., *Modernism and Music: An Anthology of Sources*, Chicago: University of Chicago Press, 2004.

Althusser, Louis, "Ideology and Ideological State Apparatuses", in *Lenin and Philosophy and Other Essays*, tr. Ben Brewster, New York: Monthly Review, 1971.

Ambedkar, Babasaheb, 1927a. *Bahishkrit Bharata*, 3 April 1927.

———, n.d., *"Buddha or Karl Marx"*, in *Dr. Babasaheb Ambedkar: Writings and Speeches*, vol. 3 compiled by Vasant Moon, Bombay: Education Department, Government of Maharashtra, 1987.

———, "Annihilation of Caste with a Reply to Mahatma Gandhi" (1936; 1944), in *Dr. Babasaheb Ambedkar: Writings and Speeches*, vol. 1. compiled by Vasant Moon, Bombay: Education Department, Government of Maharashtra, [1979] 1989.

———, "The Untouchables: Who Were They and Why They Became Untouchables?", in *Dr. Babasaheb Ambedkar: Writings and Speeches*, vol. 7, ed. Vasant Moon. Bombay Education Department, Government of Maharashtra, [1948] 1990.

Amiya Dev & S.K. Das, eds., *Comparative Literature: Theories and Practice*, Shimla: IIAS, 1989.

Anandavardhana, *Dhvanyāloka of Ānandavardhana*, 1974, tr. & ed. K. Krishnamoorthy, Delhi: Motilal Banarsidass, 2nd edn., 1981.

———, *The Dhvanyāloka with the Lochana of Abhinavagupta*, tr. Ingalls, Masson and Patwardhan, Harvard Oriental Series, vol. 49, 1990.

Anderson, Benedict, *Imagined Communities: Reflections on the Origin and Spread of Nationalism*, London: Verso, 1983.

Anirvan, Shrimant, "Vedic Exegesis", in *The Cultural Heritage of India* (*CHI*) Series, vol. I, Calcutta: Sri Ramakrishna Mission Institute, 1958, 1st edn. 1937.

Antin, David, "Modernism and Postmodernism", *Boundry*, 2, 1, 1972.

Appiah, Anthony, "Is the Post in Post-modernism the Post in Post-colonial?," *Critical Inquiry*, 17, Winter 1991.

Aristotle, In *Aristotle: Poetics; Longinus: On the Sublime; Demetrius: On Style*. tr. W. Hamilton Fyfe, Cambridge, MA and London: Harvard University Press/Heinemann, 1965.

———, *Poetics* and *Nichomachean Ethics*, in Jonathan Barnes, ed., *The Complete Works of Aristotle*, Princeton, N.J.: Princeton University Press, 1984.

Aranya, Swami Hariharananda, *Yoga Philosophy of Patanjali*, tr. P.N. Mukherjee, Calcutta: University of Calcutta, 1963.

Ashcroft, Bill, Gareth Griffiths, Helen Tiffin, *The Empire Writes Back*, London: Methuen, 1987.

Aurobindo, Sri, *The Renaissance in India*, Pondicherry: Sri Aurobindo Ashram, 1920.

———, *The Human Cycle*, Pondicherry: Sri Aurobindo Ashram Publication, 1943.

———, *Sri Aurobindo Birth Centenary Library Edition of Collected Works*, 30 vols., Pondicherry: Sri Aurobindo Ashram, 1970-72, *The Future Poetry* in vol. 9.

———, *India Rebirth: A Selection from Sri Aurobindo's Writings, Talks and Speeches*, Paris: Institut de Recherches Evolutives, Mysore: Mira Aditi, 1993.

Bagchi, Yogendra, *The Art of Philosophical Disputation*, *CHI*, Calcutta: Shri Ramakrishna Mission Institute, 1937.

Bagul, Baburao, *Dalit Sahitya: Aajche Kranti Vigyan*, Nagpur: Buddhist Publishing House, 1980.

Bakeless, John, *The Tragical History of Christopher Marlowe*, vols. I & II, Hamden Conneticut: Archon Books, 1964.

Bakhtin, Mikhail, "From the Prehistory of Novelistic Discourse", *The Dialogic Imagination: Four Essays* (1981), tr. Caryl Emerson and Michael Holquist. Also in *Modern Criticism and Theory: A Reader*, ed. David Lodge, London & New York, 1988, pp. 125-65.

Bana, *Harsa-Charita*, tr. E.B. Cowell & F.W. Thomas, Delhi: Motilal Banarsidass, 1968.

Barabash, Yuri, *Aesthetics and Poetics*, Moscow: Progress Publishers, 1977.

Barthes, Roland, "The Death of the Author", in *Modern Criticism and Theory: A Reader*, ed. David Lodge, London & New York, 1988.

Bayart, J.F., "Finishing with the Idea of the Third World: The Concept of the Political Trajectory", in *Rethinking Third World Politics*, Harlow: Longman, 1994.

Beardsley, Monroe C., *Aesthetics*, New York: Harcourt, Brace and World, 1958

———, "The Metaphorical Twist", in *Philosophy and Phenomenological Research* 22 March, 1962.

———, "Metaphor" in *Encyclopedia of Philosophy*, ed. Paul Edwards, New York: Macmillan, 1967.

Belvalkar, S.K. tr., *Kāvyādarśa*, Poona: Oriental Book Agency, 1924.

Benedict, Ruth, *Race and Racism*, London, New York: G. Routledge, 1942, p. 175.

Benjamin, Walter, *Illuminations*, London: Fontana, 1973.

Berger, M., "The End of the Third World", *Third World Quarterly*, vol. 15, no. 2, 1994.

Berggren, Douglas, "The Use and Abuse of Metaphor", in Review of *Metaphysics*, 16, 2 December 1962; 3 March, 1963.

Bernheimer, Charles, *Comparative Literature in the Age of Multiculturalism*, Baltimore: Johns Hopkins University Press, 1995.

Bhagavad-Gītā, Gorakhpur: Gita Press, 1997 (with Hindi commentary & analysis).

Bhāmaha, *Kāvyālaṁkāra*, with English translation & Notes by P.V. Naganatha Sastry, Tanjore: Wallace Printing House, 1927 (Sanskrit).

Bhandarkar, R.G., *Vaishnavism, Shaivism and Other Minor Sects*, Pune: Bhandarkar Research Institute, 1928.

Bharata, *Nāṭyaśāstra*, with the commentary *Abhinavabhāratī* by Abhinavagupta, Gaekwad Oriental Series, 36, 68, 124, vol. I, 1926; vol. II 1934; vol. III, 1954, Baroda, 1926-54.

———, *Nāṭyaśāstra*, tr. Manamohan Ghosh, Calcutta: Asiatic Society, 1950.

Bhartṛhari, *Vākyapadīya*, with Bhāvapradīpa Sanskrit Commentary and Notes by Pt. Sri Suryanarayana Sukla, ed. with Hindi Commentary by Pt. Sri Ramagovinda Shukla, Varanasi: Chaukhamba Sanskrit Prakashan, 1975.

Bhatt, Mira, *Saat Pagla Akash Man*, Bhavnagar: Sarvodaya Sahitya Mandir, 1989 (Gujarati).

Bhattacharya, Kalidasa, "Traditional Indian Philosophy as Modern Indian Thinkers View It", in *Indian Philopsophy: Past and Future*, ed. S.S. Ram Rao Pappu, and R. Puligandla, Delhi: Motilal Banarsidass, 1982.

Bhattacharya, Vishnupati, *Bharatiya Bhakti Sahitya*, Calcutta: Lekhapara, 1964.

Bhojaraja, *Śṛṅgāraprakāśa*, English tr. V. Raghavan, Madras: Punarvasu, 1963.

Bhuteshananda, Swami, *Narada Bhakti Sutra*, tr. in English with Introduction, Calcutta: Advaita Ashrama, 1999.

Bibile de lahemanite, vol. V of *Oeuvres*, Paris: Bibliotheque, 1930 tr. Michel Danino.

Bies, Jean, *Les Michelet. La Chemins de la ferveur*, Terre du cief, 1995, tr. Michel Danino.

Bloom, Harold, "A New Poetics", in Review of *Anatomy of Criticism* by Northrop Frye, *Yale Review*, 47, 1957

———, *A Map of Misreading*, New York: Oxford University Press, 1975.

———, *The Anxiety of Influence: A Theory of Poetry*, 1973, New York: Oxford University Press, 1978.

———, *Agon: Towards a Theory of Revisionism*, New York: Oxford University Press, 1982.

———, "Elegaic Conclusions", in *Falling Into Theory*, ed. David Richter, Boston: Bedford/St. Martin, 2000.

Brough, John, "Some Indian Theories of Meaning", 1953, *A Reader on the Sanskrit Grammarians*, ed. J.F. Staal, Delhi: Motilal Banarsidass, 1972.

Bullough, Edward, Aesthetics: *Lectures and Essays*, ed. with an Introduction by Elizabeth M. Wilkinson, London: Bowes & Bowes, 1957.

Butler, D.C., *Western Mysticism*, London: Arrow Books, 1980.

Butler, Judith, John Guillory and Thomas Kendall, eds., *What's Left of Theory?*, London: Routledge, 2000.

Cannon, Garland, ed., *The Letters of Sir William Jones*, vol. II, Oxford: Clarendon Press, 1970.

———, *The Life and Mind of Oriental Jones: Sir William Jones, the Father of Modern Linguistics*, Cambridge: Cambridge University Press, 1990.

Carey, Eustace, ed., *Memoirs of William Carey*, D.D. Boston: Gould, Kendall & Lincoln, 1836.

Cesaire, Aime, *Discourse on Colonialism*, New York: Monthly Review Press, 1972, rpt. in Patrick Williams and Laura Chrisman, eds., *Colonial Discourse and Postcolonial Theory: A Reader*, Hamel Hempptoes Harvester Wheat Sheaf, 1993.

Chaitanya, Krishna. *Sanskrit Poetics: A Critical and Comparative Study*, Bombay: Asia Publishing House, 1965.

Chakrabraty, Dipesh, *Provincializing Europe: Postcolonial Thought and Historical Difference*, Princeton NJ: University Press, 2000.

Chanda, Ipshita, *Reception of the Received: European Romanticism, Rabindranath and Suryakanta Tripathi "Nirala": A Case Study in Inter-Systemic Literary Reception*, Kolkata: Jadavpur University Press, 2006.

Chari, V.K., *Sanskrit Criticism*, Delhi: Motilal Banarsidass, 1993.

Chatterjee, Partha, *Nationalist Thought and the Colonial World*, Minneapolis: University of Minnesota Press, 1986.

Chatterjee, Upamanyu, *English August: An English Story*, New Delhi: Rupa & Co., 1989, 1st pub. Faber & Faber, 1988.

Chaudhary, Satyadeva, tr., *Kāvyālaṁkāra* (of Rudraṭa), Delhi: Vasudeva Prakashan, 1965 (Hindi).

———, *The Nation and its Fragments: Colonial and Postcolonial Histories*, Princeton New Jerry: Princeton University Press, 1993.

Childs, Peter & R.J. Patrick Williams, *An Introduction to Post-Colonial Theory*, London: Prentice Hall, 1997.

Chomsky, Noam, "Free Trade and Free Market: Pretense and Practice", in *The Cultures of Globalization*, ed. Fredric Jameson and Masao Miyoshi, 1998.

Cohn, Bernard, "Representing Authority in Victorian India", in *The Invention of Tradition*, ed. Eric Hobsbawm & Terence Ranger, Cambridge: Cambridge University Press, 1983.

Coleridge, S.T., *Biographia Literaria*, 2 vols., ed. J. Shawcross, London: Oxford University Press, 1965.

Coomaraswamy, Ananda K., *The Transformation of Nature Into Art*, New York: Dover Publications, 1934.

———, *The Dance of Shiva*, Bombay: Asia Publishing House, 1948, rpt. 1952, "Foreword" by Romain Rolland.

———, *Essays in National Idealism*, Delhi: Munshiram Manoharlal, 1981.

———, *Time and Eternity*, New Delhi: Munshiram Manoharlal, 2001.

Crawford, D.W., *Kant's Aesthetic Theory*, Madison: University of Wisconsin Press, 1947.

Croce, B., *Aesthetic: As Science of Expression and General Linguistics*, New York: Noonday Press, 1953.

Culler, Jonathan, *Structuralist Poetics: Structuralism Linguistics and the Study of Literature*, London: Routledge and Kegan Paul, 1980.

———, *On Deconstruction: Theory and Criticism after Structuralism*, Ithaca, N.Y.: Cornell University Press, 1982.

Cunningham, Valentine, *Reading after Theory*, Oxford: Blackwell, 2002.

Dabney Townsend, *An Introduction to Aesthetics*, Oxford: Blackwell Publishers, 1997.

Dalpatram, "*Mithyābhimān*" in *Dalpatgadya* rept., ed. Madhusudan Parekh, Gandhinagar: Gujarati Sahitya Akademi, 1999 (Gujarati).

Dandin, *Kavyadarsha*, ed. With commentary by Pandit Rangacharya Raddi Shastri, 2nd edn., Bhandarkar Oriental Research Institute, Poona, 1970.

Dangle, Arjun, ed., *A Corpse in the Well: Translations from Modern Marathi Dalit Autobigraphies*, Hyderabad: Orient Longman, [1992] 1994.

Das, S.K, *Sahib and Munshi: An Account of the College of Fort William*, Kolkata, 1978.

———, *Rādhā, the Mad Lover: Essays on Medieval Indian Religious Poetry*, Calcutta: Papyrus, 1984.

———, "Prologue" (1-23) & Appendix I "Integrated History of Indian Literature" & Appendix II, (341-370), in *A History of Indian Literature*, vol. VIII: 1800-1910; *Western Impact: Indian Response*, New Delhi: Sahitya Akademi, 1991.

———, *A History of Indian Literature, 500-1399: From the Courtly to the Popular*, Delhi: Sahitya Akademi, 2005.

Dasgupta, S.N., *A History of Indian Philosophy*, vol. IV, Delhi: Motilal Banarsidass, 1988, I published Cambridge, 1922.

Dasgupta, S.N. & S.K. De, *History of Sanskrit Literature*, Calcutta: University of Calcutta, 1947.

Dave, Ishwarlal, *Sahityasamiksha*, Ahmedabad: Nutan Prakashan Mandir, 1937 (Gujarati).

Dave, Narmad, *Narmagadya* vol. I. rpt., ed. Ramesh Shukla, Surat: Kavi Narmad Yugavarta Trust, 1996 (Gujarati).

Davidson, Basil, *Africa in Modern History: The Search for a New Society*, London: Allen Lane, 1978.

Dehejia, Vidya, *Āṇḍāḷ and Her Path of Love*, New York: State University Press, 1990.

Derrida, Jacques, *Speech and Phenomena*, tr. David B. Allison, Evanston: Northwestern University Press, 1973.

———, "White Mythology: Metaphor in the Text of Philosophy", *New Literary History*, tr. F.C.T. Moore, Autumn, 1974. ("La mythologies blanche" in *Rhetorique et philosophie*, Poetique 5, Paris, Editions du Seuil, 1971.)

———, *Of Grammatology*, tr. Gayatri Chakravorty Spivak, Baltimore: John Hopkins University Press, 1976.

———, *Writing and Difference*, tr. Alan Bass, Chicago: University of Chicago Press, 1978.

———, *Dissemination*, tr. Barbara Johnson, Chicago: University of Chicago Press, 1981.

———, *Margins of Philosophy*, tr. Alan Bass, Chicago: University of Chicago Press, 1982.

———, "Structure, Sign and Play in the Discourse of the Human Sciences", *Modern Criticism and Theory: A Reader*, ed. David Lodge, London and New York: Longman, 1988.

De, S.K., *History of Sanskrit Poetics*, 2 vols. in 1, Firma K.L. Mukhopadhyay, Calcutta, 1960.

———, *Sanskrit Poetics as a Study of Aesthetics*, Berkeley: University of California Press, 1963.

Desai, Anita, *Cry, the Peacock*, Delhi: Orient Paperback, 1980.

Desai, Ichharam Suryaram, *Hind ane Britannia: Ek Rajkiya Kadambari*, with "Preface" in English, Bombay: Bomtoj Pub., 1885 (Gujarati).

Desai, Vrajrai et al., *Upayāna*, Surat: Sri Vishnuprasad Trivedi Shashthipurti Sanman Samiti, 1961 (Gujarati).

Deshpande, Shashi, "The Dilemma of the Woman Writer", and her interviews by Vanmala Vishwanath, M.D. Riti, Lakshmi Holstorm, Geeta Gangadharan and Vimala Rao published as "Appendix" in *The Fiction of Shashi Deshpande*, ed. R.S. Pathak, Delhi: Creative Books, 1998.

Devy, G.N., *After Amnesia: Tradition and Change in Indian Literary Criticism*, Hyderabad & Delhi: Orient Longman, 1992.

———, *Painted Words: An Anthology of Tribal Literature*, New Delhi: Penguin, 2002.

Dewey, John, "Ethics", *The Collected Works of John Dewey 1882-1953*, ed. Jo Ann Boydston: Carbonsdale: South Illinois University, 2008.

Dharmapal, *Despoliation and Defaming of India: The Early Nineteenth Century British Crusade*, Wardha: Bharat Peetham, Goa: Other Indian Press, 1999.

Dhruv, Saroop, "*Beejo Pag Pan Oomara ni Bahar*", "Even the other foot out of the threshold" in *Mudrankan*, 1989, translation mine (Gujarati journal).

Dirks, Nicholas B., "Foreword", *Colonialism and its Forms of Knowledge: The British in India*", Bernard S. Cohn, Delhi: Oxford University Press, 2002.

Docherty, Thomas, *After Theory*, Edinburgh: Edinburgh University Press, 1997.

Dollimore, Jonathan & Sinfield, Alan, eds., *Political Shakespeare: New Essays in Cultural Materialism*: Manchester University Press, 1994.

Drakakis, John, ed. *Alternative Shakespeare*, Routledge, 1985.

Drucker, Peter F., *Knowledge Works and Knowledge Society: The Social Transformations of the Century*, Edwin L. Godkin Lecture, 1994.

Dummett, Michael, "Matilal's Mission: A Memeorial Address", *Studies in Humanities and Social Sciences*, vol. III, no. 2, pp. 13-17.

Dutt, M. Madhusudan, "Kidderpore", *The Collected Works of Michael Madhusudan Dutt*, ed. Kshetra Gupta, Calcutta: Sahitya Sansad, 184.

Dwivedi, Rewa Prasad, *Sanskrit-Kāvyaśāstra kā Ālocanātamak Itihāsa*, Varanasi: Kalidasa Sansthana, 2007 (Hindi).

Dwivedi, Hazariprasad, *Hindi Sāhitya kī Bhūmikā*, Delhi: Rajkamal, 1991 (Hindi).

Eagleton, Terry, *Literary Theory: An Introduction*, Minneapolis: University of Minnesota Press, 1983.

———, *The Ideology of the Aesthetic*, Oxford: Blackwell, 1990.

———, *After Theory*, New York: Basic Books, 2003.

———, *How to Read a Poem*, London: Blackwell, 2008.

Eco, Umberto with Richard Rorty, Jonathan Culler, Christine Brook-Rose, *Interpretation and Overinterpretation*, ed. Stefan Collini, Cambridge & New York: Cambridge University Press, 1992.

Ehtesham, Manzoor, *Sookha Bargad*, Delhi: Rajkamal, 1986, translation of the epigraphical excerpt mine (Hindi).

Eliot, T.S., "Tradition and Individual Talent", *The Norton Anthology: Theory and*

Criticism, ed. Vincent B. Leitch et al., New York and London: W.W. Norton and Co. Ltd., 2001.

Fanon, Frantz, *Black Skin, White Masks*. London: Pluto Press, 1965.

———, *Black Skin, White Mask*, tr. Charles Lamm, New York: Grove Press, 1967.

———, *The Wretched of the Earth*, tr. Constance Farrington, London: MacGibbon and Kee, 1976, p. 33.

Foucault, Michel, "What is an Author?" in *Modern Criticism and Theory: A Reader*, ed. David Lodge, London & New York, 1988.

Fish, Stanley, *Is there a Text in this Class? The Authority of Interpretative Communities*, Cambridge, Mass.: Harvard University Press, 1980.

Friel, Brian, *Translation*, London: Faber & Faber, 2000, 1st pub. 1981.

Frye, Northrop, *Fables of Identity: Studies in Poetic Mythology*, New York: Harcourt, Brace & World, 1963.

———, *The Stubborn Structure: Essays on Criticism and Society*, London: Mathuen, 1970.

———, *Anatomy of Criticism: Four Essays*, 1957, Princeton: Princeton University Press, 1973.

———, *The Critical Path: An Essay on the Social Context of Literary Criticism*, 1971, Bloomington: Indiana University Press, 1973.

———, *Spiritus Mundi: Essays on Literature, Myth and Society*, Bloomington: Indiana University Press, 1976.

———, *The Great Code: The Bible and Literature*, Toronto: Academic Press, 1982.

Fukuyama, Francis, *The End of History and the Last Man*, New York: Free Press, 1992.

Fuller, Thomas, *The History of the Worthies of England*, vol. III, London: Thomas Tegg, 1840.

Gaekwad, Baburao, *Drishtikshep*, Aurangabad: Parichay Prakashan, 1986. (Marathi)

Gallagher, Catherine & Greenblatt, Stephen, *Practicing the New Historicism*, University of Chicago Press, 2000.

Gandhi, M.K., "Foreword" to K.M. Munshi, *Gujarat and its Literature: A Survey from the Earliest Times*, Calcutta: Longman Green & Co., 1935.

———, *Evil Wrought by the English Medium*, ed. K.N. Prabhu, Ahmedabad: Navjeevan Publishing House, 1958.

———, *Hind Swaraj* or *Indian Home Rule*, Ahmedabad: Navjeevan Publishing

House, 2003. 1st edn., 1938. Written in Gujarati as *Hind Swaraj*, 1908, published subsequently in Gujarati and English, Ahmedabad: Navjeeven Trust, 1963 edn.

———, *The Selected Works of Mahatma Gandhi*, vol. III, *Satyāgraha in South Africa*, Ahmedabad: Navjeevan Press, 1994, 1st edn. 1968.

———, *Swa. Mohandas Karamchand Gandhinu Bhasan: Barami Gujarati Sahitya Sabha Parishad: Ahmedabad, October-November, 1936*, "Address to Gujarati Sahitya Parishad", in *National Issues and Native Responses: Indian Renaissance Prose Writing*, ed. Avadhesh Kumar Singh & Kamal Mehta, New Delhi: Creative Books, 2004.

———, "On Art: Excerpts" in *Critical Discourse and Colonialism: Indian Critical Discourse in the Colonial Period in Hindi, Gujarati and English*, ed. Avadhesh Kumar Singh & Sanjay Mukherjee, New Delhi: Creative Books, 2005.

Gardner, Brian, *The East India Company: History*, London: Hart Davis, 1971.

Garg, Mradula, "They Could not Stomach a Guilt Free Woman", *The Express Magazine*, 22 July 2001 (tr. mine).

Garg, Nirmala, "Meri Bahne (My Sisters)", *Hans*, November 2000 (Hindi).

Garg, Nirmala, "Kyā le Jāun Navjāt Bachche ke Liye (What Should I Carry with Me for the Newly-born Girl?)", *Hans*, January 2000, 154 (Hindi).

Garten, Jeffery, *A Cold Peace*, New York: Times Books, 1992.

Geoffrey, Hartman, *Criticism in the Wilderness: The Study of Literature Today*, New Haven: Yale University Press, 1980.

Ghalib, Mirza, *Ghalib: Life, Letters and Ghazals*, ed. Ralph Russell, Delhi: Oxford University Press, 2003.

Gnoli, Raniero, tr. *The Aesthetic Experience according to Abhinavagupta* (*Abhinavabhāratī*), Varanasi: Chowkhamba Sanskrit Series, 1985.

Ghosh, Manmohan, tr. into English, *Nāṭyaśāstra*, Calcutta: Asiatic Society, 1950.

Gomperz, Cp. Th., *Greek Thinkers*, Book V, Chapter 11, 482. Cited from the German edition by Popper.

Gopal, Madan, *Munshi Premchand: A Literary Biography*, Mumbai: Asia Publishing House, 1964.

Goswami, B.K., *The Bhakti Cult in Ancient India*, Calcutta: B. Banerjeee & Co., 1922.

Graddol, David, *The Future of English*, London: Glenton Press, 1997.

Grady, Hugh, *The Modernist Shakespeare*, Oxford University Press, 1994.

Greenblatt, Stephen, *Shakespearean Negotiations: The Circulation of Energy in Renaissance England,* California University Press, 1991.

———, *Marvelous Possessions: The Wonder of the New World,* Chicago: University of Chicago Press, 1991.

Griffith, Gareth, "Language and Action in the Novels of Chinua Achebe", in C.I. Innes & Bernth Lindford ed. *Critical Perspectives on Chinua Achebe,* London: Heinemann, 1979.

Habib, M.A.R., *History of Literary Criticism from Plato to the Present,* London: Blackwell, 2005.

Harishchandra, Bhartendu, *Bharatendu Samagra,* ed. Hemant Sharma, Varanasi: Hindi Pracharak Publications, 2000, 4th edn.

———, "*Nātak*" translated from Hindi to English by Prabhat Kumar Pandeya, in *Critical Discourse and Colonialism*, Delhi: Creative Books, 2005.

Hawkes, Terence, *The Shakespeare Rag,* Manchester University Press, 1988.

Hebdige, Dick, *Hiding in the Light: On Images and Things,* London: Routledge, 1988.

Heidegger, Martin, *What is Philosophy?,* tr. W. Kluback & J.T. Wilde, New Haven: College and University Press, 1956. (*Was ist das — die Philosophie?* Pfullingen, Neske 1956, 3rd edn. 1963.)

———, *On Time and Being,* tr. Jona Stambaugh, New York: Harper and Row, 1972 (Zur Sache des Denkens Tubingen, Niemeyer, 1969).

Heimann, Betty, *Indian and Western Philosophy: A Study in Contrast,* Delhi: Aman Publishing House, 1994, 1st pub. London: George Allen & Unwin, 1937.

Hensman, C.R., *The Problems of Revolt: From Gandhi to Guevara,* Allen Lane: Penguin, 1969.

Hemachandra, *Kāvyānuśāsanam,* Kavyamala, 2nd edn., Bombay: Niranya Sagar Press, 1934.

———, *Kāvyānuśāsanam* (ed. with Introduction and Translation in Gujarati by Tapaswi Nandi, Ahmedabad: Lalbhai Dalpatbhai Bharatiya Sanskrit Vidyamandir, 2000.

Hiriyanna, H., *Art Experience,* Mysore: Kavyalaya Publishers, 1954.

Holderness, Graham, *The Shakespeare Myth,* Manchester University Press, 1988.

Hopkins, Thomas J., "The Social Teaching of the Bhāgavata Purāṇa", in Milton Singer, ed., *Kṛṣṇa: Myths, Rites and Attitudes,* Chicago: University of Chicago Press, 1964.

Isher, Wolfgang, *The Act of Reading: A Theory of Aesthetic Response,* Baltimore: Johns Hpkins University Press, 1978, 1st edn. 1976.

Insha, Ibne, *Urdu Ki Akhiri Kitab* (The Last Book of Urdu), Transcription from Urdu edition by Abdul Bismillah, Delhi: Rajkamal Prakashan, 1996, 1st edn. 1988.

Iyengar, K.R.S., *Indian Writing in English*, Delhi: Sterling, 1962.

Iyer, Subramania, ed. & tr., *The Vākyapadīya of Bhartṛhari with the Vṛtti,* Chapter 1 of *Vākyapadīya*, Poona: Deccan College, 1965.

———, "Bhartṛhari on the Primary and Secondary Meaning of Words", In *S.M. Katre Festschrift*, vol. 1, Poona: Deccan College, 1968.

———, tr., *Bhartṛhari: A Study of the Vākyapadīya* in the Light of Ancient Commentaries, Poona: Deccan College, 1969.

———, ed. & tr. *The Vākyapadīya of Bhartṛhari,* Chapter 3, part 1 of *Vākyapadīya,* Poona: Deccan College, 1971.

———, ed. & tr. *The Vākyapadīya of Bhartṛhari* with the Prakīrṇa Prakāśa of Helārāja. Chapter 3, part 2 of *Vākyapadīya,* Poona: Deccan College, 1973.

———, ed. & tr. *The Vākyapadīya of Bhartṛhari*, Chapter 2 of *Vākyapadīya*. Delhi: Motilal Banarsidass, 1977.

Jagannatha, *Rasagaṅgādhara,* with "Marmaprakāśa" by Nāgeśa, edited with Sanskrit Commentary and Hindi translation by Madhusudana Shastri, 3 vols., Varanasi: Banaras Hindi University (BHU), 1964-70.

Jagannatha, Pundit, *Rasagaṅgādhara*, English tr. Madanmohan Jha, Varanasi: Chaukhamba Vidya Bhavan, 1969.

Jameson, Fredric, "Postmodernism or The Cultural Logic of Late Capitalism", in *New Left Review*, 146, 1984.

———, "Notes of Globalization as a Philosophical Issue", in *The Cultures of Globalization,* ed. Fredric Jameson and Moasao Miyoshi, Durham, NC: Duke University Press, 1998.

Jauss, Hans R., *Towards an Aesthetic of Reception,* tr. T. Bahti, Hemel Hempstead: Harvester Wheatsheaf, 1982.

Jha, Madanmohan, ed. & tr., *Rasagaṅgādhara,* Varanasi: Chowkhamba Vidya Bhawan, 1987 (Hindi).

Jha, Ganganath, *Śloka Vārttika*, Calcutta: Asiatic Society of Bengal, 1924.

Jhaveri, Mansukhlal, *History of Gujarati Literature,* New Delhi: Sahitya Akademi, 1978.

Jones, William, *The Complete Works of Sir William Jones*, vol. XIII, Delhi: Agam Prakashan, 1971.

Joshi, Suresh, *Chintayami Manasa*, Ahmedabad: Sadbhava Prakashan, 1982. (Gujarati).

Joughlin, John J & Malaps, eds., *The New Aestheticism*, Manchester: Manchester University Press, 2003.

Judd, Denis, *The Lion and the Tiger: The Rise and Fall of the British Raj*, New Delhi: Oxford University Press, 2004.

Kālidāsa, *Abhijñānaśākuntalam*, tr. into English Gajendra Gadkar, Girgaum, Bombay: Standard Publishing Co., 1920.

———, *Raghuvaṁśa: A Study*, Padma Ranganathan, New Delhi: The Gondals Press, 1964.

_______, *The Raghuvaṁśa of Kālidāsa*, Gopal Raghunath Nandargikar, Motilal Banarsidass, Delhi, 4th edn., 1971.

Kane, P.V. ed. & tr., *Sāhityadarpaṇa*, Bombay: Nirnaya Sagar Press, 1951.

———, *History of Sanskrit Poetics*, Delhi: Motilal Banarsidass, 1961.

Kant, Immanuel, *Critique of the Faculty of Judgement*, tr. James Creed Meredith, Oxford: Clarendon Press, 1952.

"Kant", *Siddhānta Sar nu Avalokan*, Mumbai: K.J. Cheetalia, Hind Sewak Samaj, 1920 (Gujarati).

Kapadiya, Kundanika, *Saat Paglaa Akaash Maan*, Ahmedabad: Navbharat Sahitya Mandir, VIIth edn., 1994, Gujarati (tr. mine).

Kapoor, Kapil, "Some Reflections on the Interpretation of Texts in the Indian Tradition", *Structures of Signification*, vol. 1, ed. H.S. Gill, Delhi: Wiley Eastern Ltd., 1990.

———, *Literary Theory: Indian Conceptual Framework*, Delhi: Affiliated East-West Press, 1998.

Kaviraj, Sudipta, "The Sudden Death of Sanskrit Knowledge", *Journal of Indian Philosophy*, vol. 33, no. 1, February 2005, pp. 119-42.

Keith, A.B., *The Sanskrit Drama*, Oxford: Clarendon Press, 1924.

Kejariwal, O.P., *The Asiatic Society of Bengal and the Discovery of India's Past 1784-1838*, Delhi: Oxford University Press, 1989.

Kermode, Frank, *The Classic: Literary Images of Permanence and Change*, Cambridge: Harvard University Press, 1983.

Kipling, Rudyard, "Yoked with an Unbeliever", in *Plain Tales from the Hills*, 1886, Oxford: Oxford University Press, 1987.

Kopf, David, *British Orientalism and the Bengal Renaissance: The Dynamics of Indian Modernization 1773-1835*, Berkeley: University of California Press, 1969.

Kosambi, D.D., *The Culture and Civilization of Ancient India,* New Delhi: Vikas Publishing, 1970.

Koshi, K.A., ed., *Towards Comparative Indian Literature,* Aligarh: Department of Modern Indian Language, AMU, 1987.

Krishna, Daya, *India's Intellectual Traditions*, Delhi: Motilal Banarsidass, 1987.

———, *Indian Philosophy: A Counter Perspective,* Delhi, 1996.

Krishnamoorthy, K., *Essays in Sanskrit Criticism,* Dharwar: Karnatak University Press, 1964.

———, *Studies in Indian Aesthetics and Criticism,* Mysore: D.V.K. Moorthy, 1979.

———, tr. *Vakroktijīvita,* Dharwar: Karnataka University, 1977.

———, tr. *Dhvanyaloka,* Delhi: Motilal Banarsidass, 1981.

———, *Indian Literary Theory: A Reappraisal,* Delhi: Meharchand Lachhmandas, 1985.

———, tr. *Locana*, Delhi: Meharchand Lachhmandas, 1988.

Kṣemarāja; *Pratyabhijñāhṛdayam: The Secret of Self-Recognition,* tr. Jaideva Singh, Delhi: Motilal Banarsidass, 1982.

Kṣemendra, *Aucityavicāracarcā,* English tr. Suryakanta, Poona: Oriental Book Agency, 1924.

Kulkarni, G.M. "Prastavana", in Anand Yadav, *Gramin Sahitya: Swarup ani Samasya,* Pune: Mehta Publishing House, 1984 (Marathi).

Kunjunni Raja, K. *"The Theory of Meaning according to the Buddhist Logicians", Adyar Library Bulletin* 18: 178-95, 1954.

———, "Akanksha: The Main Basis of Syntactic Unity", *Adyar Library Bulletin* 20: 282-95, 1957.

Kuntaka, *The Vakroktijīvita*, ed. Sushil Kumar De, Calcutta: Firma K.L. Mukhopadhyaya, 3rd rev. edn. 1961.

———, *Vakroktijīvita of Kuntaka,* tr. & ed. K. Krishnamoorthy, Dharwad: Karnataka University, 1977.

Lal, Deepak, *In Praise of Empires: Globalization and Order,* Palgrave, 2005.

Lamartine, *Opinion sur Dieu, le bouheu et l'eternite d'pres les livres sacres de l'Inde,* Paris: Sand, 1984, tr. Michel Danino.

Lentricchia, Frank, *After the New Criticism*, Chicago: University of Chicago Press, 1980.

Levinson, J., ed., *Aesthetics and Ethics*, Cambridge: Cambridge University Press, 1998.

Lewisohn, Ludwig, *The Story of American Literature*, New York: The Modern Library, 1939.

Limbale, Sharan Kumar, "Dalit Sahitya: Swarup aur Prayojan", *Hans*, January 1997, 52-55 (Hindi).

———, *Dalit Sāhitya kā Saundaryaśāstra*, tr. Ramanika Gupta into Hindi from Marathi, New Delhi: Vani Prakashan, 2000.

Luttwak, Edward, *The Endangered American Dream*, New York: Simon and Schuster's, 1993.

Macaulay, T.B., "T.B. Macaulay on India (9.3.1843)", in Dharmapal, 1999.

MacIntyre, Alasdair, *After Virtue: A Study in Moral Theory*, University of Notre Dame Press, 1984.

Macwan, Joseph, *The Stepchild*, tr. Rita Kothari, New Delhi: Oxford University Press, 2004.

Mādhavācārya, *Sarva-Darśana-Saṁgraha*, tr. & ed. K.L. Joshi, Ahmedabad: Parimal Prakashan, 1981. I tr. E.B. Cowell & A.E. Gough, 1878.

Mahimabhaṭṭa, *Vyaktiviveka* with Ruyyaka's Commentary, ed. with Hindi translation, by Rewa Prasad Dwevedi, Varanasi: Chowkhamba Sanskrit Series, 1964.

Majumdar, A.K., *Bhakti Renaissance*, 1st edn., Bombay: Bharatiya Vidya Bhawan, 1965.

Mammaṭa, The *Kāvyaprakāśa* of Mammaṭa with English tr., rev. edn., ed. Ganganath Jha, Delhi: Bharatiya Vidya Prakashan, 1967.

Mammaṭa, *Kāvyaprakāśa*, tr. R.C. Dwivedi, *Poetic Light: Kāvyaprakāśa of Mammaṭa*, Delhi: Motilal Banarsidass, 1969.

———, *Kāvyaprakāśa*, tr. Ganganath Jha, Allahabad: The Indian Press, 1925.

Mane, Laxman, *Upara: An Outsider*, tr. A.K. Kamat, New Delhi: Sahitya Akademi, 1997.

Manilal, *Sudarśangadyāvalī*, ed. Himmatlal Pandya, Pranshankar Joshi, Jambusar, 1909 (Gujarati).

Mann, Thomas, *The Transposed Heads: A Legend of India*, tr. Helen T. Lowe-Porter, Vintage Books, 1959, 1st pub. 1940.

Manu, *Manusmṛti*, Compiled with translation in Hindi by Srimat Raskrishna, Delhi: Mahmoodulamataba Murza Hambeg Publishers, Saṁvat 1941.

Mardhekar, B.S., *Two Lectures on an Aesthetic of Literature*, Bombay: Karnataka Publishing House, 1948.

Marshall, Brenda K., *Teaching the Postmodern: Fiction and Theory*, New York & London: Routledge, 1992.

Matilal, Bimal Krishna, *The Character of Logic in India*, Albany: State University of New York Press, 1998.

———, *The Collected Essays of Bimal Krishna Matilal: Mind, Language and World*, vol. 1, ed. Jonardan Ganeri, New Delhi: Oxford University Press, 2002.

———, *The Collected Essays of Bimal Krishna Matilal: Ethics and Epics*, vol. II, ed. Jonardan Ganeri, New Delhi: Oxford University Press, 2002a.

Mathur, Anurag, *The Inscrutable American*, Delhi: Rupa, 1991.

McClintock, Anne, "The Angel of Progress: Pitfalls of the term "Postcolonialism", *Social Text* 31/32, 1992.

McQuillan, Martin et al., eds., *Post-Theory: New Directions in Criticism*, Edinburgh: Edinburgh University Press, 1999.

Mead, Walter Russell, "On the Road to Ruin", *Harper's*, March 1990.

Meghani, Zaverchand, *Saurashtra ni Rasadhar*, Bhavnagar: Prasar Bharati & Lokmilap Trust, 1997 (Gujarati).

Mehta, J.L., *Martin Heidegger: The Way and the Vision*, Benares: MLBD, 1967.

Memmi, Albert, *The Colonizer and the Colonized*, New York: The Orcan Press, 1965.

Mestrovic, Stjepan Gabriel, *Coming Fin de Siecle: An Application of Durkheim's Sociology to Modernity and Postmodernism*, London, New York: Routlege, 1991.

Miller, J. Hillis, "The Critic as Host", in *Deconstruction and Criticism*, New York, London: Seabury Press/Routledge & Kegan Paul, 1979.

Mir, Taqui Mir, *Mir Taqui Mir: Selected Poetry*, English tr. K.C. Kanda, New Delhi: Sterling, 1997.

Mishra, Vijay and Bob Hodge, "What is post(-)colonialism?", *Textual Practices* 5, 3, 1991.

Mukherjee, Sushil K., *The Story of the Calcutta Theatres 1753-1980*, Calcutta: K.P. Bagachi, 1982.

Muktibodh, Gajanan Madhava, *Muktibodh Rachnavali*, ed. Nemichandra Jain, vol. IV, Delhi: Rajkamal, 1985.

Max Müller, Friederich, *India: What Can it Teach Us?*, New Delhi & New York: Penguin Books, 2000.

Munro, Thomas, *Towards Science in Aesthetics: Selected Essays*, New York: Liberal Press, 1956.

Nabhadas, *Bhaktamal,* ed. Rupakala, Lucknow: Nawalkishor Press, 1960, 2nd edn.

Nagarajan, S. & S. Vishwanathan, eds., *Shakespeare in India,* Oxford: Oxford University Press, 1987.

Nagendra, *Bhāratīya Kāvyaśāstra kī Bhūmikā,* Delhi: National Publishing House, 1963, 2nd edn., 1st edn. 1956 (Hindi).

———, *Bhāratīya Kāvyaśāstra,* 2 vols., Delhi: National Publishing, 1975.

———, *Literary Criticism in India,* Meerut: Sarita Prakashan, 1976.

Naimishray, Mohan Dass, "Stree Aarambh se Ant tak Dalit Hee Hai" (Woman is a Dalit from Beginning to End), *Hans,* September, 75, 1993 (Hindi).

Nandinath, S.C., *A Handbook of Vira Shaivism,* South India: Literary Committee, L.S. Association, 1941.

Nandy, Ashis, "Towards a Third World Utopia", in *Tradition, Tyranny and Utopias: Essays in the Politics of Awareness,* Oxford: Oxford University Press, 1992.

———, *The Intimate Enemy: Loss and Recovery of Self under Colonialism,* Delhi, Oxford University Press, 1983, 1st paperback edn., 1983.

Narmad, *Dharma Vichar,* ed. Ramesh M. Shukla, Surat: Kavi Narmad Yugavarta Trust, 1998 (Gujarati).

Navalram, *Navalagranthāvalī,* ed. Narhari Parikh, Ahmedabad: Navjeevan Press, 1966 (Gujarati).

Neelkanth, Mahipatram, *Sasu Bahu ni Ladai,* Gandhinagar: Gujarati Sahitya Akademi, 1984, 1st pub. 1866 (Gujarati).

Nemade, Bhalchand, "Marathi Novel" (1950-75), *Setu,* vol. I, 1986.

Newman, D., *Harold Laski: A Political Biography,* London: Macmillan, 1939.

"Nirāla", Suryakant Tripathi, *Nirālā Racanāvalī,* vol. 5, *Ālocanā Ravindra-Kavitā-Kānan aur Ālocanātmaka Lekha evam Sampādakīya Ṭippanīyaṅ,* ed. Nandkishor Naval, Delhi: Rajkamal Prakashan, 1999. [Translation from Hindi into English taken from Ipshita Chanda.]

Ogden, Charles Kay & Ivor Armstrong Richards, *The Meaning of Meaning,* 1923, London: Routledge & Kegan Paul, 8th edn., 1946.

Ohmann, Richard, "The Function of English at the Present Time", *Falling into Theory,* ed. David Richter, Boston: Bedford/St. Martin, 2000, pp. 89-95.

Omvedt, Gail, *Dalit and Democratic Revolution: Dr. Ambedkar and the Dalit Movement in Colonial India,* New Delhi: Sage, 1994.

O'Neill, Eugene, *Long Day's Journey into Night*, Delhi: B.J. Publications, 1981.

Page, James, *Peace Foundation: Exploring Ethical and Philosophical Foundation*, Charlotte: Information Age Publication, 2008.

Pandey, K.C., *Indian Aesthetics*, Varanasi: Chowkhamba Sanskrit Series Office, 1959.

Pandya, Navalram, *Navalgranthavali*, ed. Narhari Parikh, Ahmedabad: Navjeevan Press, 1966 (Gujarati).

Paranjape, Makarand, ed., *Nativism: Essays in Criticism*, Delhi: Sahitya Akademi, 1995.

———, "Coping with Post-colonialism", *Interrogating Post-colonialism: Theory, Text and Context*, ed. Harish Trivedi and Meenakshi Mukherjee, Shimla: IIAS, 1996.

———, "Theorising Postcolonial Difference: Culture, Nation, Civilization", *SPAN, 47, October 1998.*

Parikh, Ramesh, *Swagat Parva*, Ahmedabad: Rannade Prakashan, 2002 (Gujarati).

Parishad Pramukhona Bhashano, Ahmedabad: Gujarati Sahitya Parishad, 1941 (Gujarati).

Patanjali, *Yoga-Sutra*, ed. T.K.V. Desikachar, New Delhi: Affiliated East-West Press in association with Rupa & Co., 1987.

Patel, Bholabhai & Anila Dalal, eds., *Vrundavanman Morali Vage Chhe*, Ahmedabad: Gujarati Sahitya Parishad, 2007 (Gujarati).

Payne, Michael & John Shad, eds., *Life. After. Theory*, London: Continuum, 2003.

Peerandina, Saleem, *Contemporary Indian Poetry in English: An Assessment and Selection*, Madras: Macmillan India, 1972. (The poetic extracts of Mamta Kalia, Gauri Deshpande and Kamala Das are from this anthology.)

Phillips, Caryl, *Crossing the River*, London: Picador, 1993.

Phadkule Nirmalkumar, *Kabi Rang: Kabi Resha*, Pune: Mehra Publishing House, 1986 (Marathi).

Phule, Mahatma Jyotirao, *Writings and Speeches*, 2 vols. Bombay: Government of Maharashtra, 1991.

Plath, Sylvia, "Daddy" in *Twentieth Century Verse: An Anglo-American Anthology*, ed. C.T. Thomas, Madras, 1979.

Plato, *Plato: Complete Works*, ed. John M. Cooper, Indianapolis: Hackett Publishing Company, 1997.

Pollock, Sheldon, "The Death of Sanskrit", *Comparative Studies in History and Society*, vol. 43, no. 2, pp. 392-426, 2001.

———, ed., *Literary Cultures in History: Reconstructions from South Asia*, Berkeley: University of California Press, 2003.

Popper, Karl, *The Open Society and its Enemies*, vol. II: *Hegel & Marx*, London & New York: Routledge, 1945.

Poulain, A.S.J., *The Graces of Interior Prayer*, St. Louis: B. Herder Book Co., 1975.

Prawer, S.S., *Comparative Literary Studies*, Gerald Duckworth & Co., 1973.

Premchand, Munshi, *Karmabhumi*, New Delhi: Diamond Books, 2003. 1st published in 1931. (All page numbers are maintained in the books of text of the paper.) (All translations are mine.)

———, "Upanayas", translated from Hindi into English by Avadhesh Kumar Singh in Avadhesh Kumar Singh, & Sanjay Mukherjee, eds., *Critical Discourse and Colonialism: Indian Critical Discourse in the Colonial Period in Hindi, Gujarati and English*, New Delhi: Creative Books, 2005.

Priyamvada, Usha, *Rukogī Nahīṁ Rādhikā* (Wouldn't You Stop Rādhikā?), Delhi: Rajkamal, 1984 (Hindi).

Pufendorf, Samuel, *On the Duty of Man and Citizen According to the Natural Law*, tr., M. Silverthorne, ed., J. Tully, New York: Cambridge University Press, 1991.

Rabate, Jean-Michel, *The Future of Theory*, Oxford: Blackwell, 2002.

Radhakrishnan, S. tr. *Bhagawadgita*, London: George Allen and Unwin, 1948.

______, tr. *The Ten Principal Upanisads*, London: George Allen and Unwin, 1956.

Raghavan, V., "The Sixty-four Arts", in Bhoja's *Śṛṅgāra Prakāśa*, tr. & ed. V. Raghavan, Madras: Punarvasu, 1963.

Raghuramraju, A., *Debates in Indian Phiosophy, Classical, Colonial & Contemporary*, New Delhi: Oxford University Press, 2006.

———, *Enduring Colonialism: Classical Presences, and Modern Absences in Indian Philosophy*, New Delhi: Oxford University Press, 2009.

Raha, Kironmoy, *Bengali Theatre*, Delhi: National Book Trust, 1978.

Rajan, Chandra, tr., *The Complete Works of Kalidasa*, 2 vols., New Delhi: Sahitya Akademi: 2007.

Rājaśekhara, *Kāvyamīmāṁsā*, ed. C.D. Dalal, & F.S. Ramaswami Sastri, Baroda: Oriental Institute, 1934.

———, *Kāvyamīmāṁsā*, tr. Kedarnath Sharma Saraswata, Patna: Bihar Rashtrabhasha Parishad, 1965.

Ramakrishnan, E.V., "The Games of Fiction: Search for a Postmodernist Mode in the Malayalam Fiction of 1990s", *Critical Practice*, vol. III, no. 1, January 1996.

Ramanujan, A.K., *Hymns for the Drowning*, tr. into English from Tamil, Delhi: Penguin, 1993, Princeton University Press, 1981.

Ranade, R.D., *Pathway to God in Hindi Literature*, Madras: Adhyatma Vidya Mandir, 1954.

Rao, Raja, "Foreword", *Kanthapura*, 1938, New York: New Direction, 1963.

Rayan, Krishna, *Suggestion and Statement in Poetry*, London: Athlone Press, 1972.

______, *Text and Sub-text: Suggestion in Literature*, Delhi: Arnold Heinemann, 1987.

The Hymns of Ṛgveda, tr. T.H. Griffith, Varanasi: Chaukhamba Prakashan, 1963.

Richards, I.A., *Principles of Literary Criticism* (1925), London: Routledge and Kegan Paul, 1974.

Richter, David (ed.), *Falling into Theory*, Boston: Bedford/St Martin, 2000.

Roy, Arundhati, *The God of Small Things*, Delhi: India Inc., 1997.

Roy, Raja Rammohun, *The English Works of Raja Rammohun Roy*, Delhi, 1984.

Rudraṭa, *Kāvyālaṁkāra*, ed. with commentary of Namisadhu by Durgaprasad and V.L. Sastri, Bombay: Nirnaya Sagar Press, 1928.

———, *Kāvyālaṁkāra*, Hindi tr. Satyadev Chaudhary, Delhi: Vasudev Prakshan, 1965.

Rushdie, Salman & Elizabeth West, ed., *The Vintage Book of Indain Writing 1947-1997*, New York: H. Holt & Co., 1997.

Russell, Bertrand, "On Denoting" (1905), in *Logic and Knowledge: Essays, 1901-1950*, London: Allen & Unwin, 1956.

Russell, D.A. & M. Winterbottom, eds., "Aristotle's Theory of Aesthetic Pleasure", in *Classical Literary Criticism*, Oxford & New York: Oxford University Press, 1972.

Said, Edward, *Orientalism*, New York: Pantheon Books, 1978.

———, *The World, the Text, and the Critic, 1983*, London: Faber & Faber, 1984.

———, "Intellectuals in a Post-colonial World", *Salmagundi*, 70-71, Spring/Summer, 1986.

———, *Culture and Imperialism*, London: Vintage, 1994, 1st pub. by Chatto & Windus, 1993.

Sarasvat, Pt. Kedarnath Sharma, tr., *Kāvyamīmāṁsā* (in Hindi), Patna: Bihar Rashtra Bhasha Parishad, 1954.

Sastri, P.S., *Ananada K. Coomaraswamy*, New Delhi: Arnold Heinemann, 1974.

Sastry, P.U. Naganatha ed. & tr., *Kāvyālaṁkāra*, Delhi: Motilal Banarsidass, 1970.

Satchidanandan, K., "The Laughing Medusa or the Raging Draupadi", *Indian Literature*, September-October, 1993.

———, "Nativism and its Ambivalences", *Critical Practice*, vol. III, no. 1, January 1996.

Saussey, Haun, *Comparative Literature in the Age of Globalization*, Cornell University Press, 2006.

Saussure, Ferinanand de, *Course in General Linguistics*, tr. Wade Baskin, eds. Perry Meisel and Haun Saussey, New York: Columbia University Press, 2011.

Scharf, Peter, *Ramopakhyana: The Story of Rama in the Mahabharata*, London & New York: Routelege Curzon, 2003.

Schopenhauer, Arthur, *The World as Will and Representation*, tr. from the German by E.F.J. Payne, 2 vols., Courier Dover Publications, 1966.

Schwab, Raymond, *The Oriental Renaissance: Europe's Discovery of India and the East 1680-1880*, tr. into English from French by Gene Patterson-Black & Victor Reinking, New York: Columbia University Press, 1984.

Sehwab, Raymond, *The Oriental Imagination: Europe's Rediscovery of India and the East*, New York: Columbia University Press, 1984.

Sen, Amartya, "A World of Extremes: Ten Theses on Globalization", *The Times of India*, 16.7.2001, p. 12, 1st pub. in *Los Angeles Times Syndicate International*.

———, *The Argumentative Indian: Writing on Indian Culture, History and Identity*, London: Penguin Books, 2005.

Seth, Vikram, *A Suitable Boy*, Delhi: Penguin, 1993.

Seturaman, V.S., ed., *Indian Aesthetics: An Introduction*, Madras: Macmillan India, 1992 edn.

"Shabnam", Padmavati, *Mīrā, Bṛahat-Pada-Saṁgraha*, Banaras: Lok Sevak Prakashan, VS 2000.

Shah, Natwarlal Gokuldas and Jethalal G. Shah, *A Bird's Eye-View of Puṣṭimārga*, Ahmedabad: Pushtimargiya Vaishnava Mahasabha, 1930.

Shakespeare, William, *The Tempest*, ed. A.W. Verity, London: Cambridge University Press 1962.

———, *Hamlet*, ed. Nigel Alexander, London: Macmillan, 1982.

———, *Othello*, ed. Celia Hilton and R.T. Jones, London: Macmillan, 1984.

Shamasastri, R. tr., *Arthaśāstra*, Mysore: Wallace Press, 1930.

Sharma, Hemant, *Bhartendu Samagra*, Varanasi: Hindi Pracharak Sansthan, 1989 (Hindi).

Sharma, Ramvilas, *Paramparā kā Mūlyāṅkan*, New Delhi: Rajkamal Prakashan, 1981 (Hindi).

———, *Bhāratīya Sāhitya kī Bhūmikā*, Delhi: Rajkamal Prakashan, 1996.

Śaṅkarācārya, Ādi, *Saundarya Laharī*, tr. Swami Tapasyananda, Chennai: Ramakrishna Math, 1987.

Sharpe, Jenny, *Allegories of Empire: The Figure of the Woman in the Colonial Text*, Minneapolis: University of Minnesota Press, 1993.

Shohat, Ella, "Notes on the Post-Colonial", *Social Text*, 31/32, 1992.

Shourie, Arun, *Missionaries in India: Continuity, Changes, Dilemma*, Delhi: Harper Collins, 1997.

Showalter, Elaine, *A Literature of their Own: British Women Novelists from Bronte to Lessing*, Princeton, N.J.: Princeton University Press, 1997.

Shukla, Acharya Ramachandra, *Hindi Sāhitya kā Itihāsa*, Delhi: Prakashan Sansthan, 2003, 1st pub. Saṁvat 1986 (Hindi).

———, *Rasa Mīmāṁsā*, ed. Vishavanath Mishra, Varanasi: Kashi Nagari Pracharani Sabha, Samvat 2006.

Singer, Alan & Allen Dunn, eds., *Literary Aesthetics: A Reader*, Oxford: Blackwell, 2000.

Singh, Avadhesh Kumar, "Renaissance" Self-(Re)fashioning and Colonialism: A Comparative Study of the 19th century Gujarati and Hindi "Renaissance" Prose Writings, *South Asian Review*, vol. XXV, no. 1, 2004.

———, ed., *Ramayana through the Ages*, Delhi: D.K. Printworld, 2005.

———, "Preface", *Interventions: Literary and Critical Discourses*, Delhi: Creative Books, 2007.

———, "What is English Doing in India?: Responses to an Awkward Question", in *Indian English and Vernacular India*, ed. Makarand Paranjape & G.J.V. Prasad, New Delhi: Pearson Publications, 2010.

Singh, Kashinath, *Kāśī kā Assi*, Delhi: Rajkamal, 1994 (Hindi).

Singh, Jyotsana, *Colonial Narratives and Cultural Dialogues*, London & New York: Routledge, 1996.

Singh, Namvar, *Itihas aur Alochana*, New Delhi: Rajkamal Prakashan, 1962, 1st edn. 1957 (Hindi).

———, *Dūsarī Paramparā kī Khoj*, New Delhi: Rajkamal Prakashan, 1971 (Hindi).

———, *Vād, Vivād aur Saṁvād*, New Delhi: Rajkamal Prakashan, 1991, 1st edn. 1989 (Hindi).

———, "The Novel of English Type and Indian Novel", *Critical Practice*, vol. I, no. 1, 1994.

———, "The End of the Century and Post-modernism", *Critical Practice*, vol. no. 2, June 1995.

———, "Namvar Singh in Conversation with Avadhesh Kumar Singh", *Indian Literature*, July-August, 192, 1999.

———, "*Samakālīn Samālocanā kī Samasyāyeṅ*" (Problems of Contemporary Criticism), *Ālocaka ke Mukh Se*, Delhi: Vani Prakashan, 2010 (Hindi).

Singh, Prem, "Rethinking History of Linguistics: Saussure and the India Connection", in *Language and Text: A. Kelkar Festschrift*, ed. R.N. Srivastava, Delhi: Kalinga Publishers, 1992.

Singh, Sunny, 2001, "Where Men Sought Glory and Women Went to Fiery Pyres" (an interview), *Critical Practice*, vol. VII, no. 1, January 2001.

Sinha, Jadunath, *The Foundation of Hinduism*, Calcutta: Sinha Publishing House, 1955.

Slemon, Stephen, "The Scramble for Post-colonialism" in Tiffin and Lawson, pp. 15-32.

Solomon, Esther A., *Indian Dialectics: Methods of Philosophical Discussion*, vols. I & II, Ahmedabad: B.J. Institute of Learning & Research, 1978.

Spivak, Gayatri Chakravorty, "Can the Subaltern Speak? Speculations on Widow Sacrifices", *Wedge*, 7-8, 1985.

———, "Neocolonialism and the Secret Agent of Knowledge", *Oxford Literary Review* 13, 1-2, 1991.

———, *Outside in the Teaching Machine*, London: Routledge, 1996.

Subhāṣita-Ratna-Sandoha, Bombay: Nirnaya Sagar Press, 1930.

Shukla, Acharya Ramachandra. *Rasa Mīmāṁsā*, Varanasi: Nagari Pracharani Sabha, 1947 (Hindi).

Sreekantaiyya, T.N., *Indian Poetics*, tr. N. Balasubramanian, New Delhi: Sahitya Akademi, 2001.

Suleri, Sara, *The Rhetoric of English India*, Chicago: University of Chicago Press, 1992.

Sunder Rajan, Rajeswari, *Real and Imagined Women: Gender, Culture and Post-colonialism*, London: Routledge, 1993.

Suryakanta, tr., *Aucityavicaracarca*, Poona: Oriental Book Agency, 1924.

Swami Tyagisananda, ed. & tr., *Śvetāśvataropaniṣad*, Madras: Sri Ramakrishna Math, 1964.

Tagore, Rabindranath, *Nationalism*, Macmillan, 1917, Delhi: Rupa, 1992.

Talwar, Veer Bharata, *Rassākaśī*, New Delhi: Saransh Prakashan, 2002 (Hindi).

Thakore, Ajit, "Post-modernist Gujarati Short Story", *Mīmāṁsā*, vol I, no. 1, 1996.

Taylor, Philip Meadows, *Seeta*, London, Henry S. King & Co, 1872.

Tharu, Susie, and K. Lalita, *Women Writing in India: 600 BC to the Early Twentieth Century*, vol. I, Delhi: Oxford University Press, 1991.

Thatte, Yadunath, *Yugvani*, April-June, 1990 (Marathi).

The Challenges to the South: The Report of the South Commission, London: Oxford University Press, 1992.

Thurow, Lester, *Head to Head: The Coming Economic Battle Among Japan, Europe and America*, New York: Morrow, 1992.

Tiffin, Chris and Alan Lawson, eds., *De-scribing Empire: Post-colonialism and Textuality*, London: Routledge, 1994.

Tholkappiyam, in English with critical studies by S. Ilakkuvanar, Madras: M. Neelambar Educational Publishers, 1994, 1st edn. 1963.

Tolstoy, L., *What is Art? And Essays on Art*, tr. Alymer Maude, London: Tolstoy Society & Oxford University Press, 1929, Tolstoy Centanary, 1929.

Trevelyan, Charles, *On the Education of the People of India*, London: Orient Longman, 1838.

Tripathi, G.M., *Saraswatichandra*, part I, Mumbai: N.M. Tripathi, 1988.

Tulsidās, Goswāmī, *Rāmacaritamānasa*, Gorakhpur: Gita Press, Saṁvat, 2054. 54th edn (Hindi).

Upadhyaya, Baldev, *Bhāgavat Sampradāya*, Kashi: Nagari Pracharini Sabha, Vikram Saṁvat 2010.

Vajpayee, Sri Kishoridas, *Hindi Śabdānuśasana*, Prayag: Nagari Pracharini Sabha, 1958 (Hindi).

Vālmīki, Maharshi, *The Rāmāyana*, tr. from Sanskrit to English by Ralph T.H. Griffith, Varanasi: Chowkhamba Sanskrit Series, 1963.

Valmiki, Om Prakash, *Joothan: A Dalit's Life*, tr. Arun Prabha Mukherjee, Kolkata: Samya and New York: Columbia University Press, 2003.

Vamana, *Kāvyālaṁkāra*, English tr. Ganganatha Jha, Poona: Oriental Book Agency, 1928.

Ved Vyāsa, *The Mahābhārata*, tr. M.N. Dutt, Delhi: Parimal Publications, 1997.

Verma, Dhirendra, *Aṣṭachāpa*, Allahabad: Ramnarayana Bookseller, 1950.

Verma, Nirmal, "Sanskrit, Samaya aur Bhāratīya Upanyāsa", in *Hindī Sāhitya kā Itihāsa*, ed. Nagendra, Delhi: Mayur Paperbacks, 1993 (Hindi).

Veeser, H. Aram, *The New Historicism Reader*, Routledge, 1994.

Vishwanath, *Sāhitya-Darpaṇa*, tr. into English by J.K. Ballantyne & P.K. Mishra, Delhi: Motilal Banarsidass, 1967.

Vishwanathan, Gauri, *Masks of Conquest: Literary Study and British Rule in India*, NewYork: Columbia University Press, 1989.

Vivekananda, Swami, *The Complete Works of Swami Vivekananda*, Calcutta: Advaita Ashram, 1992, vol. VIII.

———, *The Complete Works of Swami Vivekananda*, vol. III, Calcutta: Advaita Ashrama, 1994.

Warder, A.K., *The Science of Criticism in India*, Madras: Adyar Library & Research Centre, 1978.

Wallerstein, I., in *The Oxford Companion to Politics of the World*, ed. Joel Krieger, New York: Oxford University Press, 1993.

Watchel, E., "Eleanor Watchel with Chinua Achebe", *The Malahat Review*, 113, Winter 1995, p. 55.

Wankhede, M.N., *Dalitanche Vidrohi Wangmay*, Nagpur: Prabodhan Prakashan, 1981 (Marathi).

Wellek, Rene and Austin Warren, *Theory of Literature, 1949*, New York: Harcourt, Brace and World, 3rd edn., 1956.

Wheelwright, Philip Ellis, *Metaphor and Reality, 1962*, Bloomington: Indiana University Press, 1968.

———, *The Burning Fountain: A Study in the Language of Symbolism, 1954*, Bloomington: Indiana University Press, rev. edn., 1969.

White, Hayden, *Tropics of Discourses: Essays in Cultural Criticism*, Baltimore: Johns Hopkins University Press, 1978.

Whittey, Steve, "English Language as a Tool of British Neocolonialism", *East Africa Journal*, 8, 1971.

Wilhelm, Halbfass, *India and Europe: An Essay in Understanding*, Albany: State University of New York Press, 1988-89.

Wilson, Richard & Dutton, Richard, eds., *New Historicism and Renaissance Drama*, Longman, 1992.

Woechlcke, Manfred, cited in Lester Venter, *When Mandela Goes: The Coming of South Africa's Second Revolution*, Johannesburg: Doubleday, 1997.

Woods, Tim, *Beginning Postmodernism*, Manchester & New York: Manchester University Press, 1999.

Woolstonecraft, Mary, *A Vindication of the Rights of Women* (1972), Oxford: Oxford University Press, 1994.

Wordsworth, William. "Preface" to Lyrical Ballads" (1800), Rev. in 1802, *The Norton Anthology: Theory and Criticism*, ed. Vincent B. Leitch et al., New York and London: WW Norton & Co., 2001, pp. 648-68.

Yankowsky, S.V., ed. & tr., *The Brahmin, Episode*, St. Ambrose's Version of the Colloquy between Alexander the Great and the Brahmins of India, Ansback, 1962, p. 47.

Zelliot, Eleanor, "Stri Dalit Sahitya: The New Voice of Women Poets", in Anne Feldhaus, ed., *Images of Women in Maharashtrian Literature and Relgion*, Albany: State University of New York Press, 1996.

———, "Sant Sahitya and Dalit Movement", in Meera Kosambi, ed., *Intersections: Socio-cultural Trends in Maharashtra*, Hyderabad: Orient Longman, 2000.

Zimmer, Heinrich, *The King and the Corpse*, Princeton University Press, 1971, 1st pub. 1948.

Zvelebil, Kamil, *The Smile of Murugan*, Leiden: E.J. Brill, 1973.

Index